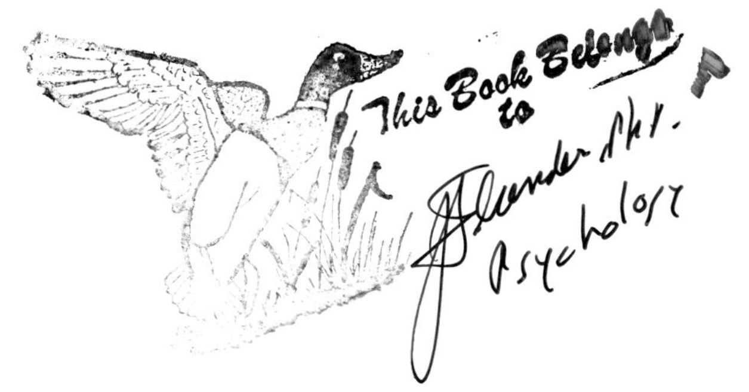

Impossible Worlds

Impossible Worlds

Birkhäuser, Publishers for Architecture
Basel – Boston – Berlin

August, London

A CIP catalogue record for this book is available from the Library of Congress, Washington DC, USA

Deutsche Bibliothek
Cataloguing-in-Publication Data

Impossible worlds / Stephen Coates and Alex Stetter (ed.).
– Basel ; Boston ; Berlin :
Birkhäuser, 2000
ISBN 3-7643-6317-7

Printed on acid-free paper produced from chlorine-free pulp. TCF ∞

ISBN 3-7643-6317-7

9 8 7 6 5 4 3 2 1

Editors: Stephen Coates and Alex Stetter
Art director: Stephen Coates
Publishing director: Nick Barley

Production co-ordinated by:
Uwe Kraus GmbH
Printed in Italy

Publisher's acknowledgements:
Fiona Bradley, Katrina Brown, Lise Connellan,
Diana Eggenschwiler, Werner Handschin, Jonathan Heaf,
Ally Ireson, Joe Kerr, Bettina von Kameke, Nigel Prince,
Silke Roch, Anne Odling-Smee, Peter Odling-Smee,
Elisabeth Scheder-Bieschin, Robert Steiger, Sandy Suffield,
Gavin Wade

Contents

Introduction
Alex Stetter

Everyone can picture a perfect world. It could be based on a memory of a place once visited, or an image once seen, or perhaps it only exists in the imagination – but it is unlikely to bear much direct resemblance to the world we live in. We are brought up on stories that take place in worlds quite unlike our own, and it is only natural for this fascination to continue. Some people take things further, creating their own detailed plans, thinking through all the practicalities until they come up with a model that looks as if it can work. But it takes a particular belief in the value and viability of this idea and a very strong will to turn it into reality, to go and *build* that personal vision of utopia rather than let it stay on paper.

The belief that there might be a better way of living, and that it is achievable if the right circumstances are created, is perhaps the only characteristic which is common to architects and ecological activists, Quakers and Communists, urbanists and DIY enthusiasts. The methods may be as different as the motivation, which can range from the philosophical and the social to the political and the financial, but the goal is the same: to create a world that is significantly better than the one we live in now.

Every utopian scheme is inextricably bound up with the reality of its creator. Representing either a radical response to, or a refinement of prevailing conditions, any such project is inevitably developed in direct relation to the situation it is designed to replace. No matter how wide-reaching their scope, utopian schemes are concerned with the way people live on a daily basis. To qualify as truly utopian, the dream must involve some form of wider community, however select. While building the house of our dreams in the ultimate location – a place where we could live in our own personal, perfect world – might be very satisfying, setting up one isolated, ideal household in an otherwise flawed environment could never amount to a utopian project.

By far the most effective method of creating an instant new community involves simply imposing one's will on others, so that they have no option but to live by newly established guidelines – be it because they are subjects, employees or tenants. While undoubtedly effective, this approach does also bring with it a huge burden of responsibility. Building a new settlement is about much more than simply providing shelter, it necessarily involves an element of prescribing a whole way of life. The Quaker family, for instance, who built the town of Bournville on the outskirts of Birmingham for the workers in their chocolate factory, provided exemplary housing, schools and parks for the employees and their families – but no pubs. At the time, the residents may well have been happy to go along with their employer's strict moral code, but times have changed, and today's tenants would be likely to make rather different demands of their immediate environment.

Before the advent of cinema, architects played a key role in making visible a possible future, by presenting grand schemes and models of brave new worlds, ideas that pushed people's expectations of how they could live. Even if they were never built exactly as imagined, these plans helped shape the cities that did follow. This may be because, by necessity, it is impossible to sustain an idea of such grand plans if one is constantly held back by the details and practicalities. In many instances, utopian schemes can most usefully be regarded as 'best case scenarios', an example of what could be possible if all the myriad elements that come into play in the creation of a community were all working in the project's favour. These projects have helped drive societal change because, unless people are shown inspirational alternatives, when it comes to the built environment most will tend to stick to what they know.

Unlike storytellers and painters, architects do not have the luxury of total control over the execution of their ideas: their creations are all too easily compromised by outside factors like money, time, politics, climate, geology, and above all people. Although these factors are the very elements that help bring a scheme to life, they contribute

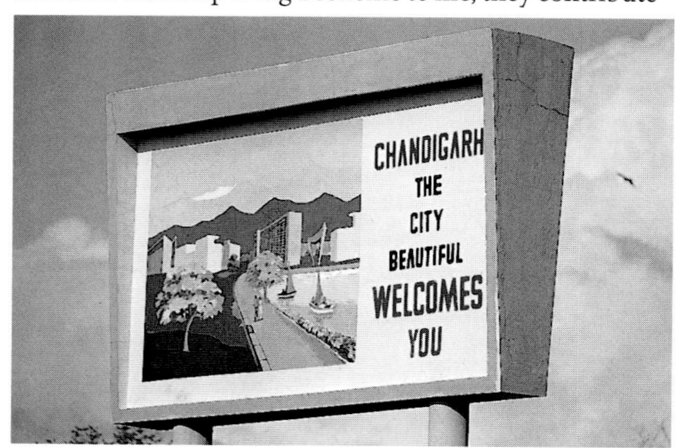

to the inevitable gap between the original vision and the built reality. So, for example, the Jewish architects seeking safety from persecution in Israel in the 1930s soon found that the balconies and large windows so beloved of Modernism were much less well-suited to the hot climate of their adopted home. And those who have attempted to introduce new ideas for living to Britain since 1945, have frequently had to watch their visionary communal schemes founder in the face of a peculiarly English reluctance to deviate from the semi-detached ideal.

Le Corbusier spent years planning alternative versions of existing cities, re-imagining New York and Paris in the image of his own vision of the perfect place. Making radical schemes such as the Plan Voisin a reality in well-established world cities like Paris would have required a level of political influence which not even Le Corbusier could wield, but using real places as examples proved a very effective way of getting his ideas across and capturing people's imaginations. Many elements of his thinking eventually found their natural home elsewhere, outside the already over-developed Western world. Their spirit lives on in the fast-growing mega-developments of China and South-East Asia, built without much regard for what was there before and looking only to the future.

The only place Le Corbusier got anywhere near to

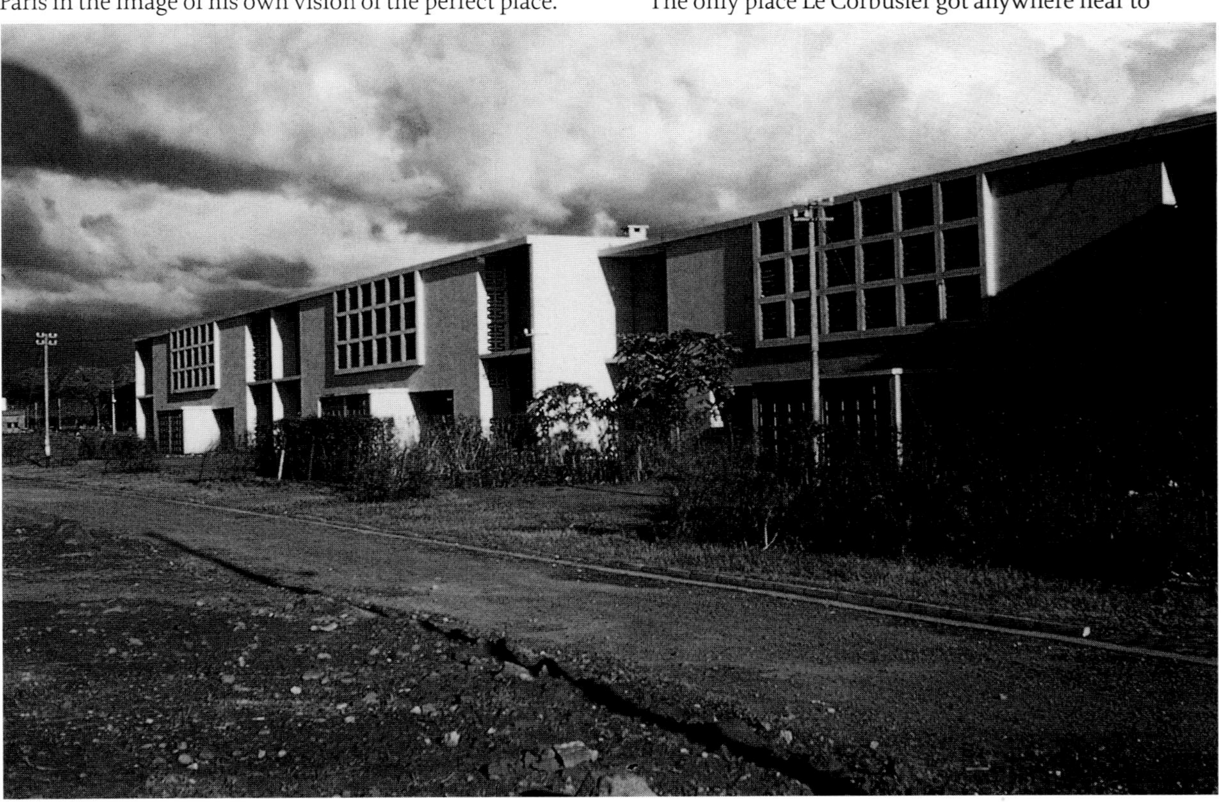

Workers' housing, Chandigarh

building his ideal city was in India, where he was given the commission to design a new capital city for the Punjab region in 1950. In India, Chandigarh is known as the 'City Beautiful', in honour as much of its clean, orderly streets, well-tended gardens and efficient water and power supply as Le Corbusier's extraordinary Capitol complex, an acknowledged high point of the latter part of his career. Yet the city is a victim of its own popularity and its designer's principles: it was originally planned to house a maximum of 500,000 inhabitants, but that number had already been exceeded by the early 1980s. Today, the population is nearer 800,000. Newcomers unable to afford land in the city have set up home in illegal settlements on the town's outskirts, creating satellite slum suburbs that do not fit in with the architect's layout out of a city consisting of 46 autonomous sectors. It has been impossible for the city's lumbering administration to reconcile the aesthetic and planning guidelines laid down decades earlier with the urgent housing needs of its less well-off new citizens. The original plan now needs to be adjusted to take the unforeseen rapid growth of city into account. It is hardly surprising that today Chandigarh is not functioning as well as it was meant to.

Fifty years after its founding, the debate about the success or failure of Chandigarh continues. Even though it is already bigger than it was ever meant to be, the city remains unfinished, but the possibility of finally constructing the Governor's palace and water gardens that Le Corbusier had envisaged as the scheme's crowning glory is still being discussed. So it can arguably be considered a work in progress: proof that just because an idea might not make the translation into reality without a hitch, that doesn't mean it's not an idea worth pursuing further. As Sir Denys Lasdun put it at a conference held to evaluate the past and consider the future of the city: 'Noble things always appear impossible at first.'

Very few people even get to attempt to build their ideal town, so most dreams of the perfect place are bound to be more domestic than civic in scale. Although most of us cannot remake the world around us to suit our ideas, we can at the very least create our little domain, beyond finding the perfect home or shaping the landscape of our garden. Even though we are increasingly likely to identify ourselves as part of a community defined by our tastes and our work, rather than by how or where we live, we can forge tentative links with potential allies and find small pockets of freedom where we can do as we please. The allotment movement is a perfect example of bringing together the personal and the communal – a federation of little utopian nation-states, founded on the premise that even city-dwellers deserve a chance of living off the land.

Another outlet for an individual's utopian aspirations is the holiday – the instant fix of a utopia for hire, but one which must usually be shared with thousands of other holidaymakers. Most people's idea of the perfect place involves getting as far away as possible from their everyday, frequently urban, reality. Many seek solace in the resolutely unmetropolitan, and utterly impractical instead. Daylight-deprived commuters dream of lazing on the iconic, endless, perfect beach familiar from countless posters and adverts. These dreams have little to do with political, architectural or philosophical ideals, but of course it is the complete absence of daily life that makes them fleetingly desirable.

Although we know, even whilst indulging our holiday fantasies, that we do not really want to spend the rest of our lives in a five-star spa resort, there is something undeniably appealing about the illusion of perfection, the homogenous enclosed world they offer. This is shared by the holiday resort's closest real-world equivalent: the master-planned community. Both entice people to buy into their version of the dream: the perfect beach, the perfect family in the perfect little house, surrounded by equally perfect other people in the perfect community. This image is undoubtedly popular, but as so often it is too good to be true, and what may seem to be the perfect holiday resort can quickly come to be thought of as an

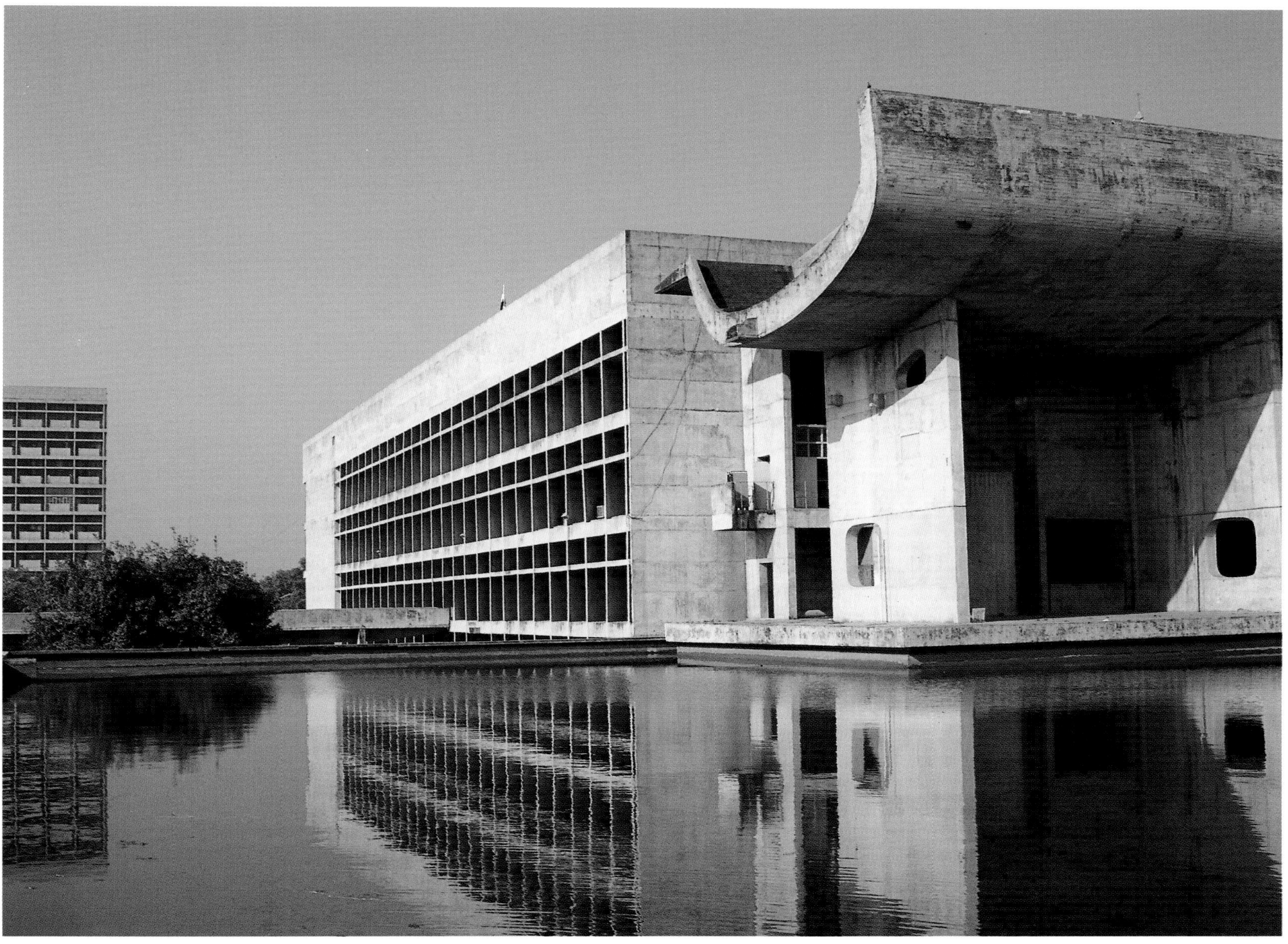

Assembly building,
Chandigarh

overdeveloped concrete beachside hell.

Nevertheless, the idea of relaxing in the sun has proved to be one of the most enduring ideals, and one which some have tried to transport into the realm of housing. Finding a way to banish the problems of everyday existence is an essential part of such schemes, and usually the veneer of perfection masks a system of rules which are every bit as invidious as the more apparent prescriptions of a Corbusian tower block. In one episode of *The X Files*, FBI agents Mulder and Scully take a break from their usual alien-chasing activities to go undercover as a normal married couple, living out the American dream in a detached house with a three-car garage. But in this particular Californian planned community, everything is not as it first seems. Any resident of the wonderfully-named 'Falls of Arcadia' who fails to conform to the standards of perfection laid down in the development's extensive rule book is messily killed by a monster that emerges from the manicured lawns, a muddy manifestation of the collective drive to maintain the community's flawless façade. Punishable offences range from failing to replace light bulbs the instant they break to spoiling the uniform look of the street by putting up a basket ball hoop in the front yard. These residents were clearly prepared to pay a particularly high price for living in their idea of a perfect world.

While a TV programme like *The X-Files* offers a tongue-in-cheek deconstruction of popular trends in housing, it also picks up on our need to belong and our fear of striking out on our own. While holiday companies sell us the idea of a life without the chores and complications of everyday living, many property developers hark back to an idealised past that never really existed, selling a dream of community, tailor-made to one's own tastes and requirements. It is not a case of 'one dream fits all': both target their wares at very specific consumers, catering for every need and income bracket. That means houses (and holidays) aimed at precisely-determined target markets – at families with young children or people planning their retirements; at hard-working, hard-playing urbanites or those seeking rural bliss; even at those who require their own aircraft hangar and access to a runway at a moment's notice. While perfectly enjoyable for a two-week period, this segregation into different life stages seems inflexible in the long run. Planned communities are defined by the very elements they exclude: those who do not meet the required criteria of age, solvency or social status. But what happens when residents' situations change? Planning a community that works in the long term means planning for that community to evolve. It will be fascinating to witness the evolution of the newly-built gated communities of white, middle class Americans such as Seaside and Celebration, as their inhabitants grow older (and presumably wealthier) and the United States which exists outside their gates becomes increasingly different. Perhaps for this reason there are already plans by those who do not wish to engage with the perceived horror of a multi-ethnic, multi-lingual future, to dream of new countries elsewhere. One of them, planned to be built on a newly-created island in the Carribean, has even been christened New Utopia.

At the other end of the political spectrum, there will always be people who do not subscribe to the notion of the safe, conventional, suburban ideal. The Centre for Alternative Technology in Machynlleth, Wales, has been developing and demonstrating more sustainable approaches to building and living since 1975. It is the centre's mission to inspire and encourage people to 'achieve positive change in their own lives', by teaching them about low-impact materials and alternative ways of providing energy, managing waste and water and building their own houses, be they straw-bale structures or wood-frame designs based on the modular building technique developed by Walter Segal. But with a building opened in September 2000, the centre has also provided a viable sustainable model for commercial buildings: the Autonomous Environmental Information Centre, designed by Pat Borer and David Lea, features structural walls and columns made of rammed earth, making it the first public building in Britain constructed using this updated version of an ancient building technique.

Today, it is easier than ever before to create new – albeit virtual – worlds, that are designed to be seen on a cinema screen or accessed via computer. Film is so much more seductive than any cardboard model or artist's impression could ever be, simply because it allows us to watch the illusion of lives lived out in a fully-imagined environment. No wonder Le Corbusier thought of film as the ideal way to spread the word about Modern architecture: it is the perfect utopian medium. Every scheme can be presented in the best light, and every element controlled – not just the appearance of the building itself, but also the way people react to and use the space. All the elements that are normally outside the architect's control can suddenly be harnessed to work in his or her favour. Rem Koolhaas wrote film scripts before he became an architect and found 'that there is little difference between the two', and in many ways film makers, game designers and architects are working with the same set of tools. We can even interact with the worlds into which they invite us, moving through perfect recreations of real or imagined places.

Computer renderings of as yet unbuilt buildings are so convincing that when the real thing is finally completed it can seem a bit of a disappointment, looking almost exactly like it did on screen. On the other hand, the same technology, and the ease with which images can be dispersed around the world, means that buildings don't even have to be realised to make an impact. They exist in the imagination, in an alternative reality where competition-winning designs actually get built and funding is never an issue.

Many schemes that would have appeared to belong to the realms of science fiction a few years ago seem increasingly viable in real life. It is not only a question of the technology being available to turn radical plans into reality, but also the rather more complex matter of getting the official go-ahead, sorting out the legalities and making sure the funding is in place. While it is one thing perfecting these big ideas on screen, the real challenge lies in finding out how they will work when taken out of the carefully-controlled on-screen environment. Once built, the houses or the cities might look just as their designers intended, but the true test lies in finding out if they can successfully be inhabited by real human beings.

The crux of the matter lies in the challenge – some might say the impossibility – of ever truly creating a well-functioning real-life community from scratch. And, as starting all over again is usually not an option with established major cities anyway, perhaps the best approach is to think smaller and try to improve on the flawed organically-grown models we have already. That means creating small but viable new elements that can be integrated into existing schemes, that can act as examples and that will eventually add up to something bigger; changing people's attitudes and expectations so they are no longer happy to settle for what they are given, but start to work towards getting what they want.

We are surrounded by built evidence of other people's hopes, fears and dreams, the visible legacy of the utopian thinking of previous generations. Looking at some of the now unloved public buildings and dysfunctional housing estates that were once hailed as the way of the future, evidence of a pure ideal behind the flawed reality can be difficult to identify. But it is too easy to mock utopian views of the past – all are unavoidably of their time, and arose out of the realities in which their creators found themselves. Their refusal to settle for the status quo and their belief that things could be different are the qualities that lend to their enduring usefulness. It is possible to find faults with every visionary project, whether it is Le Corbusier's plan to raze the heart of Paris, or smaller-scale attempts to build sustainable, eco-friendly communities. But without such visionary projects, many other widely-acknowledged architectural successes would almost certainly not have happened.

Ecstacity
Nigel Coates & Doug Branson

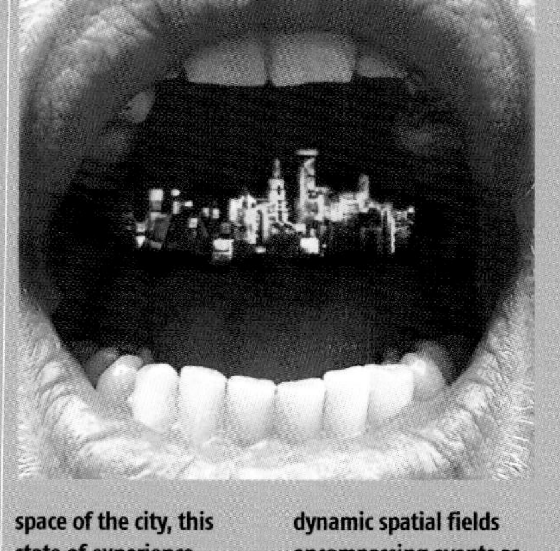

Ecstacity is a map of the conditions and attitudes of the contemporary city. Described by its designer Nigel Coates as 'a reading of the world we're in now', it is an imagined urban environment built up from elements of seven existing cities – London, Bombay, Tokyo, New York, Rio de Janeiro, Rome and Cairo – wrapping them round the image of two human forms to create a topologically-remastered reading of urban experience. This is not so much a utopian project, as a manifesto for an architecture which immerses itself in the experiential; a manifesto for the city as a series of episodes rather than an accumulation of buildings.

Coates first exhibited Ecstacity in London in 1992, but this new series of images was created for the 2000 Venice Architecture Biennale. As well as providing a medium in which to display many of Branson Coates' own design projects and realised buildings, Ecstacity sets itself out as a series of encounters from which those buildings can be seen to have arisen. It is a dialectical approach to urbanism which places buildings, people and their urban context in a state of dynamic tension. Coates expresses the tension in six set piece encounters, which are revealingly titled Tuning In; Locking On; Undressing; Letting Go; Cranking Up; and Flipping Out. It all adds up to Ecstacity.

TUNING IN (opposite)
'As the pyramids are to Cairo, so the body is to Ecstacity.'
The state of anticipation, epitomised by the postcards, souvenirs and trinkets that precede the experience of the destination itself. From Big Ben to the Guggenheim Bilbao, these places are better known by representational icons than by the three-dimensional space they occupy – and our experience of them begins as we read about them in the in-flight magazine or at the airport souvenir shop.

LOCKING ON (above left)
'Seven zones blend seven cultures... together they make one city that thrives on diversity.'
The awareness of cultures – or of a person – characterised in Ecstacity by buildings such as the Parc de la Villette in Paris, or London's Tate Modern. Acting as markers which allow us to connect the city's spaces with its cultural activity, these sites or buildings are also 'ports, open to your immediate desires and long term vices.'

UNDRESSING (cover image)
'It's important to undress – not literally – but to unmask the fashion side of your existence enough to unleash a new energy.'
The body carries its own architecture with it, existing in a dialectical tension with the city that has both created it, and been created by it. The boundary between public and private space, this encounter includes buildings such as the London Eye and Frederick Kiesler's Endless House, or in Branson Coates' work the Body Zone and Oyster furniture. As Kiesler said in 1961, 'If art could be accepted like sex and sex like eating, men and women would not feel like perverts, shamelessly obscene in the presence of modern art or architecture.'

LETTING GO (below)
'The space of the flâneur, wandering, idling and subject to contrasts of experience and scale.'
Allowing the chaotic space of the city to enter the body, and the body to enter the chaotic space of the city, this state of experience amounts to a set of invisible spatial flows which permeate the city. It is characterised in real cities by buildings such as the Jewish Museum in Berlin.

CRANKING UP (overleaf)
'Like liquid it spreads between hills, through tunnels, under freeways.'
The outer (sub)urbs of the city are linked to the centre both by dynamic spatial fields encompassing events as well as buildings. Events can be experienced as buildings or asmore abstract concentrations of energy, ebbing and flowing according to desires. 'Caesar's Palace is building new satellites as part of the Agip gas stations across the urbs of Ecstacity.'

FLIPPING OUT (above)
'Finally architecture is the product of the mind, and as such subject to its quixotic nature.'
The built environment in dialogue with the body, this space describes the flipping and compressing of extremes of scale. Just as our body occupies the city, so the city is inside our head and body, transported there through electronic data maps, the net, WAP and myriad hyper-communications.

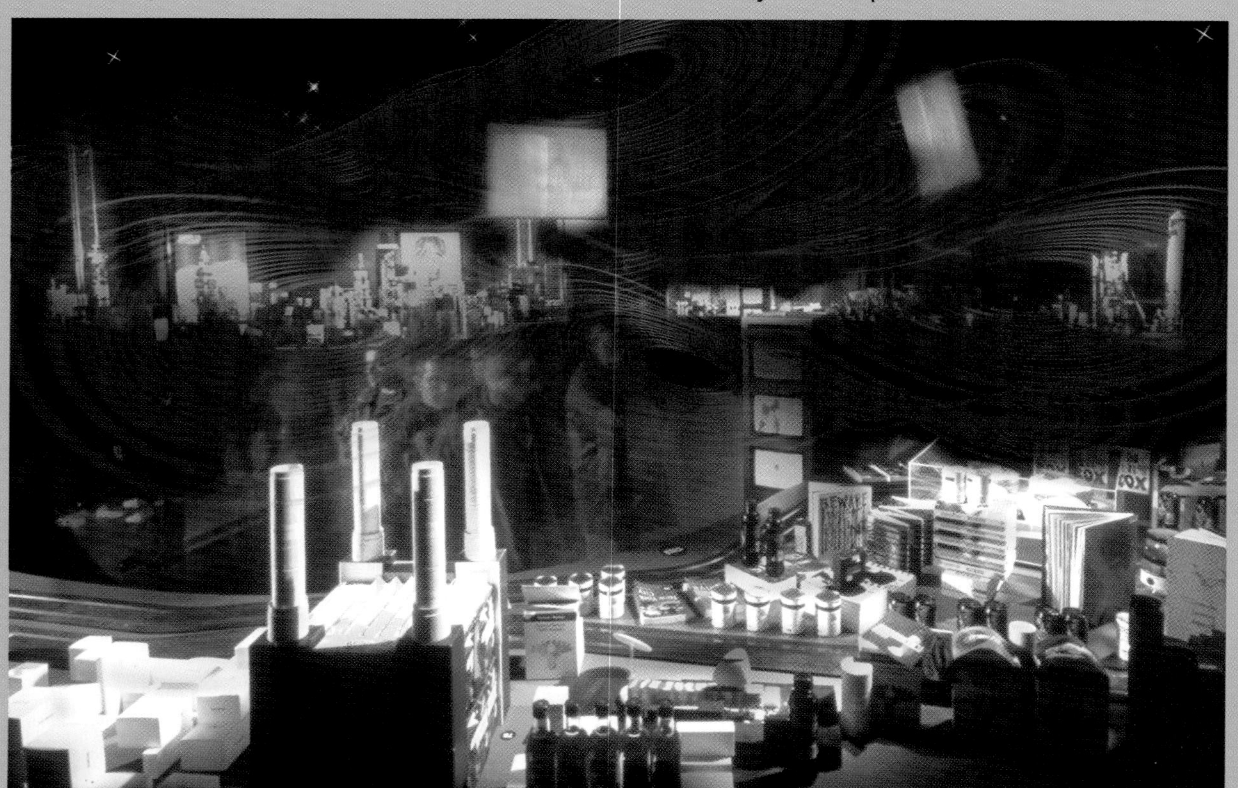

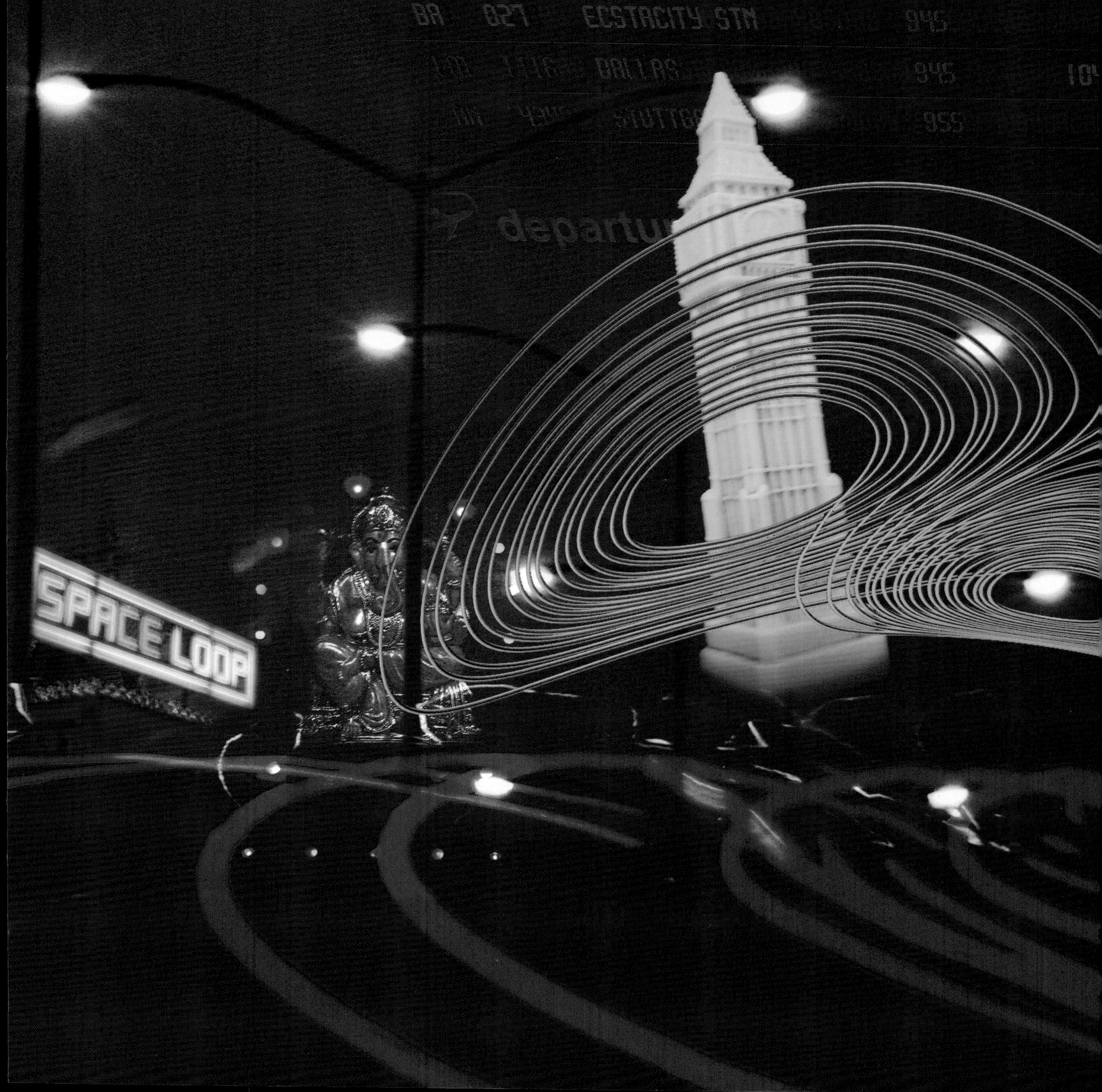

BA 027 ECSTACITY STM 945
DALLAS 945
departur
SPACE LOOP

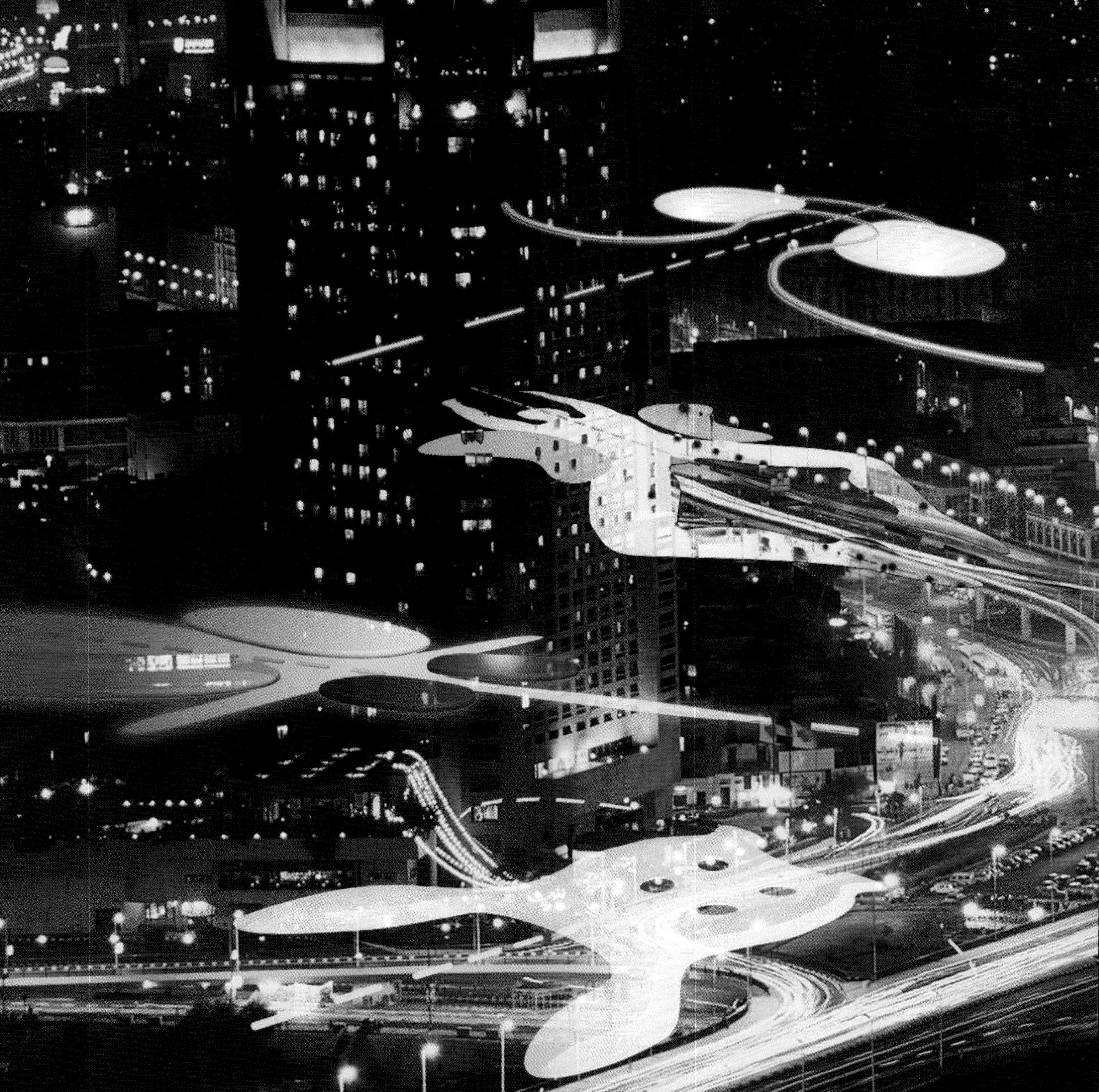

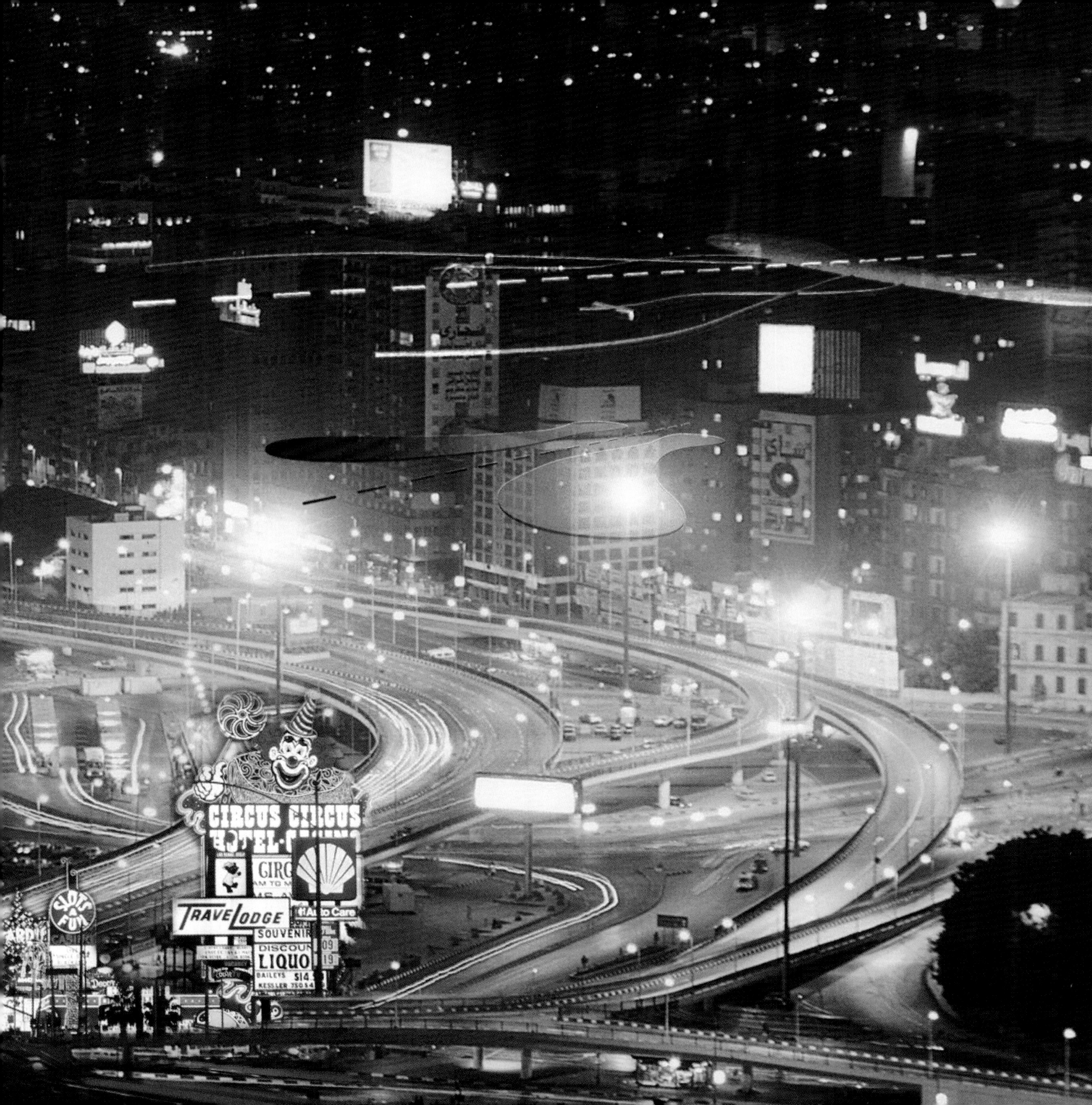
CIRCUS CIRCUS
TraveLodge
SOUVENIR
Auto Care
BAILEYS
KESSLER

Dome over New York City
Buckminster Fuller

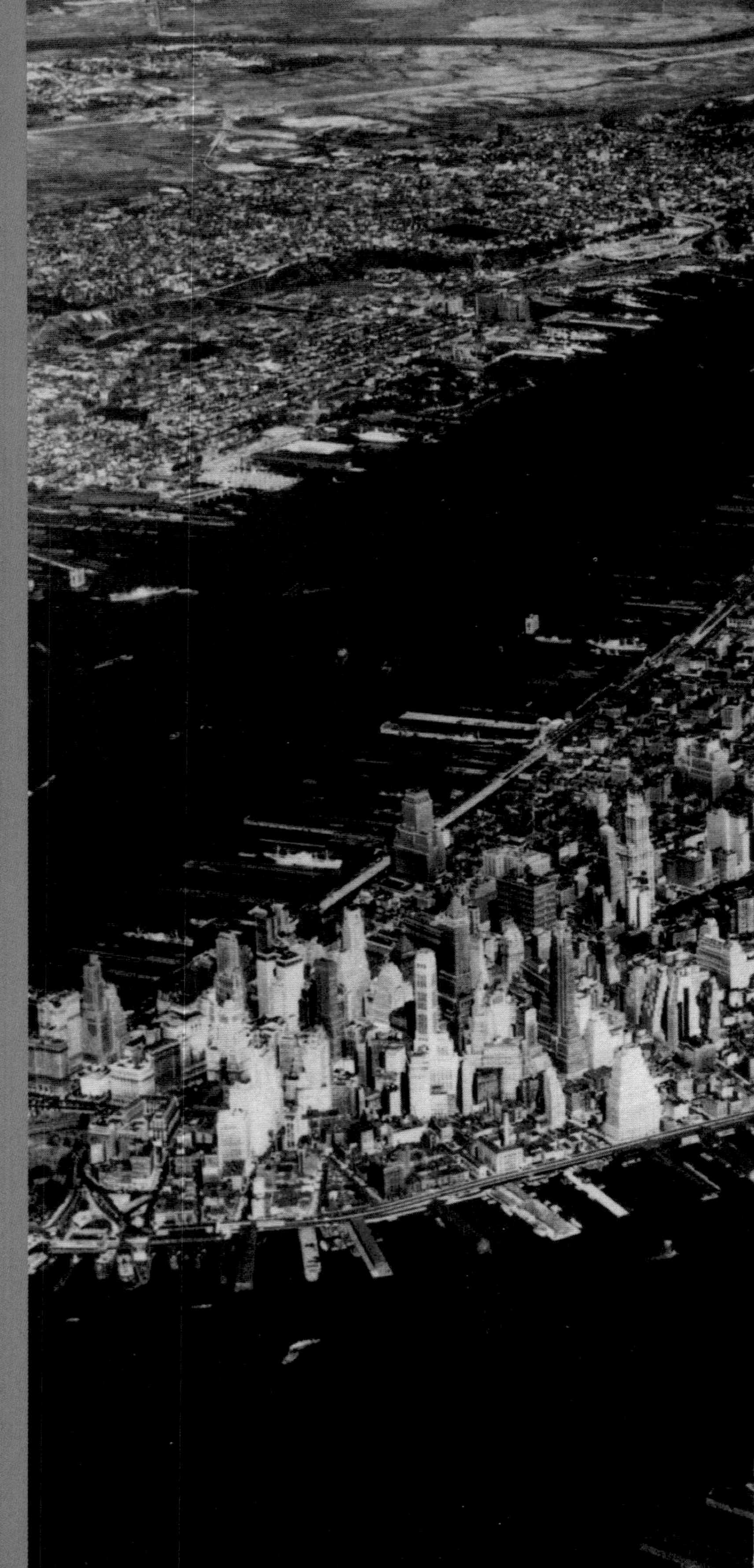

Buckminster Fuller took his study of geodesic dome structures to extraordinary levels. This photomontage, right, shows his plan devised in 1950 for a dome over Manhattan. With a span of more than three kilometres from 22nd Street in the south to 62nd Street in the north, the dome would have signalled the end of automotive traffic in this part of the city. According to the architect's calculations, the proposed dome's surface area would have been just 1/85th of the total area of the buildings it would cover, thus making enormous savings in energy costs and supposedly obviating snow removals. Buckminster Fuller calculated that the building could withstand hurricanes and heavy snowfalls, with the resultant cost savings paying for the construction costs within 10 years of its installation. Moreover, he believed that the atmosphere inside the structure would be little short of idyllic:

'From the inside there will be uninterrupted contact with the exterior world. The sun and moon will shine in the landscape, and the sky will be completely visible, but the unpleasant effects of climate, heat, dust, bugs, glare, etc. will be modulated by the skin to provide Garden of Eden interior.'
Buckminster Fuller, 1977

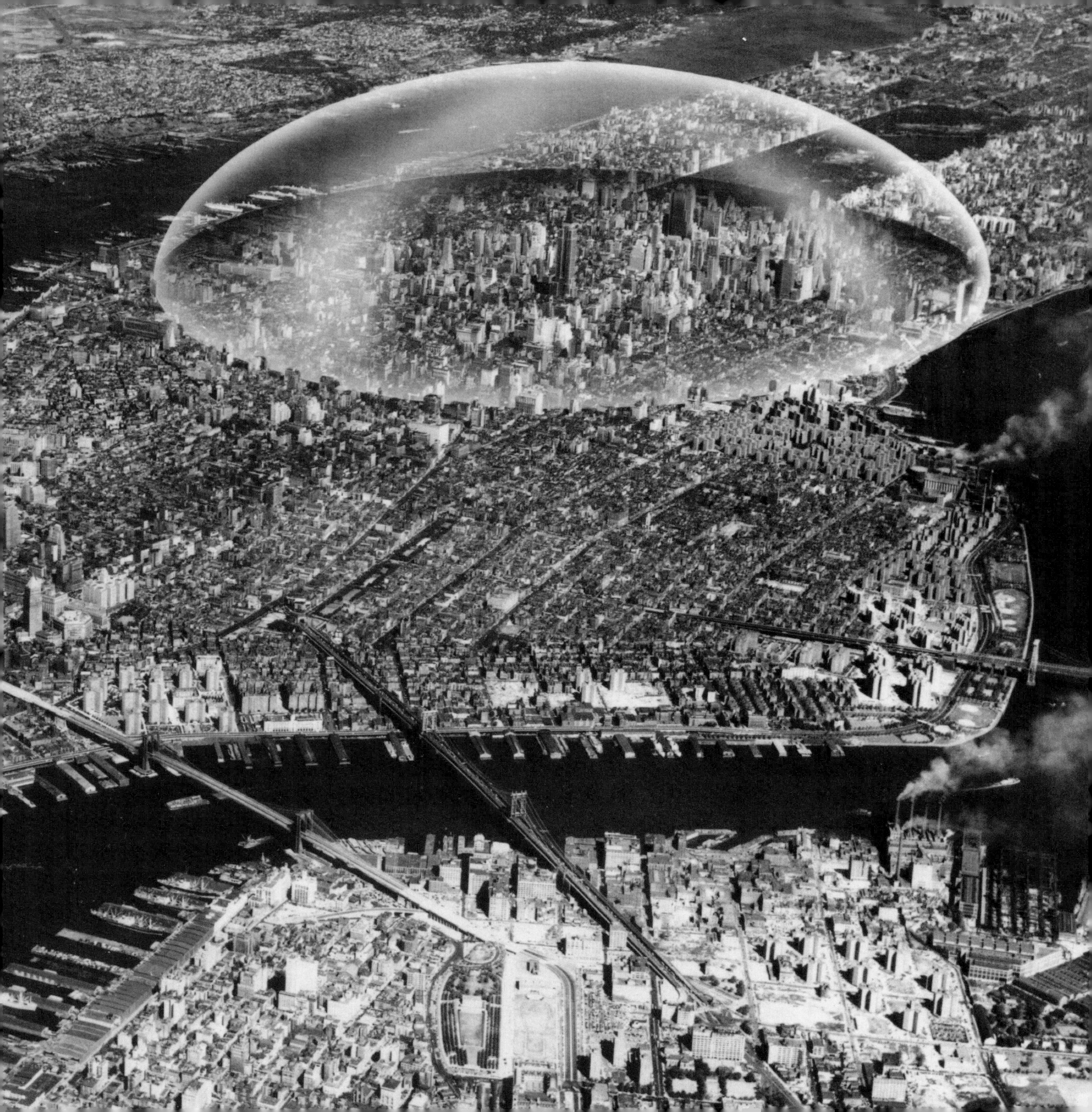

Executing God
Zaha Hadid

'This is a city of extremes, where the major obsessions are spirituality, shopping and television. A city of paradox, of voodoo and skyscrapers, magic and technology, sorcery and science. This is TotalCity, a seething fusion of Los Angeles, Mexico City, Bombay and Tokyo. Meta corporations employ teams of clairvoyants and psychics, astrologers and chaos theorists to define stock market strategy and to curse rivals. All traditional notions of civic structure have collapsed. TotalCity is ruled by market forces. Anarchic and chaotic, it is a pirate utopia. It's our future and it's gorgeous."

When it is released, *Executing God* will contain images of Zaha Hadid's first design for a complete city. Hadid was asked by film producers Marc J Hawker and Ishbel Whitaker to prepare a backdrop for the feature film which is now in development. Hadid and her team created what is perhaps their most extreme example to date of the ideas about bundling, folding and looping that Hadid has been exploring in her work for more than five years.

Meanwhile, Hawker and Whitaker commissioned Japanese designer Hideyuki to overlay images which take the pure formalism of Hadid's design and transform it into the utopia/dystopia as it will appear in the film (see pages 21–23). Total-City.com is also being developed, which Hawker and Whitaker describe as 'a pioneering 3D persistent on-line environment.'

CREDITS
Zaha Hadid
Design Team
Bergendy Cooke, Oliver Domeisen, Jee-eun Lee, James Lim, Thomas Knuevener, Caroline Voet
Photography
Edward Woodman

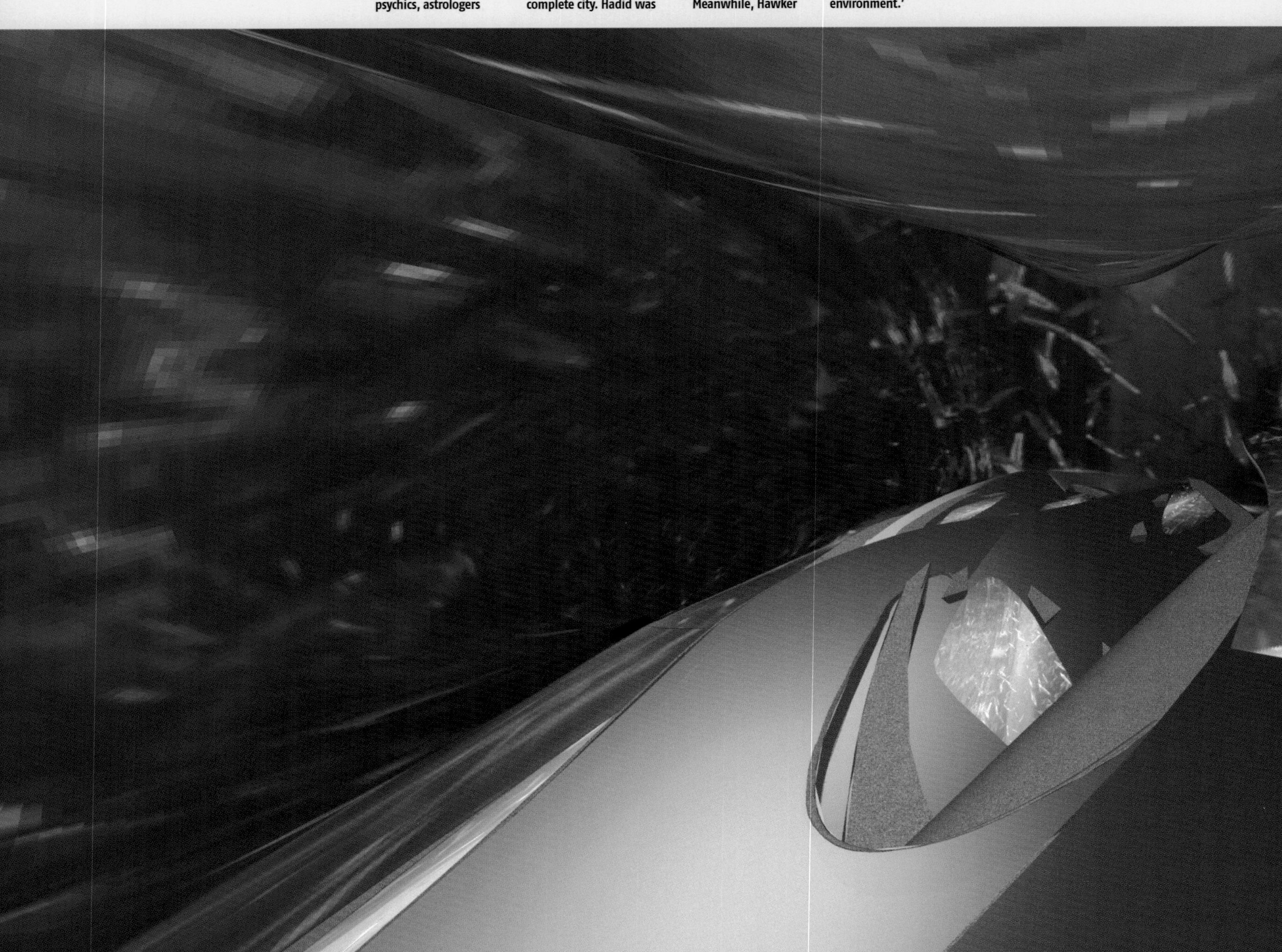

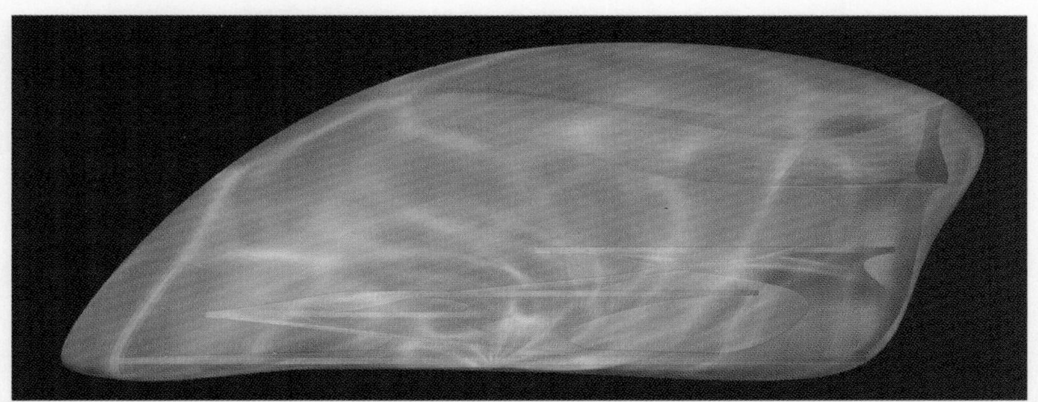

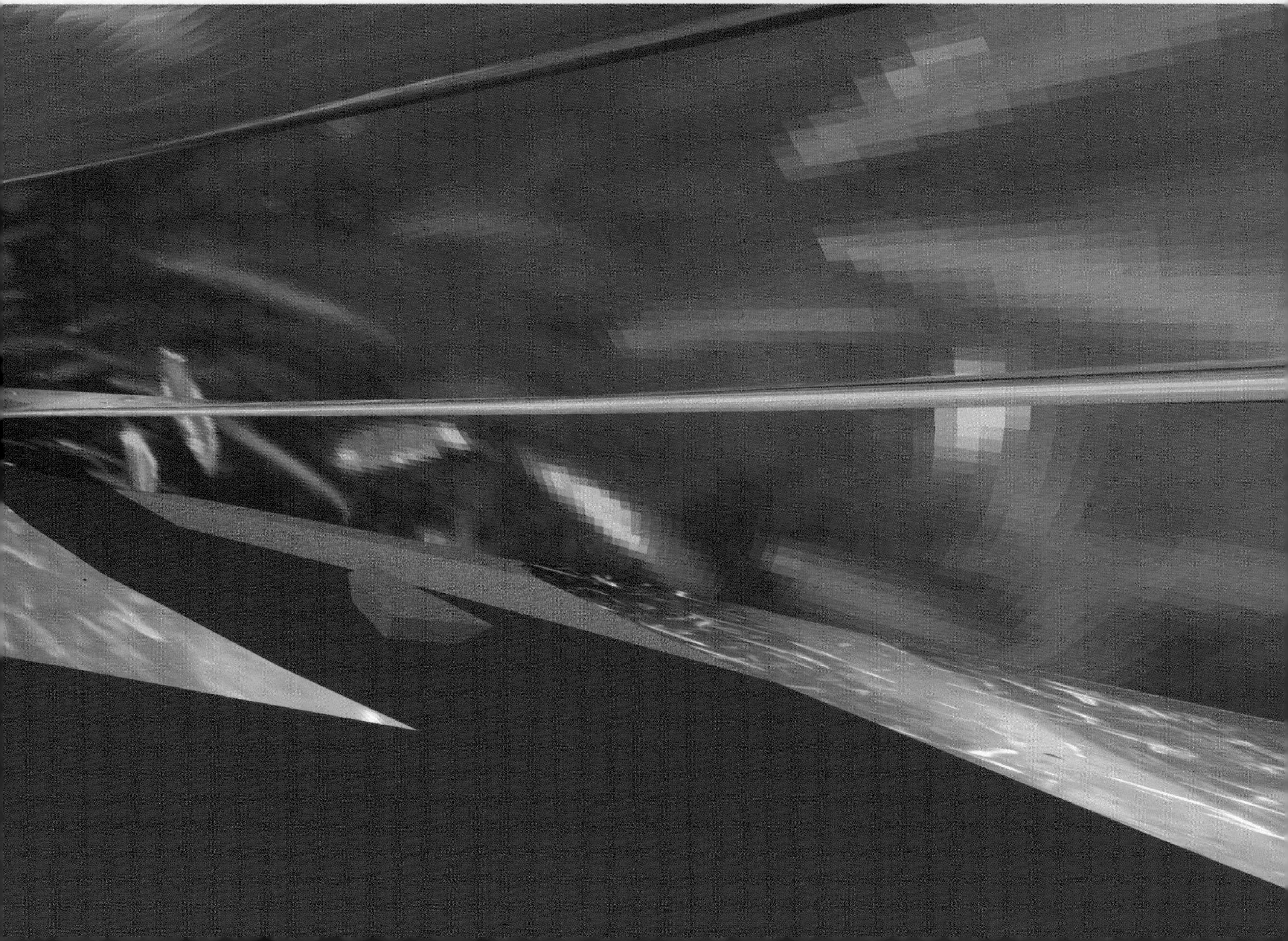

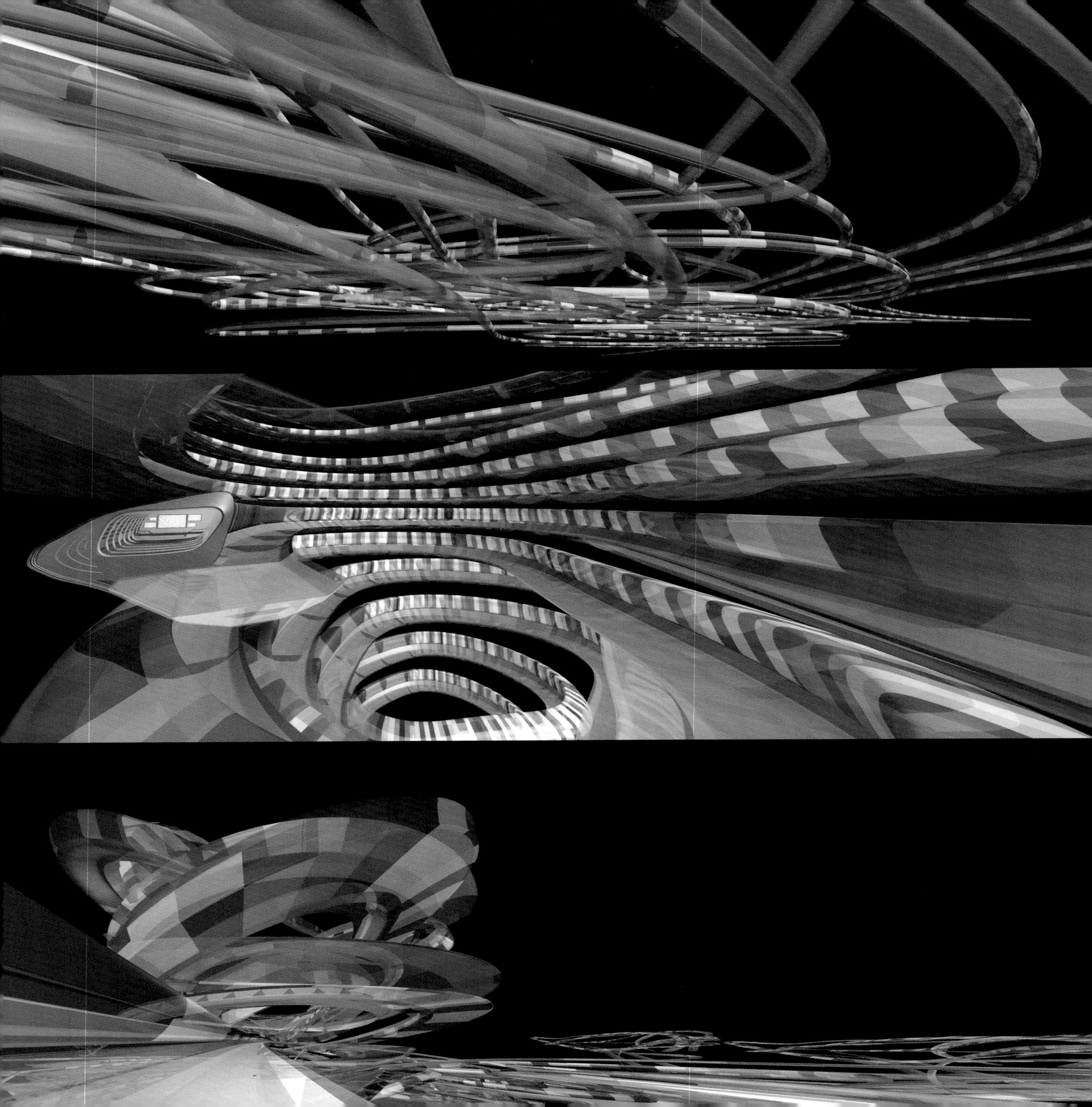

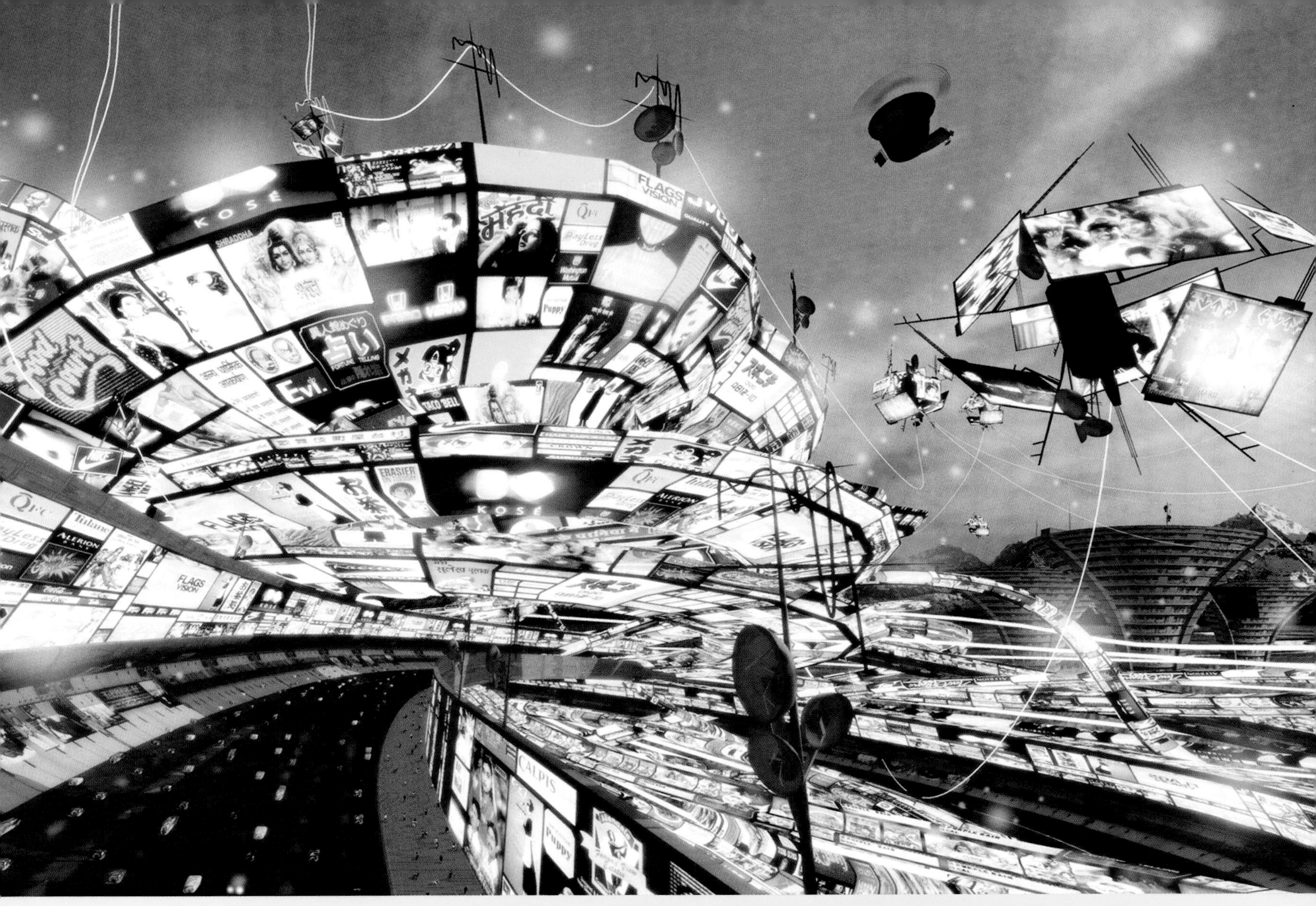
KOSÉ
FLAGS VISION
SHRADDHA
FORTUNE TELLING
Evi.
TACO BELL
ERASIER
KOSÉ
FLAGS VISION
ALERION
CALPIS
Puppy

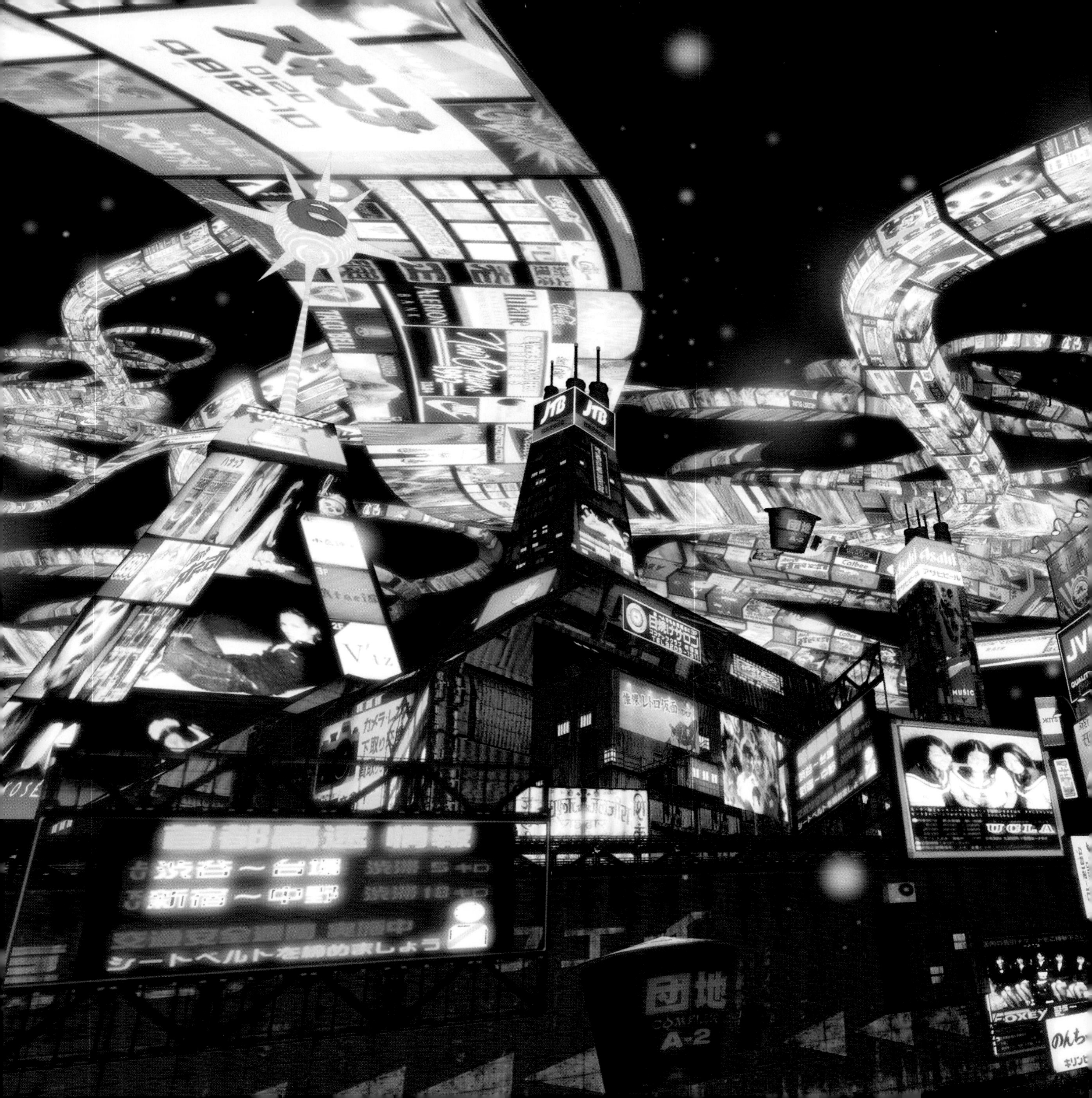

JTB
JTB
Asahi
アサヒビール
Tulane
TACO BELL
Calbee
V'tz
JVC
MUSIC
UCLA
FOXEY
首都高速 情報
渋谷～台場
新宿～中野
交通安全週間 実施中
シートベルトを締めましょう
団地
COMPLEX
A-2

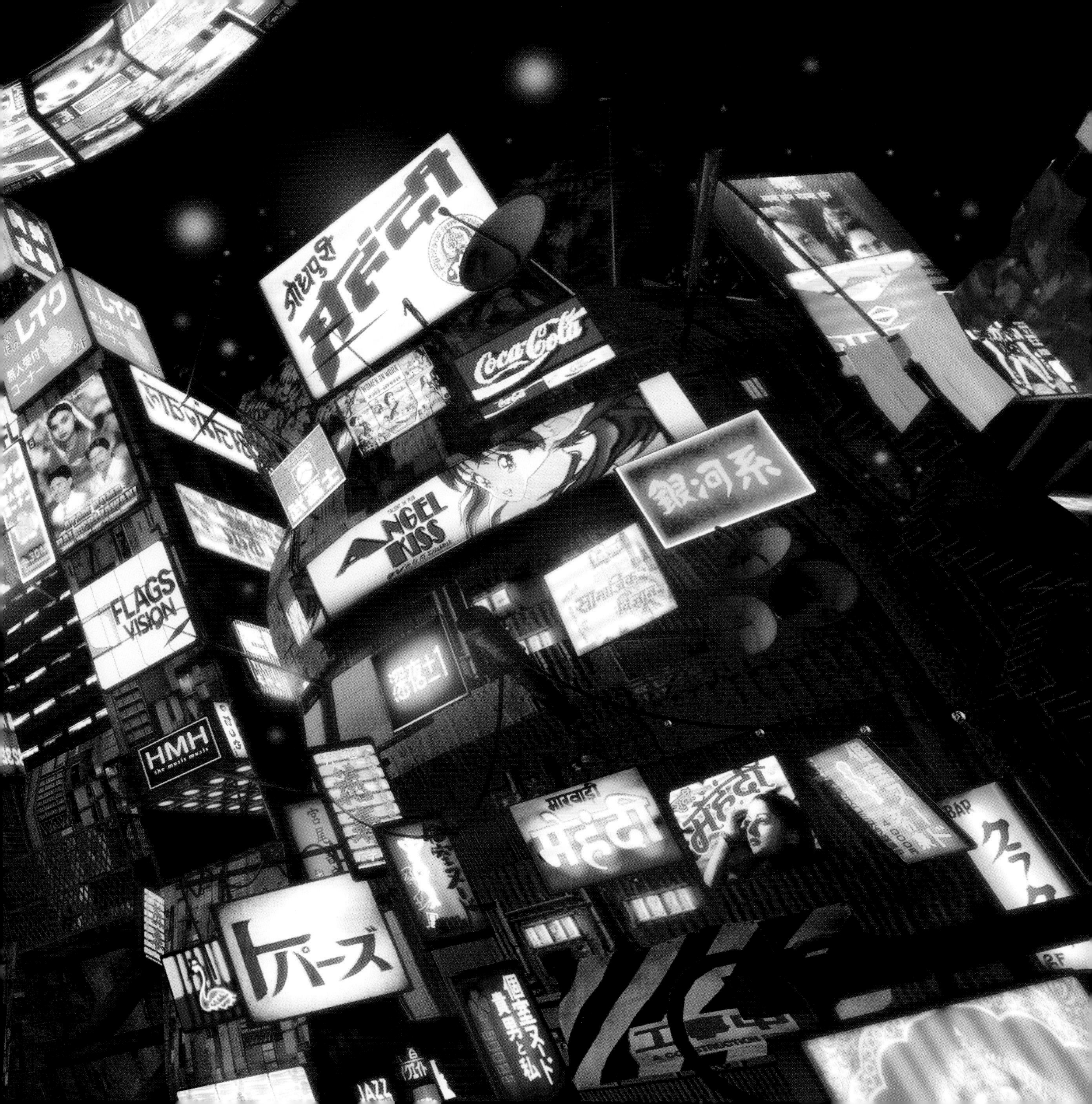

レイク
無人受付コーナー
Coca-Cola
WOMEN ON WORK
銀河系
ANGEL KISS
FLAGS VISION
深夜+1
HMH
the music music
मारवाड़ी
मेहंदी
BAR
トパーズ
個室ヌード
貴男と私
A CONSTRUCTION
JAZZ

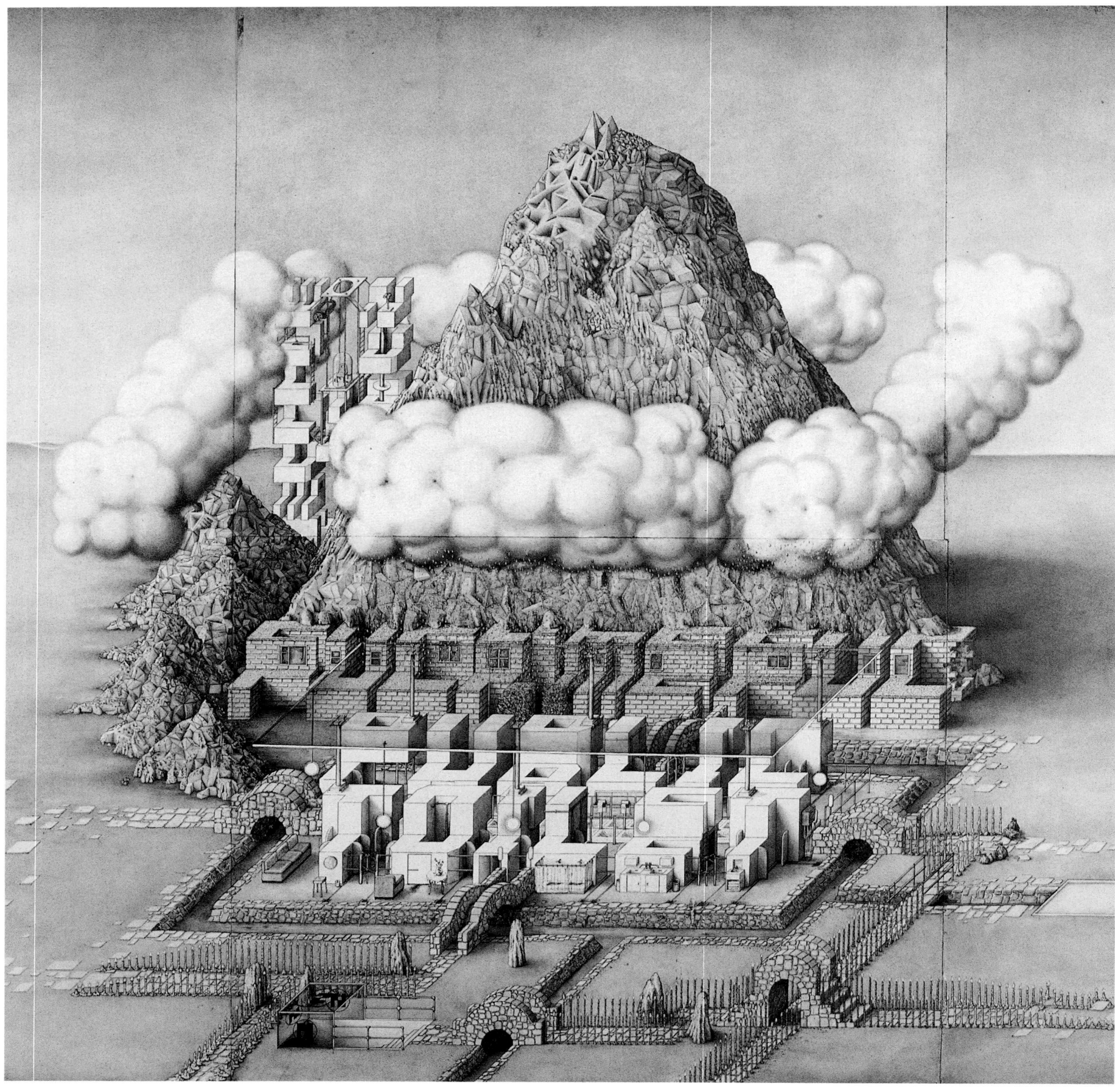

Alphabet City
Paul Noble

Paul Noble describes his work as 'an exercise in self-portraiture via town planning'. Nobson Newtown offers a vision of a community living under a cloud of dreary utilitarianism – all of the notional town's block-built monochrome buildings are constructed in the rigorously standardised shape of letters that spell out their function. Hundreds of large-scale drawings detail examples of Nobson's architecture, infrastructure and local geography: a job club, a prison, a light-industry plant, a quarry.

Noble's extensive narrative about the origins of his strangely unpopulated 'model' community describes how it was built on the site of an older town. Nobson is the product of a harshly literal knock-it-down-and-start-again school of planning, with facilities being decided on the basis of a survey of its citizens, carried out before existing buildings were demolished. The written account of Nobson Newtown's development acknowledges the extreme nature of this approach, suggesting that the plan was 'perhaps inspired by Nicolau Ceaucescu's single-mindedness in rebuilding Bucharest to accommodate his People's Palace'. With no enthusiasm to elect a government, Nobson ended up with no council offices or a town hall, and by unanimous vote, saved its former synagogue for conversion into a shopping mall. This building acts as a focus for Nobson's 'uncentre', a partially-derelict zone designed by the planners to express the residents' definition of their town as 'peripheral', and which by coincidence shares a real-life twin in Detroit. Paul Noble's project is marked by its use of architecture and planning as a metaphor in this way – with echoes of wry, Swiftian critiques of social and governmental planning. Taken together, the accumulation of antiseptic visions which make up Nobson Newtown seem to create a visual allegory warning of the dangers of allowing an excessively controlling individual vision to exercise itself on a community and the people that live in it. As the named architect of this urban scheme, Paul Noble awards himself 'Paul's Palace', a beachfront residence which is the only building in Nobson that looks as if it was designed for pleasure.

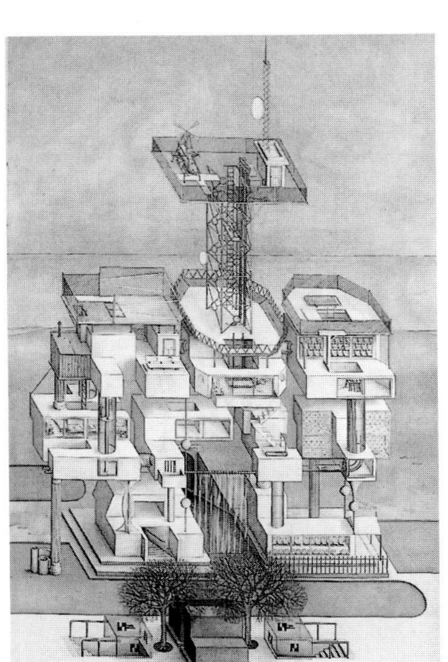

Opposite: *Public Toilet*, 1999. Above: *Dump*, 1997/8. Right: *Nobspital*, 1997/8. All pencil on paper. Courtesy Maureen Paley/Interim Art

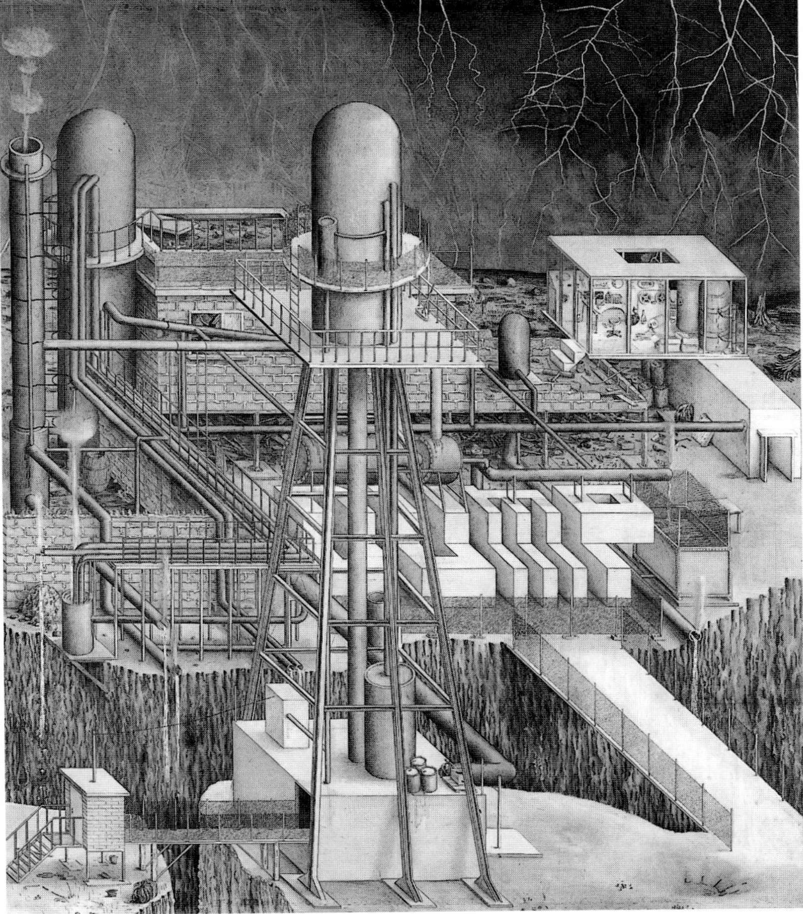

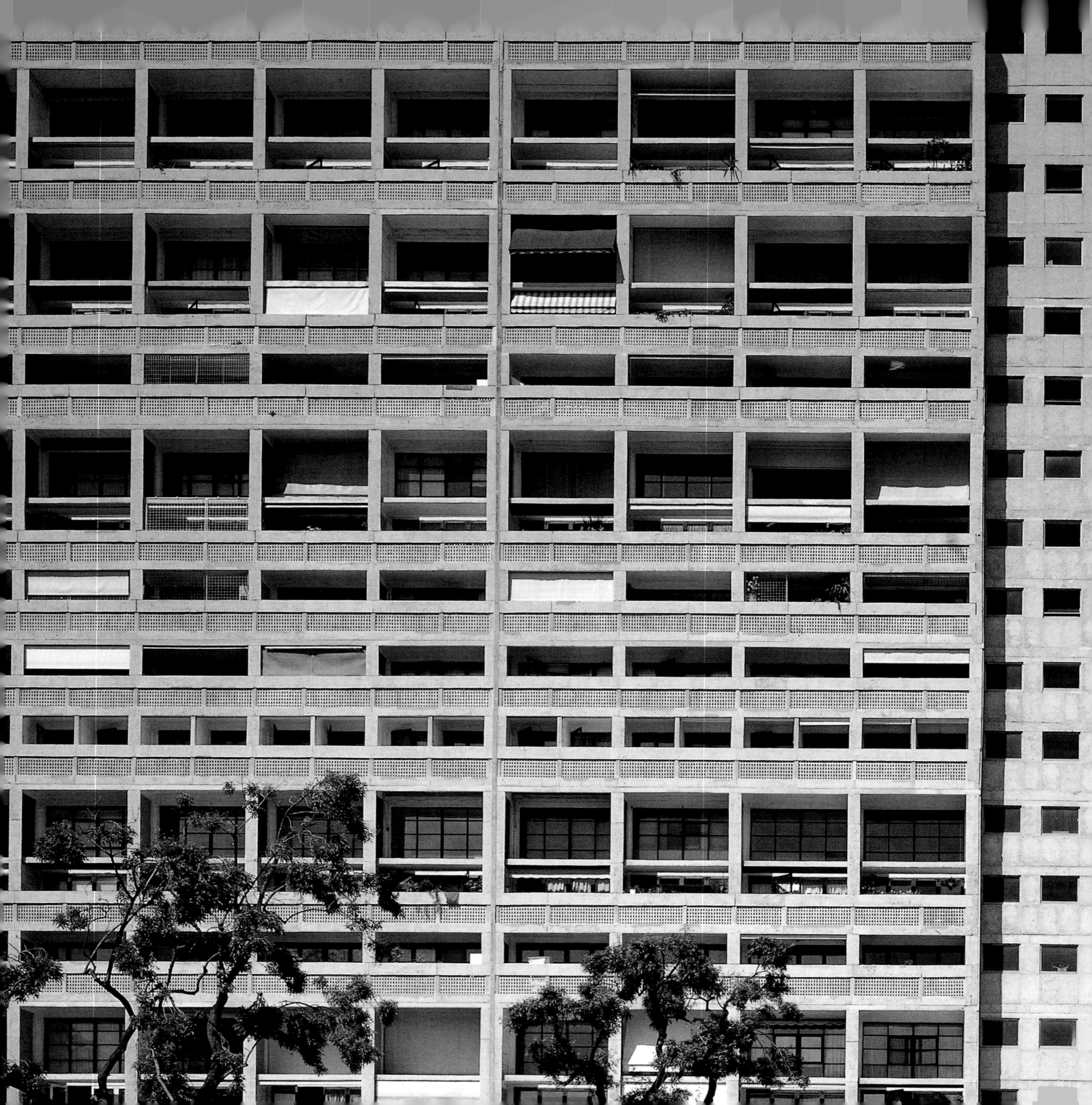

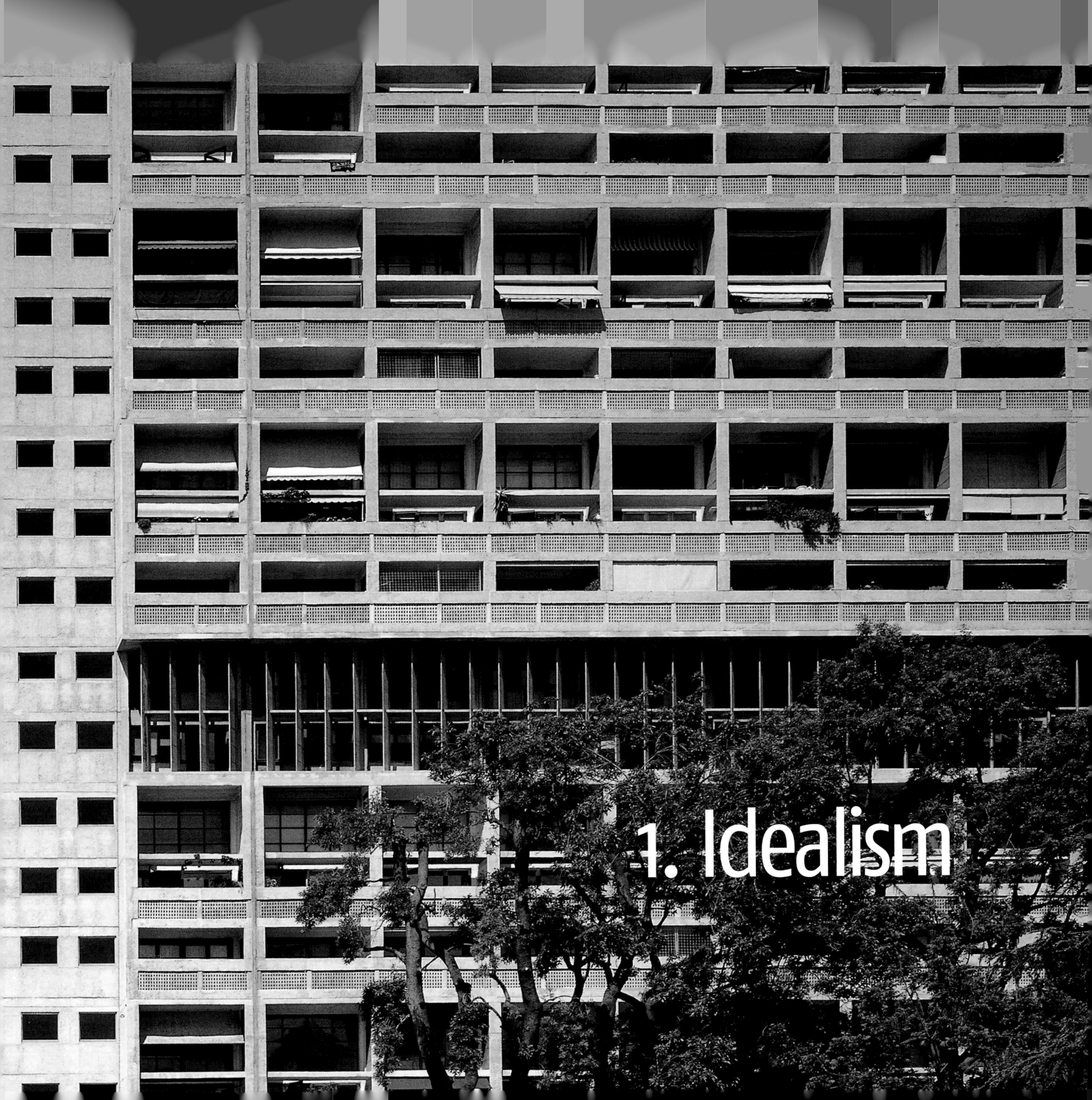

1. Idealism

Living together
Hilary French

'The house of a civilised people should convey something more than the callous commercialisation of the speculative builder, and should be arranged on some better principle than that which merely aims at crowding as many as possible into a given space.'[1]

The 'developers' semi' is a familiar sight throughout England – the two-storey, three-bedroom house, sitting in its own plot of land, with a garden front and back, 'detached' from its neighbours, can be spotted in countless dormitory towns and suburbs around the country. Its design has changed little in 100 years and, according to estate agents and developers, is set to remain unchanged for the foreseeable future, representing as it still does the favoured 'desirable residence' of many house buyers.

This ubiquitous twentieth-century phenomenon exists in sharp contrast to the ordered and dense rows of eighteenth and nineteenth-century terraced houses that make up large parts of most cities. However, ever since the idea of the individual 'family house' was first developed in the late-nineteenth century, questions have been raised as to the appropriateness of this type of housing for certain sections of the community. Alternatives such as communal houses, co-operatives and collectives have all been proposed by philanthropists and housing reformers, architects and town planners. Generally based on socialist principles, their schemes' claims for a healthier and better life are to be derived from satisfying the minimum or essential requirements of real need. Practical and social benefits for both the poor and for more affluent residents, as well as the financial benefits for property developers, house builders and financiers, have all been used to justify these ideas, driven as they are by changing economic and social circumstance. While very different from each other in philosophy and approach, the following ideas and proposals do have one thing in common: a desire to find a better way of 'living together'.

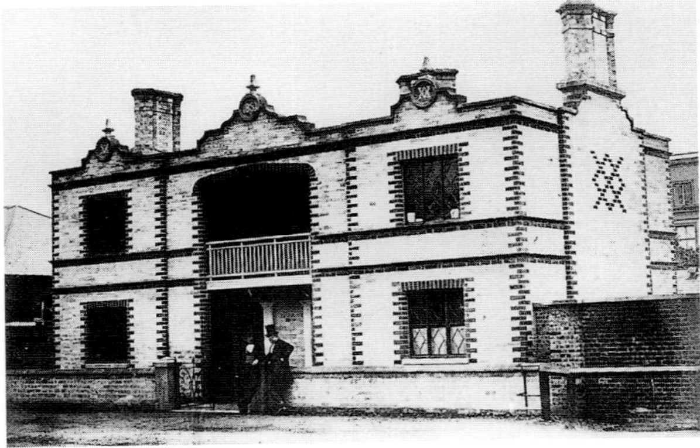

Henry Roberts' model cottages, above, were designed for the Great Exhibition of 1851, the first of the grand international fairs, whose impact on British culture reverberated for many decades after the Exhibition closed. Roberts' cottages were rebuilt in London's Kennington Park, where they remain today.

The Nineteenth Century

The images we have of London during the nineteenth century are grim: insanitary slum conditions aggravated by flooding, with rotting rubbish and excrement in the streets and a high incidence of disease, all the inevitable result of overcrowding due to rapid population growth. As people moved to the cities during the nineteenth century to be closer to industry and employment, the population of London grew from one million to six million; that of Manchester from 75,000 to 600,000, while Paris went from 500,000 to three million inhabitants. In America, growth was yet more dramatic: the population of New York expanded from 33,000 in 1801 to 3.5 million by 1901 while Chicago went from 300 people in the 1830s to two million by 1901. Legislation in the form of Public Health Acts was introduced to deal with rubbish collections, sewage disposal, water supply and maintenance of roadways, followed by Slum Clearance Acts and the Housing of the Working Classes Act (1890) to deal with provision of decent housing for the poor.

The debate about finding more suitable types of housing covered not only the question of how best to provide for the physical wellbeing of the poor, but also took their mental wellbeing into account – according to some, there was a question of morality to consider as well. In his essay 'Rookeries and Model Dwellings', Robin Evans suggests that the intention behind the first model cottages designed by Henry Roberts for the Great Exhibition of 1851 (now in Kennington Park in London) was to construct 'an introverted domesticity'[2]: a family-based social structure designed to keep people away from pubs and other gathering places and the temptations of drunkenness and debauchery – and away from each other. Surveys of living conditions at the time were shocking: in many cases, several families might be sharing one room, mixed sexes were sharing the same sleeping accommodation and there was freedom of movement between lodgings as 'the street doors are not always kept closed'[3], the implication being that such disorder and unhealthy proximity would not only breed disease but also lead to corruption of the mind and a lowering of moral standards.

Henry Roberts' new model dwellings established the idea of the single family house as a regulated domestic unit. In contrast to the usual three- or four-storey houses with one or more families per floor, the new models divided and organised in order to provide each family unit with their own separate dwelling and their own front door. Dwellings were grouped in pairs, two per floor, with access via an external staircase for improved ventilation. This theme of separation and containment was further emphasised within the dwelling itself: in addition to the living space and scullery/kitchen, there are three bedrooms – one for the parents and the two others to allow children of different sexes to sleep in separate rooms. Each bedroom can be entered without having to pass through one of the others, while the parents' room is accessible from the scullery to provide further privacy from the children. The children's rooms are accessed directly from the living room, making it easier for parents to watch over their offspring. The novel level of privacy afforded by having separate rooms and the careful consideration given to their interconnection was completed by the use of hollow brick construction specifically to reduce the transmission of noise between the dwellings.

Any suggestion that people who were used to living in just one room (and claimed to prefer it that way) would consider having two living rooms and three bedrooms an unnecessary luxury was heavily criticised by the housing reformers. They firmly believed that improving the living conditions of the poor by providing them with decent housing would serve as an education in itself, and would encourage people to develop better ideas about their preferences when it came to living arrangements.

Co-operative Housekeeping and Associated Homes

In contrast to more outlandish earlier communitarian schemes such as Fourier's Phalanstères in France, or Robert

The French social philosopher Charles Fourier (1772–1837) created one of the first communitarian schemes dedicated to improving standards of living and working. A lithograph of his plan for communities that he called *phalanstères*, right, was made in 1848. It was a key inspiration for the schemes devised fifty years later by Robert Owen in New Lanark, Scotland. Each of Fourier's living units was designed to house 400 families in buildings which surrounded communal open space.

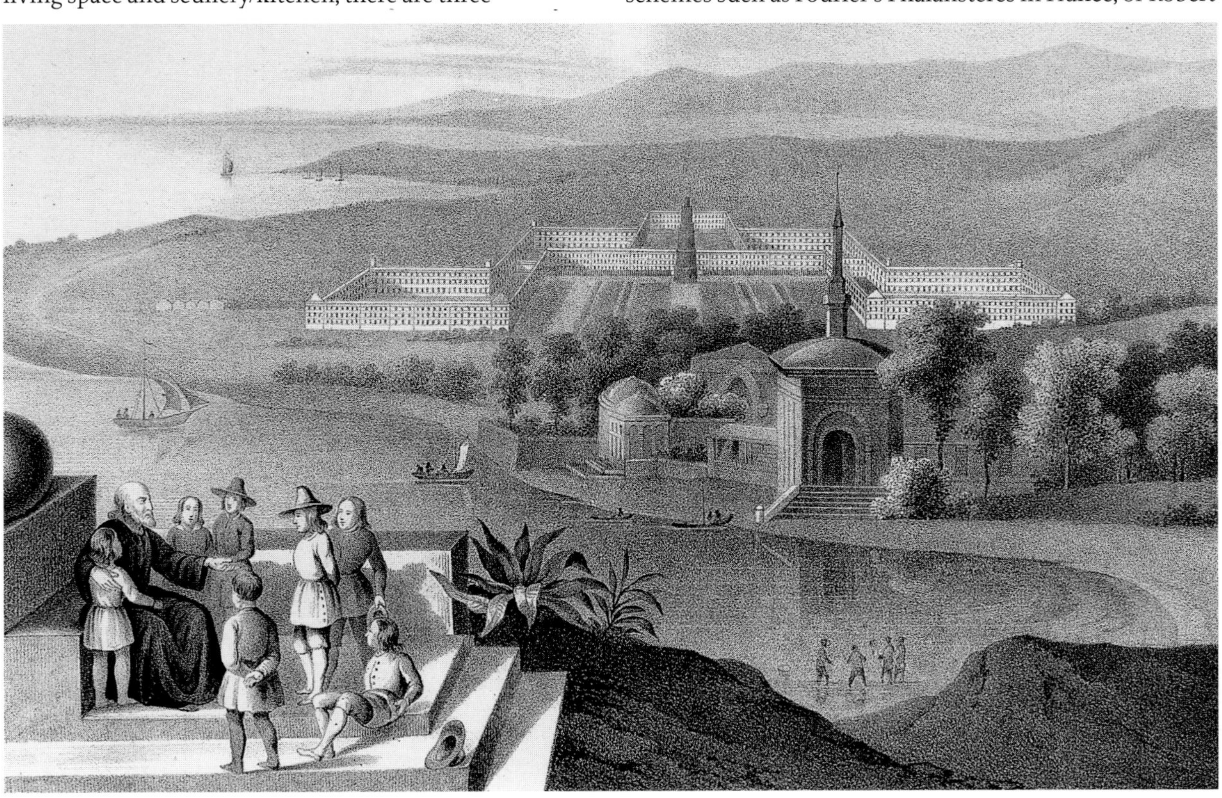

New Lanark

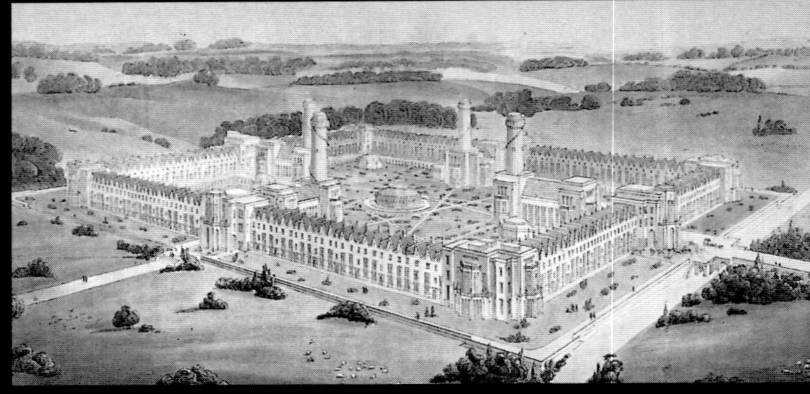

Robert Owen was one of the first social reformers of the industrial age. He held a passionate belief that all people could be improved by education that led not only to the creation of the progressive community of New Lanark in Scotland, but also to plans for a series of ideal communities which he hoped to build all over the United States.

From as early as 1810, while he was the owner of the New Lanark cotton mills in Scotland, below right, Owen was developing a plan for an ideal community. In the midst of the Industrial Revolution, Owen was campaigning for social and educational reforms, and in particular for changes to the working hours of children. When Owen purchased control of it from his father-in-law, the mill was employing around 3,000 people, with children as young as five years old working for thirteen hours a day. He immediately stopped employing children under ten and reduced their maximum daily labour to ten hours. The young children were sent to infant schools that Owen built – the first of their kind in Britain, and practising Owen's 'rational approach' to education. Some years later, in 1816, he opened the New Institution for the Formation of Character, a community education centre for the adult factory workers. Convinced that if he created the right environment he could produce rational, good and humane people, Owen pioneered ideas in management, education and human relations which were to become commonplace in twentieth-century post-industrial societies.

At the time, however, Owen's ideas were considered revolutionary, and he was forced to borrow money to buy out several of his business partners who remained convinced that his practices would reduce profits. In an attempt to persuade others to follow his example, Owen published two books, spent thousands of pounds promoting them, and sent detailed proposals to Parliament about his ideas. This resulted in an appearance before Robert Peel and an incredulous House of Commons committee in 1816, whose questions to Owen made clear their mistrust of his approach:

Committee: If you do not employ children under ten, what would you do with them?
Owen: Instruct them, and give them exercise.
Committee: Would there be a danger of their acquiring, by that time, vicious habits, for want of regular occupation?
Owen: My own experiences lead me to say, that I found quite the reverse. Their habits have been good in proportion to the extent of their instruction.
Committee: Will you state who supports the schools?
Owen: The schools are supported immediately at the expense of the establishment; they are indeed literally and truly (through surplus profits) supported by the people themselves

Not surprisingly perhaps, Owen found it hard to convince many in Britain of his ideas, and disappointed with the response to his proselytising, eventually turned his attention to the United States. In 1825 he purchased an area in Indiana for £30,000 and made plans for a new community there called New Harmony.

Since 1817, Owen had been recommending a plan to gather the poor into communities of around 1000 people and to house them in self-contained square building clusters measuring about 300 metres along each side surrounded by generous amounts of land. In the 1820s Owen's friend, the architect Thomas Stedman Whitwell prepared drawings, above, of the proposed community, and when plans to purchase the site in Indiana gathered pace, Whitwell travelled to Washington DC, where he made a presentation on Owen's behalf to President John Quincy Adams, with the proposal that such model villages be universally adopted in society.

In the end, New Harmony was never built, and Robert Owen ended his days in Britain. His influence on socialism (Owen receives a rather grudging mention in the Communist Manifesto by Marx and Engels), trades unionism and not least the Garden Cities Movement, however, were to outlive him by at least a century.

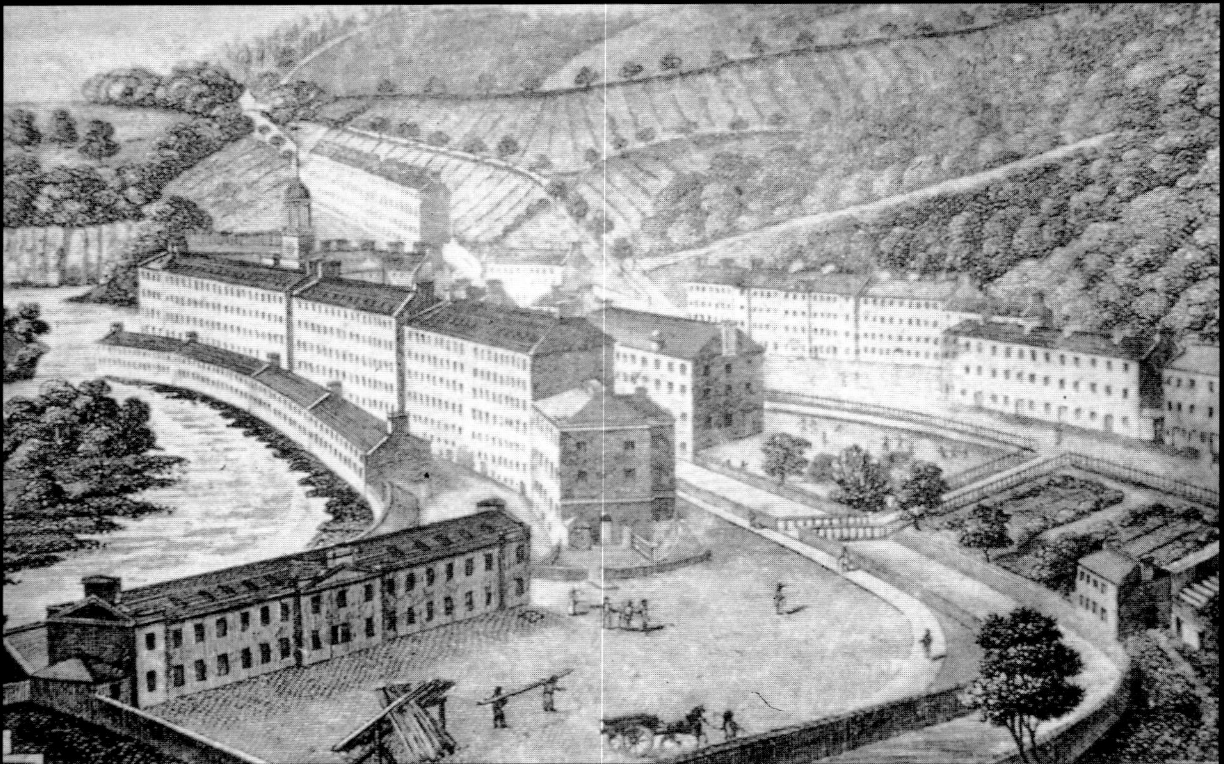

Owen's New Lanark, Raymond Unwin's (1863–1940) visions for 'happier and healthier living' at Letchworth Garden City were expected to be a real step forward in socialist housing reform. (For a detailed discussion of the Garden City Movement, see p.102). Along with growing urbanisation, the role of working women in society was changing rapidly. Educated women demanded more political and economic independence, and in a growing capitalist economy, the new opportunities for waged work in factories were far more appealing to young working women than the domestic positions that would have been their only option previously. The fact that fewer women were opting for domestic service affected the affluent families who employed them, and 'the servant question' became an important issue for feminists. For Mrs Emily King, a feminist activist, co-operative housekeeping and communal living arrangements were not only a housing solution for growing numbers of independent single women. Writing in *The Building News* in 1874, she stated that communal living would deal effectively with the shortage of domestic servants while also giving servants the 'chance of gaining, by any energy or talent they may possess a superior position in life'.[4] Her proposal for an Associated Home, with designs by the well-known architect EW Godwin (1833–86), was to have benefits not just for those who lived there, but was to represent a fundamental social reform.[5] The home she proposed is an alternative to the family house, which she describes as 'a more clumsy and costly arrangement... kept up at the expense of considerable injustice to one portion of the household.' The most obvious advantages to her scheme are that while the families enjoy the privacy of living in their own apartments, they still benefit from the economical provision for their daily needs made possible by communal living. Further advantages afforded by having a sufficient number of people available in one scheme lie in the increased opportunities for social and intellectual companionship, as well as in the scope for shared care and education of the children.

While the advantages of co-operative housekeeping are obvious – reducing the need for individual cooks, cleaners and laundry maids must save money – this makes up only half of Mrs Emily King's proposed solution to the problem of 'the servant question'. If servants were to 'go out to work' like others, they needed skills – skills which could only be gained through instruction and practice. The Associated Home could provide the perfect training ground where 'pupils or apprentices, both in cooking and housework could be taken in [...] and parents should pay for their daughters' instruction in these trades, as they now pay for their sons' in their trades.' Accommodation for servants other than a manageress and gardener is not included, and Mrs King goes further in suggesting that servants should be housed in their own Associated Homes, and go out to work for others in shifts as they would in any other type of employment. Her fundamental concern is that issues such as housekeeping, cooking and the care of children would continue to be overlooked by 'the masculine mind'. She describes the Associated Home as a 'means of pleasant and elevating social intercourse' between people of different ages and sexes; when different members of a family want to pursue different interests, living in an Associated Home would mean that 'every individual might be gratified and meet their different coteries by walking only the length of a passage'.

America and the Belief in Technology

At around the same time in the United States, feminists saw the benefits of communal living and co-operative housekeeping in the light of developing the organisation and management of the domestic environment, and not necessarily solely in relation to single or working women. In contrast perhaps to the view in England, which looked back to a medieval past as a model for the future development of towns, Americans saw the industrial city in an optimistic light – a productive and well-served community. The urban environment had changed dramatically: transport systems, water and sewerage systems, and the introduction of gas and eventually electricity had greatly improved the city. Feminists were confident that the new technologies that had so advanced the outside environment of the city would eventually reach the domestic environment.

The feminist historian Dolores Hayden quotes WL George to illustrate their enthusiasm and optimism: 'The feminist flat is revolutionary, strikes at the root of the economic system, may involve vast readjustments of land tenure, communal building and taxation. But we are not afraid of revolution, for we are the pioneers of a sex revolution.'[6] Feminists Melusina Fay Pierce and Charlotte Perkins Gilman advocated co-operative housekeeping and experimental housing schemes like the quadrangles of Unwin and Parker in England, but without financial backing most schemes remained unbuilt. The only similar developments were the bungalow courts, such as Bowen Court in Los Angeles built in 1910. Single-storey, individual houses are arranged around a central shared courtyard. It is assumed that the women living in the development would still do their own housework, but would use the central laundry building and the sewing room at the upper level which overlooks the children's playground. This scheme also included a double unit, whereby a doorway in the party wall between two units would enable a husband and wife to enjoy 'separate establishments'.

In 1919 Charles H Whittaker, editor of the *Journal of the American Institute of Architects*, called for architects to 'restudy the house itself as an industrial establishment where every unnecessary step and all useless labour are to be eliminated' and concluded with the question 'shall we dare to predict, then, that the ideal house of the future will be kitchenless?'[7] Communal kitchens had become commonplace during the war and cooked food services, dining clubs and cooperative housekeeping schemes flourished for a time. But despite support from journals and magazines, the revolution never came. Whilst Whittaker and his colleagues at the Regional Planning Association of America lobbied for state finance for building, and developed designs for workers' housing based on the Garden City Movement, speculative developers and house builders in the cities saw other opportunities: the development of the apartment house.

Enthusiasts believed that new technology, even in its most simple application, could revolutionise the apartment block. Alongside the recently introduced elevators, new equipment like gas stoves, refrigerators, electric suction vacuum cleaners, dishwashers and washing machines already in use in commercial concerns such as hotels, restaurants and commercial laundries could all be exploited in apartment blocks. Progress in heating and ventilating equipment and the ingenuity of the Pullman Dining Car kitchens encouraged an enthusiasm for the application of such technology to housing, leading for a short time to a fashion for complex gadgetry and an inventiveness in space planning. The resulting wave of 'Condensed Apartments', or 'Kitchenette Apartments' as they were sometimes called, were to solve the housing crisis, abolish housework and deal with the servant problem all at once! The reality was, of course, rather different. Basically the condensed apartment was just that, a very small apartment consisting of two rooms: one room a living room that doubles as a bedroom, complete with a bath and dressing closet, and the other a very small kitchen and breakfast room.

In addition to offering residents a complete escape from menial tasks, these apartments would provide a whole range of services extending to those normally associated with hotels. They were of great interest to developers and landlords, who could almost double the occupation of a block with such small dwellings and hence obtain vastly increased rental incomes. These schemes were, however, not popular with the building authorities, whose insistence on windows for bathrooms in residential accommodation restricted space planning possibilities. The design of the kitchenette, which included a range, sink and cabinet, was intricately detailed. Most importantly, it backed onto the wall of a service closet which was accessible from the corridor, allowing access from both sides. This cupboard was divided into three compartments, for rubbish, milk and parcels or groceries, and the access via the service corridor meant deliveries could be left without disturbing the residents, or when they were out. A clerk organised regular distribution of goods throughout the block, and ice could also be placed in the refrigerator from the rear, without having to enter the apartment. The janitor collected rubbish from the same service cupboard, where it was placed in waxed paper bags issued to the tenants, before dropping it into a chute (which doubled as the flue) into a furnace at basement level. Ventilation ducts were served a hood over the range as well as the internal dressing closet.

In the 1920s it was still almost unthinkable to entertain in the bedroom, and therefore of all the new equipment these apartments contained, the 'disappearing bed' as it was described was seen as most crucial to their success. Buildings such as The Surf Apartment Hotel and the Wrightwood Apartments in Chicago made use of collapsible beds of several different sizes that could first be folded and then pivoted into a closet, meaning one room could serve as both bedroom and living room. The use of the 'disappearing bed' was expected to spread to commercial hotels, and it was suggested that they could even be used in inexpensive summer cottages to deal with peak loading. An enthusiastic reviewer in the *Architectural Forum* suggests that these devices could even be used in small suburban houses, saying that they would not only be ideal for the studio apartment but also a perfect cost-cutting solution for institutions that need to house a large number of personnel and their wives.

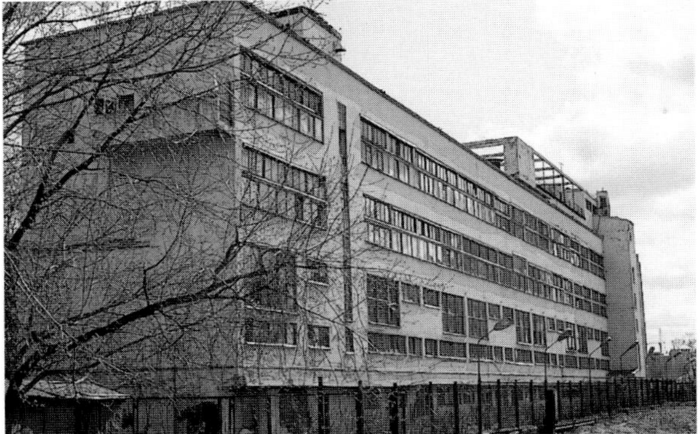

One of the earliest built projects to use the F Type split-level duplex system is Mosei Ginsburg's Narkomfin apartment house in Moscow, above, completed in 1930 and still in use today.

However, it became impossible to maintain the promised level of services and at the same time keep the rents at a realistic level. With little to recommend them visually or spatially, these apartments never had the appeal of the 'simple life' proposed by Baillie Scott (characterised by the Arts and Crafts, rustic open plan approach), nor of the more stylish version that was still to come – the modern, 'minimum dwelling'.

Modernism and the Commune House

During the 1920s and 1930s the ideas of the Garden City Movement were taken up all over Europe and in America. In Russia, in 1919, garden cities were designed near Saratov, Smolensk and Moscow. With no hierarchy of building types, they were considered legitimate models for an egalitarian society. However, in contrast to the feminist movement in the United States, the Russian state saw the liberation of women as part of intended social change. The political equality of women necessitated reform of the education and welfare systems, and women's economic independence, growing with their increasing participation in the labour force, was necessary to continuing industrialisation. A reassessment of the traditional family in social and economic terms was a necessary part of the transition to an egalitarian society. The seeds of the idea of the commune-house may have started when workers were resettled in the nationalised large houses and villas of the overthrown bourgeoisie, where several families would share one big kitchen and use the spacious entrance hall as the communal living room. The value of this initially accidental arrangement, however, was adopted by the new regime expecting housing to play an important part in

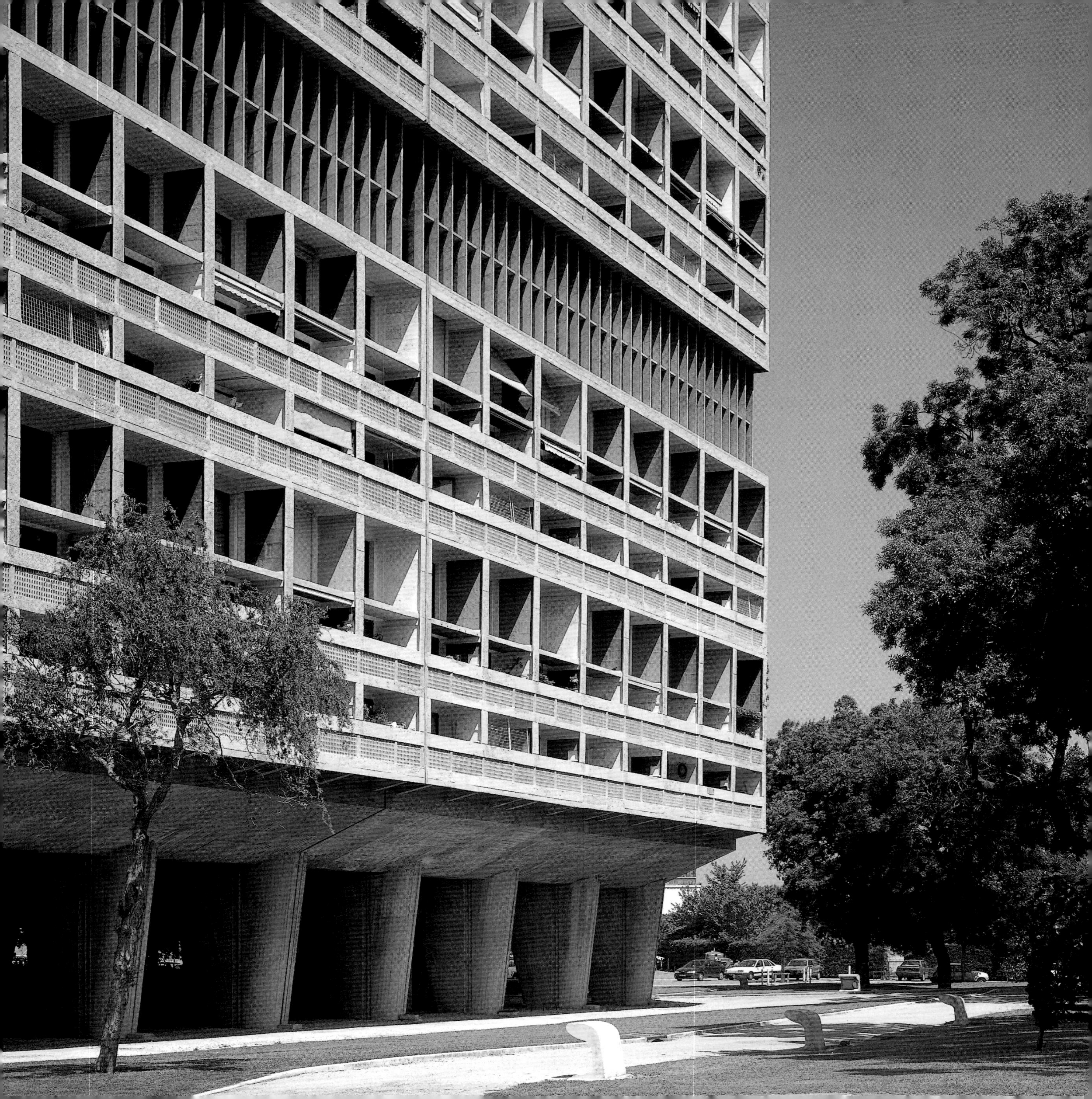

changing behaviour and consciousness. Indeed, the family as an economic unit was to cease, to be replaced with the collective economic unity. In terms of housing, therefore, each individual would need only a small private space for sleeping, reading and a sex life, all of which could easily be provided by one room. Everything else could be taken care of in communal facilities. By taking over such 'family' responsibilities, the state believed that the domestic space it provided would offer a secure environment that encouraged contentment, physical comfort and intellectual development.

Ideas and proposals for a new modern architecture that 'must legalise and crystallise the new social mode of living'[8] were taken up by a group of leading young architects, the Society of Contemporary Architects (OSA), or Constructivists, and published in their journal *SA* between 1926 and 1930. Their belief in a world of happiness and equality was based on change: a combination of trust in social progress and reliance on Western technology. As Modernists, they believed that architecture could be arrived at via an objective scientific approach, through analysis of need and functional requirements. They employed social science techniques such as user surveys to develop briefs, but loaded questions such as 'What is your opinion about communal food preparation which will free women from domestic labour?' made the desired answers very clear.[9]

A design by one member of the group, Mosei Ginsburg (1892–1946), that was published in *SA* and exhibited in OSA's headquarters in 1927, became the basis for future work on the development of designs for communal living. The scheme consisted of 'duplexes', two-storey apartments with two bedrooms, one above the other, adjoining a double-height living space that could be used as one unit or two. It also included a full range of carefully considered, socialised functions. A kindergarten at ground floor level allowed easy access both to the garden and for parents picking up and dropping off their children on their way in and out of the building. The dining rooms and reading rooms were at roof level, where terraces could be used in warm weather. Ginsburg went on to become Head of the Standardisation Section of the Construction Committee for the Russian Republic, where he designed a series of standard dwelling types which could be speedily prefabricated and built wherever housing was needed. The F Type, a split-level scheme similar to his earlier project, with a sleeping mezzanine within a double height volume, was the most popular. The Narkomfin apartment house in Moscow built in 1928–30, one of the earliest developments to use the F Type, is still in use today. Like Ginsburg's earlier scheme, there are two blocks, one containing the dwelling units, the other the communal

Le Corbusier's iconic Unité d'Habitation in Marseille, opposite and below right, arranges apartments according to the F Type split-level duplex system devised by Mosei Ginsburg in 1927 (although Le Corbusier's own 1922 studies for the Ville Contemporaine also clearly prefigure this approach). Each two-storey apartment has two bedrooms, one above the other, adjoining a double-height living space.

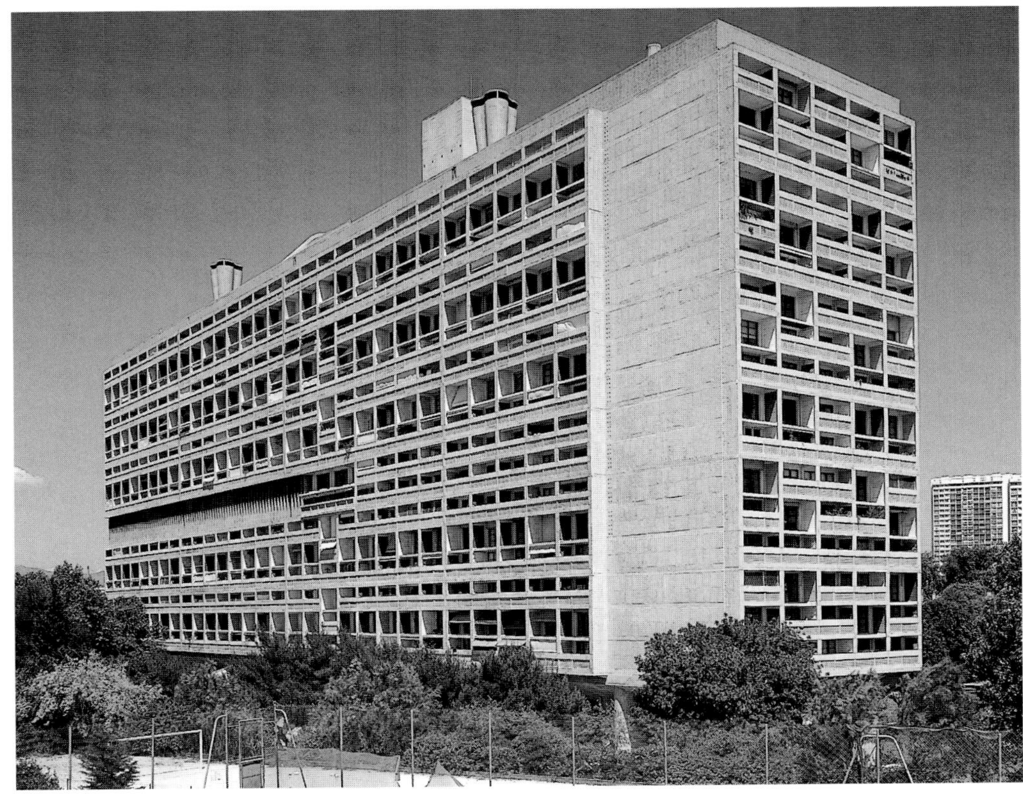

Built in 1934, the Lawn Road Flats were an attempt to bring the Modernist ideal of the communal house to London. The 'minimum apartments' designed by Wells Coates for Isokon Ltd are notable for their space-saving built-in furniture and open-plan layouts, below and opposite, as well as for the services available to residents, such as a laundry and a restaurant. During his stay at the building in 1935–36, Marcel Breuer designed the Isobar. This in-house bar and dining room, with its Breuer-designed plywood tables, was later run by Philip Harben, who became famous as Britain's first TV chef. Other notable guests included Walter and Ise Gropius.

facilities, such as kitchen, canteen, meeting rooms, and kindergarten. The different design types were published in 1929 and used in many other housing developments across Russia, Georgia, Azerbaijan and the Ukraine. The 'transitional' housing unit – so called because it was part of the 'transition to a new socially superior way of life' – became a fashionable model for European intellectuals. The most well-known application of the F Type is Le Corbusier's Unités d'Habitation built at Marseilles (1949), Nimes (1952), Nantes (1955) and in Berlin (1958).

In England, the best known version of the Modernist commune-house is the block of flats in Lawn Road, London, built by Wells Coates for Isokon in 1934. The four-storey block contains 22 one-room flats with external gallery access, plus staff accommodation for a manageress and garage space for eight cars. Most importantly, the scheme included centralised services such as a laundry and kitchen. All flats were supplied with central heating and constant hot water and additional services for the residents included bed-making, shoe polishing, the collection of rubbish and distribution of laundry. Meals could also be ordered and sent up to the flats. It was the perfect example of the 'minimum dwelling', which had been the subject of the second CIAM (Congress International de l'Architecture Moderne) in Frankfurt in 1929. At its completion, the *Architectural Review* praised the design for its efficient use of space and particularly for the built-in furniture and fittings. The minimal dwellings provided the ideal accommodation for single people with few possessions and no ties. More closely resembling college accommodation, it became popular with young intellectuals in the same way that the Russian commune-houses had. Despite the fact that the Isokon's communal kitchen lasted only two years, the value of the scheme lay, according to Nicholas Pevsner at the 21st birthday party for the building, in its message: 'The gist of the manifesto in this case is to get down to the essentials of living without the compromises with convention'.[10]

Recent Years

Modern movement ideas relating to housing of any kind had little influence in England until the Council building programmes of the 1960s. The New Towns programme, started in 1946 for satellite developments around London, were based on Garden City principles. By the early 1950s, houses in New Towns such as Crawley or Stevenage were little different from the models developed by Parker and Unwin at Hampstead. The idea that the application of science and technology could improve living conditions was still pervasive – the technology that had inspired many of the communal houses and co-operative homes had been adapted to produce a whole range of household appliances and 'labour saving' devices and, in addition, terms such as 'domestic science' and 'home economics' had been introduced in an attempt to improve the image of the work involved. In the pursuit of efficiency, time and motion studies, famously developed in Germany with Ernst May's laboratory-like Frankfurt Kitchen in 1925, were applied not only on the factory floor but to housework.

In 1954, the Building Research Establishment, who might usually be expected to test different construction methods or new building materials, carried out an experiment on housework. A mock-up of a fairly ordinary house was built at the BRE and used by a sample of ten volunteer housewives for a week each. Their activities were observed minutely, carefully monitored and analysed in some detail. How many times they went up and down stairs, how many times they went through various doorways and how much time they spent on different tasks such as tending the living room fire, cooking or making beds, were all noted and measured. The *RIBA Journal*[11] published the results of the experiment, complete with coded diagrams and charts: the picture conjured up is one of relentless drudgery and tedium. Although no firm conclusions were drawn from the study, it was expected that the information would be used by architects and designers and incorporated into their designs, thus

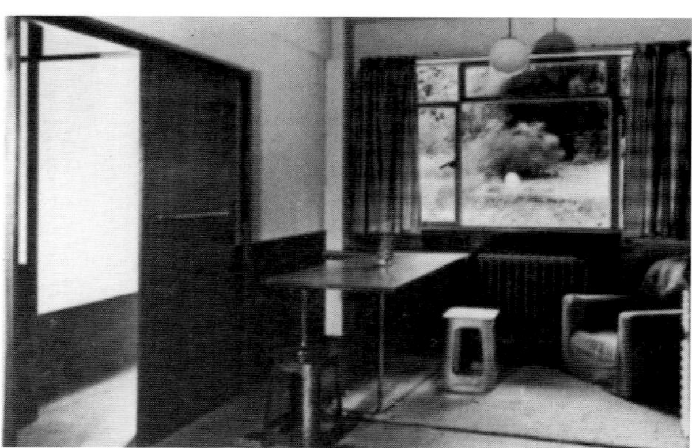

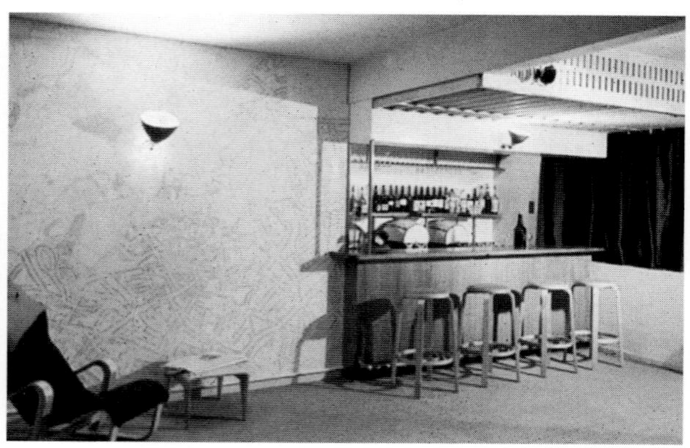

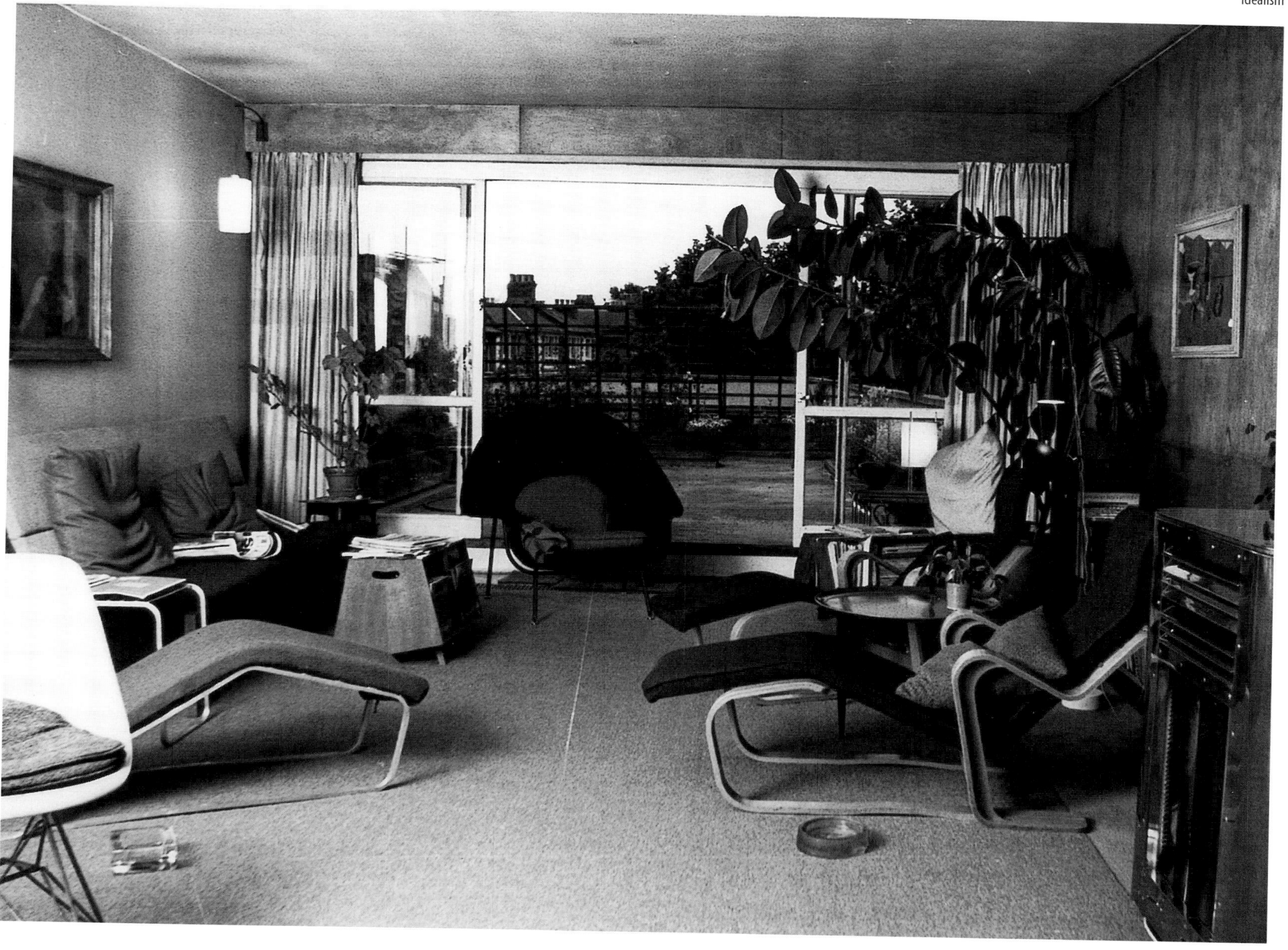

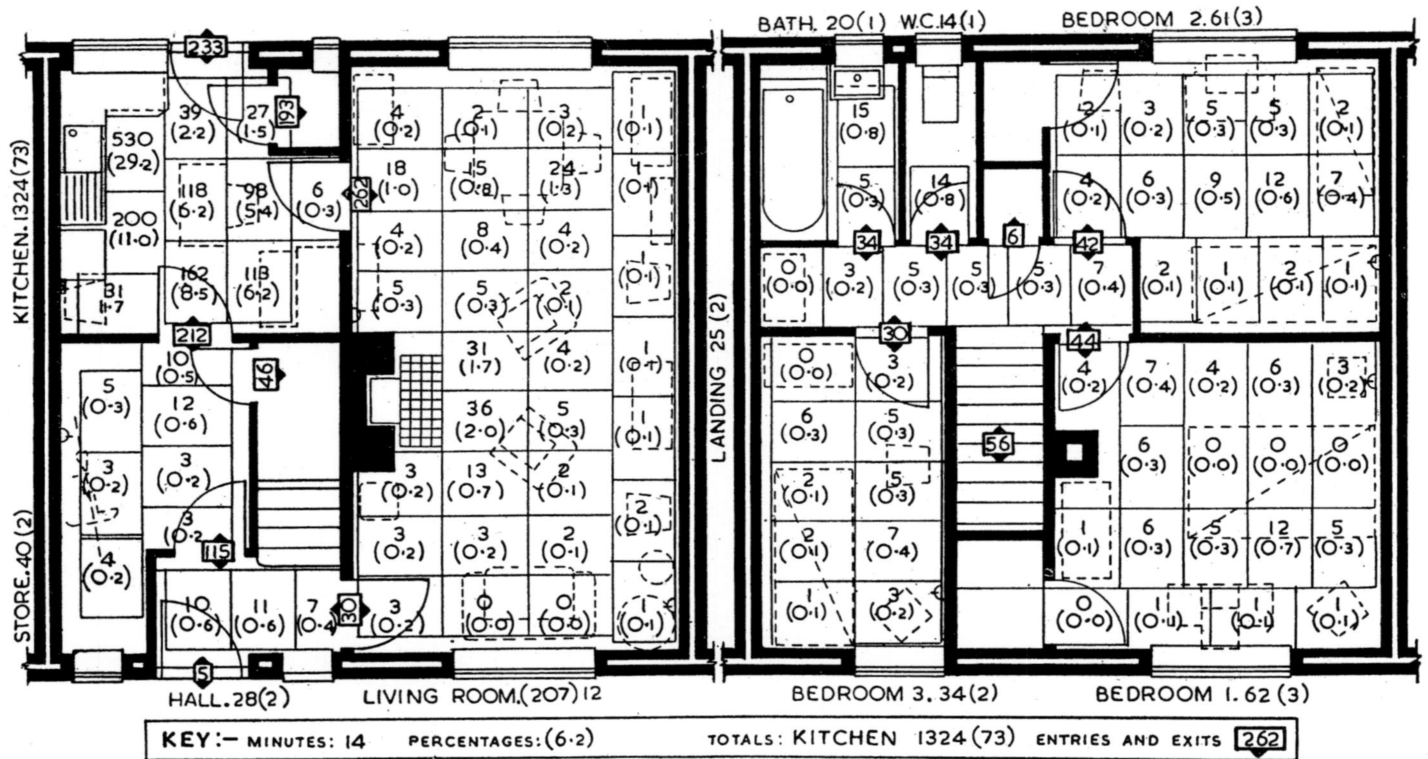
BATH. 20(1) W.C.14(1)
BEDROOM 2.61(3)
KITCHEN. 1324(73)
LANDING 25 (2)
STORE.40(2)
HALL.28(2)
LIVING ROOM.(207)12
BEDROOM 3. 34(2)
BEDROOM 1. 62 (3)
KEY:– MINUTES: 14 PERCENTAGES: (6·2) TOTALS: KITCHEN 1324 (73) ENTRIES AND EXITS 262

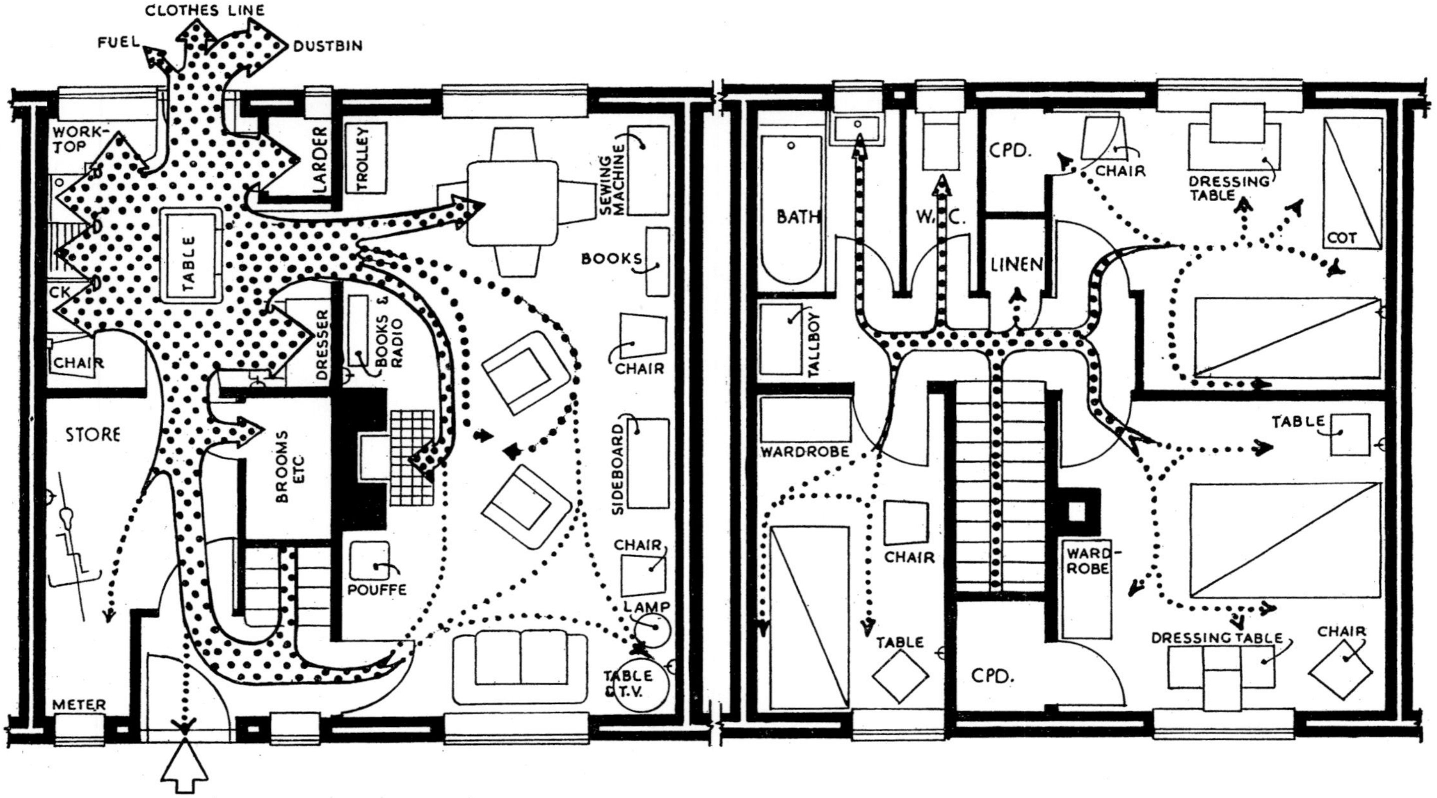

CLOTHES LINE
FUEL
DUSTBIN
WORK-TOP
LARDER
TROLLEY
SEWING MACHINE
TABLE
BOOKS
CK
CHAIR
DRESSER
BOOKS & RADIO
CHAIR
STORE
BROOMS ETC
SIDEBOARD
CHAIR
POUFFE
LAMP
TABLE & T.V.
METER
BATH
W.C.
CPD.
CHAIR
DRESSING TABLE
COT
LINEN
TALLBOY
WARDROBE
TABLE
CHAIR
WARD-ROBE
TABLE
CPD.
DRESSING TABLE
CHAIR

A 1954 Building Research Establishment experiment on the nature of housework might have promised an intriguing insight into daily life. Instead, the detailed analysis, opposite, of housewives' movement through a specially mocked-up house, painted a picture of remarkable tedium. Even hopes that the experiment would lead to better-planned interiors proved unfounded, as the conservative planners of Britain's new towns argued against the need for fundamental changes in the layout of homes.

improving the housewife's life and presumably that of her husband and children.

However, an article in *Town and Country Planning* in 1956 makes it clear that little would change. The article is based on an address given to the Council for Scientific Management in the Home by Sir Thomas Bennett, Chairman of the Crawley New Town Development Corporation, entitled 'The Extent to which the Requirements of Household work are considered in New Town Planning'. It is clear from the outset that the speaker holds a somewhat conservative position. When describing the factors that are important when making decisions about housing types, as well as mentioning obvious factors such as land use and costs he adds as a third consideration – 'the national preference for the type of dwelling'. Flats and single storey houses, he asserts, whilst having obvious advantages when it comes to housework and maintenance, are not acceptable because 'You cannot get away from the national preference for two-storey houses'. He also tells us that a survey of the preferences of single women undertaken to discover whether building self-contained 'bed-sitting-room' flats would be worthwhile resulted in a decision not to build the planned apartments. After initial enthusiasm, 'girl after girl pointed out the advantages of living as a lodger', which included mending being done by the landlady and the provision of meals at weekends as well as 'the ironing of frocks and blouses'. The only positive note in Bennett's address is his reference to a recent change in demand for two living rooms rather than one, brought about, he presumes, by the diverse activities of different members of the family, with 'some of the family listening to the wireless, children with homework to do, an adolescent studying, a courting couple who want to be segregated, even father who wants quiet to do his pools'.

Along with the general cleaning and laundry, in the 1950s the provision of food is seen as a major chore. While Bennett accepts changes in the arrangement of living rooms in order to accommodate new patterns of use, the idea of increasing the size of the kitchen to allow for dining space, or of providing the kitchen as a part of a living room, is heavily criticised as 'primitive', regardless of the fact that this approach could reduce housework and make watching over children easier. The reason given in this case is that 'In this country we have always looked to the upper classes to set our standards, and they do not live in kitchens.'[12] Again according to Bennett's informal survey, some women produced as many as six different meals every evening, starting with teas for school children at 4.30pm, followed by several supper-time meals for different age groups before ending with hot milk at 11.00pm for those returning from evening classes. Bennett's response to this heavy workload and scheduling nightmare is to suggest providing a door between the kitchen and the dining room! The subject of class is mentioned again when he states that unlike their less-privileged counterparts, middle-class women prefer serving hatches – they do not need the benefits that an open-plan or eat-in kitchen could offer, as the middle-class woman would 'manage her day rather better and she does not have these overlapping arrangements with which so often the wage-earning woman has to deal'.

Contrary to the view of social reformers in the 1850s – that improved living conditions should be provided because they would, eventually, improve behaviour – Bennett concludes that people should be provided with what they are used to: i.e. a two-storey house with two reception rooms, three bedrooms and just one bathroom. He even considers a second bathroom unnecessary as it would add to the burden of cleaning. Most shocking is that the housewife was expected to carry out all the domestic work: any idea that a different environment would promote changes in behaviour – even one as minor as children or men learning to clean a bathroom – is not considered.

One housing scheme built ten years later, in 1966, does demonstrate how it was possible to be more adventurous both socially and architecturally. The Cockaigne housing group was started by Michael Baily, a sociologist, who set out specifically to 'create a new initiative in housing design, in contrast to the existing providers of new homes... who seem to compete with each other in turning out houses which are unsatisfying; both functionally and aesthetically... to set a new pattern in development and urban renewal' and in doing so to 'provide a new source of patronage for our architects.'[13] The members of the Association he founded pooled their resources to buy a row of twelve plots of land (situated next to the railway line near Hatfield station) from the Hatfield Development Corporation, and then appointed a young architectural practice, Phippen, Randall and Parkes, to come up with a new design.

Rather than starting with a notion of the conventional or ideal house type and arranging multiples of it on the site, the architects designed a scheme closely related to the landscape, taking into account the topography of the site. They came up with a row of single-storey terraced houses that step down following the slope of the site and are staggered to give some privacy at the entrances and to take account of the curve in the road. Dense planting all round was intended to enhance privacy and the general appearance of the terrace. There are four different sizes of house, with between one and four bedrooms, all conforming to the Parker Morris minimum space standards set out in 1961. The design is of modern simplicity: the plan has a simple arrangement around a central linear 'corridor', with bedrooms and bathrooms on one side and all the living rooms on the other. In the centre of the larger houses, a patio is included on the bedroom side, allowing light into the middle of the house. The palette of materials used for the construction and finishes is limited, and surfaces and spaces are clean and uncluttered. The main (structural) walls are built in concrete block which is left natural externally and painted white internally. Timber is used extensively: varnished woodblock for flooring, softwood boarding with clear varnish for partitions and ceilings, hardwood frames for windows and glazed external doors and dark stained timber cladding completes the elevation externally.

In terms of housework and maintenance, these houses do have advantages over their more conventional neighbours. As everything is at one level, there are no stairs to consider and windows, roof and gutters are all easily accessible. The varnished timber is easy to clean and there are no picture rails, skirting boards or architraves to collect dust. The kitchen is at the front of the house, close to the front door, where there is also a cupboard that is accessible from both inside and out for rubbish bins, milk bottles and parcels. The architects have also considered patterns of occupation and allowed for some flexibility in the way the spaces might be used. Wide sliding doors separating the living spaces can be left open to maximise space, and the small bedrooms have folding partitions that can be opened up to join them to the living spaces. In the larger houses, the arrangement of two bedrooms and a bathroom at each end of the house means more privacy for parents kept at a distance from noisy children.

Whilst there are no communal kitchens and dining rooms, the scheme does include a communal garden and play space for children as well as a tennis court shared by all the owners. The most unusual aspect of the project, however, is the extra house that belongs to nobody and everybody. It contains the association club room, a shared communal space and a kitchen, that can be used for parties, meetings and suchlike and is used regularly for the nursery and youth club. It also contains a flat for guests or for a resident caretaker.

Conclusions

Perhaps part of 'the dream' did come true – housing now has everything technology can offer, with central heating and hot water, electrical appliances, every form of 'modern convenience' coming as standard. For those with money, the au pair, nanny or mother's help has taken the place of the servant and convenience foods have relieved women of the chore of endlessly providing

One of the rare British attempts to establish a more adventurous approach to the organisation of the home, this housing project at The Ryde, Hatfield, right, was designed in 1966 by the young architecture practice Phippen, Randall and Parkes. It was commissioned by the Cockaigne housing group, a collective which bought the land in order to pursue its shared vision of 'a new pattern in development and urban renewal'.

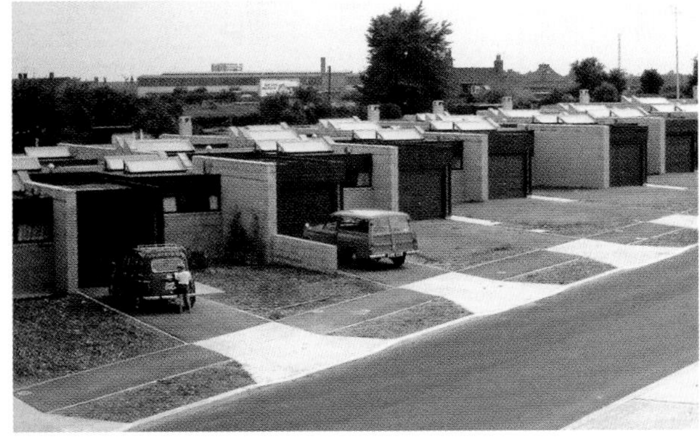

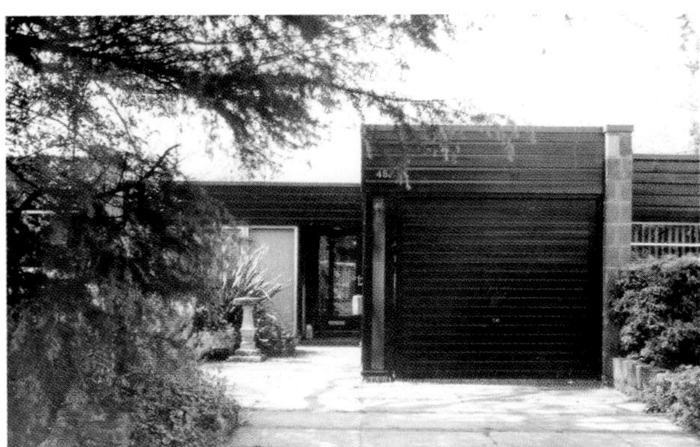

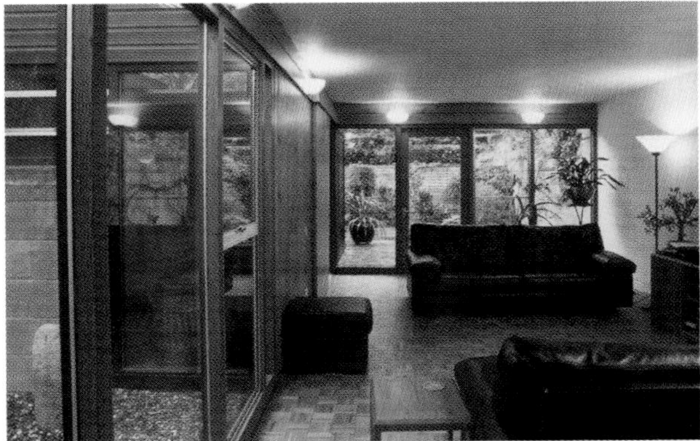

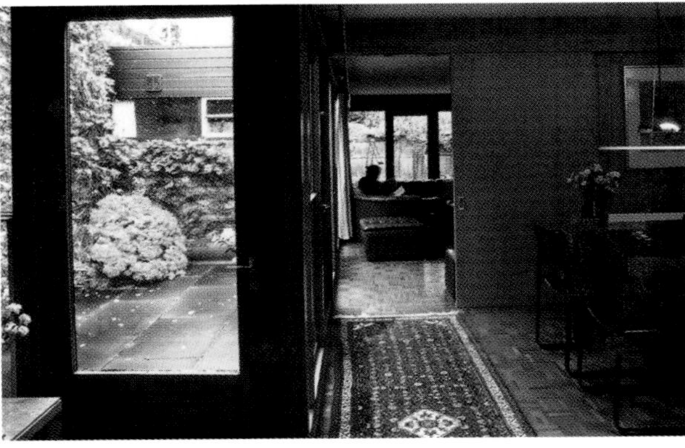

meals. TV programmes on the perhaps non-essential aspects of housing, like interior decoration and now gardening, have become the focus for home owners' dreams of a more glamorous lifestyle. But is the low-density, out-dated 'family' house that has already devoured so many acres of greenfield sites sustainable? Is the 'family' as the independent social and economic unit still the only viable model?

Housing schemes of even a marginally communal nature which are both architecturally and socially engaging as well as desirable, such as the Cockaigne Scheme in Hatfield, are rare. Despite the obvious economic benefits, the idea of communal living, or even of co-ownership of a housing block, is not as acceptable in England as it is elsewhere, for a wide range of reasons that could arguably include class, history and even inclination. It is possible that the architecture of the Isokon block was ahead of its time – simply because it did not conform either architecturally or socially to the conventional notion of the family. Today the Grade I Listed building is derelict and presents a problem for its owners, the London Borough of Camden: not only is it costly to renovate, its layout would make it unsuitable for use as family housing. From another perspective however, such an elegant building designed to suit single people without much interest in cooking or homemaking sounds the perfect proposition for many of today's Londoners – as a student hall of residence or even sheltered housing it could be ideal. It is not impossible to revive the fortunes of a seemingly failed project: Erno Goldfinger's much-maligned Trellick Tower in Ladbroke Grove (1968) found a new lease of life when the Local Authority changed their allocation policy to ensure that only those people who expressly wished to live there were moved in. As a result, the formerly run-down, unpopular high rise has become a desirable residence.

There has been little investment in alternative forms of housing since the Local Authority experiments of the

Recent attempts to break the mould of housebuilding in Britain include Walter Menteth Architects' scheme, below and right, in East London, which returns to the F Type plan of a mezzanine overlooking a double-height common area, but set in the altogether different context of a low-rise building overlooking a shared garden.

1960s. For many years now, more than 80% of new housing in Britain has been provided by property developers and private housebuilders – without the involvement of architects – to the same conventional plans first drawn up 100 years ago. Their use of open, easily accessible, greenfield sites and the repetition of standard 'family' house types ensure reliable profit margins. Architects are much more likely to be involved in schemes for difficult urban locations where more complex blocks, requiring lengthy negotiations with planners and tight budgetary controls, are built by social housing providers as an alternative to the conventional family house.

Walter Menteth Architects' scheme at Warburton Terrace, Walthamstow, for Ujima Housing Association offers such an alternative. It is one of a series of recent housing schemes in London by WMA that question accepted patterns and that are both aesthetically innovative and functionally successful. The block at Warburton Terrace stands out in contrast to the surrounding 1960s bungalows, ignoring the orientation of the rest of the street, to make maximum use of the sunlight and views and to provide a large shared garden for the residents. The plan is simple, with habitable rooms on the south side facing the garden and the service areas, shared facilities such as laundry and

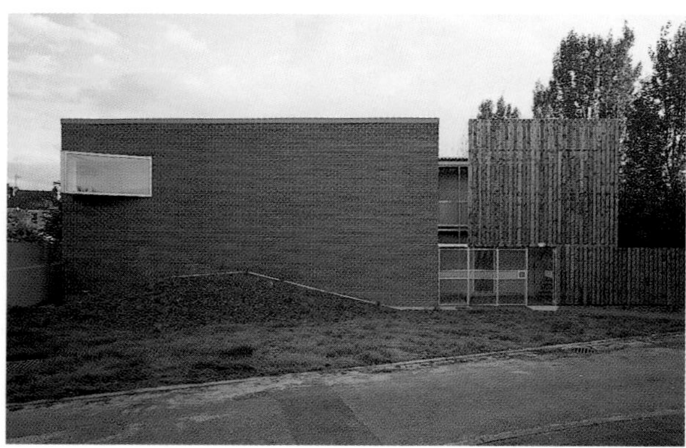

kitchen, and staff rooms on the north side facing the street. The south side block, which has integral passive solar heating panels, is painted a brilliant sunshine yellow in contrast to the more rustic north block in red brick, with a galvanised steel stairway behind a York board rainscreen. At first-floor level the corridor separating the 'blocks' terminates in a mezzanine overlooking the double height common room. The view from the mezzanine is dramatic. On the far wall there is a panel of 'brut' (Corten) rusting steel attached to exposed wind bracing, which doubles as a screen for the heating. Beyond, a high-level window lets in shafts of early morning sun. adding to the unexpected theatrical effect.

The as yet unbuilt Grass Module House turns the idea of the traditional house almost literally on its head. A direct challenge to suburban development, it has been developed as part of in-house research at de Rijke Marsh Morgan Architects to specifically address issues of 'changing lifestyle and lifetime uses, construction and flexibility, local and global ecology, air and light quality, economy, DIY, gardening and fun'. The plan, which can be occupied in a number of different ways, spirals around a central courtyard, or outdoor room, surrounded by folding glass walls. The continuously ramped roof starts at street level and follows the spiral upwards to form a garden on top of the house. The plan can be extended

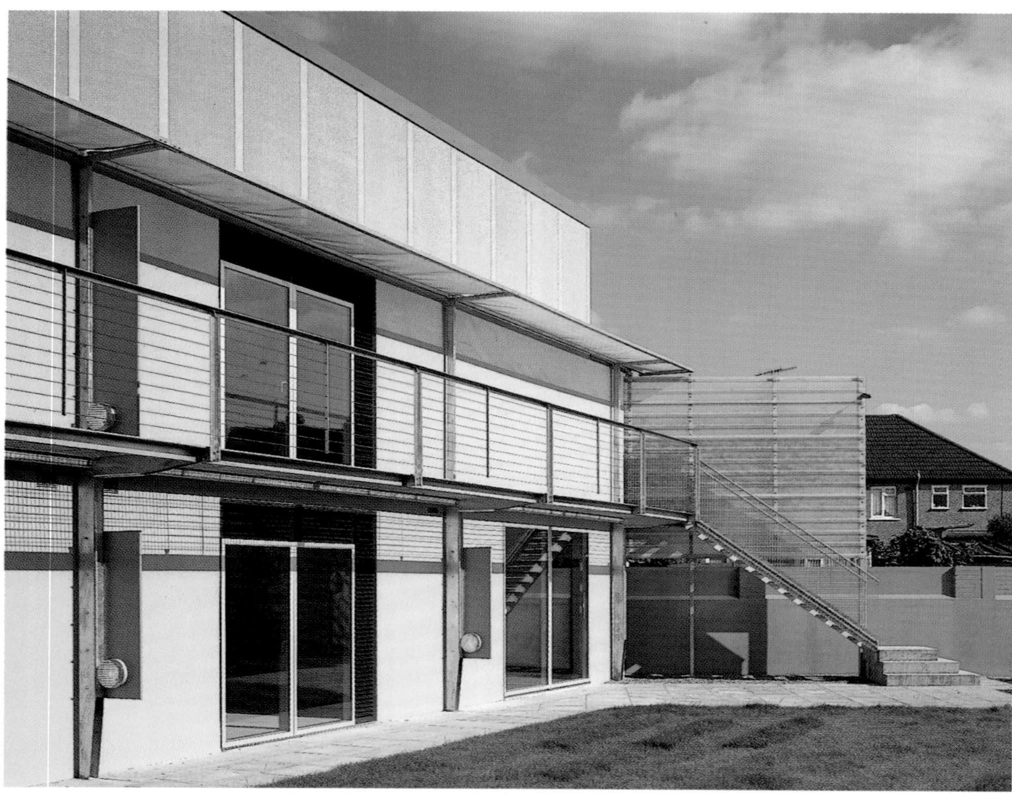

upwards centrally, and the proposed construction using a modular system of lightweight blocks of softwood timber means it can easily be done using unskilled labour. Grouped together, they form a green and undulating roofscape beneath which lies a variety of living spaces as densely occupied and richly varied as any urban block.

Social housing providers, building properties for rent, have tended to be more interested in long-term issues such as durability and maintenance than their commercial counterparts. However, current debate on housing suggests that private developers will have to start changing their ways, as ordinary purchasers increasingly demand higher levels of attention to energy efficiency and other long-term costs. According to the *RIBA Journal*, reporting on the latest Housing Design Awards, requirements for environmentally-friendly design, use of brownfield sites and a need to reduce construction costs will lead more and more developers to employ architects on their schemes. Perhaps the social aspect of housing will not be ignored, and the search for new forms of high density, innovative, sustainable development will include solutions for a whole range of occupants – lone parents, single people, older couples and those who require some care and support – people who would choose to live together outside the conventions of the nuclear family.

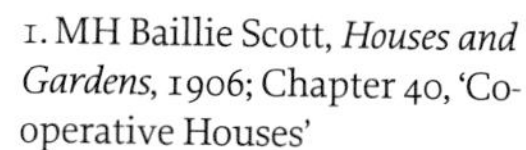

1. MH Baillie Scott, *Houses and Gardens*, 1906; Chapter 40, 'Co-operative Houses'
2. Robin Evans, 'Rookeries and Model Dwellings' *in Architectural Design*, 1978
3. Professor Kerr, 'On the problems of providing dwellings for the Poor in Towns', *RIBA Transactions*, Series 1, Vol. XVII. 1866–67
4. Emily King, 'Cooperative Housekeeping' in *The Building News*, April 24, 1874
5. ibid
6. WL George, 'Women and tomorrow', 1913, quoted in Dolores Hayden, *The Grand Domestic Revolution*, The MIT Press 1981
7. *The Journal of the American Institute of Architects* quoted in Dolores Hayden, *The Grand Domestic Revolution*, The MIT Press 1981
8. ibid
9. ibid
10. Nicholas Pevsner, in Sherban Cantacuzino *Wells Coates a monograph*, Gordon Fraser, London 1978
11. RG Bateson, 'The House and Housework, Experiments on the housewife's use of her house in the performance of routine household tasks' in *RIBA Journal*, December 1954
12. Sir Thomas Bennett, 'Housework and Town Planning' in *Town and Country Planning*, July 1956
13. *The Architects' Journal* Information Library, 12 October 1966, Housing

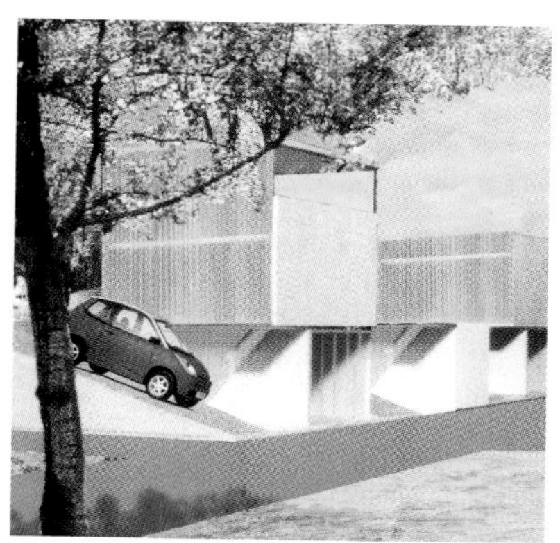

Yet to be built, the Grass Module House, above, right and on following pages, employs ramped spaces which rise around a central courtyard area, continuing upwards to form a garden on top of the house. Together, these houses designed by de Rijke Marsh Morgan would form a green roofscape.

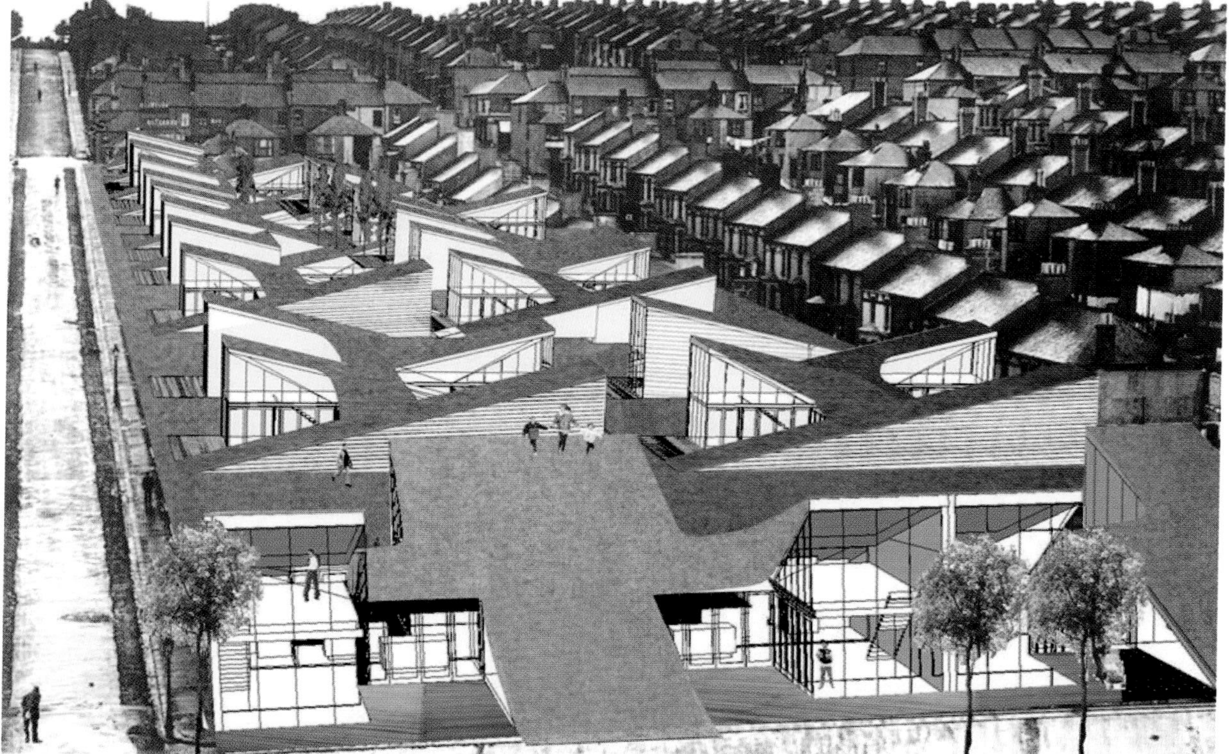

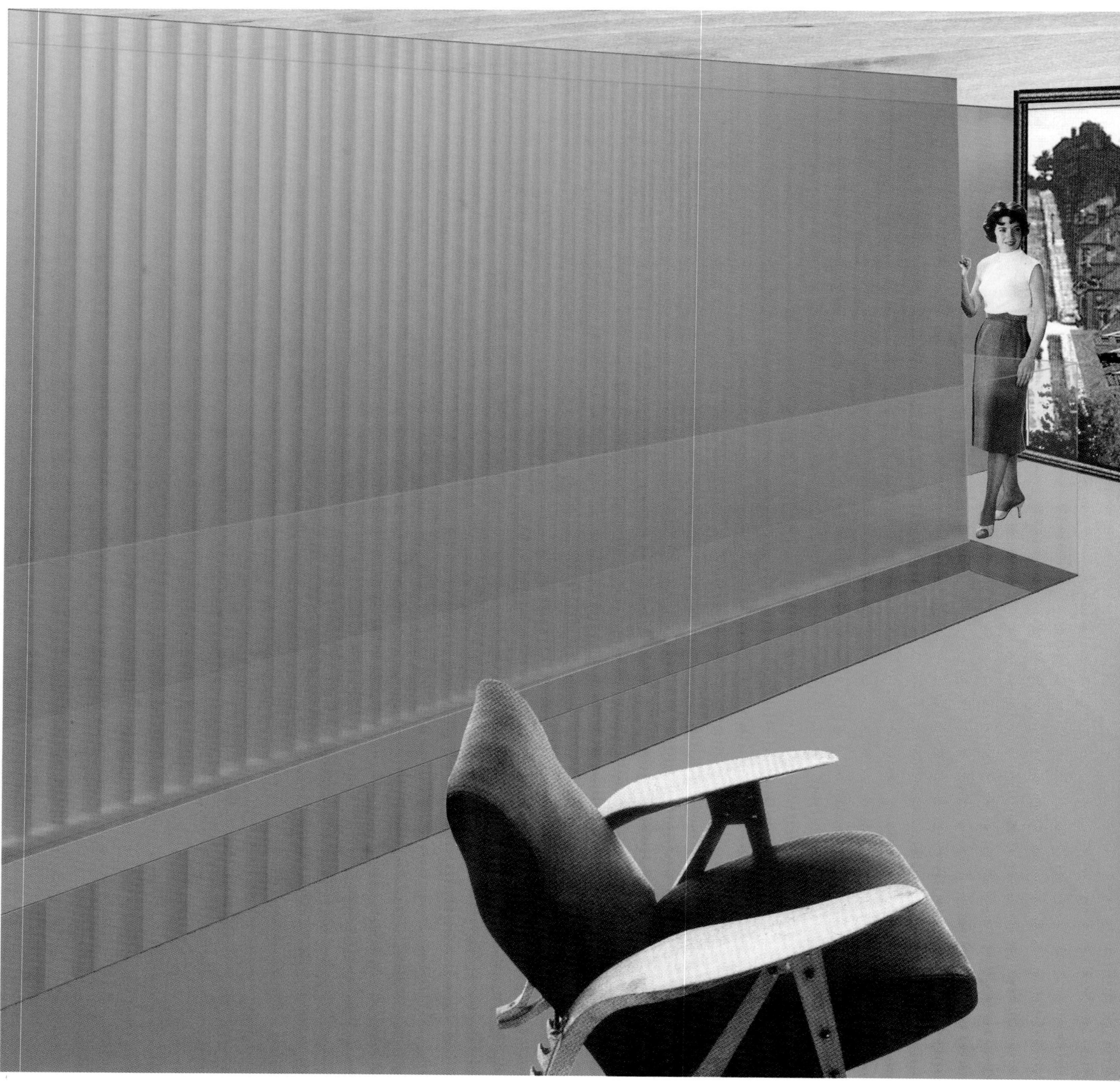

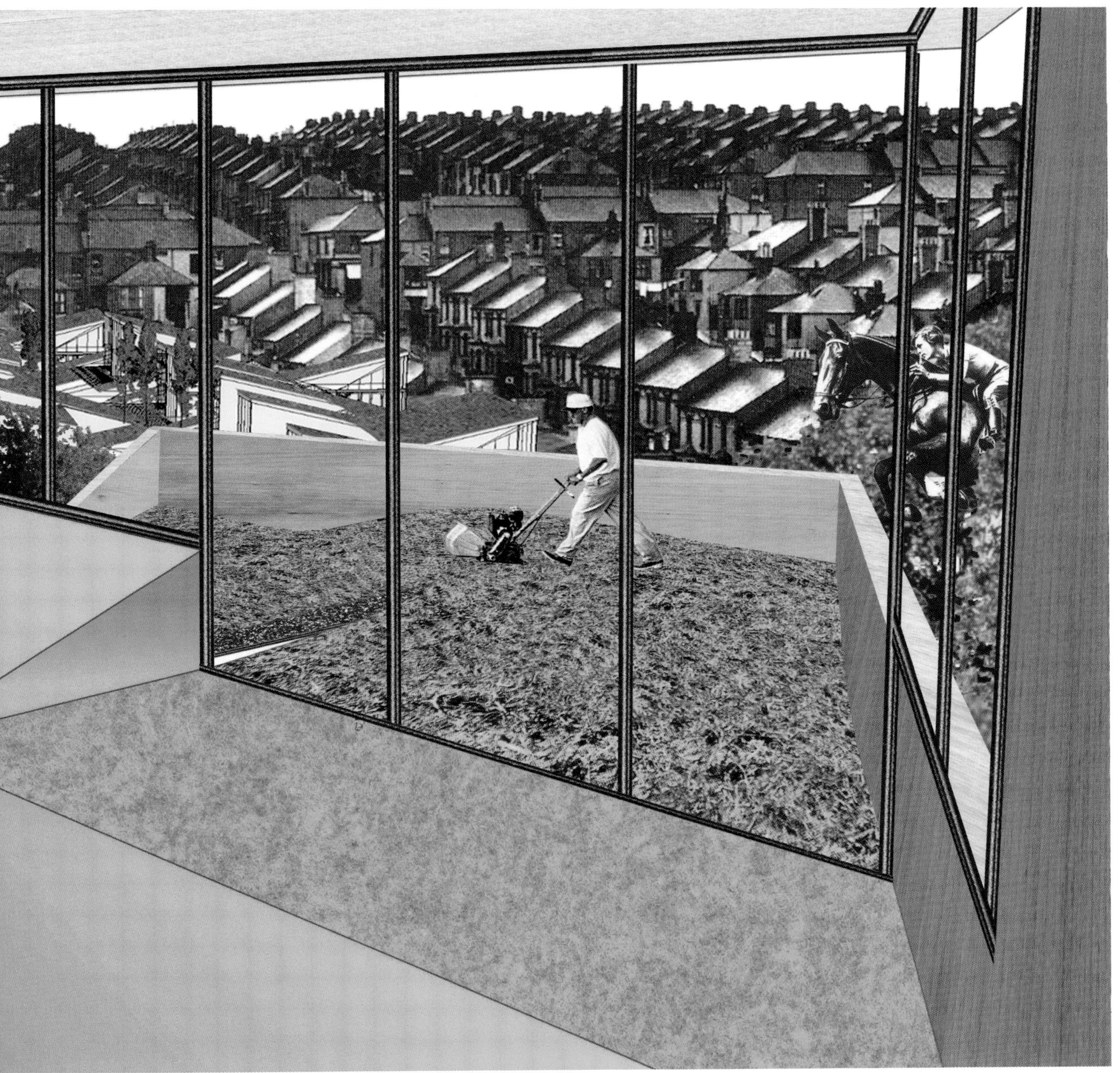

The Sims

The most successful new computer game of 2000, *The Sims* lets you play God – at least in one small, artificial neighbourhood. You can design and furnish the houses, landscape the gardens, decide on the looks and character traits of the inhabitants, and then control virtually every aspect of their lives. However. virtual omnipotence comes with a variety of responsibilities, from getting everyone to work or school on time, to making sure they don't burn down the kitchen whenever they attempt to cook dinner. If you forget to equip your house with a toilet, you will be left with an embarrassed Sim and a large puddle to clean up, and if your Sims are not given the opportunity to have fun or make friends, they will soon be too depressed to get up in the morning. But if you nurture them, they could also fall in love, get married and have children. Then again, it might be more fun to watch what happens if you make the neighbour from hell move in next door. There is no way of 'winning' *The Sims*: it is about building communities – whether they are utopian or dystopian is entirely your decision.

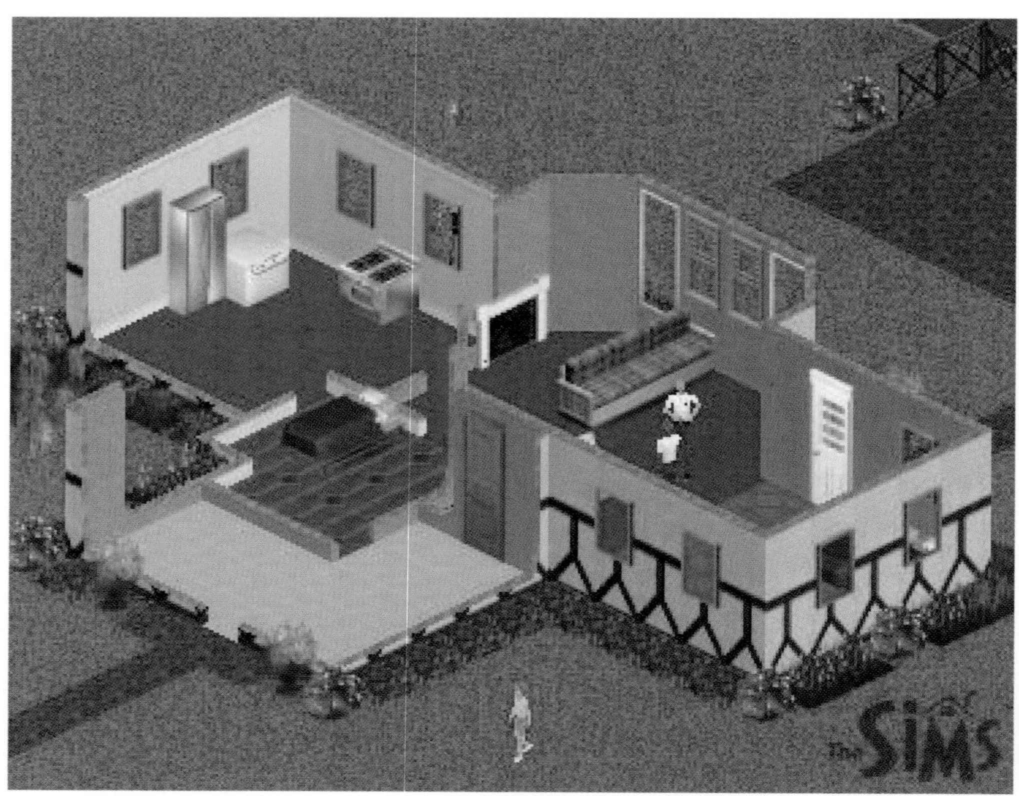

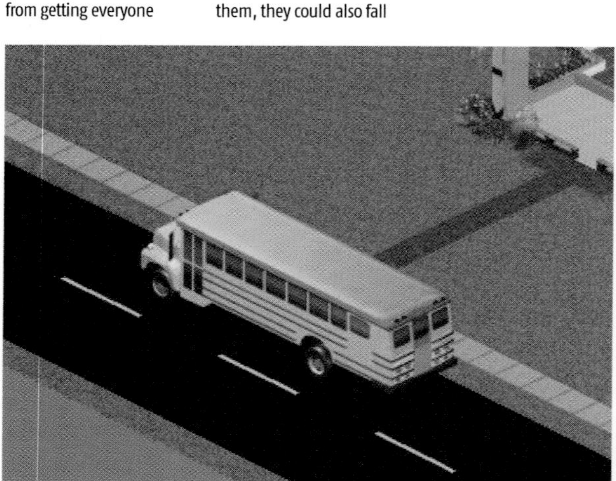

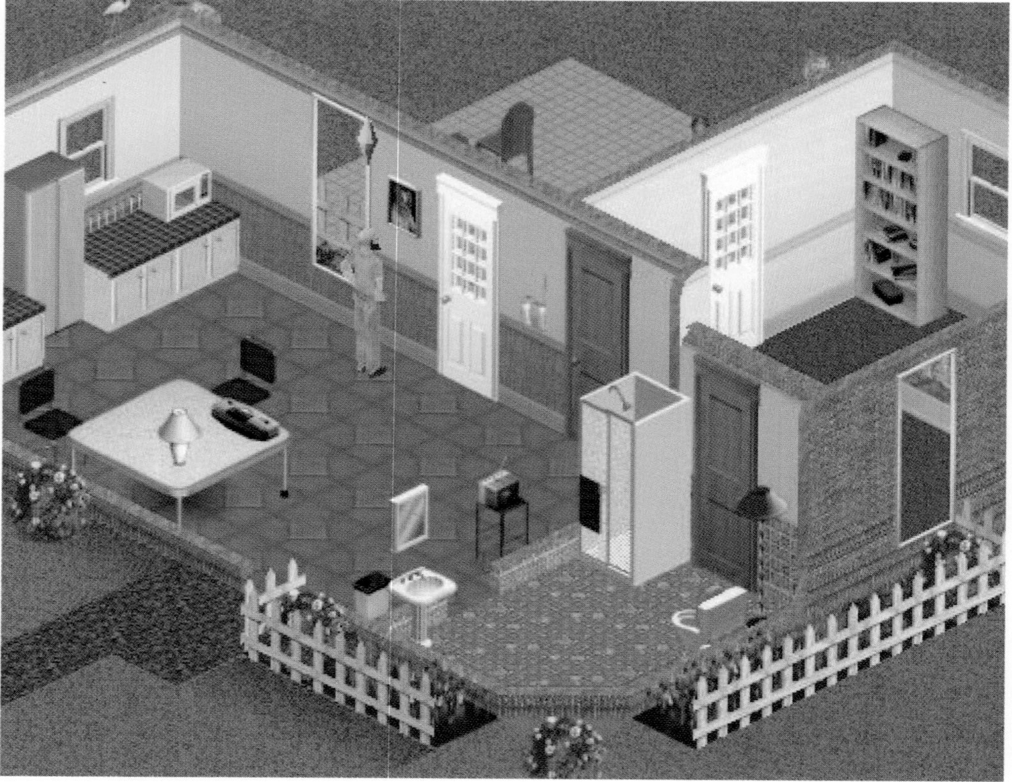

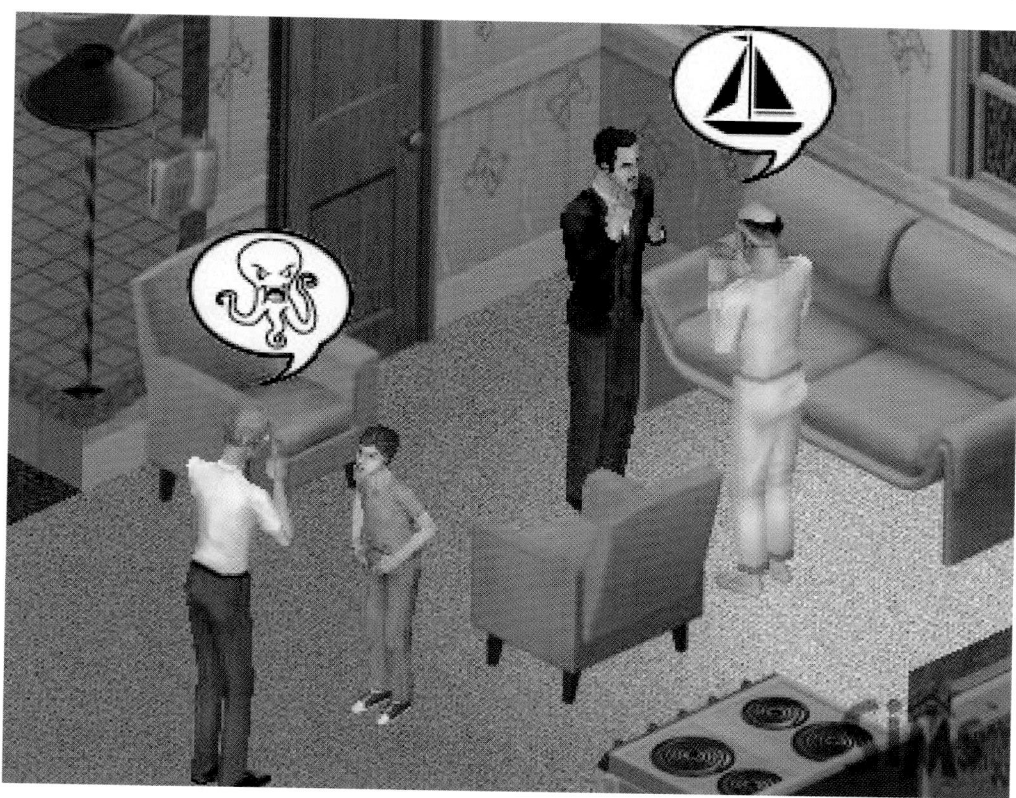

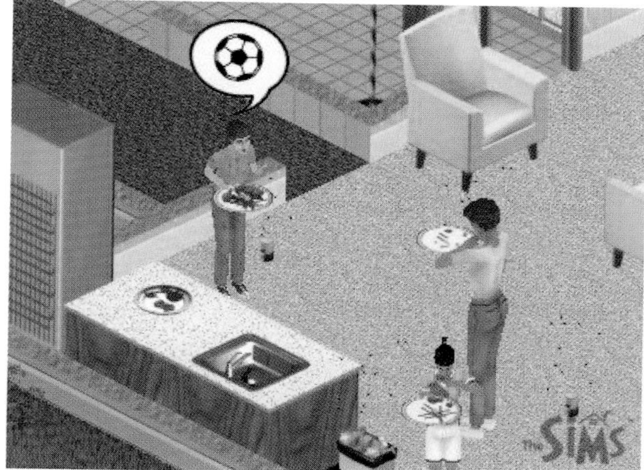

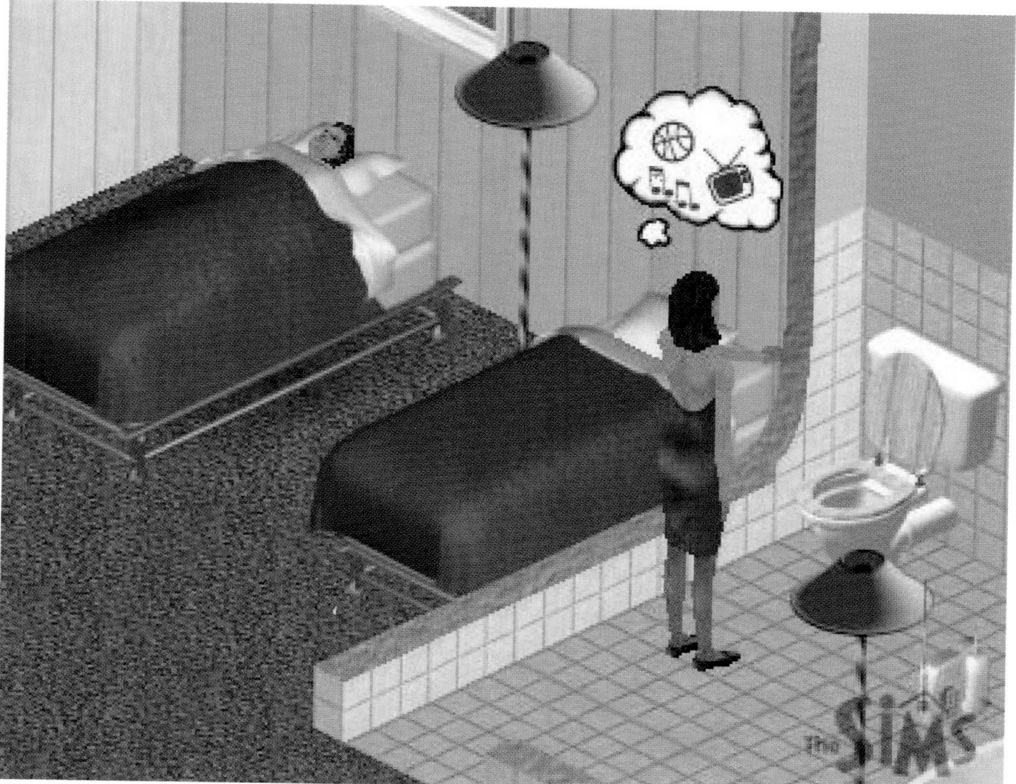

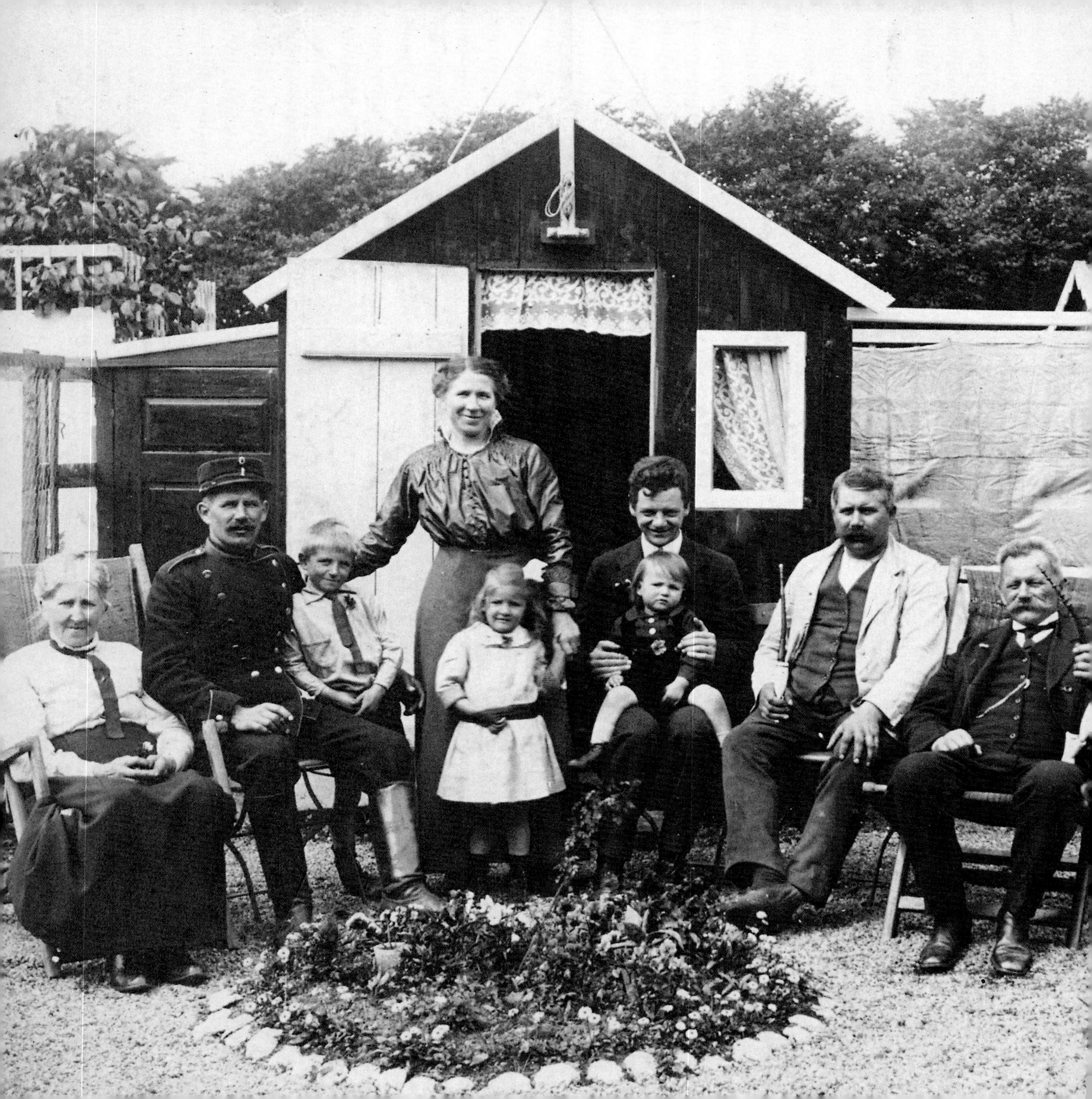

Kolonihavehus

The third most popular jukebox record in the history of Danish pop is Eva Madsen's 1978 song *Mormors Kolonihavehus* (Grandma's Garden-Colony House). The 'kolonihavehus' is a concept deeply ingrained in the Danish psyche: at the end of the nineteenth century the Danish government, keen to give factory workers the chance to escape from the cramped living conditions of the cities, introduced the 'kolonihave', or garden colony. Not far from Copenhagen, the government set aside parcels of land subdivided into small plots of 100-200 square metres which were rented out at highly subsidised prices in the hope that factory workers would work the land and supplement their diet by growing vegetables.

The first houses to be built on the 'kolonihaven' were simple sheds designed to provide temporary shelter. But as owners returned to their 'kolonihave' year after year, they began to decorate, paint and add to their small properties until each 'kolonihavehus' (house) began to develop its own identity. Towers, spires, roof terraces and balconies were added, and then porches, screens and pergolas extended into the gardens. At the peak of the kolonihave movement's popularity, there were 100,000 such houses in Denmark.

Fifty years later, the number has fallen to just 50,000 and an anxious Danish Minister of the Environment recently organised a conference at which he emphasised the cultural and economic importance of 'kolonihavehusen'. In a parallel project, Danish architecture curator Kirsten Kiser has organised a government-backed scheme in which internationally-known architects are invited to design their contemporary version of this traditional refuge. On a site in Copenhagen masterplanned by Leon Krier, the impressive list of participants included Richard Meier, Arata Isozaki, Richard Rogers, Michael Graves, Aldo Rossi, Enric Miralles, Mario Botta, Ralph Erskine, Alvaro Siza, Josef Paul Kleihues, Heikkinen-Komonen and Dominique Perrault, as well as Danish architect Henning Larsen. Of the fourteen projects, five have been completed (the others will be constructed when Kiser has raised more money), and the project has toured to Stockholm and Reykyavik as part of the European Cities of Culture scheme, picking up a new kolonihavehus design by Frank Gehry along the way. The completed schemes, set in the public land of the this suburban city park as they are, exist at one remove from the original notion of the kolonihave. Devoid of personalised decoration or whimsy, some of the structures seem to be using the language of sculpture rather than refuge. Mario Botta has built a fortress-like cube topped by wooden batons which offer the semblance of privacy to those on the roof, while Dominique Perrault's contribution is an exquisite glass box surrounding a tree, the inside of which is only accessible by ladders. Ralph Erskine's house consists of a tall tower made of thin wooden slats, out of the top of which also grows a tree, but the interior of which is accessible through a door. Some of the as yet unbuilt projects, meanwhile, are exercises in post-modernist quotation: not surprisingly, Michael Graves has made a geometric composition of interlocking cube, cylinder and gabled portico, while Leon Krier's thatched cottage is a parody of traditional vernacular styles. Meanwhile, Richard Rogers' contribution is a return to his abiding fascination with the rhetoric of Archigram.

Perhaps the most successful of these architect-designed projects are those which accept that a kolonihavehus will never be much more than a simple garden shed. Richard Meier's austere cube, Henning Larsen's elevated meditation tower and even Josef Paul Kleihues' green box are the designs which look most capable of responding to the annual challenge of holiday occupation. For the other participating architects, the kolonihavehus represents a jumping-off point: the architectural equivalent of a short story, whose ideas may well find their way into more substantial work in future. News of the project's progress can be found at www.arcspace.com

GRANDMA'S GARDEN COLONY HOUSE
The cycle wheel goes round and round;
Father is laughing and mother is cooing
It's a holiday and we are together;
The sun is shining over Sortedammen.

That was a life of idyllic bliss,
In Grandma's garden colony house;
In Grandma's garden colony house.

The house is green: It's called "Bella Vista".
The water is boiling and the primus glowing
The garden and wallpaper bloom red and green,
The sky is blue and life is wonderful.

That was a life of idyllic bliss,
In Grandma's garden colony house;
In Grandma's garden colony house.

Bent is showing Frida he can do a handstand;
Valda also wants to, but he will lose his teeth.
Grandma says it's music we need,
and she fetches her harmonica.

That was a life of idyllic bliss,
In Grandma's garden colony house;
In Grandma's garden colony house.

The sun goes down and we drive home,
Behind the town's silhouette the stars are peeping.
The town hall clock chimes the time
And this it has done many times since.

That was a life of idyllic bliss,
In Grandma's garden colony house;
In Grandma's garden colony house.

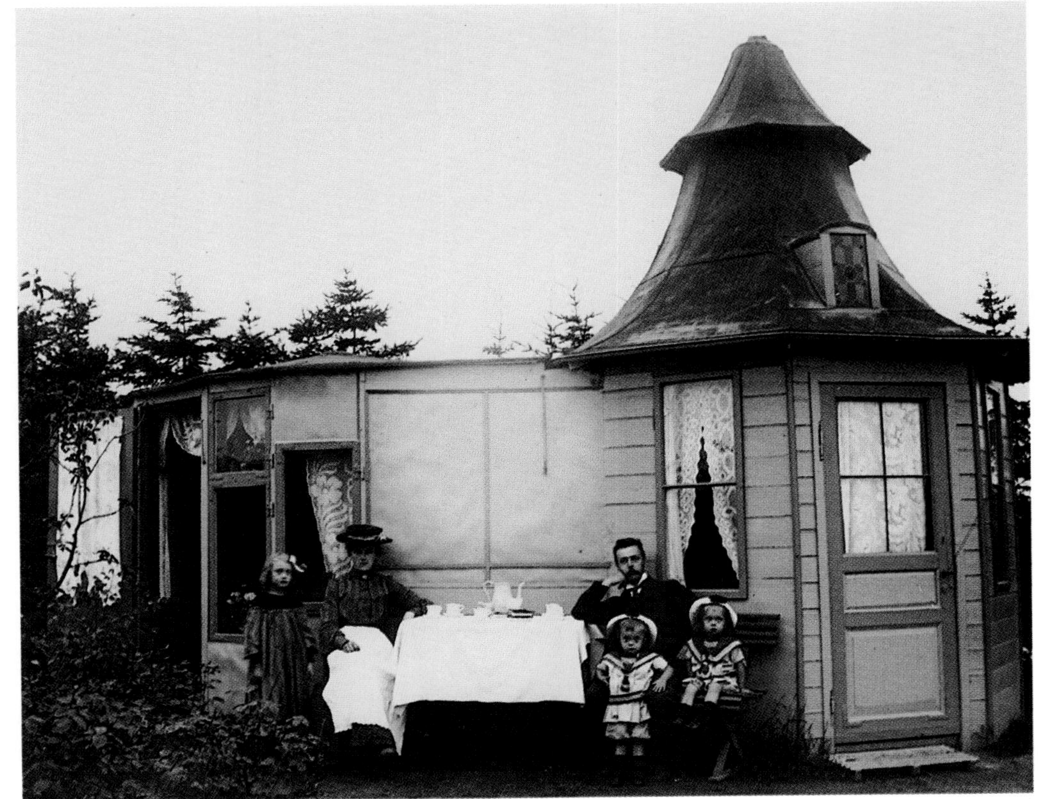

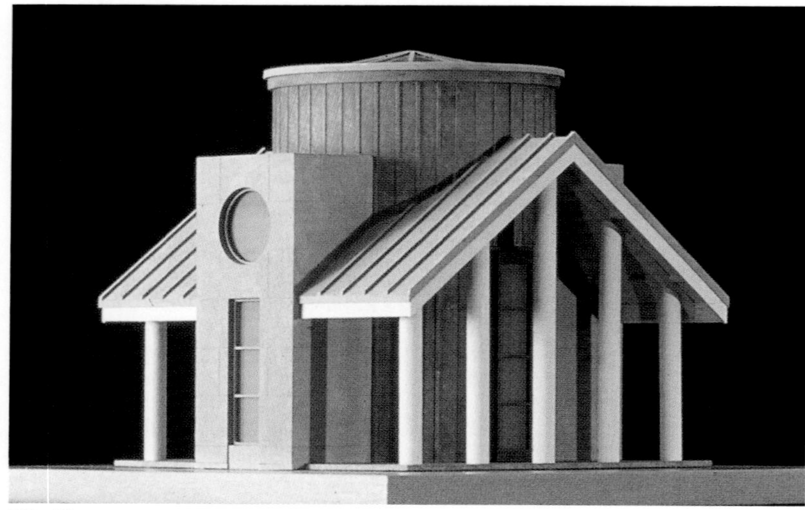

Michael Graves

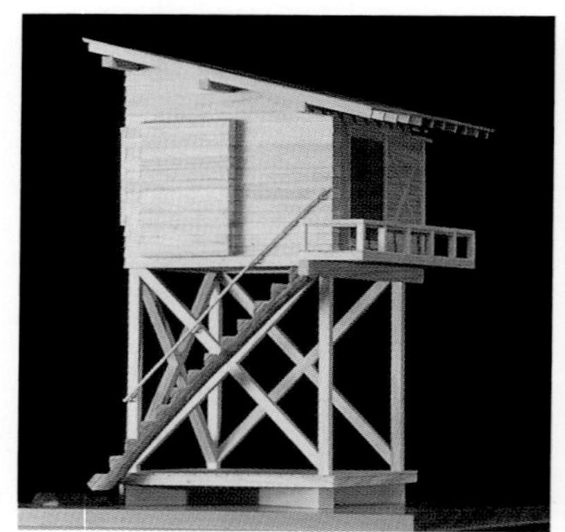

Arata Isozaki

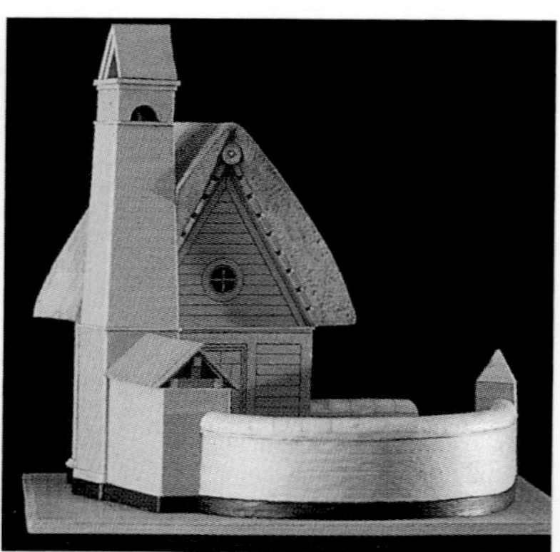

Leon Krier

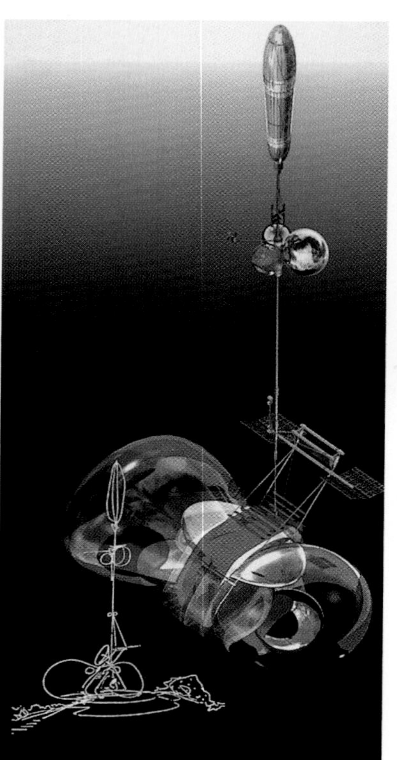

Richard Rogers

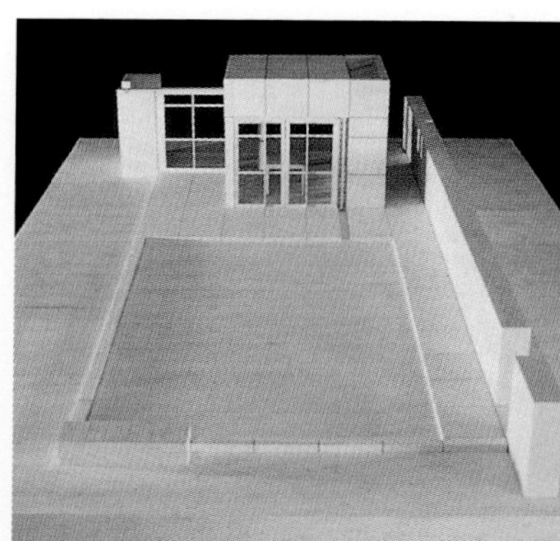

Richard Meier

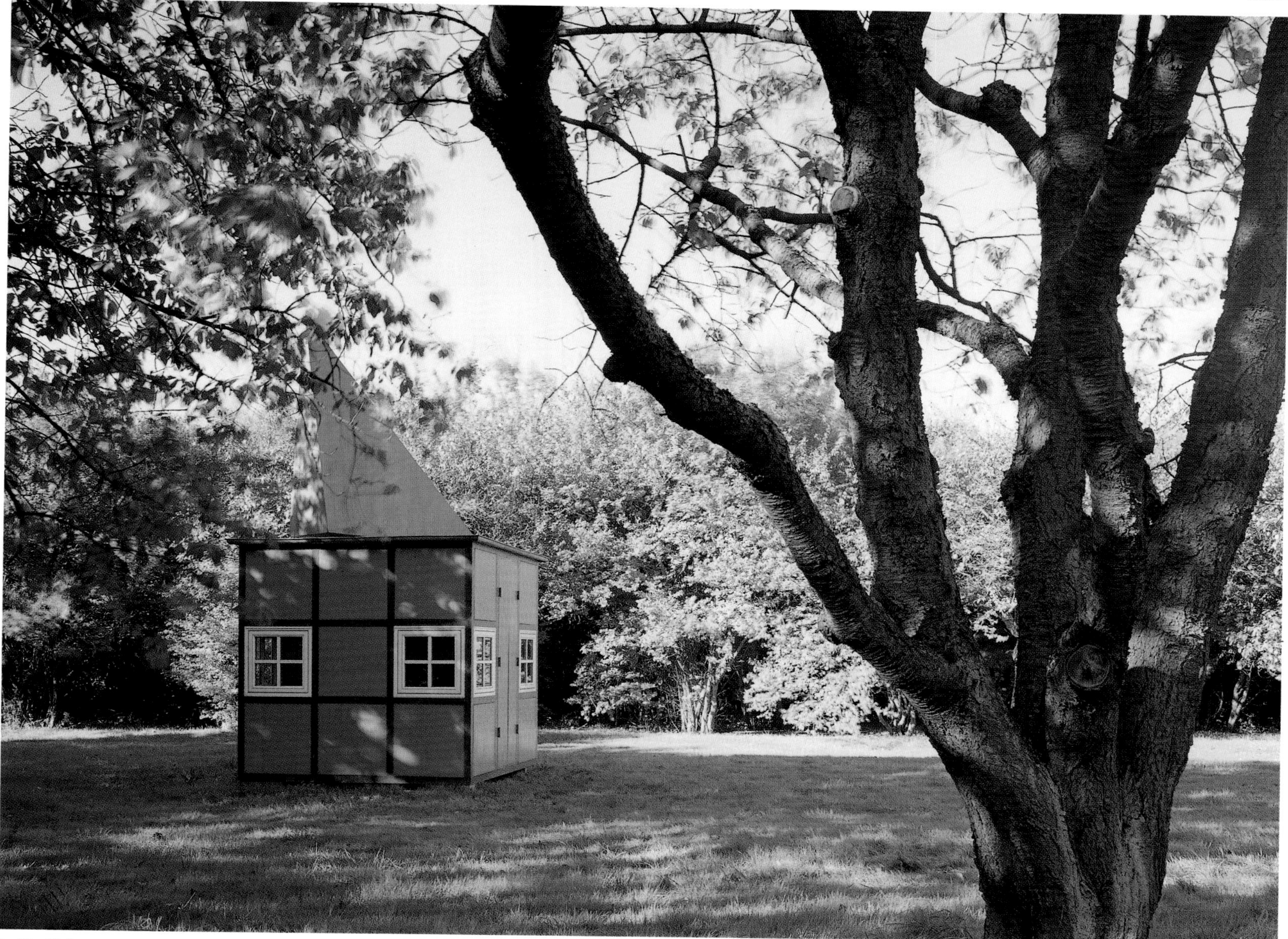

Josef Paul Kleihues

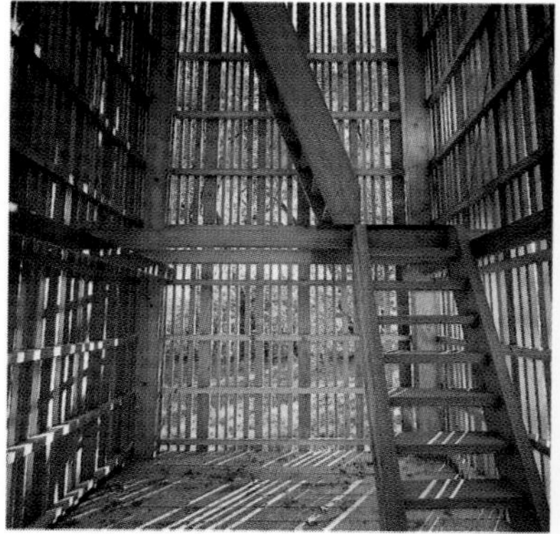

Ralph Erskine

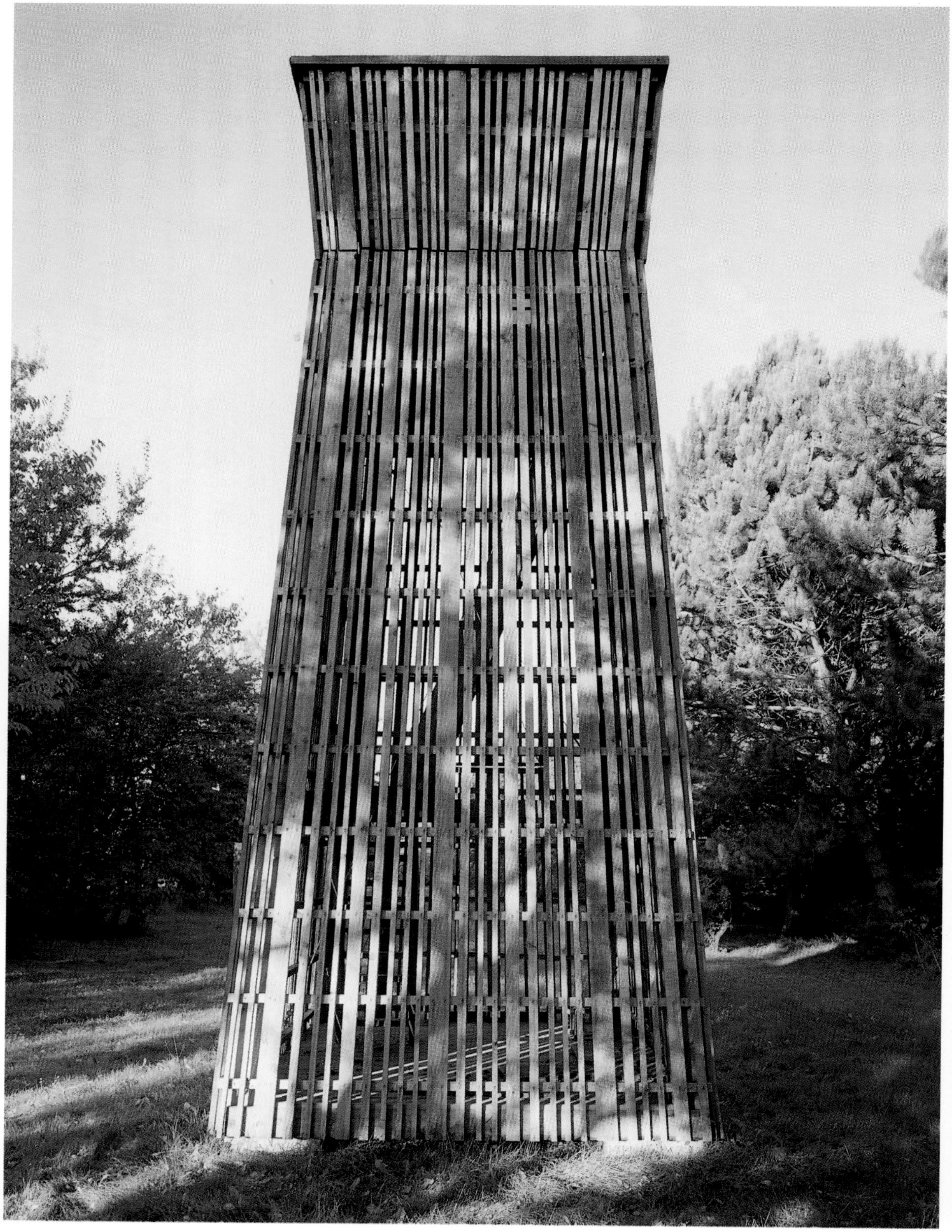

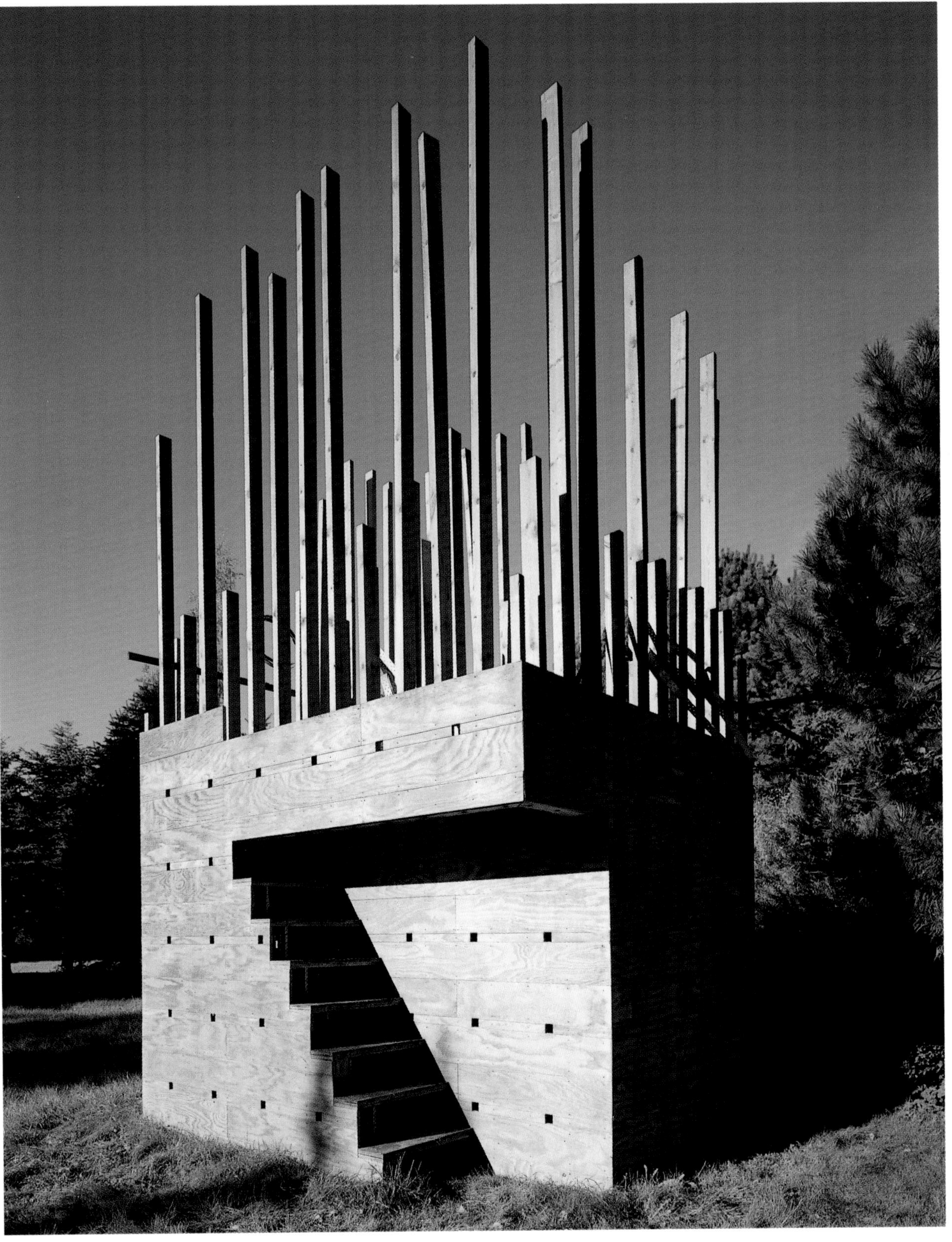

Mario Botta

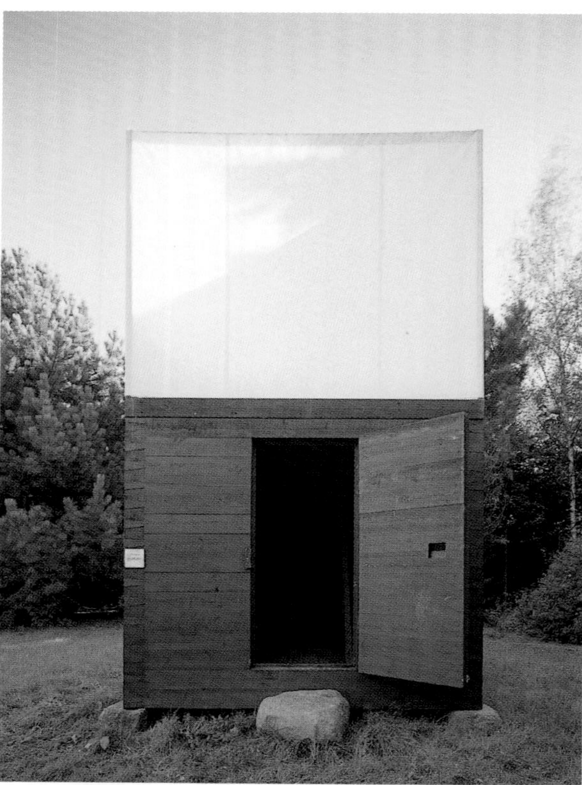

Heikkinen-Komonen

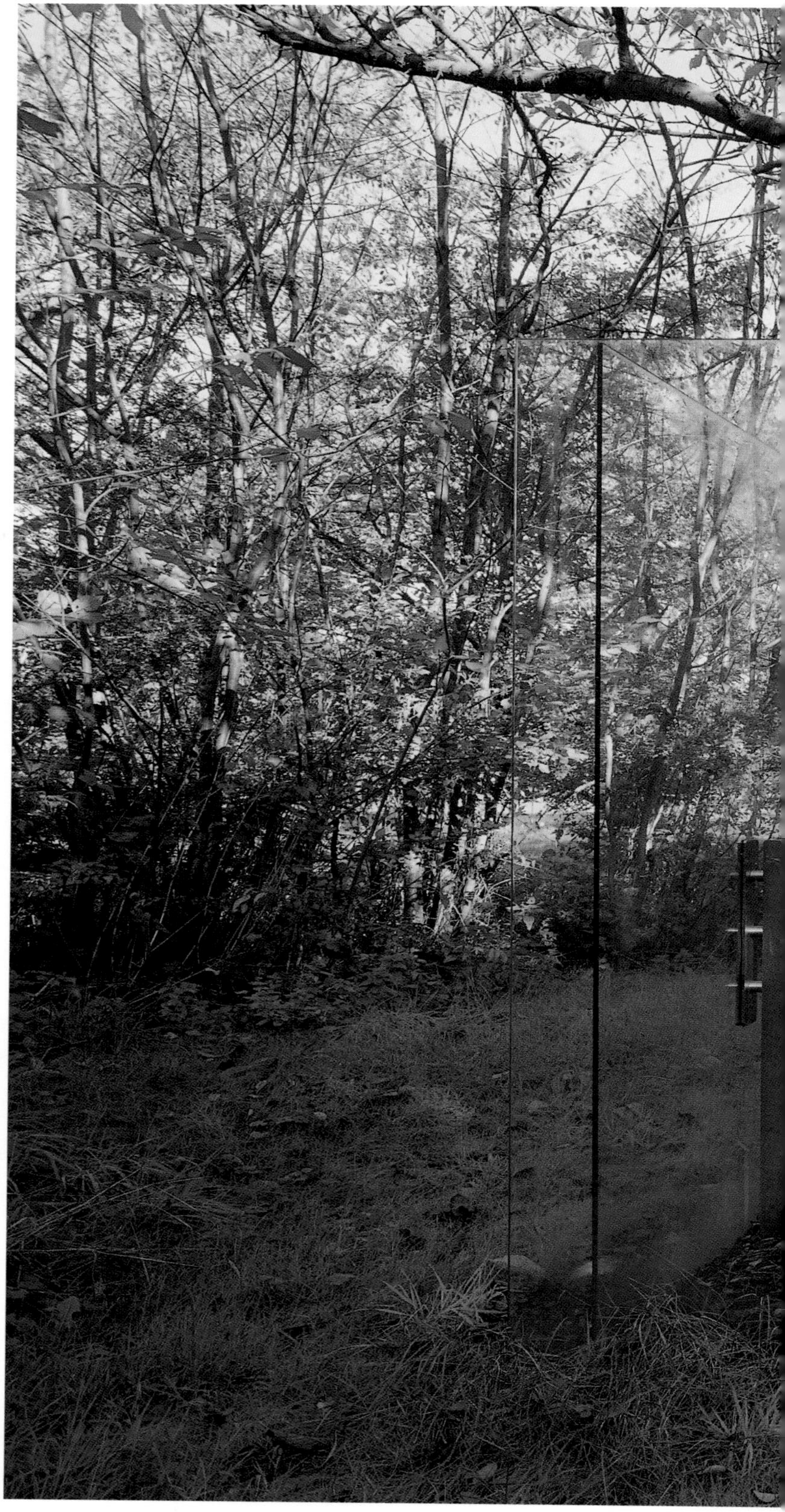

Dominique Perrault

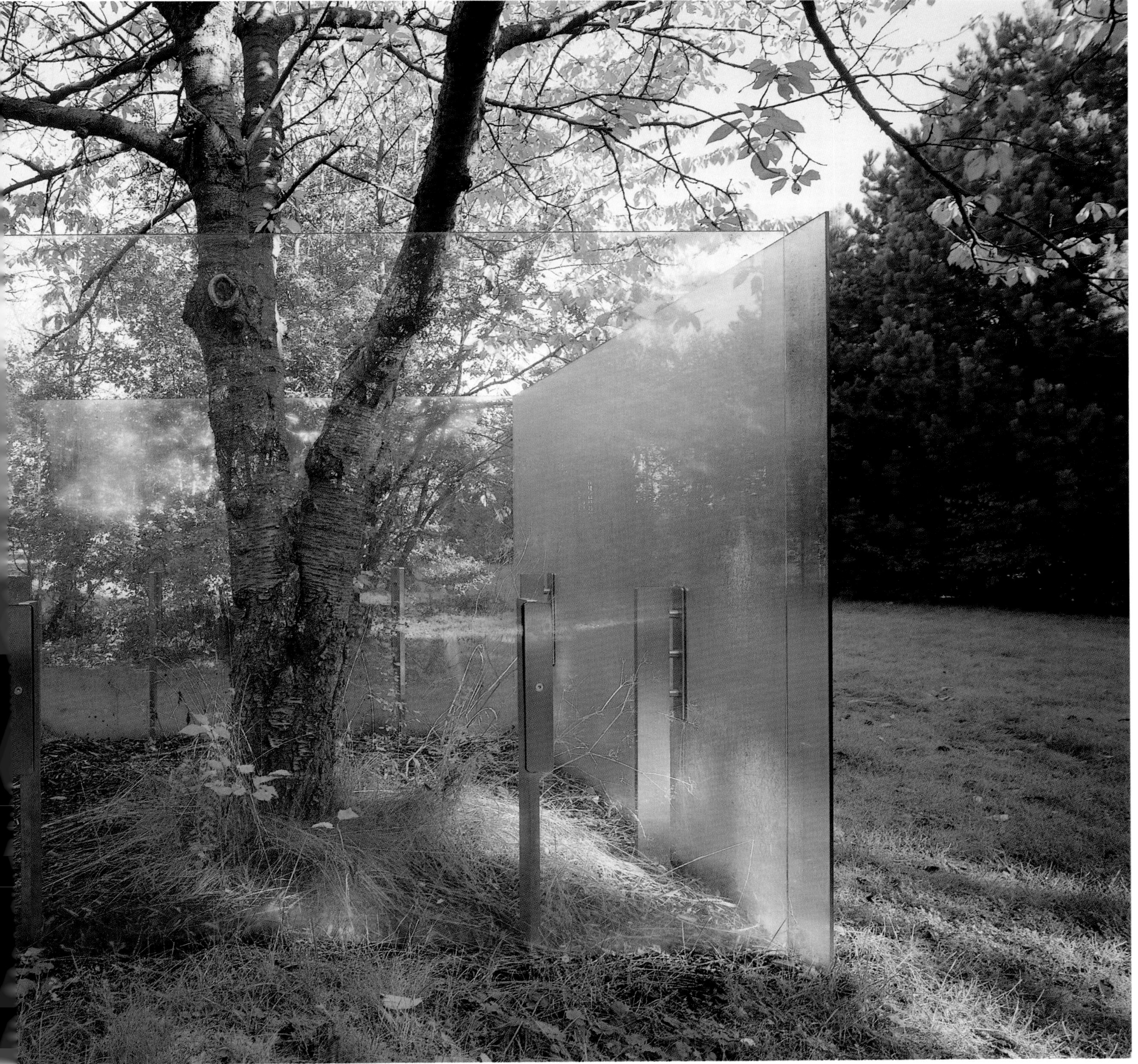

Allotment
Rick Poynor

From my window, in the room where this is being written, I can see the allotments. When I arrived here, four years ago, I didn't give them much thought. Allotments seemed like relics of some earlier austerity Britain, when the population was enjoined to plant potatoes and cabbages and 'Dig for Victory'. They were places where old boys with nothing better to do pottered about with forks and compost and flasks of tea. Today, it is raining and there is nobody there. Occasionally, on the far side, a train will pass at eye level, along a bank overgrown with buddleia and weeds, where the foxes live. The birds like the allotment, too. On a dry day they glide and swoop above the land, but now the only movement comes from the gentle rhythm of rain on leaves and the breeze that ruffles the tinfoil bird-scarers on strings. It didn't take me long to realise that unless I fitted a blind to block out this leafy rectangle, I could lose hours each day gazing out of the window at the comings and goings below.

In the last few years, the public image of allotments has changed. They are becoming fashionable among the unlikeliest groups of people. In a recent article in the *Guardian*, assorted academics explained how, to take a break from cogitation, they liked nothing better than to cultivate their own asparagus, broccoli, brassica and carrots.[1] In 1998, in its report *The Future of Allotments*, the Environment, Transport and Regional Affairs Committee concluded that there was an 'emerging renaissance' in demand.[2] Contrary to the traditional image of the plot-holder as a retired man, only 35 per cent are 65 or over; 30 per cent are 50-64 and 35 per cent are under 50. Between 1969 and 1993, the proportion of women plot-holders increased from 3 per cent to 16 per cent, but the actual figure for women allotment gardeners is likely to be considerably higher, since women often tend plots registered in a male partner's name. However, while demand apparently increases, provision continues to fall. In 1943, at the height of the war effort, there were 1,400,000 allotments. By 1970, this had dropped to around 500,000. Since then a further 250,000, most of them council-owned, have been lost.

The demand for land puts these sites under

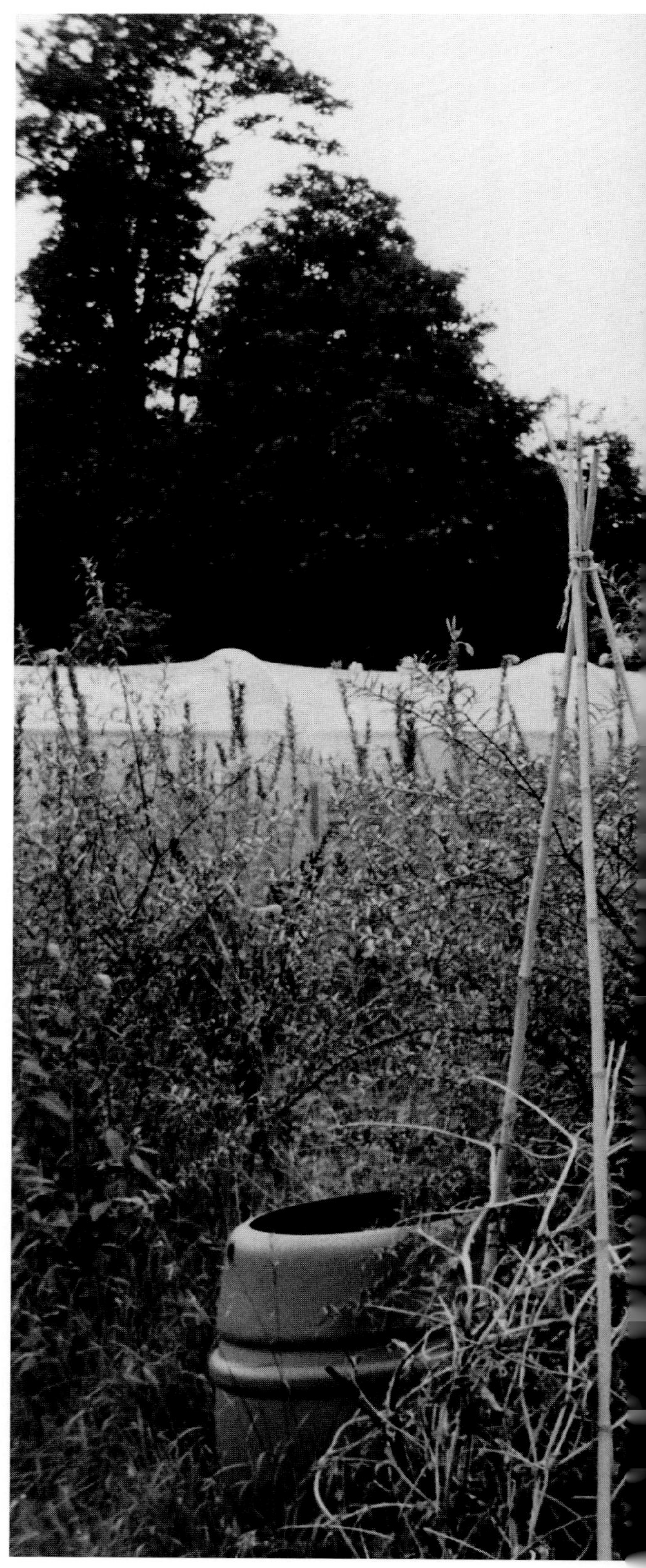

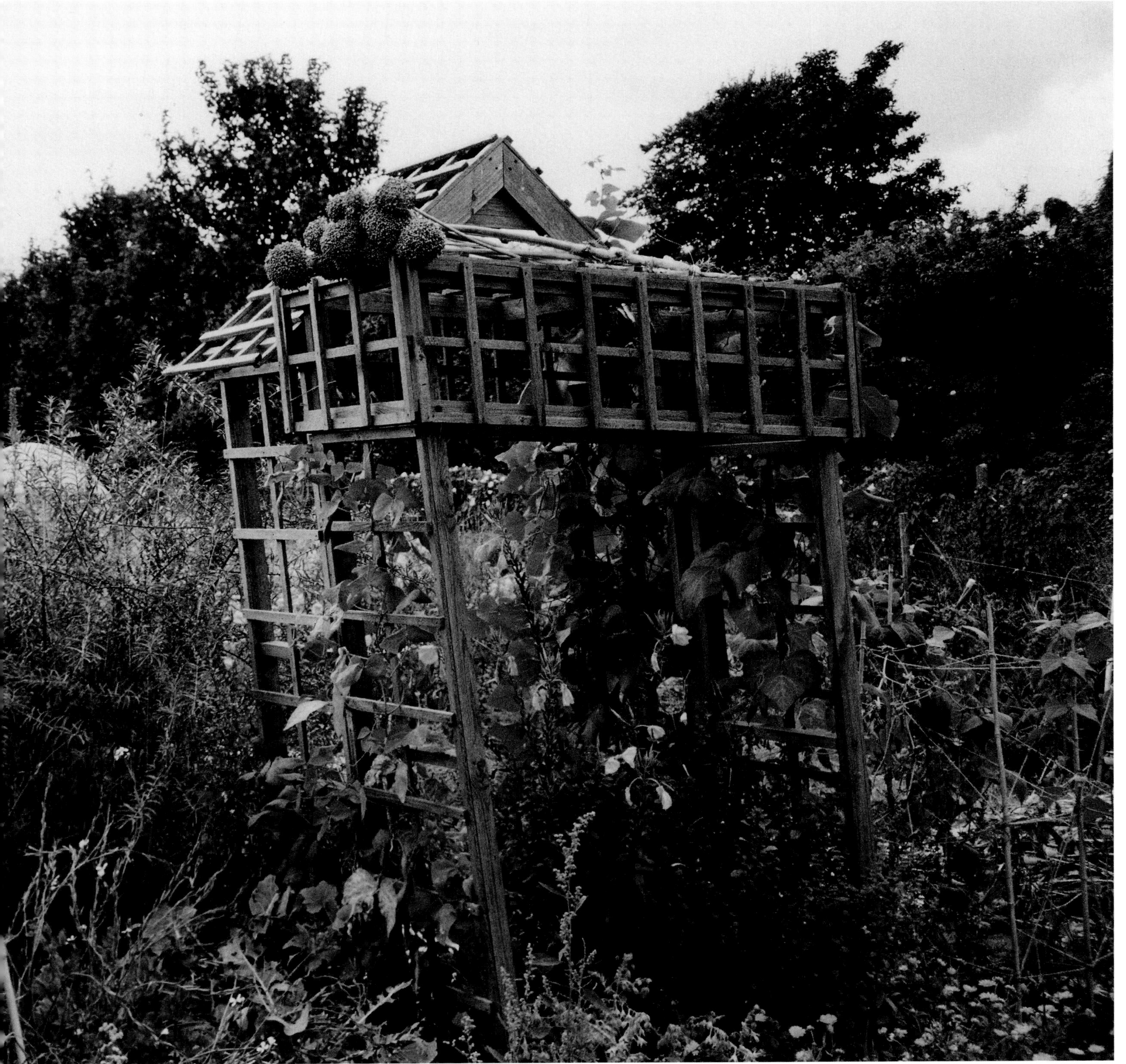

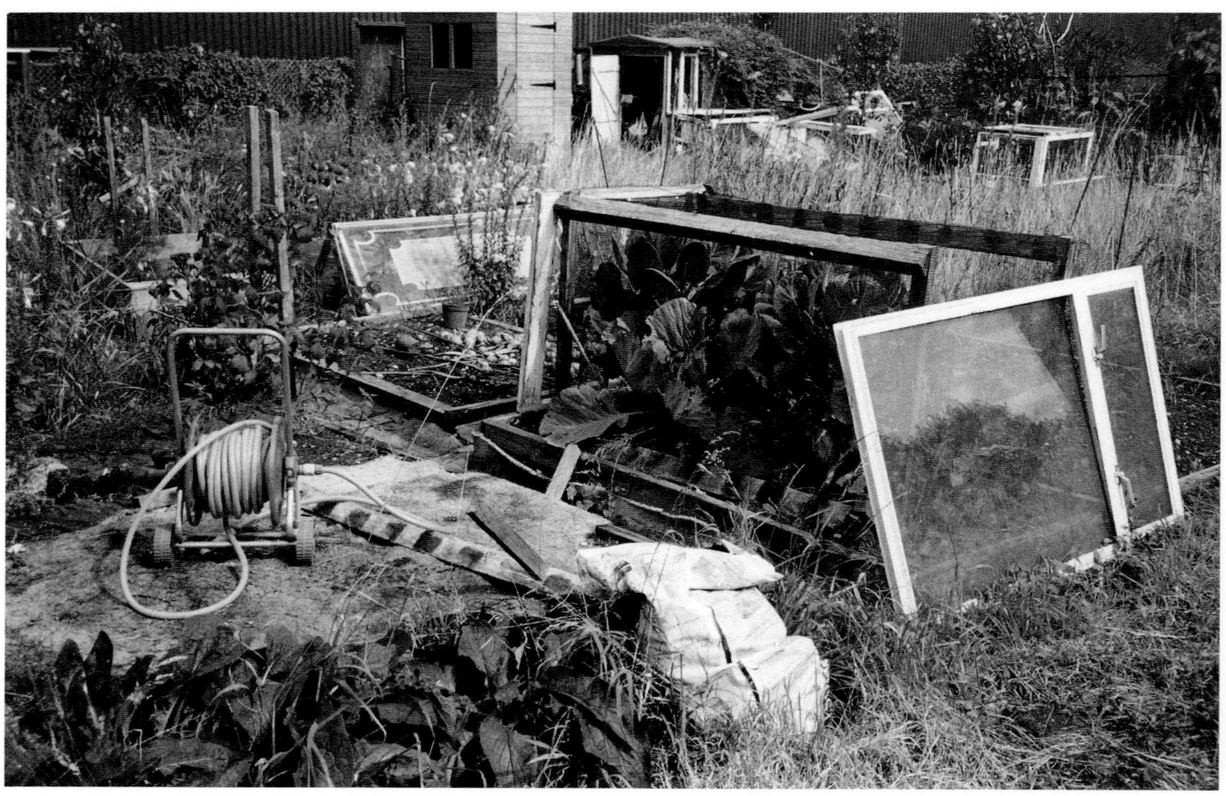

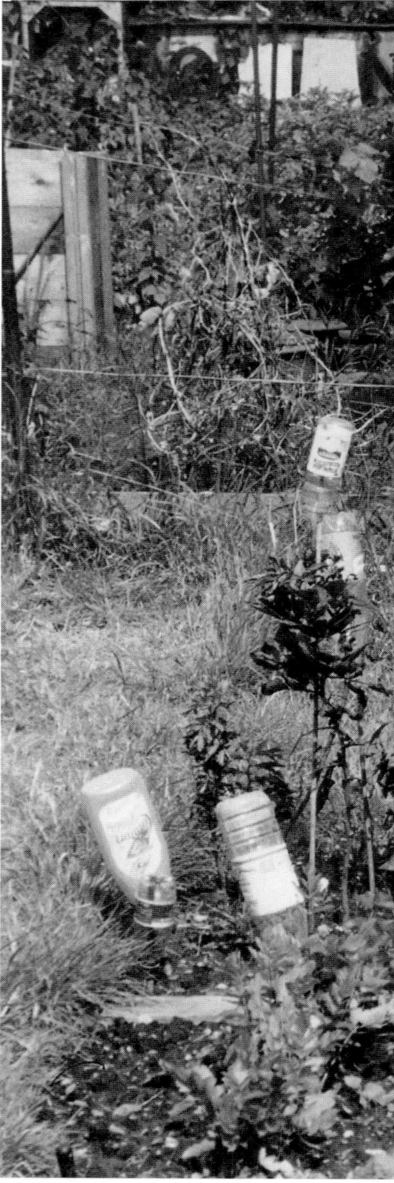

enormous pressure. The UK needs to build around 4.5 million homes in the next 15 years. Allotment sites that were once on the urban periphery are now within the limits of development, and developers eye the land hungrily. To them, it must look like potential profit frittered away. Gardeners lucky enough to occupy a plot receive an exceptional benefit for a negligible investment. In my borough, a small plot of 5 rods (approximately 125 square metres) costs the plot-holder just £22 per year and a 10-rod plot (250 square metres) costs only £44.

People are turning to allotments again in response to concerns about food safety, the high cost of organic produce sold by supermarkets, and the continuing national passion for gardening. But one of the more noteworthy aspects of allotments is the model of spatial – and therefore of social – organisation that they represent. A group of strangers occupy defined but physically borderless territories within a shared tract of land. What is planted and the way that a plot is laid out and subdivided is at the discretion of the individual (subject only to a few minor local authority restrictions). It might be argued that this is no different, in essence, from what happens on a larger scale in a street full of gardens, but gardens are privately-owned spaces held apart by fences, walls and planting. An allotment site, by contrast, is a collective space, open and permeable. Everyone is free to wander along the narrow pathways between plots and, just as crucially, the sightlines across the allotments as a whole are continuous – you cannot, politely, stare into people's back gardens. One of the great pleasures of traversing a site is the huge variety

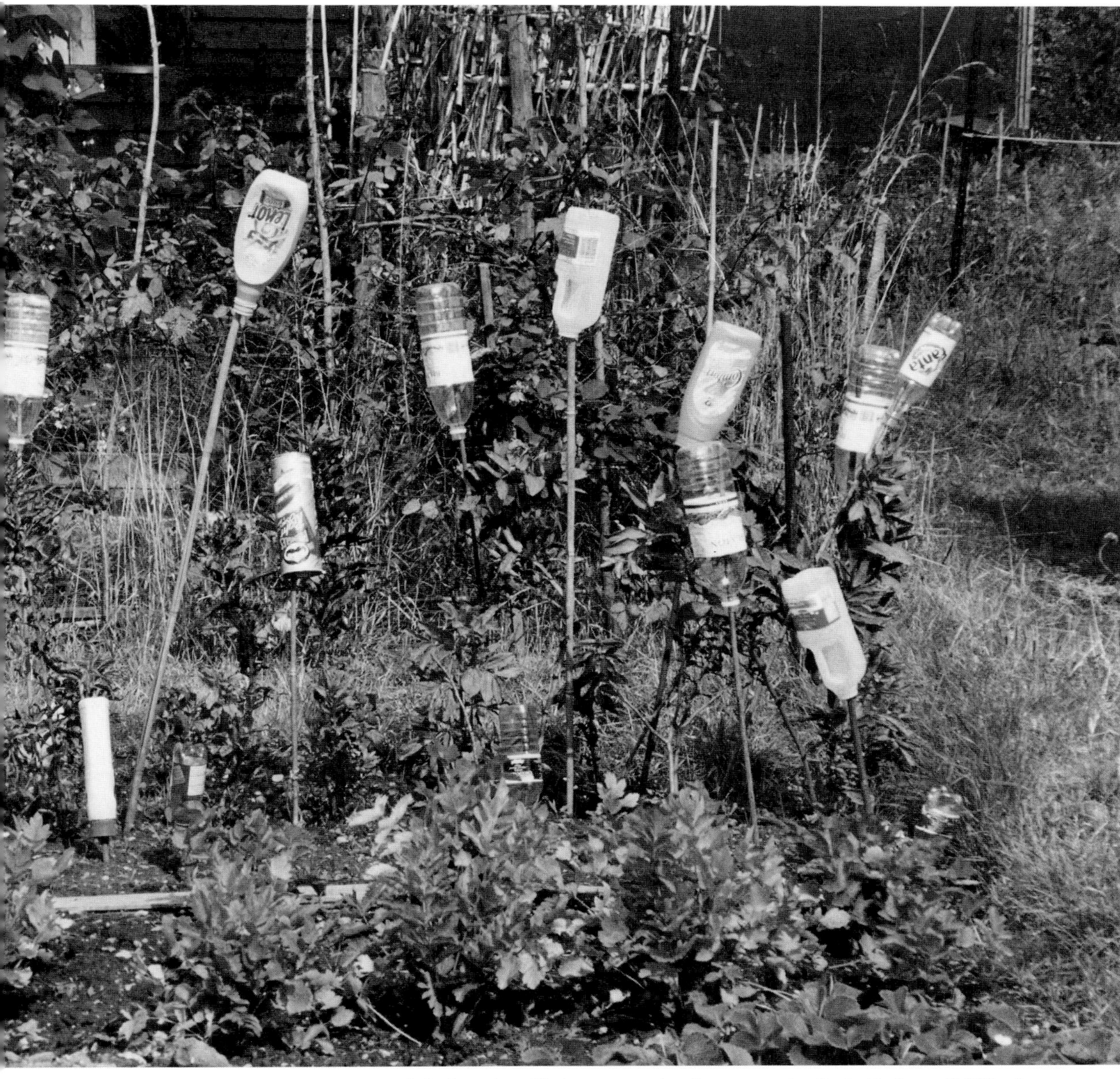

of plot layouts and features encountered within the framework of the underlying grid, and appreciating that these are expressions not of large-scale, impersonal forces, but of individual preference, taste and whim.

There is something in the open culture of allotments that encourages the way of thinking that Claude Lévi-Strauss called 'bricolage'. In folk cultures, the bricoleur 'makes do' when constructing something, and extemporises a solution from whatever materials come to hand. In modern technological cultures, however, tasks are subordinated to the availability of raw materials and tools conceived and procured for the purposes of the project.[3] The goal-directed products of contemporary engineering – garden tools, lawn mowers, Strimmers – can naturally be found on allotments, but they coexist with assemblages patched up and lashed together from humble, even degraded materials that couldn't be further removed from the decorous outdoor ornaments sold in a garden centre: a low-level barrier, not quite a fence, constructed from a thin concrete slab, a corrugated panel and a chunk of wire mesh; a rickety cage, to keep the birds away, cobbled together from bamboo poles, plastic netting, string and wooden clothes pegs; a miniature lean-to 'greenhouse' fashioned from cast-off window frames, shedding scaly flakes of paint; a do-it-yourself support structure for a raspberry bush that bristles with different weights of iron pole, like a rusting armoury of pikes and muskets. The detritus of everyday consumer culture collides with the allotment economy of recycling and bricolage to form surreal graphic totems. Empty Lenor fabric softener bottles

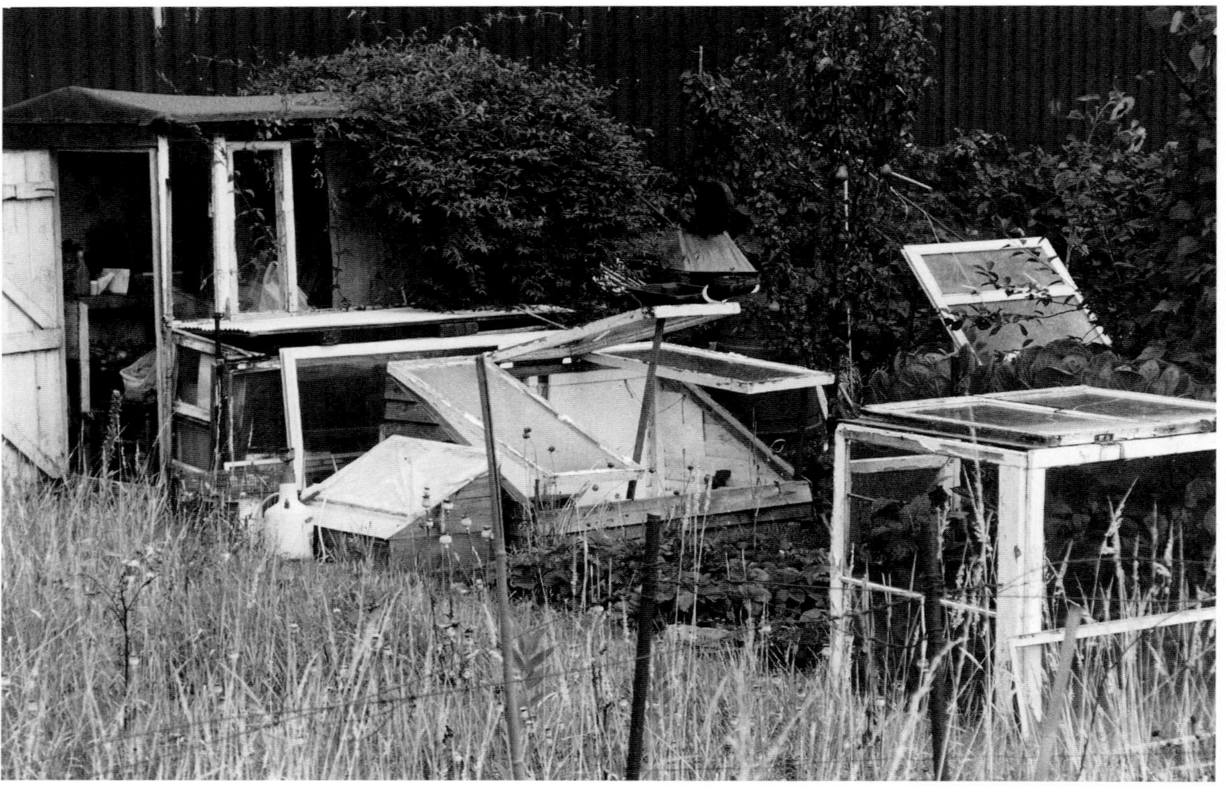

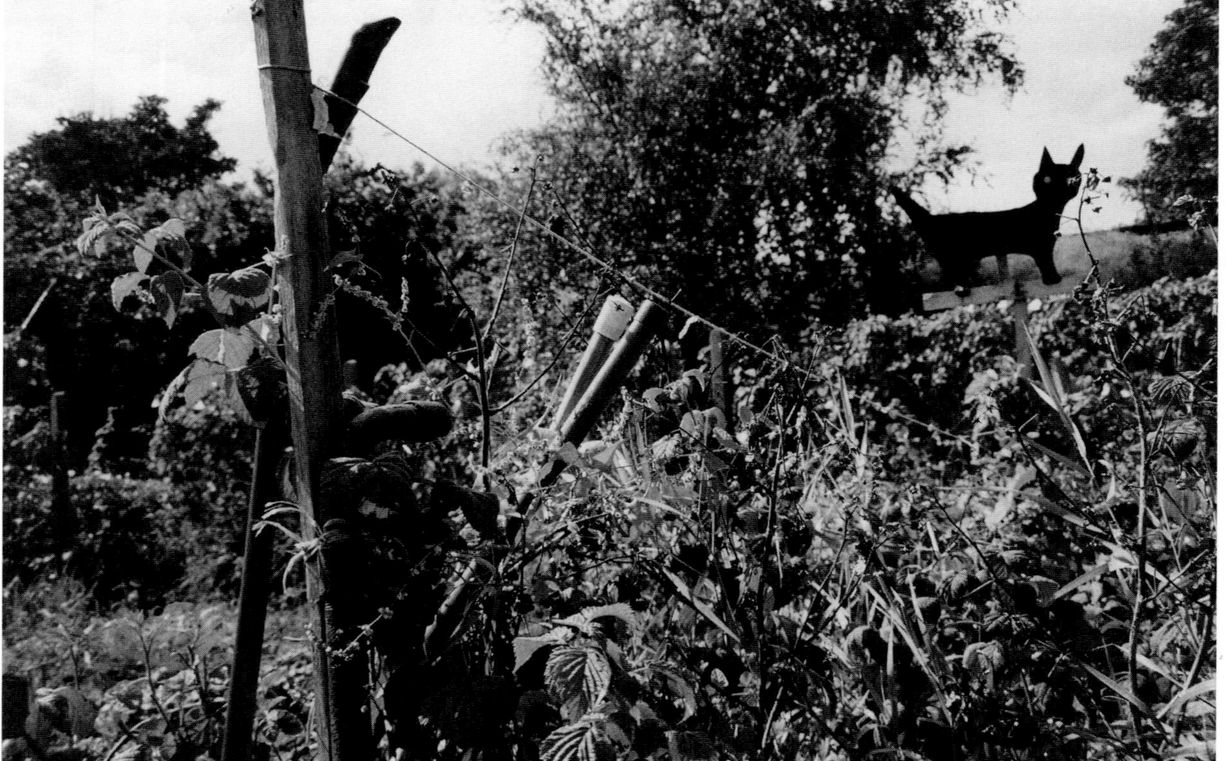

and Pringles crisp tubes jiggle on the end of bamboo canes and unwanted CD-Roms for a 10-hour Internet trial, iMac essentials and First Direct banking flutter in the wind.

In their gentle way, allotments may be one of our most subversive social spaces. The beleaguered allotment site is a small-scale, ramshackle utopia created by citizen-gardeners from all walks of life. Its values – self-sufficiency, mutual aid, inner quiet and deep communion, experienced through the body's exertion, with natural cycles of growth – are fundamentally at odds with the manufactured reality, instant consumer gratifications and atomisation of society outside the gate. Allotments are always vulnerable to break-ins and vandalism, but levels of trust among gardeners are high. Forks, hoes and trowels are left where they were last used, waiting for the plot-holder's return. Allotments are one of the few public spaces where, working alongside others in shared voluntary endeavour, it is possible to snatch a few hours away from the buzzing distractions and sensorial overload of contemporary life. Nothing would look more incongruous or misconceived on an allotment than an advertising billboard. The more insistent and vacuous the mediatised hubbub becomes, the more the allotment's unmediated simplicities are perceived as a refuge and luxury. In an era when 'intelligent' vehicles, buildings and clothing are presented as the logical next step for tool-using man, a boon to be welcomed by all, it is remarkable that such a degree of fulfilment is still to be had from fixing a piece of netting to a pole with a handful of pegs and watching your tomatoes ripen in the sun. 'It's the organicity of it, I suppose – the earthy wholesomeness – contrasted with the near sterility of professional activity,' notes Dr Chris Pinney, anthropologist and allotment-holder. 'It's the desire to escape the alienation of wage labour to temporarily inhabit this idyllic world where you control the lifecycle. It's wonderfully satisfying.'[4]

As *The Future of Allotments* recognised, for many allotment holders, their plot forms a fundamental part of their life. Long-term plot-holders develop especially deep attachments to their land. One local man has

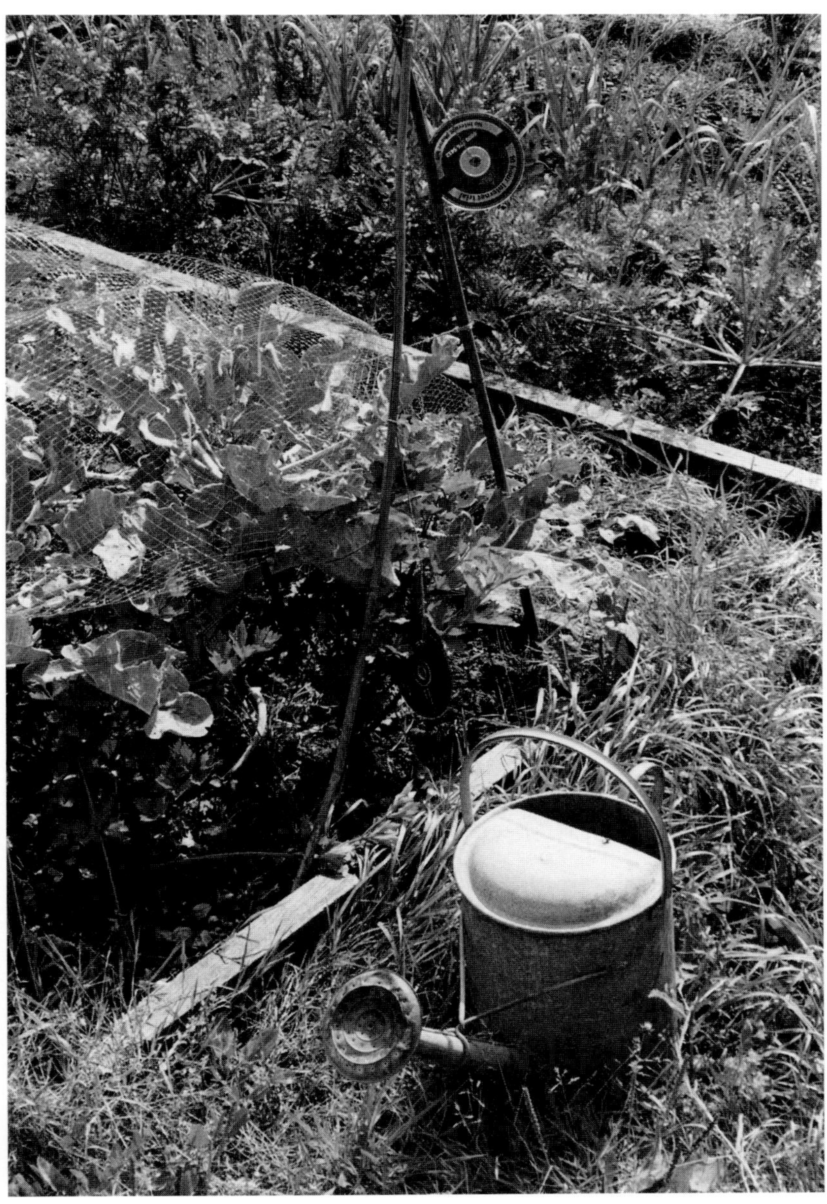

had his double-allotment for 36 years. I see him there almost every day. His father had it before him. The inner recesses of his intricately landscaped plot are a sanctuary, with a neatly trimmed strip of lawn, two apple trees and an old, lopsided wooden bench. The Select Committee's report found that allotment gardening had considerable therapeutic value and made a significant contribution to both physical and mental good health. 'I have lived in flats all my life and currently live on a busy council estate,' explained one plot-holder. 'I have no hope of ever being able to afford a garden, since my work is rather low status and underpaid ... My allotment has enabled me to find a side of myself I did not know existed and it also helps me cope with an extremely stressful job in a stressful city.'[5]

The report concluded that the benefits allotment sites provide to both allotment holders and the public mean that they have a 'critical role in modern, urban life'. It argued that there is an urgent need to protect existing sites and urged Government to clarify the role it sees for allotments in the future. Its recommendations covered changes in legislation, policy and practice and it suggested that the force of these measures would be lost if a piecemeal approach was adopted to their implementation. The Government's fence-sitting response was to endorse many of these recommendations on paper, while declining to support them in practice with new legislation.[6]

Looking out of my window, I am acutely aware of the temporality of this privileged patch of land. It has been here for decades, it's highly cultivated, yet it still feels provisional – under threat. To some ways of thinking, pockets of space like this don't make planning sense in built-up areas. Allotments don't pay their way. The site is the perfect size for a cul de sac of smart new houses. The industrial estate that borders one side would love to get its hands on it, so far without success. One day some canny developer will succeed and another green space will be expunged from London's map. The problem, as always, is that the qualities and ideas many of us most value are often the hardest to explain or justify in cost-accounting terms. What makes an area pleasant to live in for many people are the open spaces between the buildings, as much as the buildings themselves, and it is slowly becoming more widely understood that the value of housing (in both senses) is linked to the ratio of built environment to green space. I don't have an allotment, but I know that I have gained immeasurably by overlooking this site. Allotment gardening is more than just a 'worthwhile leisure activity', as the Government put it, on a par with camping or golf. Allotments are unique collective works, evolving organic tapestries to which many hands contribute. They offer a model of sustainable living, with much larger implications, at a time when this should be a national priority in a country with vision. Allotment gardeners: the new utopians? It has finally stopped raining and people are returning to their plots.

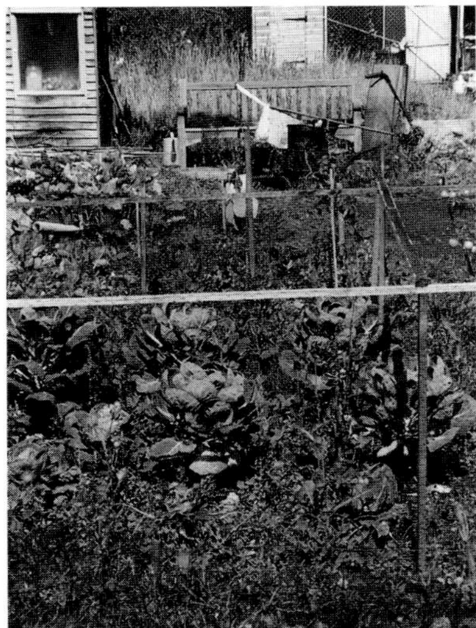

1. Simon Midgley, 'Finding the plot', *Guardian*, 4 April 2000.
2. Select Committee on the Environment, Transport and Regional Affairs, fifth report, *The Future of Allotments*, 24 June 1998.
3. Claude Lévi-Strauss, *The Savage Mind*, Oxford University Press, 1996 (first published 1962).
4. Quoted in Midgley, 'Finding the plot'.
5. Quoted in *The Future of Allotments*.
6. Department of the Environment, Transport and the Regions, The Government's Response to the Environment, Transport and Regional Affairs Committee's Report, *The Future of Allotments*, 13 November 1998. (www.regeneration.detr.gov.uk/info/env/allotments/index.htm)

Schrebergarten

Dr Daniel Gottlieb Moritz Schreber, a nineteenth-century physician from Leipzig, never set out to create a network of allotments across Germany. Instead, he wanted to establish play areas on the outskirts of town to give the children of poor families without gardens of their own a chance to spend time outdoors, which he believed to be crucial for their health.

As part of the educational nature of the scheme, the children were given small flower beds and vegetable patches to tend. These were soon taken over by their parents, who saw an invaluable opportunity to grow some fresh food for their own tables and 'family garden plots' were established. It didn't take long for garden houses and arbors to start appearing, as people spent more time relaxing in their own personal little parks. And so a new popular movement was somewhat inadvertently born as was the term 'Schrebergarten' in honour of the good doctor.

The meticulously cared for freshly-planted plots in a 'permanent garden belt' area in Hamburg, right, are the very picture of a self-contained suburban idyll. In fact, this picture was taken in May 1943.

Photographed in 1972, these allotments on the outskirts of Hamburg, below, are bordered by train tracks on one side and a busy motorway on the other, with the smokestacks of a large industrial zone in the distance. But for their owners, they represent a welcome refuge from the city.

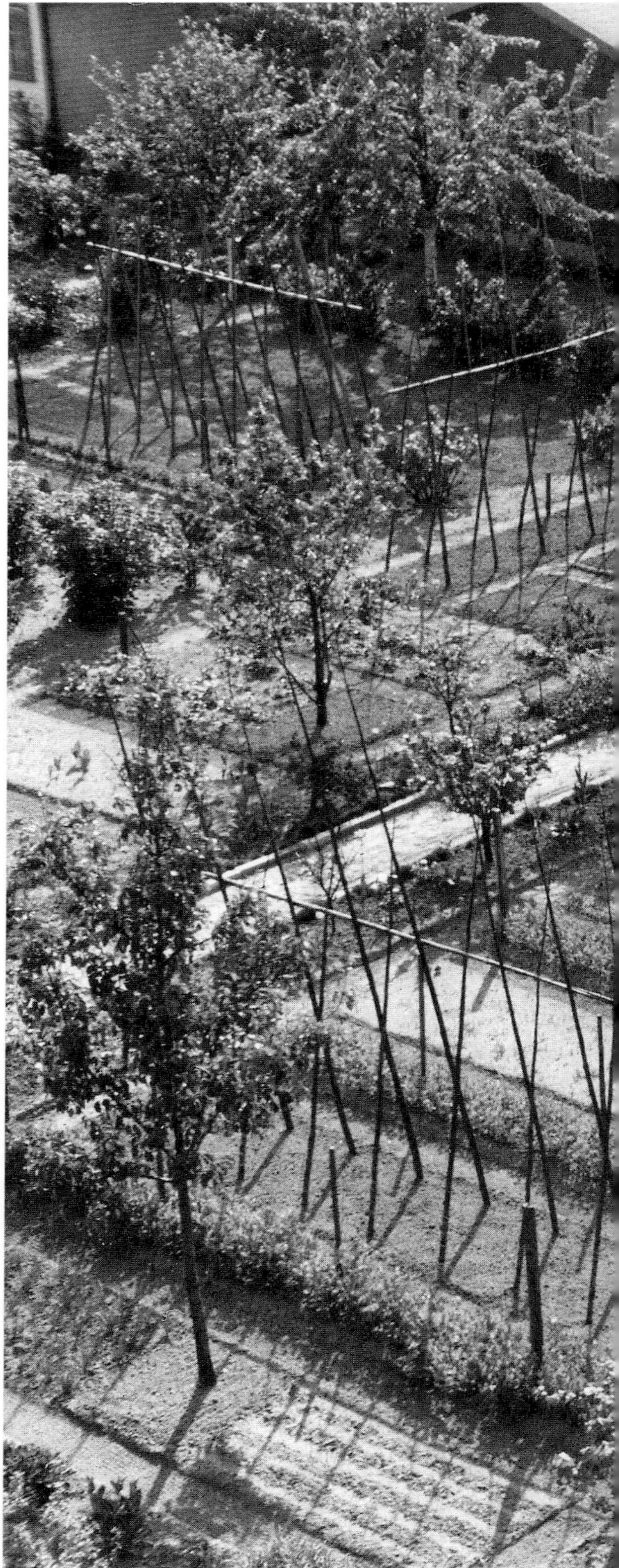

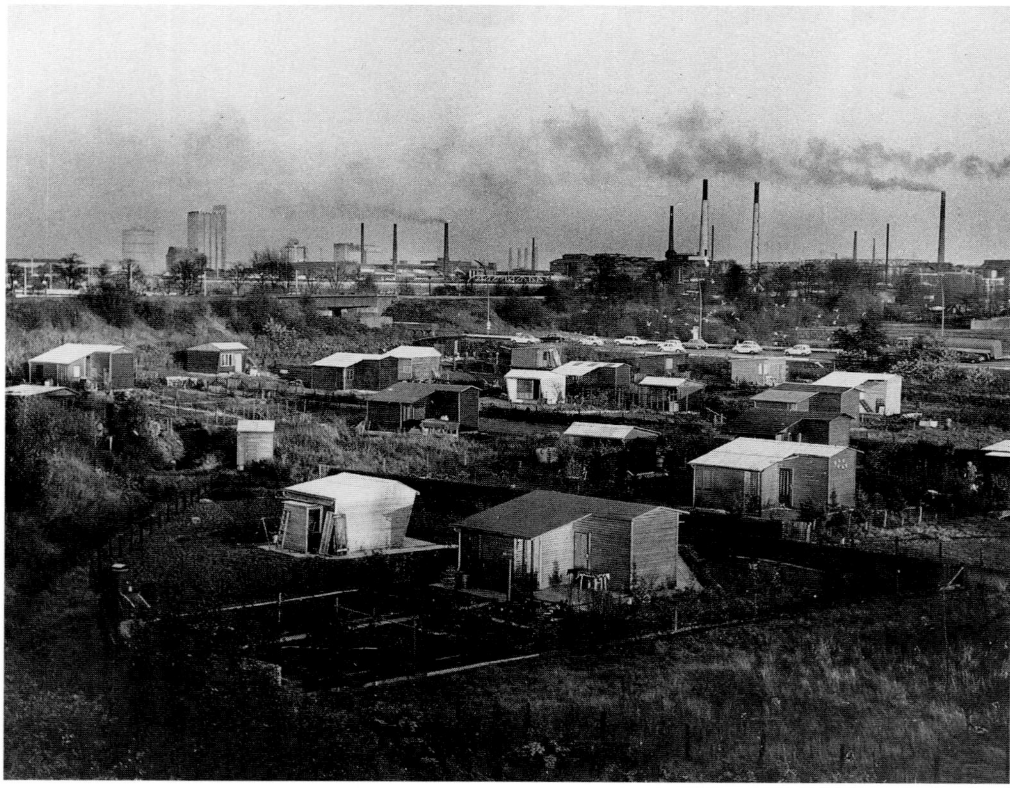

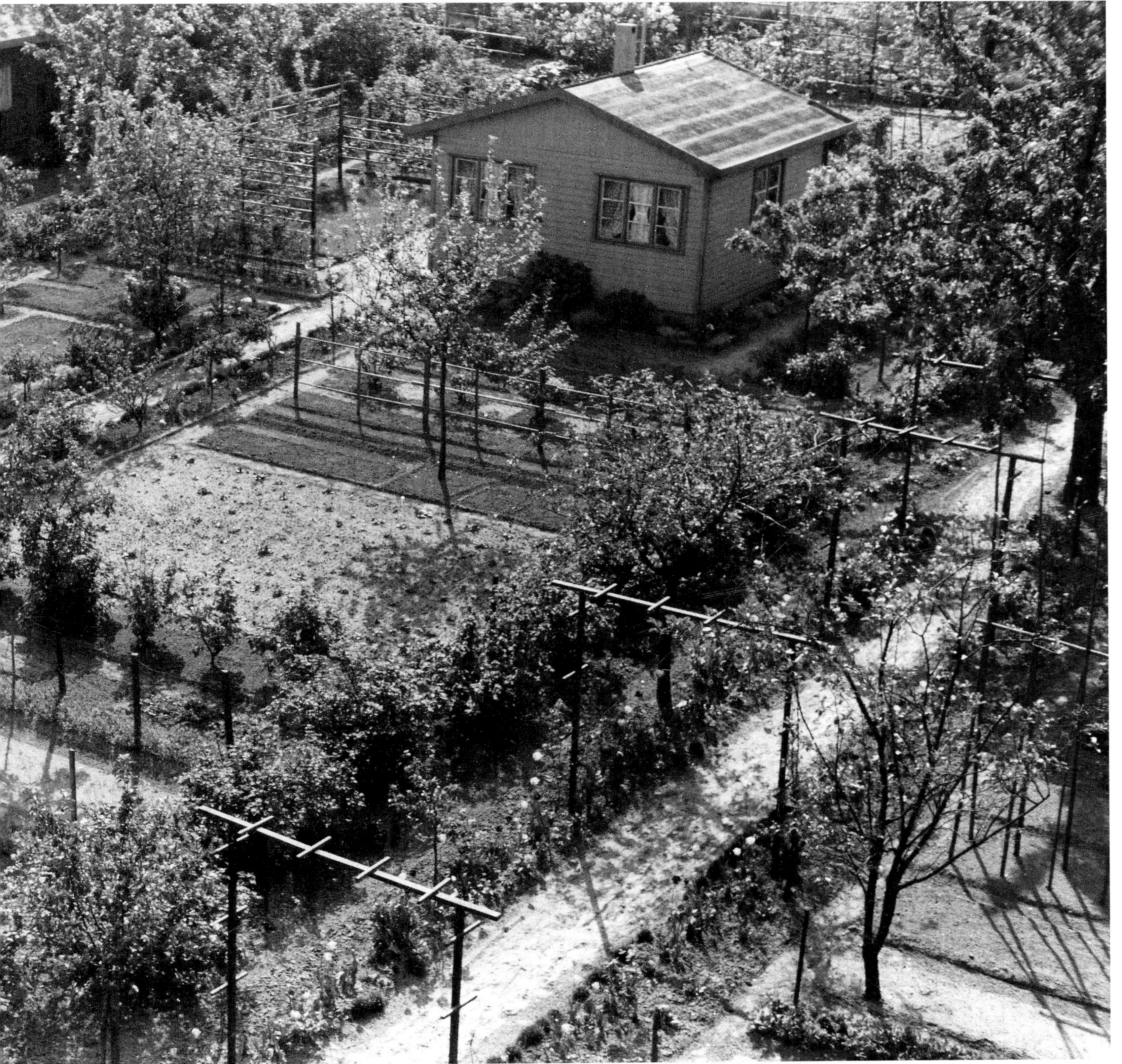

Model Railways

In the railway modeller's world, graffiti doesn't exist. Nor, for that matter, do unsightly telegraph wires, homeless drug addicts or brutalist concrete buildings. This is a world where steam trains run on time and children play happily on the village green. Here, the sun always shines and the pace of life is slow; horses pull carts along chalky lanes; and because it is always summer, the trains are never slowed down by leaves on the line. Never, that is, unless the people with their fingers on the control buttons decide to make it that way. The joy of railway modelling rests in the fact that the modeller is God: in the basements or attics of countless houses, people have lovingly created miniature worlds that are completely within their control, and not surprisingly, these fantasy worlds tend to edit out the nastier sides of life.

Yet for all their nostalgic economy with the truth, railway modellers have created a number of scenarios which are every bit as informative about a lost era of transport as the supposedly more accurate photography books from which their details have been gleaned. One of Britain's most impressive examples of model railway scenography is at the Pendon Museum in Oxfordshire. Here, scenes from the English countryside of the 1930s such as Madder Valley and Dartmoor and the Vale of the The White Horse have been lovingly recreated by a group of volunteers, faithful in many ways to

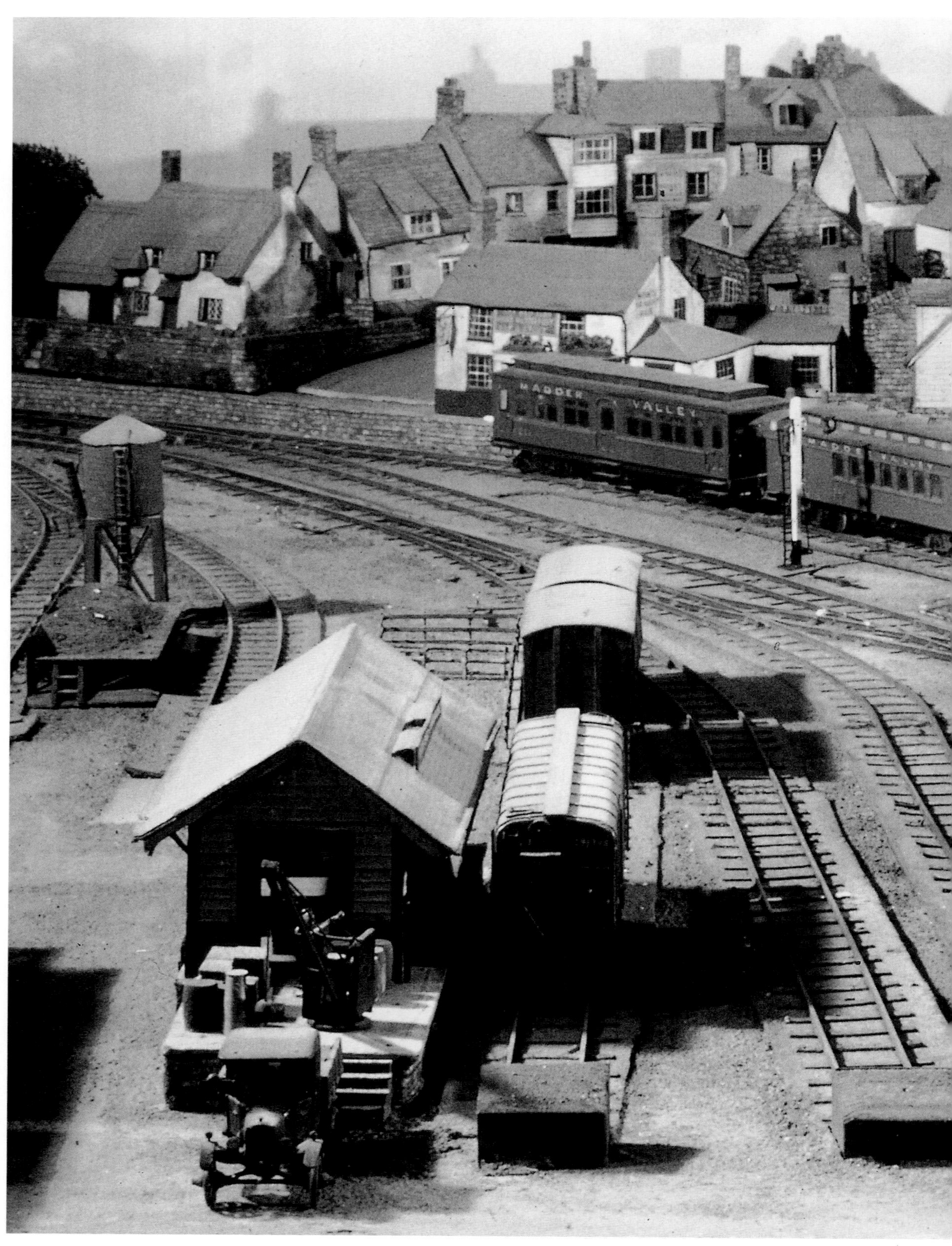

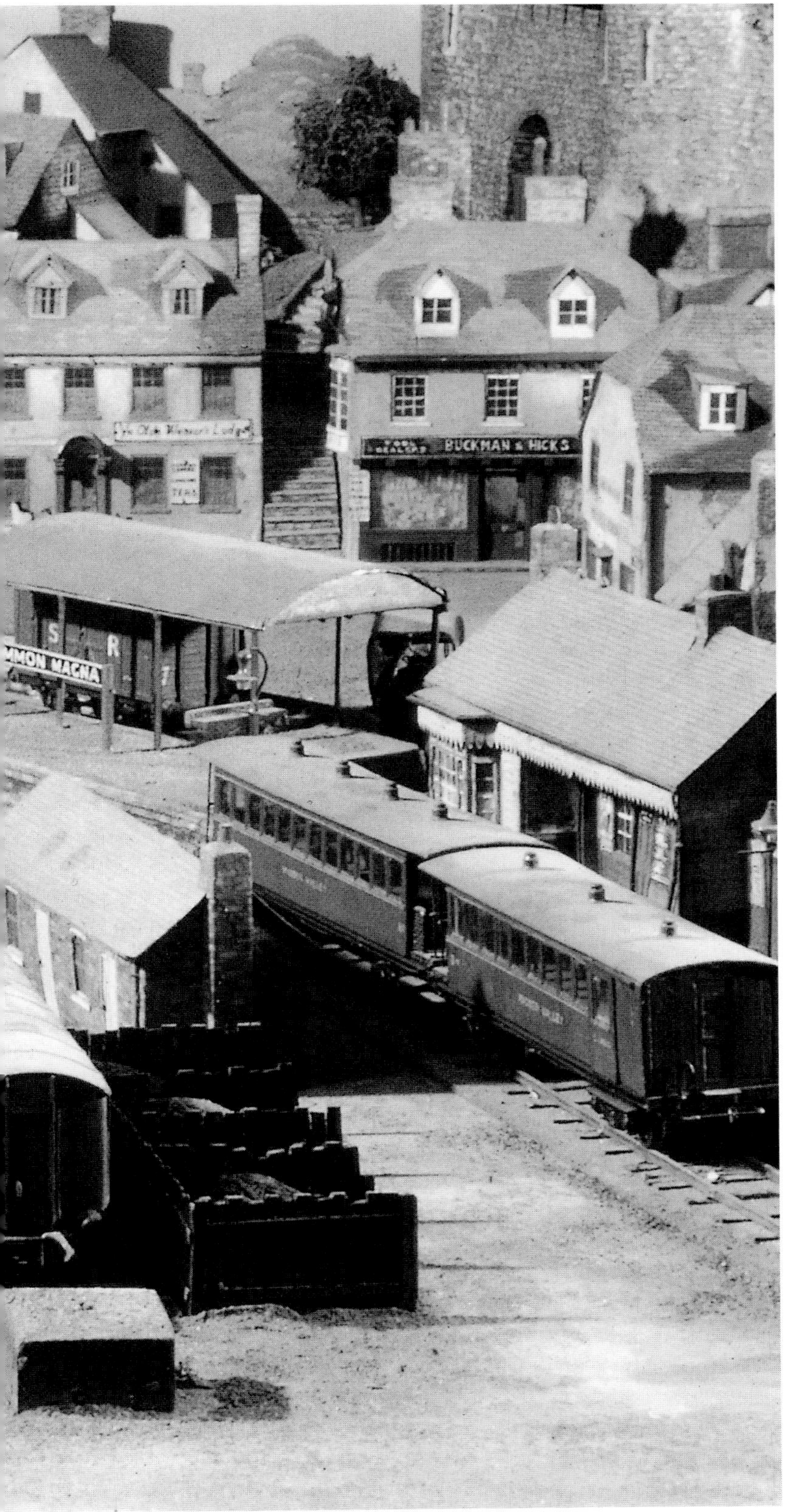

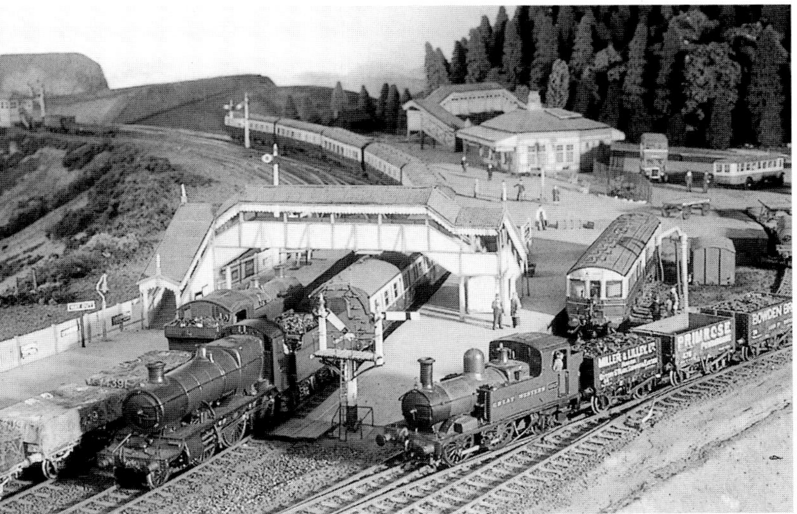
PRIMROSE

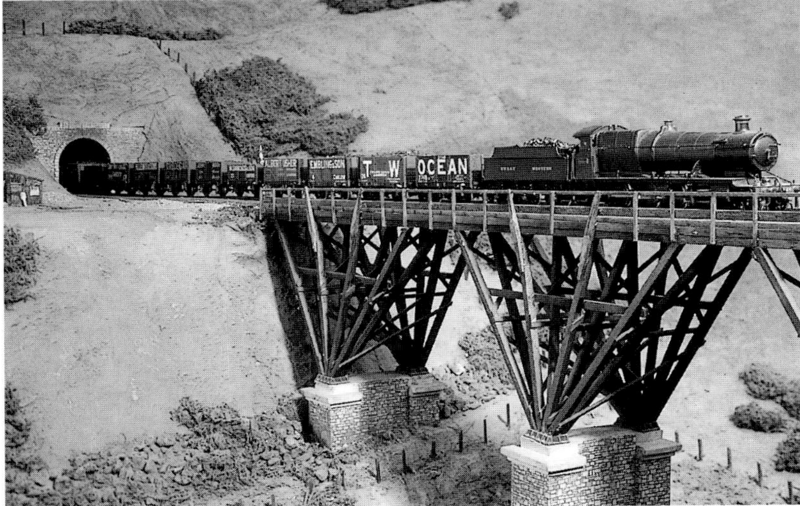
T W OCEAN

the historical details that the group has been able to unearth. Unlike the great photographers of steam trains, the modellers are not only interested in the details of the steam trains themselves but also the cultural context in which they operated. Although painting a highly partial picture of British life, the level of detailing on the model houses is extremely sensitively rendered. In Pendon Museum's 'Vale of the White Horse' scene, the modellers even make grudging concessions to the passage of time, and to the fact that the thatched roofs of some of the houses in the 1930s were increasingly being replaced by corrugated iron or asbestos. Local building styles are faithfully rendered, with the inclusion of stone buildings from the north side of the Vale (where stone is easily found), and cottages made from the local chalkstone (known as 'clunch') on the south side. Most of the cottages are thatched, in keeping with the fact that straw for thatching was the most widely available, and cheapest material at the time.

But there's the rub. The cultural and economic realities of life in the Vale are spun into a web of nostalgia, a series of highlights edited by the god-like modelling team. As the Pendon Museum Guide explains, 'Later generations have used concrete and lazy pebbledash, often disfiguring the handicraft of the past. The joy of modelling is that we can put the clock back, so that harshly modernised buildings again show their original delicate colours in sympathy with the local landscape. At Pendon, old-world gardens flourish in the mid-summer sunshine of the model scene. Nasturtiums pour over the bank above the road while hollyhocks, gladioli and sunflowers stand sentinel against cottage walls. Rabbits sit beside their burrows, and the roadside verges are alight with poppies, mallow and meadowsweet.'

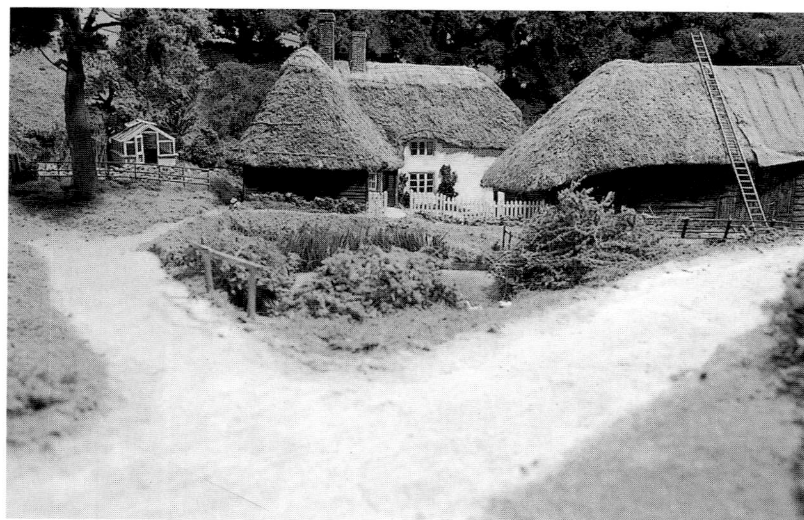

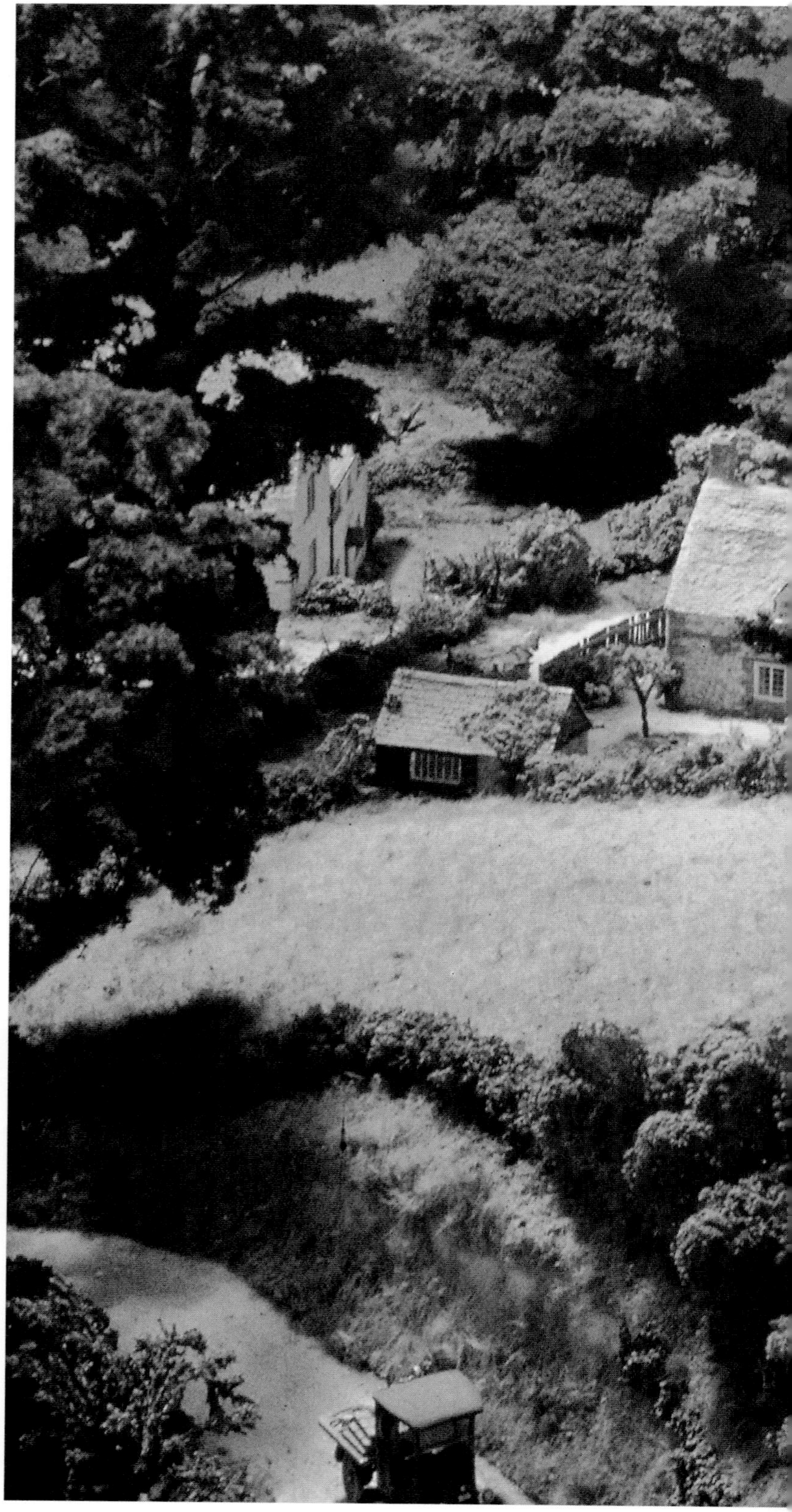

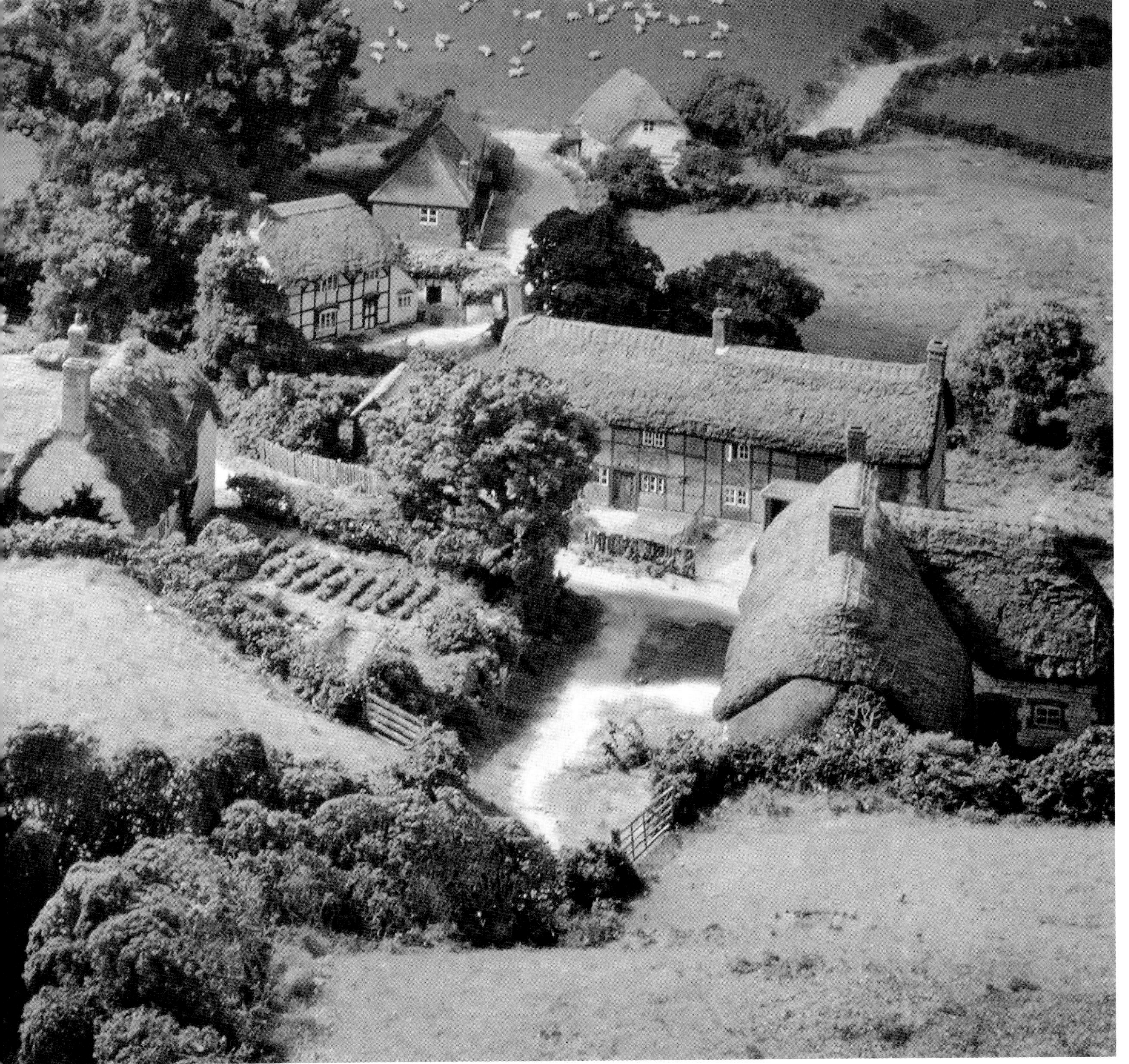

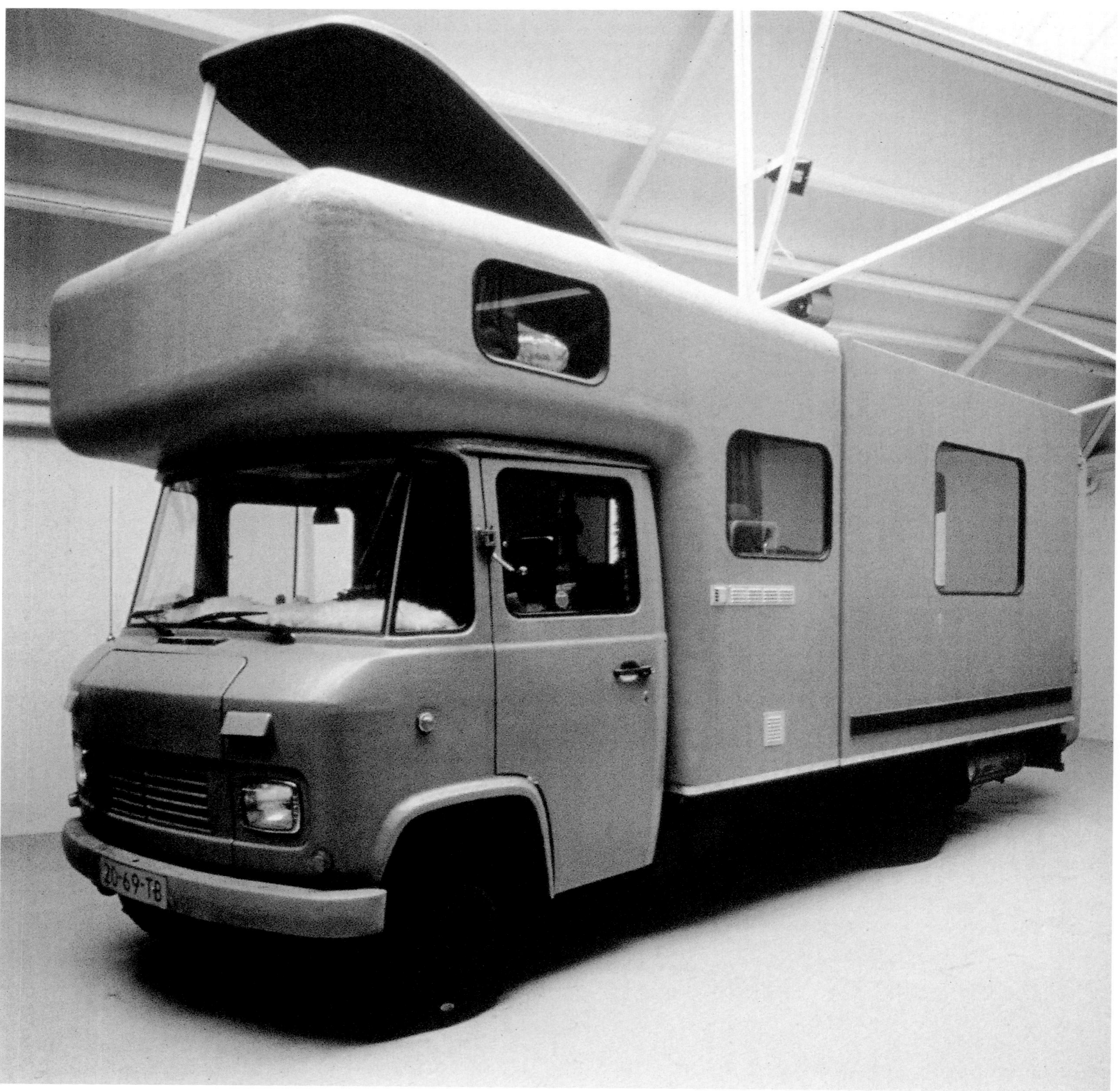
20-69-TB

AVL-Ville
Atelier van Lieshout

Atelier van Lieshout (AVL) are blurring the boundaries of architecture, art and design even more than they usually do with their latest, most ambitious project. For some time now, the Dutch studio founded by Joep van Lieshout in 1995 has been working towards the realisation of a utopian village called AVL-Ville – a free state where the people from AVL can live and work. AVL-Ville is part paramilitary survivalist compound, part hippy commune – an organic farm with an unexpected element of fun and danger.

AVL is currently in negotiations with the town of Rotterdam to realise AVL-Ville in the year 2001, when Rotterdam will be the cultural capital of Europe. The team has already identified a large site near Rotterdam airport that would be perfect for the project. But as this site still needs to be cleaned (it was previously used as a waste dump), AVL has come up with an alternative solution: in the run-up to 2001, the group is bringing together various projects that have previously been exhibited separately elsewhere to build a smaller, temporary version of AVL-Ville, located near the current AVL Studio in the docklands of Rotterdam.

Most of the artworks that van Lieshout and his team have produced over the last few years were made ultimately to function in AVL-Ville – pieces that can be used to live a more or less self-sufficient life. They range from a power plant and agricultural equipment to living and working modules made out of standardised units and refurbished shipping containers. Almost every need is catered for on site, with the provision of food, shelter, housing, work, emergency healthcare, intellectual and sexual stimulation. There is a fully equipped professional kitchen and a dining room, known as the AVL Canteen, and a simple field infirmary, housed in a 15-metre long shipping container. Apart from beds for the sick and injured, the AVL Hospital contains a nursing station, a waiting room and a rather sinister-looking operating theatre stocked with all the necessary instruments. The Atelier de l'Alcool et des Médicaments contains all the equipment needed to distil alcohol and produce herbal tonics, for either medicinal or recreational use. The Atelier des Armes et des Bombes is a workshop for terrorists, complete with welding equipment and a chemistry lab for concocting explosives from the most unlikely ingredients – in AVL-Ville, there are no restrictions on the production of drugs or weapons. Another vital element in the project is the Pioneer set – a pre-fabricated farm that can be assembled and disassembled whenever and wherever necessary, consisting of a farmhouse and several smaller outbuildings, such as a chicken coop and rabbit hutches. But the heart of AVL-Ville will be the workshop where all the studio's artworks are produced. When the village is fully realised, Atelier van Lieshout hope that it will allow a wider public to get to know their work, not only through visiting the exhibited artworks, but also by witnessing the actual process of making art. The realisation of AVL-Ville will mean the culmination of all the AVL projects that have been produced to date. It will be the ultimate artwork; their masterpiece, so to speak.

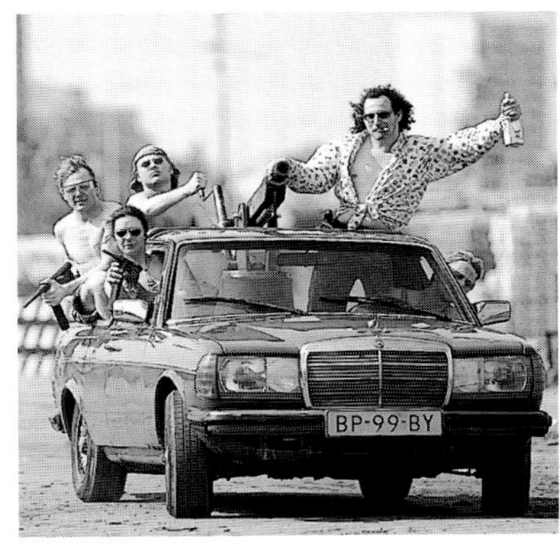

The Modular House Mobile, opposite, is AVL's take on a camper van. Even the cars in AVL-Ville are different: The Good, the Bad & the Ugly, top right, is a big Mercedes saloon that has been turned into a pick-up truck with its own 57mm cannon. A sketch for Robbers' Nest, right, suggests that further military activity is forseen.

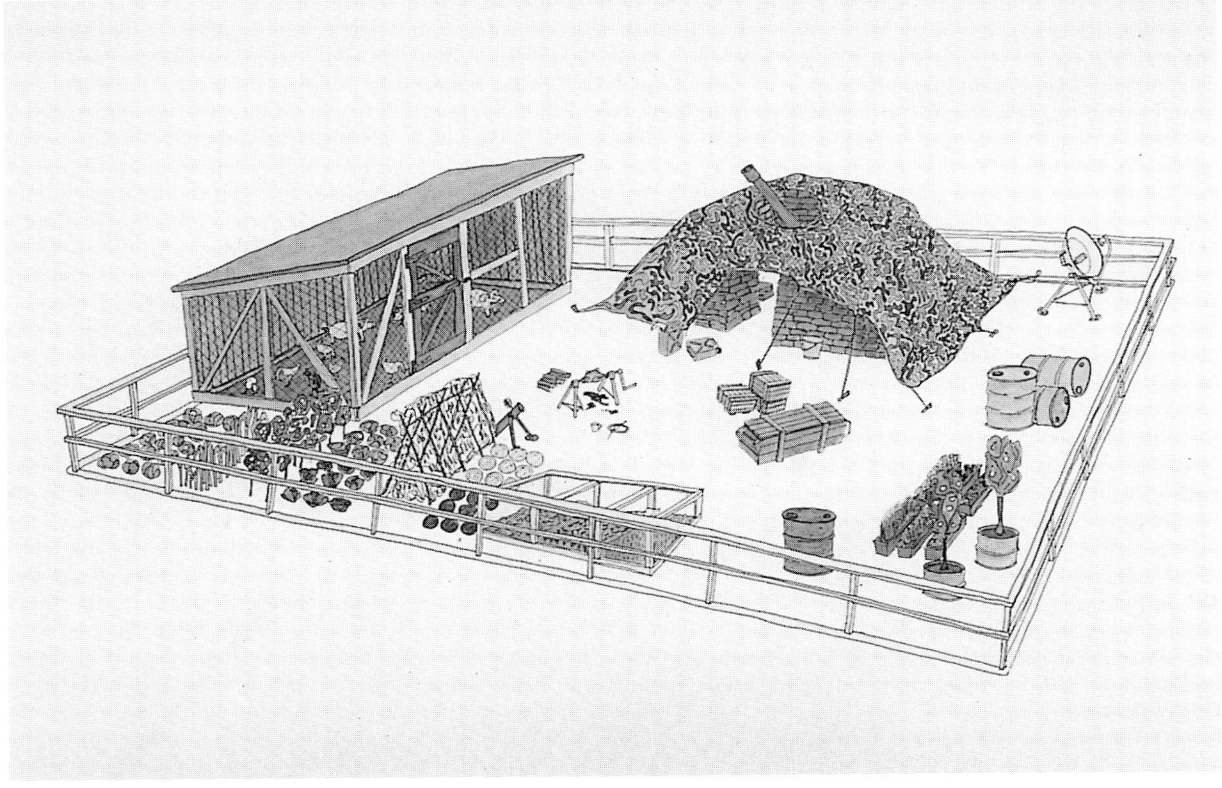

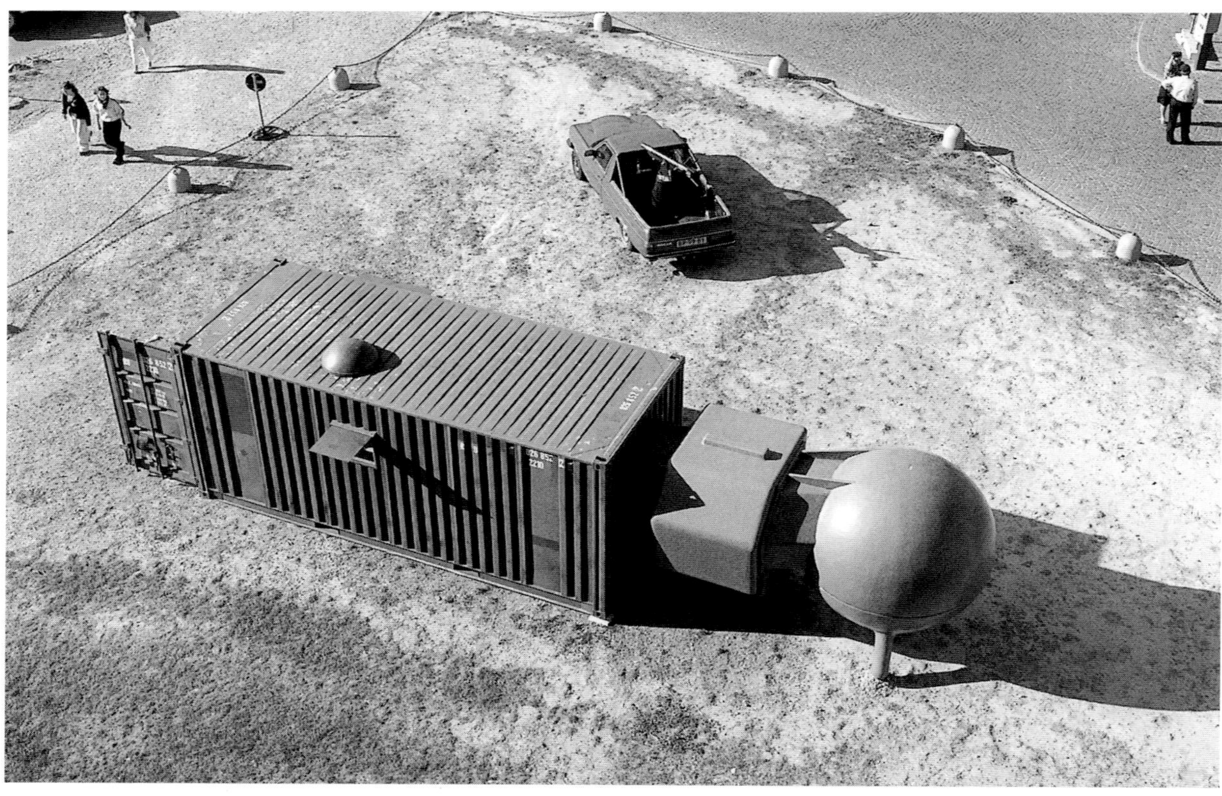

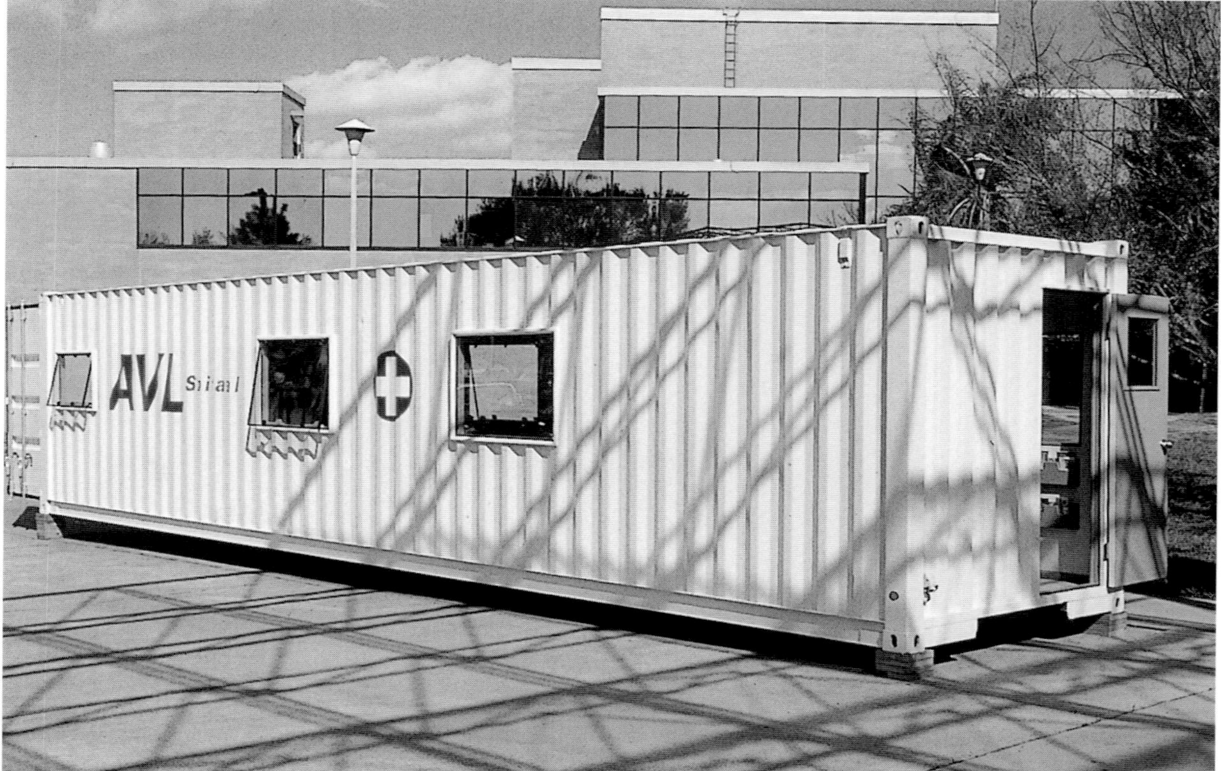

The Atelier des Armes et des Bombes, top, contains everything you could ever need to defend your territory against attack. There is an attached sleep/study ball, should the inhabitants want a break from bomb-making. The AVL-Hospital, left and opposite, is fully equipped for most medical emergencies.

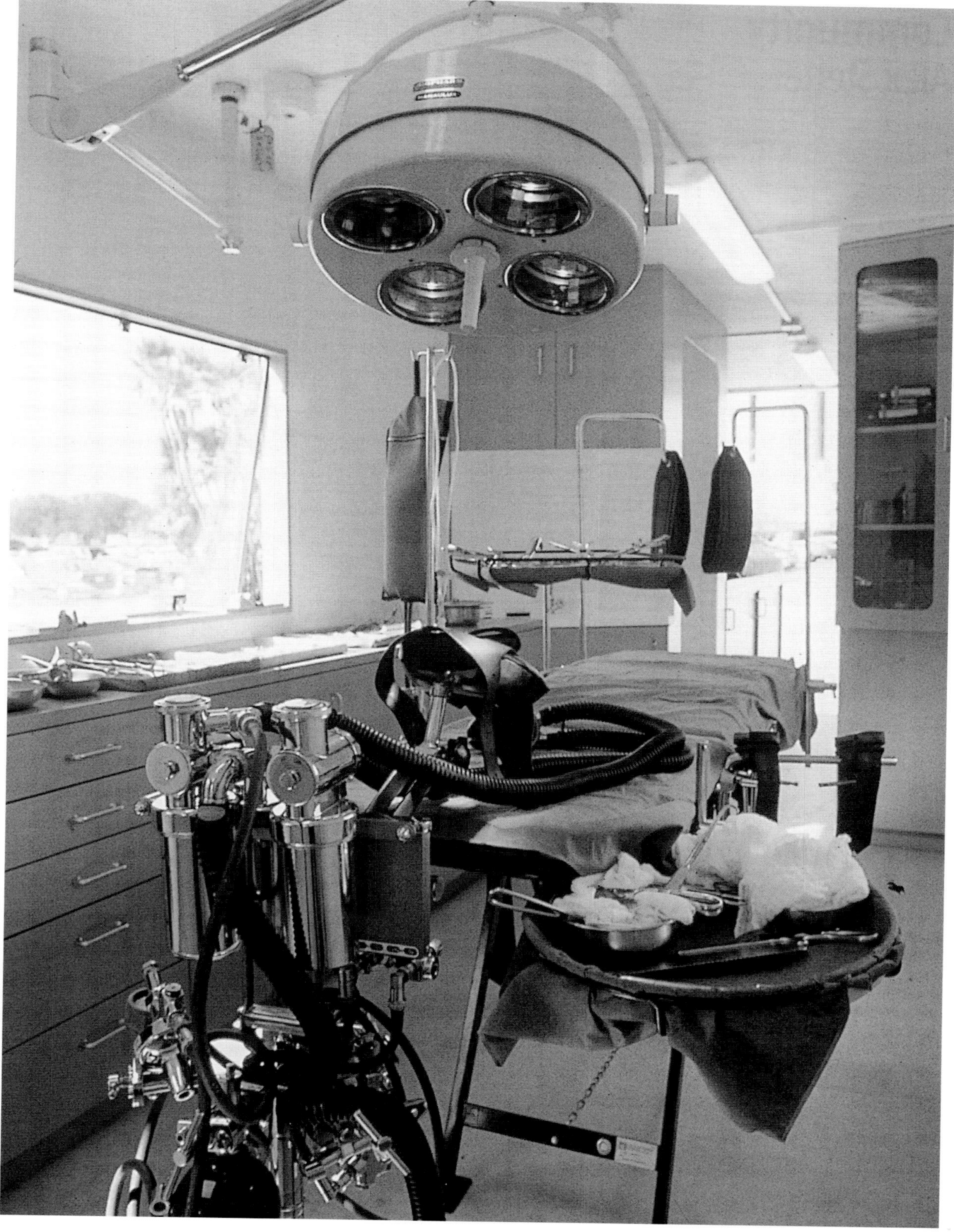

Community
Alex Stetter

In October 1998, reports began appearing in the British press about a 'lost tribe' that had apparently been discovered in West Wales. A low-flying spotter plane surveying the region for the Pembrokeshire National Park Service had noticed what looked like a reflection from a window in an area that was thought to be uninhabited. On closer inspection, this turned out to be a solar panel from an eco-community called Brithdir Mawr.

An experimental community, Brithdir Mawr is made up of around twenty adults and children who are trying to find a more sustainable way of living. Of course, the people who live there do not think of themselves as a tribe, or even as a commune – another word frequently used to describe their way of life. They are hardly lost, or trying to hide: Brithdir Mawr is not far from the neat little seaside town of Newport in Pembrokeshire, and the track that leads to the site is clearly sign-posted from one of the few roads out of town. They are not inhabiting the land illegally, as the 160 acres of land they have lived on since 1993 are owned by the community's founder, architectural historian Julian Orbach. And they don't live in jerry-built huts and primitive shelters, either, but in a variety of practical and rather beautiful dwellings, some of which are admittedly less traditional than others. But these low-impact buildings provoked the ire of Pembrokeshire County Council's planning department, and brought the group plenty of unwanted attention.

At the heart of the site is a lovingly restored stone farmhouse, surrounded by smaller buildings and barns, which provide living space for four families. The ground floor of the farmhouse is given over to a large communal kitchen and meeting space, where community members come together for regular shared meals, to which everyone is summoned with a few blasts on a large conch shell. Everyone is expected to do their share of the work, and there are weekly business meetings to deal with the running of the farm. There are also opportunities to call special meetings to discuss any non business-related matters. One of the restored farm buildings has been turned into a small hostel for visitors and walkers, the income from which pays for communal purchases like seed and animal feed. Otherwise, each household looks after itself – many community members have part-time jobs – and people have their own homes and even gardens within the site. The children don't go to school, but are educated within the community – the eldest has recently passed her A-levels. Rather than live with their parents, the teenagers have their own rooms on the second floor of the main building, where they are allowed to do as they please, even if that involves heating up convenience foods or watching TV.

The community members grow fruit and vegetables, keep chickens, ducks and goats, and rely on their woodlands for fuel for heating and cooking. A combination of wind- and water-powered generators and solar panels takes cares of most of their electricity requirements, but Brithdir is still hooked up to mains electricity as a fall-back. There is a compost toilet, housed in a little grass-roofed hut, stocked with publications about sustainable living and the principles of permaculture. The shared bathroom looks conventional enough, but taking a hot bath in iwinter, when solar power can't be relied upon to heat the water, involves chopping up a large pile of wood and firing up the Raeburn. A system of reed beds takes care of cleaning any 'grey' and waste water from kitchens and bathrooms. The community doesn't attempt to be completely self-sufficient – no-one has to go without tea, rice or tobacco – but aims to live in harmony with the land. The long-term aim is to be wholly independent of mains electricity or water, and for the farm to support all inhabitants. Horses are used around the farm to haul heavy loads, but some community members have cars, and there is a shared vehicle which has been converted to run on electricity. There are also tools it would be difficult to do without, like petrol-powered chainsaws and, in the past, JCBs have been hired in for building work. The people of Brithdir Mawr are not trying to turn back the clock or live like the Amish – they want to demonstrate that there can be a more sustainable way forward.

But the residents of Brithdir Mawr – 'large speckled land' in Welsh – are probably most famous for the buildings that got them into trouble with the local planning department when the site was first 'discovered'. The houses are built of renewable and locally found materials, including bales of straw used for constructing walls and turf for the roofs, as well as recycled window frames and glass. The buildings include a wooden geodesic dome structure by the vegetable garden, a couple of barns and stables and a large wood-framed round house, which is partially dug into a grassy bank in one of the fields. It was the solar panel outside this almost invisible dwelling that gave away the existence of the community. From some ground-level vantage

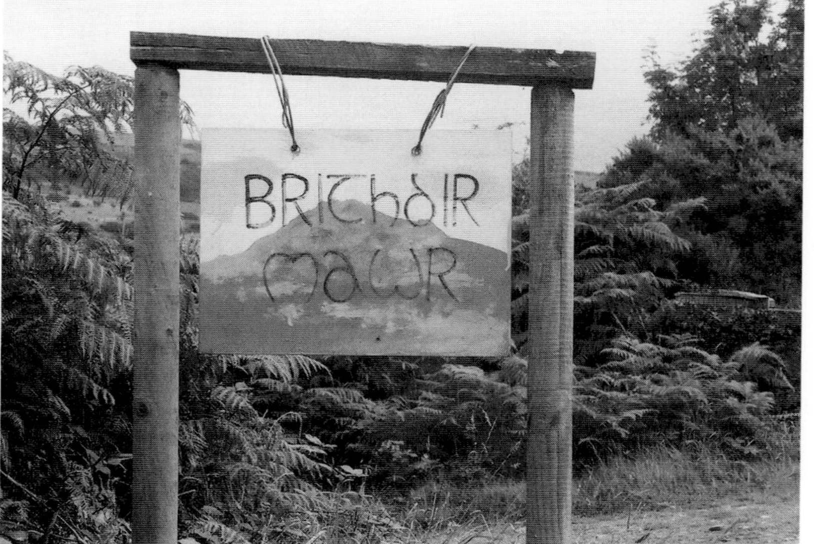

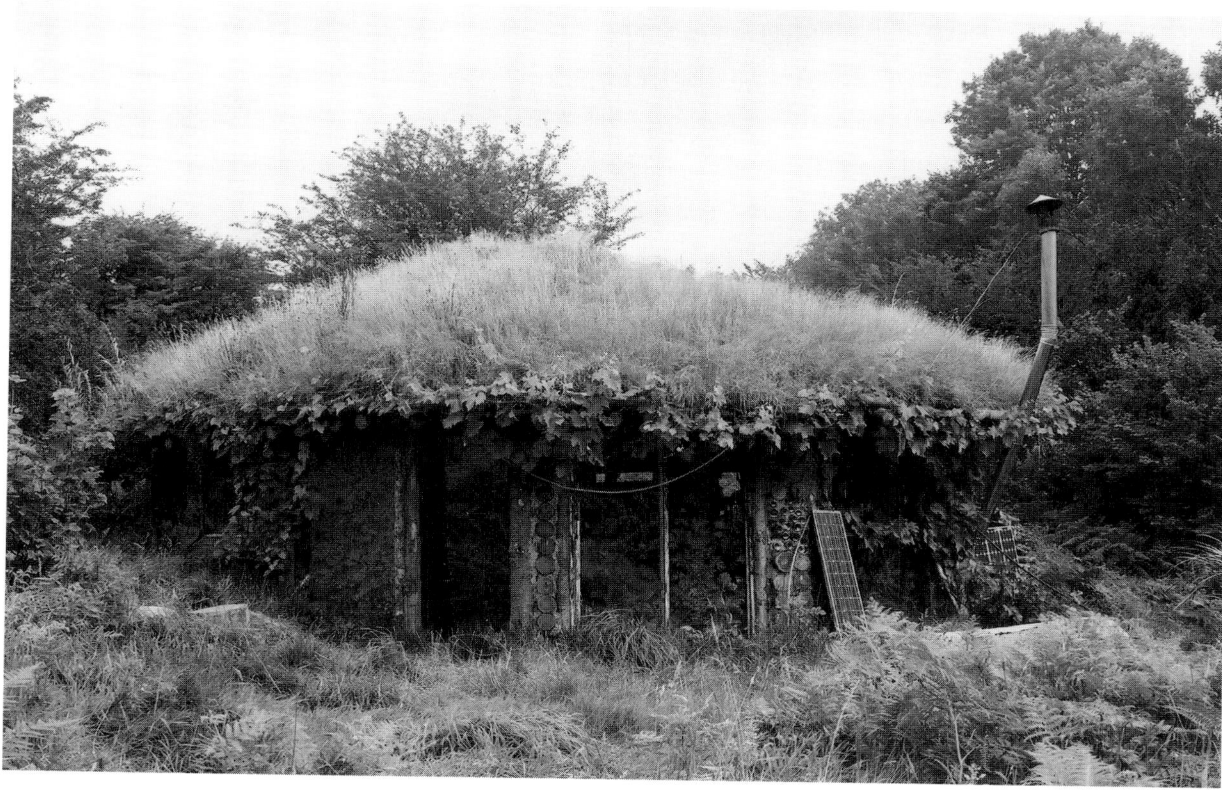

The round house at Brithdir Mawr, above and right, is a low-impact dwelling: built using only sustainable materials such as wood, straw and turf, the main structure is biodegradable. Solar panels provide electricity, running water is piped in from a nearby spring and there's a compost toilet round the back.

points, only the chimney pot sticking out of the grass- and strawberry plant-covered roof gives any indication of the surprisingly spacious home underneath. Tucked away at the far end of one of the meadows, half-hidden in the trees and tall grass, is a tiny round hut, built of clay, straw and wood. There are rugs on the floor, a small wood-burning stove with a kettle and shelves full of books, food and candles. Unlike the round house and the dome, no one lives there full-time: instead its owner uses it as an extension of her main home in one of the farm buildings, a place to sleep and be closer to nature. It is an intimate, inviting space, not much more than 2 metres across, cosy with its mud walls and clearly visible roof supports and the lingering smell of wood smoke. All you can see through the small, low windows are trees and tall grass – it feels like the kind of place you wished you could have had when you were a child, building huts out of furniture and tablecloths at the bottom of the garden in order to get some private space of your own. The hut is considered 'the best room in the house', and is used as a spare room for particularly privileged guests.

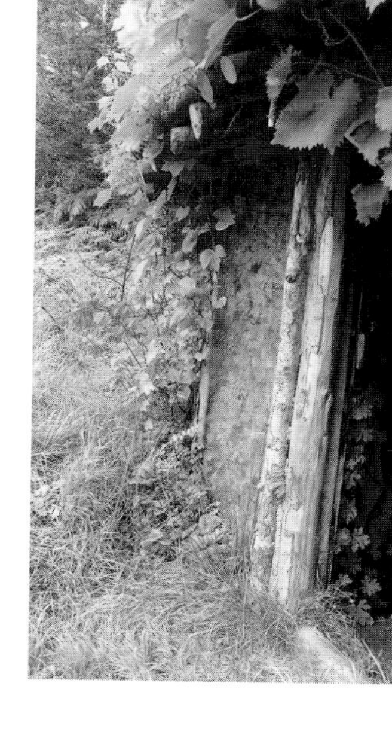

Of course buildings like these will not last forever, but then many apparently more solid structures are pulled down or abandoned long before they reach the end of their natural life span. At least houses like these will leave hardly any trace of ever having existed: they are designed to last for 30 to 40 years and then biodegrade. They are also cheap and easy to build: the Brithdir round house cost £2500, with the single most expensive component being the pond liner used to waterproof the roof. No new, sawn wood was used in its construction, only soft-wood plantation thinnings, along with straw and clay to pack out the walls. The house is surprisingly big, about eleven metres in diameter, with a great sense of space and light, thanks to there being a window in every section of the wall, apart from the part that is dug into the hill. The south-facing front section of the house is like a winter garden, with floor to ceiling glass and lush greenery both inside and out. A few metres inside the circular outside wall, an inner circle of thirteen taller posts supports the roof beams high above. These posts also screen off the central living space from the sleeping area, storage space and the kitchen located on the perimeter. High above, the main rafters of the reciprocal frame roof spiral out around a large central skylight, in a beautiful geometrical pattern that adds to the unexpectedly grand atmosphere. Structures like the round house are undeniably uplifting spaces to live and be in after spending some time in one of these welcoming, organic spaces, a conventional building seems strangely clinical.

Having little faith in the council inspectors' ability to judge elements that they were unfamiliar with, the people of Brithdir had not sought planning permission before starting the building work. They intended to invite the planners over to see the finished buildings for themselves, in the hope that they would accept that, while the structures might not match existing official criteria, they were functional, safe and designed to be in sympathy with their environment. Unfortunately, the incident with the spotter plane put an end to that idea. The people of Brithdir Mawr have spent the last two years

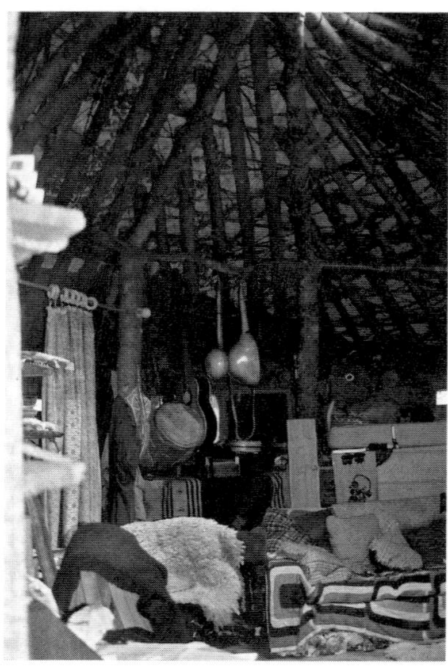

trying to ensure the future of their community, appealing against the contravention notices issued by the council. They managed to gain retrospective permission for the geodesic dome house thanks to a planning loophole – any enforcement notice has to be served with four years of a building being 'substantially completed' and capable of being occupied. They are also following the precedent set by the Centre for Alternative Technology in Machynlleth in Powys, by applying for a change of use from a farm and hostel to an educational project in sustainable living, opening up the site to the curious and the converted alike. Visitors are expected to help with the work that needs doing around the site, which gives them a chance to find out if they have the courage it takes to follow suit. The people of Brithdir Mawr believe the best way to convince others of the value of their work is to let them see and experience their way of life for themselves.

So Brithdir Mawr is now a stop on the alternative architectural Grand Tour, visited by those who are hoping to pick up some valuable tips on setting up a similar community for themselves. There is already a well-established network concerned with 'low-impact' life in Britain, and similarly-motivated sustainable communities exist around the country. They range from self-build housing schemes that ended up as a 'community' almost by default, as the participants realised that it would be cheaper and more efficient to pool their skills and tools, to people living in benders and tents in Somerset. Britain might also soon see a version of the 'earthships' made of old car tyres found in the desert outside Taos, New Mexico, that are designed to allow their inhabitants to exist 'off the grid'. The basic design can be adapted to suit different climates and environments, making it a much more viable long-term proposition for less arid zones than the teepee or the yurt, which are open to the elements. Plans and building instructions are easy to buy via the Internet, which has turned out to be the ideal way for low-impact communities around the world to keep in touch, share information and above all, spread the word to others.

Moving to a place like Brithdir Mawr is not a decision to be taken lightly. For a start, you have to know what you are doing – everyone brought skills, experience and knowledge to the project. And living here involves a fundamental reversal: rather than working in order to support the life you want to live, your life becomes closely entwined with the work you do as a member of the community – growing food, maintaining land and buildings, raising and teaching the children. There are many aspects of Brithdir Mawr that could easily be applied to other, less radical, circumstances, like the use of wind and solar power in a domestic context and some of the building techniques – but you leave the place with the distinct impression that this approach works best when all the elements are brought together. It is not just a matter of protecting the environment, but about questioning the way we live and the choices we make, about developing a different perspective on life. When one of the Brithdir Mawr children draws a picture of a house, it has the usual two square windows and a door in the middle – but the walls are definitely curved.

The basic form of the reciprocal frame roof of the round house, above, can be clearly seen in the plain wood structure, opposite, also at Brithdir Mawr. Anyone interested in building their own version of Tony Wrench's home can find out how in publications like *Low Impact News*, right, which carries information about subjects ranging from coppicing woodlands and organic farming to gaining planning permission and holding alternative wedding ceremonies.

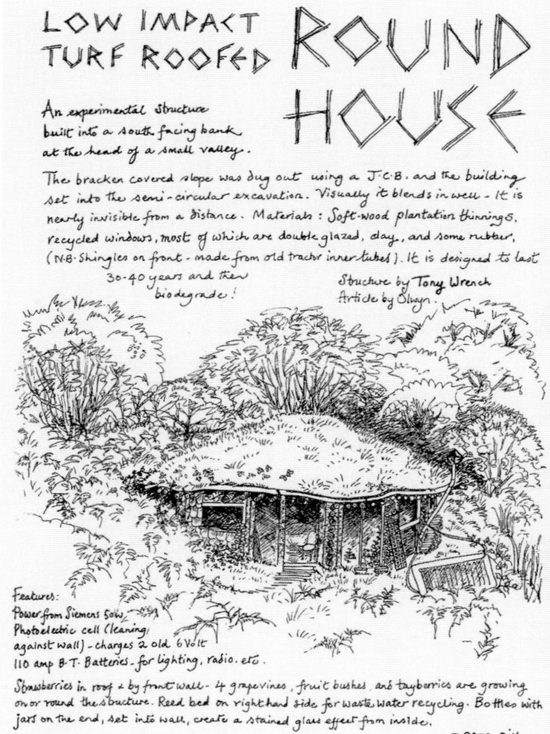

LOW IMPACT TURF ROOFED ROUND HOUSE

An experimental structure built into a south facing bank at the head of a small valley.

The bracken covered slope was dug out using a J.C.B. and the building set into the semi-circular excavation. Visually it blends in well – It is nearly invisible from a distance. Materials: Soft-wood plantation thinnings, recycled windows, most of which are double glazed, clay, and some rubber, (N.B. Shingles on front – made from old tractor inner tubes). It is designed to last 30-40 years and then biodegrade!

Structure by Tony Wrench
Article by Olwyn.

Features:
Power from Siemens 50w, Photoelectric cell (leaning against wall) – charges 2 old 6 Volt 110 amp B.T. Batteries – for lighting, radio. etc.

Strawberries in roof & by front wall – 4 grapevines, fruit bushes, and tayberries are growing on or round the structure. Reed bed on right hand side for waste water recycling. Bottles with jars on the end, set into wall, create a stained glass effect from inside.

– page six –

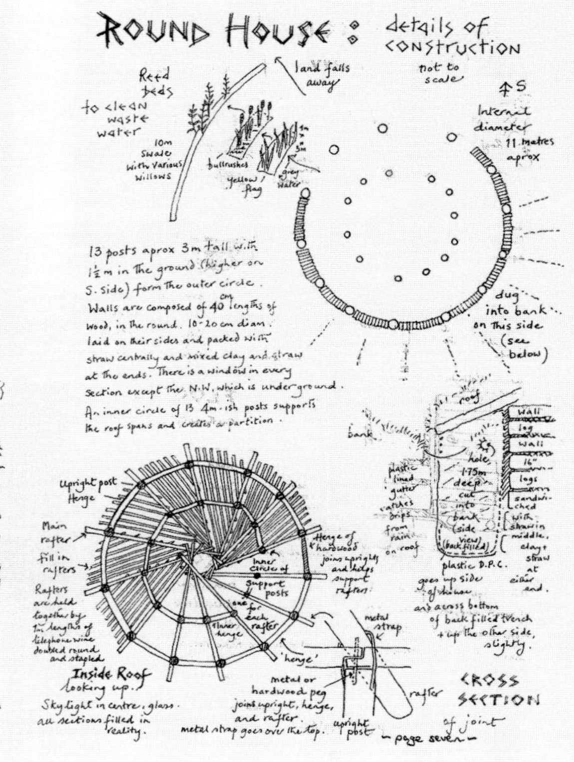

ROUND HOUSE: details of CONSTRUCTION

13 posts aprox 3m tall with 1½ m in the ground (higher on S. side) form the outer circle. Walls are composed of 40 cm lengths of wood, in the round. 10-20 cm diam. laid on their sides and packed with straw centrally and mixed clay and straw at the ends. There is a window in every section except the N.W. which is underground. An inner circle of 13 4m-ish posts supports the roof spans and creates a partition.

– page seven –

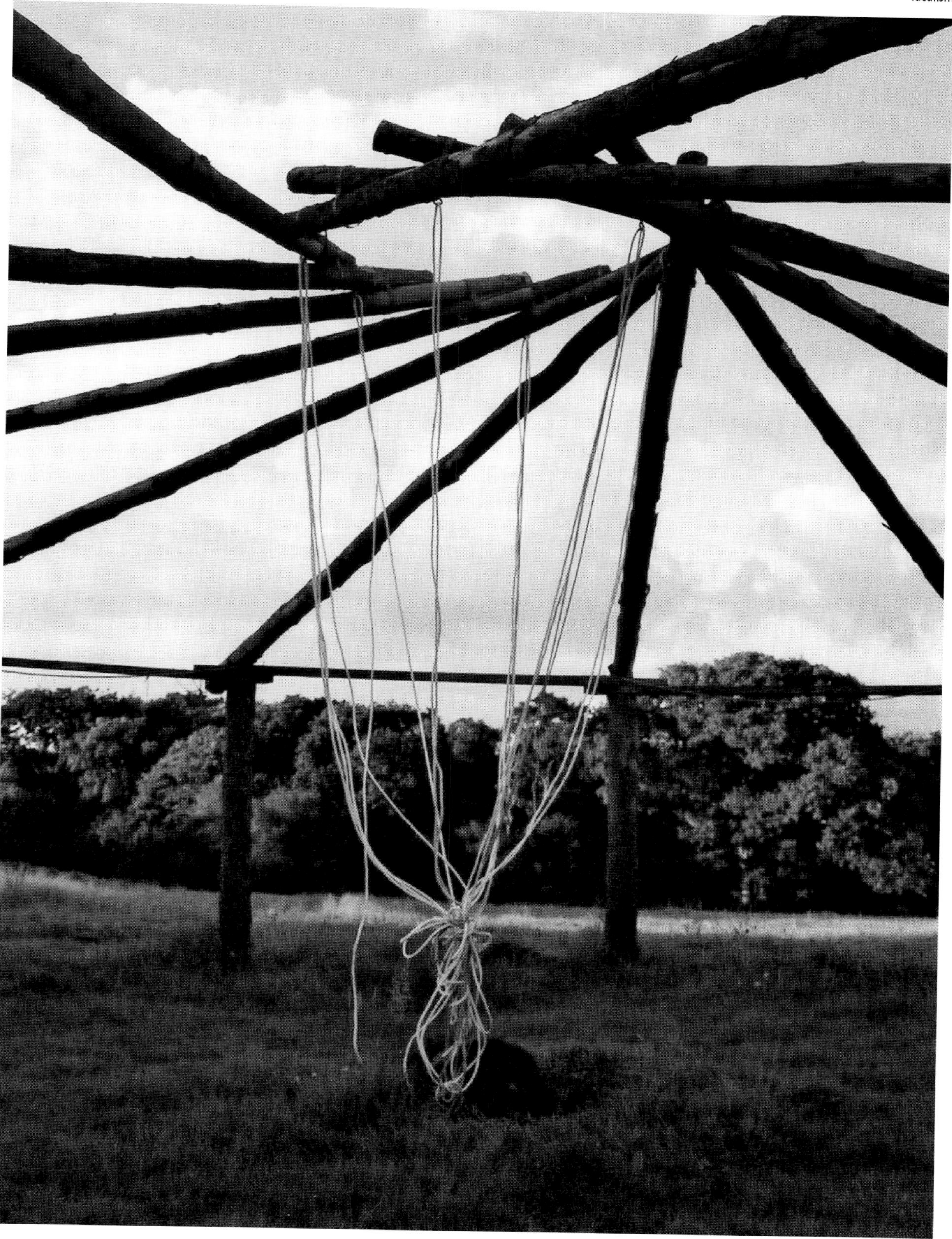

Schullandheim

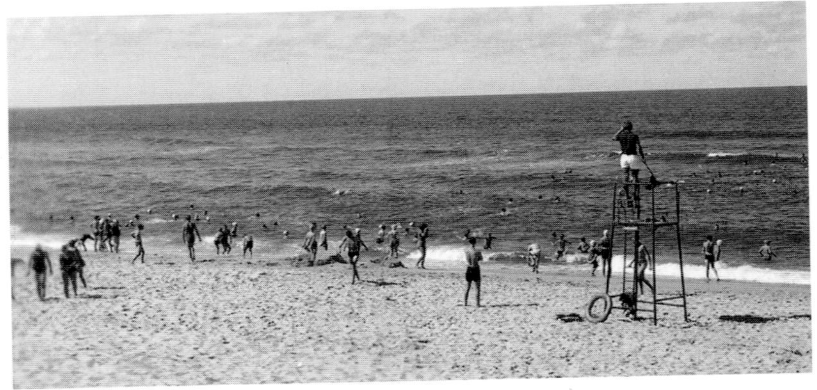

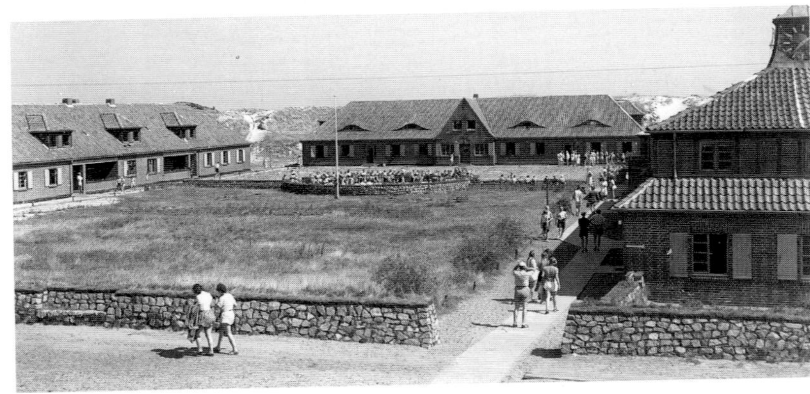

These archive photographs taken in the early 1950s show holiday camps on the island of Sylt, off the coast of northern Germany, where generations of children have been sent to get out of the city and onto the beach.
There are still hundreds of such places in Germany today, not just by the sea but also in the mountains, on lakes or in the forest. Some focus on fun outdoor activities, but the idea of the 'Schullandheim' is to provide visiting school groups with a wholesome but educational break from their usual routine – an open-air class room.

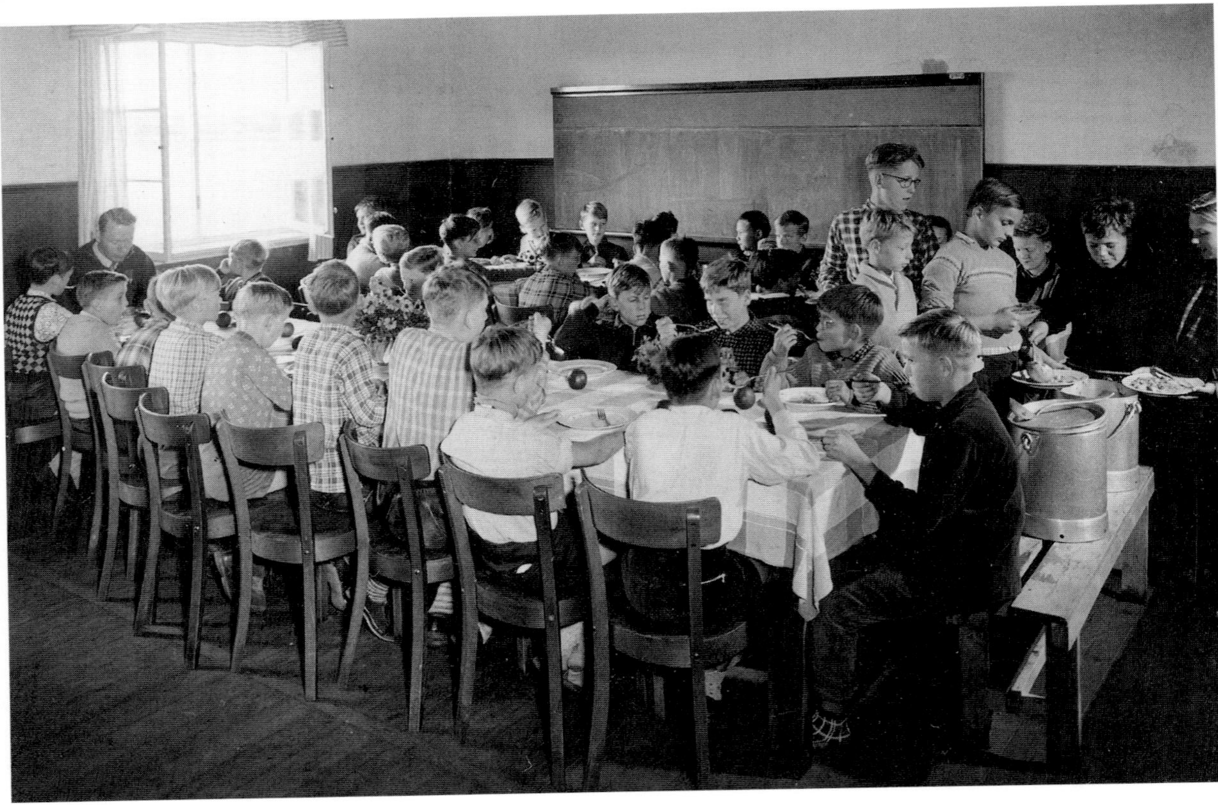

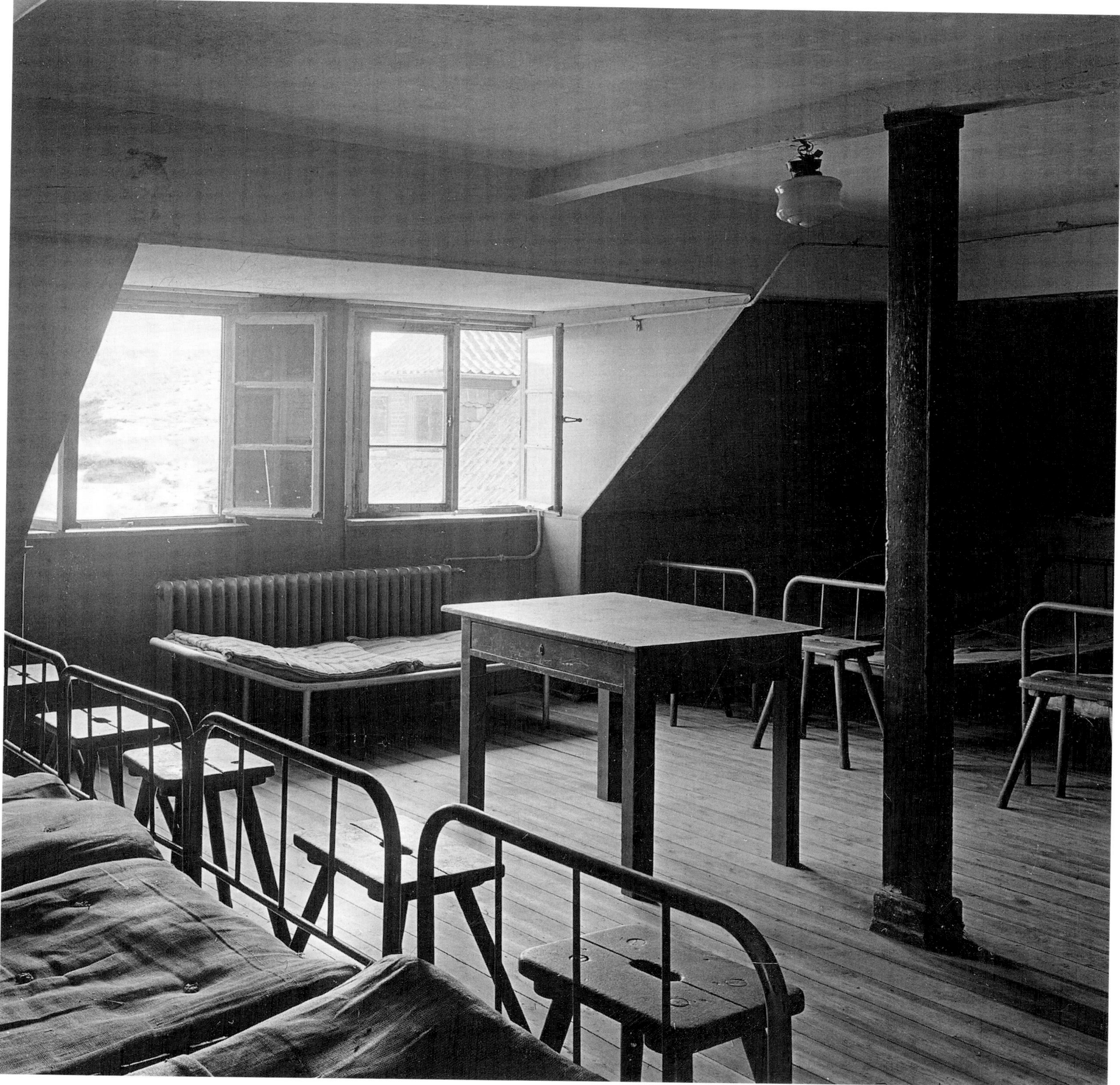

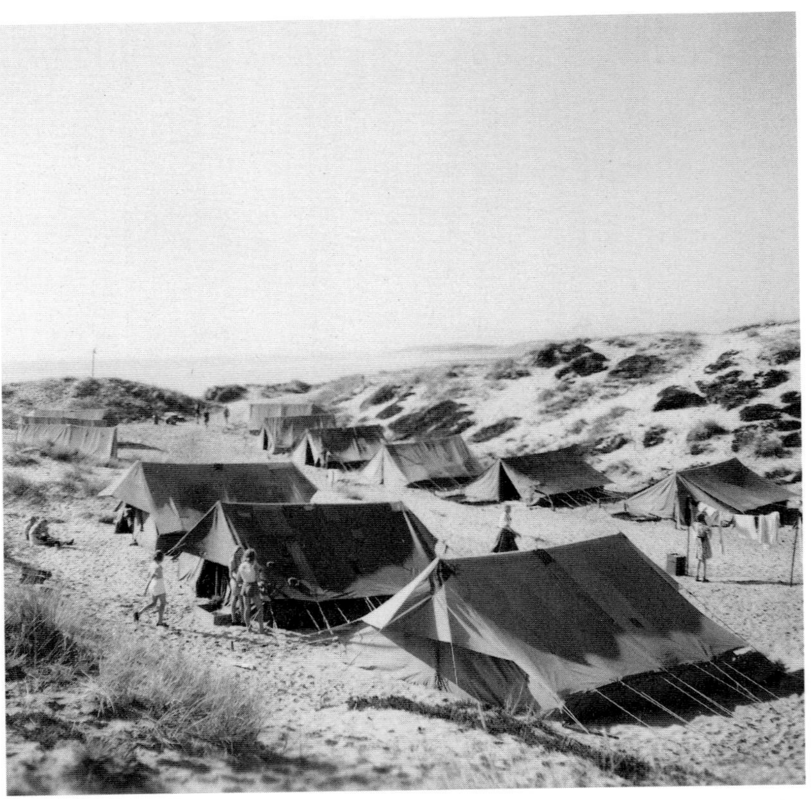

Tents pitched in the sand dunes on the island of Sylt, in the early 1950s.

Beach
Andy Martin

In the South Seas, in the second half of the eighteenth century, a terrible virus which is still abroad today was first transmitted. In the encounter between European and Polynesian, in the passage from carrier to host, its power became hugely magnified. It is not necessarily fatal, but it has warped and contaminated the lives of vast populations ever since. This virus is a consuming passion for the beach.

The classical attitude towards the beach had been elegantly summarised in a single line in Racine's tragedy, *Phèdre*, written in 1677: 'Wounded by what love did you die deserted on a barren shore?' The beach was like an elephant's graveyard where star-crossed lovers went to die. It was dripping with broken hearts. Mythic monsters were always liable to pop up out of the foam and carry you off. The sea was a sea of troubles. In 1719, Daniel Defoe in *Robinson Crusoe* conceived the beach, beyond the line of the palm trees, as a place of savagery and horror. It was a place you needed to be rescued from. Captain Cook was killed and offered up in sacrifice to the gods on the beach. The beach was a borderline with only the abyss, the maelstrom, on the far side.

It took the French explorer, Louis-Antoine de Bougainville (who brought Bougainvillaea to Europe) to transform the beach into an erotic paradise in the eighteenth century. The brief but decisive period that de Bougainville spent on the island of Tahiti contained nearly the entire spectrum of pleasures and perils that the beach affords. In one tumultuous week in the sixties – the 1760s – the Enlightenment was unhinged by Romanticism and the whole moral architecture of Judaeo-Christianity flooded by tropical hedonism.

In de Bougainville's work *Voyage autour du monde*, published in Paris in 1771, Tahitian women threw themselves willingly at French sailors, rather than the other way round, thereby becoming sirens to generations of anthropologists and sexual tourists. Despite a couple of dead bodies, mass impotence on the part of the French, and revisionist theories to the effect that in the course of this orgy Tahitian womanhood was merely being bartered for nails and buckets, the beach was decisively installed as the locus par excellence of dangerous liaisons with the Other. If it was still a desert (Alain Corbin's short history of the beach, published in 1990, is entitled *The Territory of the Void*), it had now acquired a resident Dionysian mirage.

Rather spoiling the party, Diderot denounced the French for spilling blood on the sand in the *Supplément au Voyage de Bougainville* he wrote in 1772. In the nineteenth century, Charles Fourier projected de Bougainville's beach into the harmonious realm of his 'phalanstery', turning it into a fully-fledged utopia in which everyone could enjoy multiple affairs, regular public orgies and a sexual AA call-out service for emergencies. But Faurier's *Le Nouveau monde amoureux*, written in Paris in the early nineteenth century but not published for almost 150 years, was the high-tide of fantasy. At the end of the century, Paul Gauguin bravely retraced de Bougainville's original journey to Tahiti, but was doomed to discover Mormon missionaries, shapeless sack dresses and concrete houses. His paintings are nostalgic evocations of a lost world, crumbling fragments of a dream built on sand. But that very experience of disappointment, so central to the myth that is the beach, has prompted heroic endeavours of invention in the quest for a sinless state of nature. It has fallen to the Club Mediterranée to try to rectify reality in accordance with our desires and promote the beach as the natural habitat of the id, undressed and unrepressed, a site of maximum exposure.

Byron hymned the virtues of getting wet while Wordsworth, more buttoned-up, could still 'see the children sport upon the shore/ And hear the mighty waters rolling evermore'. The eruption of Krakatoa in 1883 constituted a massive alarm-call and an irresistible invitation. Just when people were beginning to think it was safe to go back in the water, and a hydrotherapeutic culture was establishing itself in England[1], the biggest tsunami ever recorded, some 135-feet high, a 'wave that echoed round the world' as Tennyson put it, reared up out of the deep and smashed down on the beach. A major land mass was converted into several cubic miles of flying debris, 36,000 inhabitants islanders were drowned and a steamer, the *Berouw*, anchored peacefully off Sumatra, was

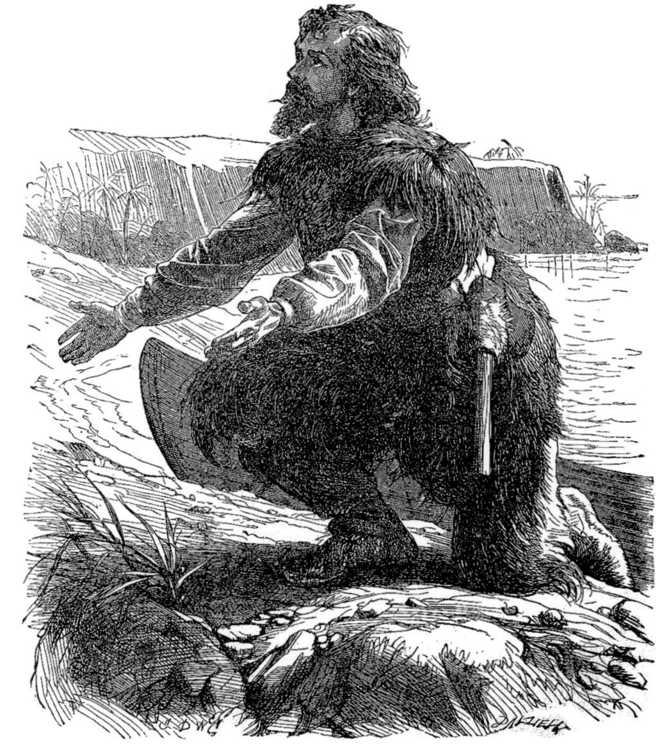

CRUSOE RETURNS THANKS FOR HIS DELIVERANCE

dumped a mile and a half inland. There could hardly be a more effective 'Keep off the Beach' warning sign.

Even without San Andreas and the plausible scenario of the whole of California floating off into the Pacific, the global beach is already marked out by a visible fault line: at the point where the solid earth collapses and sinks into the sea, catastrophes are a common occurrence. I used to fantasise about a giant tidal wave hitting London and carrying off teachers and parents alike. It was a bitter day for me when the Thames flood barriers were installed.

Napoleon, for one, had no illusions about the beach. Long before Nelson sailed over his horizon, he saw the beach as the scene of conflict and disaster. Otherwise fearless, he had a morbid phobia of the sea. He was heir to that ancient Mediterranean tradition which extolled the hills over the shore as a secure refuge from pirates, storms, and, above all, successive waves of invaders (Carthaginians, Romans, Phoenicians, Trojans, Barbarians, French). He was always in a hurry to escape from islands: Corsica, Elba, and – finally and sepulchrally – Saint Helena. The beach aroused premonitions of doom and thoughts of suicide. And still, at once horrified and seduced by the raw power of nature, he couldn't resist the call. 'Go down to the edge of the sea,' he wrote in an early work (nominally on the subject of happiness, but mostly dwelling on unhappiness), 'look at the setting sun majestically plunging into the heart of infinity, and melancholy will overmaster you: you will surrender yourself totally to this emotion.'

The beach has become practically inescapable. In one of Jung's archetypal dreams, a man is standing on dry land when suddenly there is a flood and the man who thought himself so secure now finds he is on the beach after all, surrounded by the collective unconscious, lapping at the shores of his rational mind. The beach, this indeterminate, ambiguous zone between earth and water, raked by sun and blasted by wind, is a battlefield where conflicting elements fight it out for the possession of our souls. Aeons ago we crawled up out of the primordial seas and headed for dry land. Eventually we may acquire fins and webbed feet and go back down again. But in the intermediate and amphibian period we occupy, we are locked into the landscape of the beach.

The broad historical syntax of the twentieth century, punctuated by wars and revolutions, is familiar. And yet cutting across it, undermining it almost, is an alternative sunburnt and sand-encrusted history. Around the time of Gallipoli, while all of Europe was digging itself into trenches, Duke Kahanamoku went to Sydney. He was Hawaiian, a two times Olympic swimming champion, a waterman so strong it took the future Tarzan, Johnny Weismuller, to beat him. On 15 January 1915, Duke left the public baths where he beat his own world record for the 100 yards freestyle, went down to the beach at Manly, carved himself a board straight from a tree, and paddled out and caught a handful of waves, finishing with a head-stand. As if by a miracle, a god-like man walking on water, Australia had been converted into a surf-going nation.

Kahanomoku defined surfing, which had come out of Tahiti a millennium before, as the quintessential post-historical beach exercise. You weren't going anywhere, but you rose and you fell in accordance with the rhythms of the ocean; you weren't doing, but being. The surfer was at once a compelling Biblical parable, riding the flood aboard his personal ark, and a bronzed neo-pagan metaphor in shorts, a being with an unconquerable lusting after the tube, but subject to the ultimate law of the wipeout and death.

Haunted by some potent mix of images involving Brigitte Bardot, coconuts and ice-cream, I was inevitably lured to the beach as a child. But, in truth, the beach is no picnic. It is an opportunity for an existential crisis. Meursault, Albert Camus' 'outsider', shoots a man dead on an Algerian beach because the sun is in his eyes, while Jean-Paul Sartre's Roquentin, strolling along some Atlantic shore, suffers an attack of nausea as he contemplates the tranquil water and falls to wondering: what horror is lurking beneath the surface?

But this is why we keep going back to this primeval origin, this ruined wilderness by the water: we desire what we fear, we derive pleasure from terror, we find a reminiscence of Tahiti even in the midst of Krakatoa. The beach is a jungle, the arena of a perpetual struggle for survival and optimum muscularity. The beach is a desert, where we wander like saints or initiates, buoyed up by visions, hallucinations, and madness.

1. 'No persons could be really well or in a state of secure and permanent health without spending at least six weeks by the sea every year.' From Jane Austen's unfinished novel *Sanditon* (1817), in which the young heroine, visits a small seaside resort.

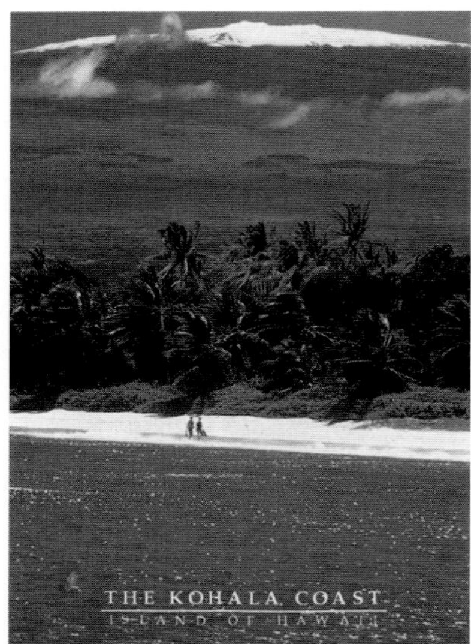

Postcard from Honululu: 'This magic coast of the Big Island is alive with contrast. Sunshine days… snow-capped mountains… and beaches… a glimmering ocean and dazzling resorts. The way the world is supposed to be.'

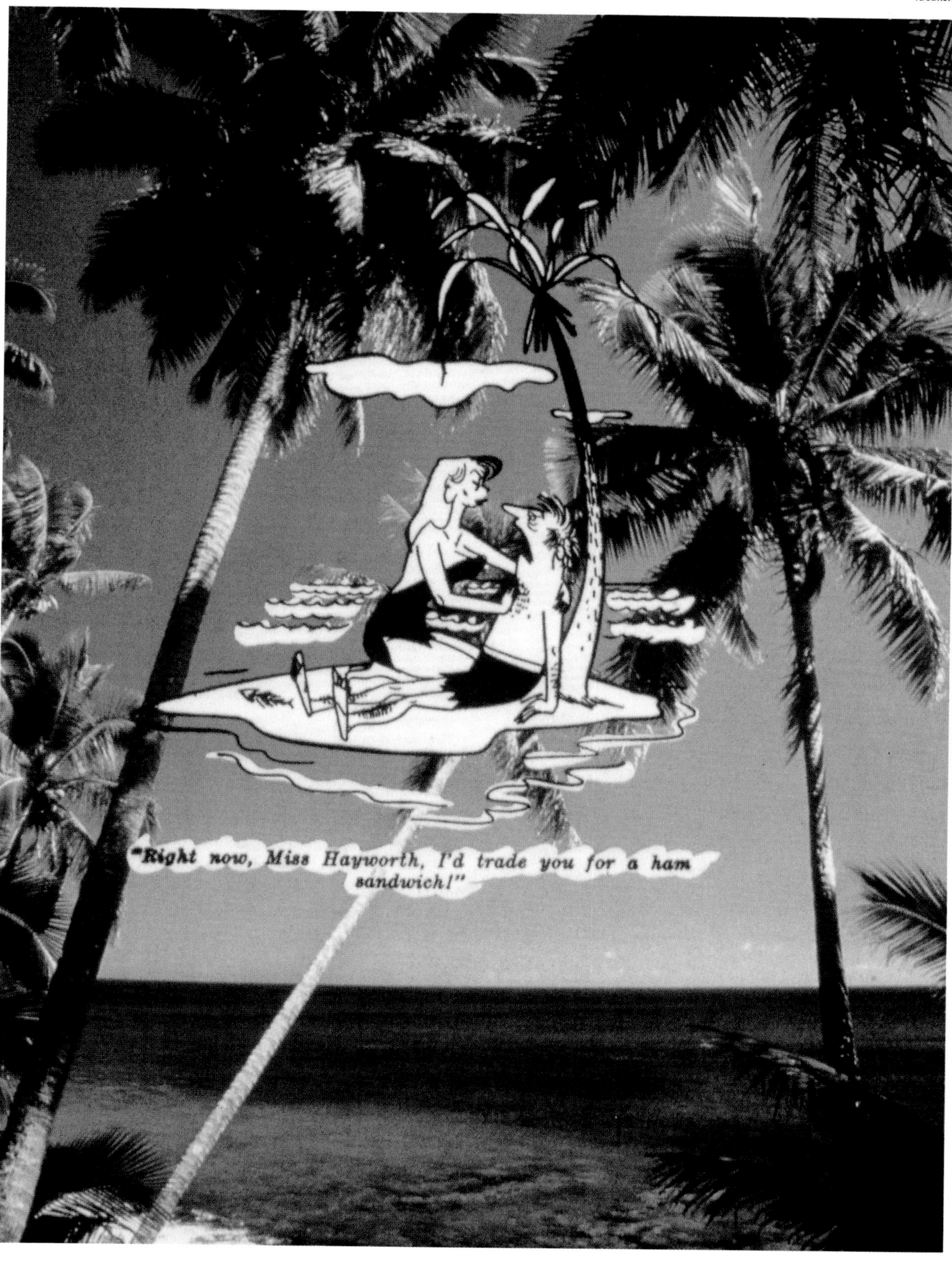

Richard Prince, right, *Untitled (Desert Islands)*, 1986, detail. Courtesy Barbara Gladstone

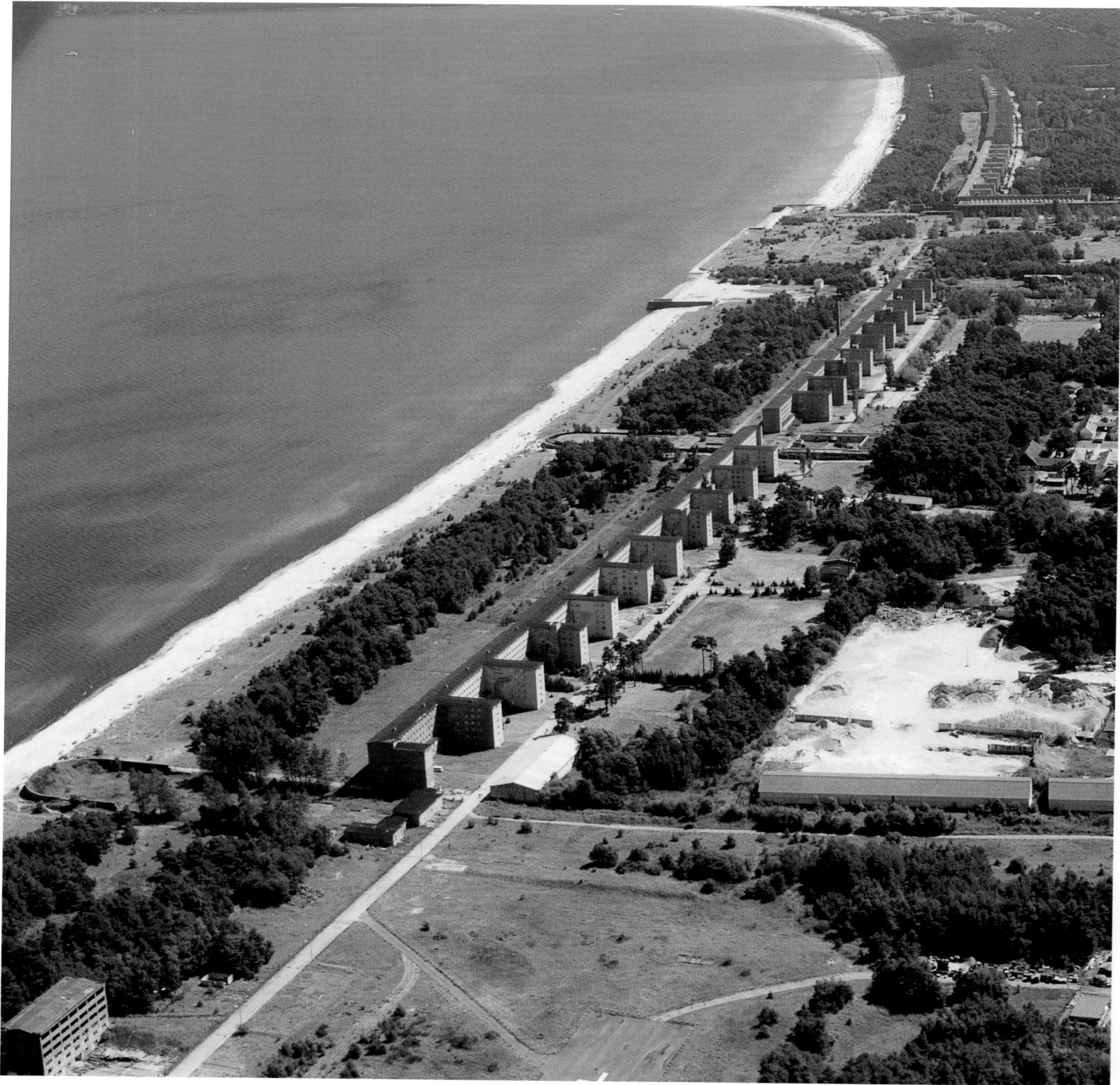

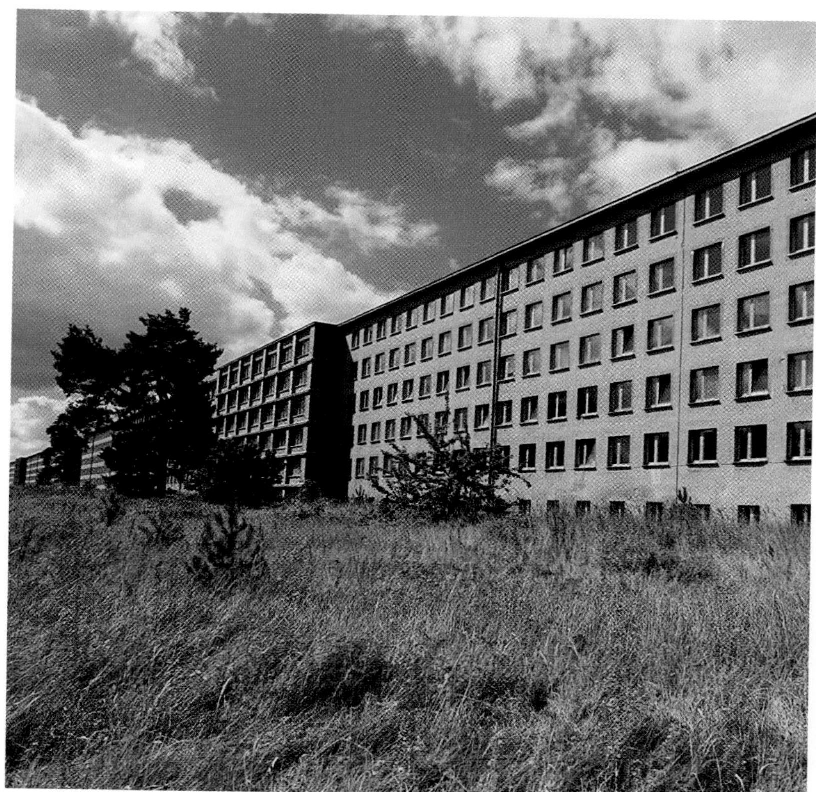

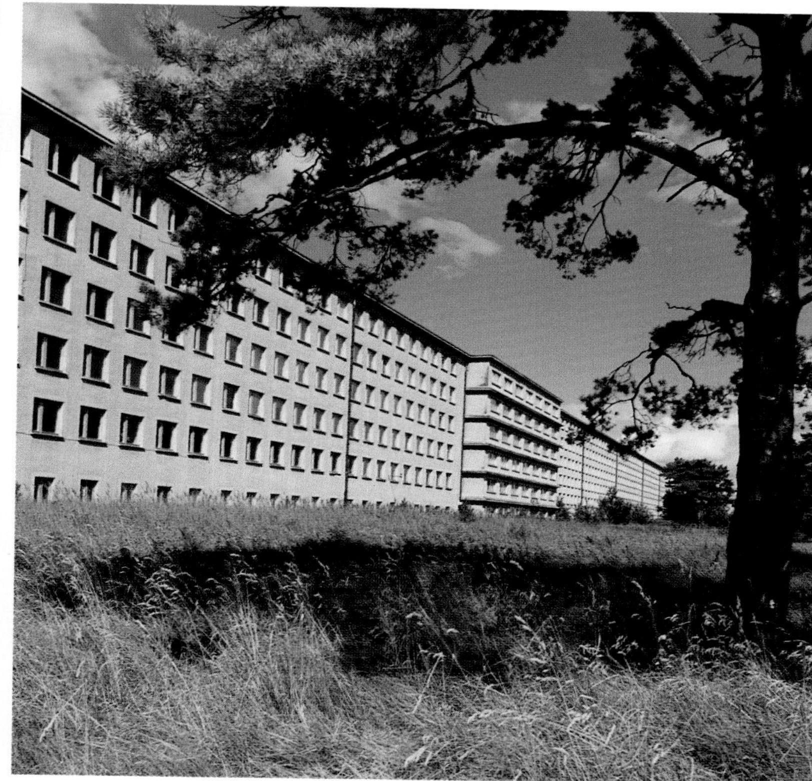

Prora
Gunnar Knechtel

In May 1936, the foundation stone was laid for what was to be the first of five planned holiday resorts on Germany's Baltic coast. Each of these resorts was to accommodate 20,000 'Volksgenossen' sent there on package holidays run by the 'Kraft durch Freude' (strength through joy) welfare organisation. Prora, on the island of Rügen, was the only one to be built.

Eight monolithic blocks, six stories high and 500 metres long, follow the curve of a beautiful sandy bay. At the centre of this four kilometre stretch of concrete there was to be a grand hall, large enough to contain all the visitors. The actual guest rooms are small and plain, but very democratic in that everyone gets the same sea view. In a way, it's a totalitarian version of the banks of hotels that blight the major tourist resorts of the Costa Brava: the holiday resort as an expression of political power rather than as a reflection of commercial exploitation. But Prora wasn't built to give the workers of northern Germany a chance to lie on a beach for two weeks, the intention behind the 'Kraft durch Freude' movement was to create a stronger, healthier people – the kind of population it would take to build a thousand-year Reich.

There would be no chance of ever being bored at Prora, not with the relentlessly timetabled activities organised by the KdF. But no holidaymakers ever did get to enjoy music, dancing, theatre, sports and other improving activities in these wholesome seaside surroundings, as Prora was never completed. The start of the Second World War put a stop to building work, so the swimming pools (which were to be the first in Europe with wave machines) were never built, and neither was the 'Festhalle' where all the holidaymakers were to have gathered to listen to uplifting political speeches. The façades of the hulking blocks, which were supposed to be painted white, remained bare concrete.

It would have been unthinkable to complete the unfinished resort after the war, but destroying it wasn't an affordable option. The Russian troops who tried to blow the place up in 1945 quickly realised that it would take an inordinate amount of explosives to make any kind of impact on the reinforced concrete colossus – Prora was clearly built to last. Instead, the buildings were used as a base by the East German army, the Nationale Volksarmee. Up to 10,000 soldiers and officers were stationed here until German reunification in 1990, in a huge military compound that, despite its vast size, did not appear on any maps of the surrounding area.

But now that the army has moved out for good, no one quite knows what to do with this all too solid reminder of an era that everyone would rather forget. In 1994, a preservation order was placed on the original structure, followed by a feasibility study looking into the resort's potential for redevelopment. So far, no suitable buyer has come forward.

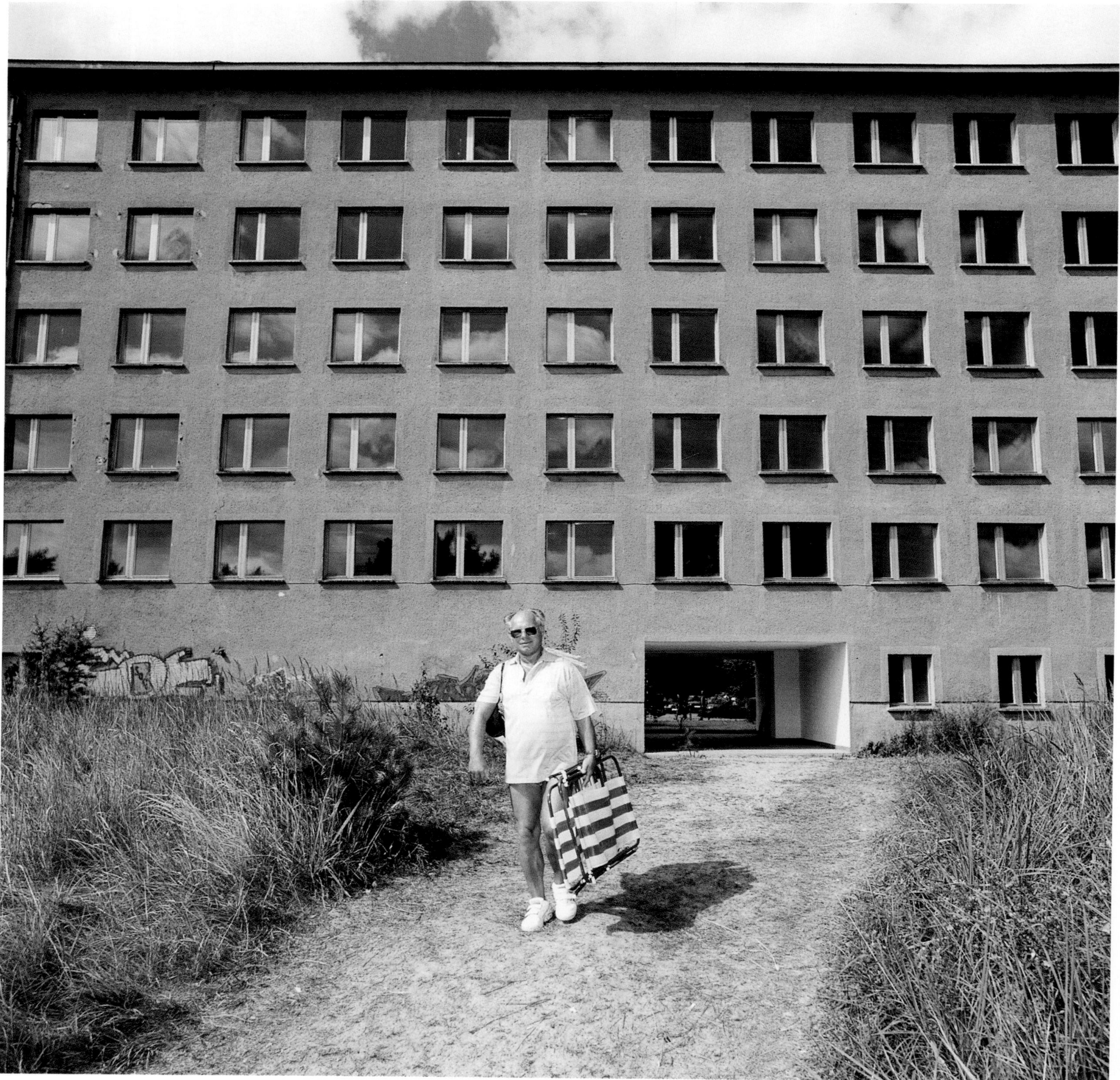

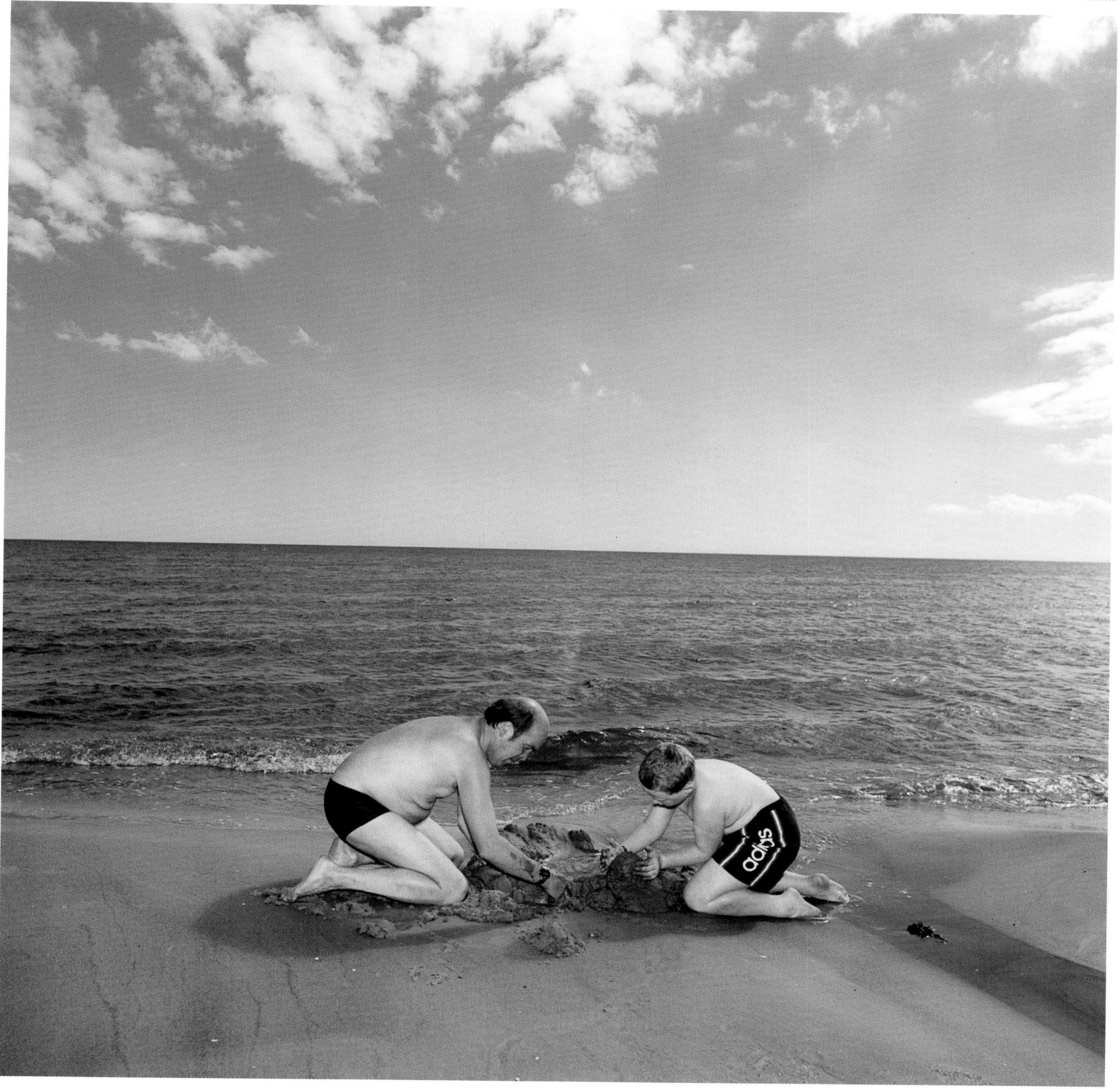

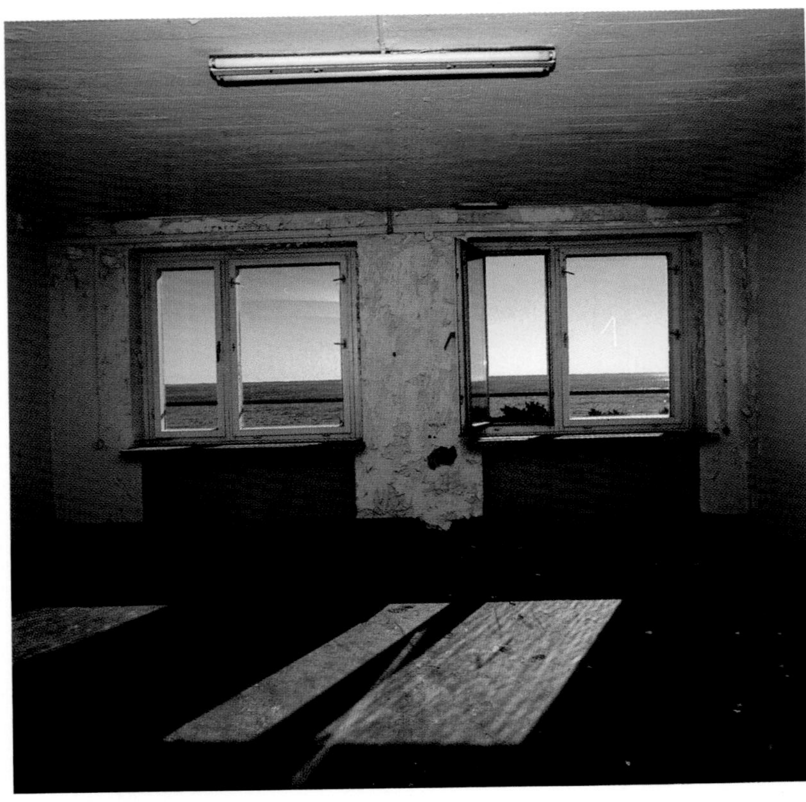

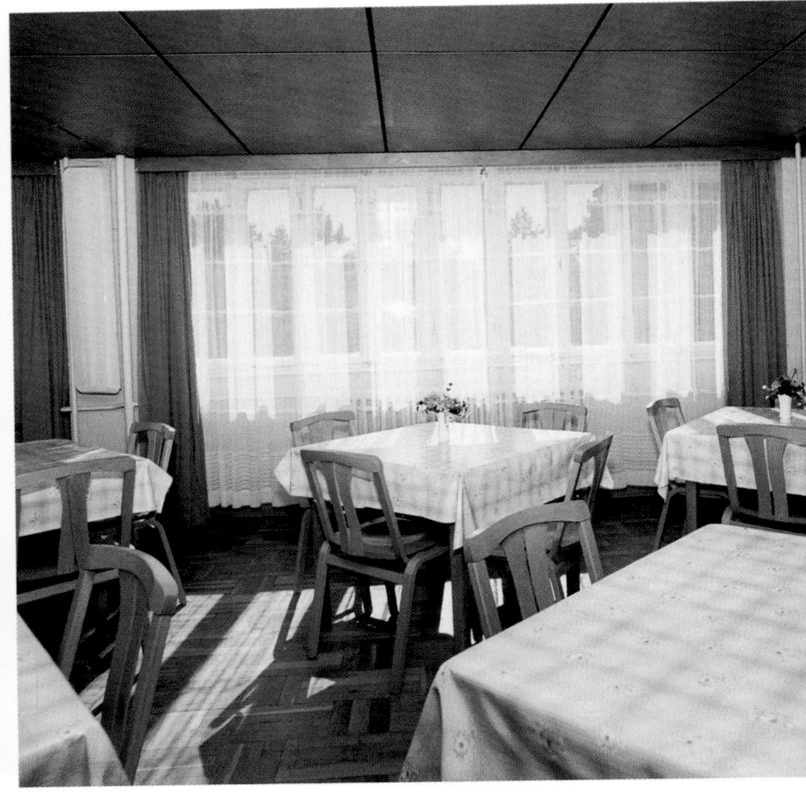

The rooms may have been small and spartan, but at Prora, everyone had the same sea view, above. While the hotel rooms built to house 20,000 visitors are empty and derelict, the small youth hostel, above right, with a maximum capacity of 150 people, is still going strong. The only clues to how the complex was meant to have looked are offered by model on a wall, opposite, which shows the great hall at the centre between the two banks of accomodation blocks.

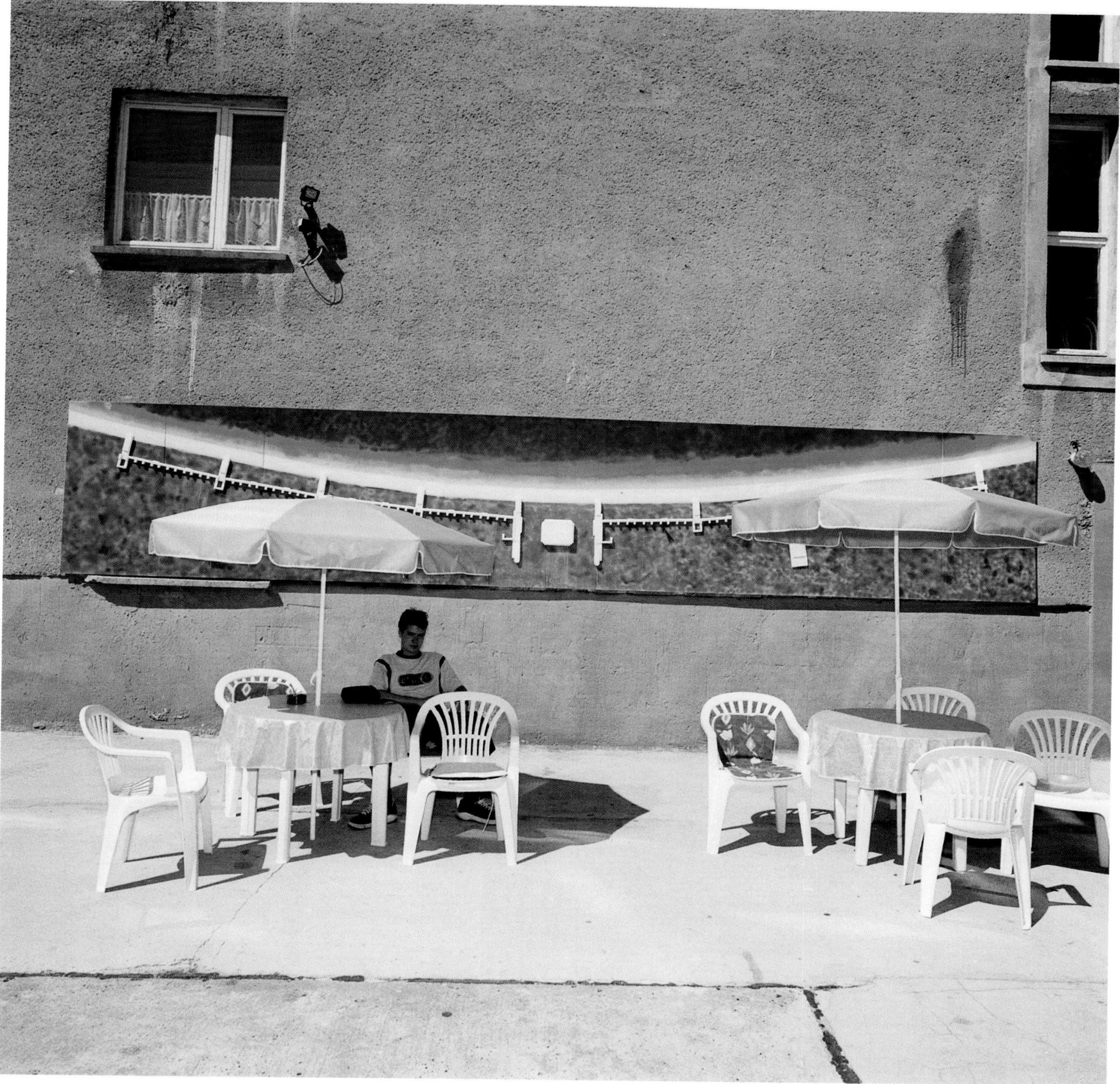

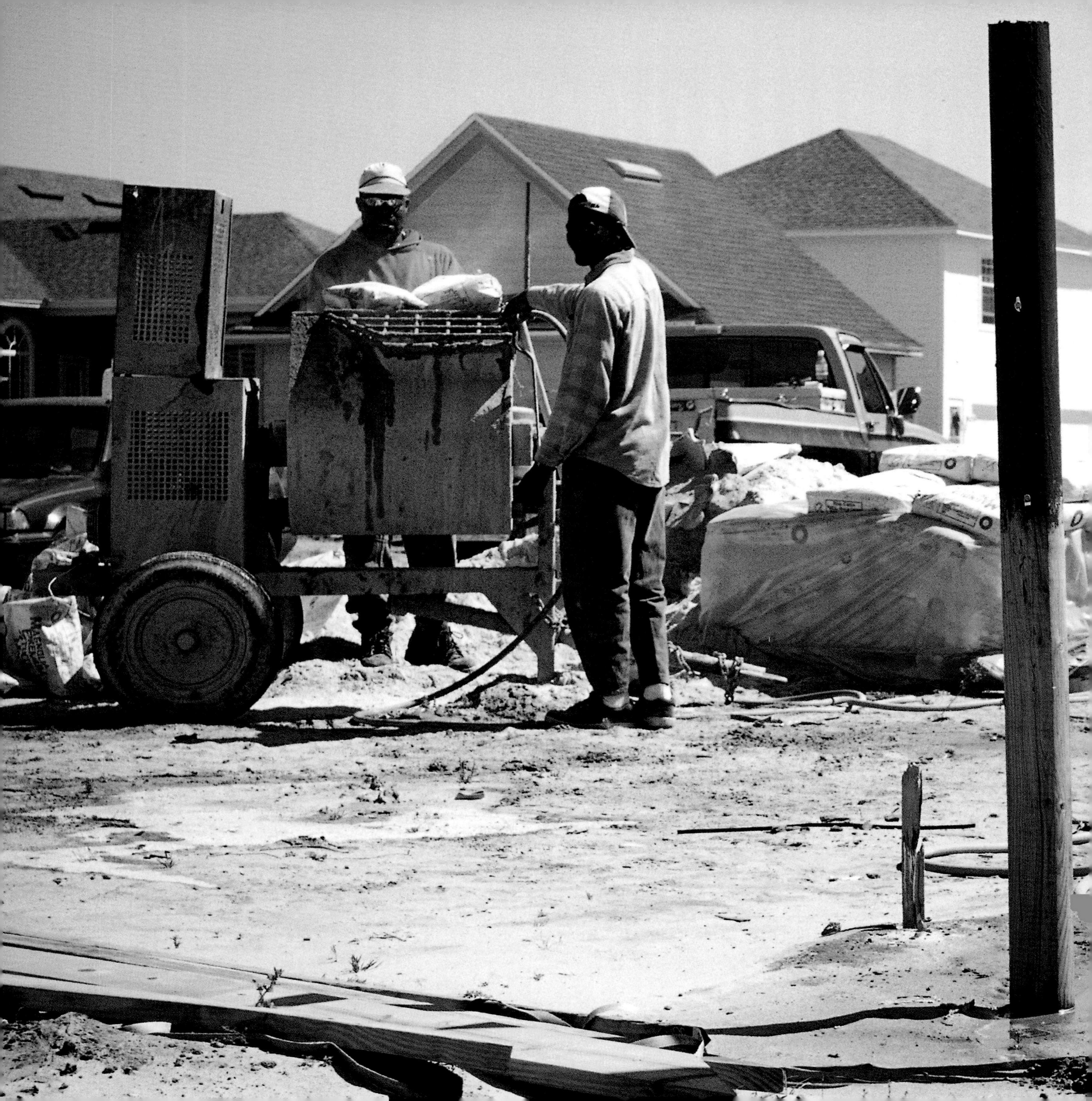

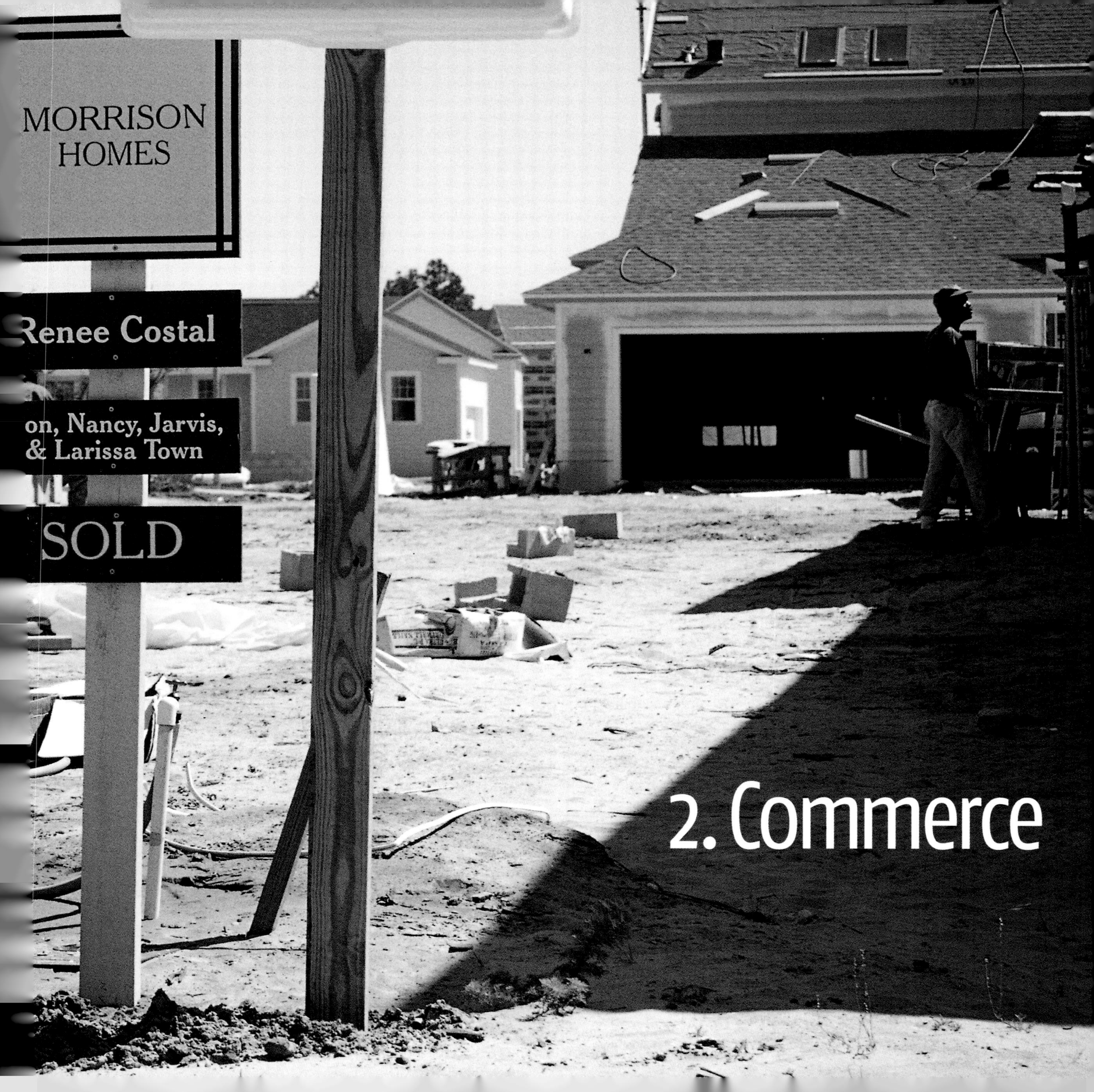
MORRISON
HOMES
Renee Costal
on, Nancy, Jarvis,
& Larissa Town
SOLD

2. Commerce

Back to the future
Joe Kerr

'A nice woman but proud of being a philistine – has no idea much beyond a window box full of geraniums, calceolarias and lobelias, over which you see a goose on a green.'

Thus the distinguished architect Sir Edwin Lutyens described Mrs Henrietta Barnett, while working on the design of her great utopian community, Hampstead Garden Suburb, in 1909.[1] Barnett was one of the most formidable philanthropists in Britain, who for more than thirty years had lived and worked in her husband's East End parish of Whitechapel, one of the poorest in the land, before embarking on the creation of this pioneering social development. But the patrician Lutyens was no enthusiast for what he termed 'do-goodery', and he had little sympathy with the wholesome image of Barnett's model community. His spiteful jibe about window boxes and village greens contained more than a little truth about Barnett's urban vision, and echoed many contemporary suspicions about the woolly idealism of the garden city movement, whose adherents were often characterised as bearded, sandal-wearing vegetarians – and yes, Hampstead Garden Suburb really had a village green, complete with maypole and stocks, provided by the residents with more than a hint of self-parody.

But to mock the village-like vision of community so vividly expressed at Hampstead was to make light of a very real tradition of utopian thought, that had its roots in Victorian English architectural theory, but was to remain influential throughout the twentieth century, and whose inspiration can still be read in ideal planned communities of today. The Modernist model of the future city, as epitomised by Le Corbusier's theoretical schemes of the 1920s, has tended to dominate conventional histories of architecture and planning. This is hardly surprising, as many of these histories were written by supporters of the Modern movement. Also, the wholesale adoption of the Corbusian vision by the architects of post-war reconstruction has largely served to obscure other traditions. However, the perceived failure of the Modernist determination to plan future cities that owed nothing to the past, and that employed rationalist precepts rather than sentiment and subjectivity to ensure the greater good of industrial society, has gradually refocused architectural and public attitudes on the possibilities offered by an older dream; one that firmly located an ideal future in a romantic vision of old-fashioned village life.

So why exactly has the vision of the 'goose on the green' retained such a durable and widespread potency to focus the dreams of utopian urban planners? The ambition of this essay is to explore some episodes in the life of this particular utopian impulse, from its origins amongst the satanic mills of Victorian Britain to its contemporary manifestations on the shores of Florida. This journey from one side of the Atlantic to the other in the course of a century and a half is not an accidental one, for although the influence of the village ideal as a palliative for urban misfortune can be seen in planned communities throughout the West, it had a particular hold on the imaginations of architects and planners in the English-speaking world; and indeed there is a rich history of cross-fertilisation of ideas and people between Britain and America throughout this whole story.

For this reason the narrative of this essay is constructed around episodes that have unfolded in these two countries, pausing only occasionally to note how Barnett's dream was translated into other cultures and ideologies (including the nascent European Modern movement). It is not a continuous, seamless tale, but one that loosely falls into two parts: the first traces the history of the 'village-community' as an antidote to the perceived ills of the nineteenth-century industrial city, which might be briefly summed up as brutal overcrowding, physical and cultural impoverishment, aesthetic starvation and class segregation as rigid as any apartheid system. The common thread throughout this first story is that these ideas were promoted by social reformers – whether enlightened industrialists, influential philanthropists, or state sponsored professionals – and were intended as exemplars for the advancement and improvement of society as a whole. It is this belief in the image of pre-industrial communal life as inspiration for the reform of industrial society, without recourse to violent revolution, that identifies these ideas as utopian, and requires that they be treated every bit as seriously as the *tabula rasa* solutions to the city promoted by their Modernist counterparts. Indeed, it must be remembered that these ideas belong to the era of modernity every bit as much as the heroic, futurist city plans of Sant' Elia, Garnier or Le Corbusier.

The second strand of this narrative, and one that is pre-eminently American in ownership, concerns the appropriation of the village ideal as a reactionary restatement of traditional societal values – 'the American way of life' – prompted by the fear of the modern city that has haunted the conservative imagination in that country for at least the last fifty years. Specifically the kinds of urban terror addressed by the modern American variant of the village ideal are: the violence and general lawlessness that have prevailed following the wholesale abandonment of downtown areas, the loss of community through suburbanisation and excessive mobility; and the challenge to old-fashioned constructions of national identity that cultural and ethnic diversity threatens for a whole class of affluent urban exiles. This essential pessimism about the future of American urban society is serious enough to be labelled in a recent book by exponents of the so-called *New Urbanism* as 'the Decline of the American Dream'.[2]

In the sense that this planning tradition was also developed as a considered response to widespread problems in American society, it can be described as utopian. But the critical difference from earlier planning movements is that the intended beneficiaries of *New Urbanism* could only ever constitute a tiny, self-selecting elite. This might make for a more realistic utopianism than the universalising prescriptions of the garden city movement, but it is certainly more open to the criticism of exacerbating rather than reconciling the divisions in society that it is reacting to. The inhabitants of Seaside or Celebration, the two Florida communities examined below, have no desire for a reconciliation of classes or races. Quite the opposite: their idyllic communities were established as safe refuges from the frightening realities of modern American life.

Scenes from a Golden Age

There were very clear reasons why the key to the future seemed to lie in the very distant past for many different Victorian reformers and architects. Britain was the first industrialised society, and so was the first to develop a considered response to the problems that industrialisation

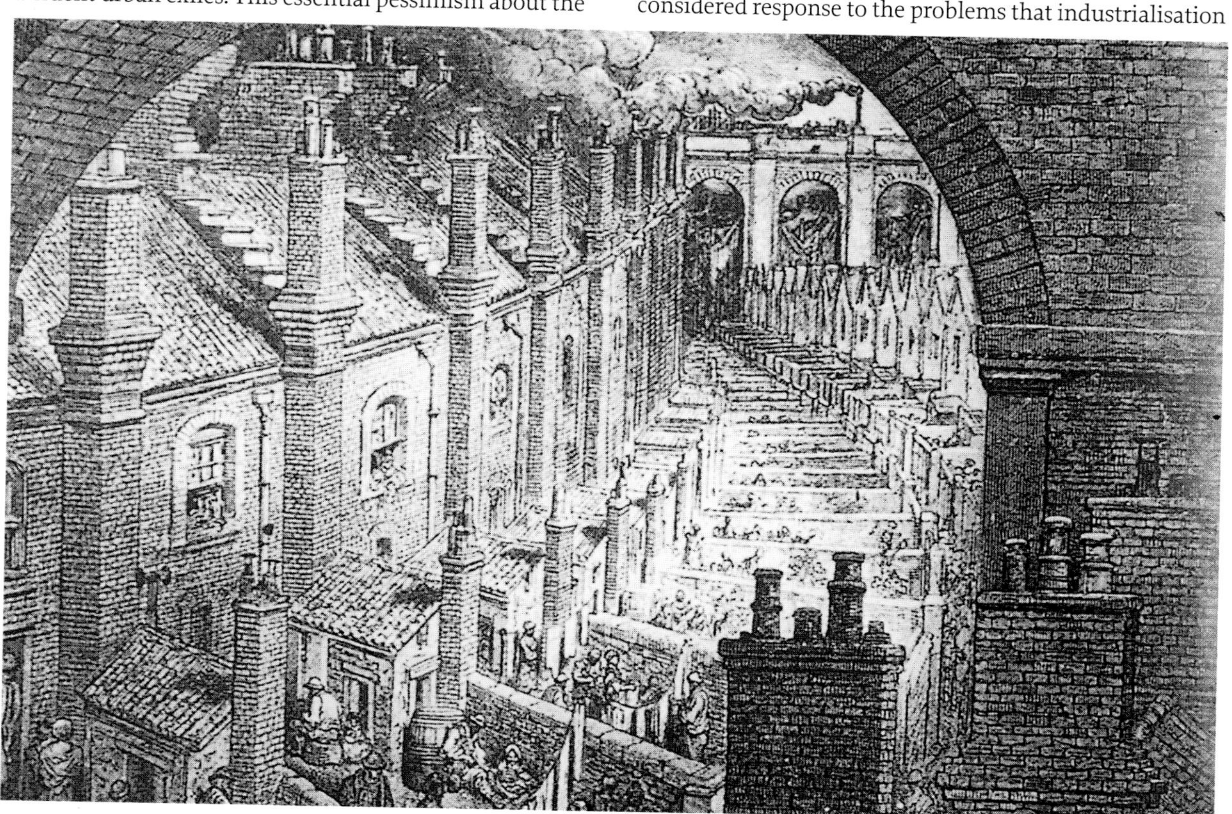

This drawing by Gustave Doré, entitled *London: a pilgrimage* (1872), is a sensationalist take on the grim reality of urban life in but it captures the horrors that galvanised the social reformers of the nineteenth century.

and the rise of capitalism brought in its wake. First and foremost of these was the problem of urban life, as cities rapidly grew beyond comprehension and control, and the few visibly profited at the expense of the many. London, the largest city in the world, became the byword for alienated urban existence and depressing ugliness, as luridly depicted in Gustave Doré's *London: A Pilgrimage of 1872*. As the growth of capital accumulation seemed to be at the root of the problem, then ergo life must have been better in pre-capitalist society. Not only that, but to a nineteenth-century audience feudal, village life implied a bond between people and nature that had been utterly destroyed by the urbanisation of the vast majority of the population.

Furthermore, the romantic vision of harmonious medieval society could be shared to some extent by almost all strands of opposition to the dominant ideology of Liberal, laissez-faire capitalism. Thus on one extreme Tory paternalists, fed on the novels of Sir Walter Scott and the ideas of Cobbett's *Old England*, were inspired to view pre-reformation England as a golden age, when society remained uncorrupted by materialism, secularism and egalitarianism. But equally on the opposite political wing, socialists and even Marxists could maintain a romantic regard for feudal society, which in England especially became the basis for an artistic as well as a political creed through the ideas of John Ruskin and William Morris.

But dreaming of an idyllic society was a very different matter from actually trying to recreate it. It was Morris in particular who was instrumental in translating an abstract attachment to the medieval village into an actual programme of social reform. His own peculiar mixture of anti-industrial arts-and-crafts idealism and radical socialism led him to see architecture as a powerful agent of social revolution: through the practice of a new architecture, a new society could be created. It was Morris who 'first translated into architectural terms the urge to escape from the grim squalor of the industrial slums'.[3] His vision of a reformed social order, based on the communal life of the village, was spelled out in the utopian novel *News from Nowhere* of 1890, in which a nineteenth-century traveller is bewildered to find himself in a future in which the great cities have been demolished, to be replaced by tranquil countryside and harmonious village settlements.

New Jerusalems

But even before Morris had inspired architects to reject the reality of contemporary city in favour of his vision of pastoral bliss, elsewhere a few of the very barons of industry whom he held responsible for the wanton destruction of proper communities in their search for profit, had themselves started to look to the old English village as a model for a productive industrial society. Many new factories had been built away from traditional centres of population, and in their desire for a stable workforce, many industrialists had built housing for their factory hands and their families, seeing it as a sound economic investment in terms of the projected benefits it would bring. In effect, they were simply maintaining the system of paternal ties represented by the estate village that served the country houses of the aristocracy. But not surprisingly, they tended to interpret their actions in terms of a higher moral purpose. For example, when in 1859 Edward Ackroyd, a successful textiles manufacturer, began a pair of model villages in open countryside, he ascribed to them a clear social programme:

> A clean, fresh, well-ordered house exercises on its inmates a moral no less than a physical influence, and has the direct tendency to make the members of a family sober, peaceable, and considerate of the feelings and happiness of each other[4]

Ackroydon, the more ambitious of the two villages was designed by the eminent Gothic revivalist Sir Gilbert Scott as a formal composition of picturesque stone cottages built around a village green complete with cross, the very picture of bucolic harmony. But the philanthropic intentions claimed by such industrialists actually had a

The Quaker Cadbury family built the town of Bournville to house the employees of their chocolate factory. Some cottages were built in the 'Dutch style', right, while others where more traditionally English in their appearance, overleaf.

"After a pause, I said: 'Your big towns now; how about them? London, which – which I have read about as the modern Babylon of civilization, seems to have disappeared.'

'Well, well,' said old Hammond, 'perhaps after all it is more like ancient Babylon now than the "modern Babylon" of the nineteenth century was. ...'Time was when if you mounted a good horse and rode straight away from my door here at a round trot for an hour and a half, you would still be in the thick of London, and the greater part of that would be "slums", as they were called; that is to say, places of torture for innocent men and women; or worse, stews for rearing and breeding men and women in such degradation that that torture should seem to them mere ordinary and natural life.'

'I know, I know,' I said, rather impatiently. 'That was what was; tell me something of what is. Is any of that left?'

'Not an inch,' said he."[5]

William Morris, *News from Nowhere*, 1890

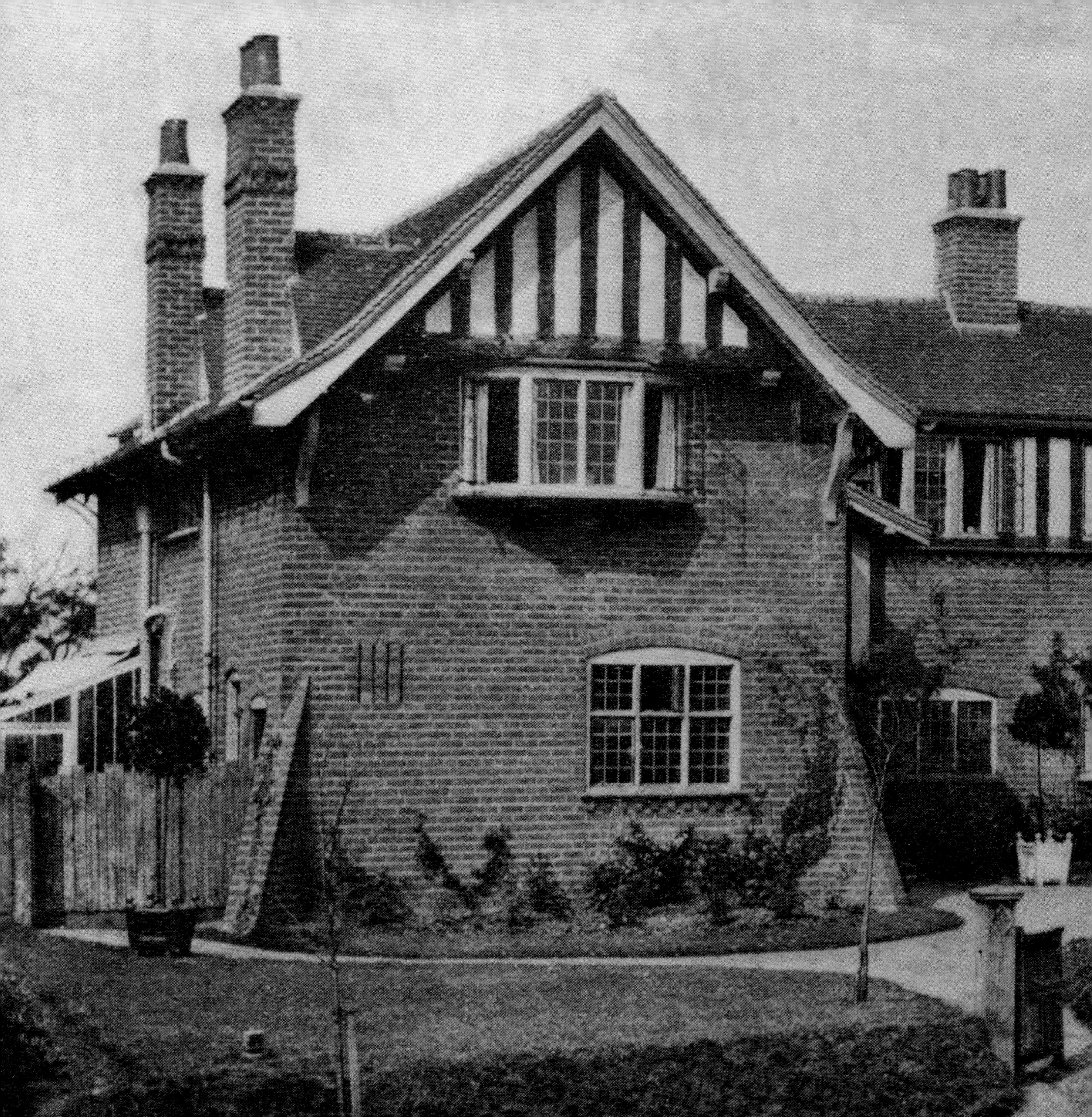

Bournville
Cornford and Cross

Built thanks to the philanthropy of chocolate-maker Joseph Cadbury, the model village of Bournville was one of several communities in Britain in the late 19th century to create better living conditions for the employees of a wealthy factory owner. Like the communities at Saltaire, Port Sunlight and New Lanark, Bournville certainly provided significantly-improved living conditions for its occupants, despite the fact that residency carried with it a number of strict conditions imposed by the landlord. Bournville's utopian vision grew out of a Quaker belief system which still has adherents today, but many of its prescriptions were resolutely of their time.

One such prescriptive gesture concerned the sports and recreational grounds so generously built for the workers by Cadbury, but segregated by gender. The mens' field, a grand space close to the factory, and taking the form of a closely mown square pitch, is highly suitable for field sports such as cricket or rugby. By contrast, the Women's Recreation Ground is situated on the other side of a road from the main factory site, shielded by a row of trees and only accessible from the factory by a long tunnel which conveniently allowed women to reach it from their changing rooms without revealing themselves to the men. The womens' field takes the form of a gently undulating meadow, with longer grass than the mens' and with a generous sprinkling of trees, making it suitable only for taking long, improving walks.

At one end of the Women's Recreation Ground, Joseph Cadbury installed a pavilion in which women might have been expected to sit and relax; and next to this small structure he built an ornamental water pool. Beautifully landscaped and designed to give the impression of a secret glade, this epitome of meditative tranquility in fact stood just a few metres from the hullaballoo of men's team sports across the road.

During the twentieth century, however, the women's pavilion fell into disrepair. By 1999, when curators Nigel Prince and Gavin Wade staged an art exhibition called *In the midst of things* on the site, the pavilion stood derelict and the pool empty, whereas the mens' sports field remained in constant use. As part of the exhibition British-based artists Cornford and Cross chose the now-derelict water feature as a site for their work. In addition to restoring the poolside paving and its immediate surrounding landscape, the artists filled the pool with water once again. On this occasion, however, the water was coloured with a food dye so as to make it the particular purple colour of Cadbury's famous corporate identity. By installing two new fountains in the pool, Cornford and Cross transformed the tranquil location into a celebratory reminder of the real reason for its existence. Like the chocolate-scented splendour of the Cadbury World visitor attraction a few hundred metres away, the artists' magnificent restoration has made the Women's Recreation Ground a Bournville destination once again. At the same time Cornford and Cross have drawn a parallel between the with-profits beneficence of the company that is now part of a multinational food and drinks group, and the same conditional utopianism which drove Joseph Cadbury to build the site in the first place.

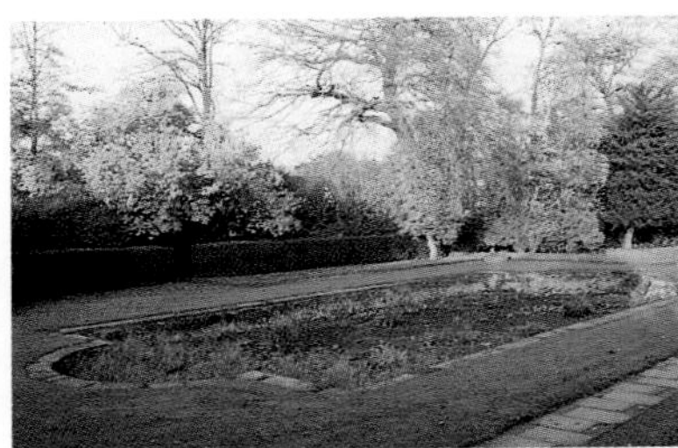

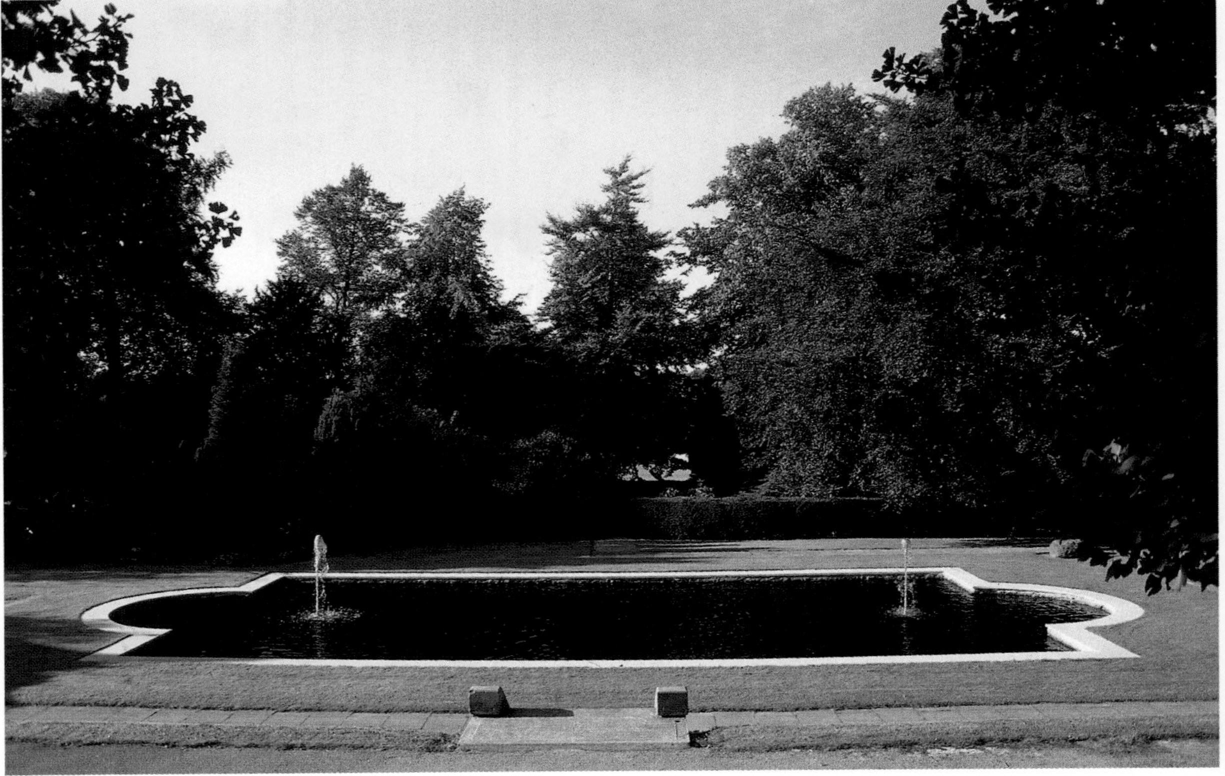

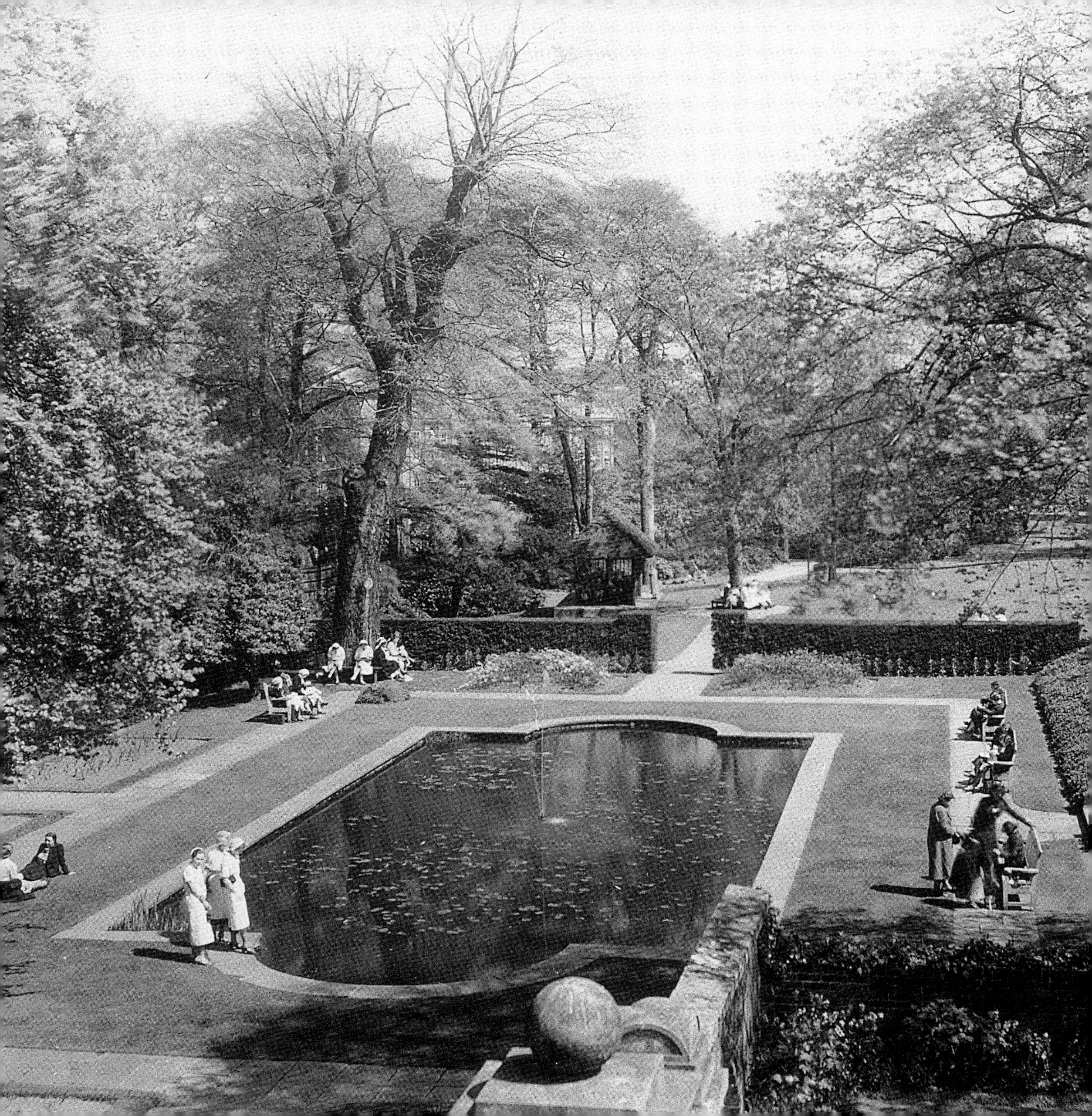

solid base in economic self-interest. For of course when mill hands were housed at the behest of their employer, at a great distance from any alternative employment or accommodation, they became in effect a captive workforce. As architectural historian Mark Swenarton explained:

> Since the early days of the Industrial Revolution, factory owners had known that their power over their workforce could be greatly increased if they controlled, not just the jobs, but also the houses of their employees. For instance, in building his factory-village at Copley, outside Halifax, Colonel Ackroyd's motive was primarily to make his mills 'secure against the sudden withdrawal of workpeople'.[6]

There is no doubt that the housing and facilities provided by such industrialists as Ackroyd, or Titus Salt who built the contemporary village of Saltaire to serve his enormous alpaca mills, were of an appreciably higher standard that conventional industrial urban housing. But it would be inappropriate to award them the accolade of utopian planners, given their straightforward economic motives. However, later in the century a small group of industrialists commenced building model villages that were far more ambitious in their social programme. They believed that humanitarian motives were wholly compatible with sound business sense, arguing that by dramatically improving the living standards of their employees they could establish a contented and stable, and therefore productive, workforce. The costs of creating and maintaining such communities would be more than repaid in terms of raised productivity and diminished industrial discord. Once again therefore, their ultimate ambition was guided by self-interest, but by successfully demonstrating that improving the lot of the working classes was in the best interests of industrial society as a whole, they laid the basis for the great phases of housing reform that followed.

The spectacular industrial village of Port Sunlight was established by the Lever Brothers in 1888 to serve their soap factory, which they had relocated the previous year from Warrington to a new rural site on the shores of the River Mersey. Built to the designs of William and Segar Owen, it eventually comprised 720 houses in a picturesque domestic style, complete with structural half-timbering, set on curved roads and around open space, and built at a very low density, recreating all the essential features of the old English village. Port Sunlight still offers today a seductive image of the village ideal, and remains a highly desirable place to live for all sectors of the local population. It can deservedly be described as the first successful exemplar of how reform of the physical

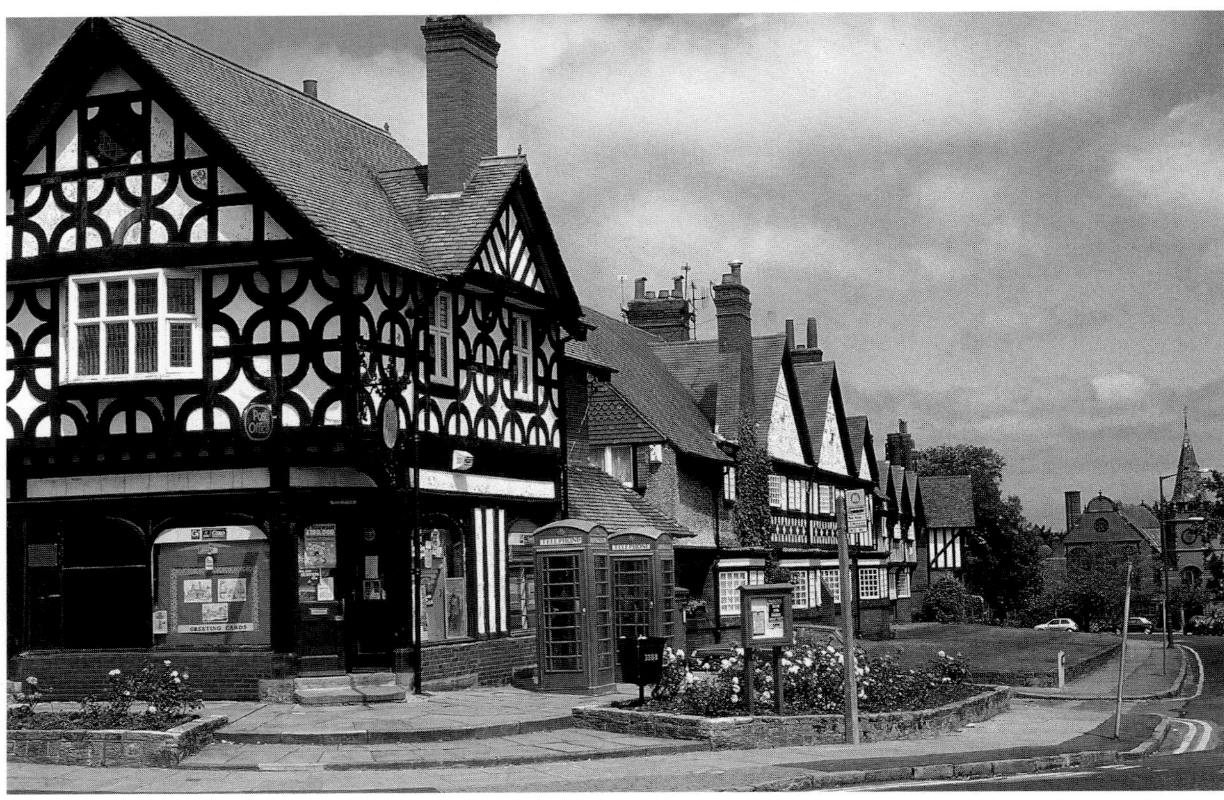

environment might lay the foundations for a more enlightened industrial society.

A Peaceful Path to Reform?

Such communities as Port Sunlight, or the famous village of Bournville built by the Quaker Cadbury family in 1895, are deservedly described as the beginnings of the garden city movement. But in 1898 that movement entered a new and theoretical phase with the publication of Ebenezer Howard's *Garden Cities of Tomorrow* (originally published as *To-Morrow: a Peaceful Path to Real Reform*). Howard was not an industrialist but a social reformer who was writing in response to widespread anxiety about the state of Britain's cities. He was also not an architect or a planner, and so his proposals for the garden city were presented in diagrammatic form, and not as a concrete urban plan that might be built – a limitation recognised by *The Times* which observed 'the only difficulty is to create such a city, but that is a small matter to Utopians'.[7] Neither was he a political radical, and it is important to appreciate that 'Real Reform' addressed the consequences of capitalist production rather than its mechanisms.

But what is significant about Howard's vision is its utopian scale of ambition: for it was intended to achieve the wholesale reformation of British society, through the construction of an entire network of planned communities of a strictly limited size, that would serve to decentralise and disperse urban society. At the heart of Howard's diagram for the new 'social city' was the village green, clearly betraying his affinity to the well-established model of the small rural community as the ideal paradigm for a new society. He ideas also reflect the widely held belief amongst philanthropists and reformers that an attachment to the land was morally beneficial, not least because it kept the working man away from the pub (it was impossible to buy a drink in Bournville or at many later planned communities).

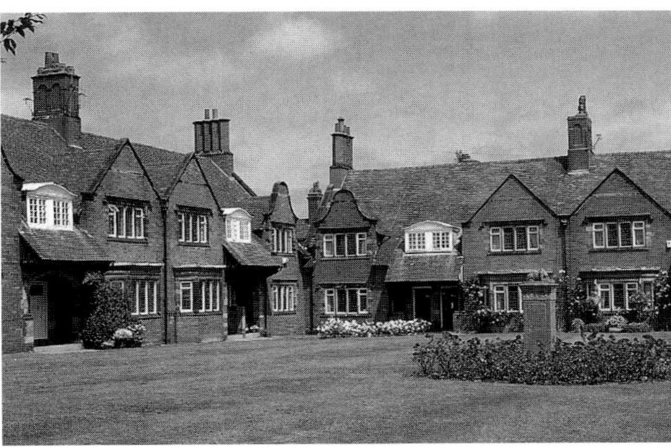

Established in 1888, Port Sunlight was built by Lever Brothers when it moved its soap factory to a new site on the Mersey. The designs, by William and Segar Owen, hark back to the days of 'Merrie England', with picturesque village greens and low density housing.

But Howard was not simply advocating the resettlement of the urban population into conventional village developments, for he appreciated that life was far from ideal in many rural communities. Instead, as his diagram of the 'Three magnets' shows, he was proposing an entirely new kind of rural city, 'the creation of a pure organism that combines the advantages of both city and countryside'.[8] Furthermore his garden cities were not simply enlarged industrial villages for the benefit of the urban proletariat alone. For at the heart of the whole movement was the desire to achieve a utopian reconciliation between the classes. It was only when all sectors of society were represented in a community that reform could really be achieved.

The first of what was intended to be an indefinite chain of garden cities was established at Letchworth, a short distance north of London, in 1903. (In the event only one other was ever established, at Welwyn in 1920, which indicates how successful the movement eventually was at least on its own terms). But at Letchworth the social vision of Howard was united with the architectural vision of the architect Raymond Unwin, who with his partner Barry Parker attempted to put into practice the arts-and-crafts and socialist ideals of William Morris. Seldom has a planning concept been so influential as the one produced by this marriage of theory and design, that created the concrete expression for Howard's social vision of community life.

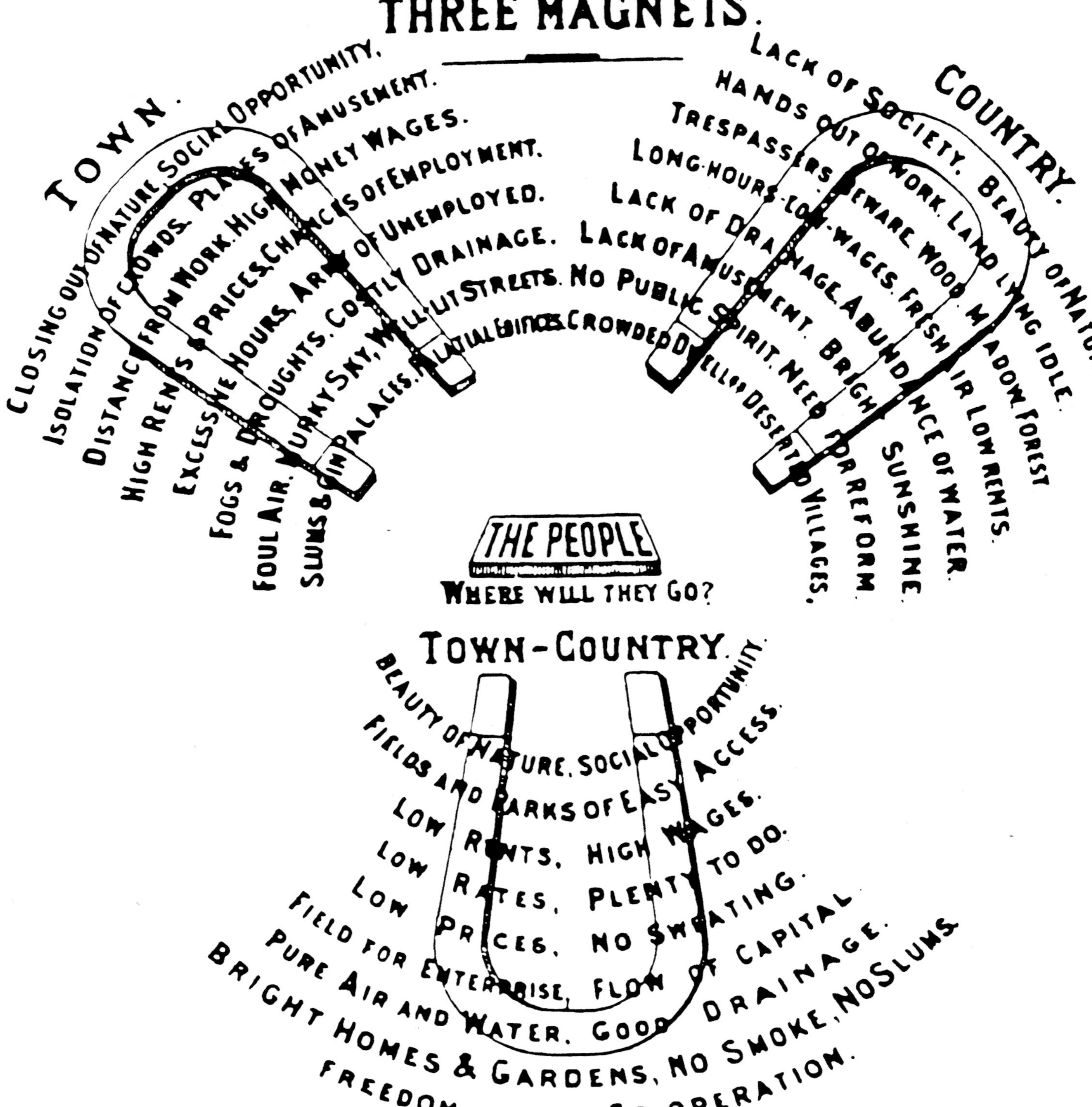
THE
THREE MAGNETS.
TOWN.
CLOSING OUT OF NATURE. SOCIAL OPPORTUNITY.
ISOLATION OF CROWDS. PLACES OF AMUSEMENT.
DISTANCE FROM WORK. HIGH MONEY WAGES.
HIGH RENTS & PRICES. CHANCES OF EMPLOYMENT.
EXCESSIVE HOURS. ARMY OF UNEMPLOYED.
FOGS & DROUGHTS. COSTLY DRAINAGE.
FOUL AIR. MURKY SKY. WELL-LIT STREETS.
SLUMS & GIN PALACES. PALATIAL EDIFICES.
COUNTRY.
LACK OF SOCIETY. BEAUTY OF NATURE.
HANDS OUT OF WORK. LAND LYING IDLE.
TRESPASSERS BEWARE. WOOD, MEADOW, FOREST.
LONG HOURS-LOW WAGES. FRESH AIR. LOW RENTS.
LACK OF DRAINAGE. ABUNDANCE OF WATER.
LACK OF AMUSEMENT. BRIGHT SUNSHINE.
NO PUBLIC SPIRIT. NEED FOR REFORM.
CROWDED DWELLINGS. DESERTED VILLAGES.
THE PEOPLE
WHERE WILL THEY GO?
TOWN-COUNTRY.
BEAUTY OF NATURE. SOCIAL OPPORTUNITY.
FIELDS AND PARKS OF EASY ACCESS.
LOW RENTS. HIGH WAGES.
LOW RATES. PLENTY TO DO.
LOW PRICES. NO SWEATING.
FIELD FOR ENTERPRISE. FLOW OF CAPITAL.
PURE AIR AND WATER. GOOD DRAINAGE.
BRIGHT HOMES & GARDENS, NO SMOKE, NO SLUMS.
FREEDOM. CO-OPERATION.

In his diagram of The Three Magnets, opposite, published in *Garden Cities of To-Morrow* in 1898, Ebenezer Howard put forth his visionary ideas for new cities that combined the best elements of town and country. When planning Hampstead Garden Suburb, Raymond Unwin set out to make the 'imaginary village', right, illustrated in his book *Town Planning in Practice*, published in 1909, a reality. This idealised view of the Suburb, below, as a place where the town meets the country, was drawn by one of Unwin's many collaborators, Charles Wade, in 1909.

As the illustration from Unwin's classic 1909 text *Town Planning in Practice* shows, his architectural and planning ideas derived directly from an aesthetic reading of the old English village, one that was intended as the absolute antithesis to conventional speculative urban housing developments of endless straight terraces of identical houses, built to a very high density – the so-called 'by-law' houses that were built in huge numbers up until the Great War. In 1907, Unwin moved on from Letchworth, which was struggling to establish itself as an independent community, to plan Henrietta Barnett's Hampstead Garden Suburb, and there his work achieved a real maturity, creating one of the most influential visions of twentieth-century architecture: 'the great exemplar – a model of inestimable importance',[9] as the architectural historian Andrew Saint has described the scheme.

Of course planned residential suburbs were by no means a new idea, but Hampstead is unique in terms of its handsome provision of amenities and in its ambition to accommodate people with a wide range of incomes and occupations. It was planned to include a village green, complete with clubhouse, two churches, and tea-shops, as well as shops, playgrounds, allotments, schools, homes for single women and for the elderly, as well as cottages and houses of different sizes 'as it was Mrs Barnett's intention that the various social classes should benefit from proximity, as in the traditional English village with its squire, parson, doctor, lawyer, banker, brewer, miller and tenants. But public houses were to be excluded'.[10] The idealised drawing of Hampstead reproduced here was executed by one of Unwin's small army of architectural collaborators, Charles Wade. It clearly shows that the new suburb drew both its social and its aesthetic inspiration from a mediaeval walled hill town (the wall was actually built!), with winding streets of picturesquely asymmetrical houses fronted by gardens leading up to the prominent civic and ecclesiastical buildings on the summit of the hill.

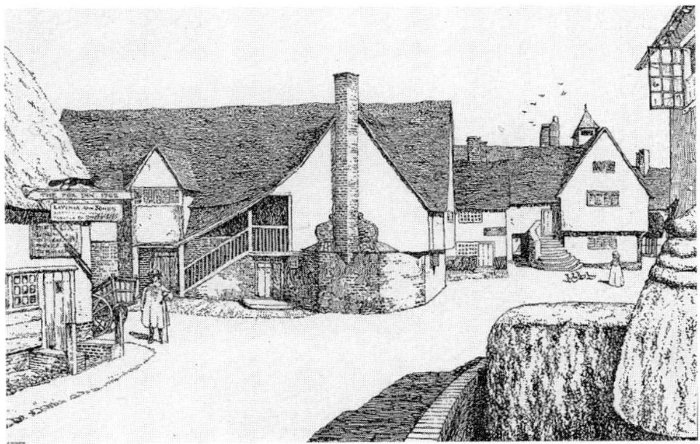

It is, in arts and crafts parlance, a total work of art, in which every detail has been carefully considered as part of a harmonious whole. Unwin planned the residential areas of the suburb, and then closely supervised the designs of the buildings. which were executed by a variety of architects. In this way he managed to achieve the extraordinary variety of the multitude of different house designs, while maintaining a strong visual unity across the whole suburb. The houses, like the plan, were inspired by pre-industrial examples, successfully so to judge by the contemporary comment that they 'were getting back something of the old English village life'.[11] The archivist to Hampstead Garden Suburb noted more recently in language wholly appropriate to the subject, that 'the medieval mantle had fallen strongly on Parker and Unwin. It shows in the Suburb in great ways and small – in the Merrie England, village green atmosphere of Willifield Green as originally planned; in the suffixes of the street names – close, way, chase, lea, holm, garth ...[in] the Great Wall along the north side of the Heath Extension, which states architecturally "here ends the country and begins the town"'.[12]

Hampstead Garden Suburb belongs to the early years of the twentieth century, and it seems to both suffer from the limitations of a specifically Victorian vision of social reform but also to hold the promise of urban reforms that

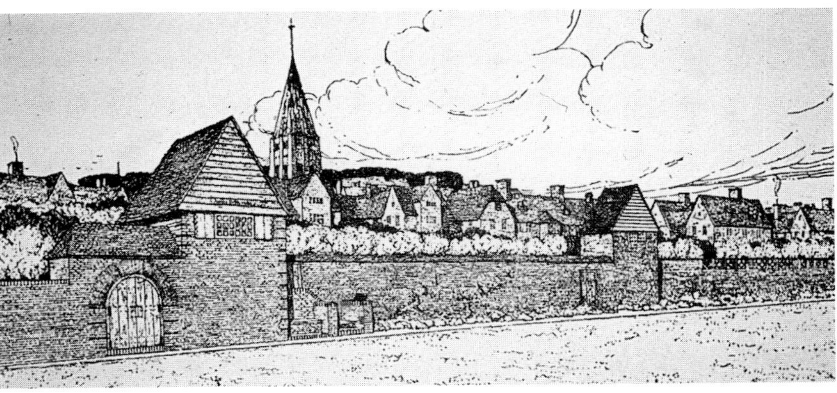

The Garden City
Hilary French

The intention of the Garden City Association founded in 1899 by Ebenezer Howard (1850–1928) was not just to resolve the problems of overcrowding in cities but also to provide a new socio-political model for the future. New satellite cities surrounded by a green belt, with a maximum population of 23,000 people, would be linked to the main city by railway. The economy would be based on a combination of agriculture and light industry. The first example of a garden city, at Letchworth in Hertfordshire, was started in 1904 and was followed in 1907 by Hampstead Garden Suburb on the edge of London and Wythenshaw on the outskirts of Manchester. The emphasis was on the provision of housing for families, and although the garden cities included some experimental communal schemes, the majority of building was devoted to individual family houses.The architecture of Raymond Unwin (1863–1940) and Barry Parker (1867–1941), who realised Ebenezer Howard's dream of the Garden City, was closely related to the Arts and Crafts Movement – inspired by Ruskin and William Morris and based on a pre-industrial feudal model of the medieval village. Unwin was a close associate of Edward Carpenter (1844–1929), active in the socialist movement and advocate of 'the simple life'; he believed that life was complicated by unnecessary conventions that should be put aside to be replaced with real needs based on nature. Unwin also shared the belief that an orderly arrangement of buildings on the medieval model, with forms such as quadrangles, would impress a sense of order onto the minds of the buildings' occupants.

MH Baillie Scott (1865–1945), one of the most active architects of the period, was very critical of the low densities proposed by Parker and Unwin and of the design of some of the proposed cottages and houses. His ideas about the essential function or 'real needs' of the cottage coincided with the Arts and Crafts idea of the Artistic House, or the ordinary house thought of as an architectural work, but were critical of the adoption of the second living room, or 'parlour'. Scott's Elmwood Cottages, built at Letchworth and exhibited at the Cheap Cottage Exhibition of 1905, served, he believed, as 'a protest against the merely utilitarian ideals of modern building generally'.[1] The 'open plan' ground floor has just one living room, with only the staircase acting as a divider; different activities are catered for in alcoves, recesses, fixed seating, and cupboards around the perimeter. One room is considered better than two for practical reasons, such as the need for only one fire for both cooking and heating, as well as the all-important cross ventilation deemed necessary for improved health. Having only the one room also allows for more flexibility in orientation on the site, making it easier to obtain views from the living room. On a social level, Scott believed that this layout would also help recall the convivial atmosphere of medieval times: '... in this way, even the labourer's cottage retains its hall, which has now become the kitchen, dining room and parlour'.[2]

MH Baillie Scott's design for Waterlow Court at Hampstead is a variation on another of his designs for the Garden Suburb, the Plot 400 proposal. Although not built, the Plot 400 plan is a significant of example of the architect's progressive ideas: seven large houses, of about ten rooms each, are arranged

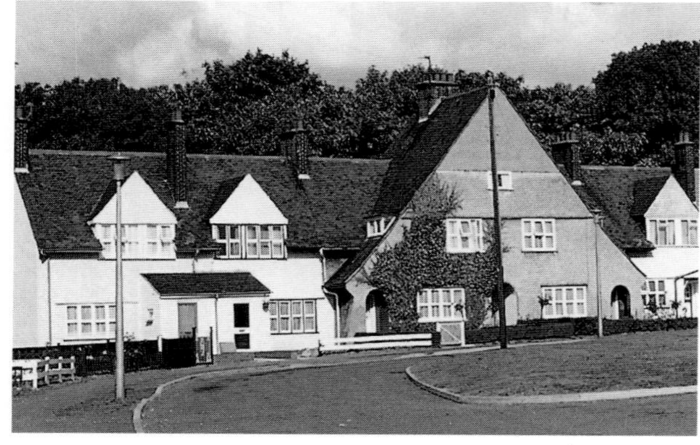

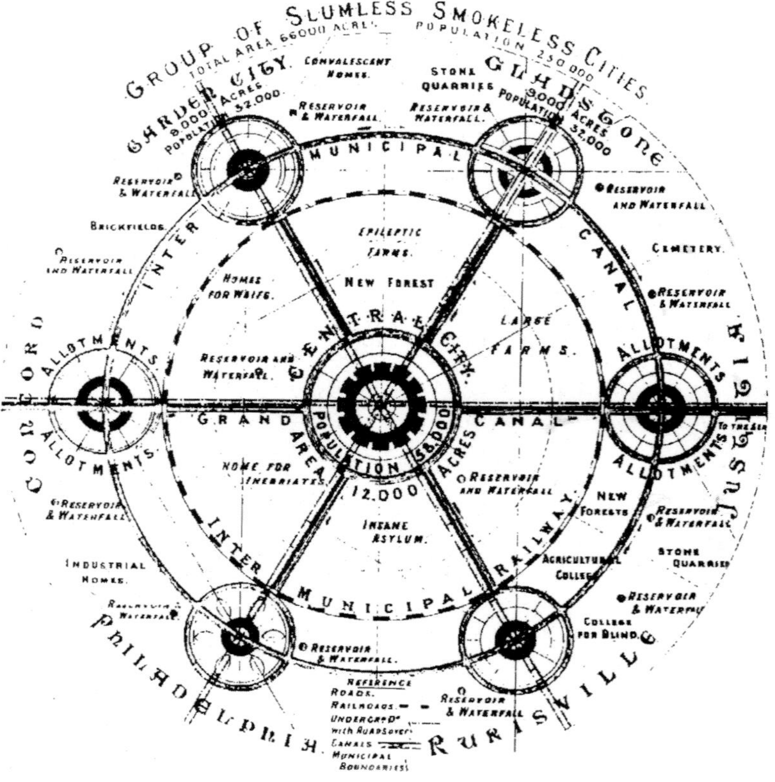

Ebenezer Howard's plan for a Garden City, right, published in *Garden Cities of To-Morrow* proposed cities of about 32,000 people carefully planned and surrounded by a permanent green belt. Letchworth, above, was the first example of a Garden City to be built.

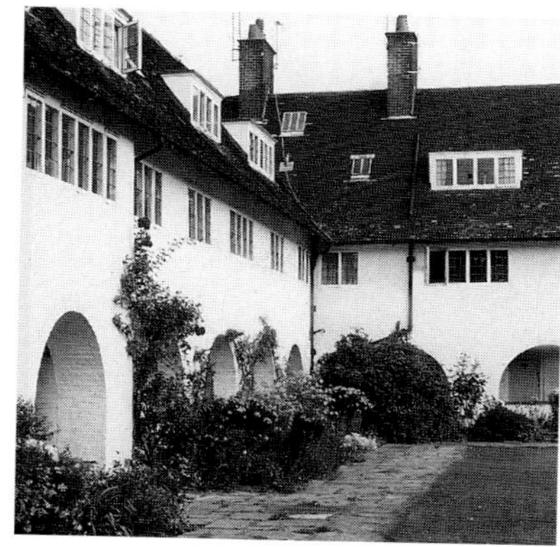

around three sides of a quadrangle on a site of around one acre. Each house is independent but part of an identifiable whole; the intention is to provide for physical community but also accommodate the psychological need for individuality. The interiors and the use of the space have clearly been considered in some detail; there are outdoor living rooms, inglenooks, alcoves for dining or study, screens in place of walls and galleries in place of corridors. The proposal is typical of Scott's work, with roughcast wall finishes and half-timbering and steeply pitched roofs above a horizontal mass.

Waterlow Court, completed in 1909, is a larger scheme than Plot 400, consisting of 50 flats of three or four rooms arranged simply around the four sides of an enclosed quadrangle. It had communal kitchens, dining rooms and lounge, as in Scott's words: 'Here it would seem that a great saving of labour and expense might be effected by centralising the functions of cooking and heating in these houses and by providing one large fire and one capable cook to take the place of a dozen miniature cooking-ranges.'[3]

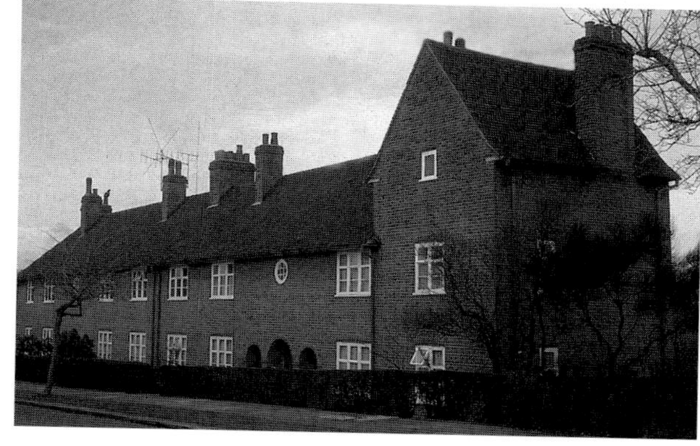

The Waterlow Court scheme is entered via a lych-gate and has a cloister running around the interior perimeter to protect the residents from the weather. Scott specifically designed the court for use by single working women: 'There are many lonely men and women living dreary lives in boarding-houses and hotels in social isolation. In the Associated Cottagers' Company they would become members of a family, and live, perhaps, a more useful social life.'[4] Another scheme of the architect's designs for multiple houses was part realised at one of the main road junctions, Meadway and Hampstead Way, where Scott insisted on the need for mass and height to mark the junction and add scale to the suburb. Although designed when there was little 'traffic', all these proposals would be very appropriate now in urban terms, when so many bay windows and front gardens face what have long since become major roads.

1. MH Baillie Scott, *Houses and Gardens*, 1906, Chapter 30, 'Six Cottages'
2. ibid
3. ibid
4. ibid

Completed in 1909, Waterlow Court in Hampstead Garden Suburb, above and overleaf, by MH Baillie Scott, was built to house single working women. The building had shared kitchens and dining rooms, and was designed to make its inhabitants feel part of a community. Raymond Unwin, who planned Hampstead Garden Suburb, designed the flats on Addison Way, above right, while his collaborators on the scheme included Sir Guy Dawbar, the architect behind No 5 Ruskin Close, right.

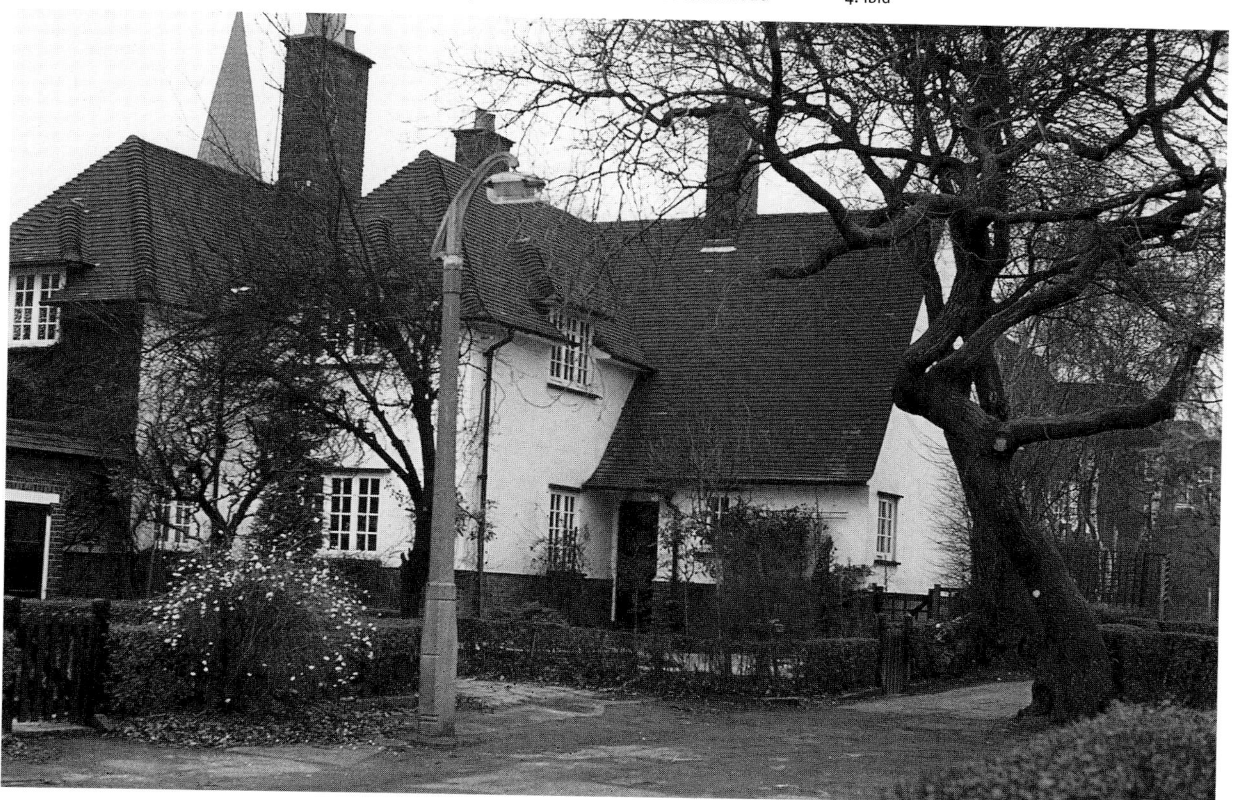

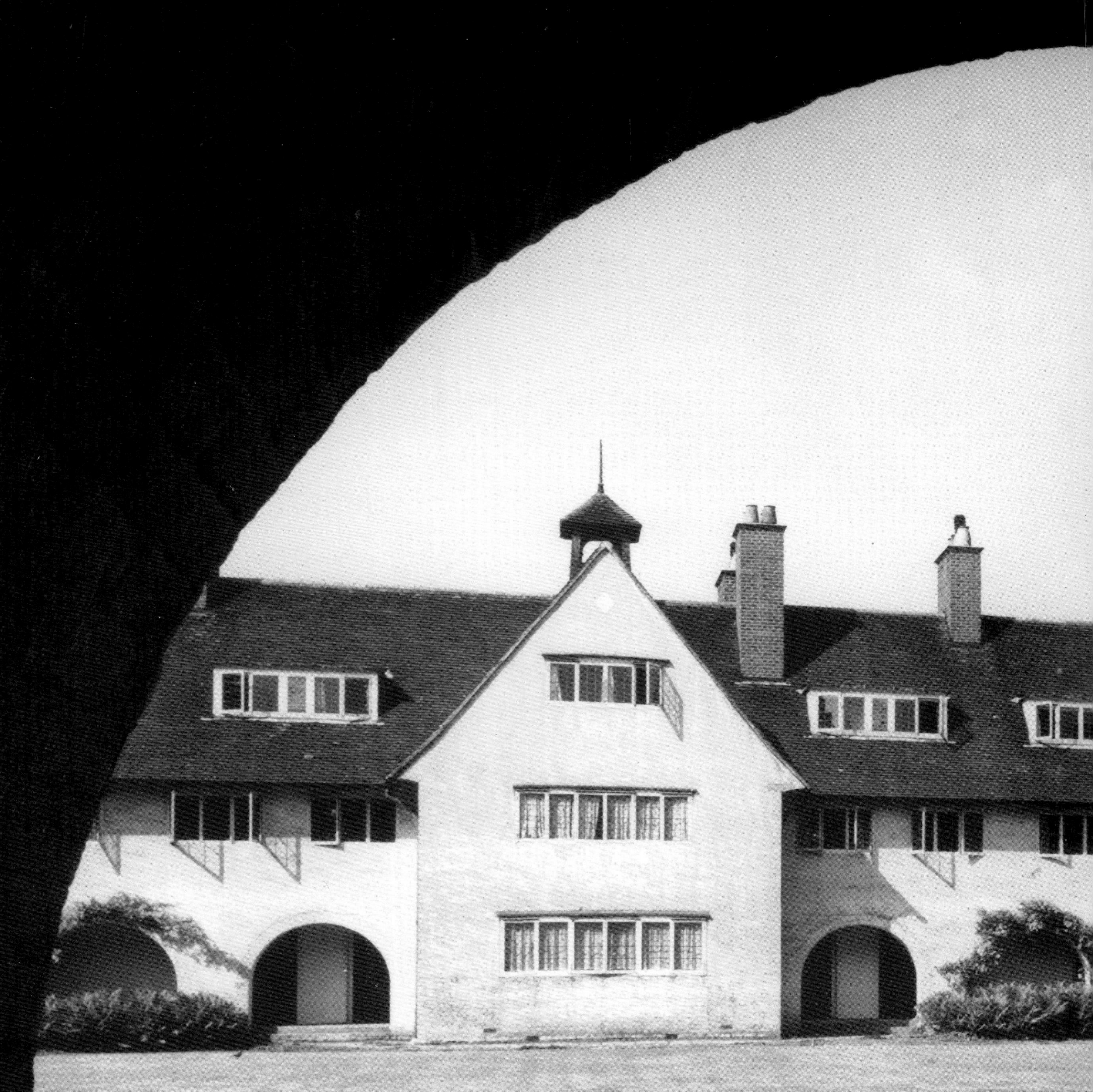

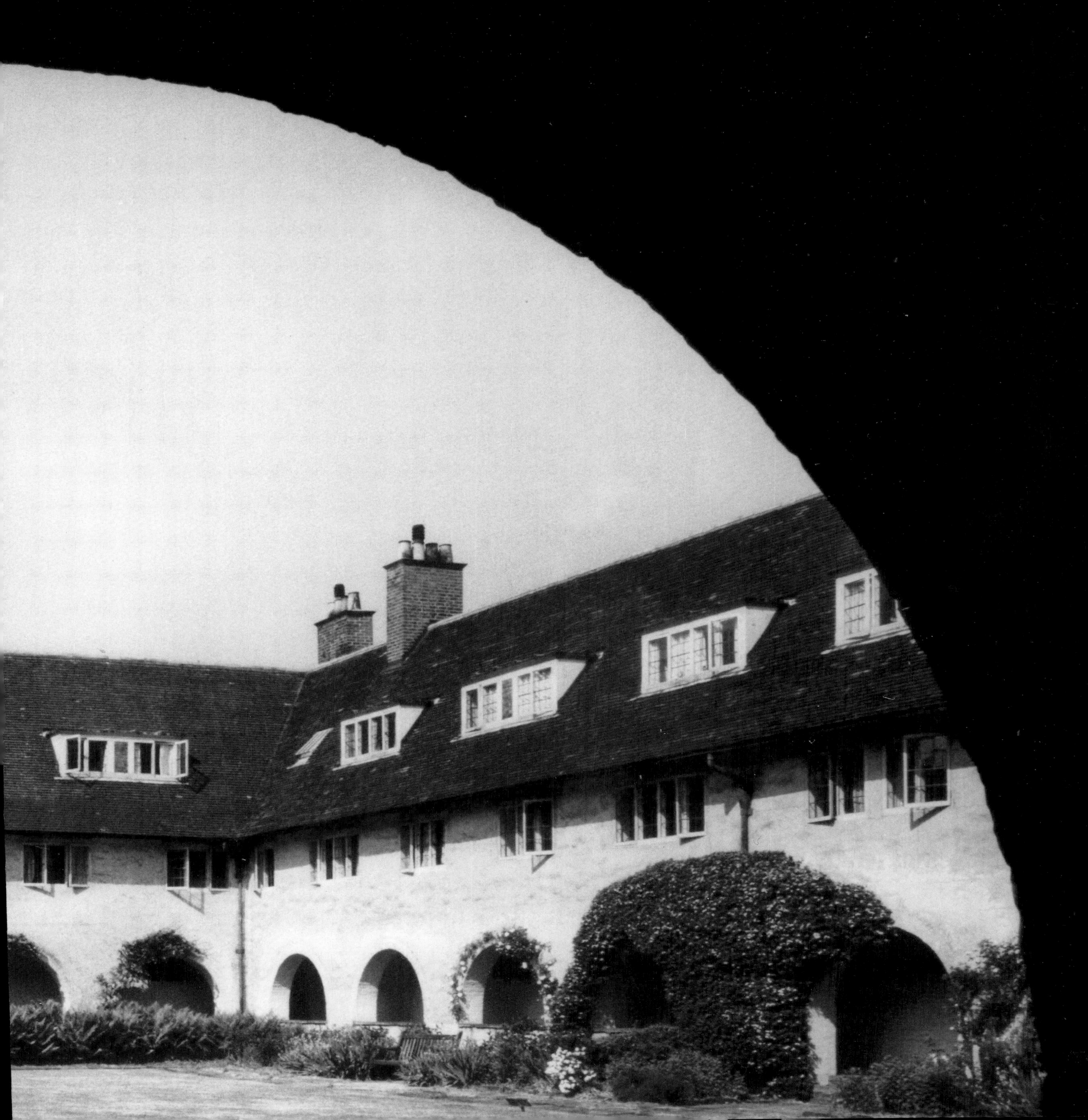

were to take effect later in the century. Thus on the one hand it failed in the short term to realise its ambition of mixing the classes, becoming eventually a wholly bourgeois enclave; but on the other hand it provided the inspiration for the first great municipal housing campaigns that followed the First World War. Likewise, its picturesque and costly architectural language was ultimately to prove unsuitable for mass housing construction without considerable simplification, yet its planning ideas were soon to become widely influential:

> Seemingly in no time at all, Hampstead Garden Suburb was being visited and imitated not just in the many garden suburbs and villages that sprung up all over Britain, only to be nipped in the bud by the First World War, but also all over Europe and the further-flung, English- speaking world. The Americans, with their boundless suburbs, were hot on it, even the French came up in double-quick time with their home-spun version of the cité jardin ... This was the period of greatest international admiration for English architecture: the Unwinian suburb, with its deft layout and gamut of simplified vernacular styles, took centre stage in that story.[13]

In England itself, the domestic revival style of Raymond Unwin was widely imitated by the speculative housebuilders who surrounded London and other cities with endless suburban developments in the inter-war years; their debased descendants of the old English cottage proved an easy target for critics of that kind of development, such as Osbert Lancaster who wryly observed that: 'when the young passer-by is a little unnerved at being suddenly confronted with a hundred and fifty accurate reproductions of Anne Hathaway's cottage, each complete with central-heating and garage, he should pause to reflect on the extraordinary fact that all over the country the latest and most scientific methods of mass-production were, only a few years ago, still being utilized to turn out a stream of old oak beams, leaded window-panes and small discs of bottle-glass, all structural devices which our ancestors lost no time in abandoning as soon as an increase in wealth and knowledge enabled them to do so'.[14]

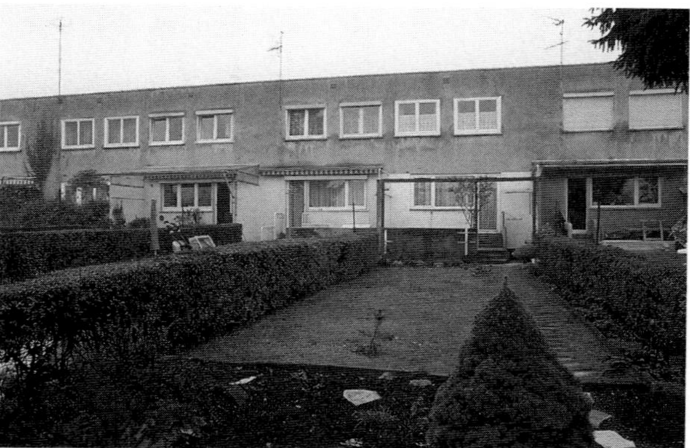

But if the revivalist architectural style employed at Hampstead deflected some English critics away from appreciating the progressive elements of this pioneering development, this was not always the case elsewhere: for instance in Weimar Frankfurt an ambitious social housing programme was placed under the control of the architect Ernst May. Although May was a disciple of Modernism, he had worked before the Great War as a student under Raymond Unwin at Hampstead, and had absorbed his ideas about low-density suburban planning. In a number of his Frankfurt *Siedlungen* of the 1920s, he laid out rows and blocks of sober workers' dwellings in a manner strongly reminiscent of an English garden city, thus providing one of the most surprising offshoots of the village ideal.[15] However it is worth pointing out that the English attachment to the symbols of pre-industrial community were taken far more seriously by the Nazis in the following decade, when they advocated the construction of village housing using traditional German forms and materials, in repudiation of the dwellings previously built in 'Das Neue Frankfurt'.

The Cottage and the Car

But by far the most significant export of the Garden City model was to America, where the increased mobility that resulted from mass car ownership, and the seemingly limitless availability of open land, provided fertile territory for the further development of these ideas. Henry Ford's success in pioneering cheap mass-produced automobiles meant that by 1928 there were more than 20 million cars on American roads, and this in turn led to an unprecedented wave of unplanned suburban expansion, resulting in what was later termed 'sprawl'. American architects and planners responded to this situation in a variety of ways. The most famous of

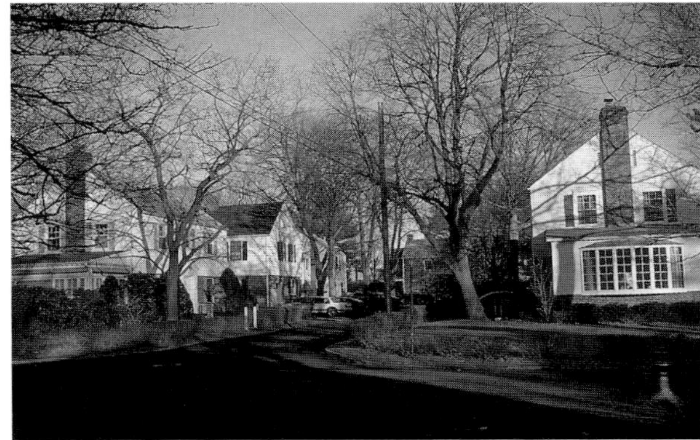

these was Frank Lloyd Wright's Broadacre City project of the early 1930s, which argued for the complete decentralisation of overcrowded cities across the undeveloped American landscape.

But more influential in real terms was the adaptation of the garden city model by Henry Wright and Clarence Stein, who designed the community of Radburn, New Jersey in 1928-29. It has often been the case that American designers have adopted European ideas, but have then adapted them to the particular circumstances of their own country, before eventually re-exporting them back to their place of origin. This is exactly what happened in the case of Radburn, which improved on Letchworth and Hampstead in that it was planned to accommodate the motor car:

> From Howard they acquired the idea that the town ought to be large enough to support local amenities like schools and shops, yet small enough to retain its own identity and allow easy access to the surrounding green belt. They also took the idea of retaining rural-like open spaces within the development. To these Garden City concepts ingeniously added the car by restricting main arterial streets to the periphery of the project, allowing access to individual homes through local dead-end streets, or cul-de-sacs. Families were free to wander through the local parks and pathways without fear of encountering heavy automobile traffic, even crossing under major streets through underpasses.[16]

The Great Depression halted the development of Radburn when only a relatively small portion of it had been completed, yet this model community had an influence out of all proportion to its size, on both sides of the Atlantic. The illustrations show how similar the small cul-de-sac streets were to their English precedents, although the vernacular style of the housing is obviously American. In fact Unwin (a regular and celebrated visitor to America, who even appeared on the front pages of the Wall St Journal voicing his criticisms of Manhattan's

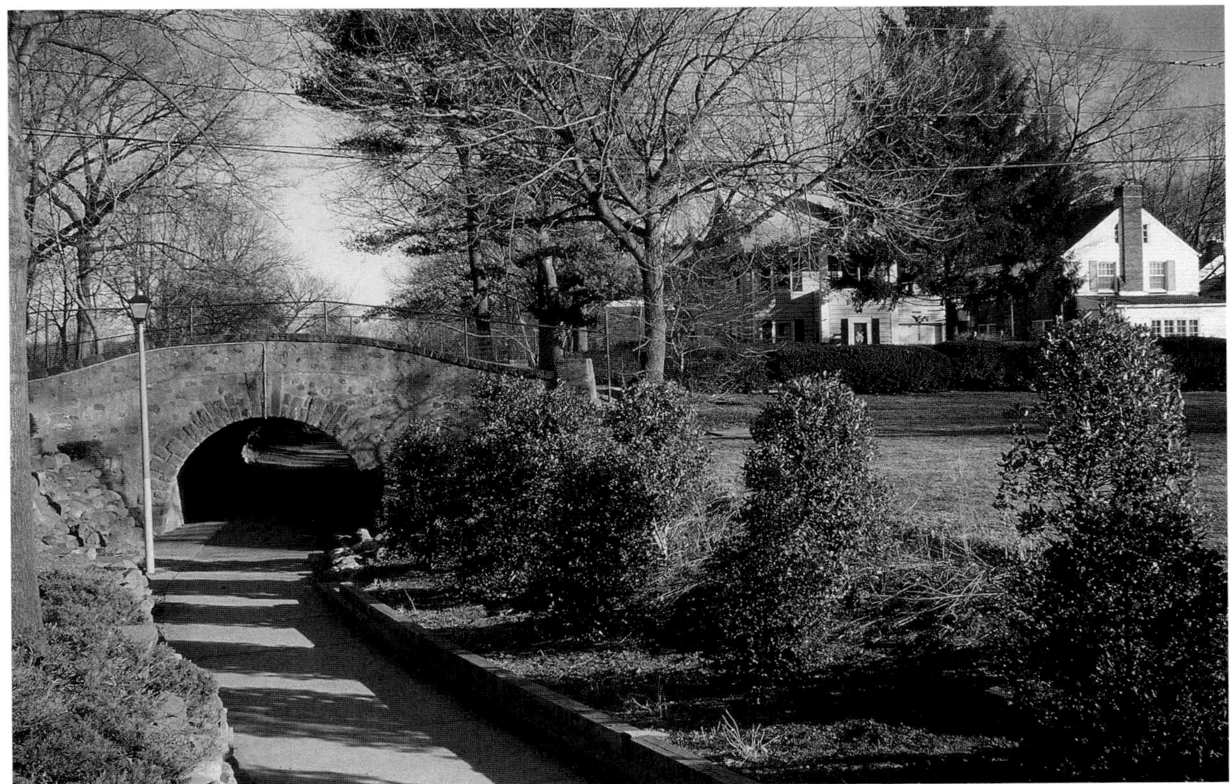

In his designs for the Römerstadt estate, opposite, in Frankfurt from 1927–28, Ernst May combined the lessons he learnt about low-density urban planning from Raymond Unwin (with whom he worked as a student), with his own Modernist ideals. Around the same time, Henry Wright and Clarence Stein were creating their own version of 'Old England' in America, with the community of Radburn in New Jersey, right. But unlike English garden cities, Radburn was planned with the needs of both pedestrians and motorists in mind, below right, as demonstrated by this underpass that keeps people at a safe distance from the traffic crossing the bridge overhead.

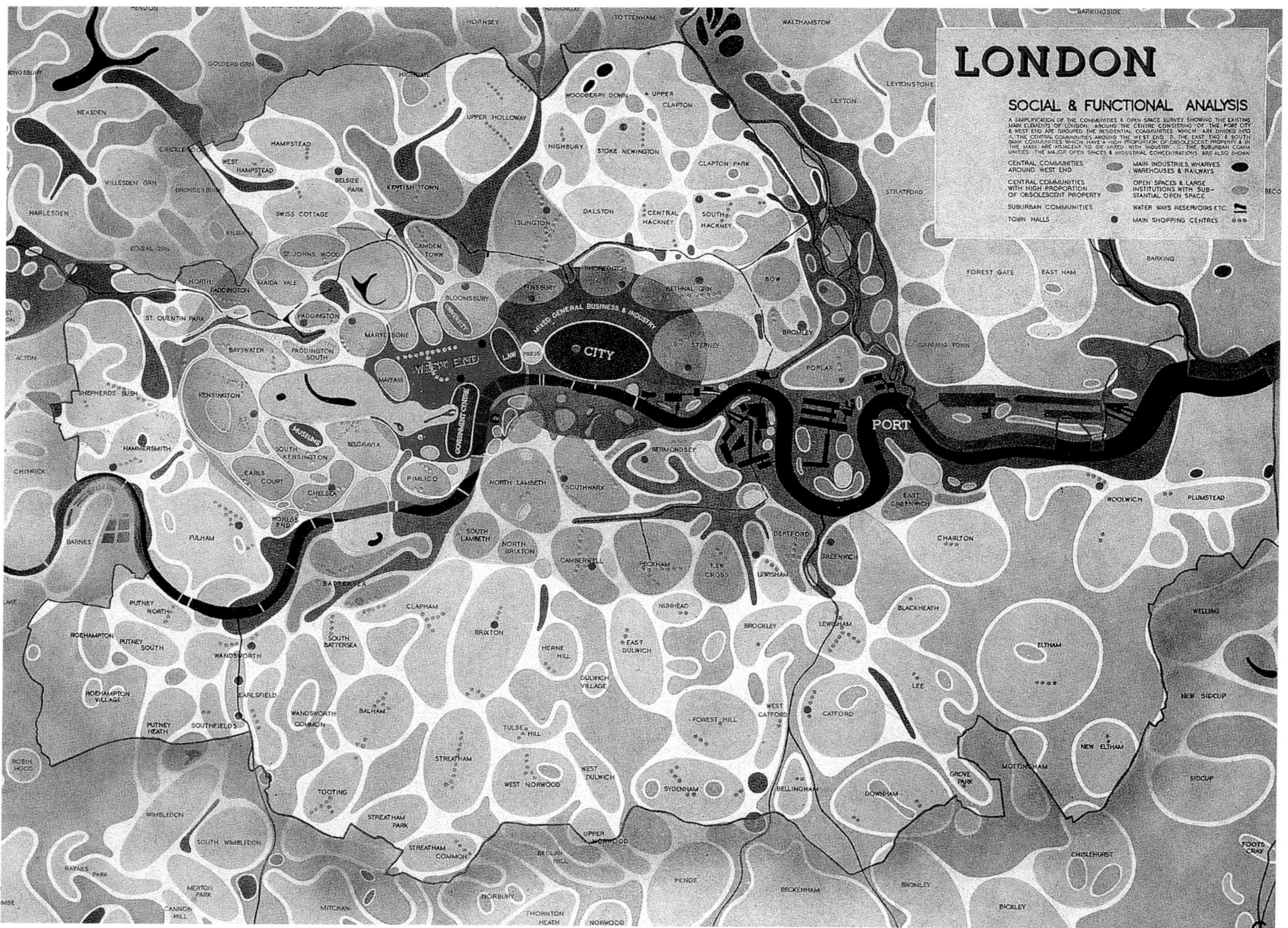
LONDON
SOCIAL & FUNCTIONAL ANALYSIS
A SIMPLIFICATION OF THE COMMUNITIES & OPEN SPACE SURVEY SHOWING THE EXISTING MAIN ELEMENTS OF LONDON. AROUND THE CENTRE CONSISTING OF THE PORT CITY & WEST END ARE GROUPED THE RESIDENTIAL COMMUNITIES WHICH ARE DIVIDED INTO A. THE CENTRAL COMMUNITIES AROUND THE WEST END. B. THE EAST END & SOUTH BANK COMMUNITIES WHICH HAVE A HIGH PROPORTION OF OBSOLESCENT PROPERTY & IN THE MAIN ARE ADJACENT TO OR MIXED WITH INDUSTRY. C. THE SUBURBAN COMMUNITIES. THE MAJOR OPEN SPACES & INDUSTRIAL CONCENTRATIONS ARE ALSO SHOWN.
CENTRAL COMMUNITIES AROUND WEST END
CENTRAL COMMUNITIES WITH HIGH PROPORTION OF OBSOLESCENT PROPERTY
SUBURBAN COMMUNITIES
TOWN HALLS
MAIN INDUSTRIES, WHARVES WAREHOUSES & RAILWAYS
OPEN SPACES & LARGE INSTITUTIONS WITH SUBSTANTIAL OPEN SPACE
WATER WAYS RESERVOIRS ETC.
MAIN SHOPPING CENTRES
CITY
WEST END
PORT
LAW
PRESS
MUSEUMS
GOVERNMENT CENTRE
MIXED GENERAL BUSINESS & INDUSTRY
HORNSEY
TOTTENHAM
WALTHAMSTOW
BARKINGSIDE
LEYTONSTONE
LEYTON
GOLDERS GRN
HIGHGATE
NEASDEN
UPPER HOLLOWAY
WOODBERRY DOWN
UPPER CLAPTON
HAMPSTEAD
WEST HAMPSTEAD
HIGHBURY
STOKE NEWINGTON
CLAPTON PARK
WILLESDEN GRN
BELSIZE PARK
KENTISH TOWN
STRATFORD
HARLESDEN
SWISS COTTAGE
ISLINGTON
DALSTON
CENTRAL HACKNEY
SOUTH HACKNEY
KENSAL GRN
CAMDEN TOWN
ST. JOHNS WOOD
SHOREDITCH
BARKING
FOREST GATE
EAST HAM
NORTH PADDINGTON
MAIDA VALE
FINSBURY
BETHNAL GRN
BOW
BLOOMSBURY
ST. QUENTIN PARK
PADDINGTON
MARYLEBONE
STEPNEY
BROMLEY
CANNING TOWN
ACTON
BAYSWATER
PADDINGTON SOUTH
POPLAR
MAYFAIR
SHEPHERDS BUSH
KENSINGTON
HAMMERSMITH
BELGRAVIA
BERMONDSEY
SOUTH KENSINGTON
CHISWICK
EARLS COURT
PIMLICO
NORTH LAMBETH
SOUTHWARK
CHELSEA
EAST GREENWICH
WOOLWICH
PLUMSTEAD
FULHAM
WORLDS END
SOUTH LAMBETH
DEPTFORD
BARNES
NORTH BRIXTON
CAMBERWELL
PECKHAM
NEW CROSS
GREENWICH
CHARLTON
LEWISHAM
BATTERSEA
CLAPHAM
NUNHEAD
BLACKHEATH
WELLING
PUTNEY NORTH
BRIXTON
BROCKLEY
ROEHAMPTON
PUTNEY SOUTH
SOUTH BATTERSEA
HERNE HILL
EAST DULWICH
ELTHAM
WANDSWORTH
LEE
DULWICH VILLAGE
ROEHAMPTON VILLAGE
EARLSFIELD
NEW SIDCUP
WANDSWORTH COMMON
BALHAM
WEST CATFORD
CATFORD
FOREST HILL
PUTNEY HEATH
SOUTHFIELDS
TULSE HILL
NEW ELTHAM
ROBIN HOOD
STREATHAM
MOTTINGHAM
GROVE PARK
WEST DULWICH
SIDCUP
TOOTING
WEST NORWOOD
SYDENHAM
BELLINGHAM
DOWNHAM
WIMBLEDON
STREATHAM PARK
UPPER NORWOOD
SOUTH WIMBLEDON
STREATHAM COMMON
CHISLEHURST
FOOTS CRAY
RAYNES PARK
PENGE
MERTON PARK
NORBURY
BECKENHAM
BROMLEY
CANNON HILL
MITCHAM
THORNTON HEATH
NORWOOD
BICKLEY

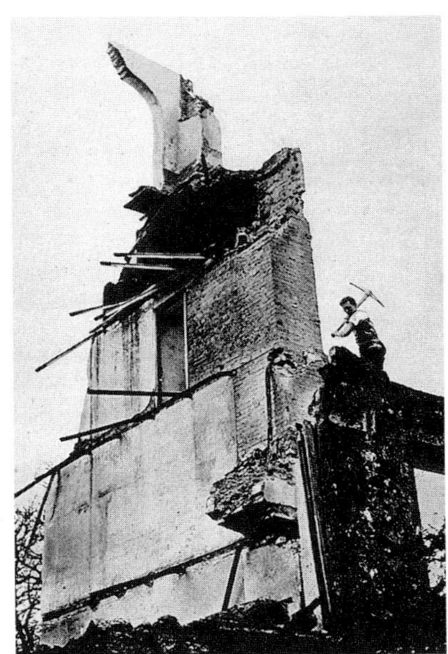

The County of London Plan of 1943, opposite, purports to be 'a social and functional analysis' of the city, showing the supposed boundaries of the familiar 'urban villages' that London is commonly thought to be made up of. The Plan addressed the need for reconstruction in post-war London, above, with bomb damage providing an opportunity for new ideas to be tested. To quote this photograph's original caption: 'In the end is my beginning.' This pedestrian underpass at Stevenage New Town, right, echoes the road layout of Wright and Stein's influential earlier New Jersey suburb – a planning debt which is also acknowledged in the name of a street in Harlow, called Radburn Close.

skyscrapers), took an active interest in Wright and Stein's work. But it is the small pedestrian underpass shown here, that was to crop up time and time again in later schemes inspired by Radburn. This was especially true of a group of communities planned and built in Britain after the Second World War, when the Garden City ideal had once more crossed the water.

New Towns for Old

In tracing the history of the Utopian village it can be seen that the vision of the ideal community was constantly being adapted in reaction to changing conditions in, and perceptions of, those urban societies which had provoked the enmity of the reformers. While the destruction of huge swathes of London during the war had caused considerable suffering to the civilian population, the need to plan for reconstruction concentrated the minds of politicians, architects and planners alike on how this opportunity might allow them to address the manifold problems of the great metropolis.

The post-war future of London was set out in the 1943 *County of London Plan*. Amongst the many problems it identified, the Plan highlighted congestion, inadequate open space, bad housing, architectural squalor, and sprawl as the major obstacles to a better London. The proposed solutions included identifying and reviving the ancient village communities which by common consent constituted the social fabric of London. The map reproduced here shows London divided up into these communities, which were then further broken down into 'neighbourhood units' as the American-derived planning jargon of the day called them, which were to be judiciously replanned, without destroying what had survived the bombing. With the exception of the Lansbury Estate, a new model neighbourhood planned as part of the 1951 Festival of Britain, this detailed level of planning was rarely ever followed through in reality. Lansbury may have been, as one historian of post-war architecture has claimed, 'a pioneering achievement of the concept of mixed development, the integration of housing and flats of varying sizes with shops and services to form a suburb that was a real community;'[17] but what seems to have constituted a 'real community' in 1951, namely this slightly shabby ensemble of picturesque, genteel architecture grouped around a traditional town square, seems a far cry from the utopian ambitions of Howard and Unwin half a century earlier.

The other major solution offered up by the post-war planners was the designation of a ring of new towns to be built around London, just as Howard had originally proposed. The first generation of these towns, at Basildon, Bracknell, Harlow, Hemel Hempstead, Hatfield and Stevenage were carefully and sensitively planned by leading architects of the day, most famously Frederick Gibberd at Harlow, and they assiduously paid homage to the ideal of the English village. For as one architect writing in the official government manual on 'Design in Town and Village' of 1953 put it, 'the English village is, I believe, among the pleasantest and most warmly human places that men have ever built to live in'.[18]

But the ancient village was not the only inspiration for the New Town planners, as these illustrations show. For the view of Stevenage shows a pedestrian underpass that strongly suggests a debt to the American automobile suburb of Radburn, while at Harlow the street name Radburn Close is an explicit homage to Wright and Stein's model community. In this particular street, in imitation of its New Jersey forebear, the English cottage is reconciled with the American motor car by providing road access at the rear of the dwelling, and a pedestrian footpath at the front.

The English New Towns represent a climax to the story of the traditional village as model for urban development, the official endorsement of Howard and Unwin's Utopian vision. But these towns are widely viewed today as dull and uninspiring environments in which to live: they were the creations of state-sponsored technocrats, who seemed to have stifled all the romance

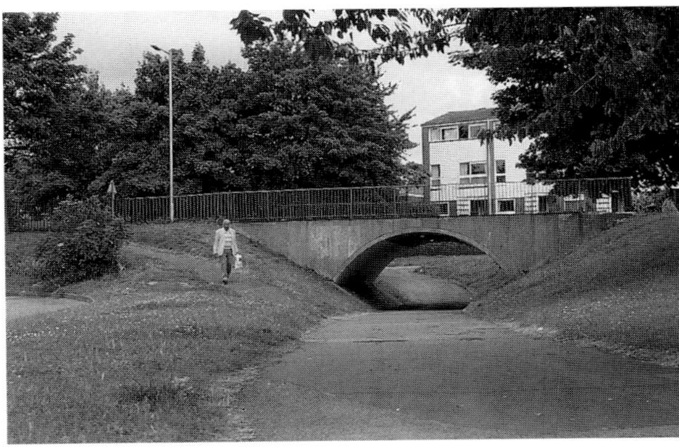

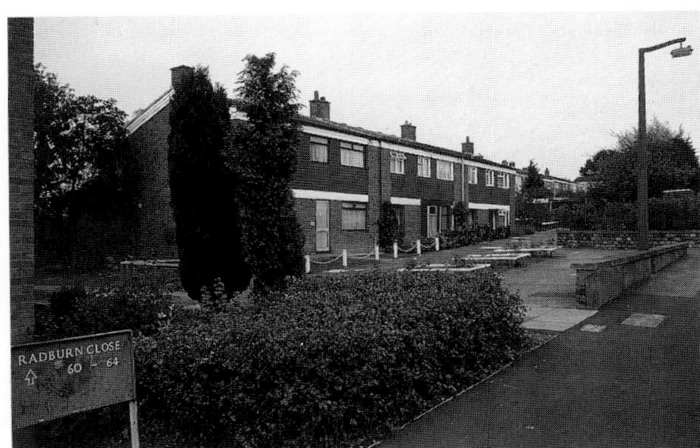

and the radicalism that once fired the Garden City movement, without correcting their worst failings:

> In his analytical book *Town Design* (1953) Frederick Gibberd, like Sitte and Unwin in their time, revealed his sensitivity to historical urban places (mostly Italian), but little of this feeling can be detected in his design for Harlow. The civic centre in this new town lacks such qualities entirely ...As in the garden cities of Letchworth and Welwyn – where breweries were banned – the new towns lacked any urban scruffiness, leaving little to do in the evening.[19]

Thus after a century of development, the utopian vision of the 'goose on the green' had become institutionalised and banal. But in America at least there have been other champions of the traditional village who have reinvested that vision with new meanings powerful enough to be at the forefront of planning debates today. The final part of this essay takes a tour of small-town America, or at least the version of it promoted by the New Urbanism movement, which has deliberately set out to supersede the automobile-based settlements of the past fifty years with more traditional patterns of development.

Exopolis

American society has rested on the horns of a dilemma for most of the last hundred years. For on the one hand the development of the mass-produced motor car in the early years of the twentieth century offered to the US citizen the prospect of almost total freedom of movement, which accorded well with the extraordinarily high value placed on the concept of freedom in American culture. But on the other hand, this new mobility also meant freedom for communities to segregate themselves by class or culture, and freedom for those who could to abandon the congestion and danger of cities altogether in favour of the new open suburbs that from the 1920s onwards began their unplanned march across the American countryside. This process was exacerbated by the prosperity that followed the end of the Second World war, and the considerable financial incentives offered to returning GIs – 100% mortgage with no down payment – to purchase a new home of their own.

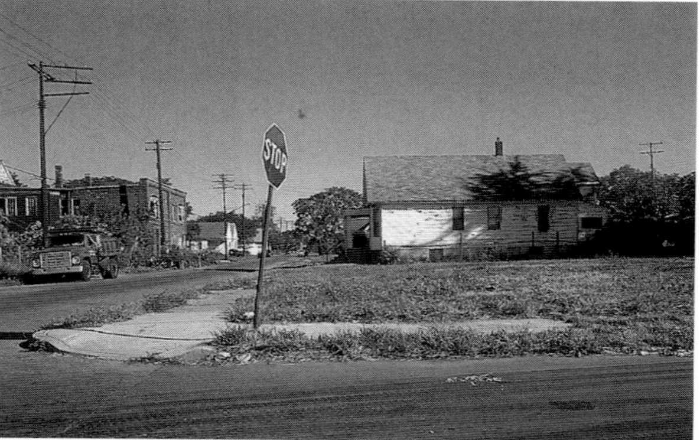

> With little to risk and much to gain, Americans in the millions bought a little piece of what by now had become the American dream. In just four years between 1956 and 1960, 11 million new homes were built in the suburbs. Owning one's own single family detached house on its own plot of land, close to nature and away from the now thoroughly evil cities; this is what many desired and could now possess. Jefferson's rural vision for America – although now much transformed – continued to drive American values and aspirations.[20]

But as people no longer lived close enough to downtown areas to shop there easily, then the shops had to come to them, creating a culture of total dependency on the automobile. Thus the price for the American Dream was the atomisation of society itself. The abject condition of the abandoned city centres, and of the poor populations that were left behind, are hinted at in the pictures of downtown Detroit. Of course the worse these cities became, the greater the desire to flee them.

But just as there had been a reaction in late nineteenth century England not only to cities but also to the sprawling suburbs that had gobbled up the countryside around them, so a hundred years later there is a new American movement that seeks to create orderly, planned communities, based on traditional forms and values, in which life can be lived without fear and ugliness.

The mythical image of the small American town, in which people know each other, and children happily play on bicycles without fear of dangerous traffic, has proved a potent one for almost as long as people have believed it to be disappearing. (That particular icon of the child on a bike has really become the contemporary 'goose on the green': one only has to think of Spielberg's sentimental use of it in small-town homages like *ET* to recognise its power

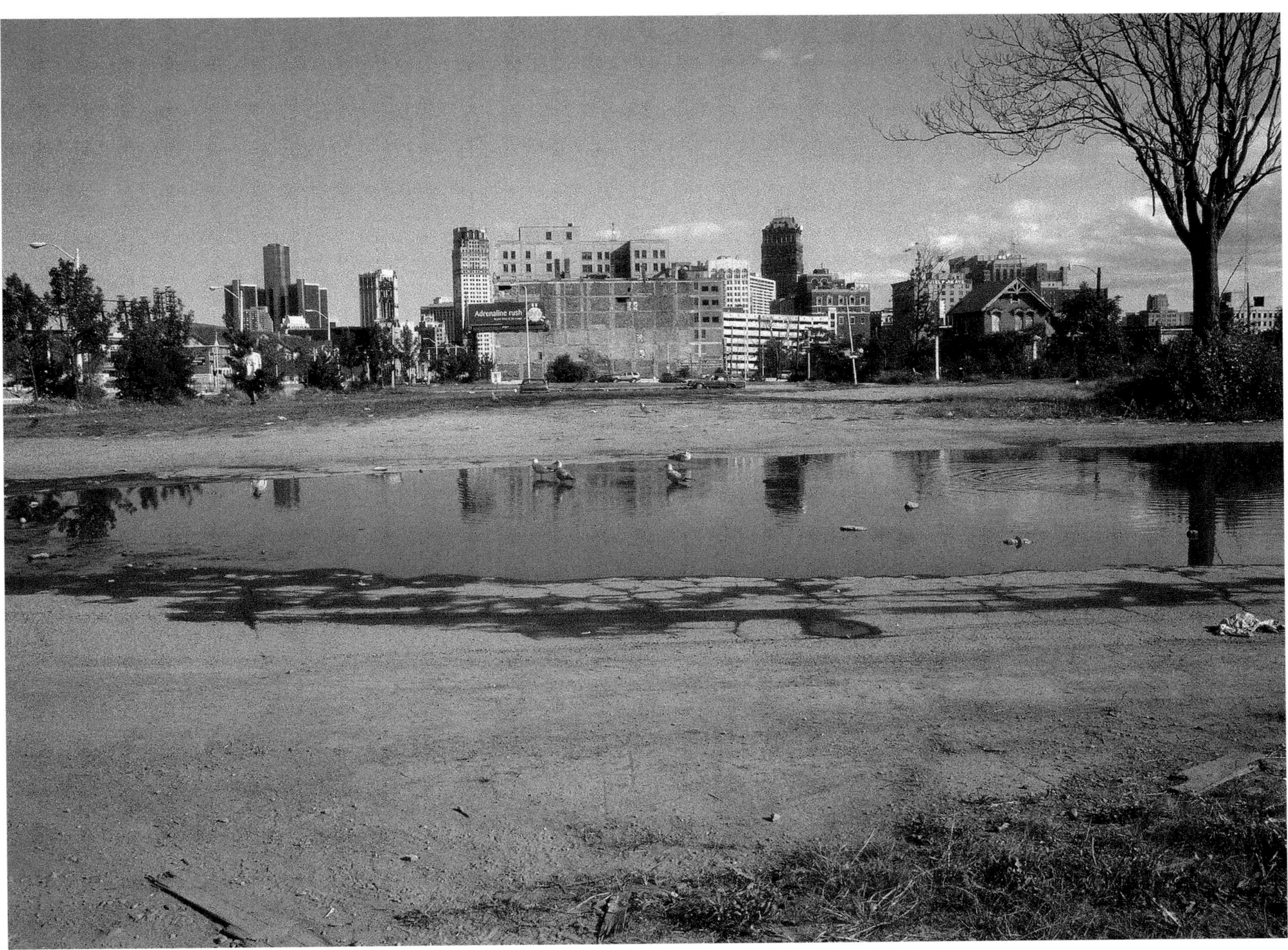

Large areas of downtown Detroit are turning into a post-industrial version of rural open space, with whole blocks disappearing in recent years. Today, the heart of the city, above, is surrounded by urban wasteland. The overgrown pavements and empty lots of this neglected eastside neighbourhood, opposite, are signs of a city that is being abandoned by all those who can afford to leave.

Designed by Albert Kahn, the power plant at Henry Ford's River Rouge factory, right, makes for a striking contrast with nearby Greenfield Village, opposite. You can still enjoy the pleasures of an old-fashioned game of baseball on the village green, opposite, but while it gives the impression of being a real town, Greenfield is in fact Ford's own tribute to American ingenuity. It features buildings brought to the site from around the United States, such as the former home of the Heinz family, below opposite, where the baked bean was allegedly invented. The plaque commemorating a Depression-era incident, below, presents another, rather less philanthropic, side to the great industrialist.

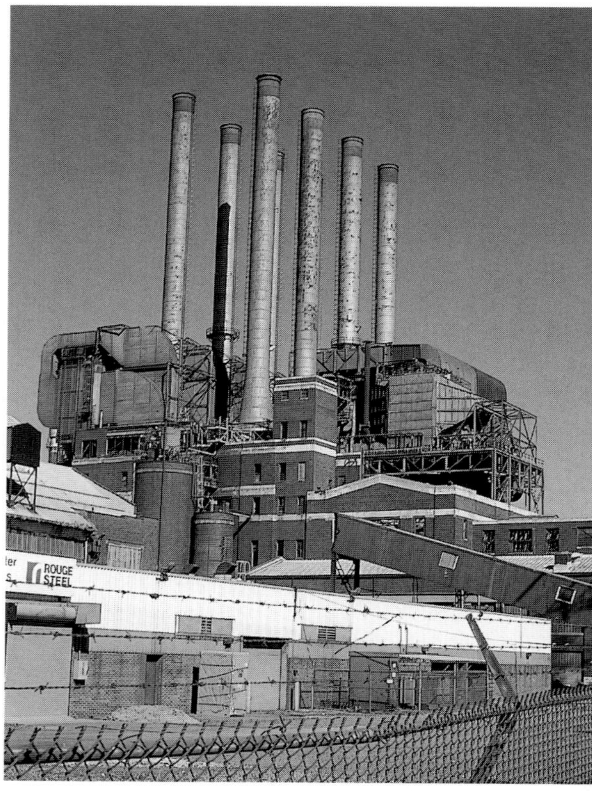

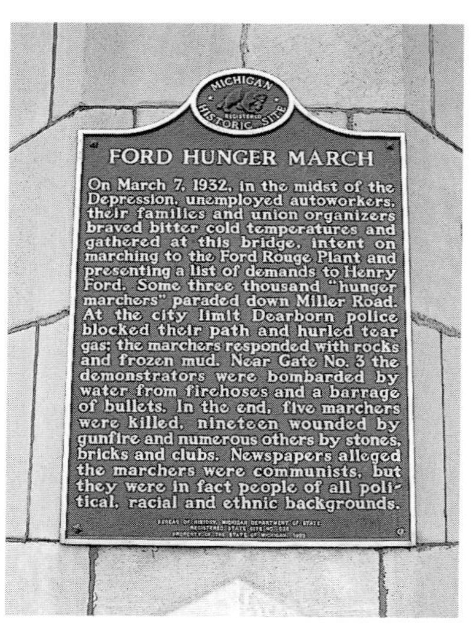

as a symbol of American domestic values) Although the planning of anti-urban enclaves is really a late twentieth century phenomenon, the construction of model communities as demonstrations of American values under threat, has a longer history.

An American Invention

Every institution is the lengthened shadow of one man
Ralph Waldo Emerson[21]

Ironically it was near to Detroit – Motor City – the home of the automobile, that Henry Ford himself made an extraordinary contribution to the story of the ideal village. In 1929 he opened Greenfield Village a short distance away from his massive River Rouge factory, then the largest industrial complex in the world, a bizarre juxtaposition that serves to emphasise the fundamental contradictions between Ford's actions as a hard-nosed industrialist, and his public persona as philanthropist and upholder of conservative morals. Greenfield was not a real village in that it had no inhabitants, but Ford's ad hoc assemblage of vernacular American housing, and buildings associated with his own pantheon of American heroes (especially Thomas Edison) , was carefully laid out in the semblance of a traditional American community. One can still participate in old-time baseball on the playing field, while waving to the 'Puffing Billy' steaming past, or congregate on the village green, which even has a church and a town hall to complete the picture of a harmonious and well-ordered community.

Ford claimed that Greenfield was his response to the furore that greeted his famous remark 'History is Bunk!' What he objected to he said was the kind of history that only dealt with politicians and battles. Here instead he curated a living museum of the ordinary lives of Americans, and particularly those ordinary Americans who had worked the land. For it was his belief that 'With one Foot On the Land and One Foot In Industry America is Safe'.[22] The enduring appeal of Ford's fantasy village, and his belief in the redemptive power of the past, is evident in the millions who visit it annually from across the United States.

Home from Home

But Ford never intended his folly to be a model for real developments, and for the next fifty years, the advance of American sprawl continued unabated. By the 1980s, there was agreement amongst both American architects and their clients that the blandly uniform housing tracts that had disfigured the post-war American landscape were no longer desirable. There was a positive sense of the importance of environmental issues and a renewed

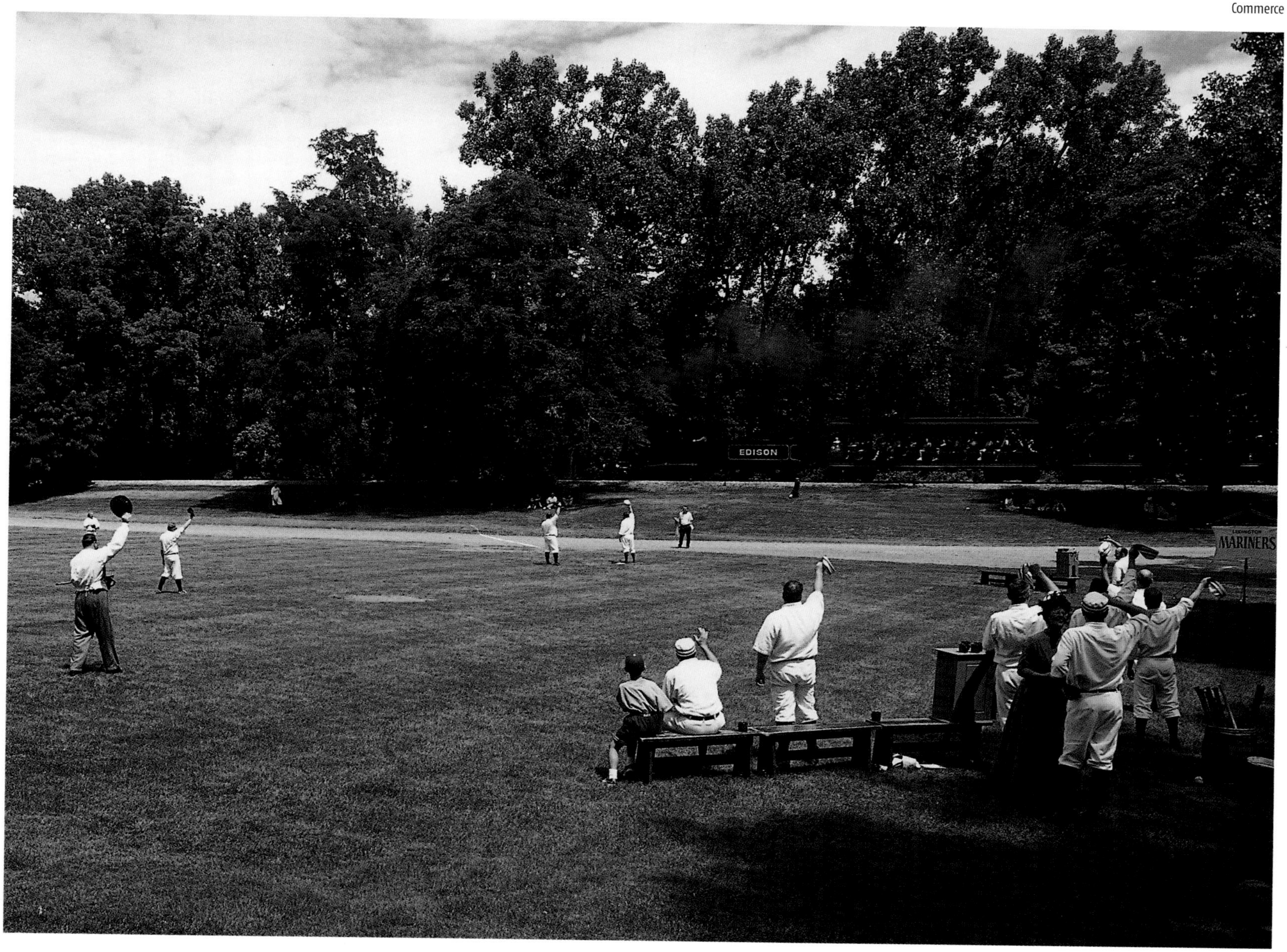

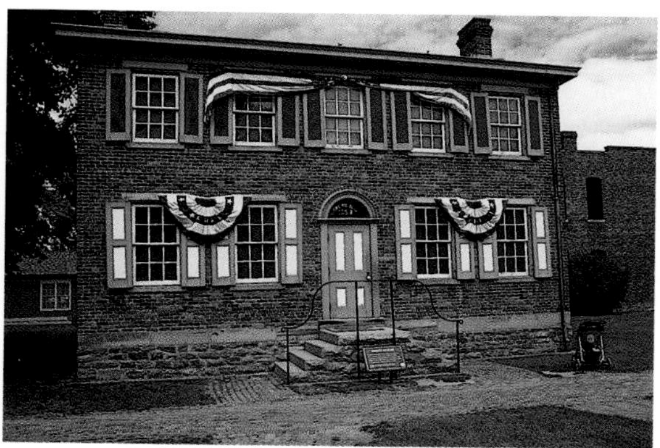

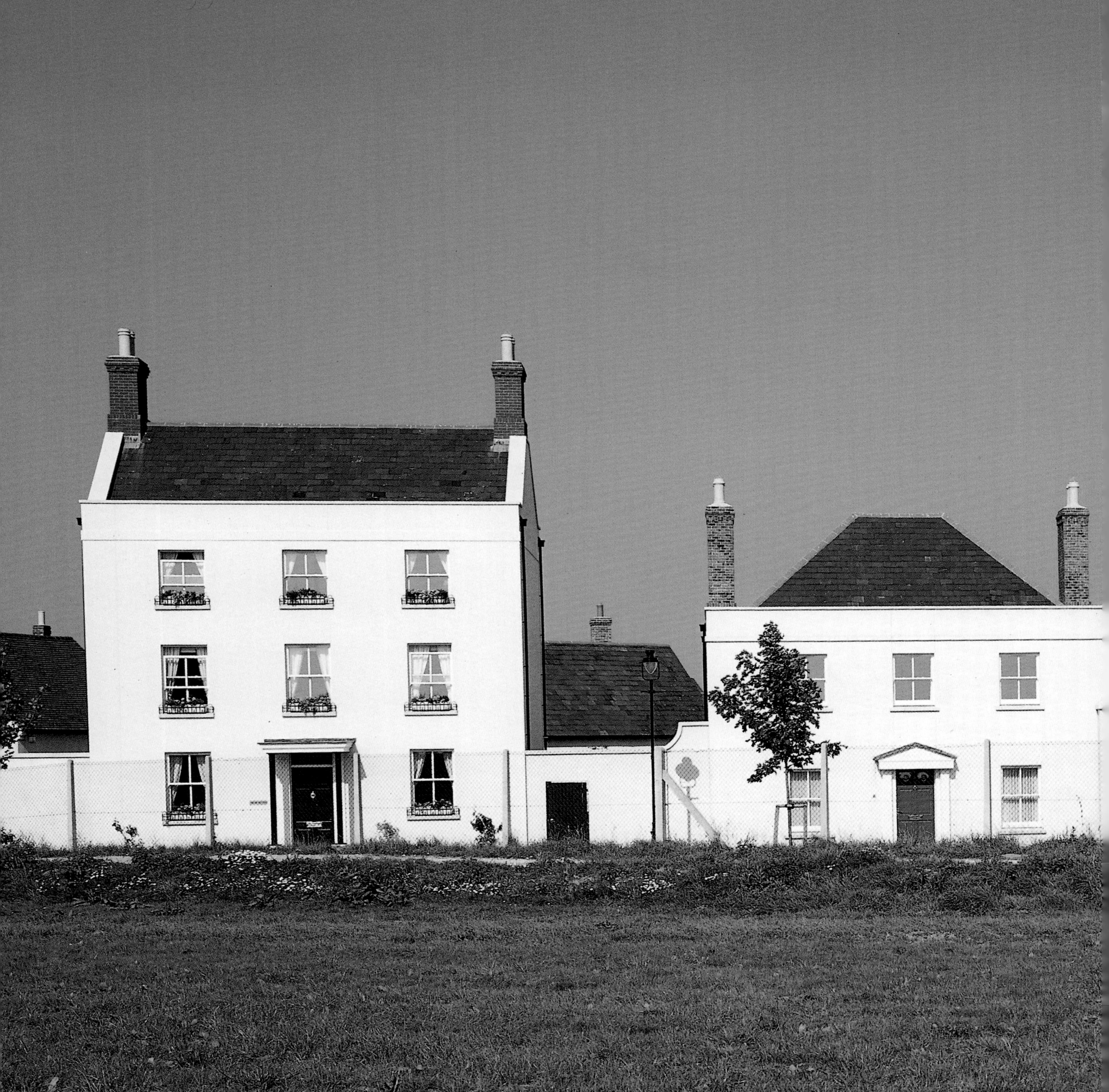

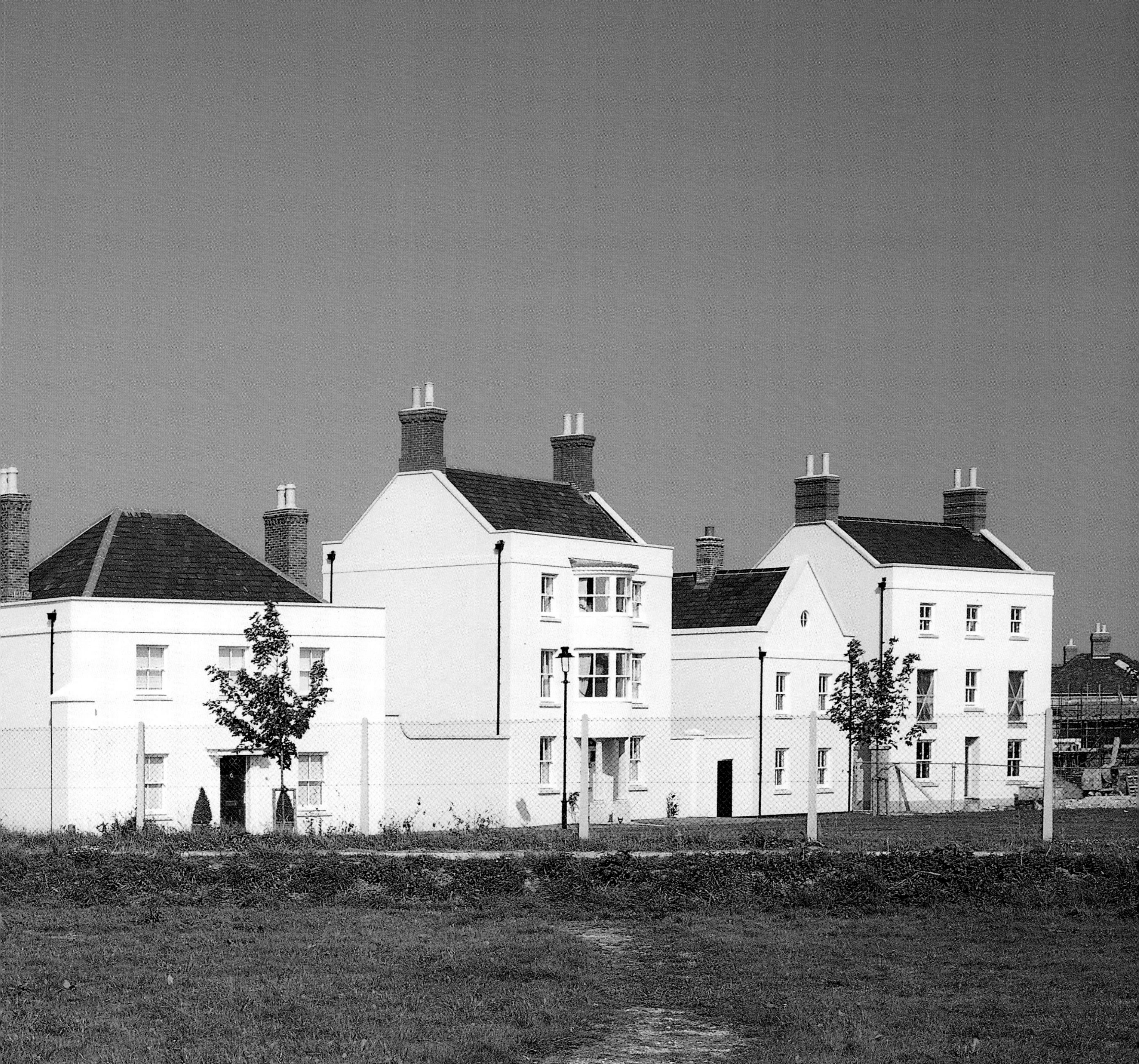

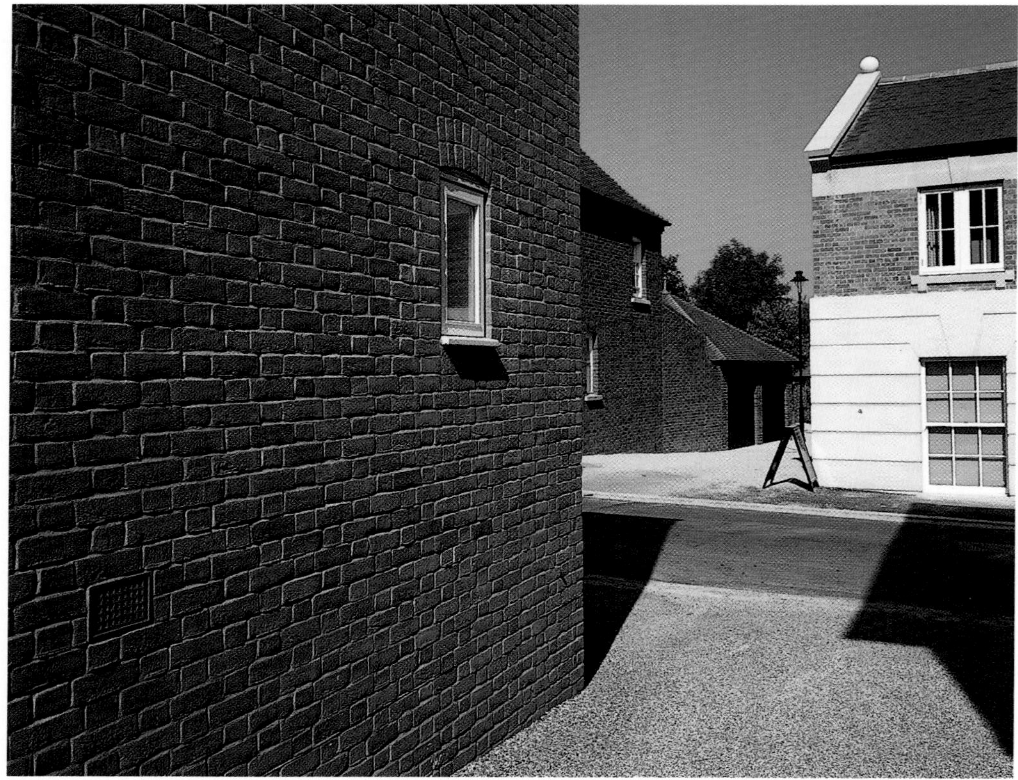

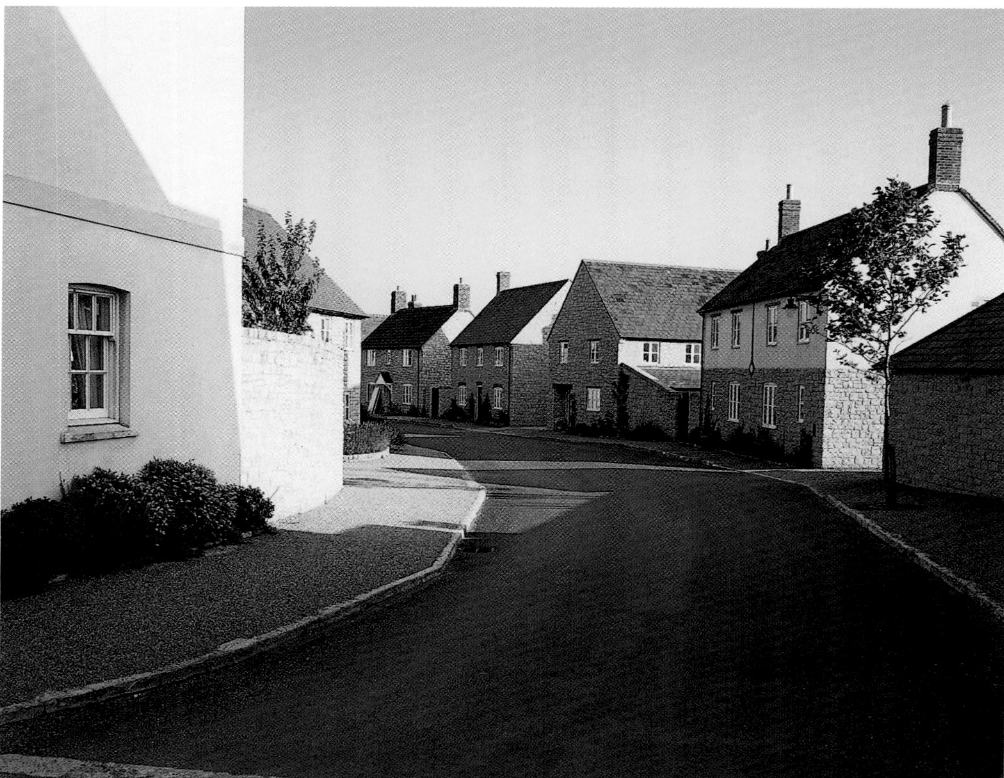

interest in a sense of place. Most developers responded to this by simply adding picturesque and regional detailing to their new houses. But at the ideal community of Seaside, Florida (designed 1982 and under construction since 1986) the architects Andreas Duany and Elizabeth Plater- Zyberk attempted something rather more ambitious. Combining the regard for the American vernacular they had learnt from the architect Charles Moore at Yale, with the anti-modernist urban ideas of the European architect Leon Krier, they developed the concept of the Traditional Neighbourhood Development (TND), by which new settlements would be based on a proper plan and a set of building codes or ordinance – much in the manner of Raymond Unwin at Hampstead. The intention was clearly to turn the clock back on American communities to the supposed golden age prior to the war:

> INTENT
> This ordinance is designed to ensure the development of open land along the lines of traditional neighbourhoods. Its provisions adopt the urban conventions which were normal in the United States from colonial times until the 1940s.[23]

Seaside, much beloved by HRH the Prince of Wales in his brief period of architectural influence in the late 1980s, was the first significant monument of the movement known as New Urbanism. It was particularly influenced by Krier's arguments about how one might restore the necessary social life of communities than modernist urban planning was capable of providing. He preached that as in the traditional town, every journey within a neighbourhood should be walkable, and that town squares and greens were provided the proper setting for people to gather and talk, and so develop a real sense of belonging to a community. Seaside, basking in the Florida sun and lapped by the waters of the Gulf, presents a seductive advertisement for the benefits and values of small-town life. This is a place where one can walk across the central green to the old-style post-office, chatting to the

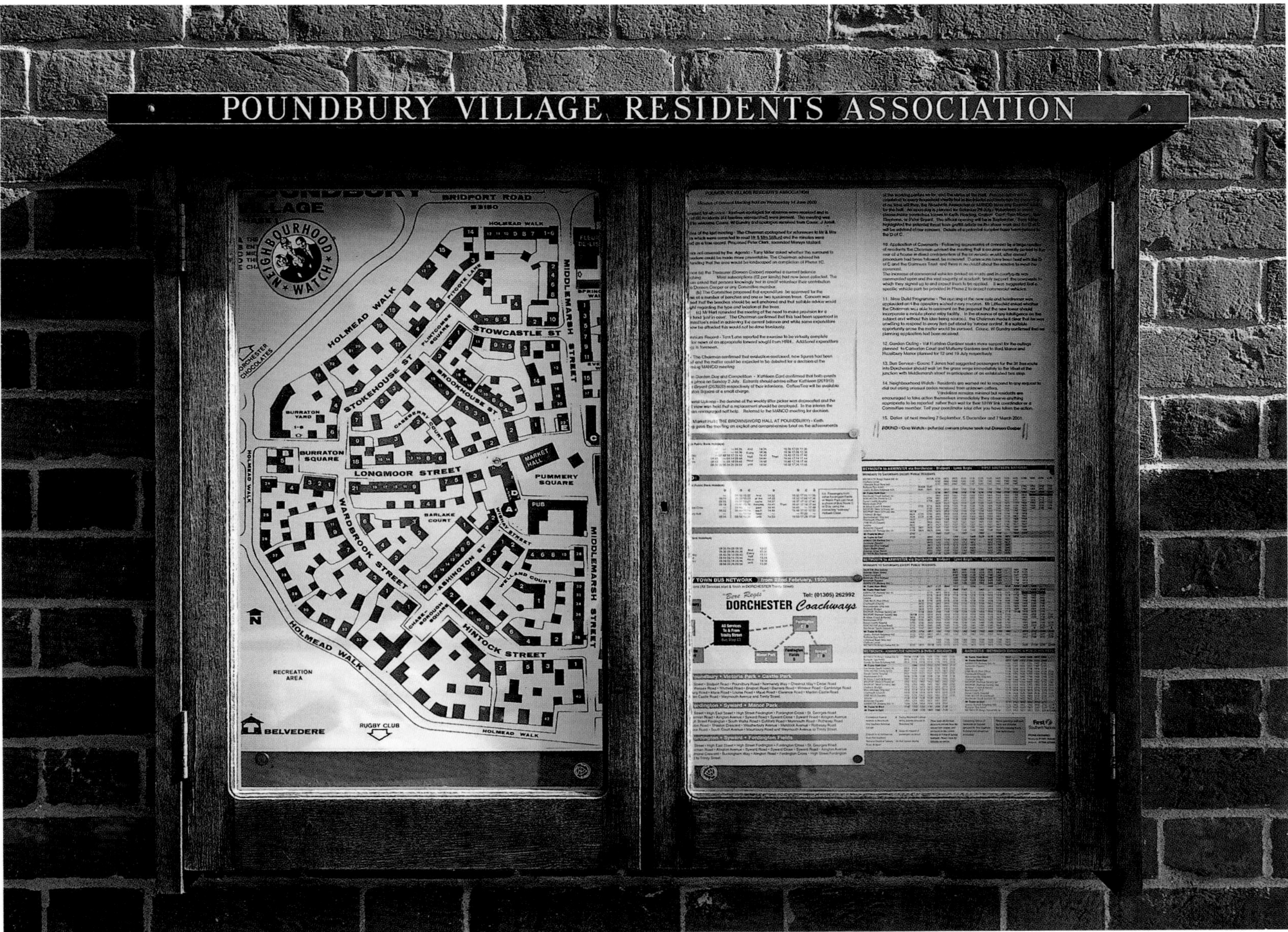

Poundbury, previous pages, above and opposite, is Britain's own answer to Seaside. It represents an ideal community as envisaged by HRH the Prince of Wales. Built on Duchy of Cornwall land outside Dorchester, the community was designed by Leon Krier to imitate a traditional English village that had evolved over time.

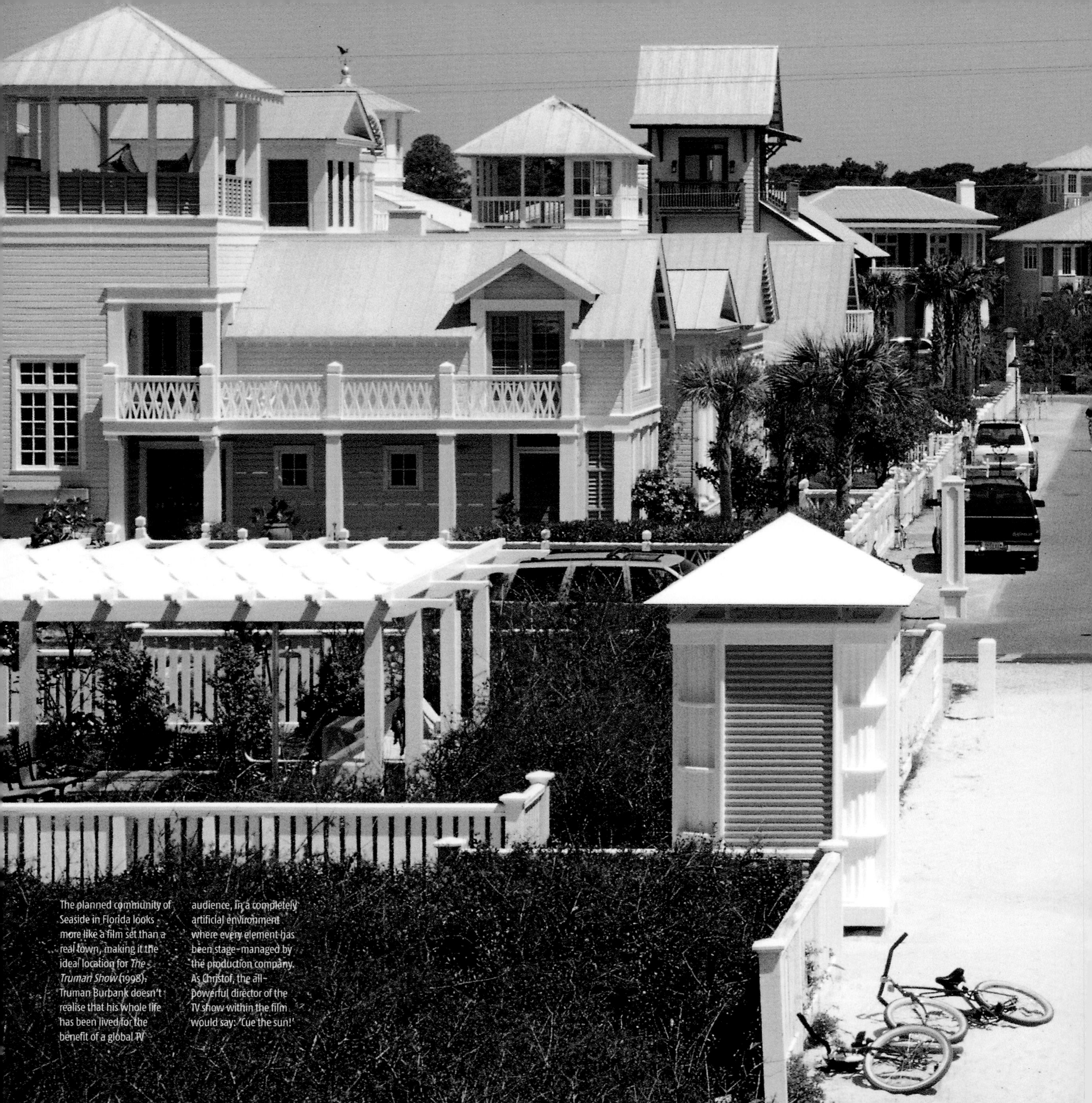

The planned community of Seaside in Florida looks more like a film set than a real town, making it the ideal location for *The Truman Show* (1998). Truman Burbank doesn't realise that his whole life has been lived for the benefit of a global TV audience, in a completely artificial environment where every element has been stage-managed by the production company. As Christof, the all-powerful director of the TV show within the film would say: 'Cue the sun!'

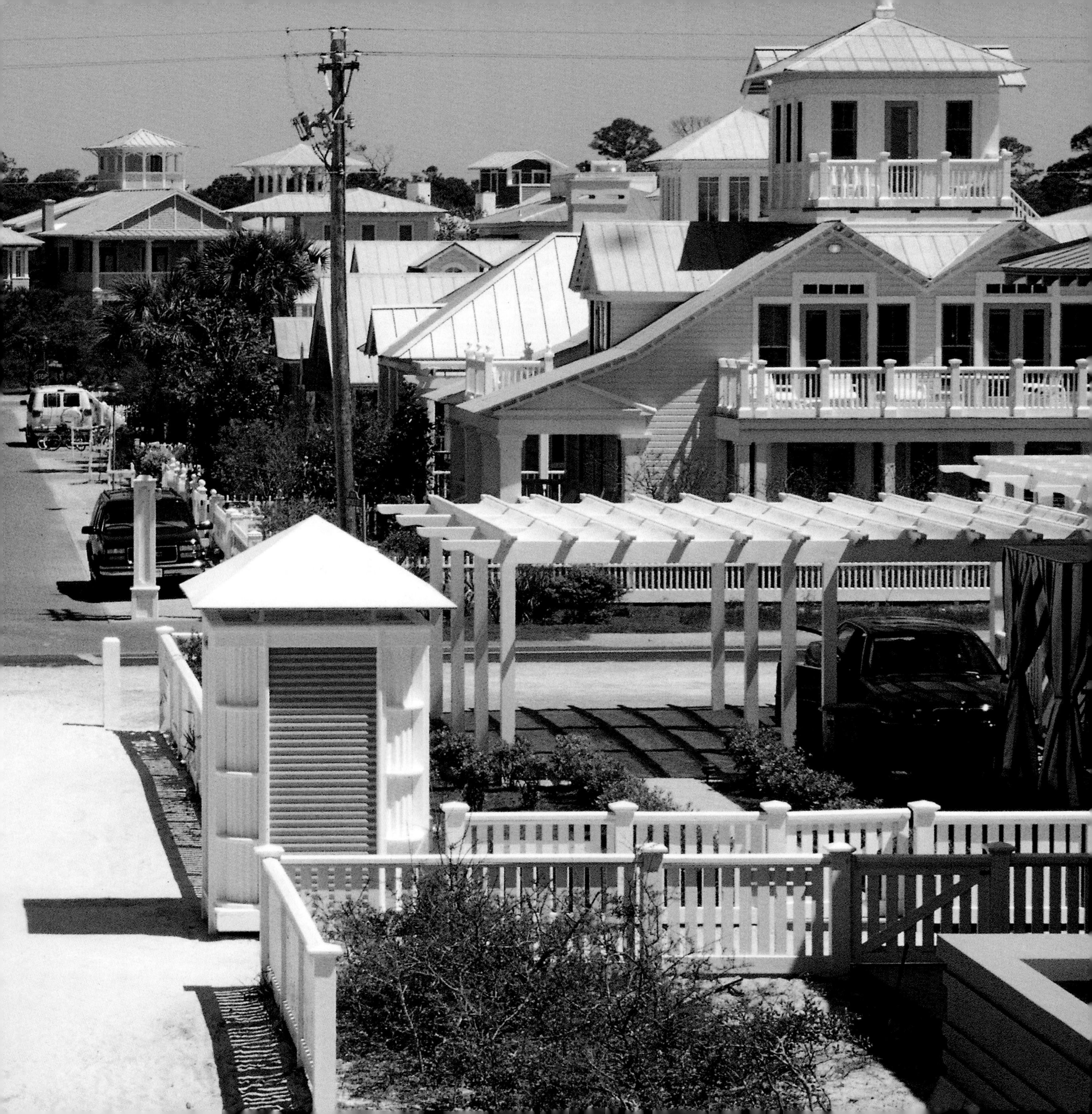

neighbours on the way. Here children can ride their bikes along quiet residential streets free of fast traffic and suspicious outsiders. But on one level the image that Seaside offers up as the perfect place to live is a false one, for in fact there is only a tiny residential population. As the name boards outside each brightly painted wooden house proudly tell you, the inhabitants, and their maids, and their pets, have actually driven there for the summer from towns across the United States.

But Seaside actually registers in the memories of people across the entire world, most of whom won't even recognise it as a 'real' place; for it was the location for the 1998 comedy film *The Truman Show* in which the central character lives in a make-believe world that is actually being watched live by million of television viewers. It is difficult not to read the film's satirical portrayal of a happy, trouble-free town that actually doesn't exist in the real world as a critique of Seaside itself.

The Retreat from the Future

Utopia, these days, is a Mickey Mouse business.[24]

But while Hollywood may have exploited Seaside as a backdrop to their fantasies, the most substantial experiment to date of New Urbanist ideals was actually created by the greatest of all the corporate image factories. In 1966 Walt Disney unveiled his plans for Epcot (Experimental Prototype Community of Tomorrow) an experimental, futuristic settlement to be built in Florida. Nothing ultimately came of EPCOT – there have even been claims that Disney was only using the scheme to secure local planning control over their land. But in 1977 the first was heard of a new model scheme proposed by Disney head Michael Eisner. But when Celebration came off the drawing boards some years later, it was not a space-age fantasy, but an essay in the architecture of a long-lost American past, with white dormered colonial houses ringed with white picket fences, surrounding substantial tracts of common land. Critics have not been shy of picking up on the alarming differences between these two highly different visions of the future:

> It depends on your notion of future and past whether you view the shift from Epcot to Celebration as a backward or forward movement. Luckily, the movie Back to the Future came out in 1985 and elided the two directions, pointing to an underlying anxiety at the heart of the Disney conception of the new town. It was necessary to go back in order to improve the future. Something had gone wrong with postwar living arrangements and turned a hopeful world sour.[25]

Celebration was planned by the distinguished American architect Robert Stern, the Dean of Yale

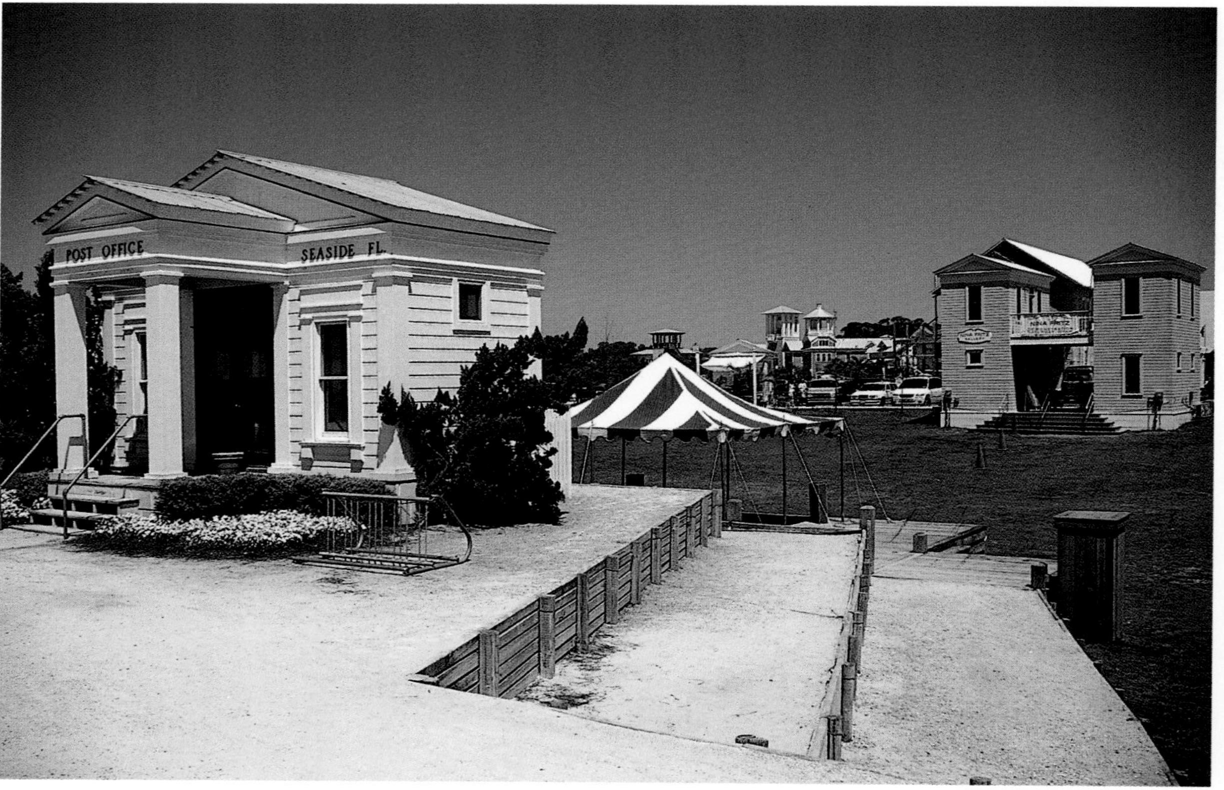

Celebration is the town that Mickey Mouse built. Masterplanned by Robert Stern, this Florida community displays the meticulous attention to detail you would expect from the Disney organisation, below, with the corporate identity even stamped on manhole covers. The village post office, opposite, was designed by Leon Krier.

Architecture School, and a strong advocate of anti-modernist planning principles. As one would expect of the Disney Corporation the execution of Celebration is stunning, creating so convincing a simulation of an old town that Disney decided at the last moment that they did not need to invent a mythical history for it. Their own publicity seems to elide the familiar, cosy world of film nostalgia with the real business of making a hoe and starting a new life. Indeed one wonders whether the readers of Disney's brochure were altogether aware of the difference:

> 'There was once a place where neighbours greeted neighbours in the quiet of summer twilight. Where children chased fireflies. And porch swings provided easy refuge from the care of the day. The movie house cartoons on Saturday. The grocery store delivered. And there was one teacher who always knew you had that 'special something'. Remember that place? Perhaps from your childhood. Or maybe just from stories ... There is a place that takes you back to that time of innocence. A place where the biggest decision is whether to play Kick the Can or King of the Hill. A place of caramel apples and cotton candy, secret forts, and hopscotch on the streets. That place is here again, in a new town called Celebration.'[26]

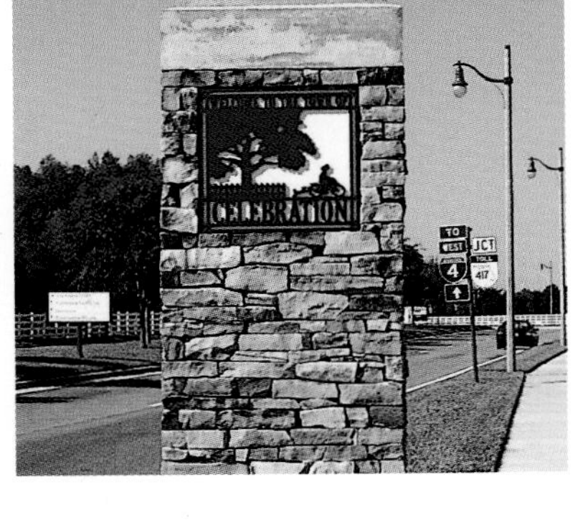

In years to come Celebration will no doubt mature as successfully as Hampstead Garden Suburb did, appearing to have been there forever. But visiting Celebration under construction, entering past the sign of the child on the bicycle, and pulling up alongside the manhole emblazoned with the corporate logo, one is made only too aware of its artificiality. There is something wholly unreal and impermanent about the sight of 'traditional' new homes emerging from under the wrappers, with Latino workers labouring to finish the dream houses of the new white inhabitants, whose names are proudly recorded on a sign at the front of the lot. It is as if this place really had been made in the dream factory, and transported on site.

But already the children playing happily in the downtown area, and the first residents sitting comfortably on the porches of their 'Churchill Colonial Revival' home, are testament to the enduring power of the old-fashioned village idyll.

What is unique about Celebration is the level of interest it has generated, not just amongst prospective supporters or buyers, but also amongst design professionals and academics, instinctively wary of the claims of such schemes. Indeed, two books have appeared recently on the town, both by people who lived there while writing.[27]

This at least has meant that some light has been exposed on the short-term success or otherwise of Disney's New Town. Not altogether surprisingly, the picture that emerges is of things not wholly running to plan, partly because Disney had not prepared for people behaving as citizens in their new community, rather than as the grateful recipients of corporate philanthropy. Disney, it is said, will not repeat the attempt to build Utopia ... at least outside of the film studio.

Neighborhoods or Nothing!

Cities have been causing us major problems throughout the last two centuries. When in Victorian Britain the appalling urban consequences of industrialisation became intolerable, one response was to look back nostalgically to a supposed golden age of community life that predated such horrors of the modern world as protestantism and capitalism. When in the next century Henry Ford contemplated the woes of fellow Americans who had not profited from his country's industrial might, he advocated a reunion between modern manufacture and the agrarian society which had founded and built the new republic. When fifty years later American architects and planners contemplated the awful, sprawling outgrowths of the American Dream, they established building codes to replicate the small-town communities that had been the mainstay of American life before 1940. So the belief that life could only be better in the future if it looked to a better

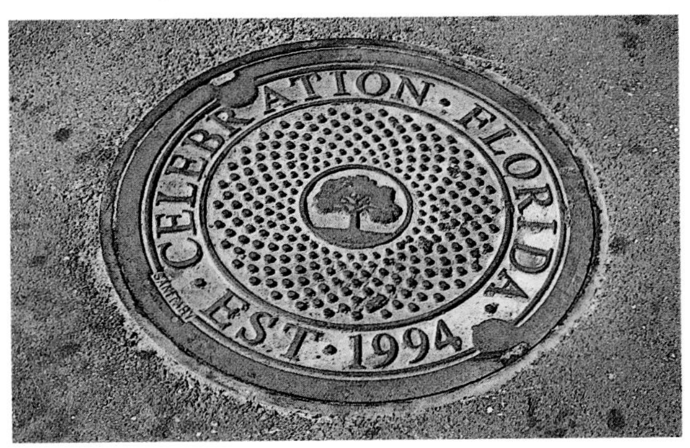

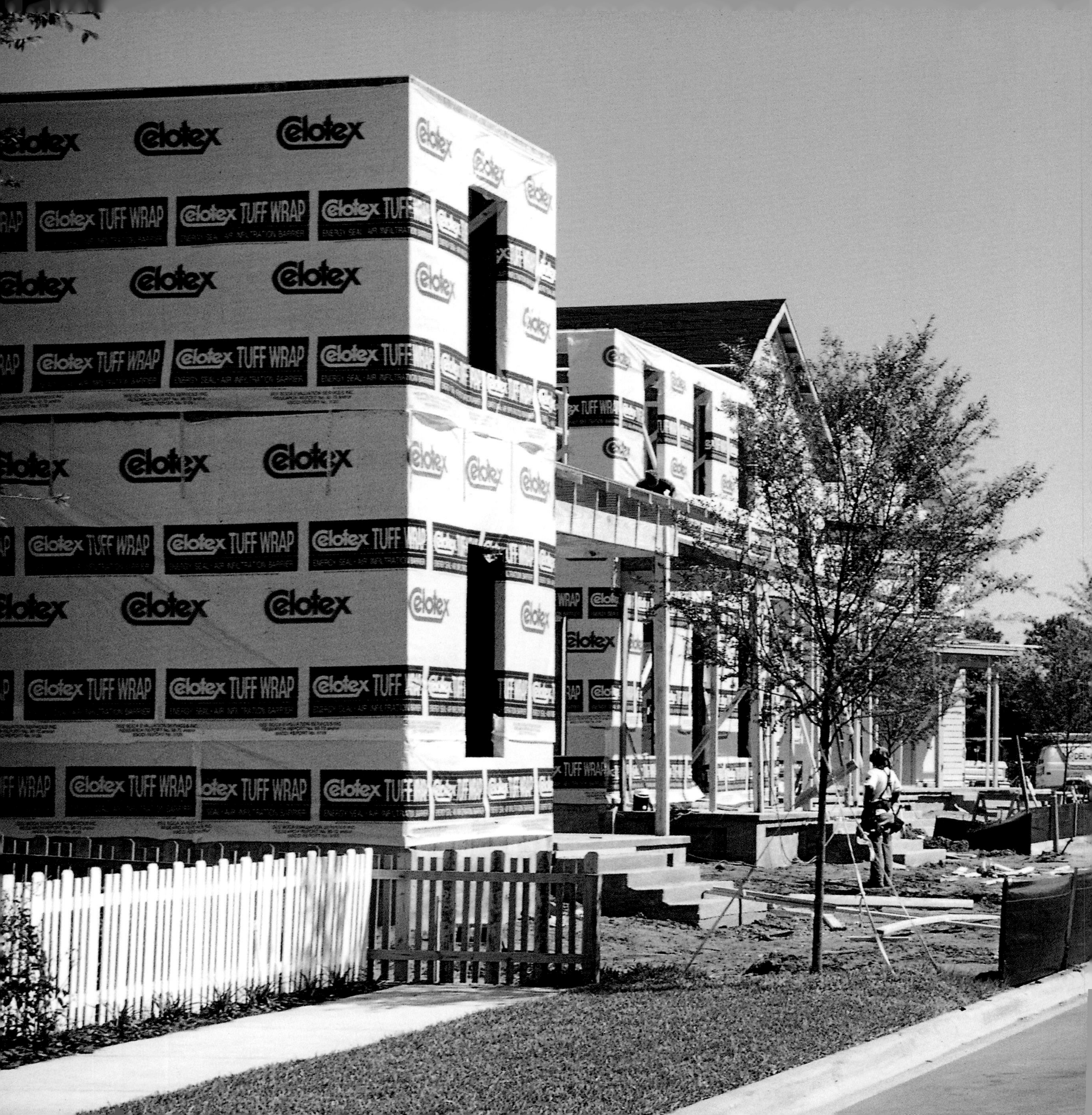
Celotex
Celotex TUFF WRAP
ENERGY SEAL · AIR INFILTRATION BARRIER

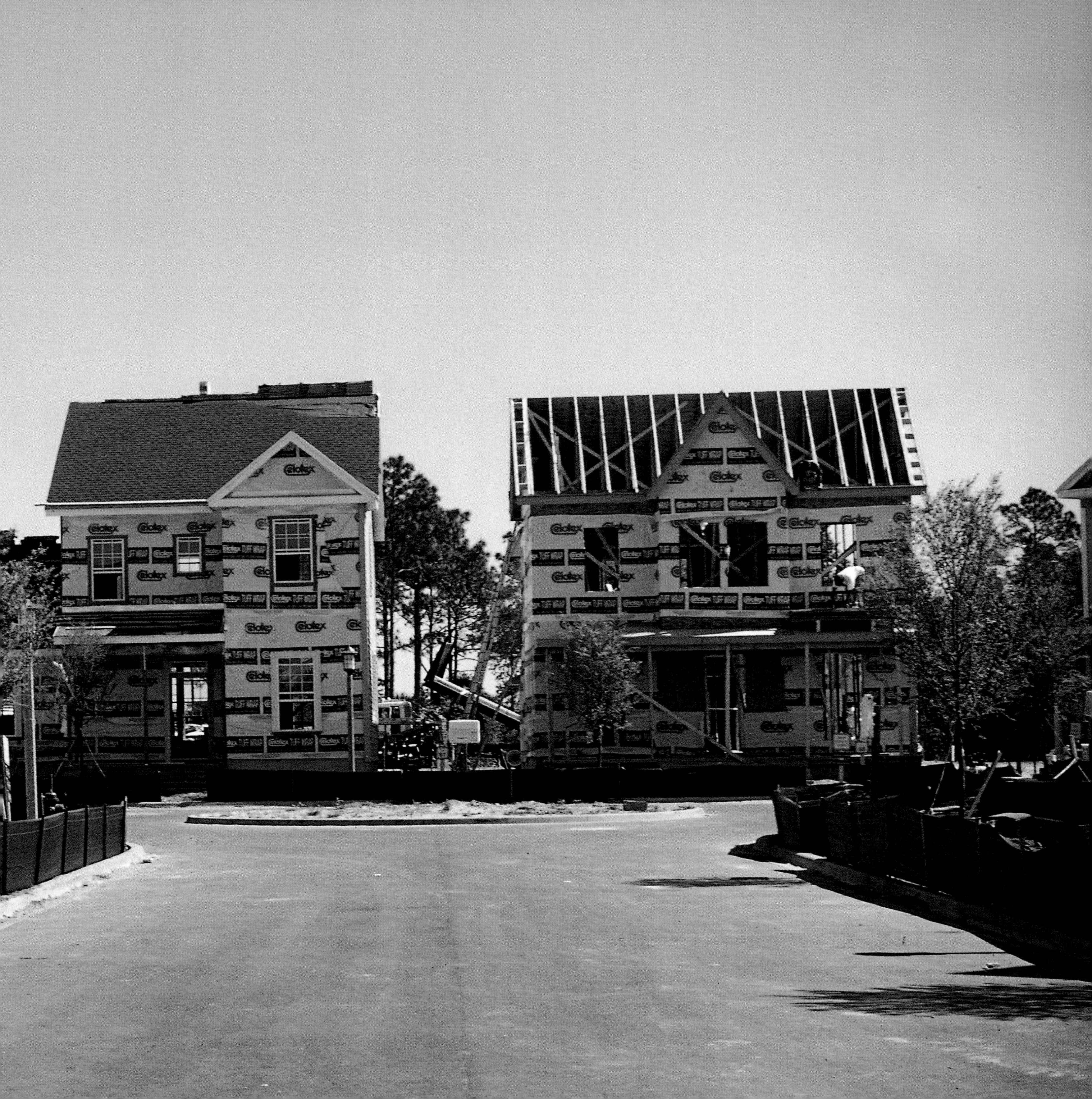
Celotex
TUFF WRAP

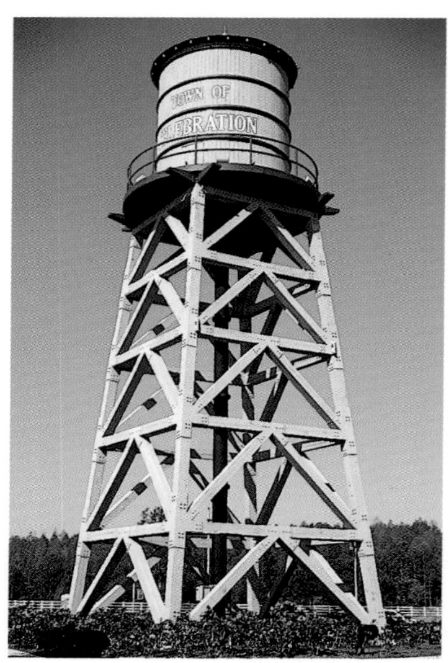

life in the past, has continued to capture the imaginations of utopian reformers – it is just when and where life in the past was supposed to have been better that varies. Even such unloved creations as the English New Towns or American Levittowns now have their enthusiasts.

Quite clearly neither none of the utopian schemes detailed here have changed the rest of the world as they had hoped, however influential they may have been. Nor have the communities that were actually built themselves ever lived up to what were unrealistic expectations about how they would function as places to live in. It is of course a tried and tested fact about Utopia, that the dream is always ruined by attempts to actually build it. But on the other hand, it would be hard to see how any of these visions of ideal village life have actually harmed their inhabitants, which is what the alternative, Corbusian model of the future is universally accused of.

What has changed throughout the period covered by this essay has been the scaling down of expectations that has accompanied each era of reformist ideas. William Morris may or may not have been serious about the replacement of London with mediaeval villages, but Howard certainly believed that his movement would bring about the transformation of the whole of urban society. But the Garden City movement was reduced to a set of technical planning formulas by the bureaucratic machinery of the welfare state. Today's New Urbanists have not tried to do much more than accommodate the dreams of affluent 'white flight' Middle America. Their published refrain concerns itself with the shape of things to come, rather than expressing any abstract social aspirations:

> No more housing subdivisions!
> No more shopping centres!
> No more office parks!
> No more highways!
> Neighborhoods or nothing![28]

But what is impressive about this whole story is the recurrent belief that if people are allowed to live in a way that permits the growth of proper social relations, then they will be capable of overcoming the relentless atomisation of human-centred society. And really, it would be hard for most of us to disagree with the proposition that life has more to offer than the soulless, anonymous environments of our contemporary cities. While only a minority of people could actually contemplate life in a garden city, let alone in a Disney town, it is likely that the unfulfilled desire to participate in a full version of community life is pretty universal. We simply need to decide where in the past we would like to live in the future.

Celebration glorifies the small-town values of America's past, even if that means putting up fake old-fashioned water towers, above, to maintain the illusion. The picture-perfect houses look out over an expanse of common land that evokes the idyll of the perfect village green, and children play happily in the fountains of the downtown commercial district.

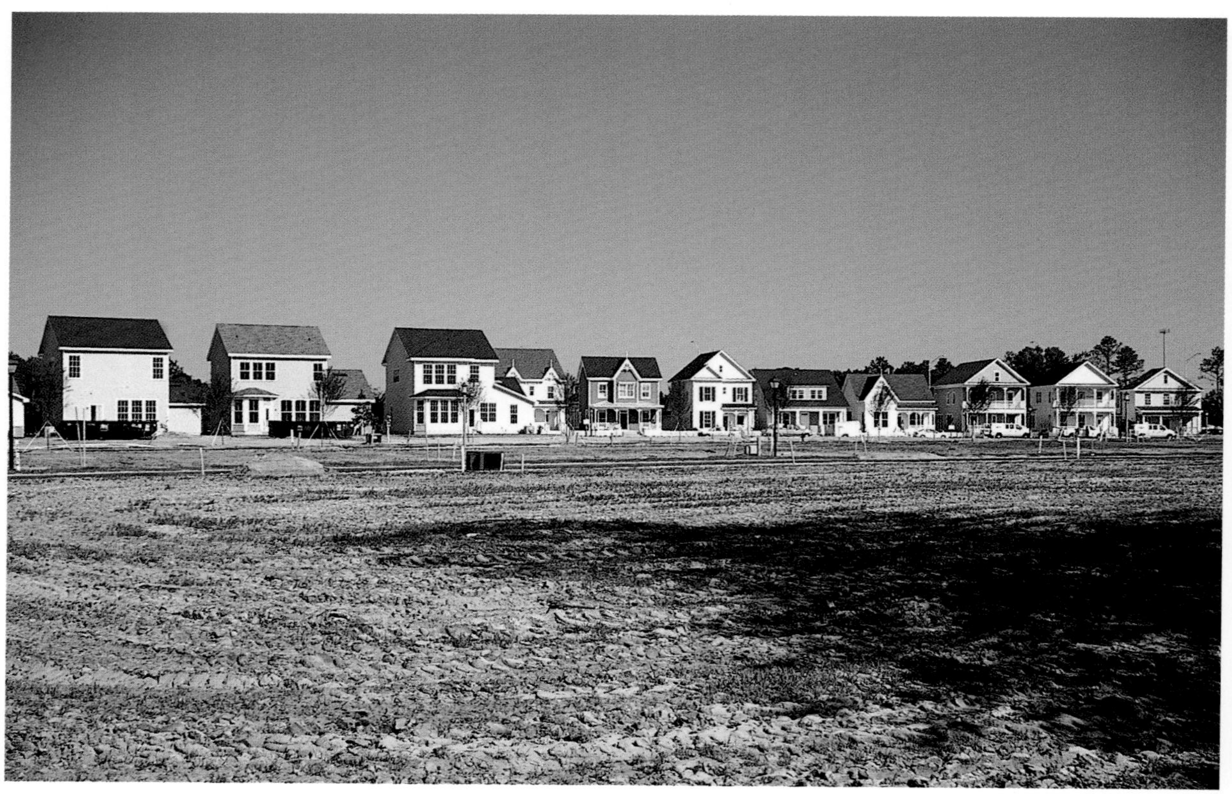

1. Letter from Lutyens to Herbert Baker, 1909. Quoted in *Lutyens: the work of the English Architect Sir Edwin Lutyens (1869-1944)* (London: Arts Council, 1981) p126
2. Andres Duany, Elizabeth Plater-Zyberk, and Jeff Speck *Suburban Nation: The Rise of Sprawl and the Decline of the American Dream* (New York: North Point Press, 2000)
3. J M Richards *The Castles on the Ground: The Anatomy of Suburbia* (London: The Architectural Press 1946; reprinted London: John Murray, 1973) p28
4. William Morris *News from Nowhere* (1890) reprinted in Asa Briggs ed *William Morris: Selected Writings and Designs* (Harmondsworth: Penguin, 1962) p 239
5. E Akroyd *On Improved Dwellings for the Working Classes* (1861) p8. Quoted in John Burnett *A Social History of Housing 1815-1970* (London: Methuen, 1980) p177
6. Mark Swenarton *Homes fit for Heroes: The Politics and Architecture of Early State Housing in Britain* (London: Heineman Educational Books, 1981) p6. The quotation comes from W Creese , *The Search for Environment. The Garden City: Before and After* (1966)
7. Quoted in A Stuart Gray *Edwardian Architecture: A Biographical Dictionary* (Ware: Wordsworth, 1988) p 24
8. Koos Bosma and Helma Hellinger "British Urban Planning – London: Continuity of the Garden City Model" in Bosma and Hellinger eds *Mastering the City II: North-European City Planning 1900-2000* (Rotterdam: Netherlands Architecture Institute, 1997) p68
9. Andrew Saint "Introduction: The Quality of the London Suburb" in *London Suburbs* (London: Merrell Holberton, 1999), p19
10. A Stuart Gray *Edwardian Architecture* p26
11. *The Garden City* vol III no 28 (May-June 1908) pp80-81, quoted in Mark Swenarton *Homes fit for Heroes* p7
12. Brigid Grafton Green *Hampstead Garden Suburb 1907-1977: A History* (Hampstead Garden Suburb Residents Association, 1977) p12
13. Andrew Saint *London Suburbs* p20
14. Osbert Lancaster *Here, of All Places: the Pocket Lamp of Architecture* (London: John Murray, 1959) p142
15. For a full discussion of this subject see Mark Swenarton "Rationality and Rationalism: the theory and practice of site planning in modern architecture 1905-1930" *Architectural Association Files* 4 July 1983 pp49-59
16. Mark Gelernter *A History of American Architecture: Buildings in their Cultural and Technological Context* (Manchester: Manchester University Press, 1999) p244
17. Elain Harwood "The Road to Subtopia: 1940 to the Present" in *London Suburbs* p138
18. Thomas Sharp "The English Village" in *Design in Town and Village* (London: HMSO, 1953) p1
19. Bosma and Hellinga *Mastering the City II* p71
20. Mark Gelernter *A History of American Architecture* p270
21. Quoted in *An American Invention: The Story of Henry Ford Museum & Greenfield Village* (Dearborn: Henry Ford Museum & Greenfield Village, 1999) pvii
22. Henry Ford, *The Dearborn Independent* reproduced in Jeanine M Head & William S Pretzer *Henry Ford: A Pictorial Biography* (Dearborn: Henry Ford Museum & Greenfield Village, 1998) P71
23. Duany + Plater-Zyberk "Traditional Neighbourhood Development Ordinance" (1989) reprinted in Charles Jencks and Karl Kropf eds *Theories and Manifestos of Contemporary Architecture* (London: Academy Editions, 1997) p191
24. Jenny Diski, "Celebrating Conformity: Disney's Mickey Mouse Utopia" *London Review of Books* August 15 2000 reprinted at www.guardianunlimited.co.uk
25. Jenny Diski, *London Review of Books* August 15 2000
26. Disney Corporation brochure quoted in Jenny Diski, *London Review of Books* August 15 2000
27. Andrew Ross *The Celebration Chronicles: Life, Liberty and the Pursuit of Property Value in Disney's New Town* (New York: Verso, 2000) – Douglas Frantz and Catherine Collins *Celebration, USA: Living in Disney's Brave New Town* (New York: Holt, 1999)
28. Andres Duany, Elizabeth Plater-Zyberk, and Jeff Speck, *Suburban Nation: The Rise of Sprawl and the Decline of the American Dream* p243

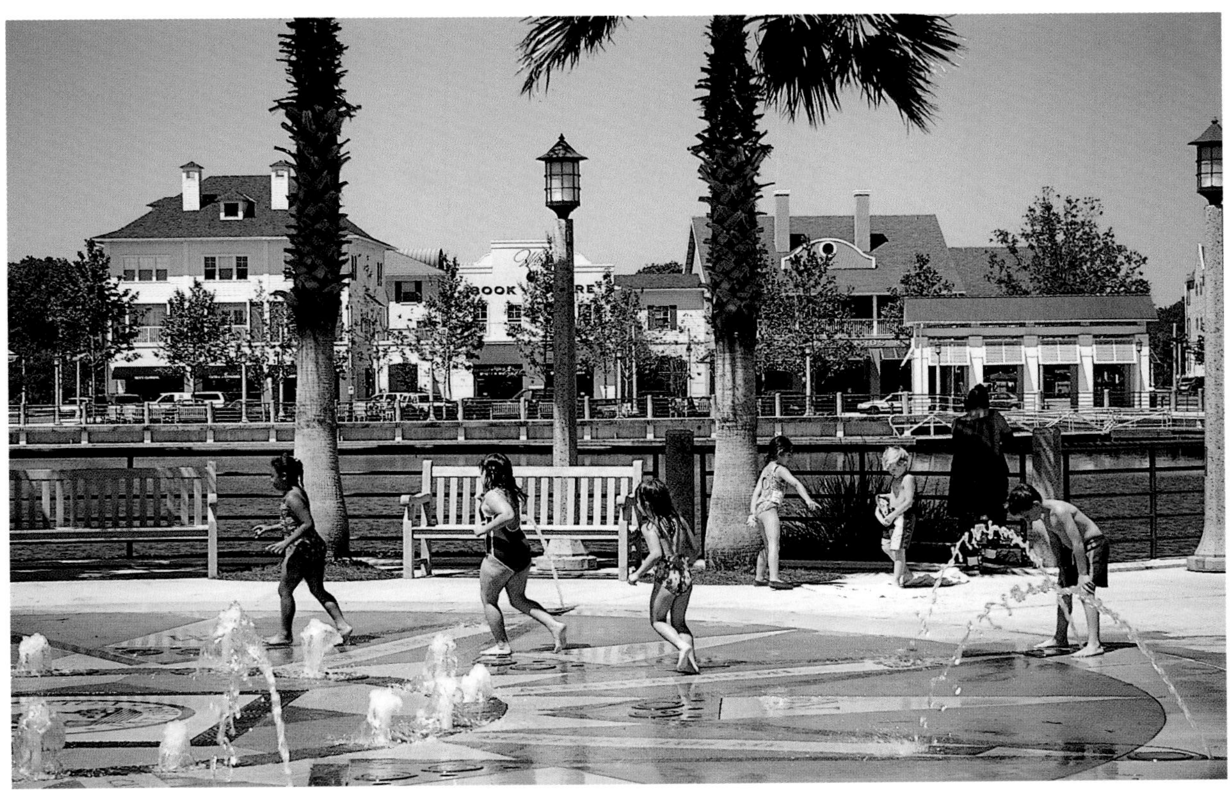

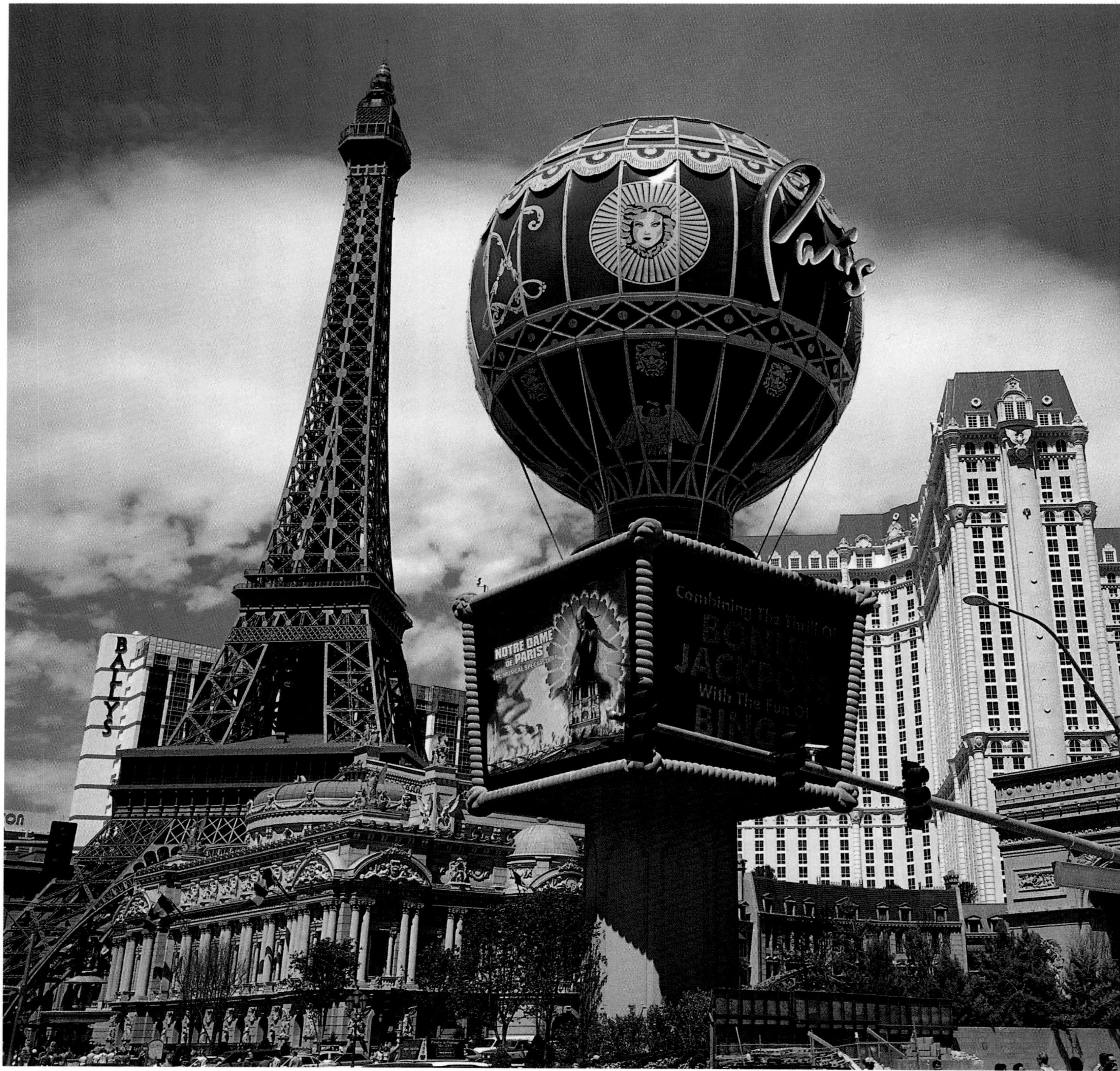
BALLY'S
Paris
NOTRE DAME DE PARIS
Combining The Thrill of
With The Fun Of

Las Vegas

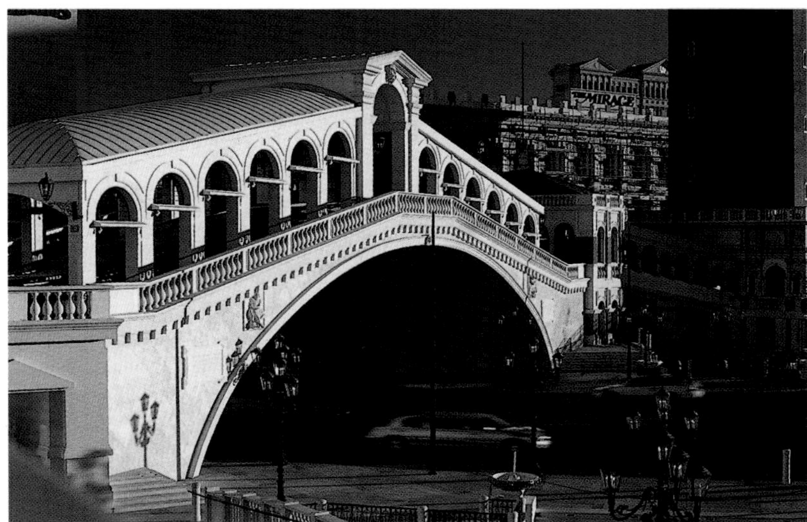

Las Vegas is trying very hard to develop good taste. Naturally enough, it is taste that has been reconstructed in a collage of images from elsewhere. The city has reinvented itself before, morphing into the ultimate family holiday destination with a string of hotels based on child-friendly themes like castles, pirates and the circus, complete with spectacular pyrotechnic displays that turned parts of the Strip into outdoor theatre. Now, just a few hundred metres from the erupting volcanoes of the Mirage, Vegas is revelling in the Renaissance beauty of Venice.

The American entrepreneur behind the Venetian hotel was keen to recreate his favourite city as perfectly as possible in the Nevada desert. But he was unable to resist the odd improvement: there is an escalator over the Rialto bridge, a video screen on top of the campanile and the gondolas on the Grand Canal are motorised. The Grand Canal itself is not only indoors, under a delicately tinted artificial sky, but up on the first floor, over the casino.

Further along, the Paris hotel provokes a similar sense of dislocation: an overgrown version of a typical Haussman-era apartment block containing thousands of identical hotel rooms looms behind a scaled-down Eiffel tower, which in turn straddles a stuccoed pastiche of an elegant French mansion block. The best view of Paris is enjoyed from one of the terraces of the Bellagio across the road, which aspires to the sophistication of a luxury Italian lakeside resort. The place is filled with vast amounts of fresh flowers, has its own small but definitely real art collection and is, very unusually for Las Vegas, flooded with natural daylight. If it weren't for the water jets in the huge artificial lake, that spurt into action every half hour in a dynamically choreographed aquatic display set to the strains of Frank Sinatra's 'Luck be a Lady tonight', you could almost think you were in Europe.

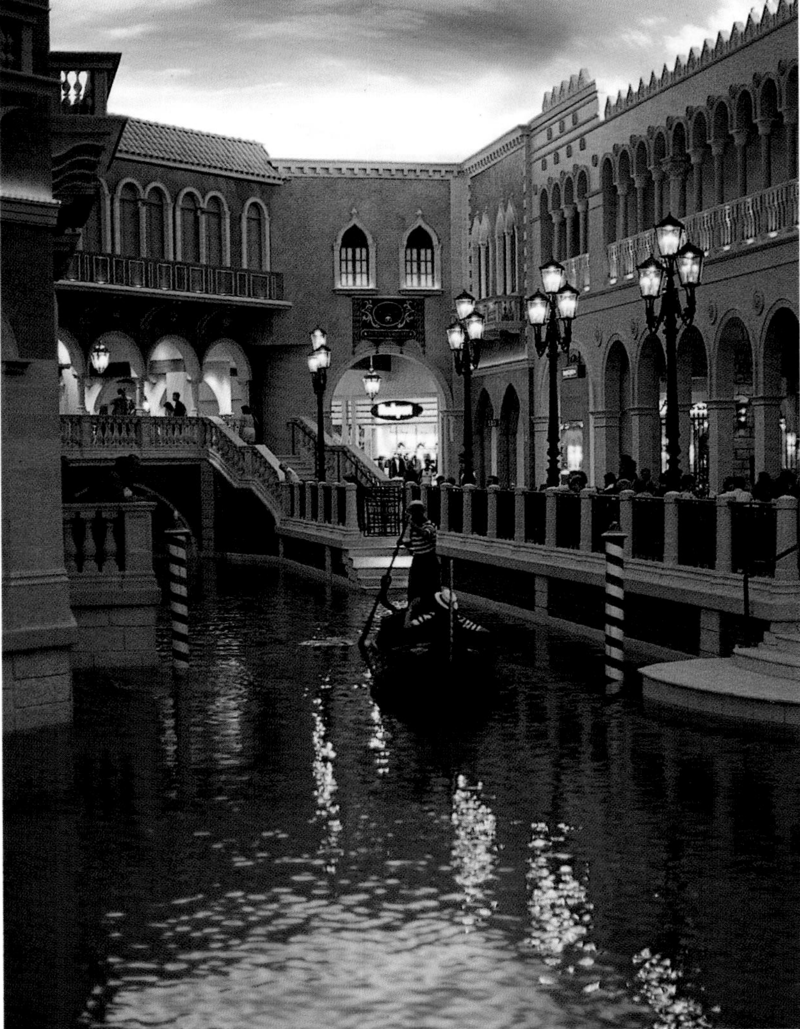

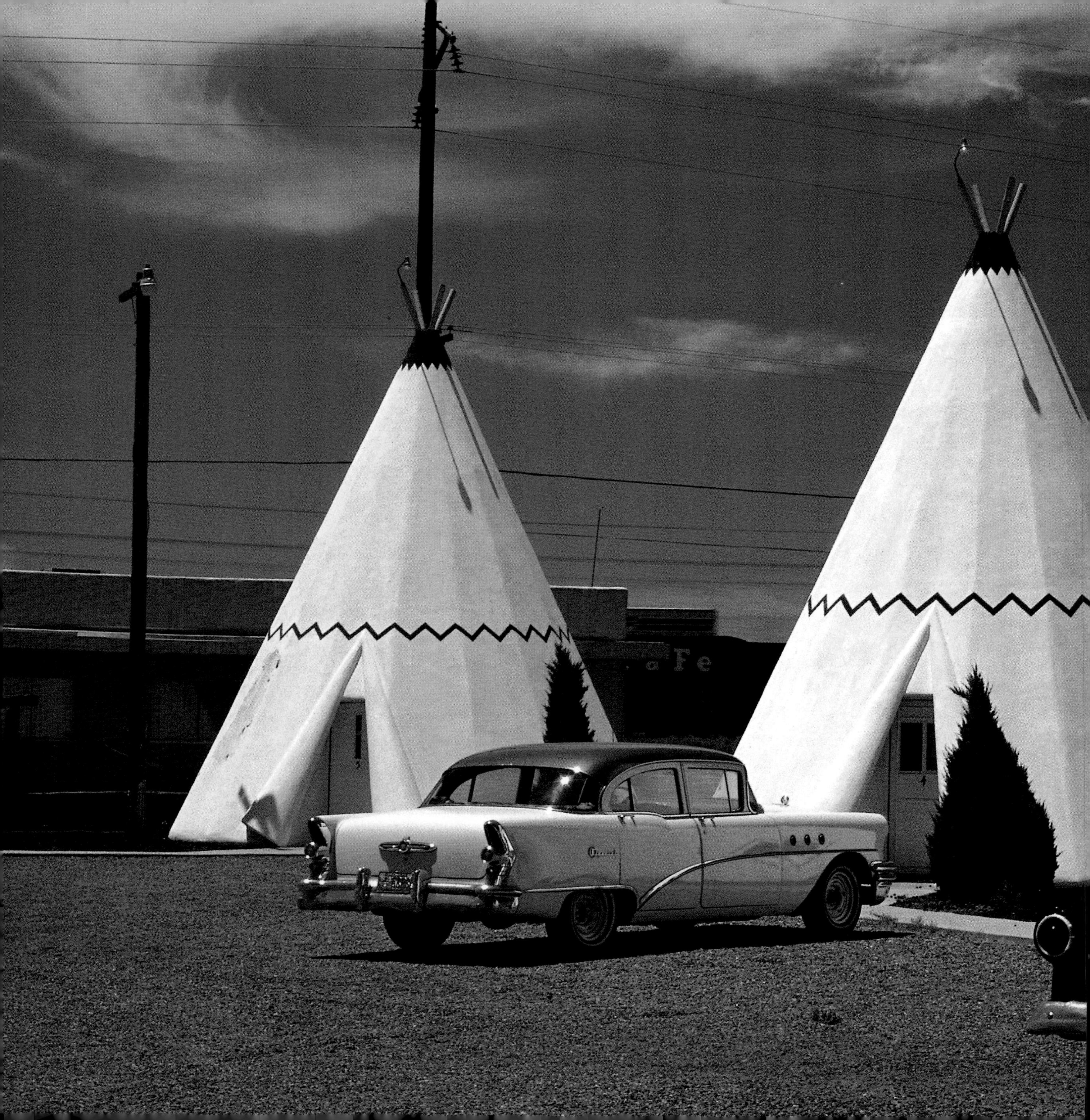

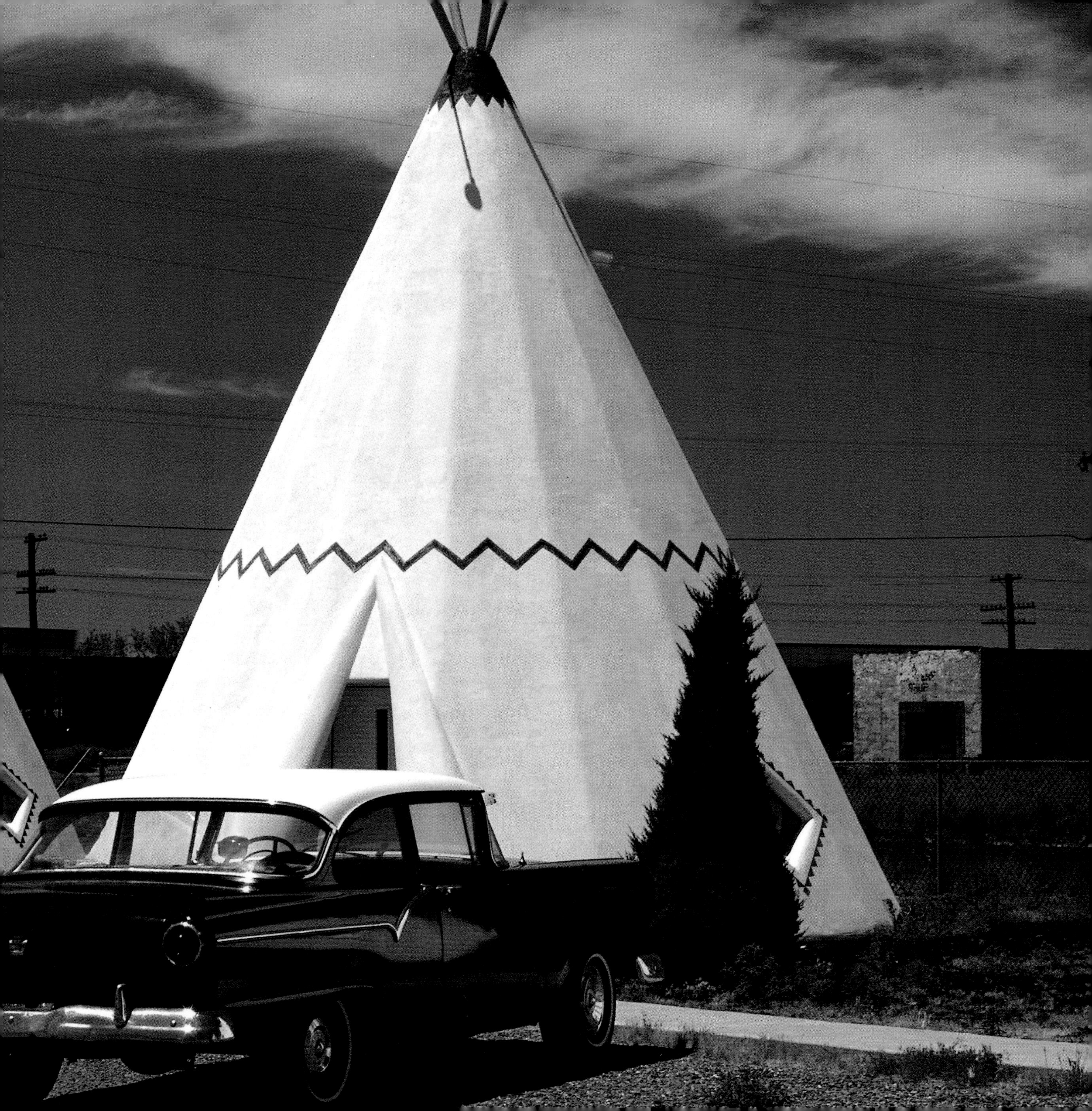

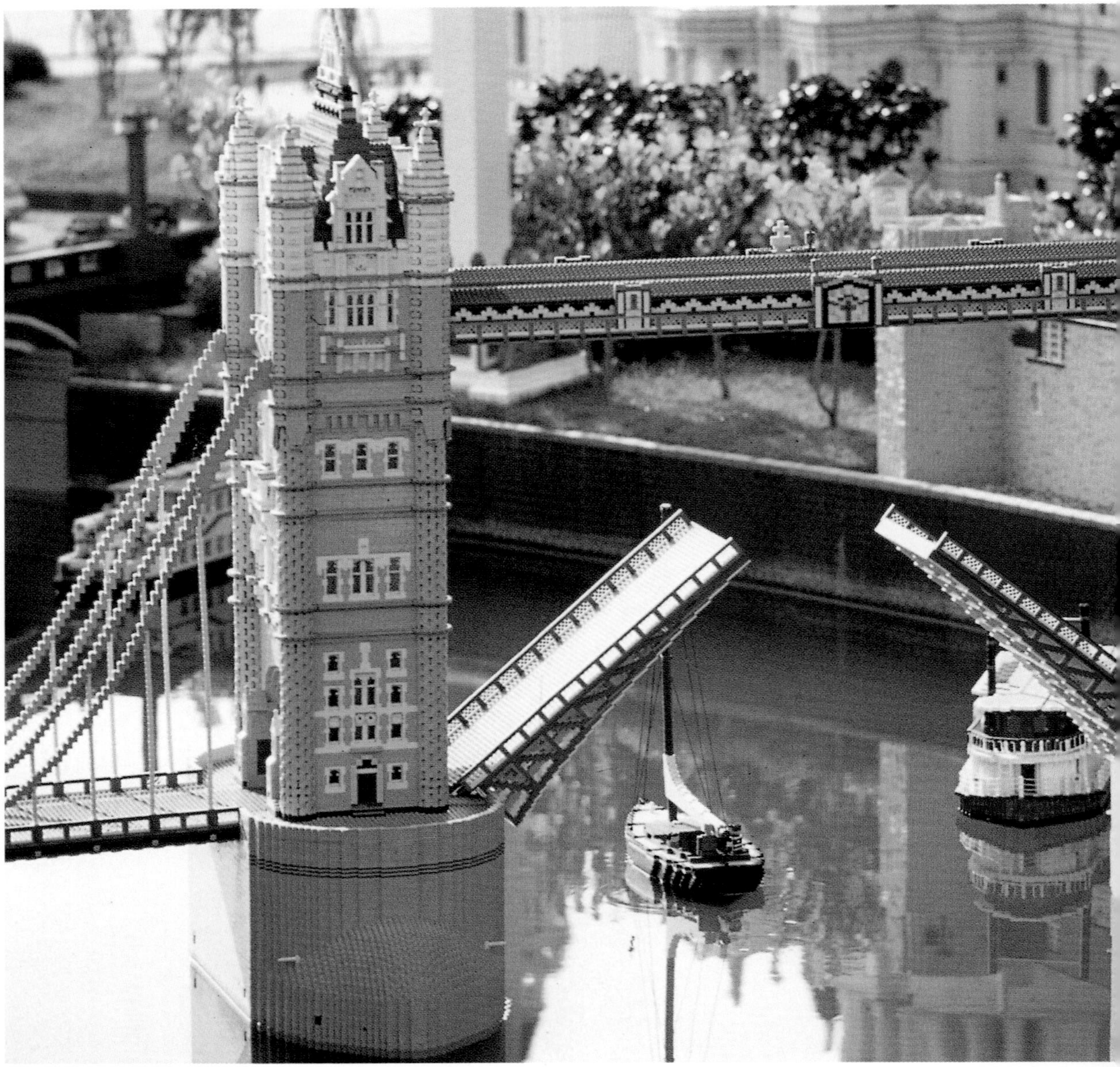

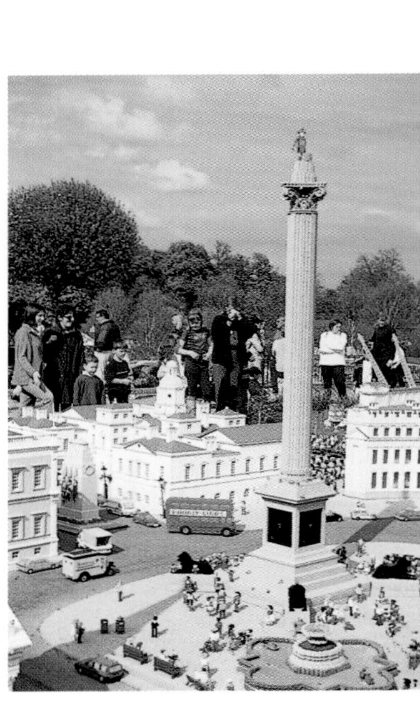

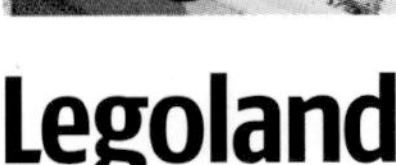

Legoland

In a section called Miniland, the Legoland theme park near Windsor brings together edited highlights from cities around Europe in a scaled-down, child-friendly format. Miniland's condensed version of London includes all the landmarks a tourist could ever wish to see, with the added bonus of being within easy walking distance of the miniaturised delights of Denmark, Holland and France as well. It's an approach reminiscent of the themed hotels of Las Vegas.

The makers of Lego are keen to stress the educational value of their product. Miniland is designed to encourage the property developer within: a wide variety of vernacular styles are achieved using the simplest of means, and are endlessly repeatable. Everything is smooth, clean and perfect, without worrying about texture, detailing or the effects of age.

But time doesn't stand still in Miniland: the new addition for 2000 was the Millennium Dome. But will the plastic brick version of Wembley Stadium, which was only added in 1999, be torn down to reflect the fate of the real Twin Towers? Norman Foster's new design for the venue would be a serious challenge for Legoland's team of modellers. The huge metal arch spanning the stadium could be difficult to recreate without resorting to specially-made elements – an act that would be anathema to the Lego purist.

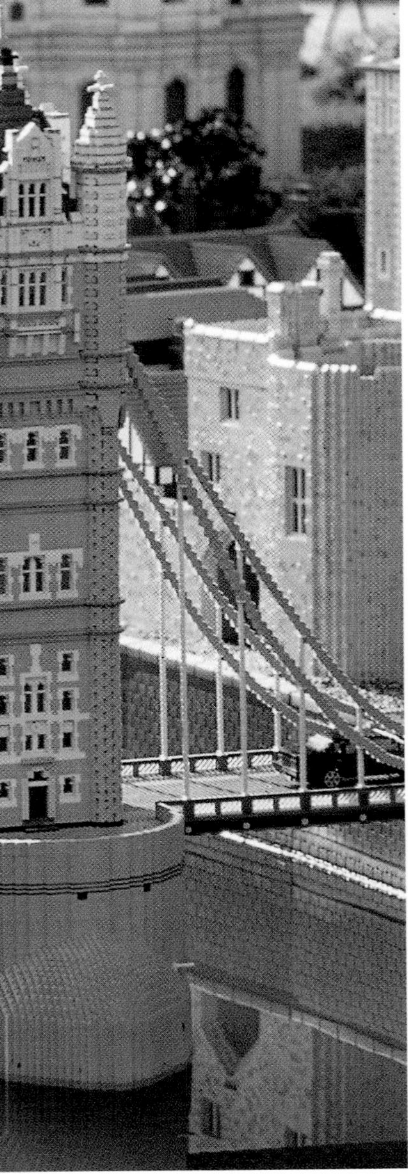

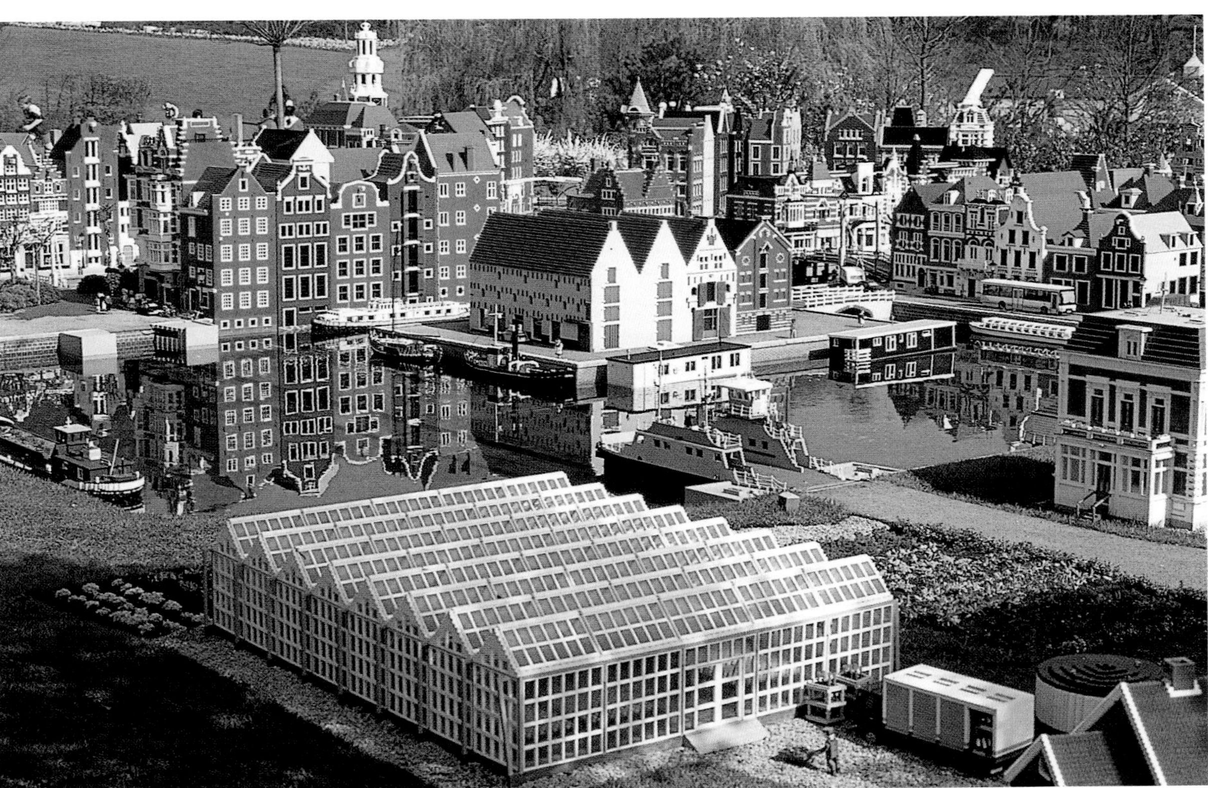

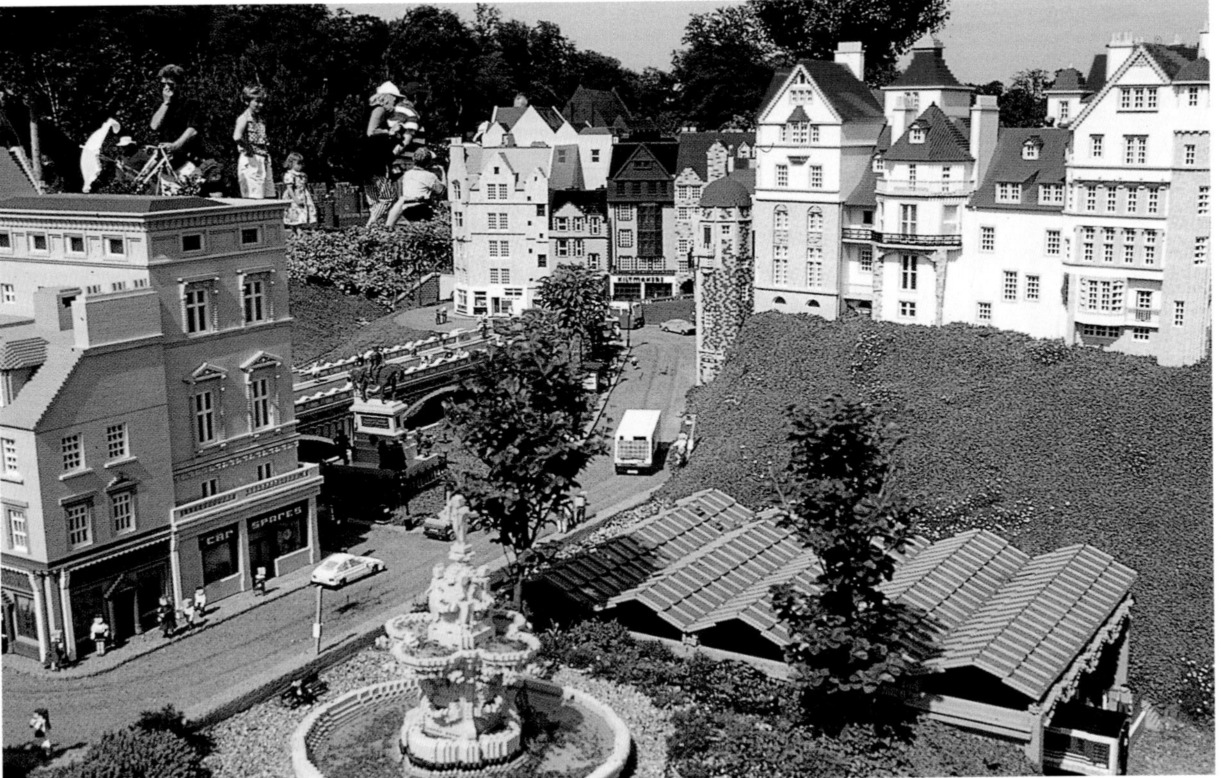
CAR SPARES

Utopia
Alex Stetter

If you are not satisfied with the country you live in and can't find one you would rather call home, why not go out and set up your own nation? A place that brings together all the best elements from different places around the world, but without any of the restrictions, a place where you make the rules and you will be surrounded by people who share your dream and your ideals. But where? The world's existing nations are unlikely to give up a piece of their landmass to you willingly (and taking some over by force is not really an option), and there are probably very good reasons why the earth's few uninhabited territories have yet to be colonised. So why not construct a country from scratch? Even a small island would suffice. And you might as well choose a pleasant location for this new nation, somewhere with a tropical climate and crystal clear waters ... It may sound like a fairy tale, but this is exactly what Lazarus Long is setting out to do: the first phase of construction of the island of New Utopia will start just as soon as the necessary finances are in place.

In true fairy tale style (with all the outmoded ideologies that this implies), New Utopia is set to be a Principality, with Long and his wife as the crowned Heads of State. In a rather more modern twist, this particular constitutional monarchy will be characterised by the freedom to make money and live in luxury for as long as possible, thanks to an absence of taxation (apart from a flat 15% import duty), minimum interference from politicians and access to a state-of-the-art anti-ageing medical centre. The philosophy behind the scheme owes a lot to the libertarian thinking of Ayn Rand: there are no plans for a welfare system, and everyone is encouraged to look after their own best interests. In other words, the Prince of New Utopia aims to model the country on the principles of an efficient, profitable business. Now in his late sixties, Long does not have much faith in the democratic process, but he is a firm believer in the power of entrepreneurial drive and imagination. Not only did he make his fortune in a variety of different business ventures, from shrimp farming to selling used generators, he also pioneered the use of human growth hormone to counteract the effects of ageing.

Long first came upon the perfect location for his capitalist paradise in the mid-1990s: a reef in international waters to the south-west of the Cayman Islands, with plateaux close enough to the surface to allow for concrete platforms supported by piles anchored in the rock to be constructed. His vision of utopia combines the watery setting and canals of Venice with the glamour of Monaco and the financial freedom of the Cayman Islands. Apart from being an irresistible proposition for anyone in search of eternal youth, New Utopia is designed to become a world centre for insurance, banking and internet businesses, while luxury hotels, casinos and a string of glitzy international events should appeal to tourists who wish to share their leisure time with the rich and the facelifted.

So far, New Utopia exists only in cyberspace, as a website run from Lazarus Long's base in suburban Tulsa, Oklahoma. But the Board of Governors appointed by the Prince to run the country is ready and waiting in the wings, and a network of Honorary Consuls around the world is busy interviewing potential citizens of Long's grand plan. Passports and citizenship papers are already being issued to the hundreds of pioneering individuals who have invested money in the project, while many others have asked to be kept informed of progress, and are just waiting for the first concrete foundations to be poured before they commit. The New Utopia Development Trust needs to raise over $200 million to start construction and put New Utopia on the map. And then all the people who want to pursue eternal youth through experimental medical procedures in a tax-free environment will finally have a place to call home.

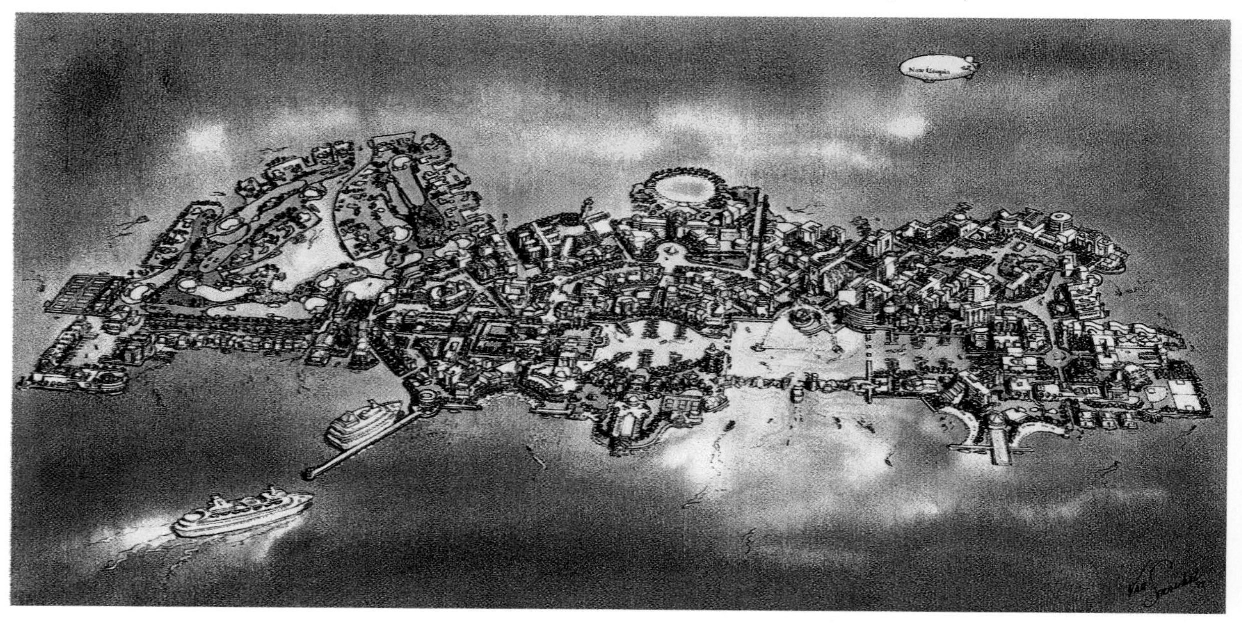

So far, the nation of New Utopia exists only in the form of drawings, right, but this artificial island in the Caribbean could easily become a reality – from a technical standpoint, at least. As with so many grand schemes, it's a matter of getting the funding in place before this particular dream can come true. And money is in many ways at the heart of the project: a key feature of life on the island will be freedom from taxes.

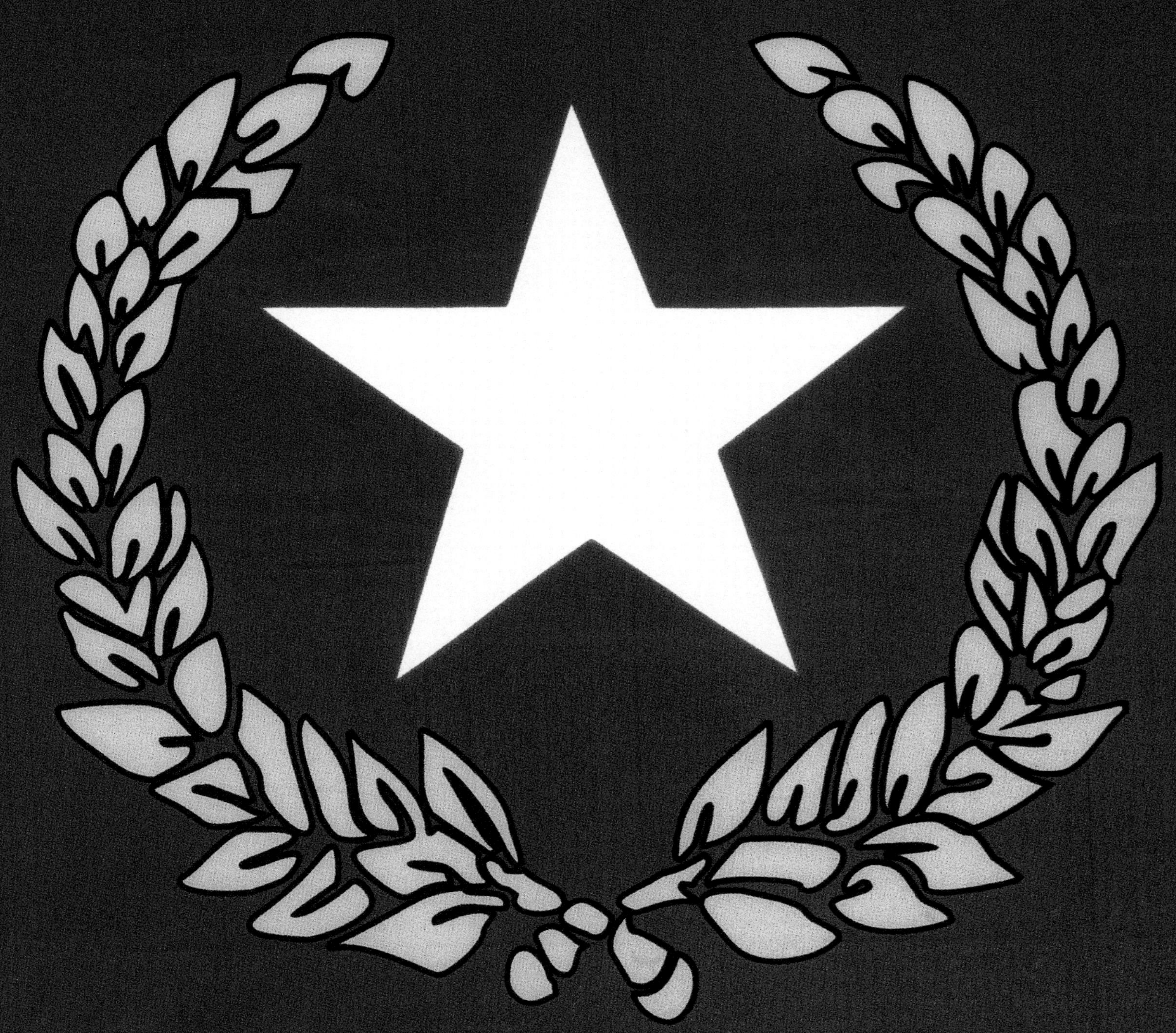

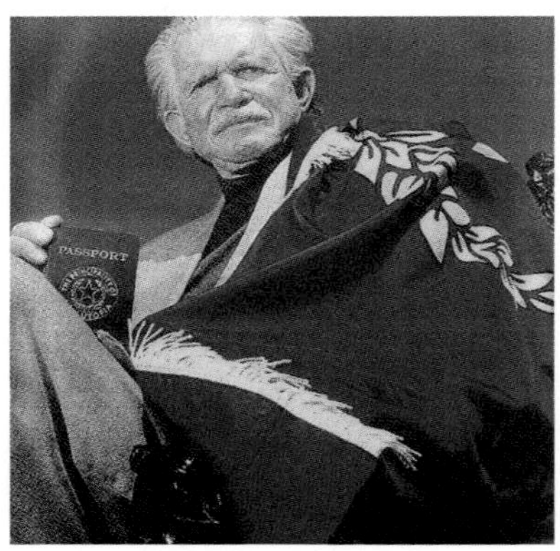

At the moment, Lazarus Long, above, is a Prince without a Principality. But even though his country has yet to be constructed, all the trappings of nationhood are already in place, including a flag and some fully-fledged citizens, with passports and papers to prove it. The designs for the island, right, combine the canals of Venice with the glamour of a top-class resort on the French Riviera. There will also be casinos, to bring in revenue and tourists.

A statement from Lazarus, Prince of New Utopia:

'Imagine a city state in the middle of the Caribbean, made possible by twentieth-century technology and surrounded by, and interspersed with, canals of clear, blue water, a clean and beautiful place to live and raise families. Visualise, if you will, an oasis in the middle of the ocean: office buildings, hotels, theaters and shopping centers, sitting slightly above the sea in neat rows surrounded by greenery and flowers. This is a new country, which will be built in a moderately tropical sea, a perfect climate, a paradise: Utopia!

There have been a number of delays, as any project of this magnitude can expect, but now we are getting ready to begin with the construction which is expected to start in July/August 2000. This will be the staging area where the building materials can be received for the construction of the first phase of the city proper. This area will also eventually be the home of the airport docks and port authority. There will also be an airport hotel in this area which will provide accommodations for those who want to visit and make plans before moving to New Utopia.

We already have over 1,200,000 square feet of office/retail space committed, and over 1,300,000 square feet of apartments/condos, another 1,000,000 square feet for hydroponics farms, plus the airline, medical center, the medical teaching university, the first hotel/casino and much more.

A contribution ($1,500 minimum) to our new country is required in order to be invited to become a citizen. Passports and documents for family members are $24 each. Charter Citizens will have preferential treatment for housing and space for businesses. It is not necessary that people be disenchanted with their government to move to New Utopia, but only that they want a fresh start. Like any vacation spot on the ocean, the prices will range from moderate to expensive, but New Utopia is not being built just for the wealthy – like any other resort area there will have to be many people to man the shops, restaurants and service companies. They in turn should live better and accumulate more in New Utopia than they could anywhere else. The industrious will prosper; those who are slothful will exist like they do everywhere.

Some years ago, we determined that the gradual loss of freedoms and the constant increased intrusiveness of government into every area of our lives is the direct responsibility and fault of politicians. Every politician runs for office on a platform of change, designed with only the possibility of his being elected in mind. Otherwise you would leave the incumbent in the office. If he is elected by 60% of the voters, this means that 40% are disenfranchised because the change is made without their endorsement. None of the politicians are able to live up to all of their promises of change, but all do manage to implement some change. Multiply all the small changes election after election, at city, county, state and federal level, and you have the reason for the increasing government intrusiveness.

Therefore we want a minimum of politicians in New Utopia. So what kind of government should we have? We decided on a constitutional monarchy, a constitution to protect the citizens against abuse and a monarchy to guarantee stability. In New Utopia the only vote the citizens have is on any change which impacts their freedoms, which must pass by at least 2/3. Other than that the government will operate like a well run company.

We could sit there with a stiff upper lip kind of government, like all the other little countries in the Caribbean and we would die aborning. We must toot our horn, dance in the streets, make some noise to attract tourists and immigrants which will be the only factor which will impact the growth of New Utopia.

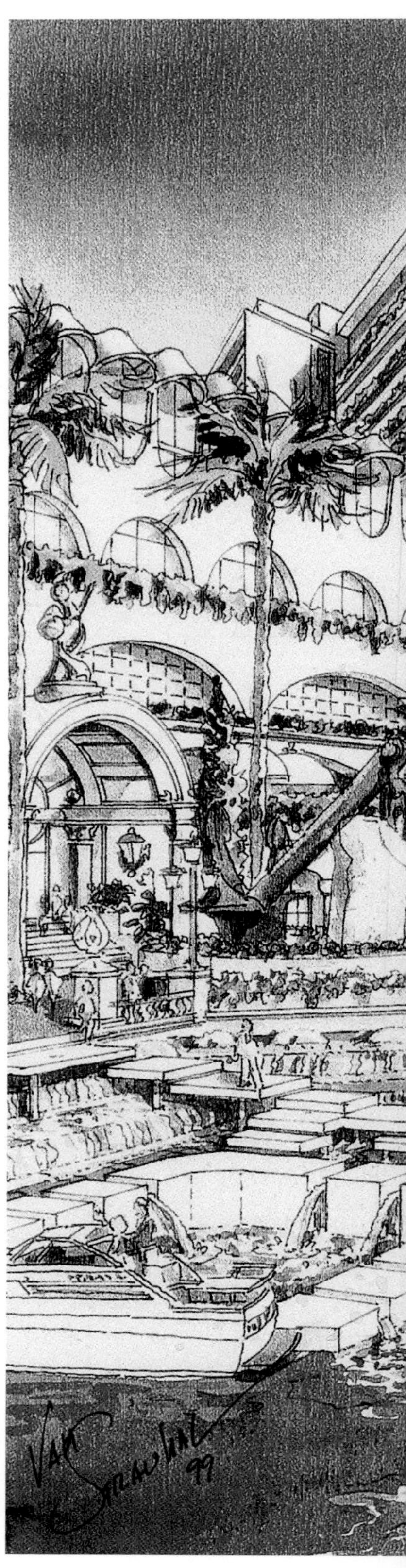

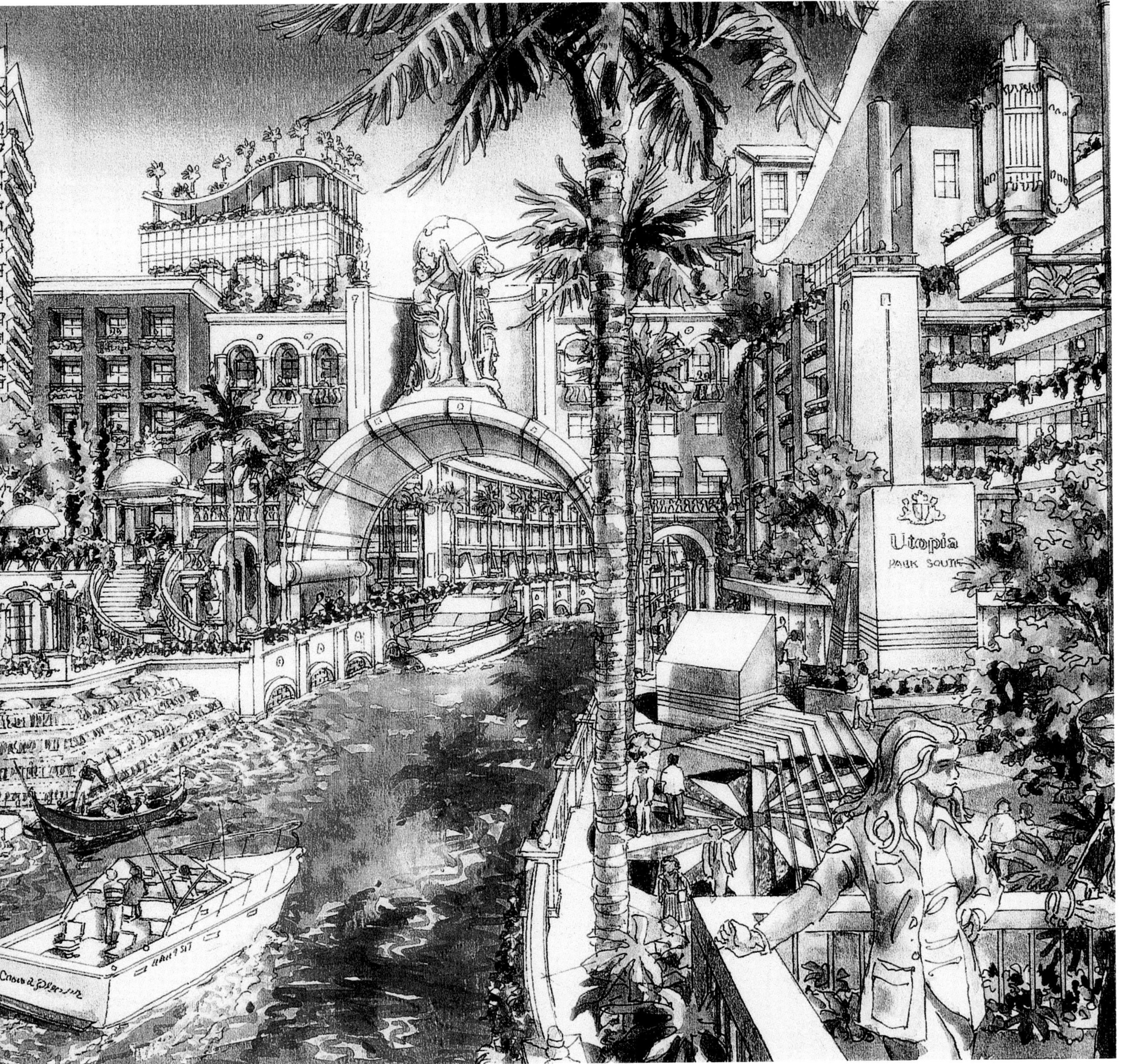
Utopia
PARK SOUTH

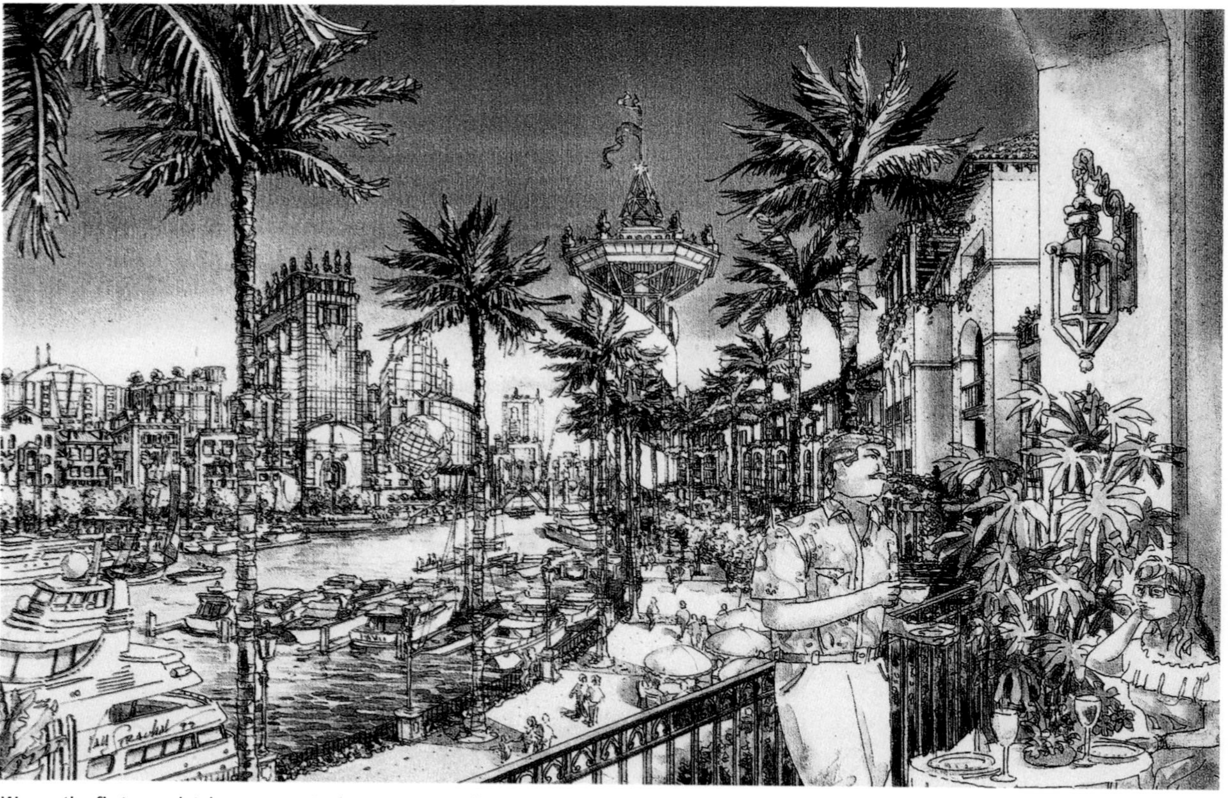

We are the first completely new country in hundreds of years, we intend to capitalize on this. We are also the first new monarchy in a even longer time, and half of the world is enamoured with royalty.

Nothing gets as much press coverage as a royal wedding or any other function, in fact the changing of the guard at Buckingham Palace in London is directly responsible for hundreds of millions of dollars spent by tourists who visit London with this as one of the criteria for their visit. We will capitalize on this as well, with pomp and pageantry to attract the tourists. A genteel circus for the masses, if you will, on the one hand, and a stable profitable government on the other. We will be able to attract much more than what would be considered our fair share of tourists, bringing their money to the merchants who will make the growth of New Utopia a certainty.

In keeping with this theme we will have 4 annual galas, a grand prix with boats instead of cars, a birthday celebration such as Pirate week in the Cayman Islands which draws thousands of visitors every year, a Mardi Gras celebration which will become a real competitor for the one in New Orleans, and a winter festival featuring the arts and culture. New Utopia, with its wonderful tropic climate, will attract those visitors who want to escape the snow. There will also be world class golf courses and tennis courts, and tournaments that compete with the best the rest of the world has to offer. Our "Venice of the Caribbean" with its waterways instead of roads and gondolas and water taxis instead of cars will be an attraction like no other in our part of the world.

With the only tax being a 15% import duty, the same for everything, there should be much more disposable income whatever your circumstance. If you have a business this means that much faster growth is possible. New Utopia will become a world center for Internet business of every kind because every city, state and country in the world is trying to find a way to tax them, and they will. By our constitution no tax can ever exist but the 15% import duty. No income tax, no sales tax, no fuel tax, no property tax, no death tax, no wealth tax. NO TAXES.

Even young people just beginning their lives and careers need to take this into consideration. The other thing is the most beautiful place in the world, the most perfect weather, the fastest growth area that has ever existed. This makes for an energy and excitement which should appeal to the youth who will become the movers and shakers of the world of tomorrow. The fact that it will also attract the best in entertainment and the arts of every kind will make it a magnet for their peers from every other country.

A submerged mountain plateau makes up the territory of New Utopia. It is interesting to note that the area where we will start construction is almost all a flat rock surface with a dusting of sand. The plateau covers almost 400 square miles – the depth ranges from 15 to 60 feet – and is very solid rock. This is part of an underwater mountain range which runs from the southern part of Cuba through where the Cayman Islands are (they are on peaks of the same range) – we are on the other end of it.

Unlike the Pacific and the New England coast, the water where we are is very calm,

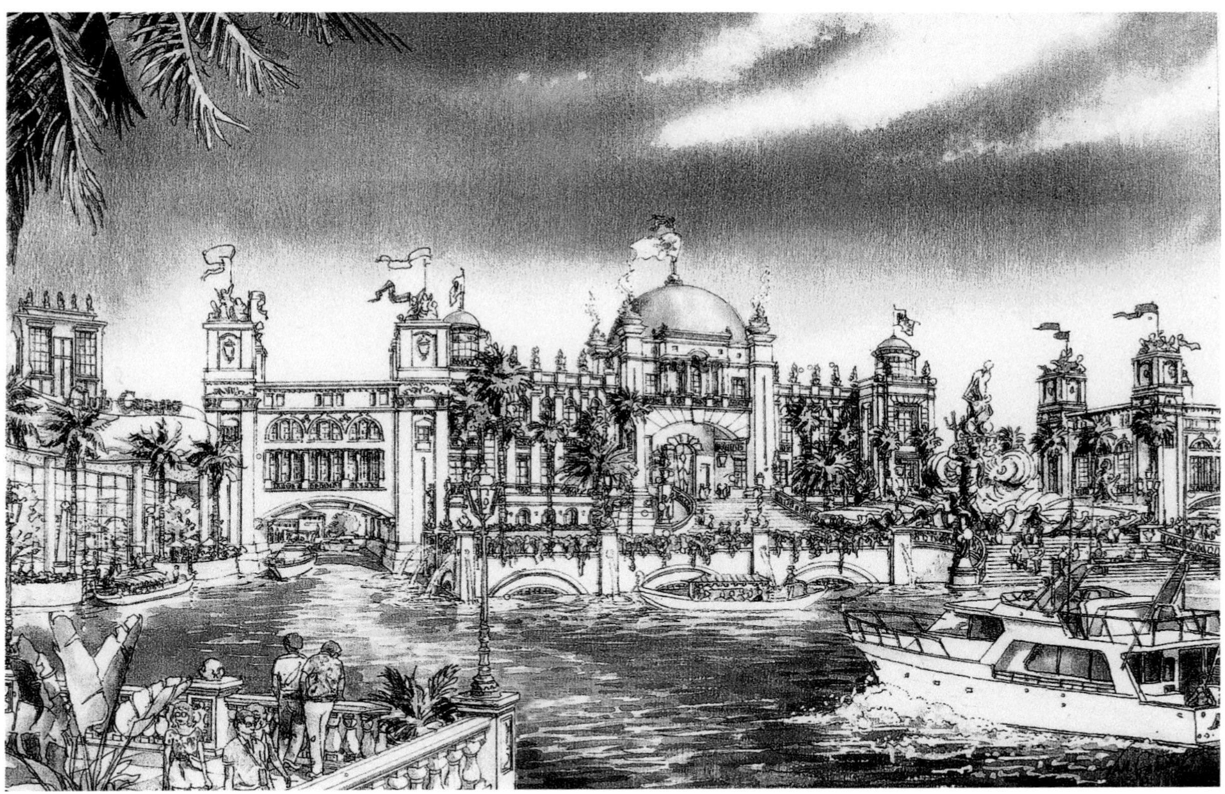

like glass most of the time. Our high tide is between 6 and 10 inches depending on the season. Hurricanes, as a worst case, can be expected on average of once every 7 years, (we have tracking charts dating back to 1834) but the wind and rain have no bad effect on the concrete and steel buildings. Think of the worst news story you ever saw about hurricane damage: the high rise office and condo buildings were not what was damaged. They (the hurricanes) can't cause floods or mud slides where we are, like those which devastated Central America. The platforms will be 10 feet above the surface so if there are storm surges they will pass under them. The Cayman Islands, 130 miles to our east, went 60 years between their last two hurricanes. So the once every 7 years is conservative. Having said that, yes, the buildings must be designed to withstand the wind, but that is the responsibility of the architects and engineers who design a given building for the developer who will build it. The technology is the same as a freeway bridge over a river, with a lot less abuse than all the traffic.'

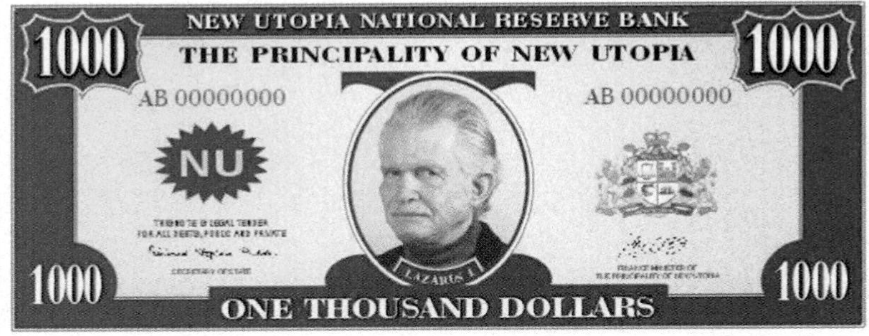

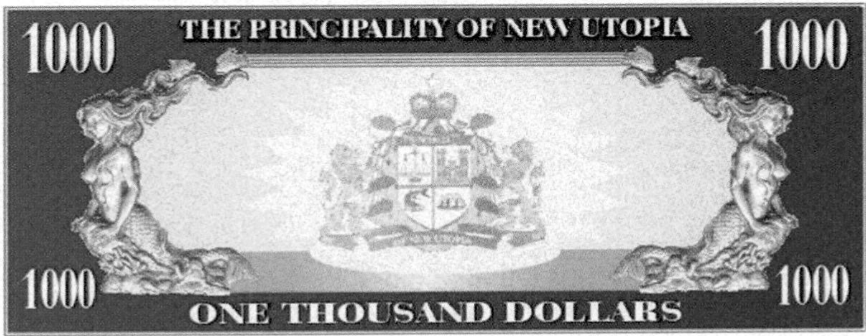

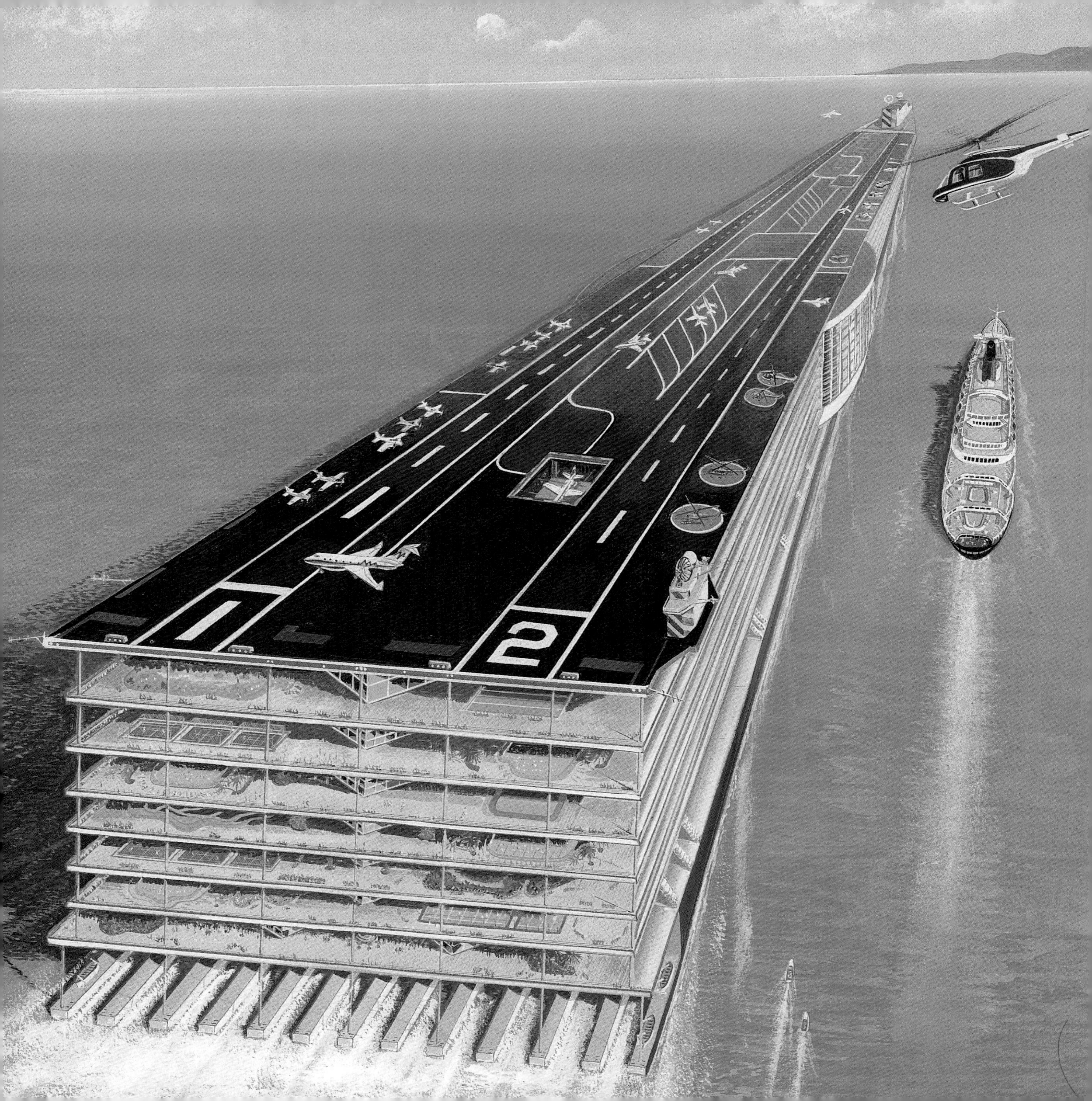

2

Freedom
Alex Stetter

The idea of seeing the world without ever leaving home is undoubtedly appealing. The Freedom Ship will allow you – and 40,000 other people – to do just that. At over a mile long and 25 stories high, this floating city will be six times larger than any vessel ever built. But anyone keen to become a member of this 'Community on the Sea' is likely to be just as interested in making money as in joining a holiday cruise that never ends. The Freedom Ship's primary objectives include creating 'a vigorous commercial community whose privately owned and operated on-board enterprises will sell their products and services world-wide and operate totally free of local taxes and duties'. In practice, this translates into a water-borne tax haven with a massive duty-free shopping mall, open to residents and day trippers alike.

If talk of an enormous, luxurious ship, the like of which has never before been seen on the world's oceans, brings to mind just one word – Titanic – you will be reassured by the thought that this vessel will have more in common with oil drilling platforms than the average cruise liner. The Florida-based engineering company behind the Freedom Ship originally planned to turn the expertise gained towing the elements of modular chemical plants halfway around the world before assembling them at sea towards building a floating artificial island. Instead, the firm decided to apply the same principles to something a little more mobile. But the Freedom Ship is designed for stability rather than speed, and won't be doing that much cruising: the plan is to spend 70% of the time lying just offshore from the world's more prosperous coastal resorts.

Apart from offering a range of elegant living quarters (as usual, a seaview comes at a premium) and abundant retail opportunities, the ship will also feature 200 acres of landscaped park and every sporting and recreational facility its inhabitants could possibly desire. But not everyone on board will be a super-rich tax exile – there are the needs of the thousands of members of staff and their families to take into account, as well. So the ship also has to accommodate the usual infrastructure needed to run a more conventional city of this size: that means education, healthcare and even transport facilities. There are plans for electric trams to move people around the ship as well as speed boats and planes to take people onboard and off. The ship's designers are also very sensitive to accusations that it will contribute to the pollution of the oceans, and promise that the vessel will be a model of environmental responsibility

Even though Freedom Ship's inhabitants will be making their homes in international waters, their vessel will be flying the flag of an existing country (exactly which country is still under consideration). So the ship will not constitute a whole new nation in itself: instead, the captain will have the authority to enforce the laws of the nation whose flag they will be sailing under. The safety of life on board is a key element of the ship's appeal to prospective wealthy inhabitants, and will be ensured by the deployment of a 2000-strong private security team. So in one sense at least, the Freedom Ship seems rather inappropriately named – it looks as if things will be strictly controlled. The question is whether the greatest threat to the stability of life at sea is likely to come from outside, in the form of terrorist attack, or from within the community. Who knows what will happen if you bring together thousands of people from different cultures in one place – will they really come together as a community, the way the ship's creators imagine they will?

With almost a quarter of the available residential units already spoken for, the idea of the Freedom Ship has clearly captured people's imagination. Maybe it's the romance

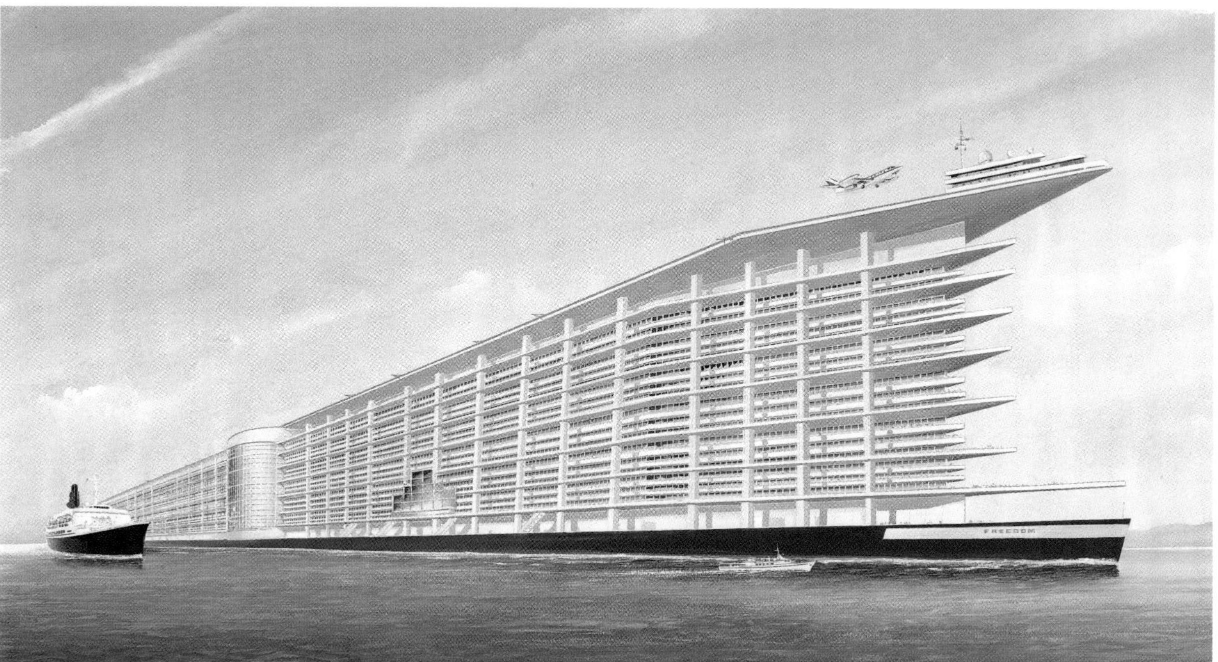

of running away to go to sea, or maybe it's just the appeal of living in a mobile luxury resort with added financial benefits: either way, this particular utopian project is gathering support all around the world. Whether that's enough to raise the estimated $6 billion needed to build the ship in Honduras remains to be seen. Even though construction hasn't even started on the first one, the Freedom Ship consortium is so sure of success that three more ships are already being planned. They look forward to meeting you on board in 2003.

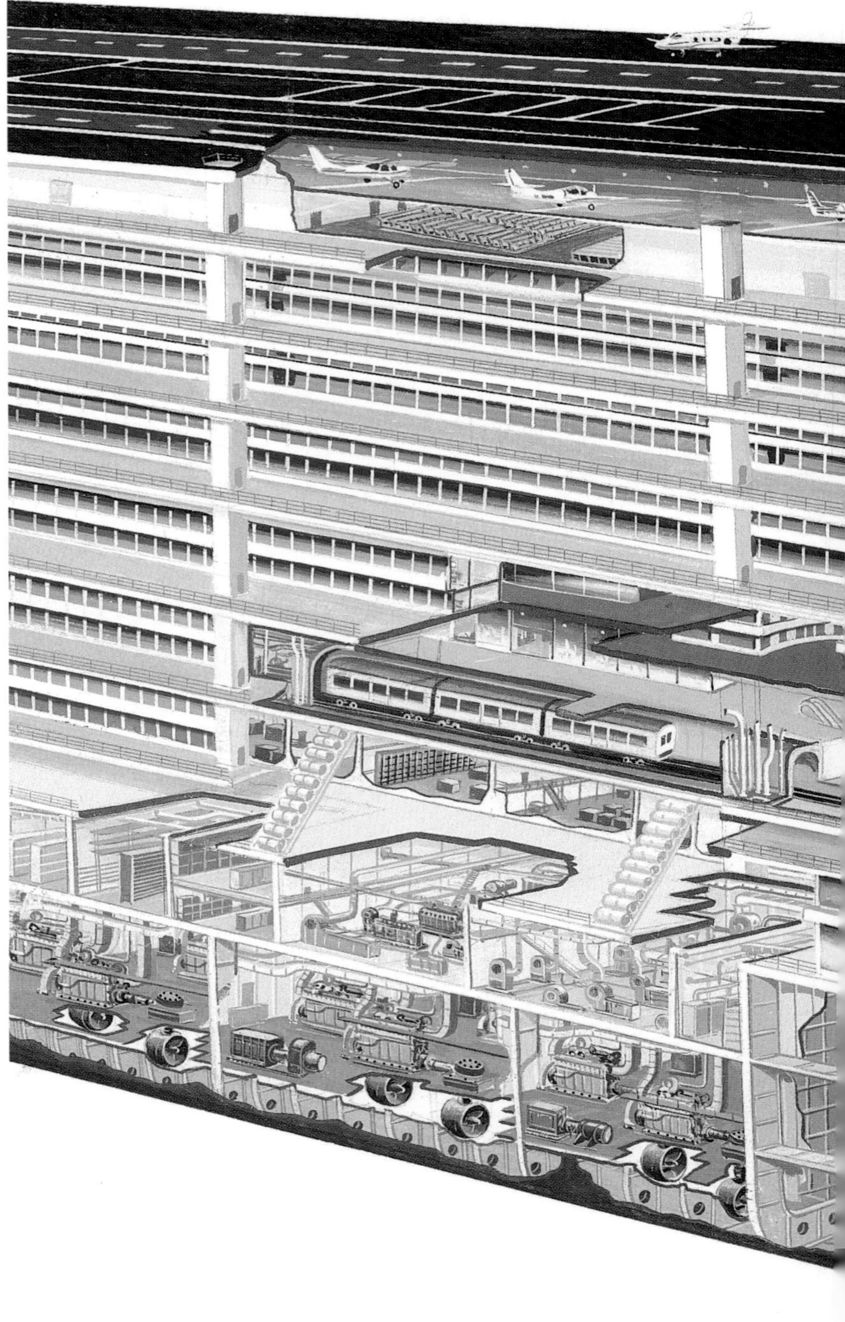

Statement from Norm Nixon, CEO, Freedom Ship

'Hello, this is Norm. I was requested to give you a one-minute description of the Freedom Ship, but this is not possible. A good understanding of the Freedom Ship would require about two hours of reading on your part. So let me pass along a little information. Let me tell you what the Freedom Ship is *not*. This will also answer numerous questions we have received. Freedom Ship is not just about the creation of a massive ship, but about the creation of a community. A community that offers its residents a new, exciting and unheard-of lifestyle. We designed the community, calculated the required square footage and backed it to the size of the ship. And the ship itself is not a high-tech breakthrough: the structural engineers could have designed a high-tech steel structure, but we chose a simple flat-bottomed barge, utilising steel technology used in this country for more than fifty years. This was done in order to lower the cost of the units and increase the structural integrity. The ship is not a fragile creation subject to damage by severe weather – the vessel can withstand force 5 winds and the most severe hurricanes. Since the mission of the ship does not require movement at high speed, we were able to sacrifice speed in exchange for unprecedented structural integrity in the design of the ship. The ship will not be an easy target for common criminals or terrorists of any variety. With a twenty-eight-year-old FBI agent directing a 2000 man security force, the ship will be the safest place you will ever reside.'

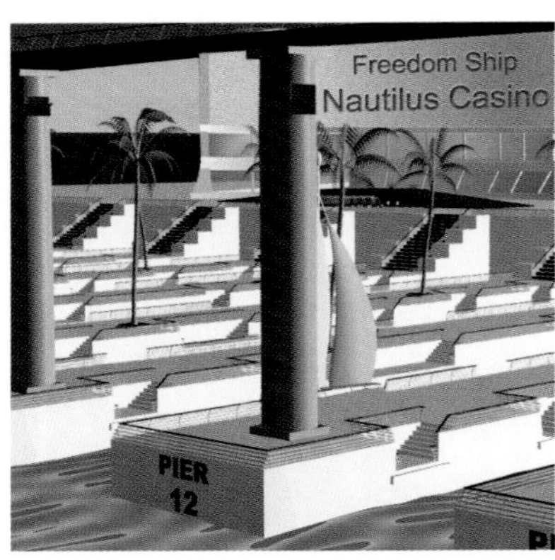

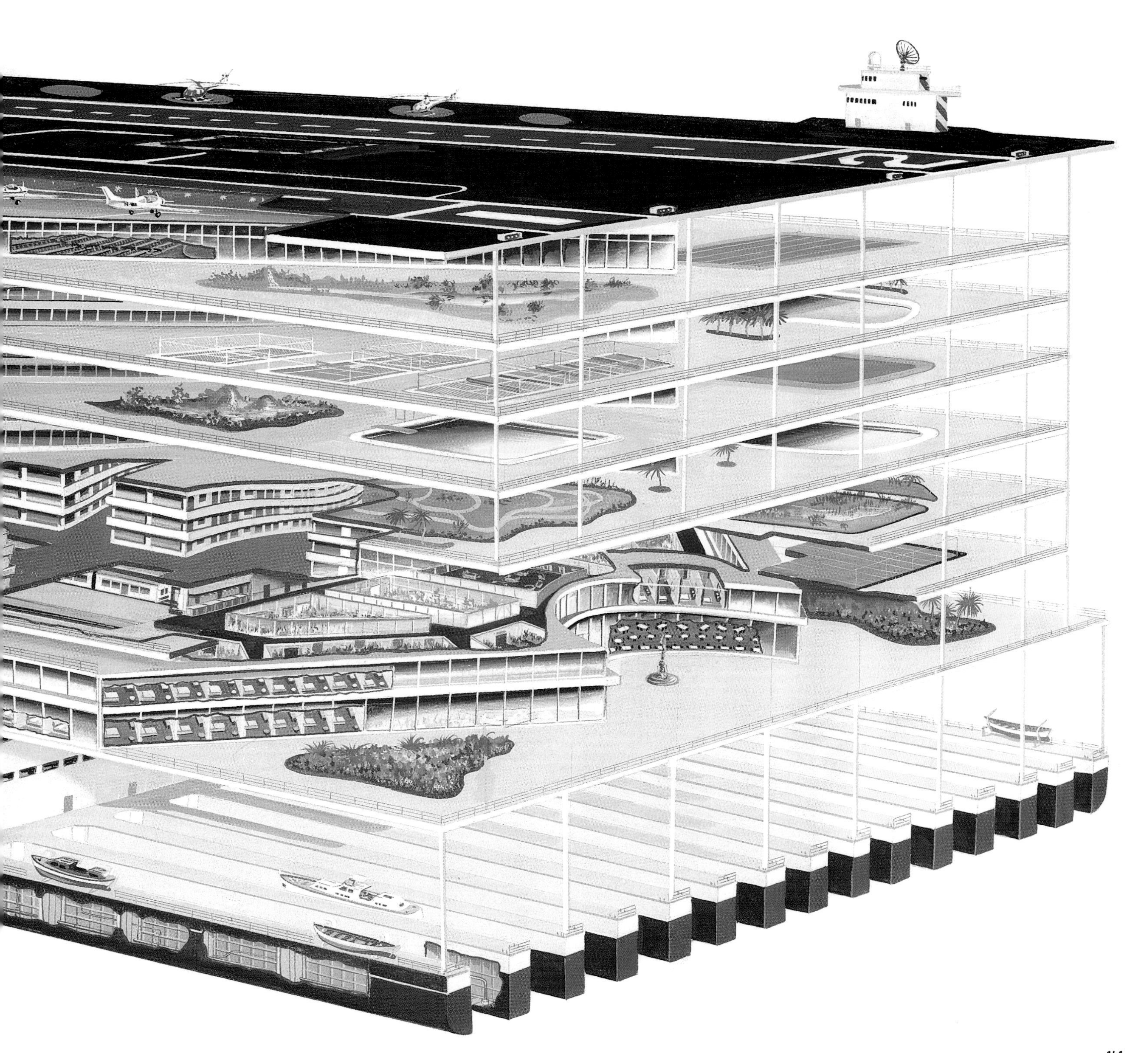

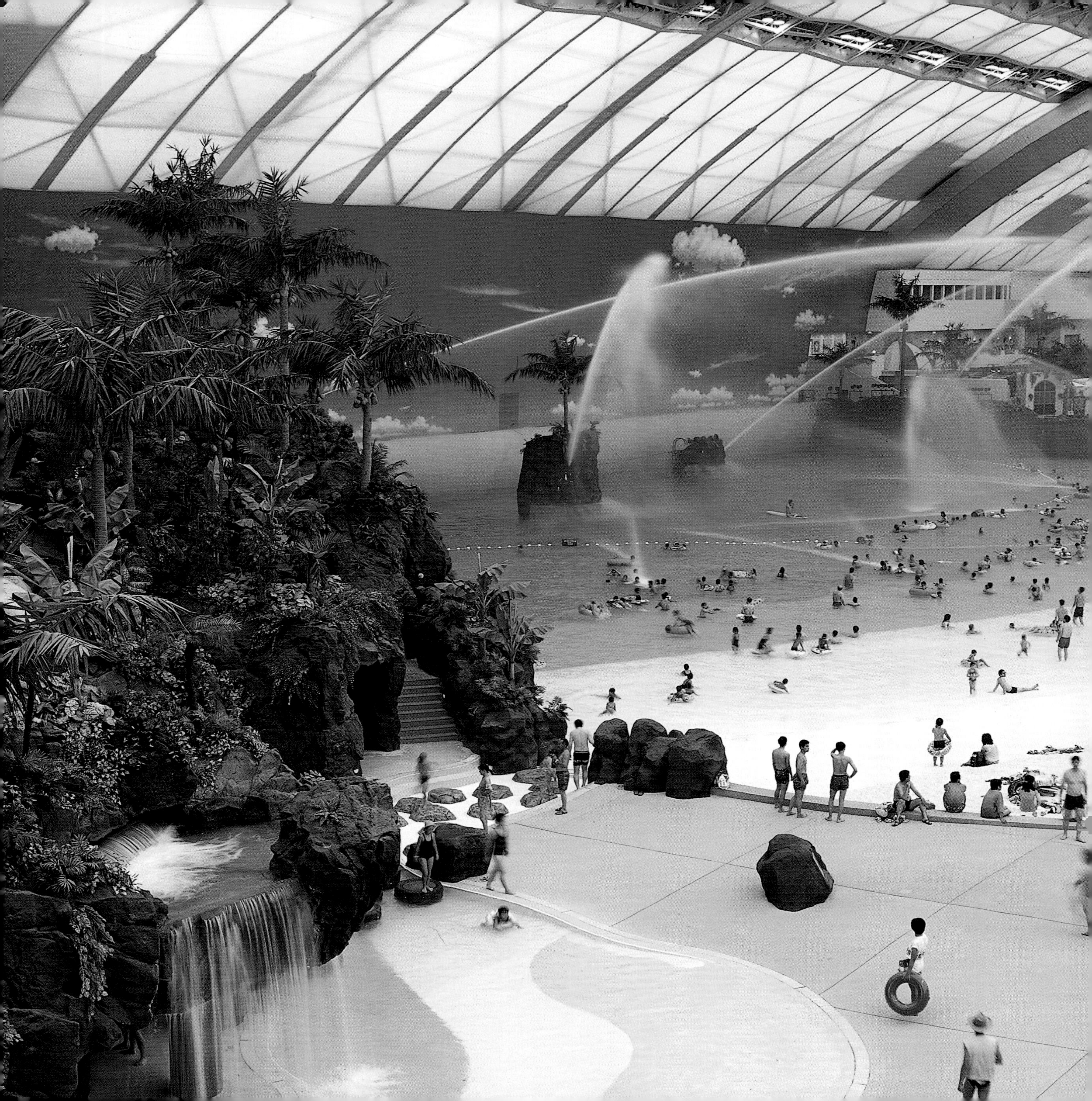

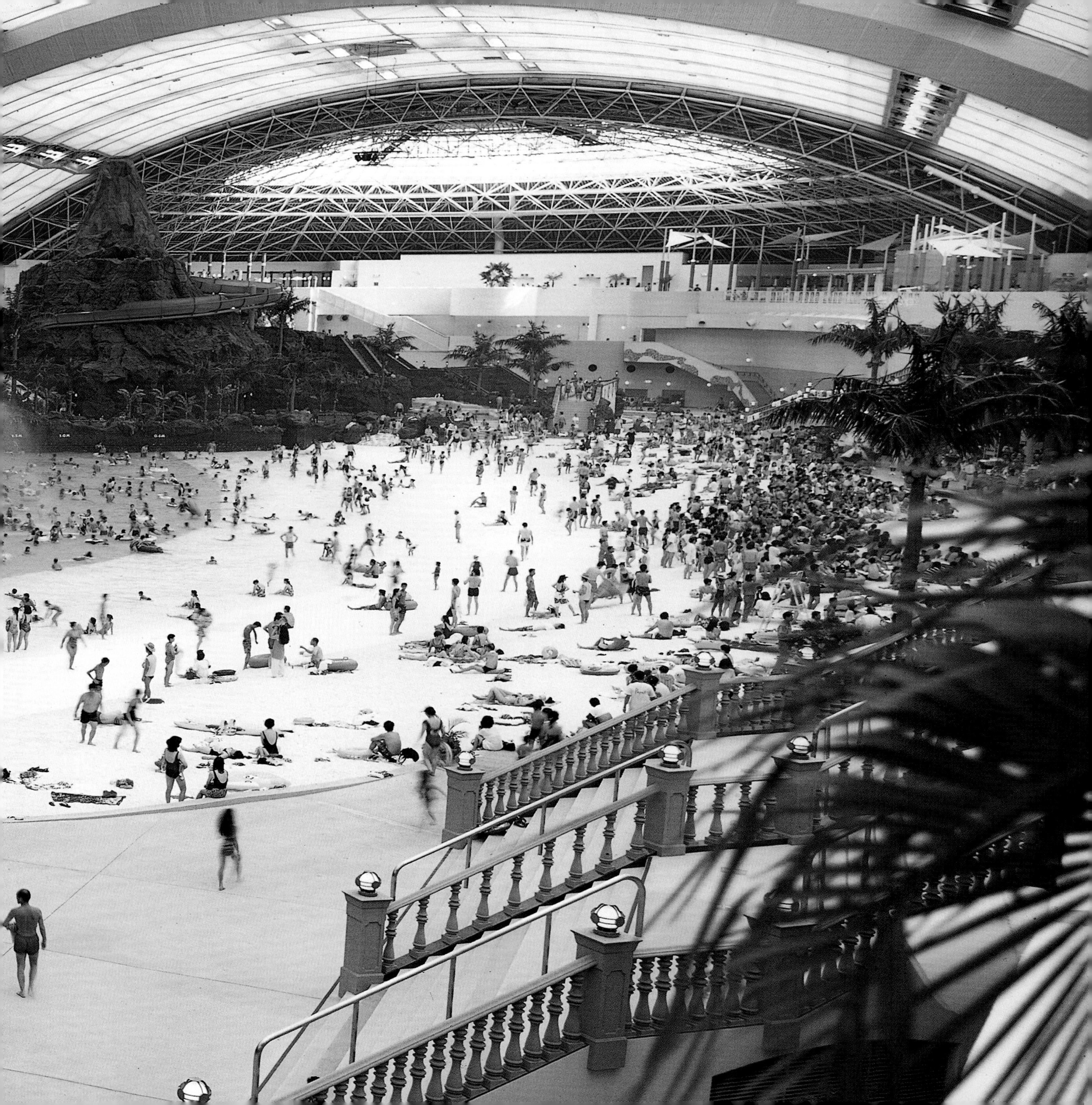

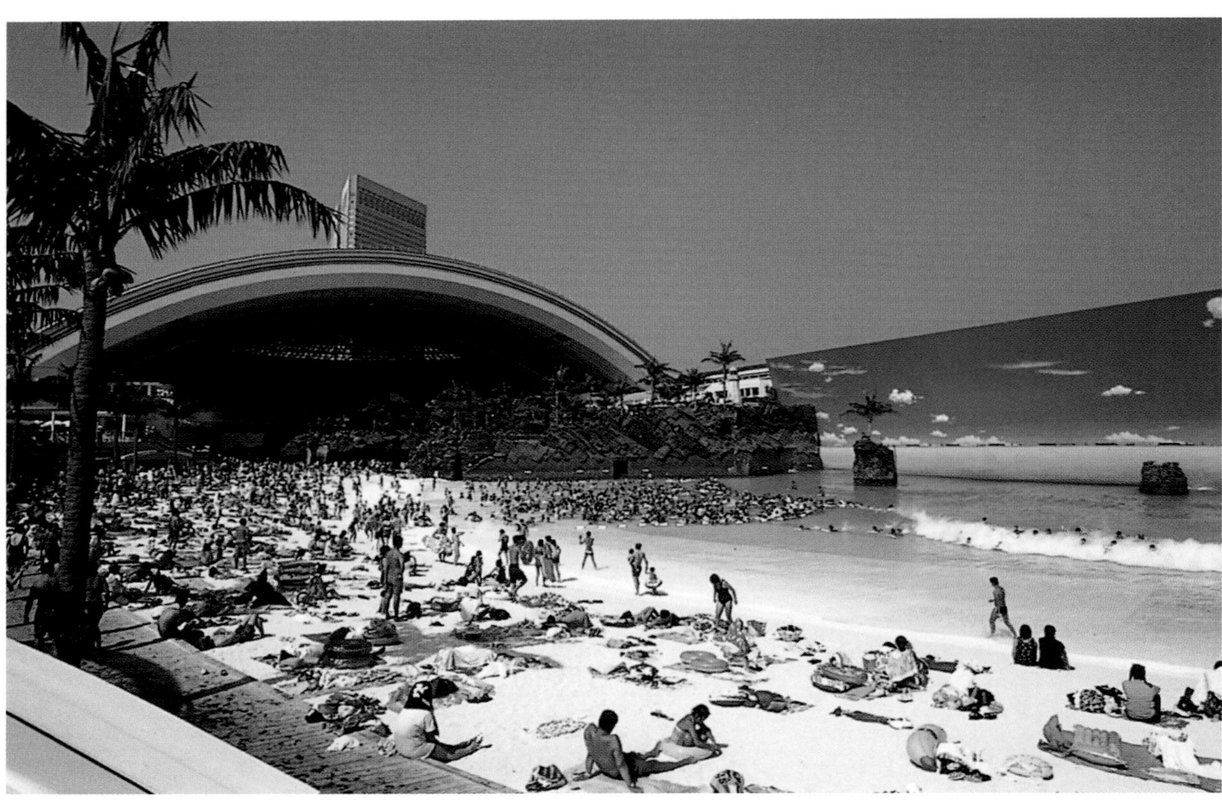

Oceandome
Miyazaki, Japan

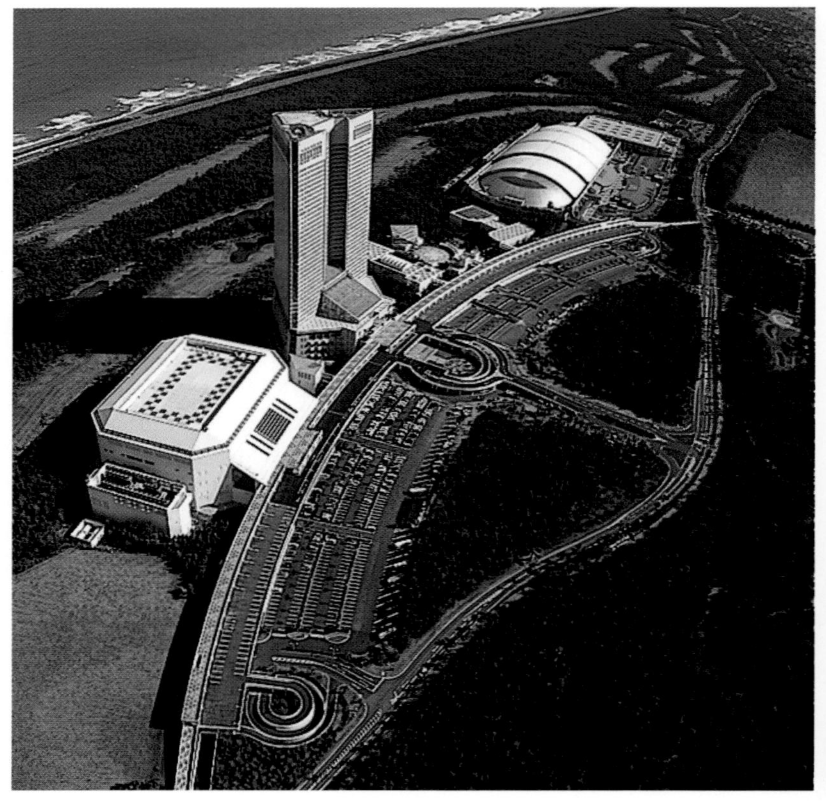

Imagine a place where the temperature is a steady 30°C and the water is always perfect, where there are no sea urchins on the beach, no sewage pipes spewing filth into the waves just up the coast and there is not the slightest risk of rain ever spoiling your fun. It does not exist, obviously, but the Oceandome in southern Japan is probably the closest you can get. It is the world's biggest indoor water park, with a retractable roof and a wave machine powerful enough to make surfing an indoor activity for the first time. Oceandome is part of the huge Seagaia resort in Miyazaki, which includes half a dozen hotels, a golf course, a zoo, a tennis club, a bowling alley and a high-tech amusement complex with all the latest games machines.

It is also the home of Japan's largest international conference centre, which played host to the Meeting of the Foreign Ministers at the G8 summit in July 2000. And if the provision of all these facilities starts to feel a little too much, you can escape to the real beach just a few hundred metres away.

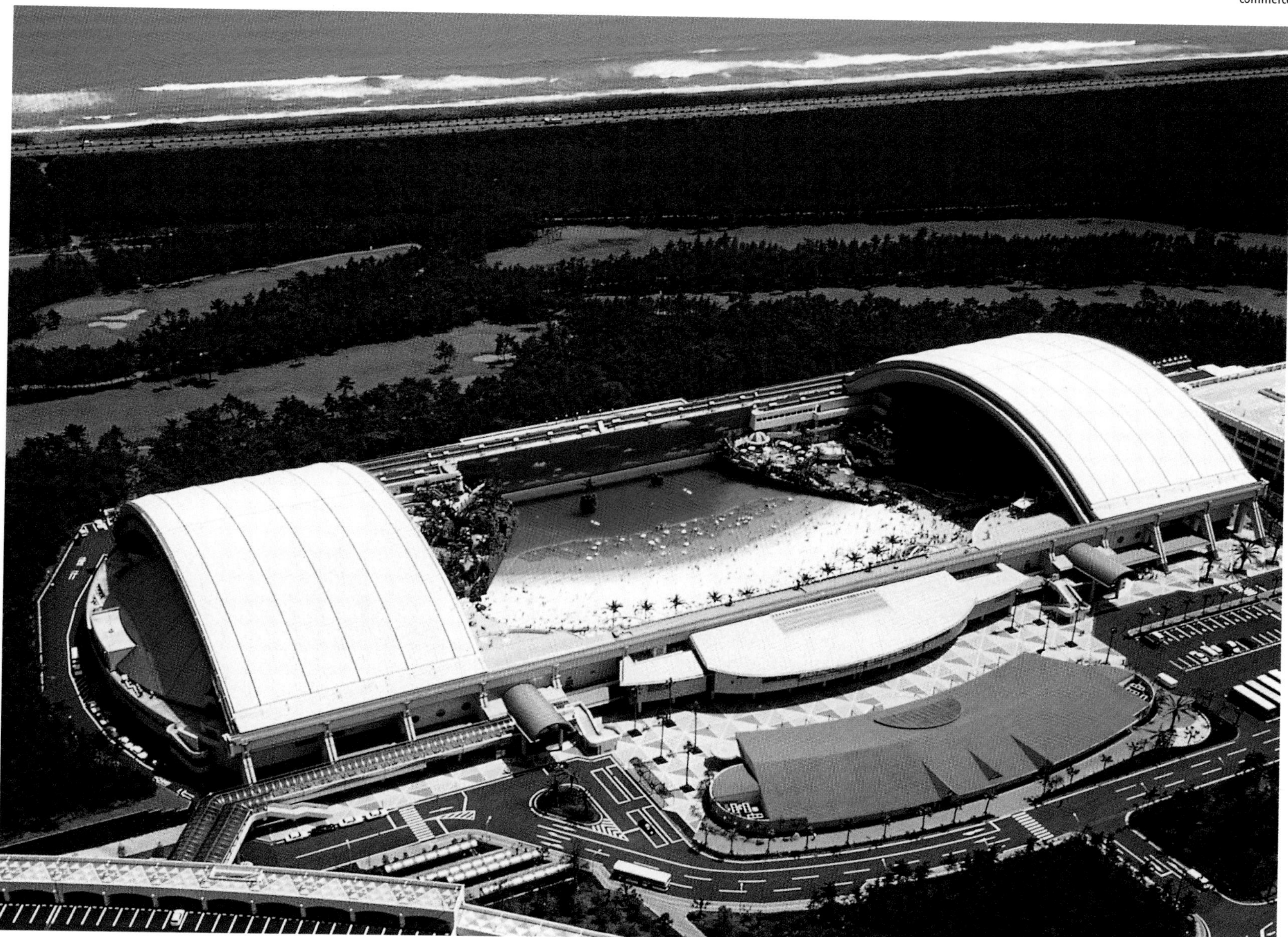

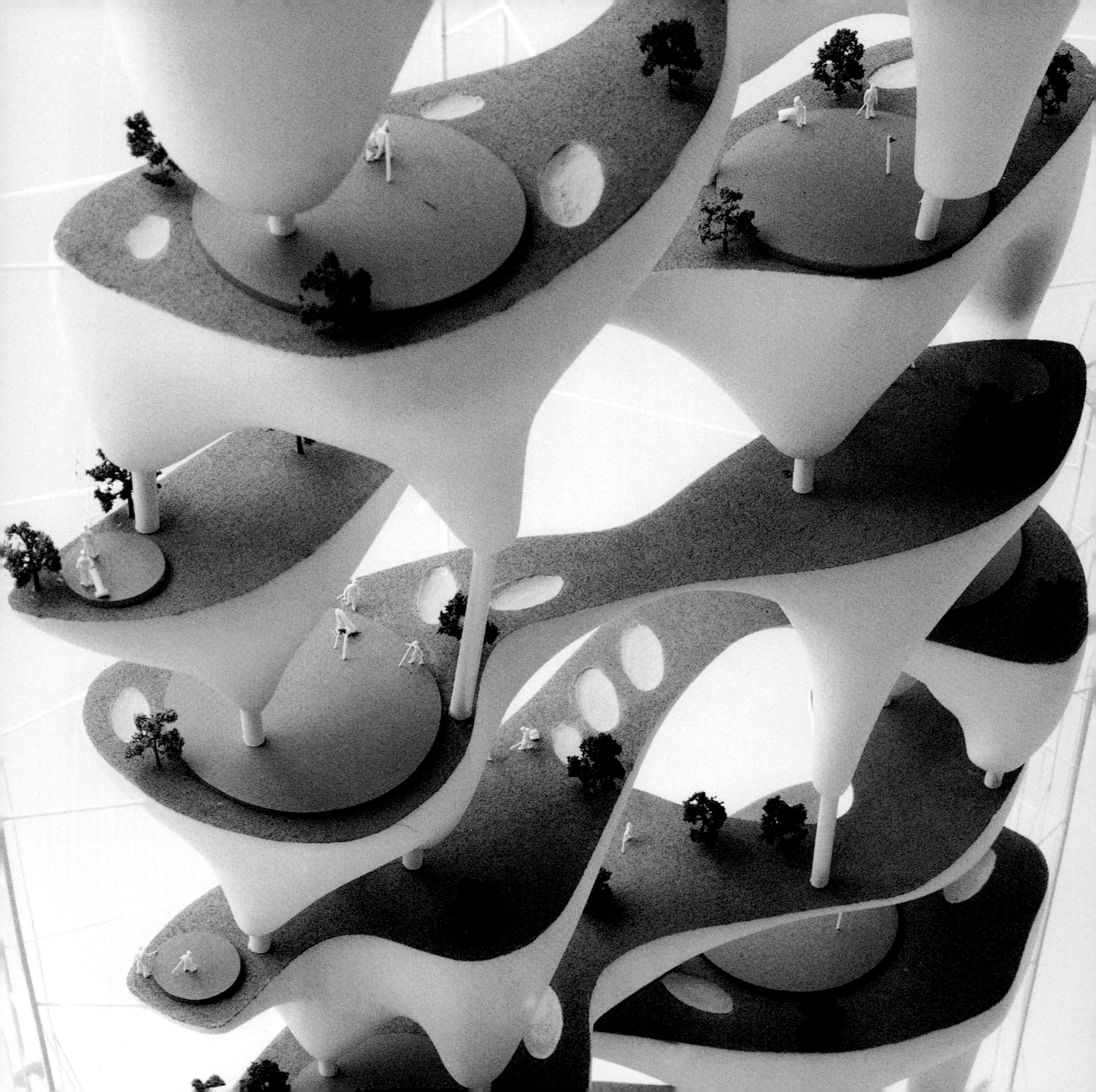

Vertical Golf Course
Harty and Harty, 1999

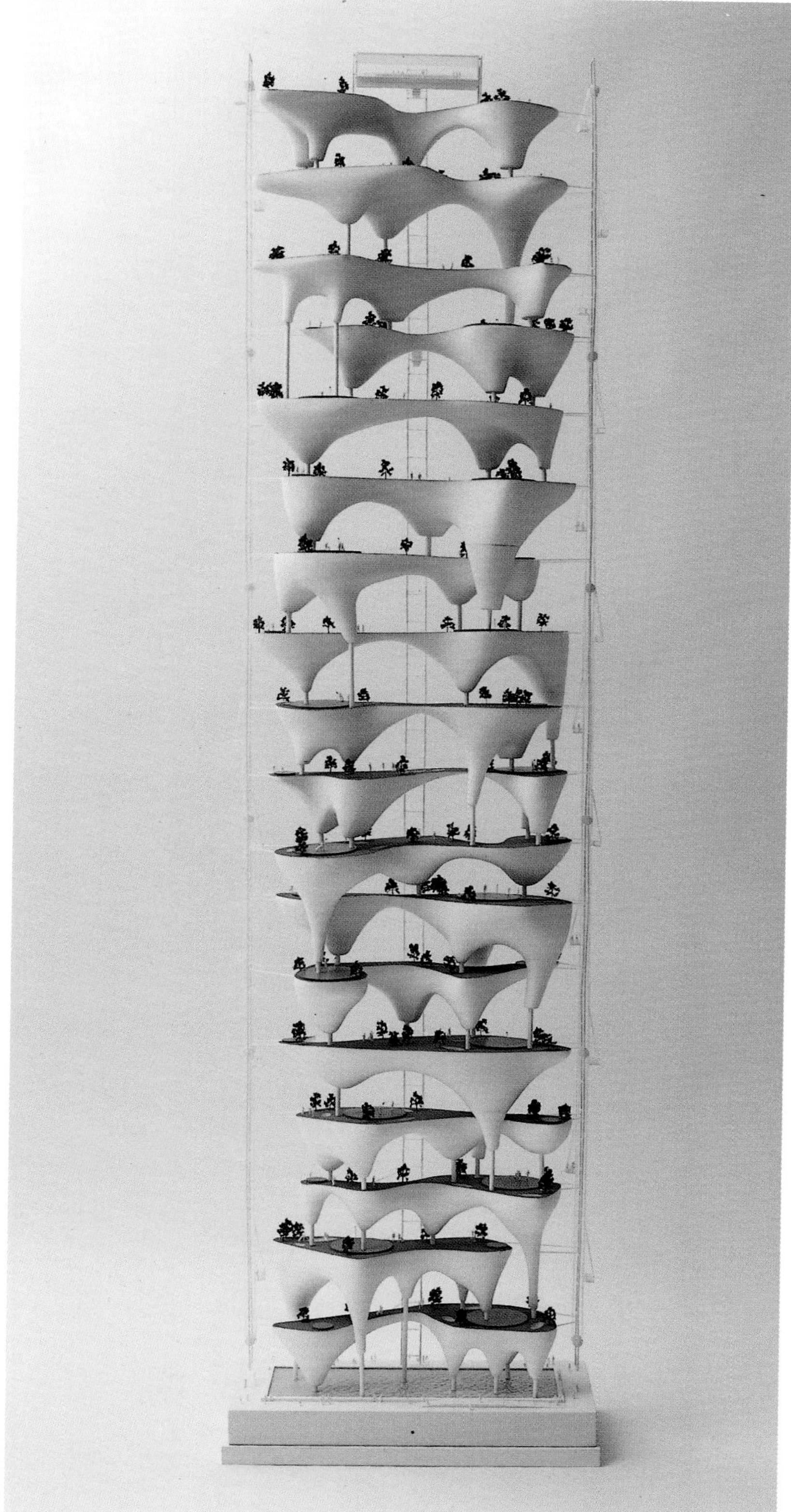

Strange though it may seem, the high-rise golf course is probably not far from the realms of possibility. The growth of the world's most upwardly-mobile pastime has done more than almost anything else in the past ten years to transform rural areas on the edge of major cities all over the world. In Britain alone, 560 new golf courses were built during the 1990s, and at 7 kilometres of playable length for each course (in other words, roughly 60 hectares of playable space), the transformation of land from countryside to golfing sprawl adds up to nothing short of an invasion.

In Japan and East Asia, the pastime has grown even more quickly. Today, there are courses in Bahrain, Burma, China, India, Japan, Korea, Malaysia, the Philippines, Singapore, Sri Lanka, Taiwan and Thailand. Already, due to the large land area required by courses, Japanese golfers have resorted to practising on driving ranges, whose triple-decker driving tees are surrounded on all sides by high netting.

Given the huge levels of investment into golf course architecture it is surprising that the traditional layout of the course has remained fundamentally unchallenged for so many years. London-based architects Harty and Harty have devised the vertical golf course as a logical conclusion to the expansive trend: 'As architects we seize the opportunity to question, from first principles, traditional models of architecture; what was horizontal and sub-urban becomes vertical and urban.'

The notion of the stacked golf course is not in fact so different from the idea of high-rise housing, a building typology whose invention at the beginning of the twentieth century must have seemed equally challenging to conventional ideas about public and private space.

Blur
Diller and Scofidio

This artificial cloud in the middle of a Swiss lake is an intervention by Elizabeth Diller and Ricardo Scofidio which does more than simply defy architectural convention; by denying the norms of architectural practice it aims to reinstate the idea of the body as a fundamental consideration in spatial design.

'Architecture typically enters into a role of complicity, to sustain cultural conventions', Diller and Scofidio argued in a 1993 lecture. According to their thinking, technological and political reconfigurations of the contemporary body mean that all such conventions must be questioned, and they have devoted a number of years to conceptual research into a new set of priorities for architecture. Until recently, an influential installation for MoMA in New York and a much-published design for a seaside house have been the most important built manifestations of their thinking. The cloud project in Switzerland, to be completed in time for Expo 02, will see their work realised on a much larger scale. Using mist generated by thousands of computer-controlled spray nozzles, Diller and Scofidio will create formless architecture; a cloud which hovers over the lake, concealing its interior spaces from the outside world. Beneath the mist, a complex of bars and restaurants will cohabit together with a graphic collage of screen grabs and electronic abstraction fed directly from the Internet and projected in a darkened chamber.

Highly visible but apparently immaterial, the project embraces the surrealist notion of formlessness posited by Bataille in his *Dictionnaire Critique* in 1929. Bataille's discussion of the 'informe' explores the apparent inability of people to exist without systems. Bataille argued that without them, the world opens into an abyss of formlessness: 'Something like a spider or a blob of spittle'.
If it is true that we have a tendency to overlay simplifying systems onto the innate formlessness of matter, then for Diller and Scofidio architecture has developed into one of the most rigid systems of all. With their mysterious cloud, the system is undermined, and the only means of comprehending its formlessness is active human participation.

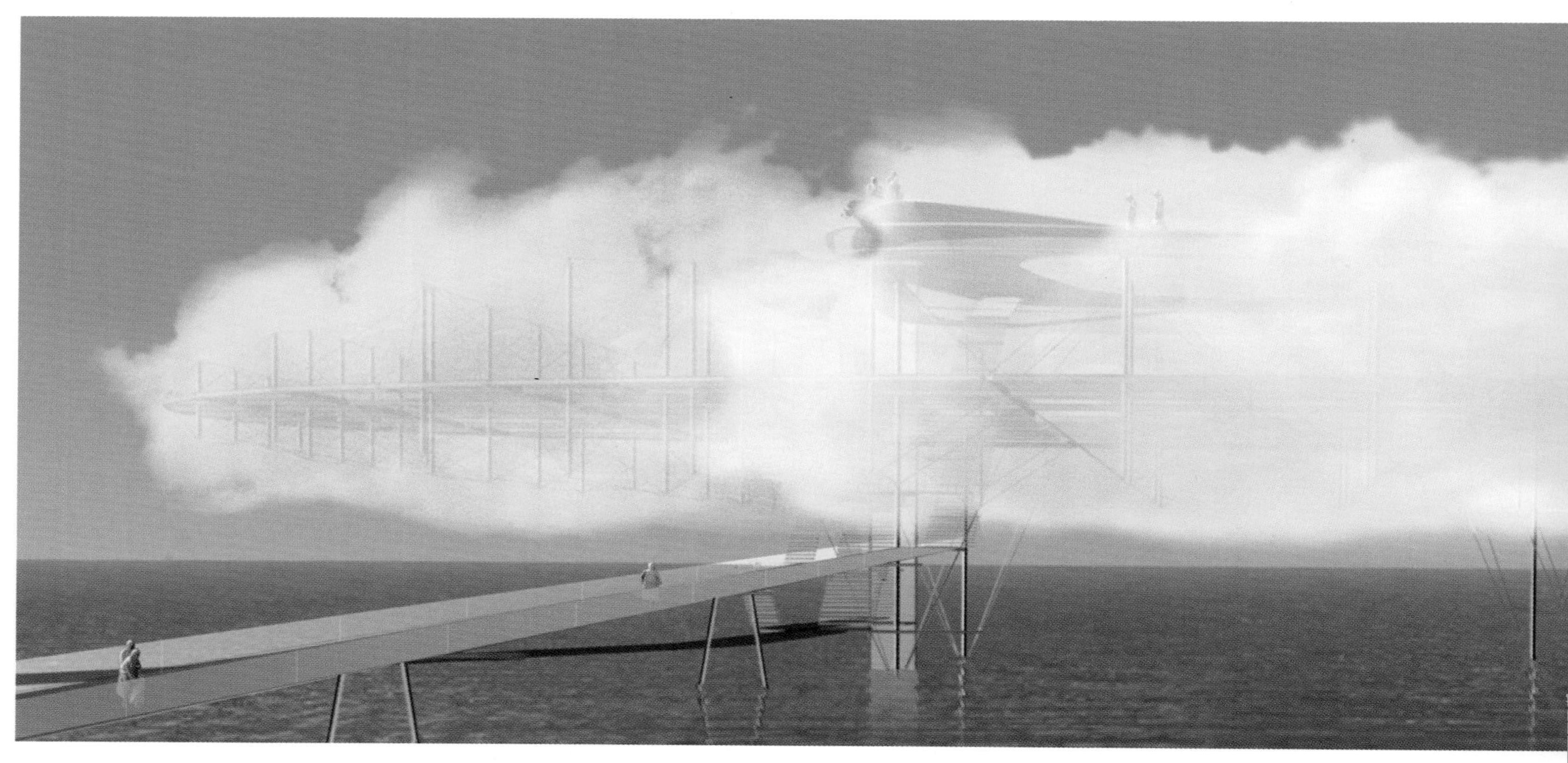

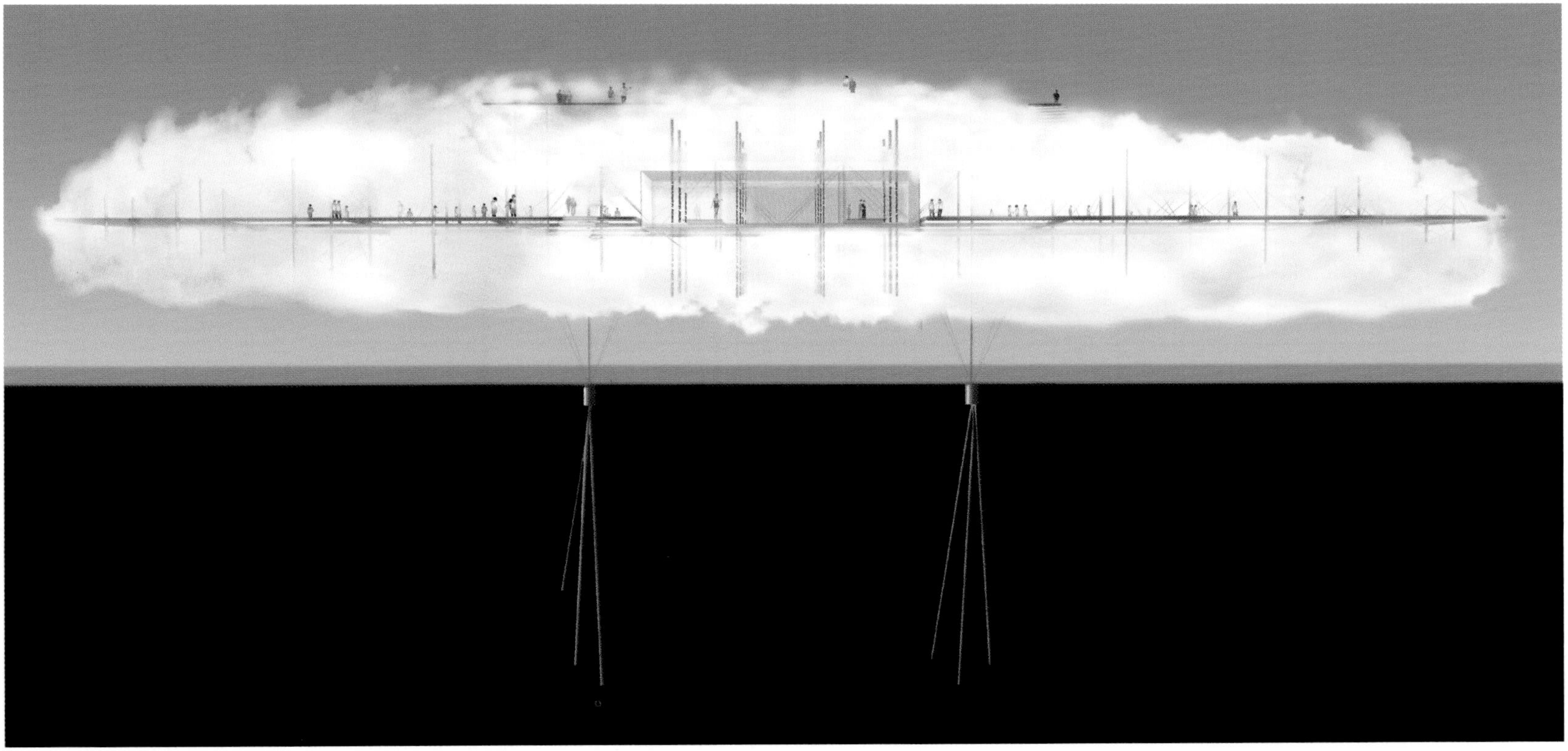

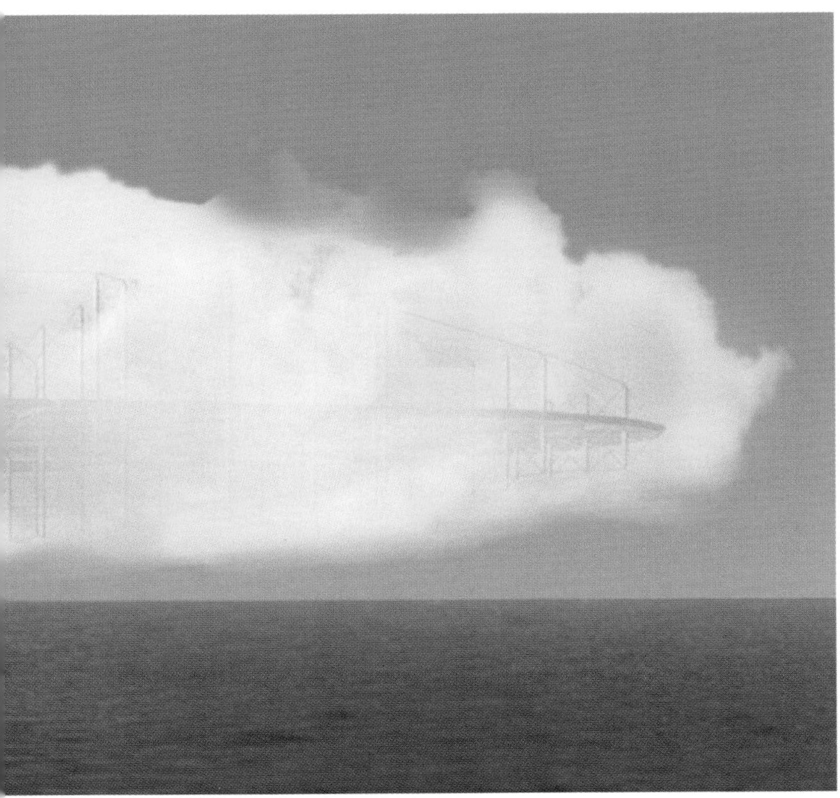

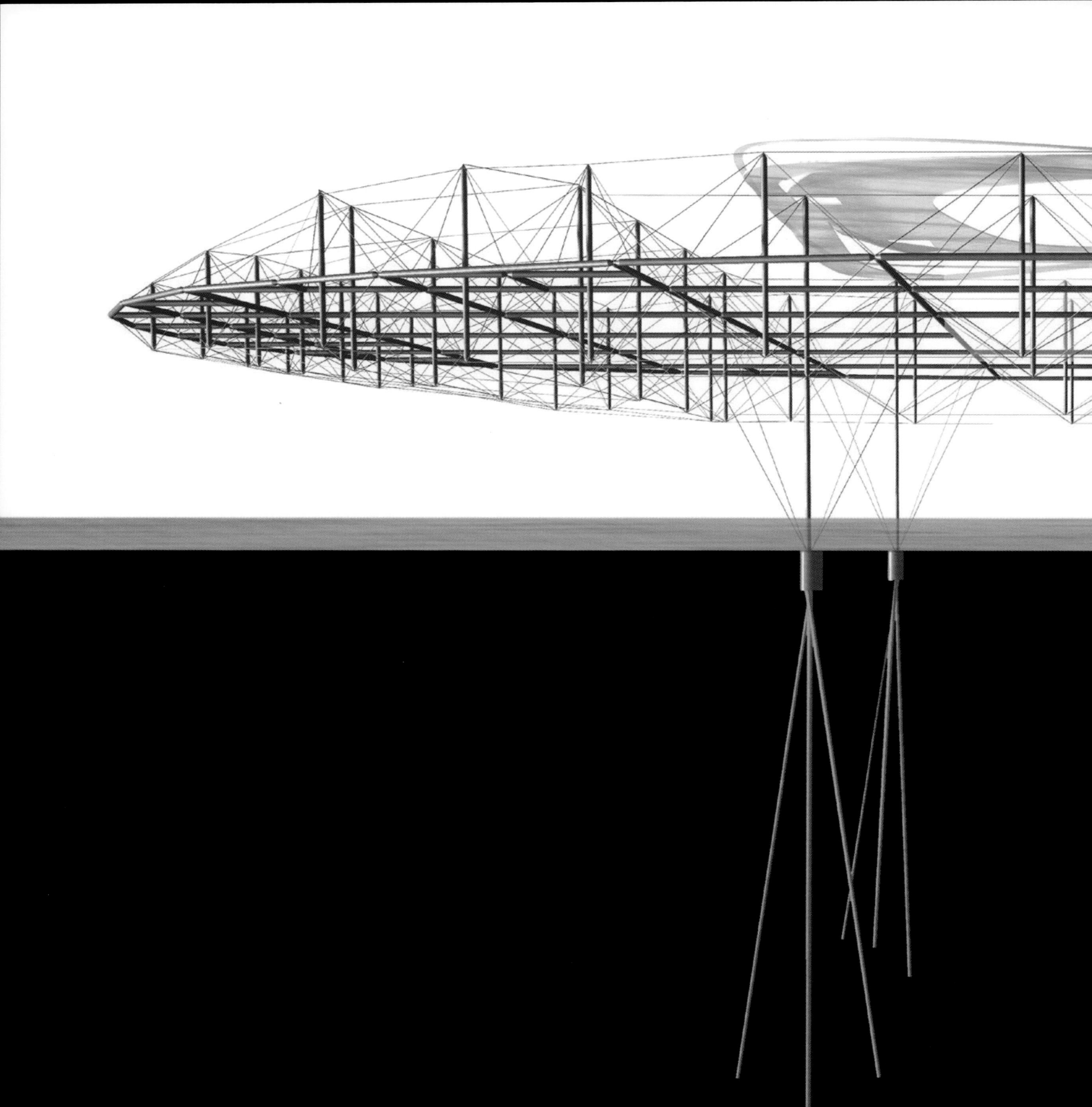

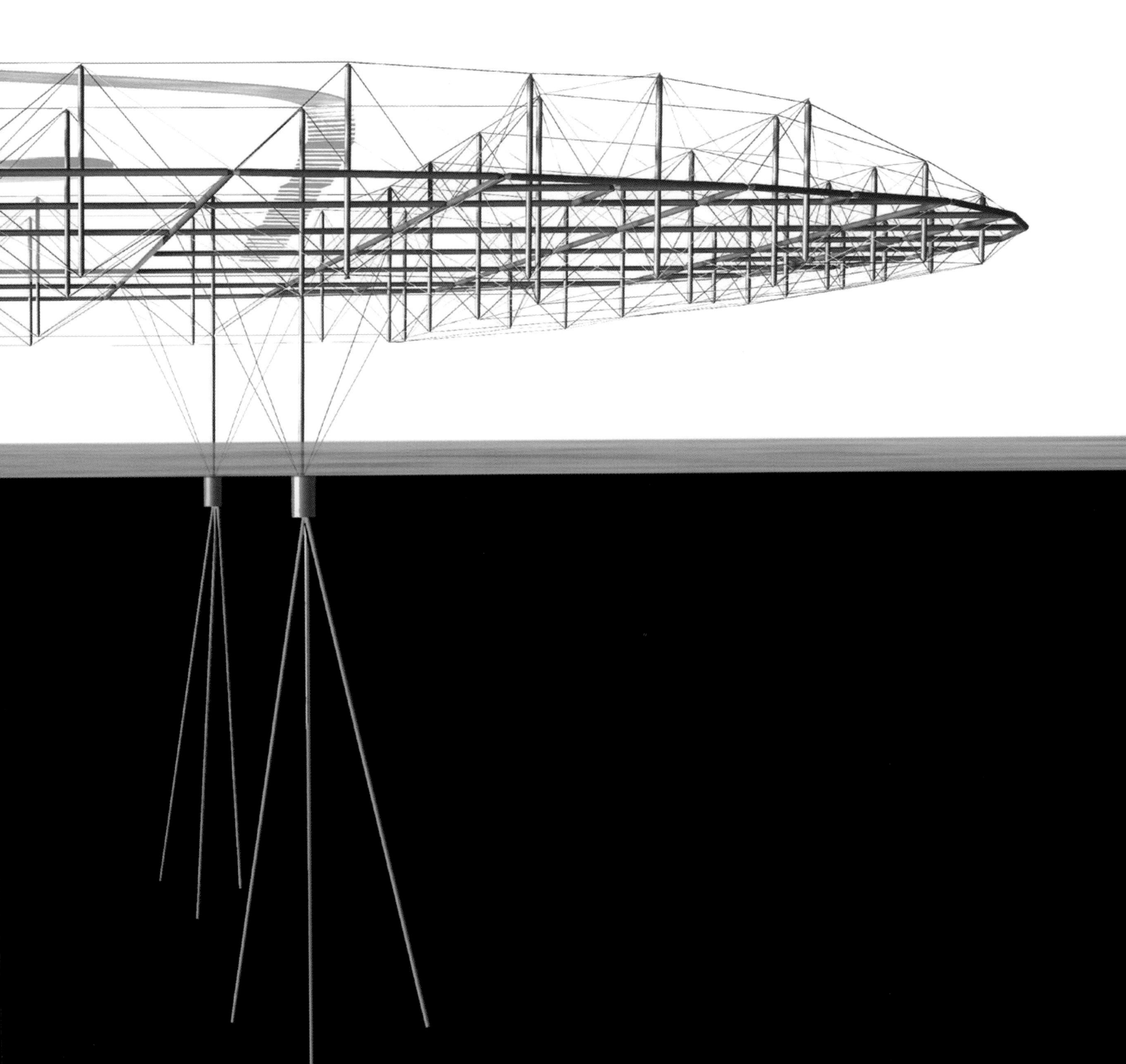

Resort
David Spero

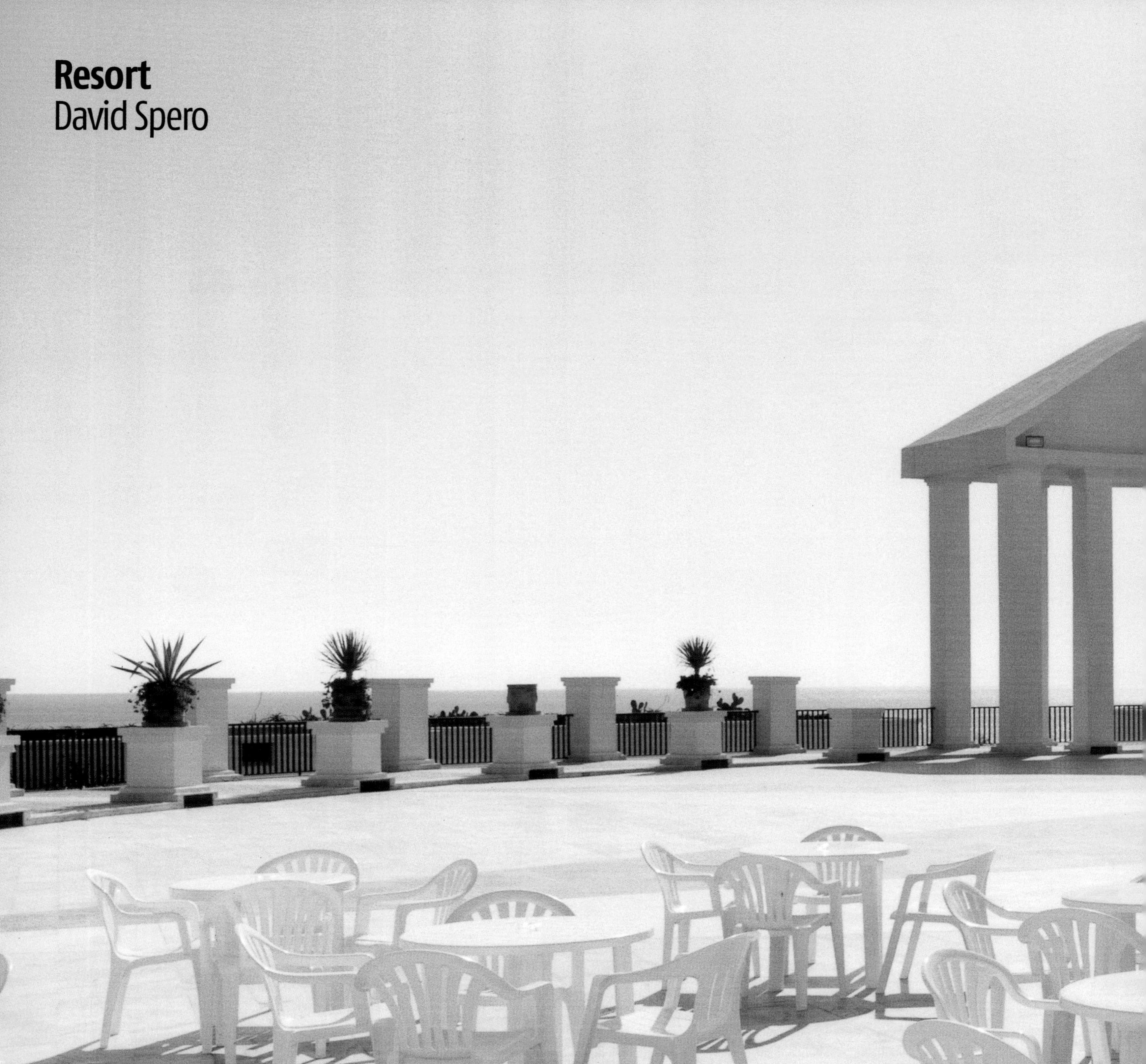

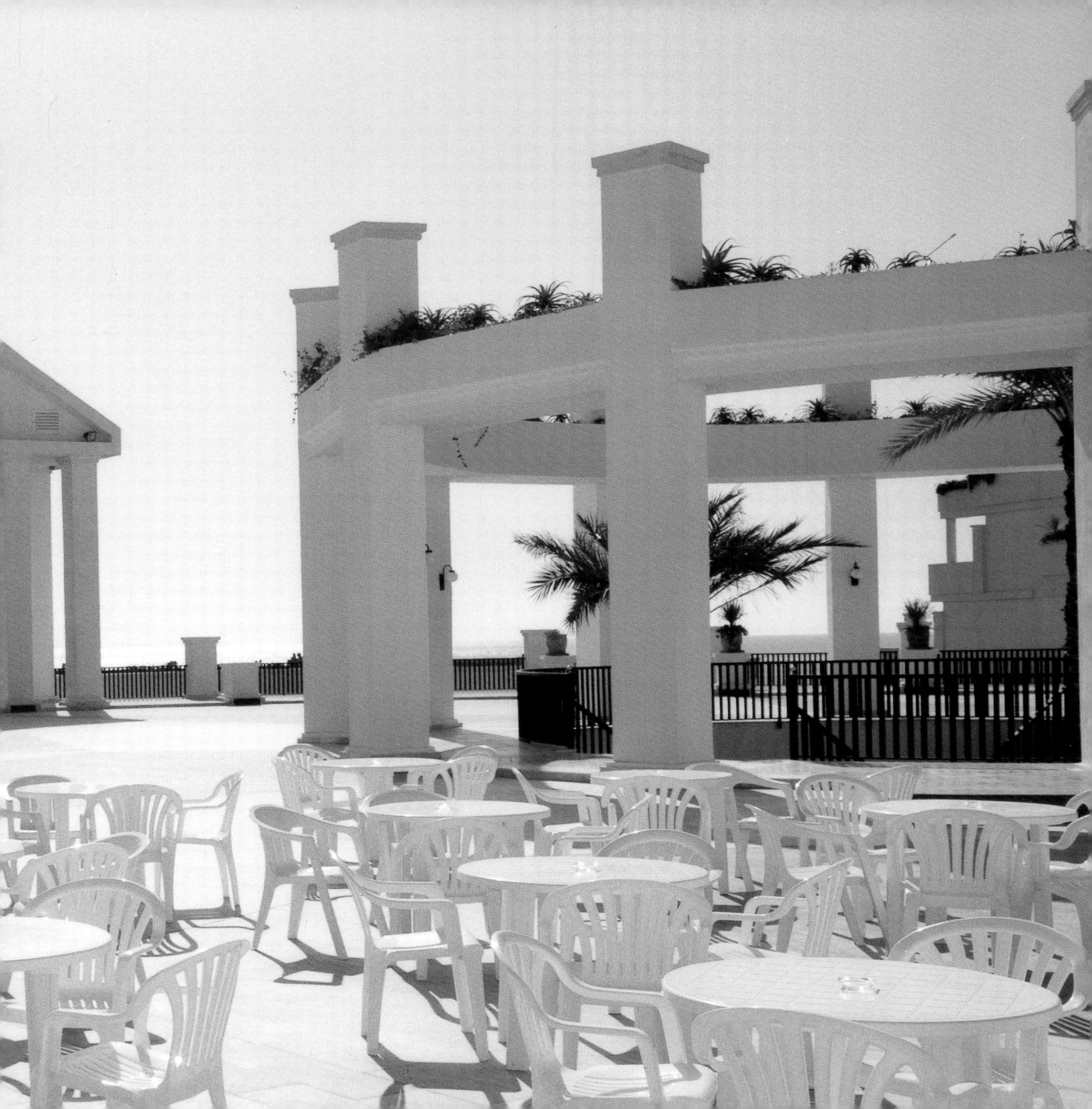

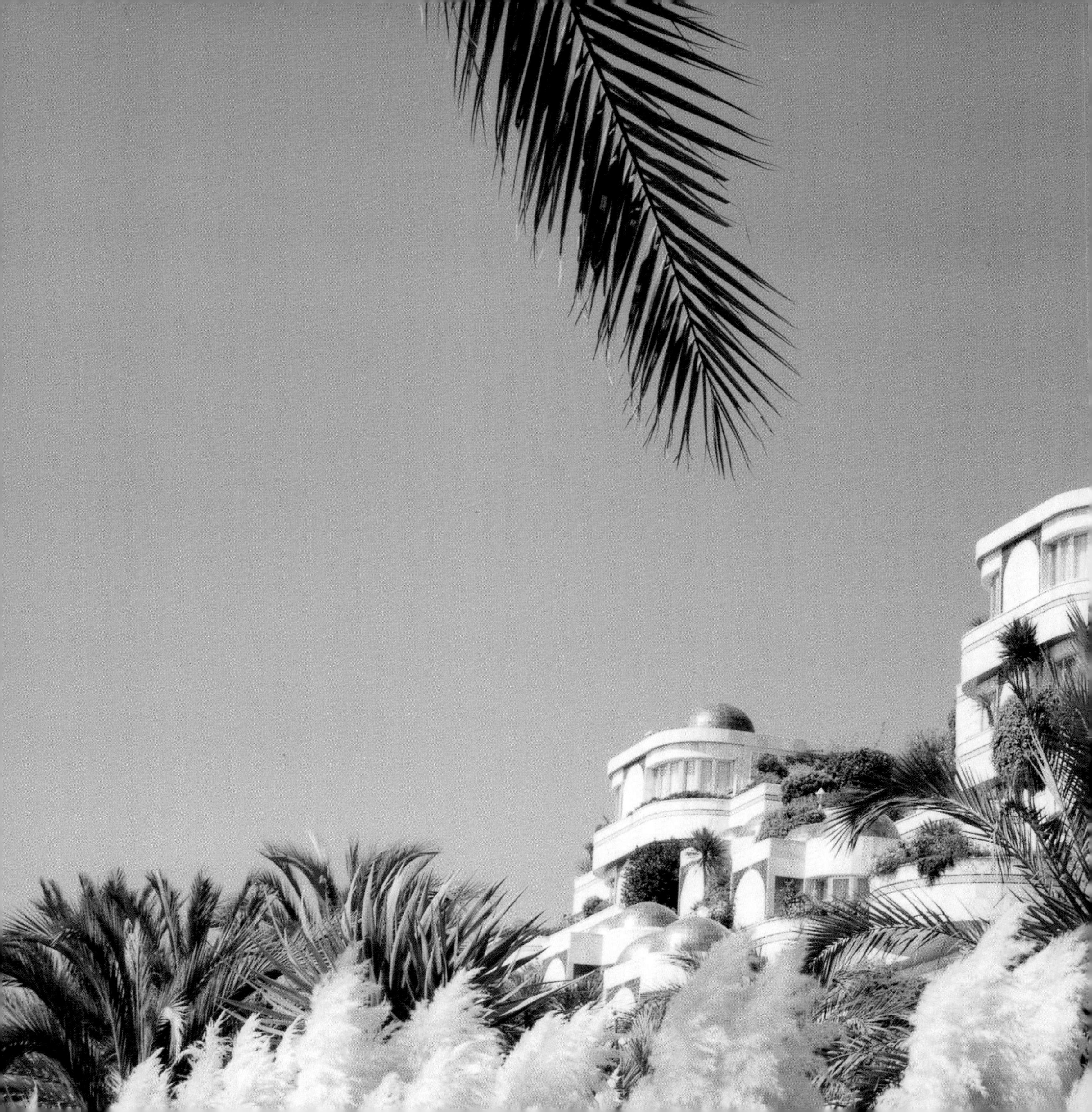

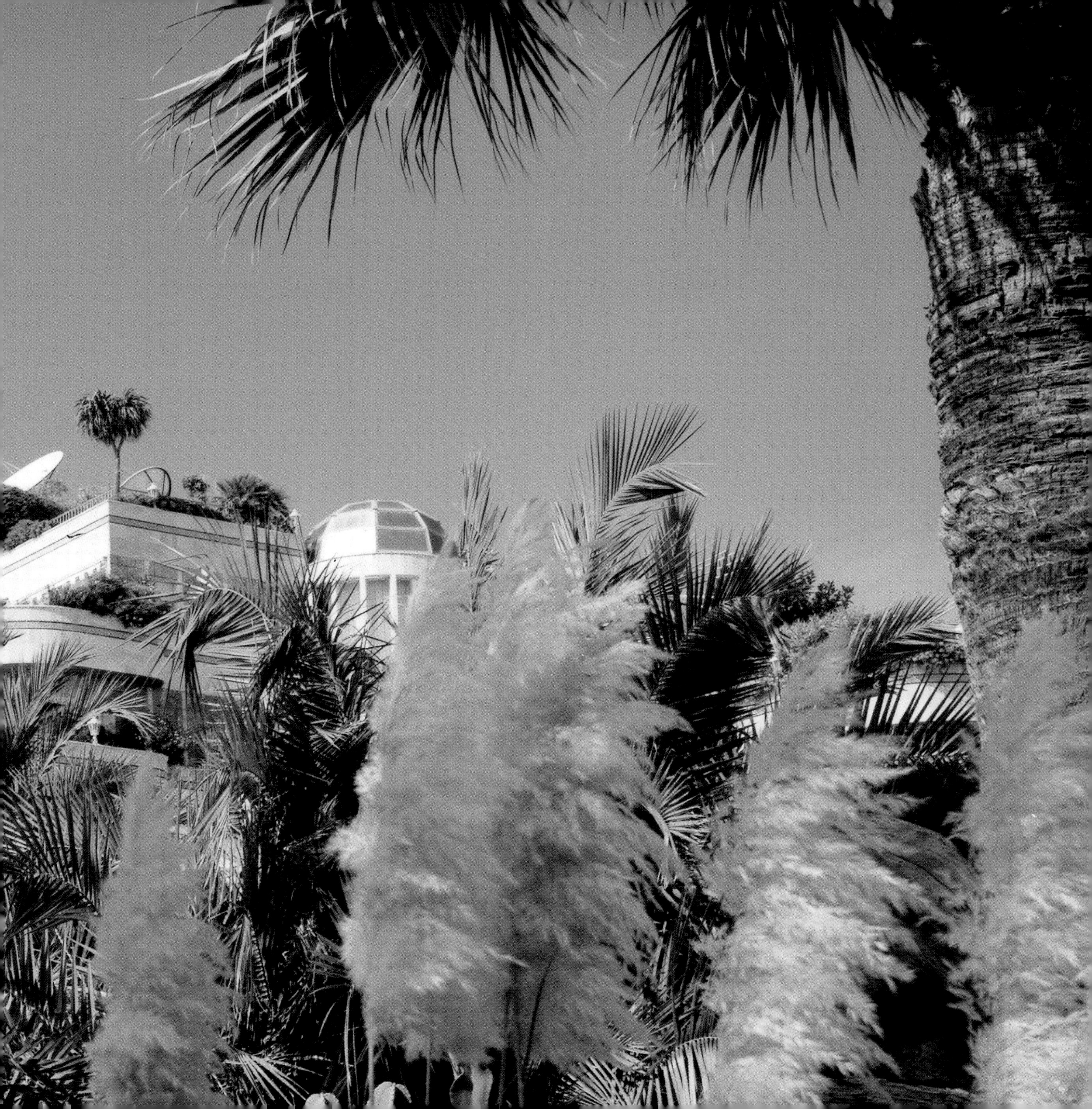

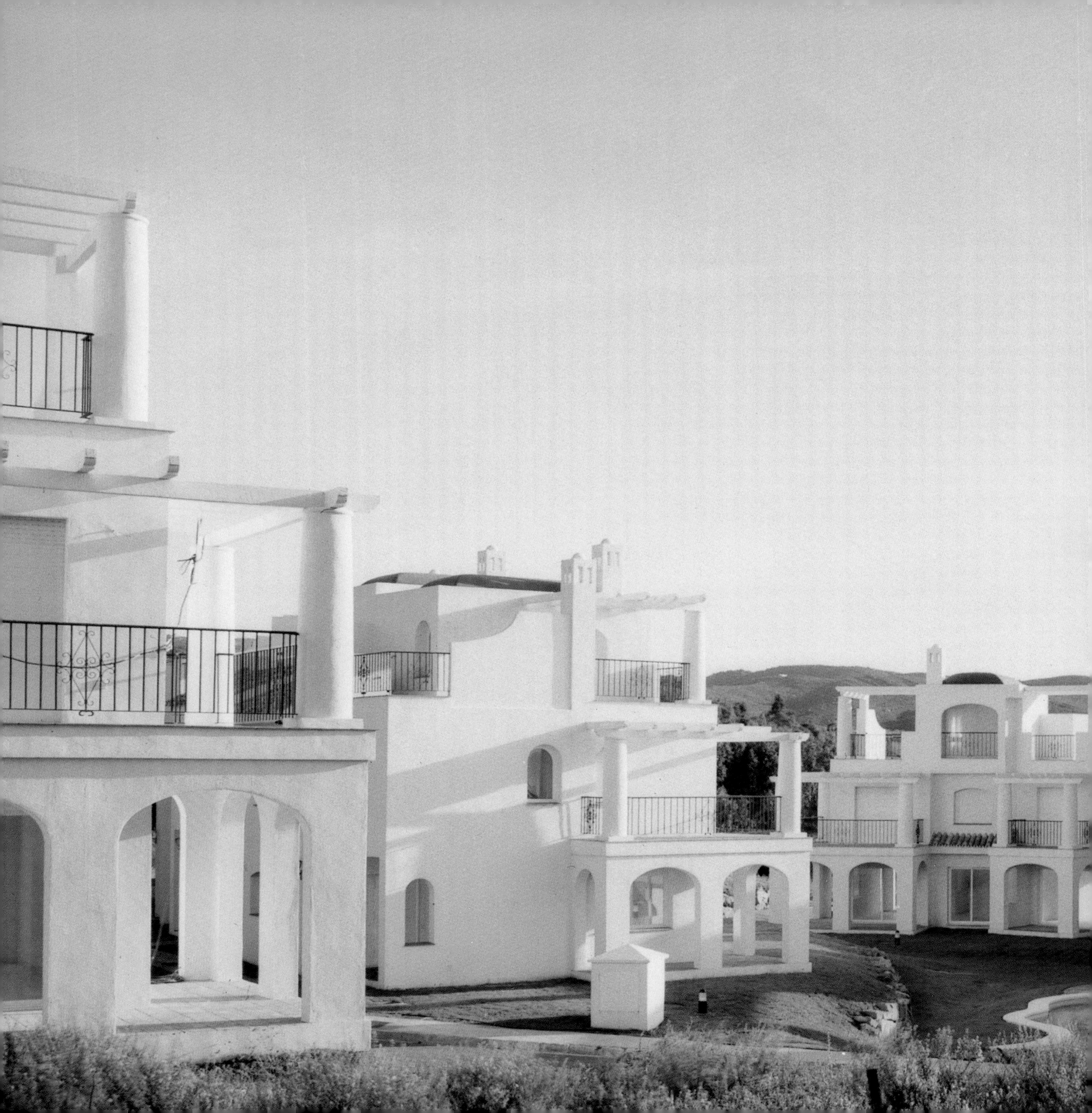

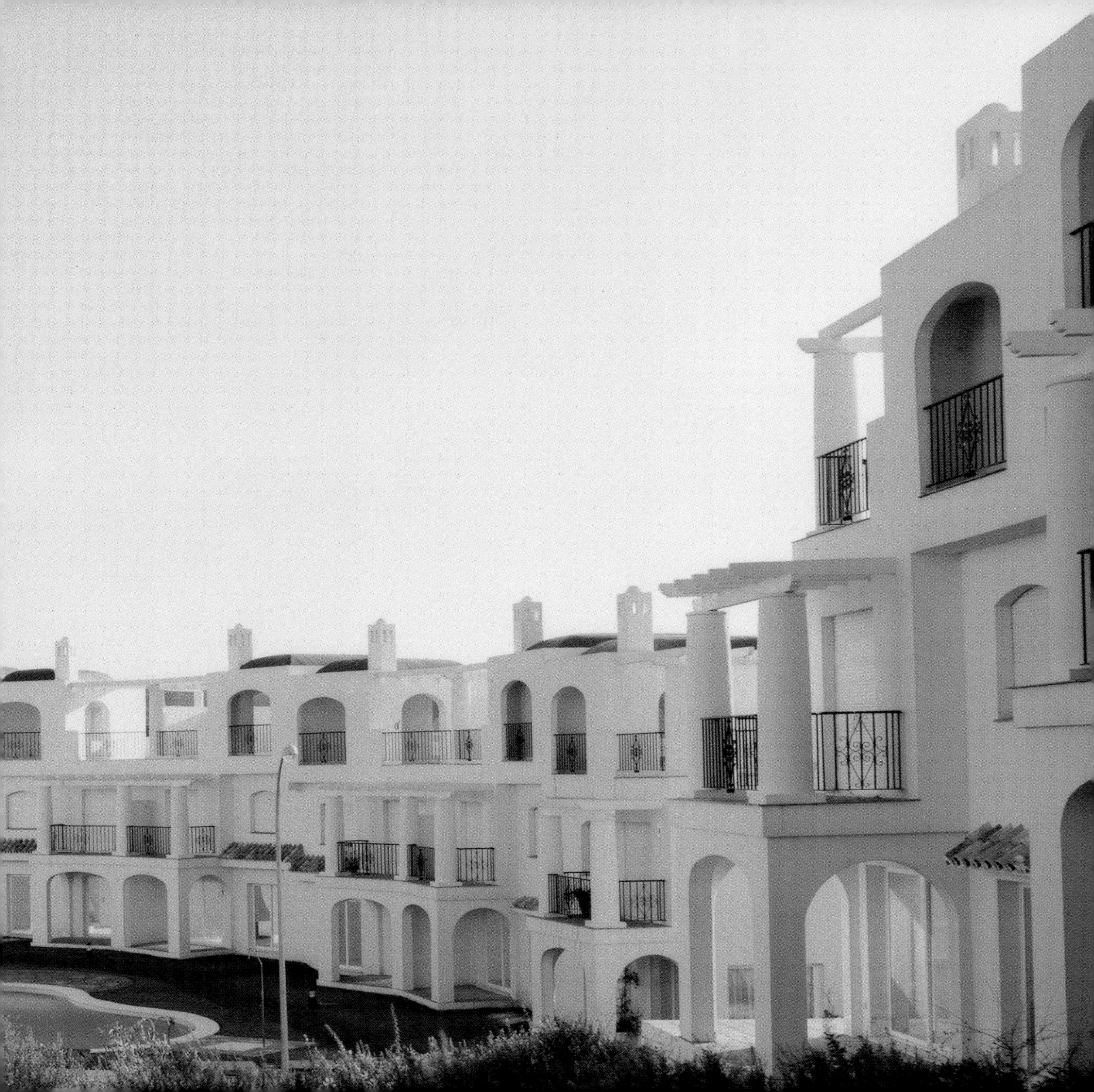

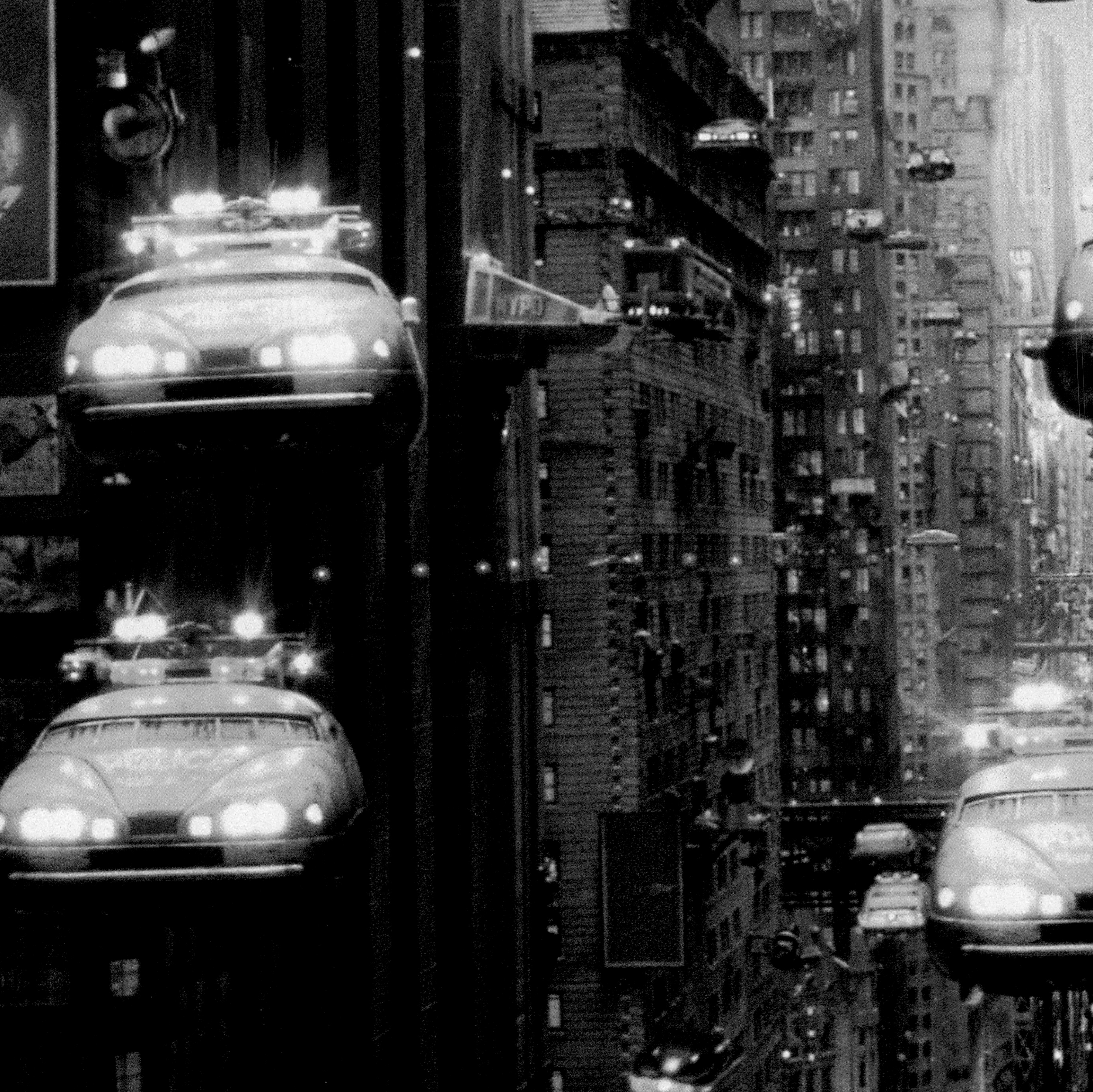

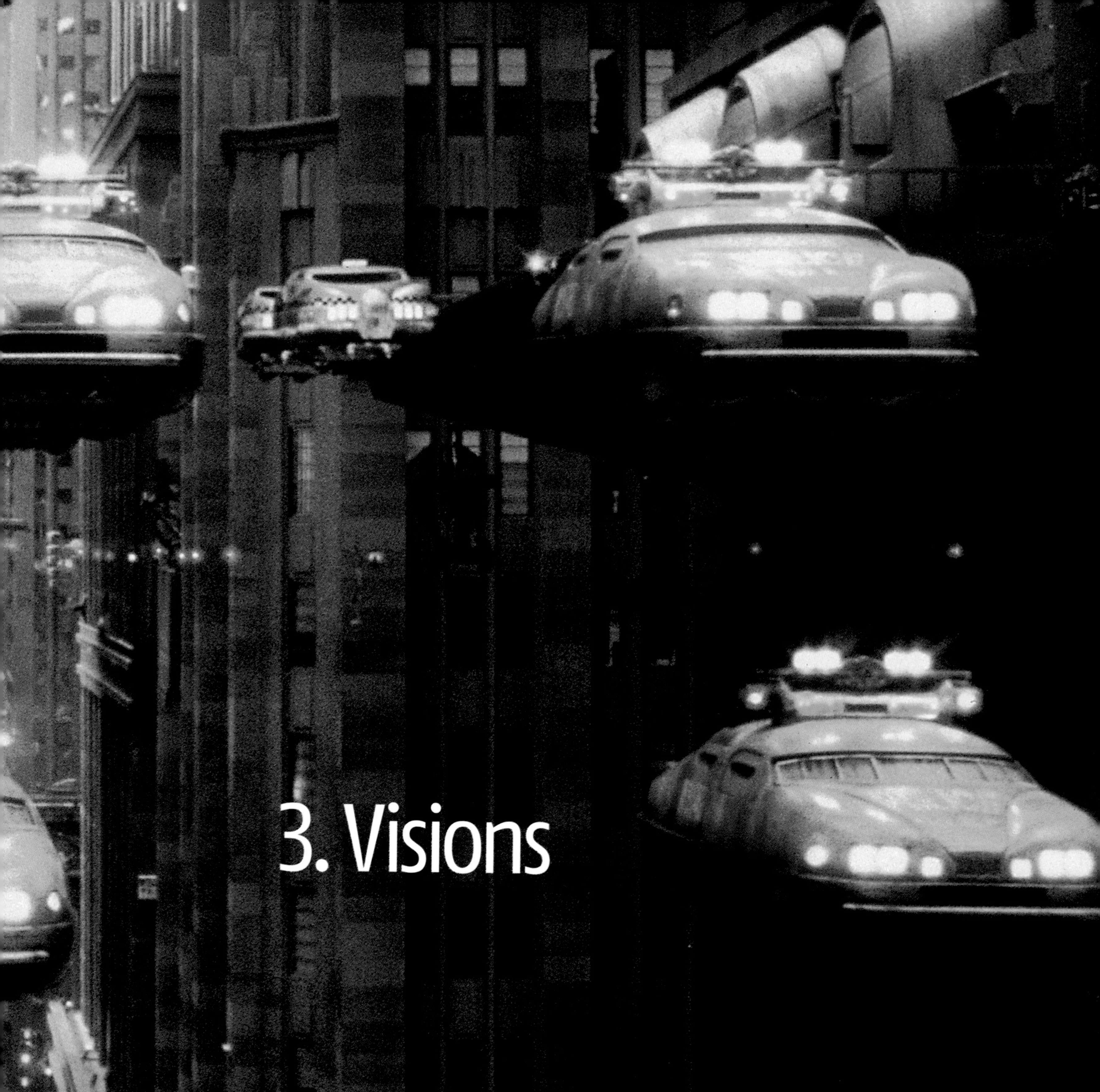

3. Visions

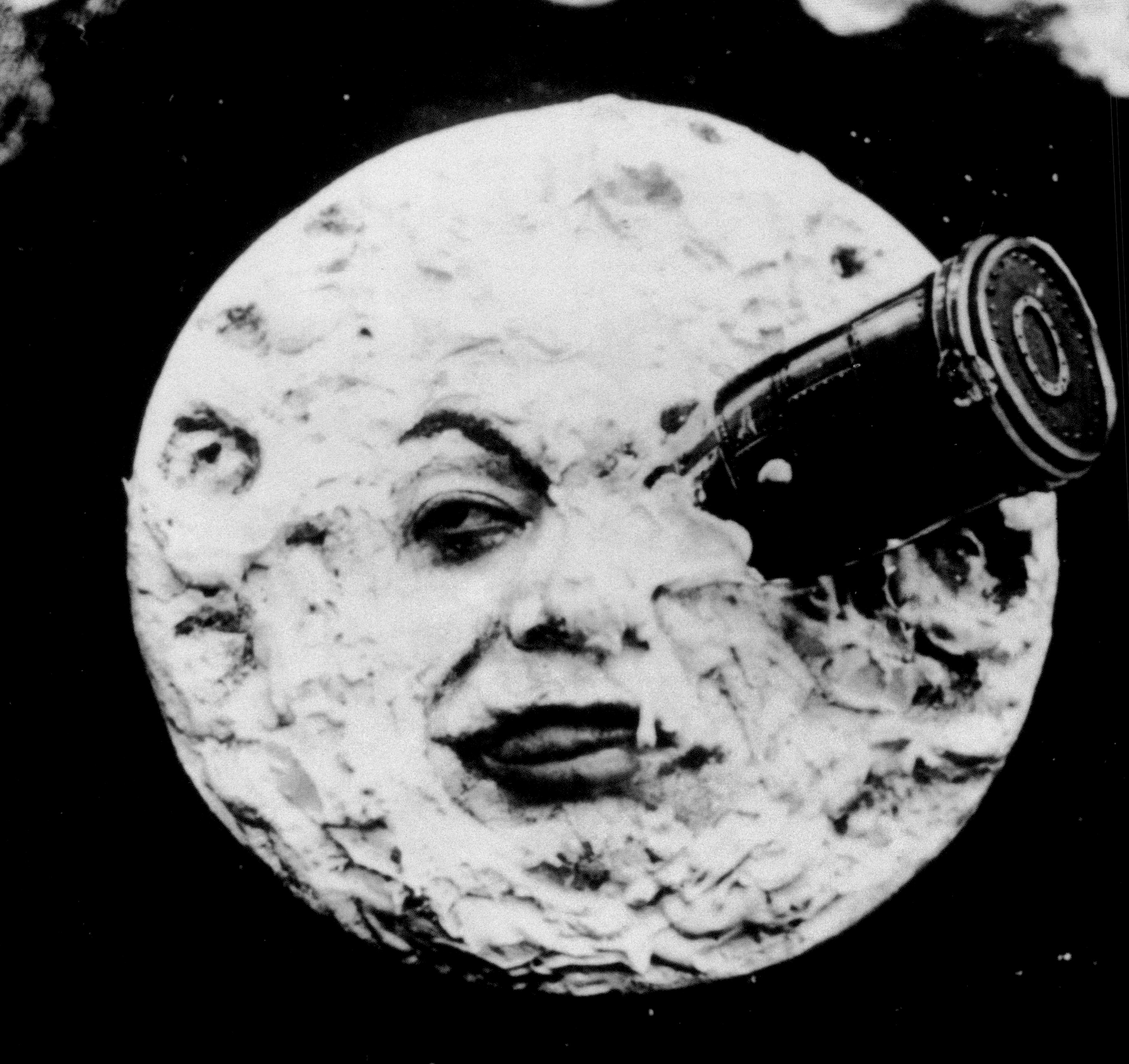

Utopia/Dystopia
Maureen Thomas

Miranda: O Wonder! How many goodly creatures are there here! How beauteous mankind is! O brave new world, that has such people in't!
The Tempest, William Shakespeare, Act V, Scene 1

'Moving pictures' on film only became viable in the late nineteenth century. As a narrative medium with a comparatively short history, film borrowed directly from the stage, drama and the novel (as well as from fairground shows and illusionism) from the first, and has continued to assimilate many literary and dramatic genres. In doing so, cinema has both developed new twists on old tales and brought into being original forms of its own.

In the movies, the two-dimensional screen becomes a place, a specific location, where the activity of the performance is carried out. This intrinsic characteristic of the form is fundamental to all its narrative modes, and applies to documentary as well as to drama in live action and to animation[1]. Because the medium itself is inherently visual (though sound is often an important element), locations have a particular specificity and detail which they do not have in novels or plays. Much of the screen narrator's art lies in joining one narrative space to another in a convincing and comprehensible way: the techniques of editing which developed in the first hundred years of film history are mostly explorations of how to take the audience smoothly from place to place on the screen (whether in detailed close-ups or comprehensive wide-shots) in a way which seems to make topographical sense, but which is in fact driven by the movie's dramatic action. The silver screen, the TV screen, a monitor displaying moving images from a computer: all are frames for illusory space, non-existent worlds – and for illusory travels through that space.

In the literature which informs early screen history, the usual term for a non-existent world is 'Utopia'. Etymologically, the term 'Utopia' (or 'Eutopia'), deriving from the Greek 'ou' – not – and 'topos' – place, should simply mean 'no place'. However, Sir Thomas More (Henry VIII's Master of Requests) gave the word a positive and idealistic connotation when he published in 1516 (in Latin) his influential political satire, *The Golden Book of the authentic excellent republican state exemplified in the new island of Utopia*. In his book, More describes the (in contrast to England) Perfect State found on the imaginary island of 'Utopia'. The book was successful, and popular in Europe. It was first printed, under the supervision of Erasmus, in Louvain, it also appeared in Paris and Basle, finally being translated into English, after More's death, by Ralph Robynson in 1551. Since then, in the English language the word 'Utopia' has meant a place 'ideally perfect in respect of laws, customs and conditions' (*Oxford English Dictionary*). Though its full title echoes Plato's *Republic*,

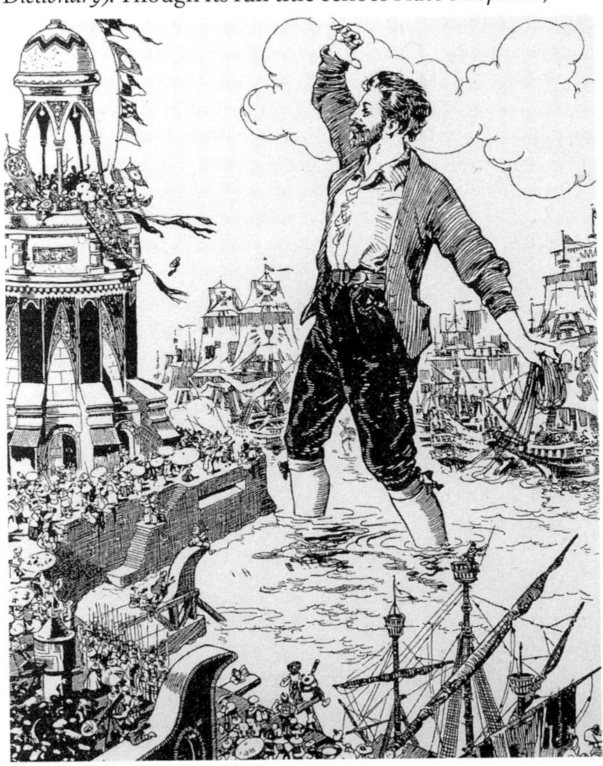

The tradition of fiction and fantasy in film-making began with George Méliès' *Le Voyage dans la lune (A Trip to the Moon)*, opposite, in 1902. A pioneer of trick and stop-motion photography, he made the first special-effects movie.

"Long live the most puissant Emperor of Lilliput!" Gulliver makes a conciliatory entrance to the royal port of Lilliput, above, while dragging the entire enemy fleet with one hand, in a 1918 edition of *Gulliver's Travels*.

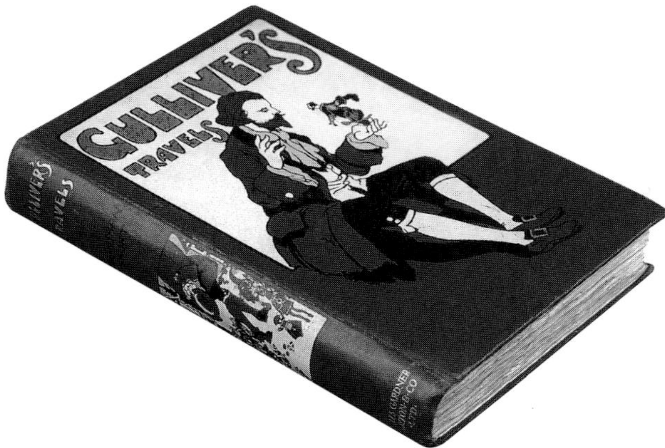

the form of More's book, where a (somewhat gullible) traveller comes upon and is amazed by a new world, was almost certainly inspired by the narrative of Amerigo Vespucci's voyages to the Americas, printed in 1507.

Since More's day, the form of socio-political satire where a traveller discovers a new, exotic world and finds in it light by which to judge more familiar environments, has become firmly rooted in European and American literary tradition. It includes such influential works as William Shakespeare's *The Tempest* (1611), Francis Bacon's *New Atlantis* (1626), Daniel Defoe's *Robinson Crusoe* (1719), Jonathan Swift's *Gulliver's Travels* (1726), Voltaire's *Candide* (1759), Samuel Johnson's *Rasselas, Prince of Abyssinia* (1759, published 1787 – no doubt inspired by his 1735 translation of Father Jerome Lobo's *Travels in Abyssinia*), to some extent Jean-Jacques Rousseau's *Emile* (1762), Jacques-Henri Bernadin de St Pierre's *Paul et Virginie* (1788), Samuel Butler's *Erewhon* (1872), William Morris's *News from Nowhere* (1891), H G Wells' *Time Machine* (1895), Charlotte Perkins Gilman's *Herland* (1915), Aldous Huxley's *Brave New World* (1936), George Orwell's *Nineteen Eighty Four* (1949), B F. Skinner's *Walden Two* (1949) and Philip K. Dick's *Do Androids Dream of Electric Sheep?* (1968).

It is striking that after the seventeenth century, the vein of dire warning begins to predominate. The majority of literary excursions into imaginary states that fall into the utopian genre – clearly reflecting the writers' own environment, caricatured and exaggerated to bring out the particular features they wish to comment upon – do not depict ideal states. They portray, on the contrary, societies where contemporary trends, particularly ugly ones, are pushed to their extreme, and the evil consequences of wicked behaviour are demonstrated. To describe this kind of literature, the word 'dystopia' (perhaps by analogy with 'dyspepsia', and alongside 'dysfunctional') was coined in the twentieth century, meaning the 'Far-from-ideal State'.

From the 1970s, the genre of 'adult fantasy' and science fiction literature started on an exponential growth curve, and utopian tales were its staple for the last three decades of the second millennium. Inspired by man's exploration of space, films of the 1960s already reflected this interest in distant, future, or conjectural worlds (often incorporating a strong technological bias), with adaptations of novels such as Ray Bradbury's *Fahrenheit 451* (1954), filmed by François Truffaut in 1966, and of the work of graphic novelists, such as Jean-Claude Forest, who inspired Roger Vadim's *Barbarella* (1968), providing models for original movies in the 1980s and 1990s.
Like Thomas More, Terry Southern, who wrote the script for *Barbarella*, once thought he had a vocation for the priesthood. Fictional Utopias are created by people whose ethical consciousness yearns to reach a wide

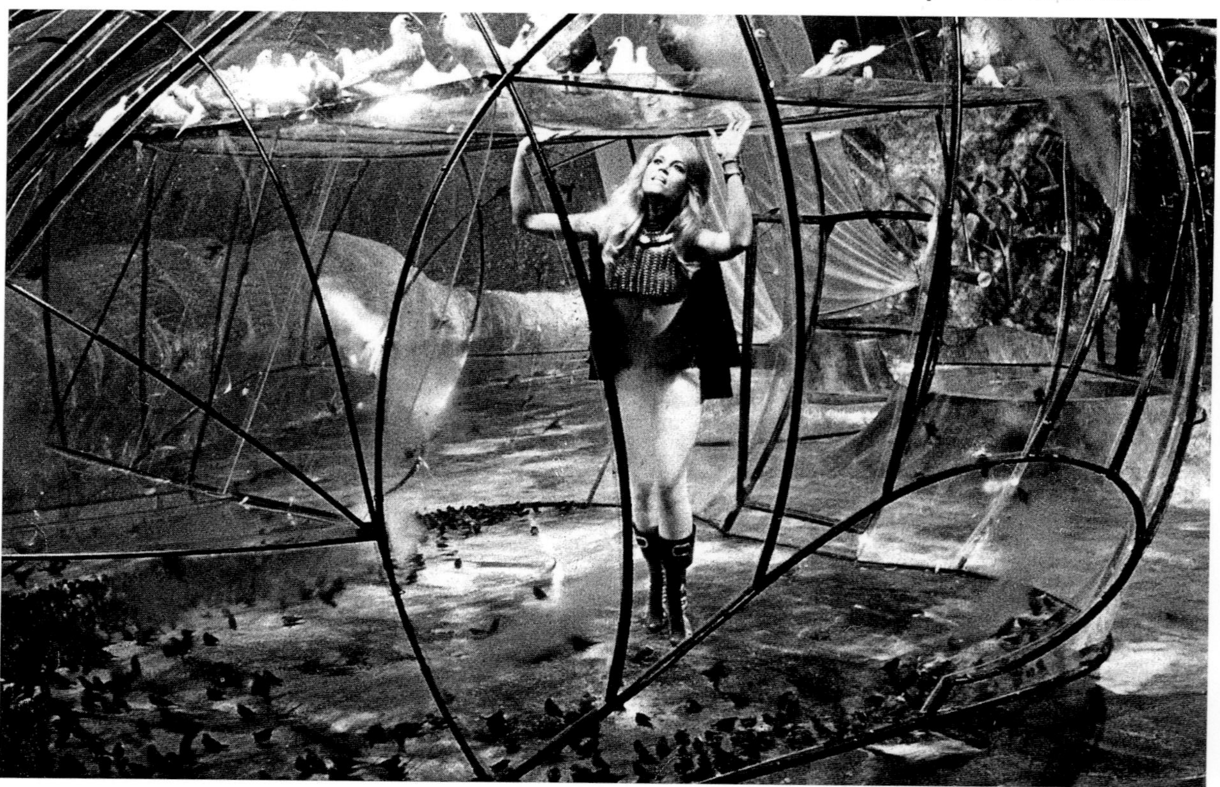

audience, and warn of the perils of this-earthly ways.

Thomas More's original Utopia was a state where cities are not allowed to grow beyond certain limits, where education is universal, all religions are tolerated, a national welfare service cares for the sick in hospitals, and the economy is not based on money. Greed for wealth does not exist. Rousseau's educational ideals in *Emile*, where healthy intellectual, spiritual and moral development is related to 'natural' man rather than his 'civilised' counterpart, also reflects the optimism of the original European American Dream; of a world, like Crusoe's or Prospero's, where the corruption of an old, hierarchical (European) system might be discarded and replaced with new (more democratic) values. Inspiring this vision was the contemporary discovery of the 'Noble Savage', the inhabitant of a remote place whose assumedly innate morality owed nothing to knowledge of Christianity and Original Sin, and who provided a phenomenon to be wondered at; who awoke ideas of idyllic and harmonious social living, untainted by the sins dogging urban, money-based economies. Pride, wrath, sloth, gluttony, and above all lust, envy and avarice – in *Utopia*, the author is ashamed to admit that these prevail in 'civilised' England, in contrast to the 'savage' island described by the traveller, Raphael. In the fiction, Raphael is one of 24 men left behind in South America by Vespucci. Fiction or not, the Seven Deadly Sins – or perhaps rather the vices which embody them – are the moral enormities which the sensitive social imagination longs to cleanse away from the Old World, and replace with Utopian virtues inspired by the New.

The voyage to Utopia and its exploration, the discovery there of a brave new world of unexpected people and novel landscapes, presents itself at once as an obviously attractive genre for cinematic narrative. The Silver Screen could provide a window upon any number of new worlds, exotic though 'real' or 'natural', and equally if not more exotic when created in studios using special effects. Georges Méliès quickly seized upon the idea of travel to a strange new world for one of his most popular and enduring movies, *Voyage to the Moon* (1902), one of the earliest narrative motion pictures. People are shown travelling through space and landing on the moon, where they deal with unexpected conditions, all seen through a haze of studio-produced lunar mist. But the heroic journey of discovery in itself – though a much-loved story form, and one which has generated some glorious screen worlds, such as that of Don Chaffey's *Jason and the Argonouts* (1963) – has a slightly different and less provocative cinematic power than does the journey to a Utopia/Dystopia.

While many films are screen adaptations of books or plays, the structure of the epic tale, in which a hero or heroes' journey (actual or metaphorical) through strange and challenging realms (physical and/or psychological) on their quest for the beautiful princess, for the talisman that will save the world, and for the right ending, is older than any written version we may find. According to Joseph Campbell – author of *The Hero with a Thousand Faces* (published in 1948, and American movie-makers Spielberg and Lucas's book of inspiration) – this genre is indeed older, possibly, than tale-telling itself, perhaps as old as the ritual performance of myth, or of the human psyche's need for individuation. The hero-journey tale underpins most of the American movies whose conventions dominate the Western world at the beginning of the

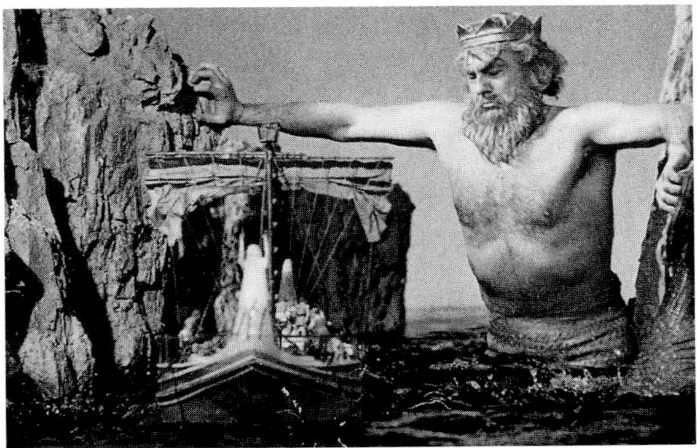

Roger Vadim tried to use Terry Southern's screenplay for *Barbarella* as a vehicle in which to mould his new young wife, Jane Fonda, opposite, into another Brigitte Bardot. The kitsch comic-book effect derived partly from Southern's interest in graphic novels and their fascination during the 1960s with space exploration.

Five years earlier, in 1963, Don Chaffey's cult classic *Jason and the Argonauts*, above, was a fantasy based on Greek mythology its allegorical power enhanced by Ray Harryhausen's fabulous special effects. Like many other utopian films, the narrative is driven by its hero's journey of discovery, and self-discovery.

twenty-first century, and it is used to tell screen stories with varying levels of allegorical or symbolic significance.

In Don Chaffey's film *Jason and the Argonauts*, the hero travels through an overtly archetypal, mythical landscape populated with larger than life creatures as he completes his quest for the Golden Fleece, and finds the wise and beautiful Medea. In the subtext, it is here that Jason learns about himself and how to be a leader, as well as about the environment where he is to rule. In episode one of the *Star Wars* saga (George Lucas, 1977), Luke Skywalker performs his epic part in the age-old Oedipal Myth in an Outer Space penetrated by black holes and populated by robots, large chitinous insects and beasties – the late-twentieth century counterpart of the Homerian landscape depicted by Chaffey, which is enlivened by the clashing rocks Schylla and Charybdis, Talos the Man of Brass, and the unstoppable skeletal Myrmidon warriors. In this film from 1962, the fabulous beasts, the Gods on Olympus who steer the mortal game of Jason's adventures and many other wonders were all realised through Ray Harryhausen's innovative filmic special effects. Like the robots, spacecraft and creatures given digital life in *Star Wars: A New Hope* in 1977, they rely on spectacle and danger, rather than moral analysis or social comment, for their impact, though they certainly provide the audience with that direct and essential cinematic pleasure – the voyage through the screen to Wonderland. However, social comment and ethical perspectives are a fundamental necessity to Utopias and Dystopias – and this is what makes these 'impossible worlds' so engaging, and enduring on the screen. Adventures don't just happen against the backdrop of an exotic location – the settings are an integral element, as they are in *Gulliver's Travels* (adapted for the screen in 1995 by British writer Simon Moore and director Charles Sturridge). Here, following Swift's lead, the environment where the story/drama unfolds is a moral, as well as a psychological and physical landscape, created by set design, lighting and camerawork – whether 'real' or 'virtual'. In the novel, this is a world of the imagination, existing nowhere but between the pages of a book. Cinema took up the challenge of making such worlds visible early on – making them real, at least, within the frame of the screen – and has pursued it triumphantly ever since. It is the tradition of creating environments which express not an objective world, but a world tinged with memory, longing, loss, regret, redemption, passion, fulfilment, love and hope that informs production design at its most exhilarating, that allows it to generate the creations of the mind, by they utopian or dystopian. These impossible worlds of the screen are built from emotion and ethical perspective, their architecture is about connotation, resonance and significance – their functionality is poetic rather than material.

Some late twentieth-century films, such as the Wachowski Brothers' cyber-fantasy *The Matrix* (1999) or Alex Proyas' adventure thriller *Dark City* (1998), are direct offspring of Huxley's *Brave New World* (1936), even though both these films were written originally as movies, and not derived from novels at all. They are not just epic adventures, but adventures where an innocent outsider finds himself entering an unknown universe and in so doing reveals the true moral nature both of himself and of his fellows. These late-twentieth century 'impossible' screen worlds are hidden beyond the everyday world, in folds of time, parallel universes or virtualities, which have to be reached by a dangerous journey through some other dimension – just as More's *Utopia*, Johnson's *Abyssinia* or Shakespeare's isle in *The Tempest* had to be reached by long and arduous voyages. This difficulty of approach is not merely a geographical or topographical one – it signifies moral toil, testing the worthiness and developing the spiritual stamina of the adventurer, whilst setting up a contrast between the domain we have left (and which we know) and the unfamiliar domain we enter. One of the earliest and most enduring movies to stage such an allegorical quest is Victor Fleming's musical, designed by Cedric Gibbons, *The Wizard of Oz* (1939), in which Dorothy (Judy Garland), after struggling her way through

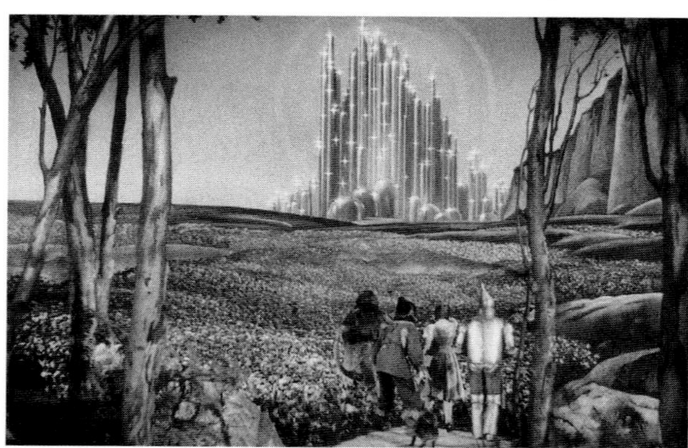

Dorothy's journey along the yellow brick road to the Emerald City, right, while conquering some self-doubts along the way, is a moral journey which has been a hit with millions of goal-oriented Americans year after year. Made in 1939, the film version of *The Wizard of Oz* has proved much more enduring than the childrens' book which inspired it, as much thanks to the messages carried by its set designs as to its acting performances. Ultimately, the Emerald City only provides a utopian vision until Dorothy has discovered her inner strength and can return to a life of true happiness in her Kansas home.

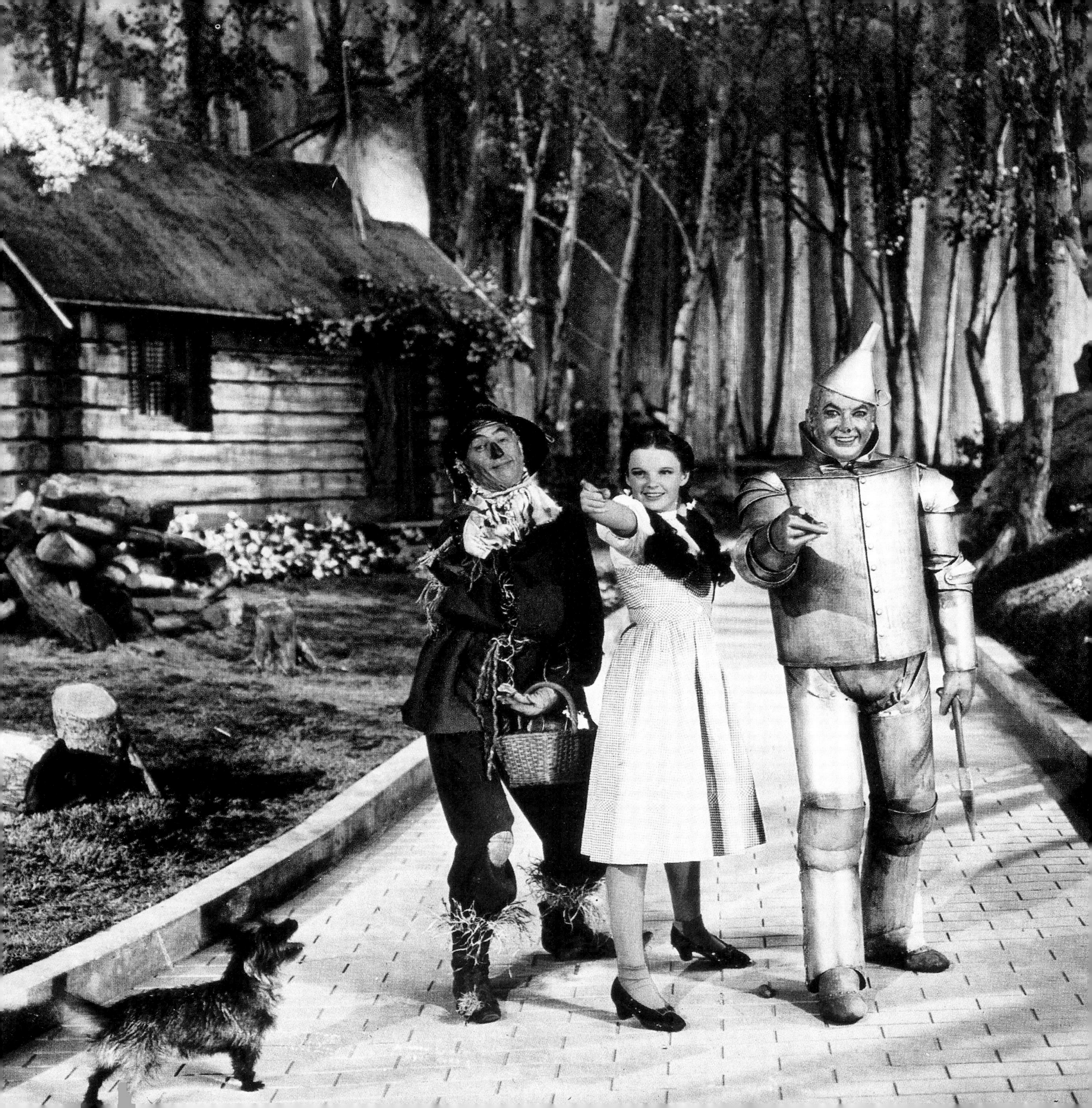

the desert, is whirled in a hurricane from a Kansas farm to the Land of Oz. Here Dorothy and the companions who join her along the Yellow Brick Road have to find the Wizard, in order to gain the qualities they need to make them complete, and eventually find their way home. This film is based on a children's book (the traditional locus for nineteenth-century fantasy), but it is the movie, not the book, which has become the modern classic, and which directly inspires *The Matrix* – 'Buckle your seat-belt, Dorothy – 'cos Kansas is goin' bye-bye,' are the last words its hero, Neo (Keanu Reeves), hears as he is strapped into a chair and his brain is 'jacked in', ready for his first trajectory into cyberspace.

Cedric Gibbons' landscape of Oz unashamedly and exuberantly exploits the emotional resonances of primary colours, with giant flowers of a size only the tiniest beings (the ones we all see ourselves as when we are children) could experience. It deftly creates the improbably colourful and smooth lines of the Wizard's 'Futurist' Emerald City, where life is an endless merry carnival varied by spine-chilling illusions. It revels in the dark, scary wood inhabited by animate trees, culminating in the mock-gothic halls of the Wicked Witch of the West's goblin-haunted castle. Starting from the world of childhood memories, fears and longings, Gibbons brilliantly deploys the elaborate repertoire of shapes, colours, light and astonishing illusions which are the stock in trade of the theatrical designer, already highly developed on the stage of the nineteenth century (and returning to favour in the late twentieth century with theatrical musical extravaganzas such as Disney's stage version of *Beauty and the Beast* – whose design in fact owes a great deal to Jean Cocteau's black and white film made in France in 1946). The form of the musical as well as the subject matter of the children's tale allow Fleming, director of *The Wizard of Oz*, to revel in a non-naturalistic visual style and to flaunt, for the colour/sound movie-screen, like a fairground showman, the fact that this is not a real world, but a fantasy world composed of screen magic in which characters can walk from solid-looking three-dimensional sets into impossibly infinite landscapes of bright blossoms and unwinking sunshine where literally anything can happen. The illusionist invites the audience to enjoy the knowledge that this is an illusion, conjured up for their entertainment. The world has the safety of a game, staged by a master, as well as the thrill and mystery of dream – an altogether more dangerous entity.

But the film *The Wizard of Oz* endures not just because it is spectacular and enchanting, or because it allows the audience to leave behind a humdrum reality in favour of a more brightly-coloured, more sensuous, more exotic screen world, but because the landscape Dorothy enters is a moral one. Its extraordinary visual qualities alone would provide a novelty rapidly experienced and discarded – but in fact they are not merely visuals, they are visuals which are inspired by, and embody with consummate artistry, a meaning. The yellow brick road of her hopeful innocence leads Dorothy through the gloom of fear and self-doubt, and in the end, fellow-feeling, moral integrity, ambition and courage triumph (as we know they will for every goal-oriented, Protestant American). Shams are shown up for what they are: the tricky inventions of the Futurist city of Oz, where roads and a press of hurrying vehicles predominate, prove to be nothing but illusions. The chief scientist, the paternal Wizard himself, turns out to be a charlatan and illusionist, and Kansas, with its farmland and family values, is revealed as the place to which we, like Dorothy, really want to get home to in the end. The Emerald City – urbane, sophisticated, scientific – is, for all its enchantment, in its way a Dystopia – and bright as Oz may seem, this 1939 movie shows that the land of childhood (curiously intertwined with the realm of Futurism and technology) can only be Utopian while it serves its purpose: that of helping human beings to grow up with steadfastness, courage, generosity and uprightness, so they can learn finally to leave Oz behind them, and go back to a culture rooted in the land, with its straightforward values. Could Kansas be populated by a

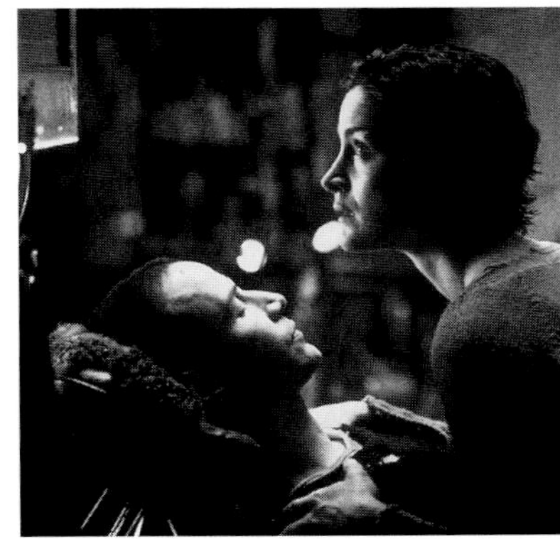

species of noble savage, a transparency for the Americas revealed by Vespucci to Europe in 1507?

The Land of Oz is the kind of impossible world the screen is uniquely able to achieve – a world where the physical location is a set, designed to bring out emotional, psychological and ethical values – an illusion, sustained through lighting, camera-work, mise en scene (staging for the camera) and editing, which effortlessly shows us the landscape of our collective moral imagination. In 1999, sixty years after *The Wizard of Oz*, the designer of *The Matrix*, Owen Paterson, transports the techniques used by Cedric Gibbons, who mixes 'real' three-dimensional shots with forced perspective and illusionist two-dimensional shots, into the digital age. He borrows three-dimensional illusions from the interactive computer adventure-game ubiquitous at the beginning of the twenty-first century to carry the hero into a screen world where characters can morph from one 'reality' into another and manifest as one 'avatar' or another. In the world of *The Matrix*, electronic technology has become so powerful that the vital energy of human beings is siphoned off to fuel the 'life' of robotic insect creatures. It is another urban Dystopia, one, like the Land of Oz, which is insidiously attractive despite its dangers – whose colours and sounds and experiences of power are greater than those you can achieve in your own body and context, a country where the mind can truly make a heaven of hell – or a hell of heaven (as Satan in Milton's seventeenth-century epic poem, *Paradise Lost*, suggests).

The Matrix works on the topos of the fearful dichotomy between 'meat' (the human body) and the cybermind, the jacked-in human brain communicating directly through biochips with the computer and other 'pure' intelligences, using infinite instantaneous electronic networks to amplify mental activity, bypassing the puny human flesh that contains it – a theme powerfully and influentially articulated by William Gibson in his novels from *Neuromancer* (1984) onwards. The world of *The Matrix* is a true Dystopia, containing its own shadow twin, the illusory Utopia, in which the unseeing human victims of the grand digital scam pass their stress-free lives. Like More comparing England, mired in sin as a result of its submission to greed for wealth, with Utopia's eugenic but nobly liberated aspiration towards universal welfare, in *The Matrix* the Wachowski Brothers compare the world of cyber-vision and effortless control with the cumbersome and chaotic world the late-twentieth century audience knows from everyday experience, but which in the film is revealed to be the illusion, not the reality (a topos perhaps first thoroughly explored in Philip K Dick's novel of paranoia from 1969, *Ubik*). The audience of *The Matrix* is asked to question its own moral and ethical values in day-

Made sixty years after *The Wizard of Oz*, *The Matrix* (USA, 1999) employs precisely the same device of a utopian/dystopian world into which its hero Neo (Keanu Reeves), above, must travel in order to bring out part of himself which will otherwise remain hidden. New computer graphics technology makes an impossible world seem terrifyingly plausible.

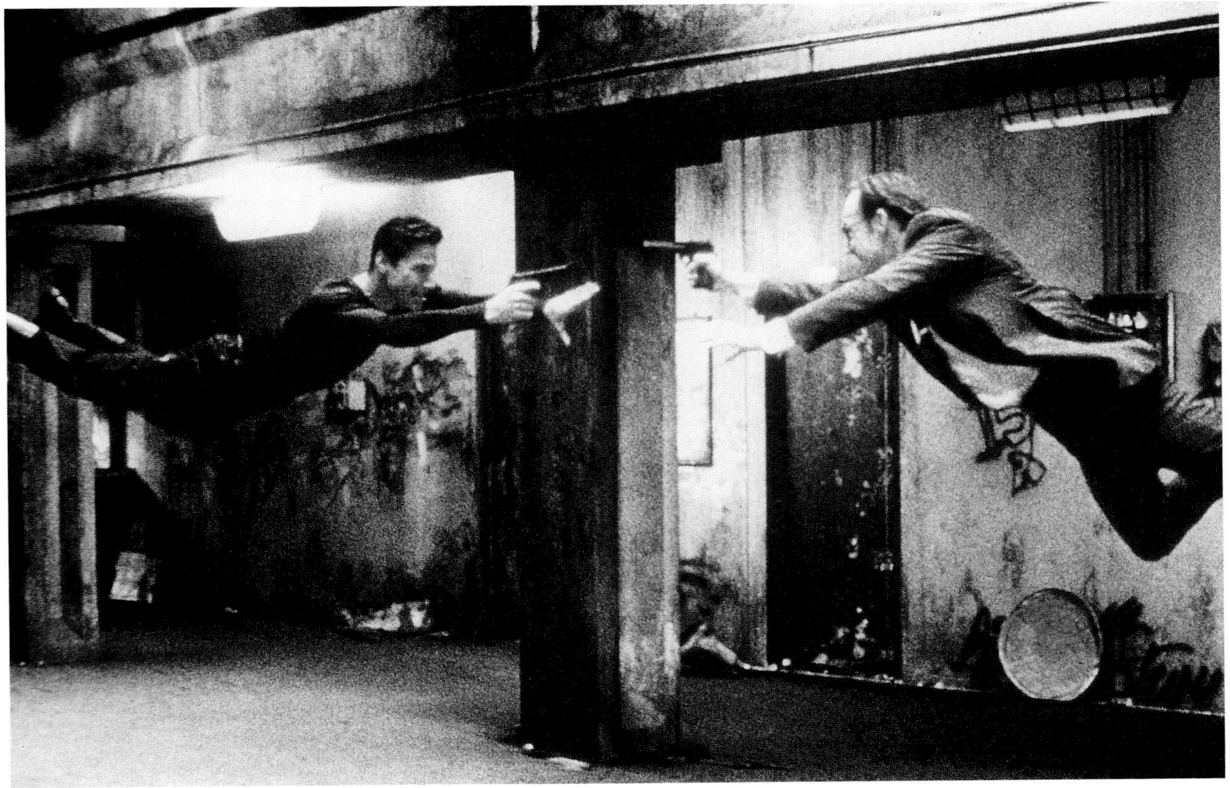

to-day life, its own position vis-à-vis electronic technologies, whilst enjoying an epic adventure. *Brave New World* is not far away, and *The Matrix* makes it clear, rather like the Emotional Engineer (Newspeak for writer or artist) in Huxley's story, that computers are not good or bad – but if the people who use them are impelled towards unethical or ignoble behaviour, electronics can certainly provide the power to amplify the consequences to a terrifying level. The bright and dark corridors of power and despair which form the set for the moral action of the drama are designed to emphasise this underlying issue. But the world of *The Matrix* can only actually be achieved in moving image and sound media, the adventure could not happen without digitally-generated visual effects – this particular message could not be delivered in any other way. *The Wizard of Oz* adapted the literary tale of the spiritual journey and made a transference of stage techniques to the two-dimensional cinema screen, extending them through film special effects, joining glass paintings and other two-dimensional backgrounds seamlessly to three-dimensional studio spaces. *The Matrix* goes farther, generating parts of the screen world inside a computer, so that they live only as moving images transferred directly from the mind of the authors through a digital generator to the two-dimensional cinema screen.

Alex Proyas does something similar in his *Dark City* (1998), a highly cine-literate work which looks back to many movies, including Fritz Lang's *Metropolis* (1927), a film which has provided architectural inspiration for many production designers, and to Chris Marker's *La Jetée* (1963) – which also inspired Terry Gilliam's *Twelve Monkeys* (1995) – as well as to the Utopia/Dystopia literary tradition of Wells' *Time Machine*. In *Dark City*, the hero, John Murdoch, is again an innocent who accidentally visits a world that is hidden from his dreaming fellows. The element of chance, which may be destiny in disguise, is often important in the Utopian tale: the traveller is storm-tossed off course, or stumbles upon the entrance to the new world by accident. Here Murdoch negotiates an environment which brings together the worlds of the two-dimensional screen and the three-dimensional navigable computer adventure-game, realisable only in the domain of moving images, using digital effects. The human race, living in a hyperdense urban congeries, is under threat from aliens who have discovered that humanity has something they want for survival – and they are trying to identify exactly what that is. With the help of a human psychiatrist (an unwilling collaborator), the aliens experiment with extracting and interchanging people's memories in an attempt to filter out the essence of humanity. By putting memory in the foreground, the film focuses attention on the significance of the human

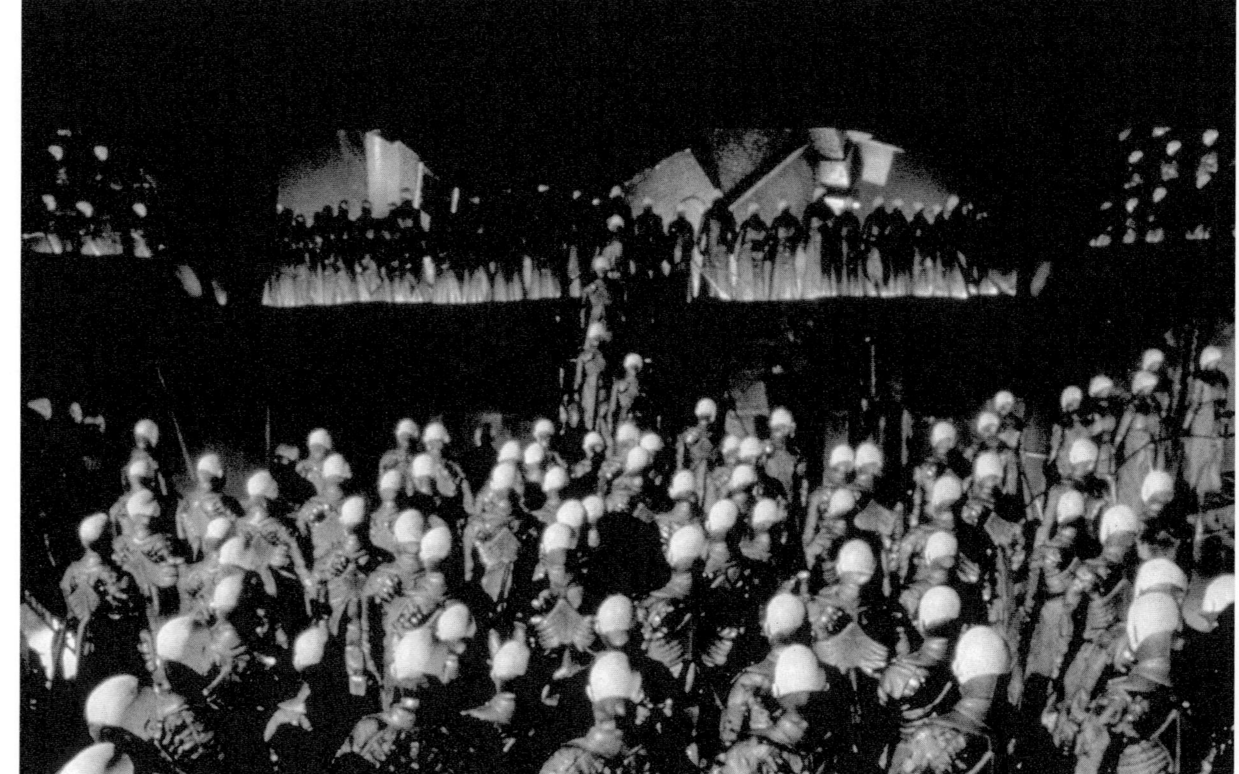

concept of time. The hero resists treatment and becomes able, like the aliens, to function in an environment without time, in the space between the seconds where his fellow humans hang in suspended animation. The concept of near-simultaneous (timeless) activity, an astonishing speed of transmission, apprehension and processing of information, where transactions are measured in nanoseconds (a conceptual framework brought to prominence by electronic communications and data processing) provides a groundbase for this film in the same way as it does for *The Matrix*. And computer life is here clearly shown as dystopian for human beings – the last line spoken by *Dark City's* hero summing up the message: humanity needs human memory, imbued with sensual and emotional significance, for personality and love – memory is not the same as data storage, understanding not the same as data processing, and only aliens, incapable of faith, hope and charity, can confuse the two. Who exactly are these faceless aliens in their long dark overcoats and Homburg hats, the audience is left asking itself? How close to us are they?

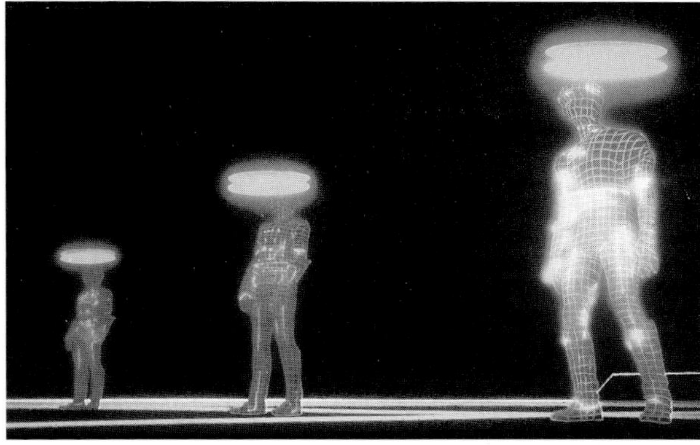

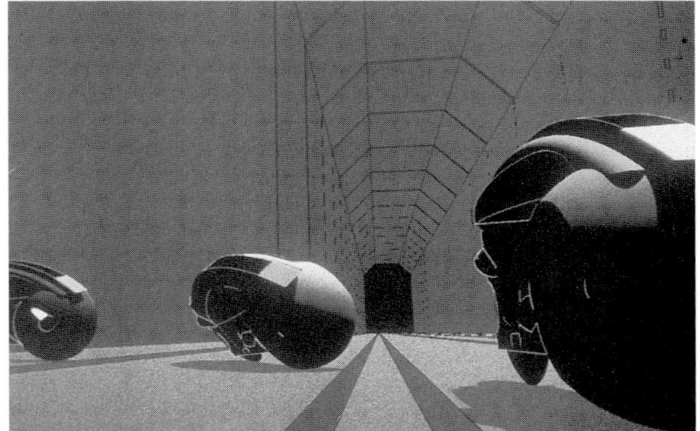

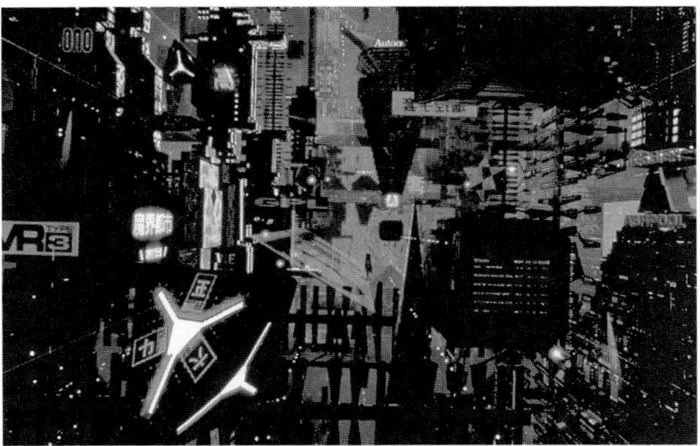

Ever since the hero of *Tron* (1982), right top and centre, embarked on an adventurous journey in a groundbreaking visualisation of cyberspace, computer games have influenced the look and feel of on-screen worlds like *Dark City* (1998), opposite, and *Johnny Mnemonic* (1997), bottom.

The visual possibilities in screen worlds for transitions from the 'meat' realm to the cyber domain were already clear in the 1980s, and first realised in Steven Lisberger/Disney's *Tron* (1982) – an adventure within an adventure, combining groundbreaking computer animation with live action, where a human being takes on the characteristics of his own software program to inhabit and infiltrate the computer-mind which is planning to supersede control and intervention by fallible humans. Rather than mixing real and animated characters in an animated environment, as *Tron* does, Robert Longo's *Johnny Mnemonic* (1997, from a cyberdrama script by William Gibson) offers, like *The Matrix* and *Dark City*, some stunning constructions combining physical and virtual sets as the locus for live action. In its movie ancestor, Ridley Scott's *Blade Runner* (1982, adapted from Dick's *Do Androids Dream of Electric Sheep?*), designer Lawrence G Paull created a future Dystopia by conflating characteristics of major dense twentieth-century cities (Los Angeles, Hong Kong, New York) with actual props and furnishings from the twentieth century, only minimally modified to create a slightly evolved look. *Johnny Mnemonic* plays on the ubiquitous late-twentieth century urban landscapes of inner city decay to create a mud-spattered lo-tech 'future' hinterland, against which the inhumanity of the multinational corporate technology-based informationocracy stands out immaculate, stark, almost omnipotent, and grim. Here, the social and political criticism is still – just as it was in Thomas More's book in 1551 – directed against the destructive and self-destructive force of greed for money,

The city which plays host to Bruce Willis in *The Fifth Element* (1995), right, is a carefully crafted parody of a New York of the future, which has become so densely populated that nearly all its open spaces have been taken over by flying vehicles, and sleep takes place in mortuary-style cubicles controlled by Gaultier-clad women.

which in the hi-tech culture equals information (not quite knowledge), which in turn equals power. Gibson's story plots how the glamour of wealth and power drags the underprivileged into its deathly wake, as it makes its inexorable progress through human history, distorting values and spreading disloyalty and weakness like a virus. In *Johnny Mnemonic*, there is a classic element of redemption, acted out through Johnny's relationship with the girl, Anna, and underlined by the dolphin whose intelligence helps solve the ultimate puzzle of the movie. Girl and dolphin, capable of affection, kindness, loyalty and love, provide the dystopian hero with 'shadow twins', who throw the evil of flourishing gangster morality in the luxurious circles of technopower into even more vivid and menacing relief. Addiction, danger, dealing for high profits (whether the commodity is drugs as we know them or electronically coded information), the moral message is clear – there is seduction in power, abuse and violence are common and easily escalate, and only the traditional redeeming values as advocated by Thomas More – integrity, faith, hope, charity and loving thy neighbour as thyself – offer a positive outlook. The material culture of Johnny Mnemonic's world (designed by Nilo Rodis Janero) is rapidly submerging in an urban squalor of discarded electronic parts, reminiscent of the ruined landscape bristling with the overthrown rusting hulks of useless steam engines and other indestructible machines, abandoned by those who recognise their destructive potential, described by Samuel Butler in his 1872 book *Erewhon* (an anagram of 'nowhere'). In *Johnny Mnemonic*, too, the impossible world of the screen offers a foretaste of the all too possible dystopian world towards which twenty-first century electronics-based culture may be propelling itself, if – the film implies – left by the ignorant in the hands of the unscrupulous.

The late-twentieth century dystopian 'impossible' screen worlds of *The Matrix*, *Dark City* and *Johnny Mnemonic* come out of a lively and colourful cinematic tradition, ranging back through Luc Besson's fantastic the

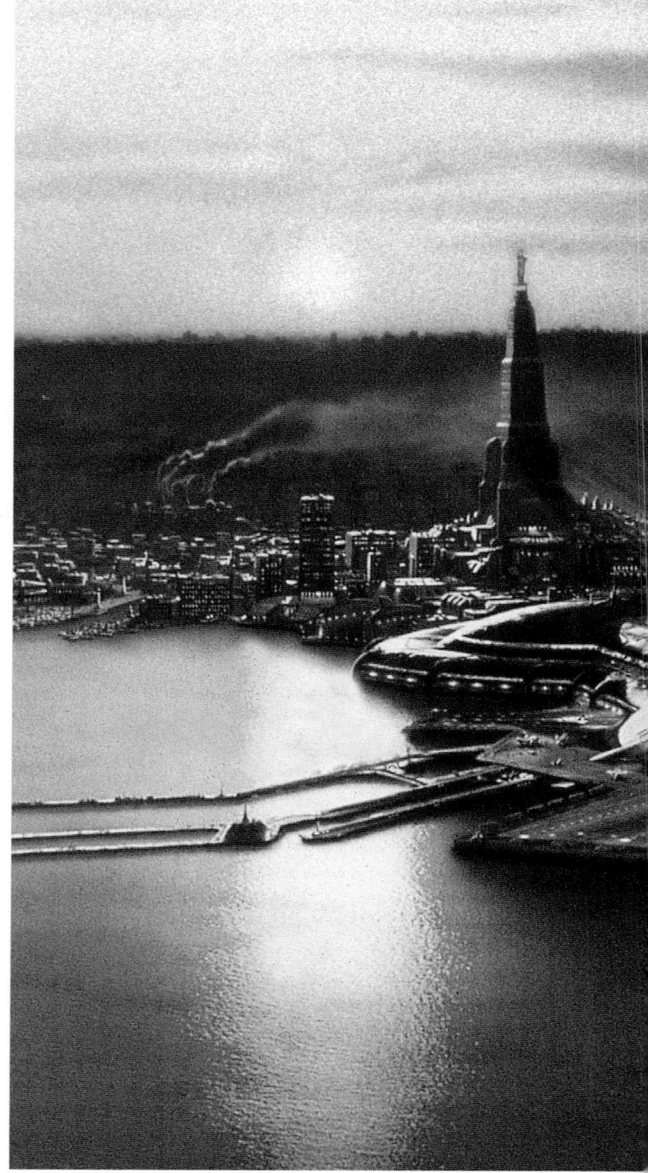

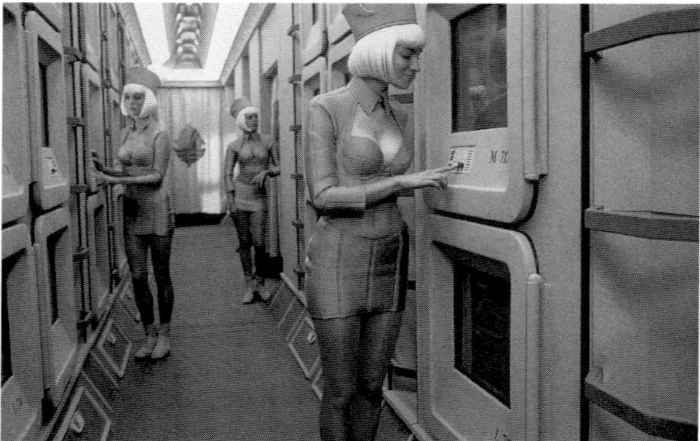

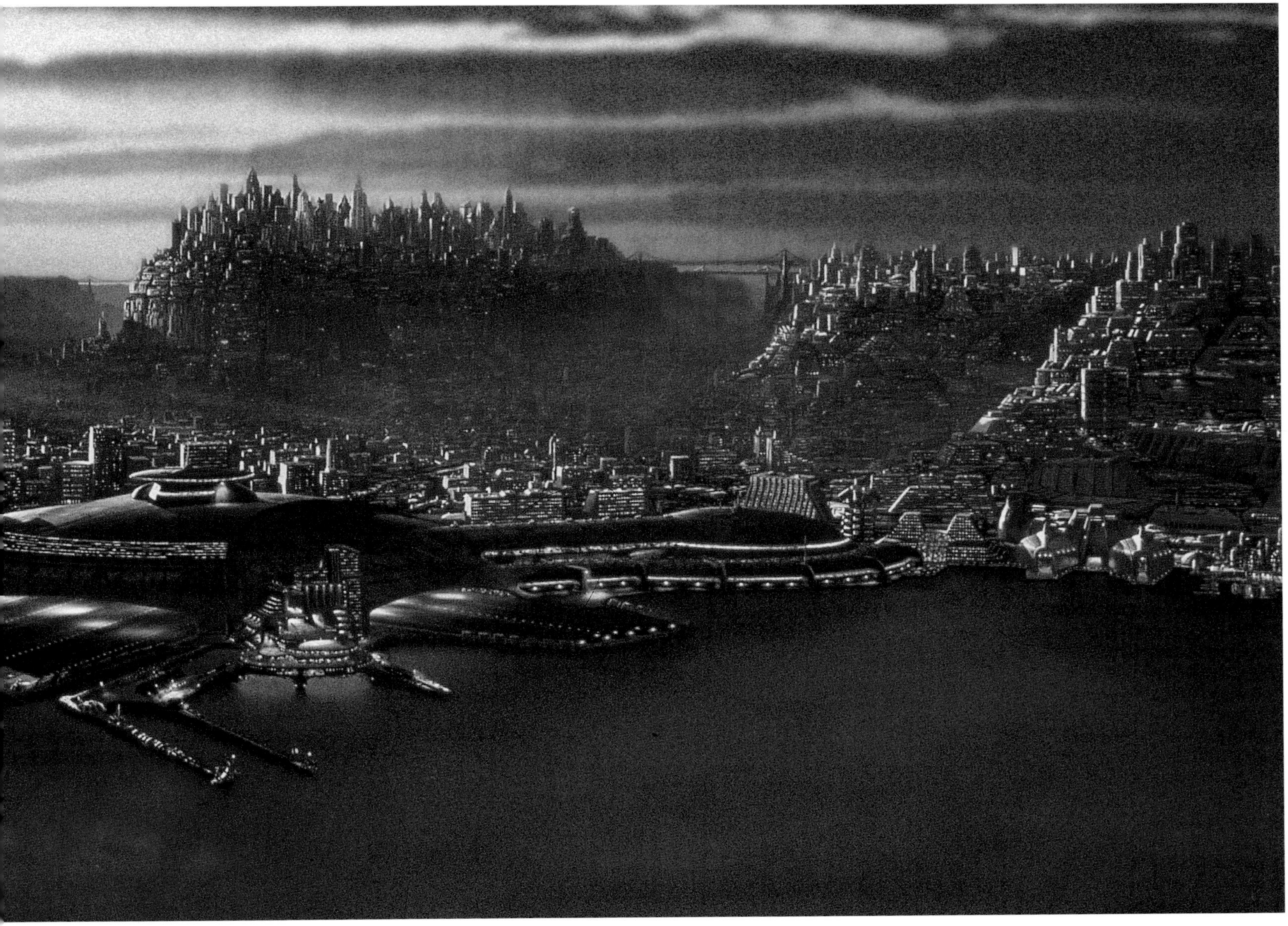

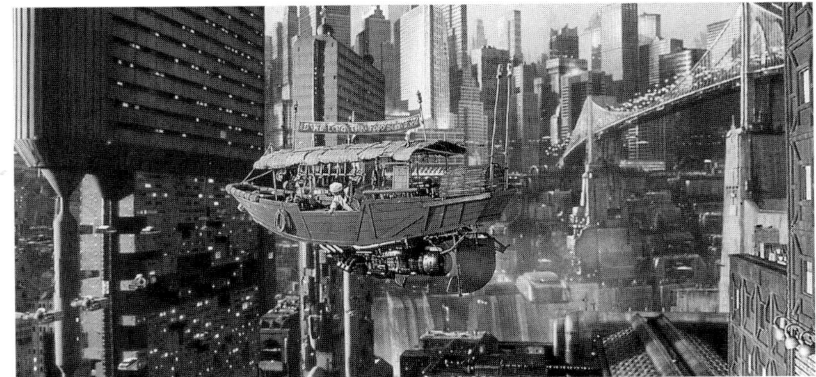

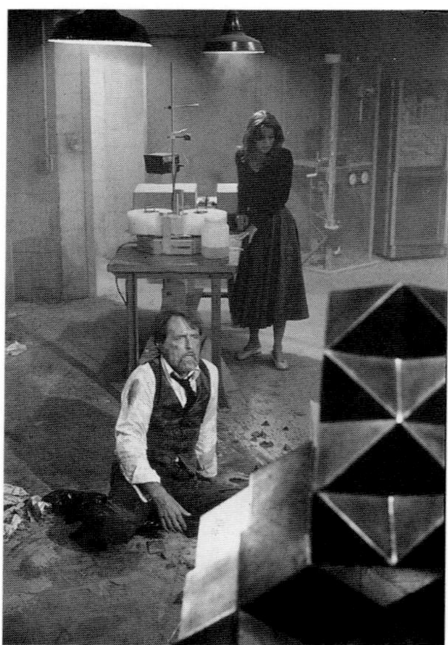

A smart domestic computer yearns for a human life – and gets it – in Donald Cammell's 1977 movie *The Demon Seed*, above. In *The Stepford Wives* (1975), right, the town's male inhabitants are replacing their wifes with robot doubles, creating a town full of compliant über-housewives in pretty floral dresses. Tim Burton's *Edward Scissorhands* (1990), opposite, is also set in suburban America: but the sensivite, strange boy from the Gothic mansion on the hill realises it will be hard for him to fit into the surrounding pastel-coloured utopian idyll.

Fifth Element (1997), Terry Gilliam's complex *Twelve Monkeys* (1995) and *Brazil* (1985), John Boorman's passionate *Emerald Forest* (1985) or his *Zardos* (1974), through Roger Vadim's playful *Barbarella* (1967) and Jean-Luc Godard's disturbing *Alphaville* (1965) to Lang's classic of social criticism, *Metropolis* (1927). It includes movies which use somewhat 'naturalistic' locations, such as *The Stepford Wives* (Bryan Forbes, 1974) where the smooth face of suburban America is exposed as a cosmetic covering for ruthless social engineering, or Donald Cammell's *Demon Seed* (1977), also set in suburban America at the dawn of the age of 'smart' domestic environments, where the computer yearns for human bio-life, and achieves it. This tradition also comprehends more stylised films, such as Tim Burton's *Sleepy Hollow* (1999) or *Edward Scissorhands* (1990), set in pastoral or suburban America but firmly in the 'Gothic' tradition, *Delicatessen* (Jean-Pierre Jeunet/Marc Caro, 1990), located in everyday France but presented at the intensity of animation rather than live-action, and *ET* (Steven Spielberg, US 1982), all about life and prejudice in suburban America but cast as science fiction, which rely heavily on non-naturalistic genres to get across their warnings of human and inhuman ignorance, gullibility, cruelty and greed. The vices (wrath, gluttony, avarice, sloth, pride, lust and envy) wage war against the virtues (prudence, fortitude, temperance, justice, faith, hope and charity), just as they do in *The Tempest*.

It is striking that the social and political critique expressed in More's original Utopia has provided the ethical basis for so many of the literary Dystopias which followed it. It is perhaps not surprising that his formula, directly inspired by the accounts of Vespucci's voyages to the Americas – to which Europe reacted with optimism and a collective sigh of relief, as the breath of fresh air from the lands of the noble savage blew across its already fetid urban landscape – has passed on the legacy of its structure to film, a medium whose paramount development has been in the USA, a nation whose founding European fathers were themselves also inspired by the moral and ethical imperatives More articulates.

The format of an innocent traveller who fortuitously discovers a distant land whose cultural and legal practices throw new light on the world from which the voyager originally comes, could have been designed for moving-image media, which have an inbuilt need to engage with viewpoint and perspective. Utopias and Dystopias, seen as they are through the eyes of the outsider – whether an astronaut, an extra-terrestrial, an android, a time-traveller, an electronic information runner, a cybernaut, or a young girl on a dream quest – provide the perfect material for screen presentation, because they offer designers, cinematographers and editors the opportunity to create expressive narrative environments which cannot exist anywhere else but on the screen, and which integrate an ethical viewpoint with the camera viewpoint. The Utopia/Dystopia as a genre contains an implicit perspective, a great strength in organising a coherent screen world. A clear viewpoint makes these 'impossible' worlds not only possible, but convincing – because they are assembled round a core of meaning.

What the screen worlds of Utopian/Dystopian movies have in common is that they are making real not just a movie continuum of locations, which is credible because the cuts joining the spaces cunningly provide an illusion of continuity in place and time – every movie does that – but that they are making real on the screen, the only place, apart from dreams, where it can exist, the landscapes of the human psyche, of the ethics of human society, the topography of choices open to human beings for the designing of the moral as well as physical landscapes of their own world. The heritage of the literary Utopia/Dystopia has successfully, fruitfully, and to great effect, colonised the screen, and opened it up to the creation of many impossible worlds, enabling all of us, like the crew of the Starship Enterprise, 'to explore strange new worlds, to seek out new life and new civilisations, to boldly go where no man has gone before', as Miranda and Ferdinand did on Prospero's Island in 1611.

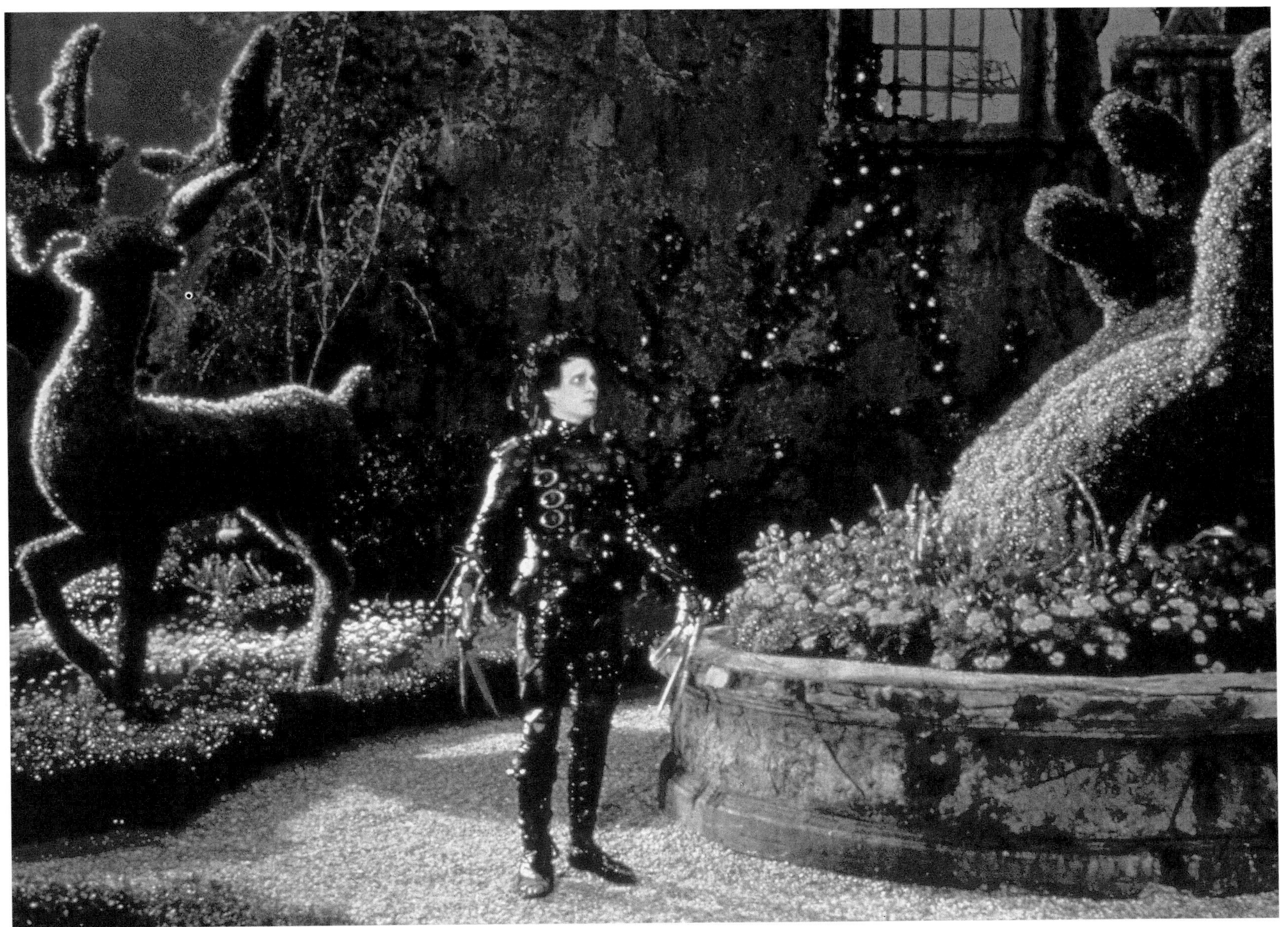

Truths/Fictions
François Penz

In 1899, Ebenezer Howard founded the Garden City Association, which went on to build England's first garden city, Letchworth in Hertfordshire. Howard's was a truly utopian vision of self-sufficient communities dispersed throughout the land, places where town and country could be combined in the most harmonious manner. His book *Tomorrow: A peaceful path to social reform*, published in 1902, had a profound impact on city planning which went far beyond the realisation of Letchworth and later Welwyn Garden City: his vision formed the basis of the great British suburban tradition and ultimately paved the way for the founding of Milton Keynes. Today, Lord Rogers and his Urban Task Force are discussing ways of increasing the density of the city as opposed to encouraging the 'sprawling' suburban alternative. This latter form of urban development may currently be unfashionable but is probably, thanks to Ebenezer Howard, deeply ingrained in the British psyche. Those aspirations and tensions are well illustrated in Ken Loach's *Family Life* (1972), and in Karel Reisz's film *Saturday Night and Sunday Morning* (1961), in particular in the last scene where Arthur (Albert Finney) and his fiancée Doreen contemplate newly-erected semi-detached houses of the type Doreen dreams of living in: 'I want a modern house, with a bathroom and everything!'

While the ideal of the Garden City may have turned into the much more prosaic reality of the type Doreen may have aspired to in the 1960s, the vision proposed by the Futurists in their manifesto a decade after Howard published his has been very influential both on and off the screen. Published in 1914 by Antonio Sant'Elia, item 7 of the manifesto of Futurist Architecture proclaims:

'That by the term architecture is meant the endeavour to harmonise the environment with Man with freedom and great audacity, that is to transform the world of things into a direct projection of the world of the spirit.' Antonio Sant'Elia (Lacerba, Florence, 1 August 1914)

In Milan, Sant'Elia and Mario Chiattone presented their scheme for the Citta Nuova – a revolutionary picture of the 'city of the future'. Sant'Elia laid out their visionary quest in a catalogue in which he pleaded for the need to radically renew Italian architecture and free it from the stranglehold of academic eclecticism. The goal of the Futurists was to create greater harmony between man and his environment in the light of the advances made in science and technology. The Citta Nuova represents an urban complex of the future, symmetrical in its construction, complete with new forms of transportation, medical facilities and many other scientific and technological wonders. The Futurist ideal of the modern city, it contained some key elements of a utopian vision, and even though it was never constructed, some of the city's innovations did materialise on screen – but perhaps surprisingly, they did not necessarily find their way onto celluloid through the Futurist cinema[2] movement, but rather in the form of Hollywood movies. A particularly good example is David Butler's film *Just Imagine* (1930), which is set in the New York of 1980 – a city in which cars have been replaced by aeroplanes and names by numbers, leading to new designations such as Single 0 and J-21.

The Modern Movement, with Le Corbusier's book *Vers une Architecture* (1923) constituting its manifesto, was the next architectural movement with a utopian dimension. Le Corbusier's fascination with the aesthetic of the aeroplane and the motor car provides a direct link with the work of the Futurists, but his vision of a new society is best encapsulated in his concept for La ville radieuse, and its corresponding reality in the shape of the Unité d'Habitation in Marseille. Built between 1947 to 1951, this structure incorporates all the theories of the 'ville radieuse' the architect had developed since 1935. The building consists of 337 apartment-villas, each with its own terrace and picture window. The block contains a hotel, post office, and an enclosed shopping street; and a gymnasium, a children's pool and a nursery school with a playground are located on the terrace roof. While Ebenezer Howard was advocating horizontal development for his garden city ideal, Le Corbusier's vision was vertical and therefore key to the birth of high rise flats. But all too often, these

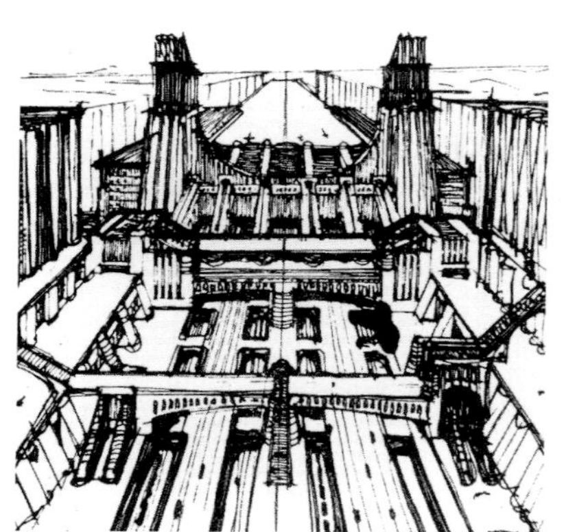

Citta Nuova, the Futurist city envisaged by Antonio Sant'Elia in 1914, left, was never built, but his preparatory drawings served as an inspiration for many celluloid 'cities of the future', including the geometric urban landscape of *Metropolis* (1927), opposite. Fritz Lang's futuristic allegorical fantasy took two years to complete, and at the time was the most expensive film ever made in Germany. Its set design and pictorial composition – if not its simplistic plot – influenced architects just as much as film-makers.

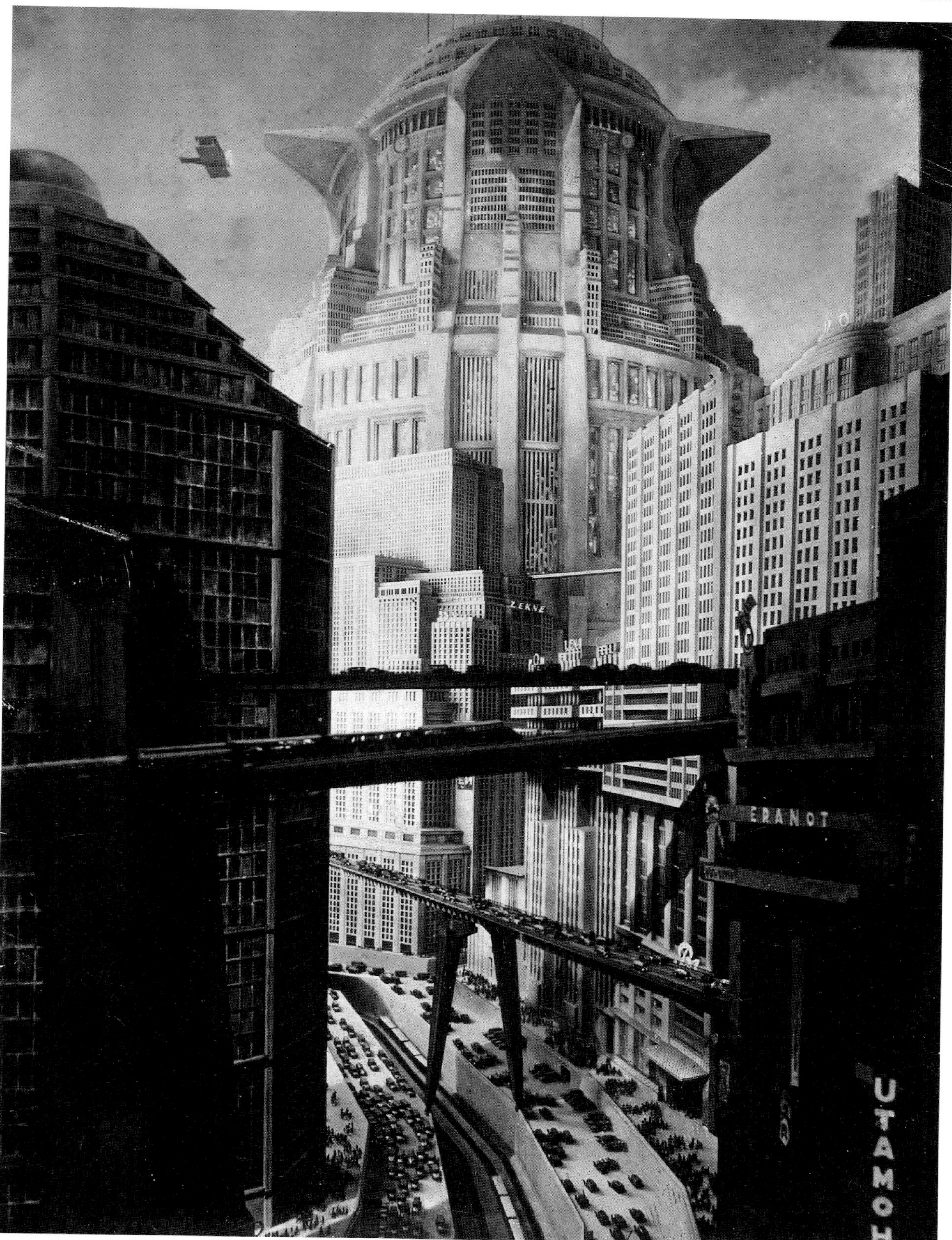
EPANOT
UTAMOH

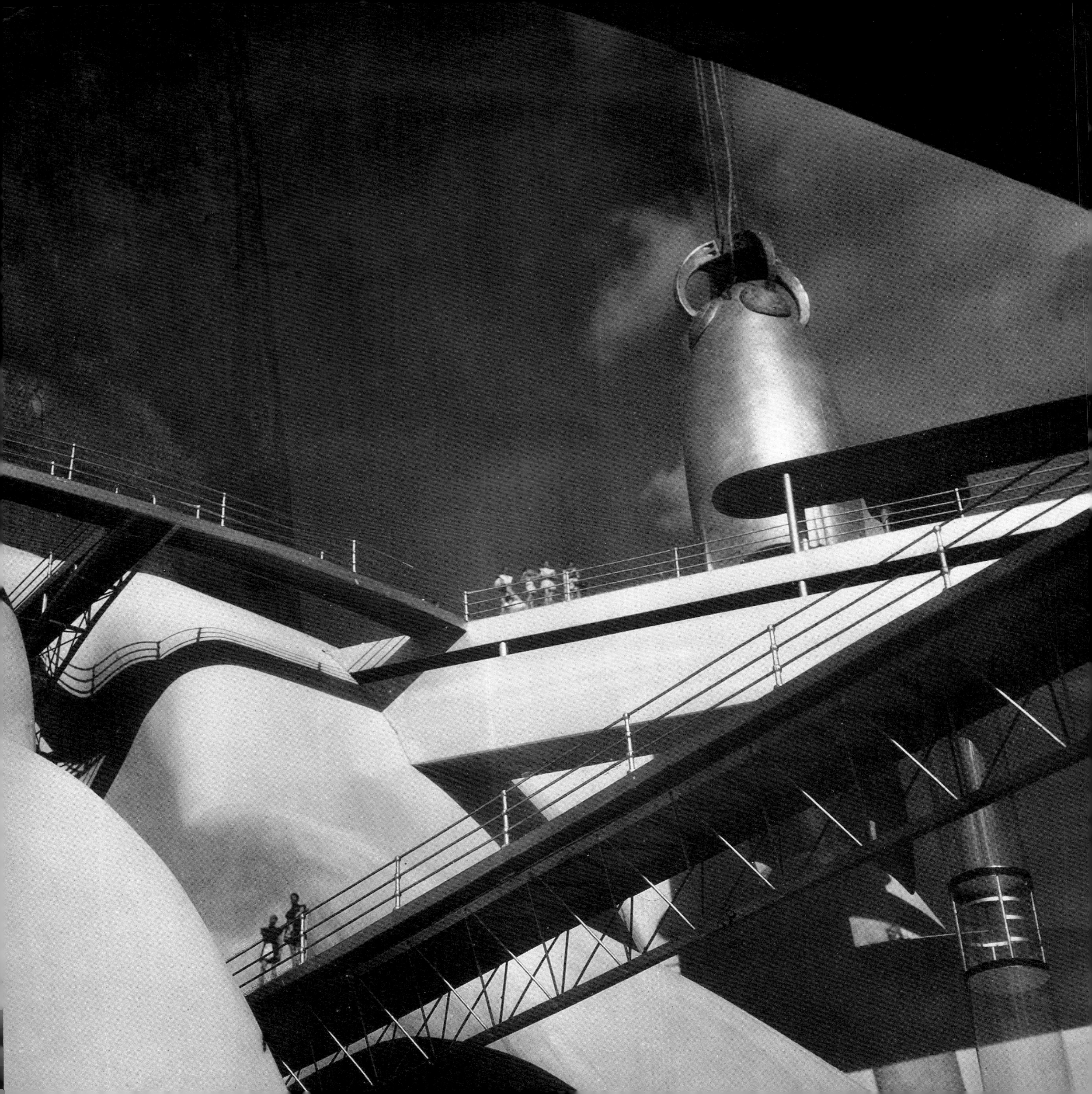

developments resulted in his utopian vision for housing being turned into a dystopian reality of often squalid towerblocks, synonymous with social deprivation rather than urban sophistication. Towerblocks started to appear in films like Tati's *Mon Oncle* (1957) and loom large in Kubrick's *A Clockwork Orange* (1971), where the Thamesmead Estate and the concrete passages of the South Bank Centre provide an expressive and sinister backdrop to the 'ultraviolence' of the Droogs.

While Kubrick's use of 1960s London architecture gives us a 'modernist nightmare', the vision developed by Fritz Lang in *Metropolis* in 1927 is in many ways not only kinder but also truer to the modernist ideal. *Metropolis* describes a vision of the German city of the future, a city inspired in part by New York and by the work of Mies van der Rohe. Fritz Lang offers us a seemingly Wellsian glance into the future, but paradoxically, HG Wells hated *Metropolis*. Partly as a result of that dislike, 1936 saw the release of *Things to Come*, a truly Wellsian vision in that Wells himself wrote the screenplay, which in turn was based on his essay, 'The Shape of Things to Come'. Set in the year 2036, the film shows the emergence of a new, subterranean world order and offers a vision of automation, artificial sunlight and state-of-the-art telecommunications technology. On a large television screen, we see a city built above ground (which looks not unlike the set of *Metropolis*) that is described as '...a city of the past, where sunlight used to be harnessed through a device called windows'.

The use of glass and panoramic windows is symbolic of the modernist vision of the world, and both elements feature in abundance in the expansive city set built for *Murnau's Sunrise* (1927). The city portrayed in this film was certainly an architect's dream made real, a collage of symbols of modern architecture used to depict a place which did not exist anywhere in the world at the time. Yet this imagined city deployed not only the grammar of the emerging modern architecture (curtain walls, horizontal protruding slabs, simple cube shapes) but also its materials (glass and concrete). The interesting thing about such a construct is that it portrays the vision of a city 'just around the corner', a city within the realms of the possible as opposed to a science-fiction view of the distant future.

The same principle would apply to the modern house portrayed in Jacques Tati's *Mon Oncle* (1957), which features a caricatured collage of futuristic culinary equipment and domestic gadgets that could all be described as being 'not quite there yet, but very nearly possible'. Tati's trademark approach to pushing the boundaries of existing technology and aesthetics reaches its culmination in *Playtime* (1967). In this film, Tati constructs and collages his own city, allowing him to twist

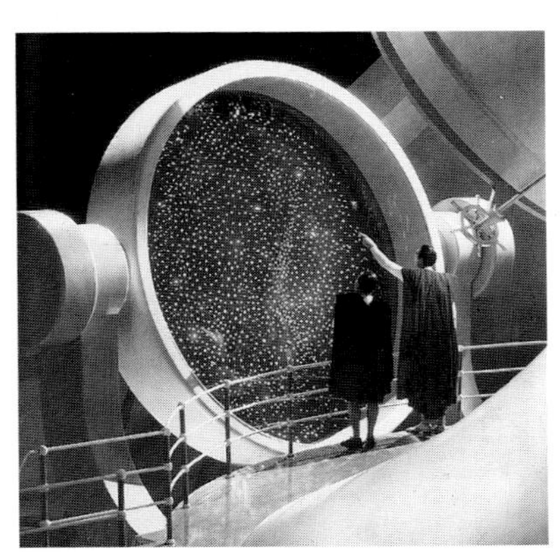

Set in the year 2036, *Things to come* (1936), opposite and above, was HG Wells' response to *Metropolis*, which he believed to be not nearly radical enough in its representation of the future. Today, the film looks like the essence of 1930s style, with its perspex furniture and ocean-liner aesthetics. In contrast, Le Corbusier's Plan Voisin for Paris, 1925, right, which shows the architect's ideas for a modern city applied to a real location, still suggests pure science fiction today – the historical heart of Paris colonised by monolithic blocks.

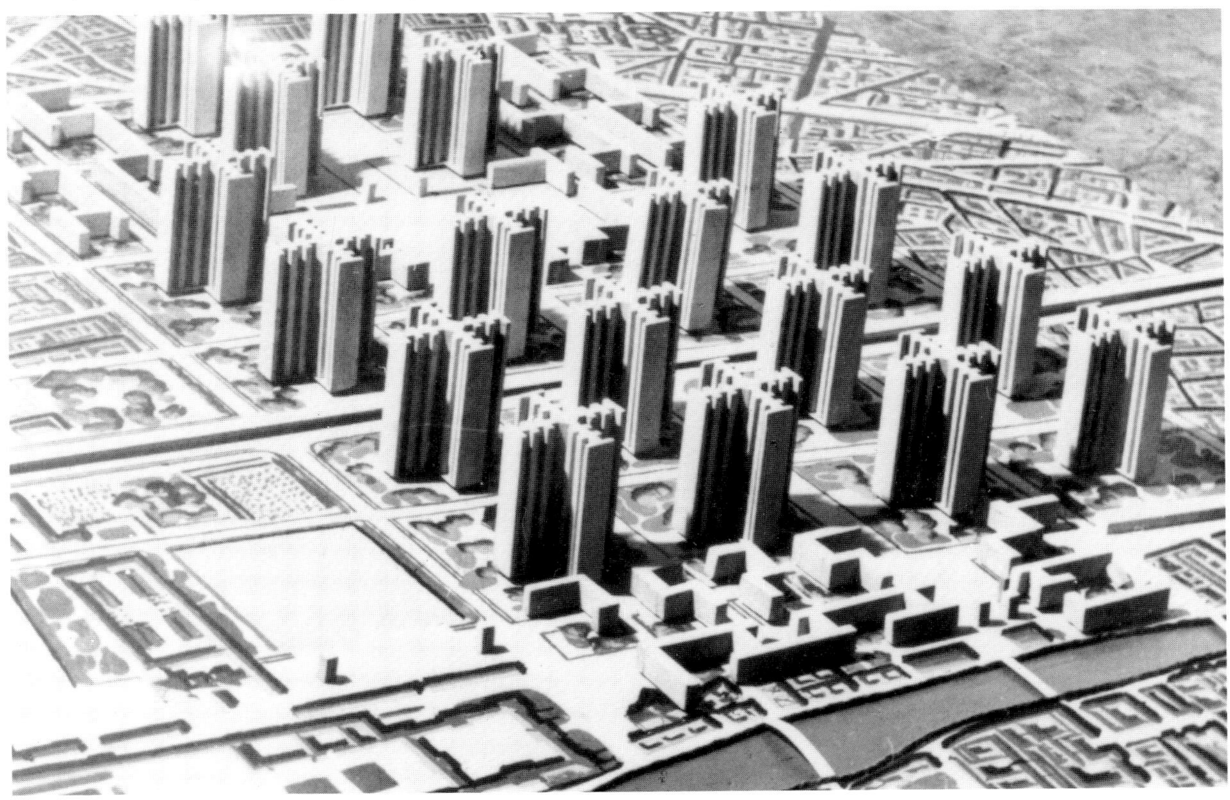

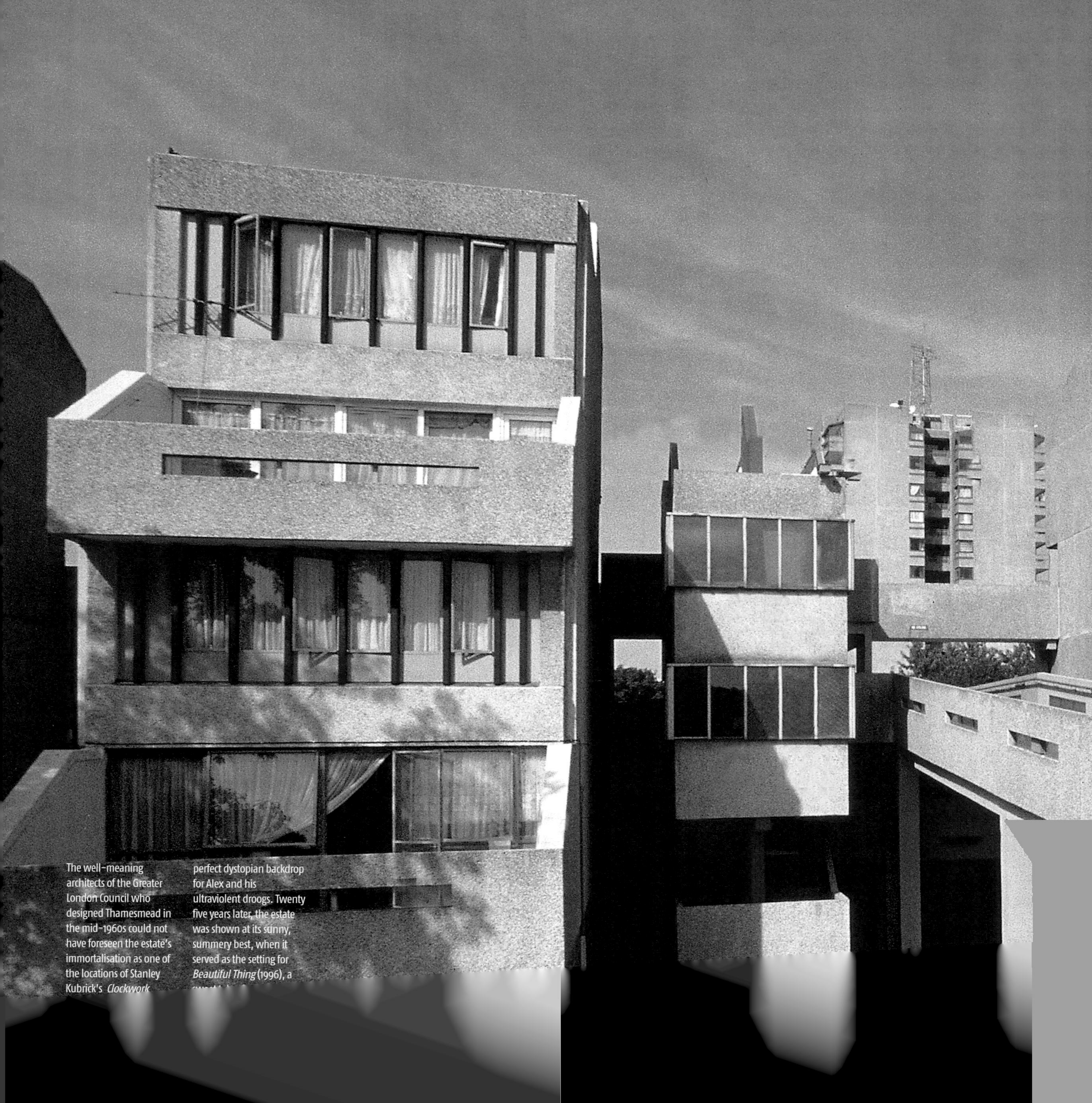

The well-meaning architects of the Greater London Council who designed Thamesmead in the mid-1960s could not have foreseen the estate's immortalisation as one of the locations of Stanley Kubrick's *Clockwork*

perfect dystopian backdrop for Alex and his ultraviolent droogs. Twenty five years later, the estate was shown at its sunny, summery best, when it served as the setting for *Beautiful Thing* (1996), a

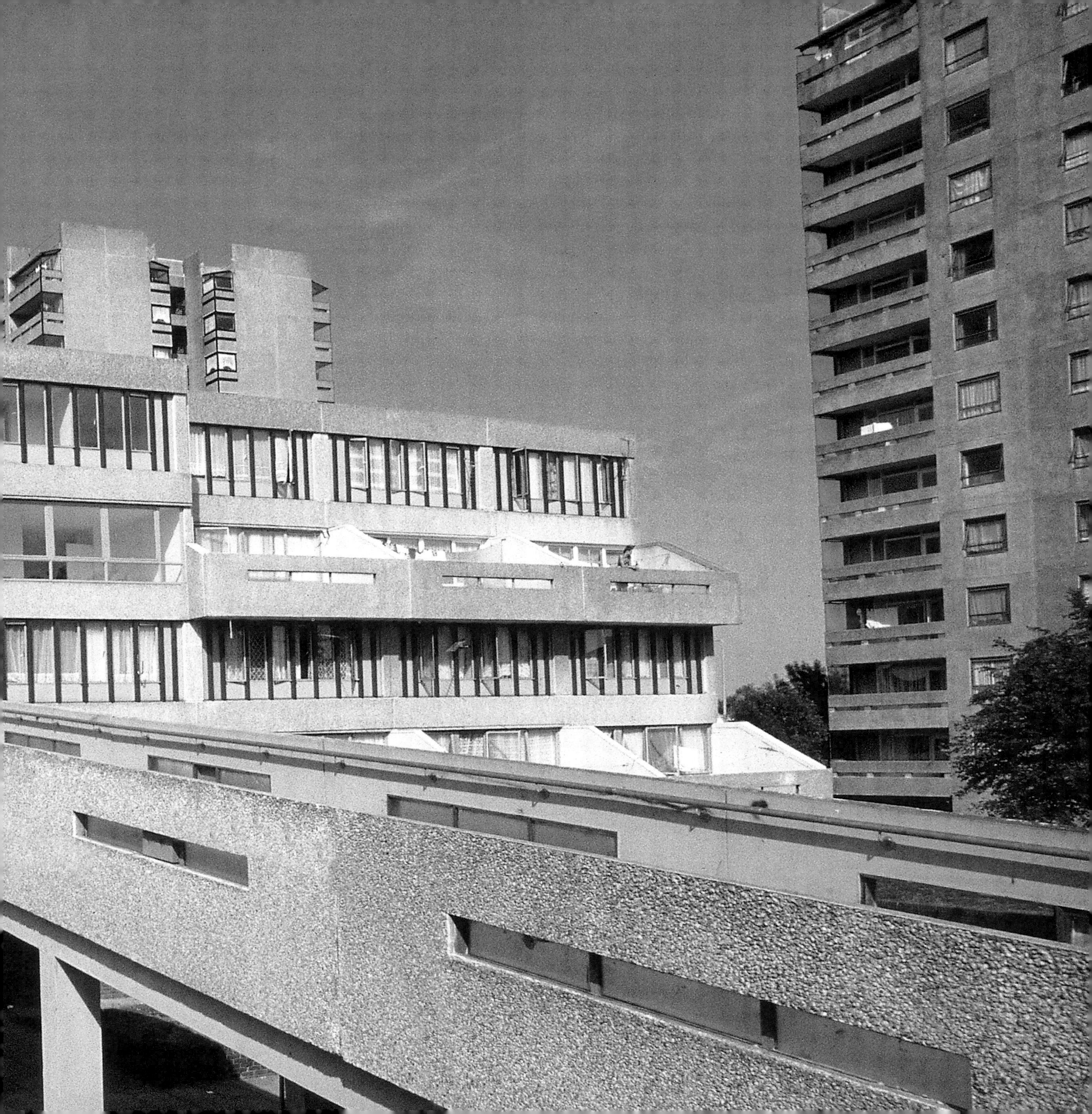

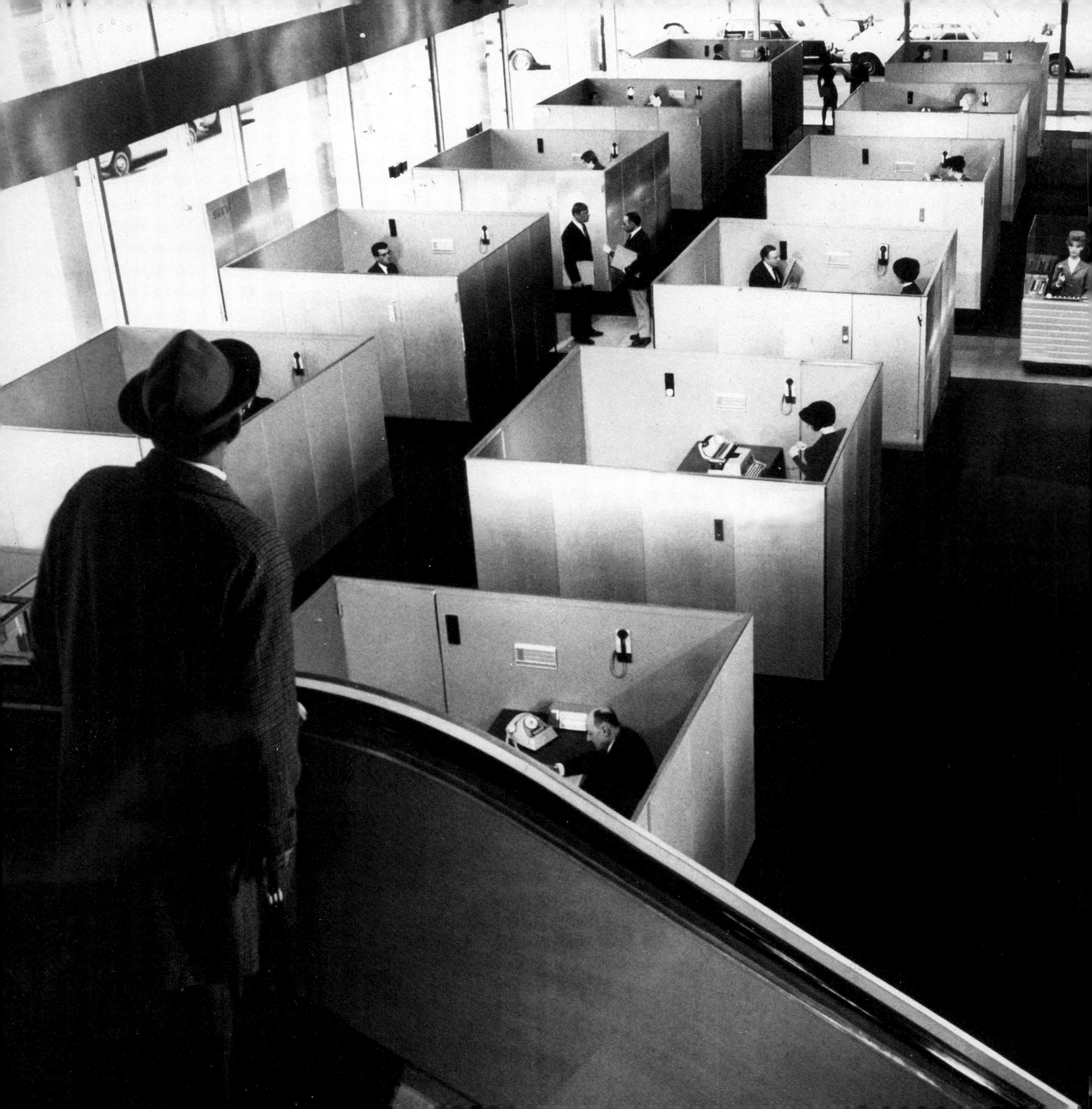

the modern style's ubiquitous use of glass to suggest a world of reflections, transparencies and ambiguity – a dystopian vision maybe, but ever so close to the emerging urban reality of the 1960s.

It is interesting to note that while the 'Tativille' of *Playtime* was actually an immense studio set, in *Alphaville* (1965) Jean-Luc Godard gave us a science fiction vision shot entirely on location in Paris. Part of the thrill of watching this movie lies in observing the economy of means used in the creation of another world, a transformation effected by the night-time darkness, the signage and the billboards, and by the surreal use of familiar locations for absurd and disturbing scenes, such as the swimming pool where state executions are performed as part of a synchronised swimming event. Perhaps the use of carefully chosen familiar and real locations for unfamiliar and unreal actions helps to create an even more profoundly disturbing and dystopian vision on the screen, not unlike the effect achieved by Kubrick in *A Clockwork Orange*. It may be rare for science fiction films to be shot on location, but *Alphaville* is not unique in its use of Paris for this purpose: René Clair's *Paris qui dort* (1923) recounts the improbable tale of a crazy scientist who uses a magic ray to freeze unsuspecting passers-by (a special effect achieved using stop-motion photography). This early example of the science fiction genre uses the near-deserted and frozen streets of Paris in a very imaginative and unexpected way. In a much more recent example, Peter Weir's *The Truman Show* (1998) features another type of imagined world – an immense, domed, city-sized sound stage where the main character is held prisoner, unwittingly living his life in a completely artificial environment. The irony here of course lies in the fact that many of the scenes that take place on this supposed 'set' were filmed on location: the holiday town of Seaside in Florida makes for an ideal 'pretend city' as it looks like no other 'real city' in the world.

So far, most of the examples cited represent some form of dystopian vision brought to life on screen. In fact, it is possible to argue that the only true vision of Utopia in the cinema comes from the worlds of dadaism and surrealism, in the shape of a documentary shot by Man Ray. In 1928, Charles de Noailles asked Man Ray to make a film for a documentary project entitled *Les Mystères du château du Dé*, about the cubist villa conceived by Robert Mallet-Stevens. Man Ray was charged not only with filming the building's architecture, interior design and collection of modern art but also with capturing the new way of life the villa represented. Initially, he suggested the idea of an essentially sporting and cultural life to his friends, but the reality of the life on show ended up becoming 'total art' instead. The film portrays a new model of society, with 'bodies' (clearly people, but as they are mostly wearing masks it is difficult to identify them as individuals) involved in carefully choreographed group activities (swimming, jumping etc.). In what amounts to a very surreal and poetic piece, the suggestion is made that the surroundings the characters find themselves in – the new architecture of Robert Mallet-Stevens – somehow act as the trigger and the catalyst for this new form of human behaviour. Curiously, a documentary shot a few years later called *Architectures d'Aujourd'hui* (Pierre Chenal, 1930) puts forward a similar vision of a sporting and cultural life, this time based around the modernist architecture of Le Corbusier. In this film, Le Corbusier's Villa Savoye (or to paraphrase the architect, La Villa Radieuse) is in part the setting for a series of athletic and gymnastic displays. In the 1930s, this film may have had sinister undertones, but the project clearly errs more on the side of the utopian vision of the good Dr Auguste Rollier, the apostle of the Heliotherapy movement, than towards the dystopian world envisioned by the evil Dr Goebbels.

While on the subject of the documentary movement, it is also worth briefly mentioning a couple of earlier examples of utopian films about cities. The first is a German town-planning film, *Die Stadt von Morgen* (1930) – *The City of Tomorrow* – which portrays the crowded contemporary city as being unhygienic and evil, and

Monsieur Hulot, the comic character created by Jacques Tati, constantly finds himself at odds with the gadget-laden, antiseptic world around him, getting lost in anonymous, labyrinthine office buildings. In films like *Playtime* (1968), opposite, Tati built elaborate sets to poke fun at the ideals of Mies and the Modernists, while Jean-Luc Godard shot his science fiction film *Alphaville* (1965), right, on location in the streets of Paris. The film, which presents a dystopian vision of a de-humanised computer age in the near future, was originally titled *Tarzan versus IBM*.

promotes the wonders of the perfect future city: a place where town and country meet, a model town that resembles Howard's ideal of the Garden City. The second is an American film based on an original idea by documentary filmmaker Pare Lorentz. *The City* was produced by the American Institute of Planners, and the celebrated American town planner Lewis Mumford helped shape the film's content. The 45-minute film offered a look at the 'perfect' city of the future, using scale models and motorised props to illustrate its thesis. The concept was to create a huge, gleaming modernistic residential development far removed from the existing slums, in order to improve the quality of life in New York, Chicago and other metropolitan communities.

Most architectural movements of the twentieth century with utopian undertones were destined to remain 'utopian on paper only'. As the vast majority of real-life architectural experiments have proved to be a social minefield, in turn their interpretation on the silver screen has been at best 'science fictional', and at worst dystopian. Paradoxically one has to turn to the realm of the documentary and the surrealist tradition to find a true utopian vision of our built environment. Here is where architecture and screen design both converge and diverge. Architects, like the authors of fictional Utopias, often aspire not to maintain the status quo, but to transform the world as we know it, to realise a dream. As the Futurist manifesto quoted above puts it, the end of architecture is 'to transform the world of things into a direct projection of the world of the spirit'. Utopian/dystopian film, from the contemporary *Metropolis* of Fritz Lang, through the *Wizard of Oz*'s Emerald City to the world of Luc Besson's *Fifth Element* (France 1995), whose towers are clearly directly inspired by Marinetti's drawings, expresses just this aspiration because their task is to do precisely what Sant'Elia suggests. Like the crew of the Starship Enterprise, the travellers in the Mayflower, Thomas More, or Shakespeare's innocent Miranda, their visions are of brave new worlds – worlds primarily of the spirit. Where the vision is dark and disturbing, the screen worlds are dark and disturbing, whether designed by architects or production designers. If you are content with the old world, if you see no reason to change it, then if you are a film-maker, you set your story in as near and bright an approximation to the environment we live in as you can devise or photograph. If you are an architect who feels no urge to change the status quo, why should you be impelled towards revolutionary manifestos, or the screen as a place to realise your dreams? Architecture and the making of utopian/dystopian movies both attract idealists and thinkers who are concerned with ethics, morality, welfare, and the way people fit into, treat and shape their environment.

Prospero, perhaps the most memorable builder of dreams, aptly evokes the final common ground between architects both of fictional and of real environments, when he says to Ferdinand (who is bewildered by the moral masque he has just witnessed) in *The Tempest*, Act IV, Scene 1:

> 'You do look, my son, in a moved sort,
> As if you were dismay'd: be cheerful, sir.
> Our revels now are ended. These our actors,
> As I foretold you, were all spirits, and
> Are melted into air, into thin air:
> And, like the baseless fabric of this vision,
> The cloud-capp'd towers, the gorgeous palaces,
> The solemn temples, the great globe itself,
> Ye all which it inherit shall dissolve
> And, like this insubstantial pageant, fade,
> Leaving not a rack behind. We are such stuff
> As dreams are made on ....'

Prospero words suggest that all our habitations, whether we build them in words on the stage, out of light on the silver screen, or out of concrete in the real world, are all as ephemeral as we ourselves are. They represent our human thoughts, our aspirations, our spirits – projected onto things.

Man Ray's film for a documentary project, *Les Mystères du château du Dé*, below, used as its subject matter the cubist villa designed by Robert Mallet-Stevens. Man Ray's brief was to capture its architecture and its interior, but also the way of life it represented.

A 'machine for living in'; a 'box on stilts', or a manifesto for the Heliotherapy movement. Whatever else was claimed for it, Le Corbusier's *Villa Savoye* quickly became a symbol of utopian possibilities in the modern age.

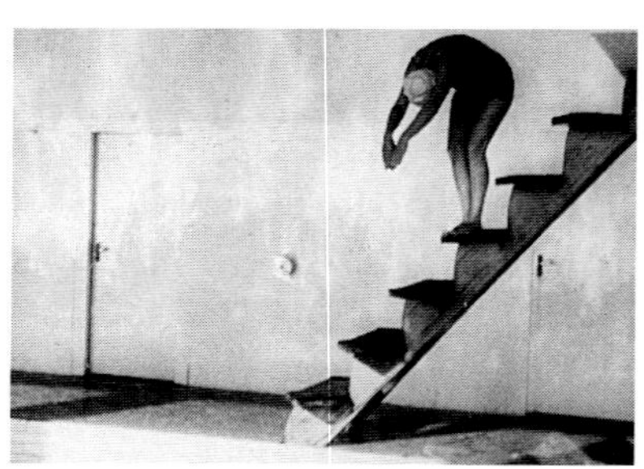

1. Animation does however also have close affinities with non-time-based pictorial and visual arts, and often does not use human characters for its protagonists or naturalistic environments for its action.
2. In 1916 the *Futurist Cinema Manifesto* by F.T. Marinetti, Bruno Corra, Emilio Settimelli, Arnaldo Ginna, Giacomo Balla, and Remo Chiti (L'Italia futurista Milan) proclaimed: 'The Futurist cinema will thus cooperate in the general renewal, taking the place of the literary review (always pedantic) and the drama (always predictable), and killing the book (always tedious and oppressive). The necessities of propaganda will force us to publish a book once in a while. But we prefer to express ourselves through the cinema, through great tables of words-in-freedom and mobile illuminated signs.'

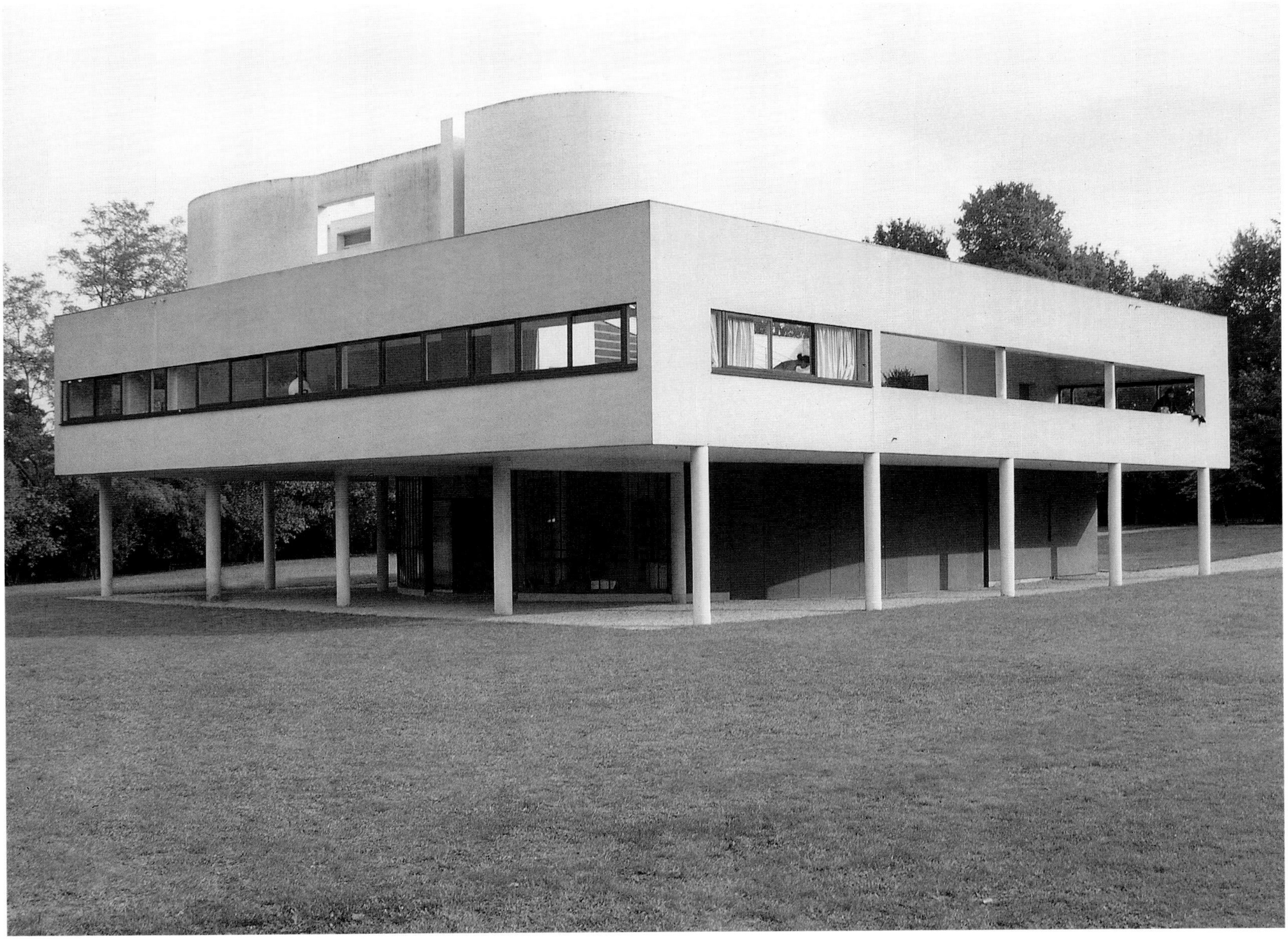

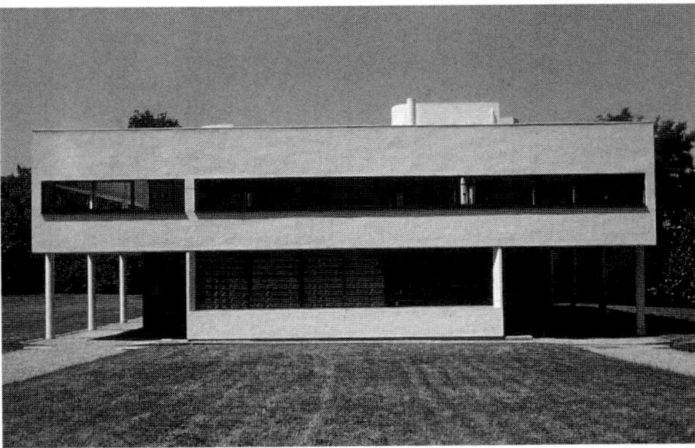

Villa Savoye
Nathan Coley, 1997

Installation with audio/slide presentation, commissioned by the Berlinische Galerie im Martin-Gropius-Bau and the Scottish National Gallery of Modern Art.

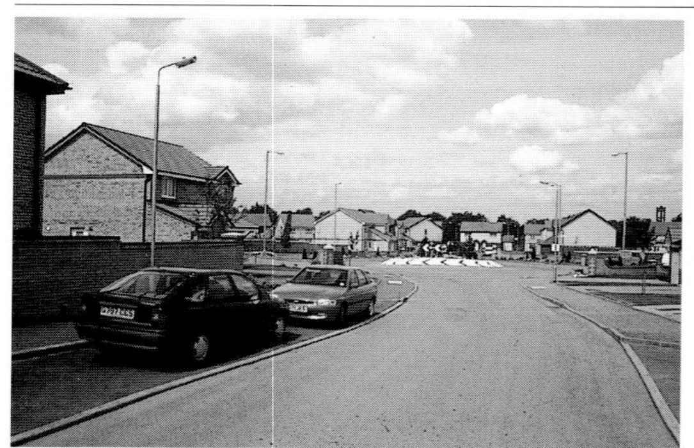

The site is expansive, bordered by trees on three sides, and has long views towards the softly rolling fields and valley.

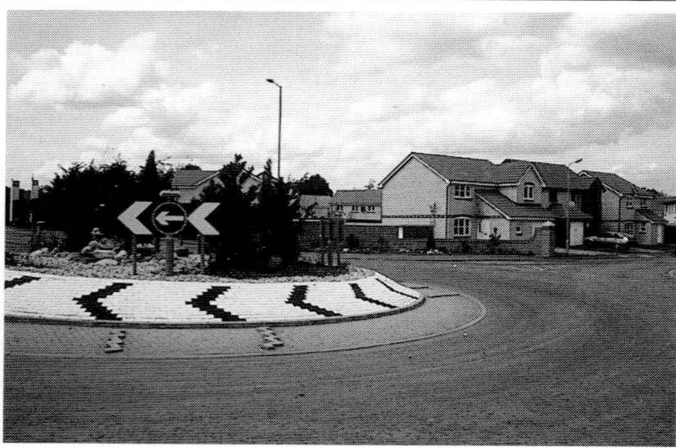

Perhaps you arrive by car, in which case you leave the road and pass by this small, white, cubic gate-house guarding the entrance to the drive.

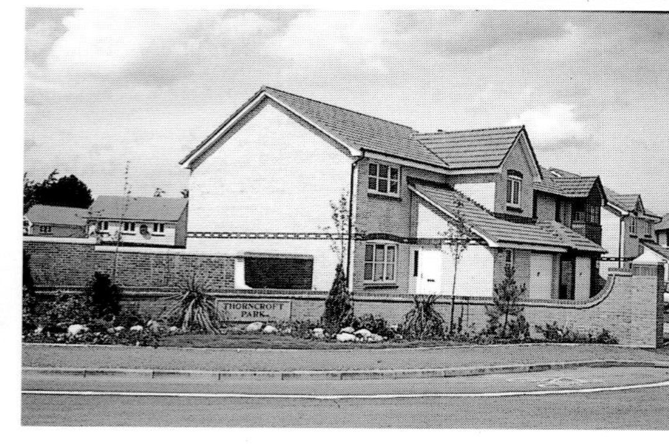

The gravel turns slowly into the trees, its destination unknown.

Then one catches this first view of the villa, standing fifty yards away towards the centre of an open meadow...

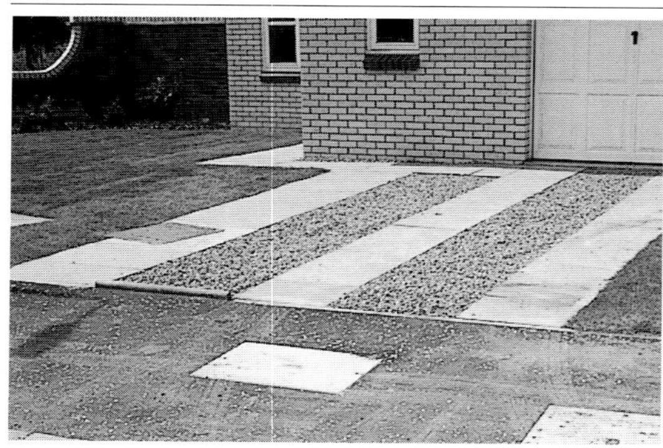

At first sight, there is a shock of recognition – a sense of formal inevitability. What could be more 'natural' than this horizontal white box, poised on pillars, set off against the rural surroundings, the far panorama and the sky?

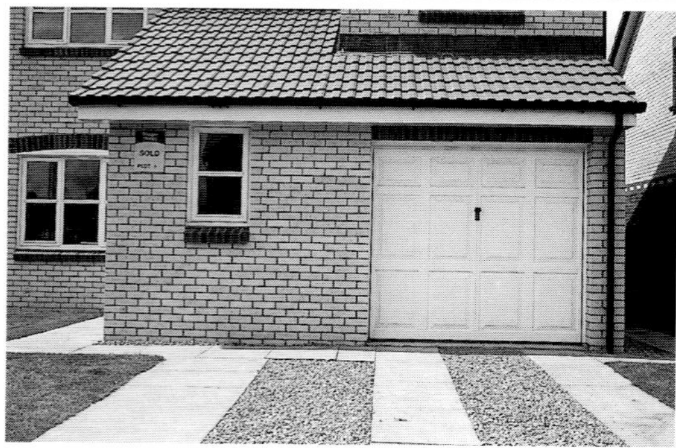

The driveway passes through the undercroft (whose walls are deep green)...

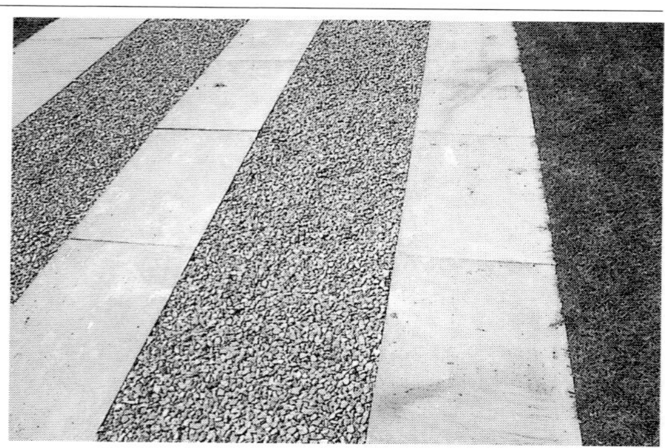

circles the building beneath the overhang... and re-emerges to return to the road on the other side.

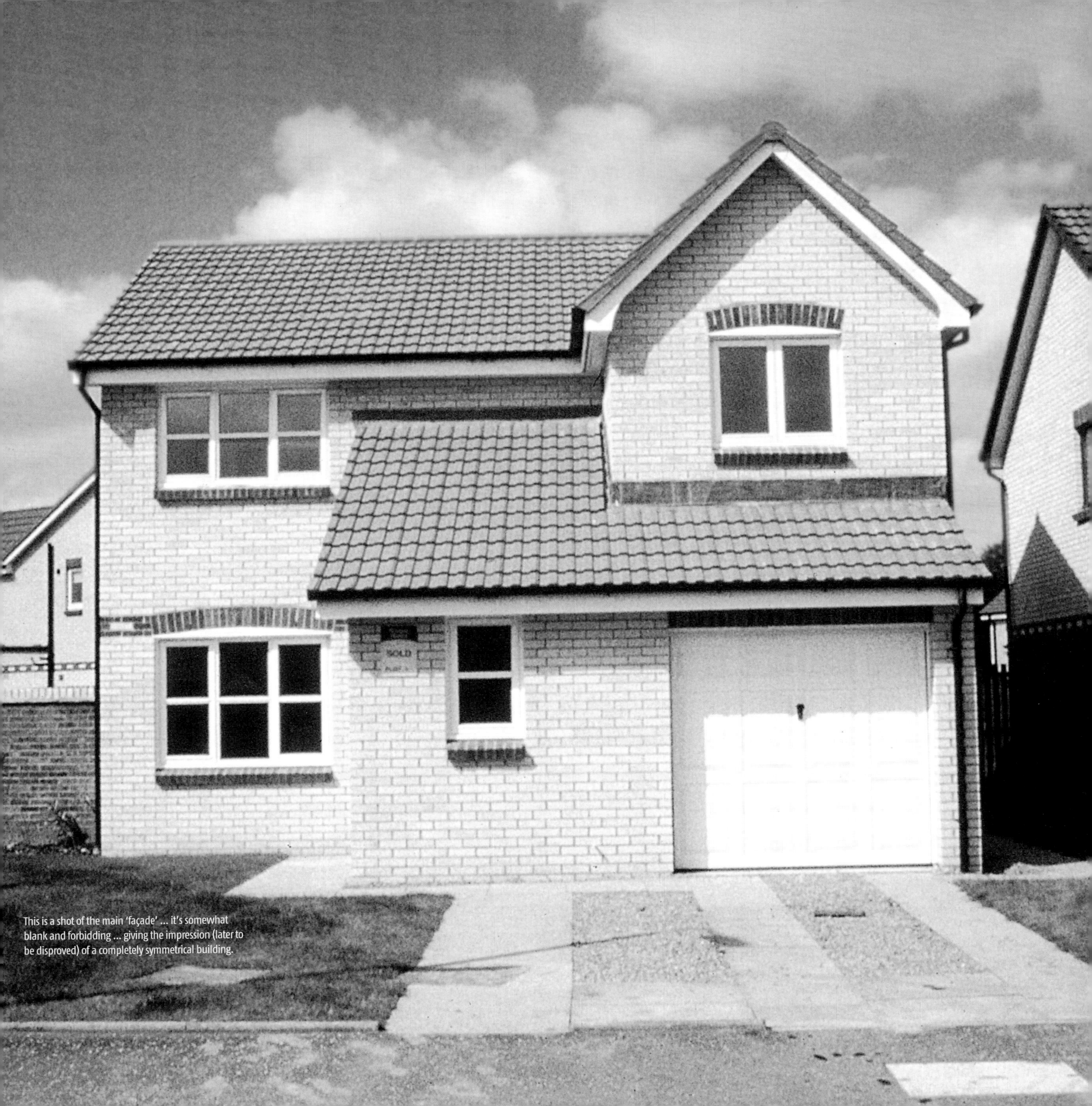

This is a shot of the main 'façade' ... it's somewhat blank and forbidding ... giving the impression (later to be disproved) of a completely symmetrical building.

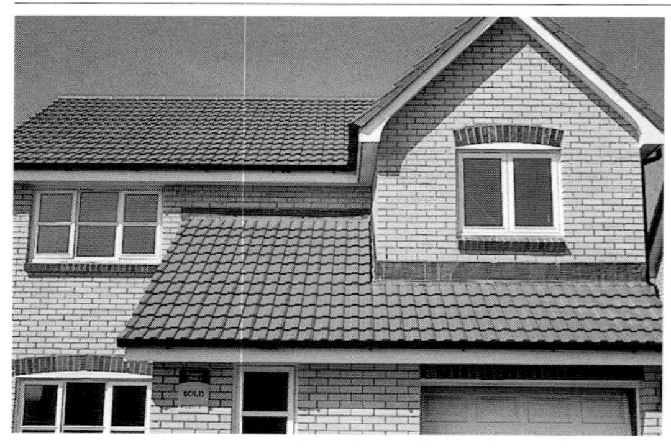

The house is not monochrome, but coloured. White paint on the pillars and on the main box stand out sharply against the green walls of the undercroft... and the pink and blue of the curves on top.

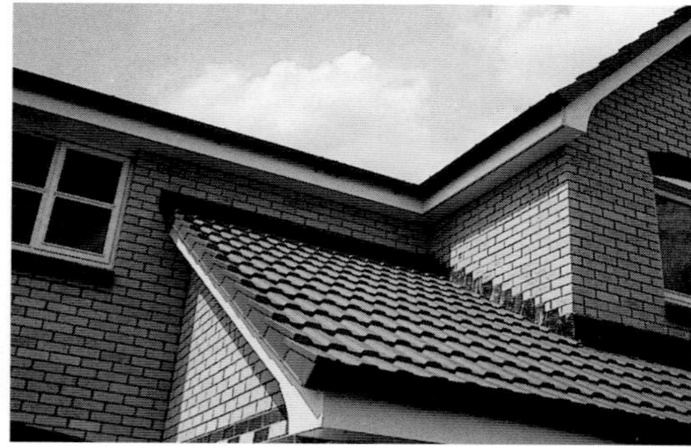

This is just a detail.

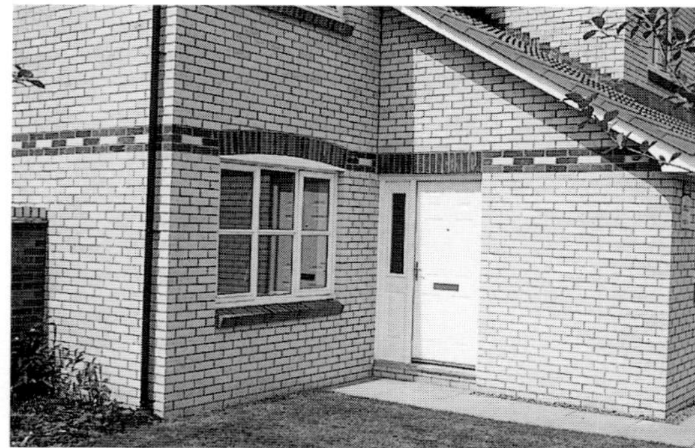

The villa is open on every side... making it a container and receptacle for sunlight.

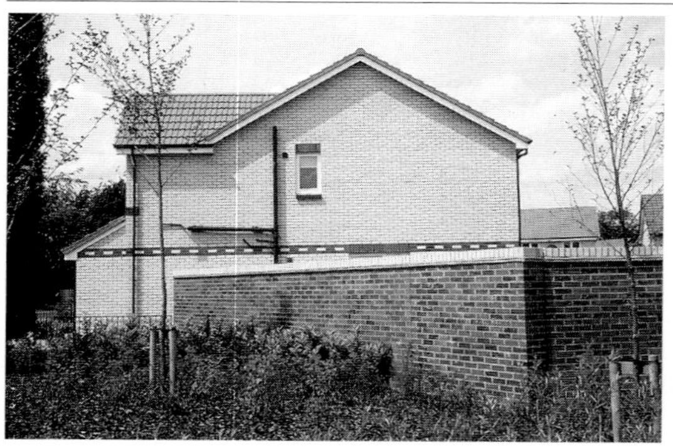

These are some details of the north...

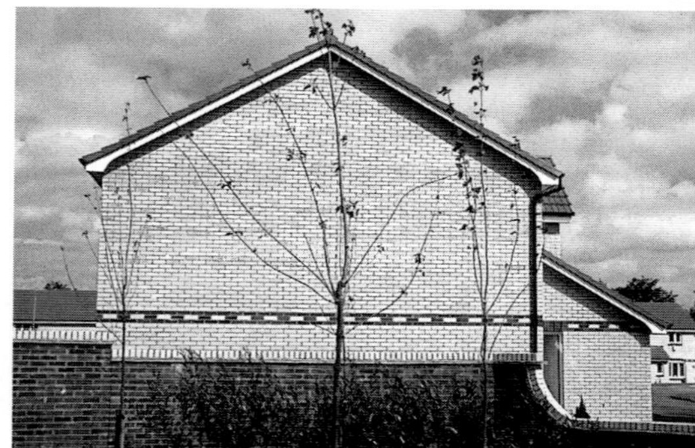

and south elevations.

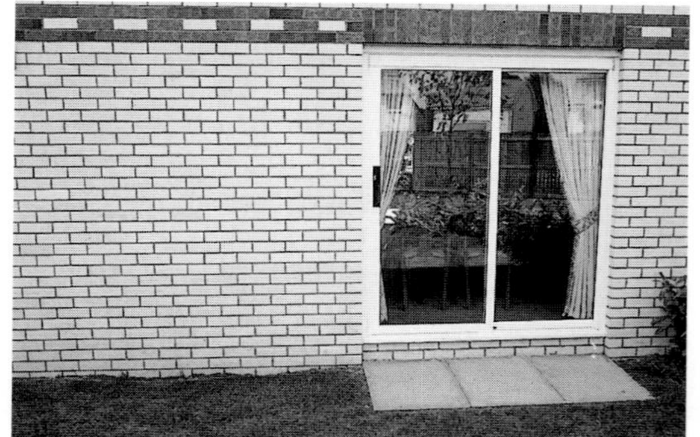

The villa is basically a cube lifted above the landscape by reinforced concrete pillars... channelling the movement of the car and accentuating the main axis.

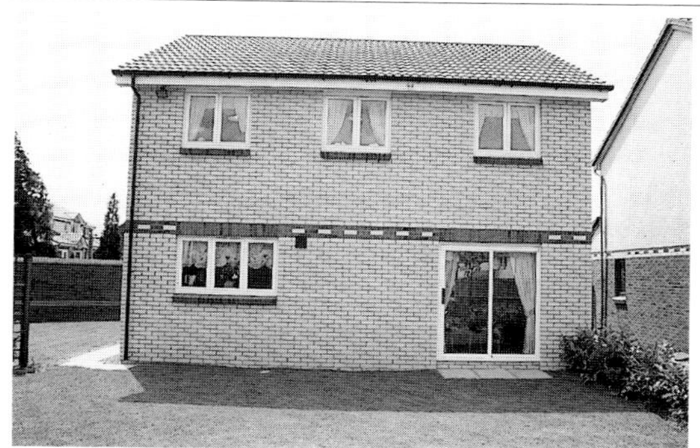

There is no façade... no front... and no back.

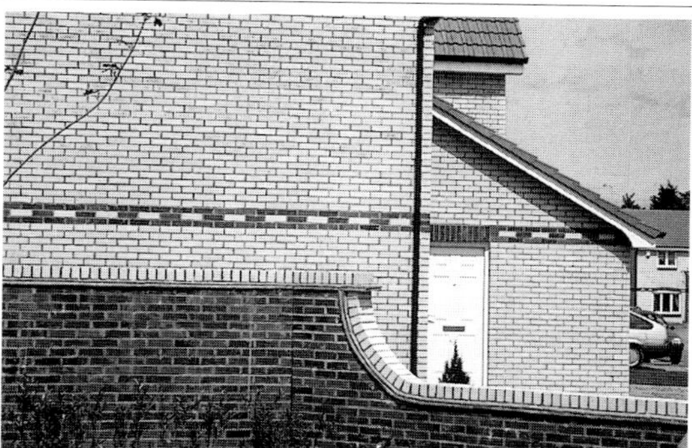

It is impossible to comprehend from any single viewpoint.

It is a kind of... 'four façade' solution.

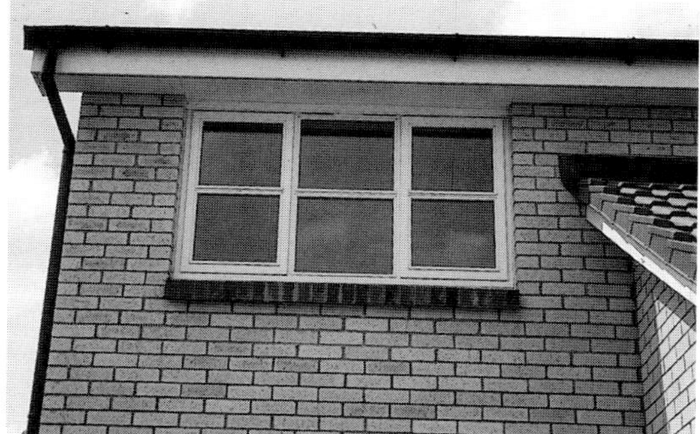

The strong horizontal emphasis is supplied by the overall shape, the single window running from one end to the other of the (main) upper level... and the repeated horizontals of the factory glazing at the lower level.

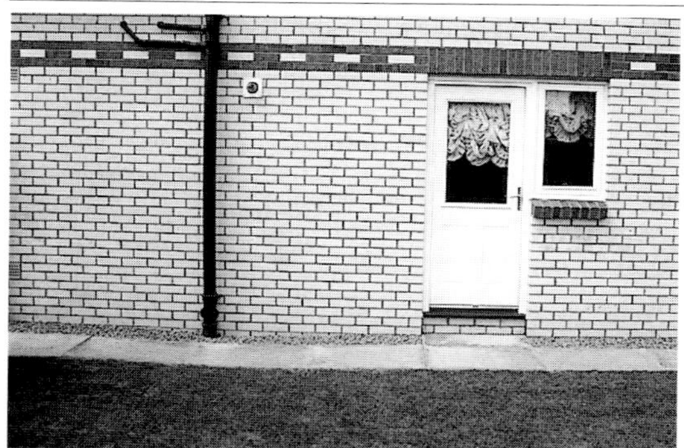

On the side of the building the pillars are flush with the façade giving a clear reading of load and support but on the front and back they are recessed under the slab creating a hovering effect as well as a slight sense of horizontal movement in the superstructure.

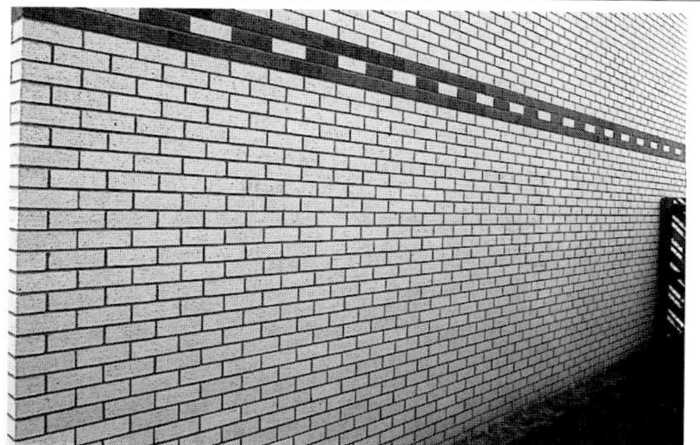

Bit by bit you gather that the villa is not as detached as it first appears. It is sculpted and hollowed to allow the surroundings to enter it... its formal energies radiate to the borders of the site and to the distant horizon.

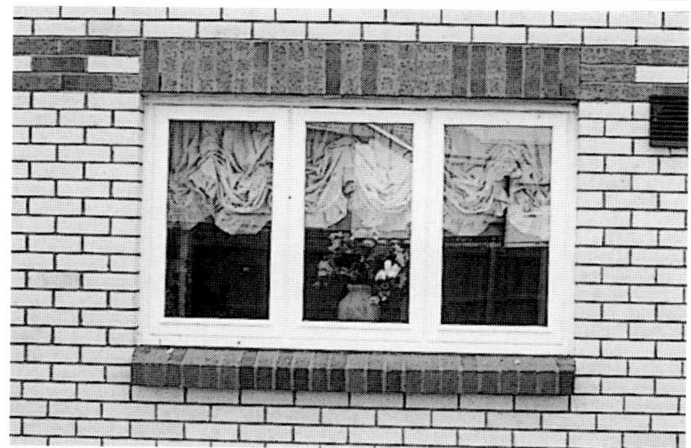

This shows you how the long window becomes part of the façade solution.

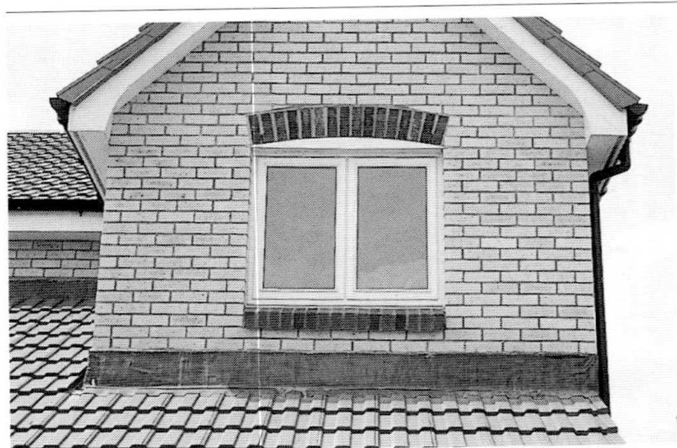

The slides don't really represent the feeling of space...the sense of rising up into an illuminating realm... or the intensive lyricism of the semi-reflective glass.

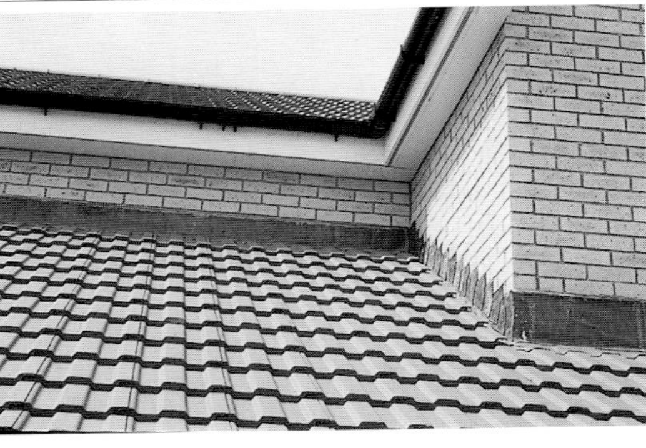

The building imposes its own order on the senses through sheer sculptural power...

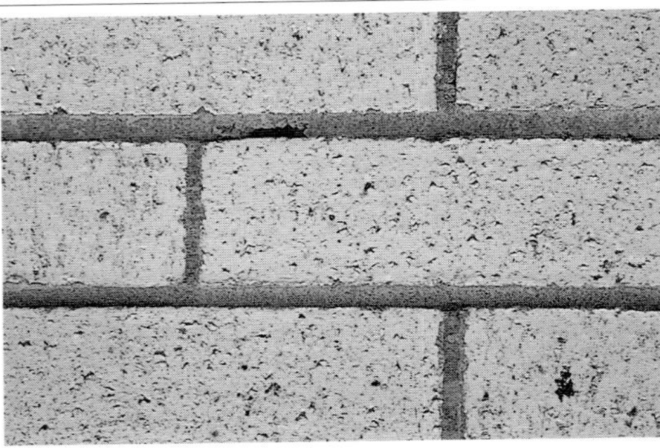

The entrance is found at the apex of a curve formed by the glazed lower level.

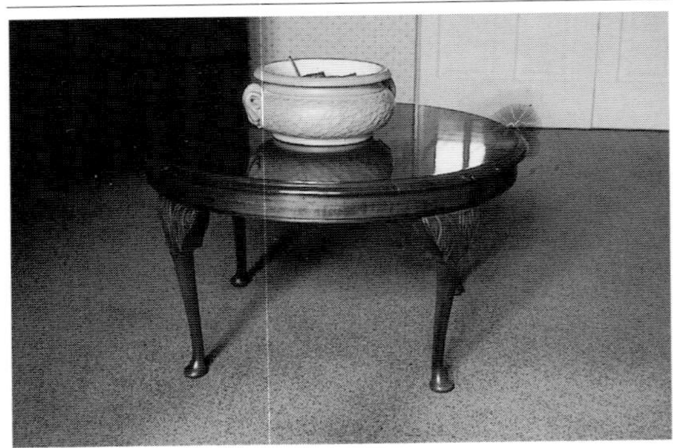

The main choices are clear. You either travel up the ramp straight ahead along the main axis of the building to the upper levels... or take the spiral stairs which link this level to the world above.

Ahead and slightly to the left this free standing wash-basin poses as an industrial 'ready-made', inviting ablutions before the ascent.

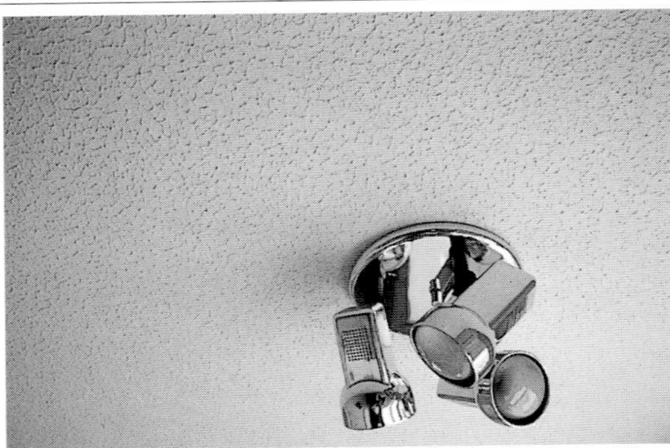

These are some details of the interior surfaces.

Brittle and smooth... the atmosphere almost clinical.

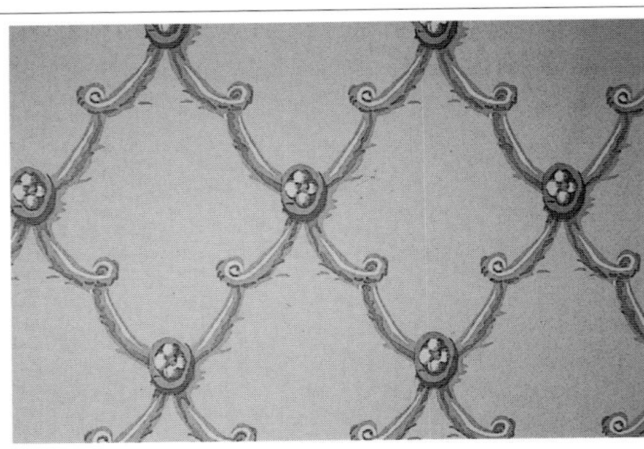

Another detail catches the eye: these small white tiles in the floor are laid out on the diagonal... and effect a subtle link between the various curves and rectangles of the building.

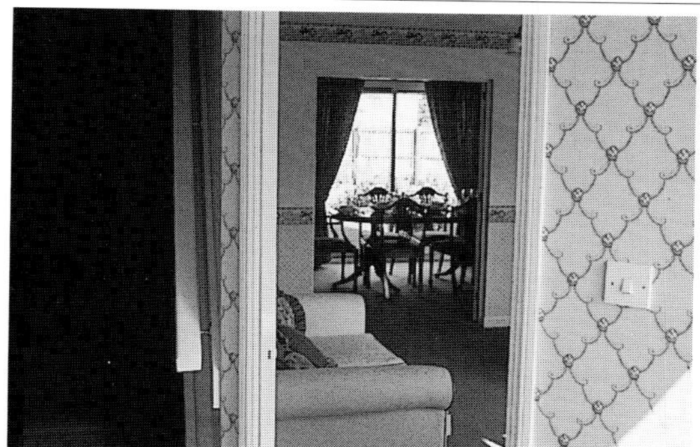

One passes through the main doors into the vestibule.

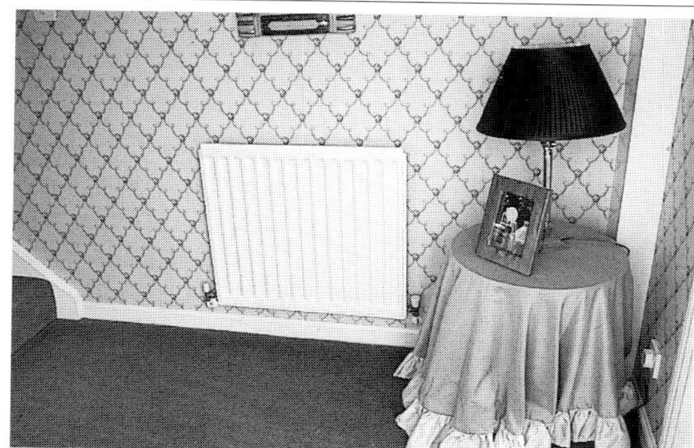

The moment one steps inside the villa one finds a new structural rhythm taking over.

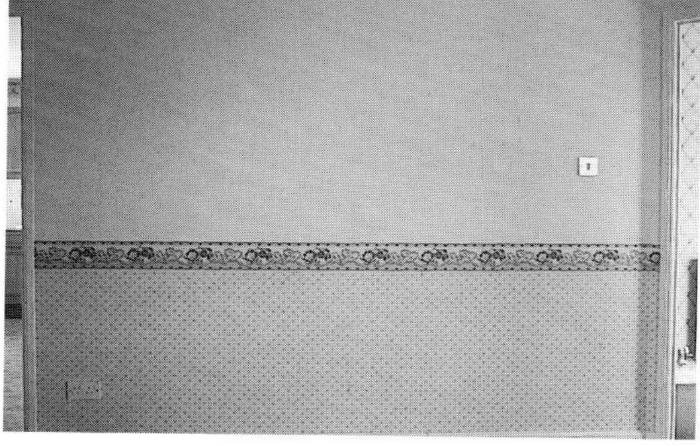

The space is defined by these curved glass surfaces on either side... and a square pier answering to the corner of the wall by the base of the ramp.

The path traced by the car is echoed by the ramp which rises up through the house as if in a continuous flow of motion.

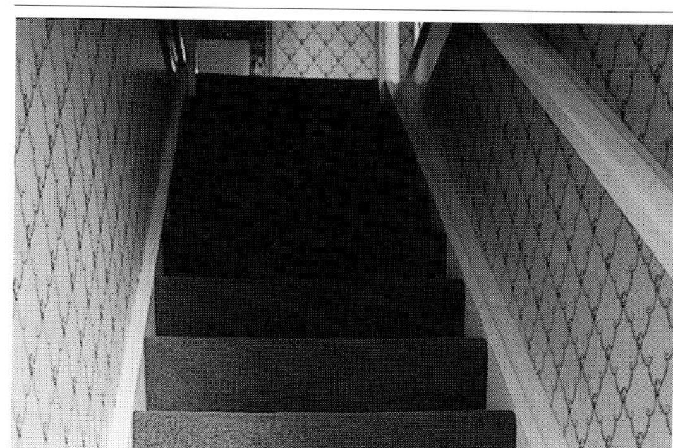

You are able to see through many layers of the villa at once: a pillar in the fore-ground might pun with a stack or the spiral stairs in the background.

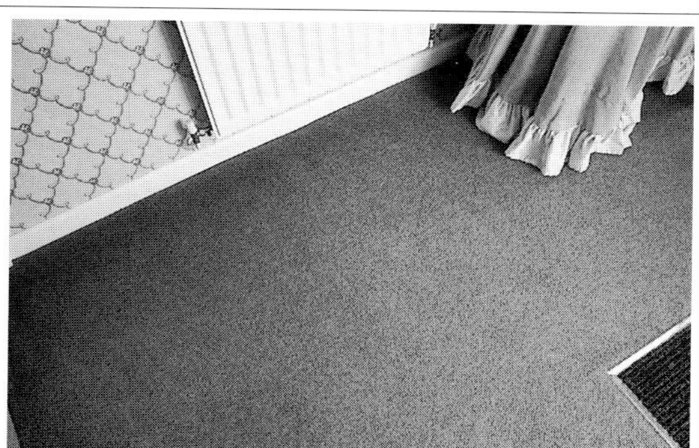

The ground floor plan is determined by the notion of a continuity between automobile transport and pedestrian circulation.

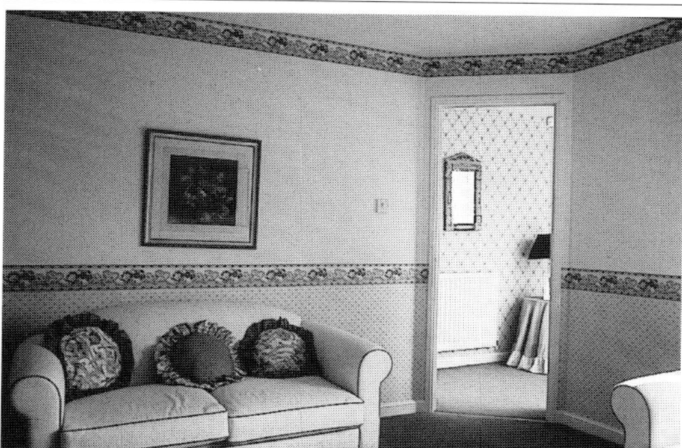

The dining room, bathroom, kitchen and other living quarters are grouped together on the piano nobile around the terrace which opens to the south and lives ambiguously as an outdoor room connected to the sky.

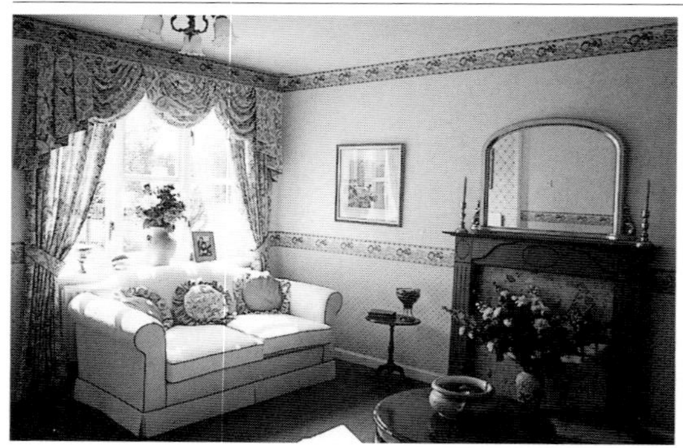

To the other two sides of the roof terrace are the more private areas... the main bedroom...

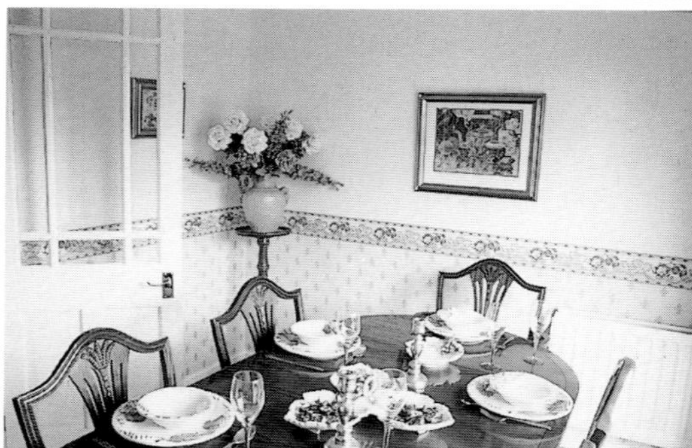

the dining room...

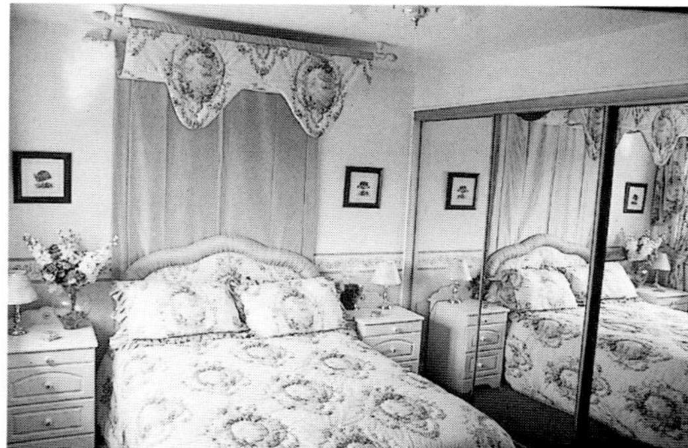

the bedroom...

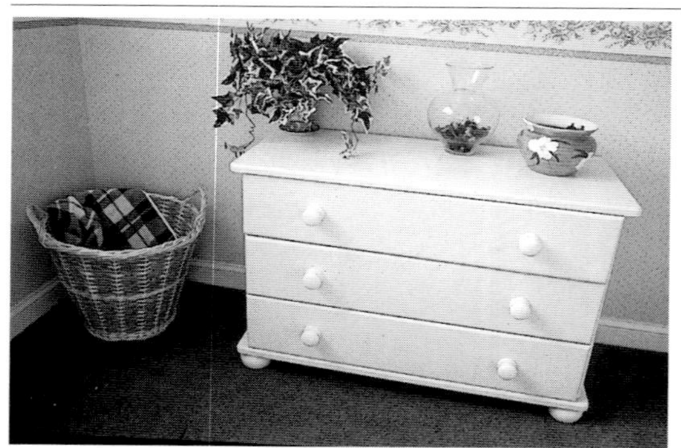

Slab-like wardrobes subdivide the space in the bedrooms.

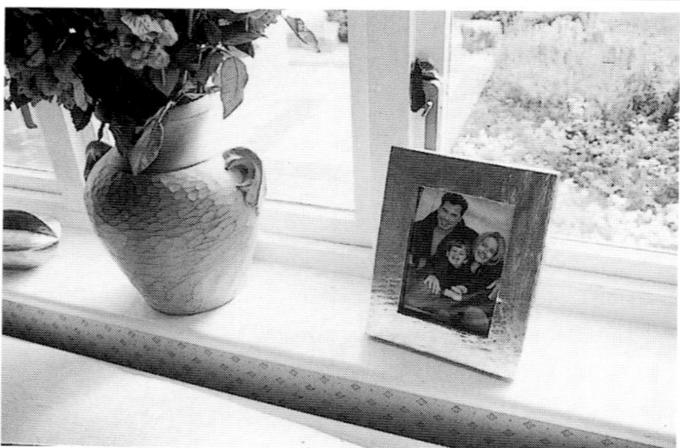

Shelves under windows and in wardrobes act as planes.

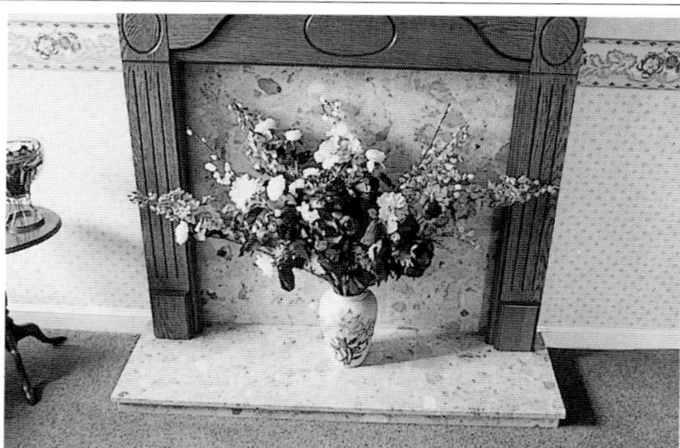

The hearth is built simply of brick, a statement of function expressed within the overall discipline.

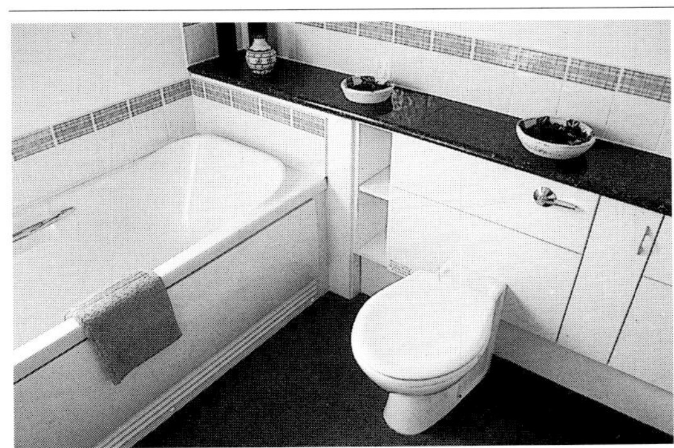

and the bathroom.

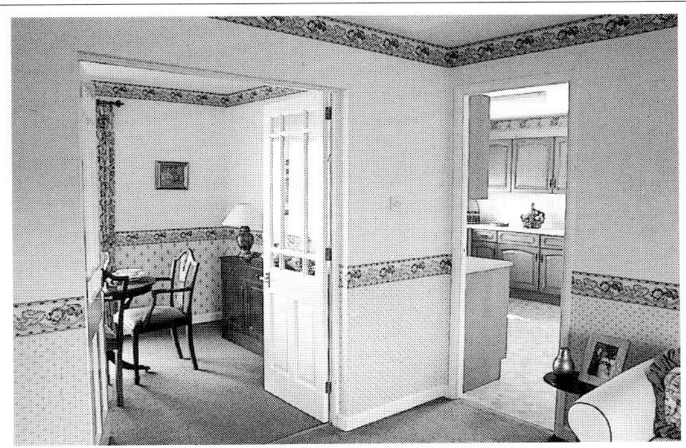

The strip windows, which appear equal on the outside, mask a variety of internal realities which are jigsawed into the plan: in places they are glazed, in other places open.

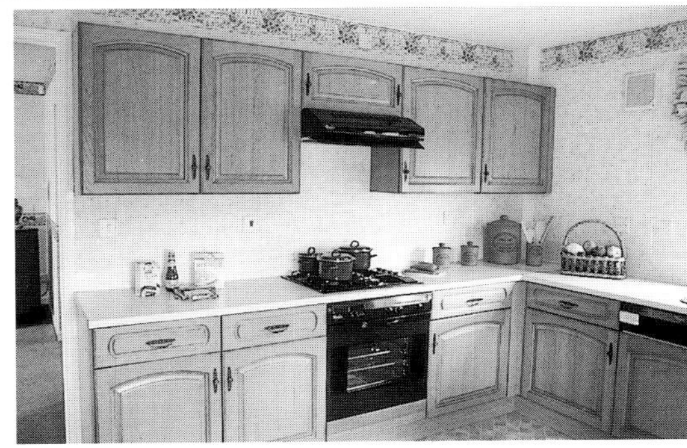

This is the bright airy kitchen with its fitted cupboards, white tiled surfaces and aluminium doors.

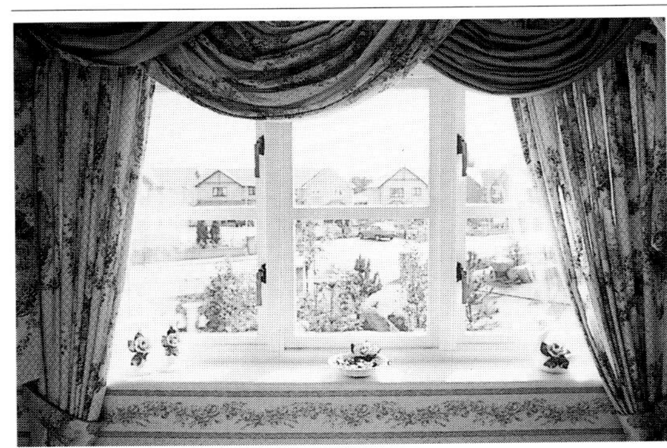

At the piano nobile level the continuous strip of glazing is echoed by the horizontal plane of the window ledge. The opening in the roof screen with its adjacent table confirms this idea.

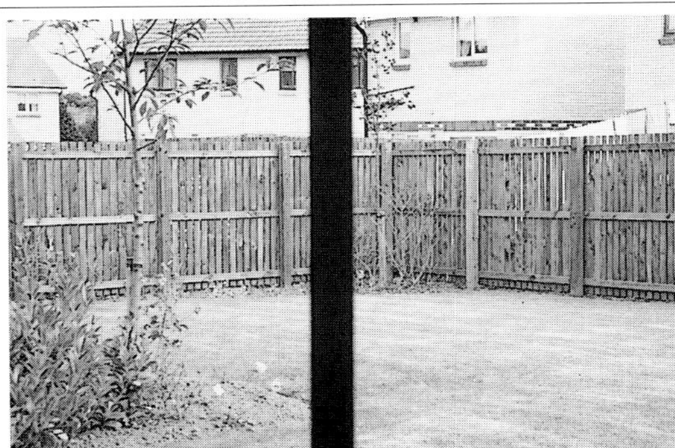

From a practical viewpoint the screen gives shelter from the north and east while admitting the afternoon sun.

It becomes clear that one is to be drawn into a modern-age ritual. The plan of the building comes from the dynamics of the curved forms within a stable perimeter.

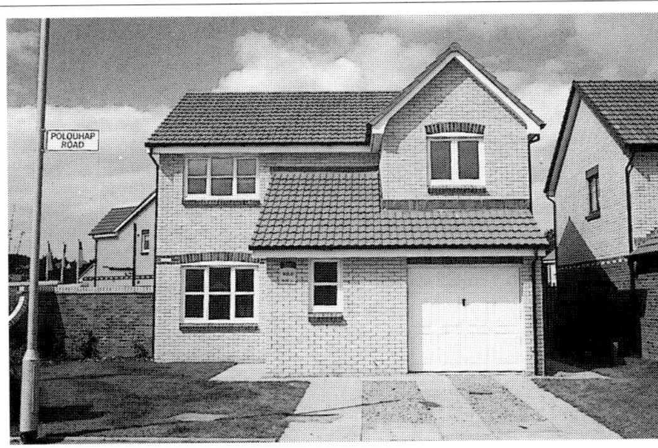

On first approaching, the building was seen surrounded by the setting; now the setting is framed by the building.

Critics have described it as a hovering spaceship, a temple, a Palladian villa. In truth it is a pristine health house open to light, sun, and views over greenery.

A house as a machine for living in.

Unbuilt Monuments
Takehiko Nagakura

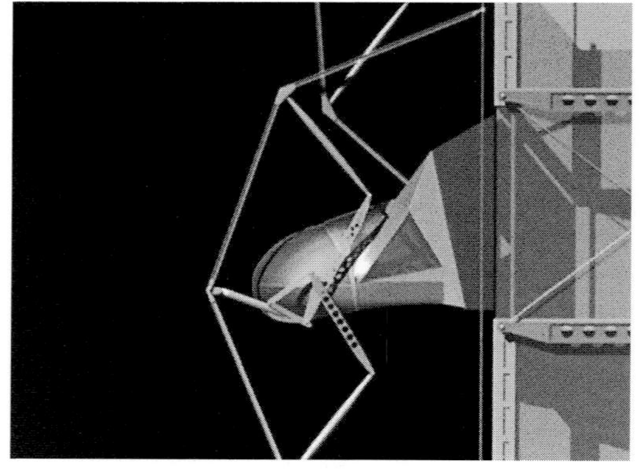

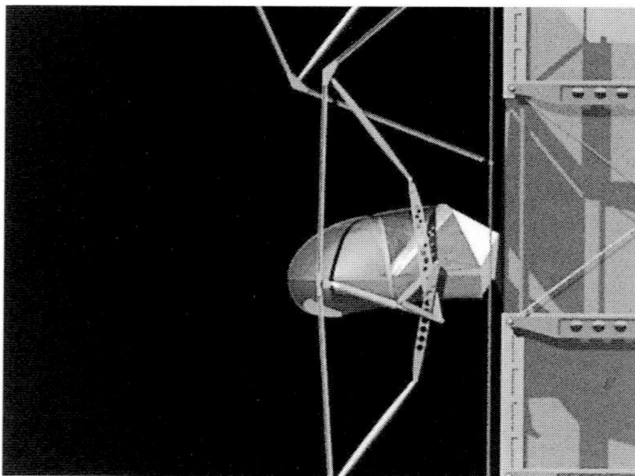

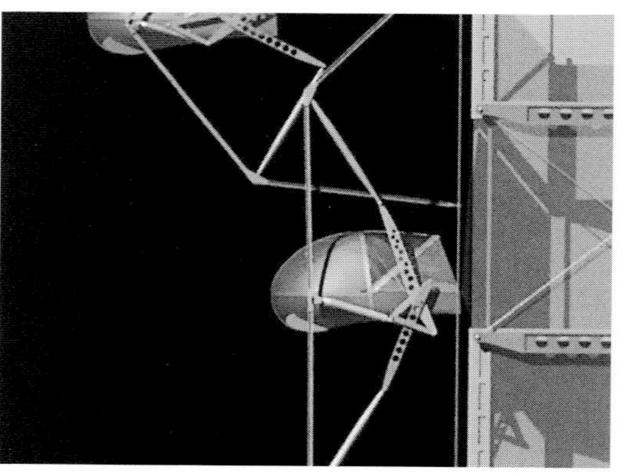

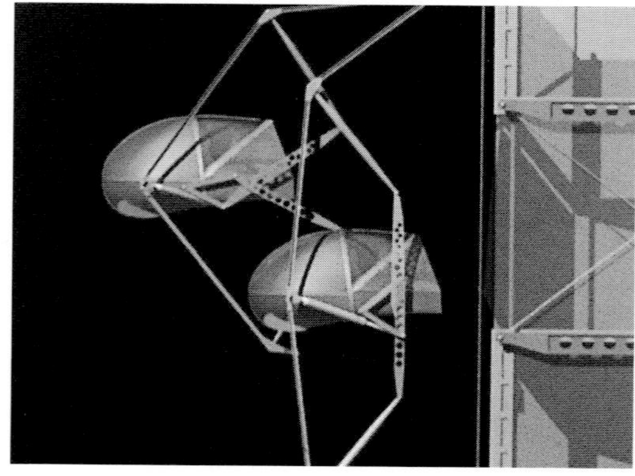

For all its technical complexity, the virtual reality architectural fly-through no longer seems, in itself, particularly special. So familiar a part of the architect's impressive marketing armoury has it become, that realistic montage photographs of mile-high skyscrapers against the backdrop of a familiar city; or of slices, curves, slashes and blobs artificially inserted into the rectilinearity of the twentieth-century city grid no longer seem any more unexpected than those after-the-fact table-napkin sketches which sustained the myth of architectural genius before the advent of computers.

Given the ubiquity of computer-rendered architectural fantasies, at first it seems surprising that Takehiko Nagakura's unbuilt monuments have generated attention from all over the world. Yet there is something irresistible about these realistic renderings of iconic architectural proposals of the modern era: something about the rusting ironwork of Tatlin's *Monument to the Third International*; the blemished concrete of Le Corbusier's *Palace of Soviets*, that sets them in a league apart.

For Nagakura, the interest in pursuing such a financially unrewarding activity lies both in the detective work required to visualise the spaces and materials intended by the architects in their often incomplete designs, and also in the creative direction required to turn his computer renderings into three-dimensional filmic reality. But while this creative conjecture gives the projects a powerful visual richness, what makes the *Unbuilt Monuments* really compelling is in Nagakura's choice of architectural designs.

Vladimir Tatlin's *Monument to the Third International* is one of the enduring icons of the Soviet revolution, a sculpture commissioned in 1919 and planned to stand taller than the Eiffel Tower. Tatlin designed it to dominate St Petersburg, the classical capital of Russia, and although the project is widely known, it only survives through abstract drawings and a sculptural model. Similarly, Le Corbusier's 1931 design for the *Palace of Soviets* would have provided an enormous addition to the Moscow skyline had it been selected by Stalin. With a curving roof suspended from a vast concrete parabolic arch, Le Corbusier's design would have been heralded as one of the most important buildings of the twentieth century, but it fell foul of the highly political selection process at a time when Soviet Communism had developed an uneasy relationship with artists and architects.

Imagining the future dominance of the machine, rather than Communism, the *Drive-in House* designed by Michael Webb of Archigram in 1968 suggested that transport and housing would be even more integrated than they are today. The project consisted of high-rise building structures with a crane on each level. At street level, inhabitants of the building would travel in specially-designed cars running on tracks. When they returned to the building, each car would be picked up by the crane on the relevant level, and plugged into the occupant's apartment. The entire process would take place without the driver having to leave the vehicle.

Despite the huge variety of these ideas, each represent versions of a future in which society would – literally or metaphorically – have been controlled by a greater machine. It is in imagining this possibility that the *Unbuilt Monuments* become more than visualisations; there is a frisson of power in the knowledge that architecture can prop up utopian ideals which turn out to be dystopian. Their verisimilitude allows us to nudge up to a dangerously exciting possibility that these things might actually have been built – extraordinary buildings without doubt, but ultimately a sophisticated backdrop for an imaginary journey into the workings (for an American or European audience) of an alien political world. Somehow, if *Unbuilt Monuments* had focused on the rejected versions of Chicago's Tribune Tower, the impact would not be the same.

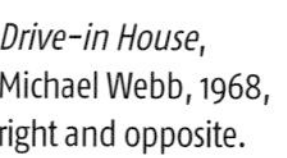

Drive-in House, Michael Webb, 1968, right and opposite.

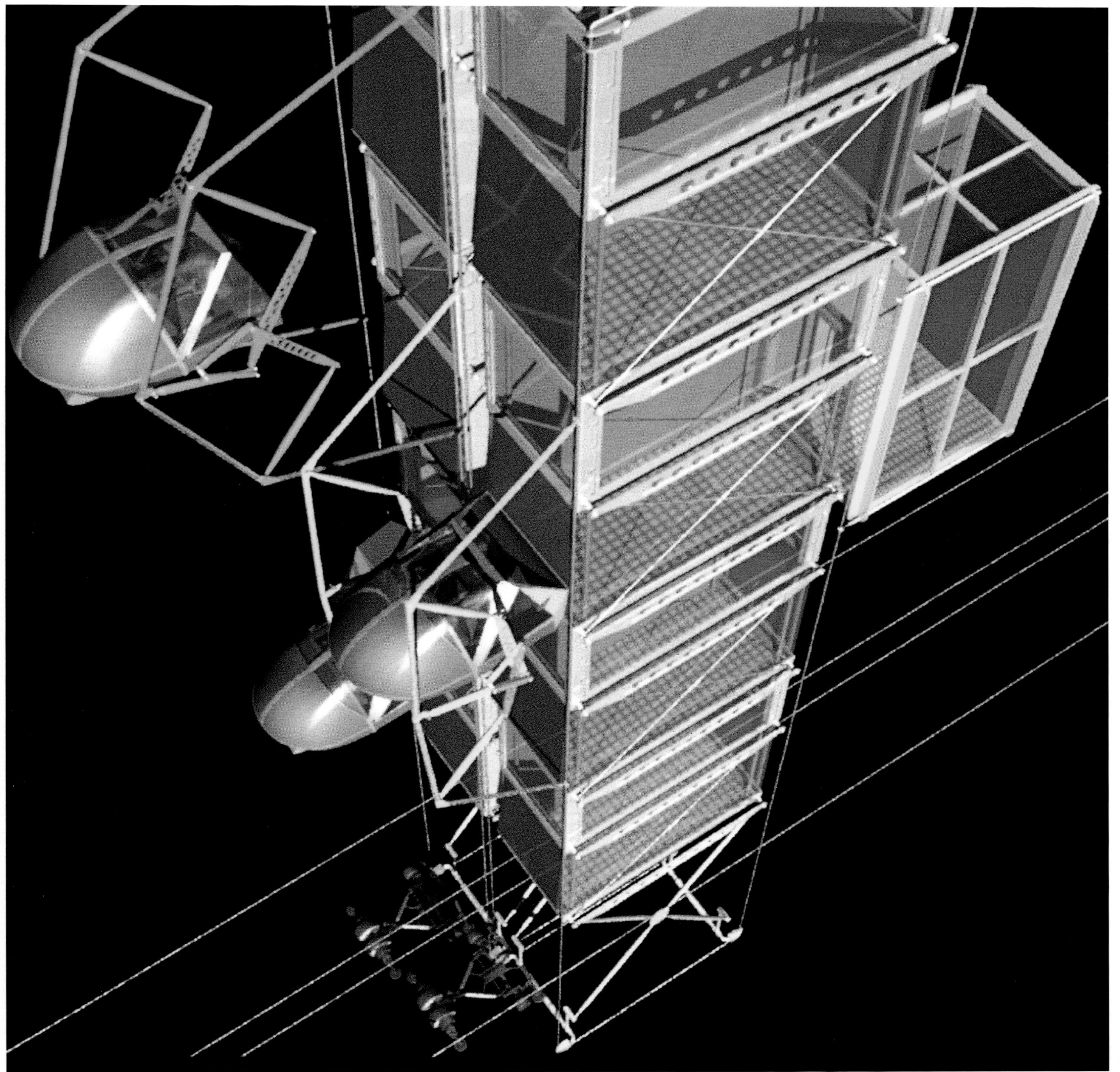

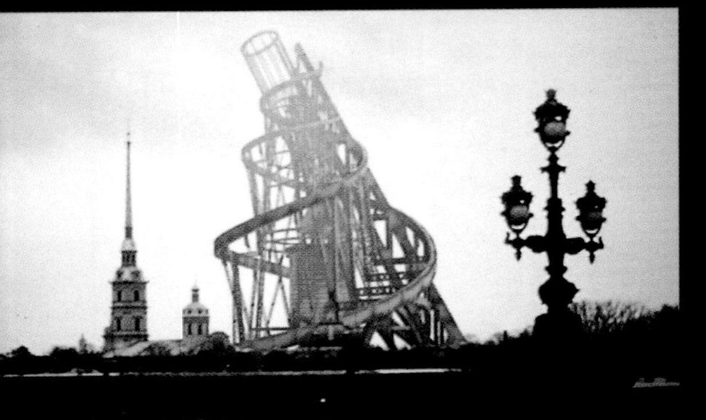

Monument to the Third International, Vladimir Tatlin, 1919, left and below.

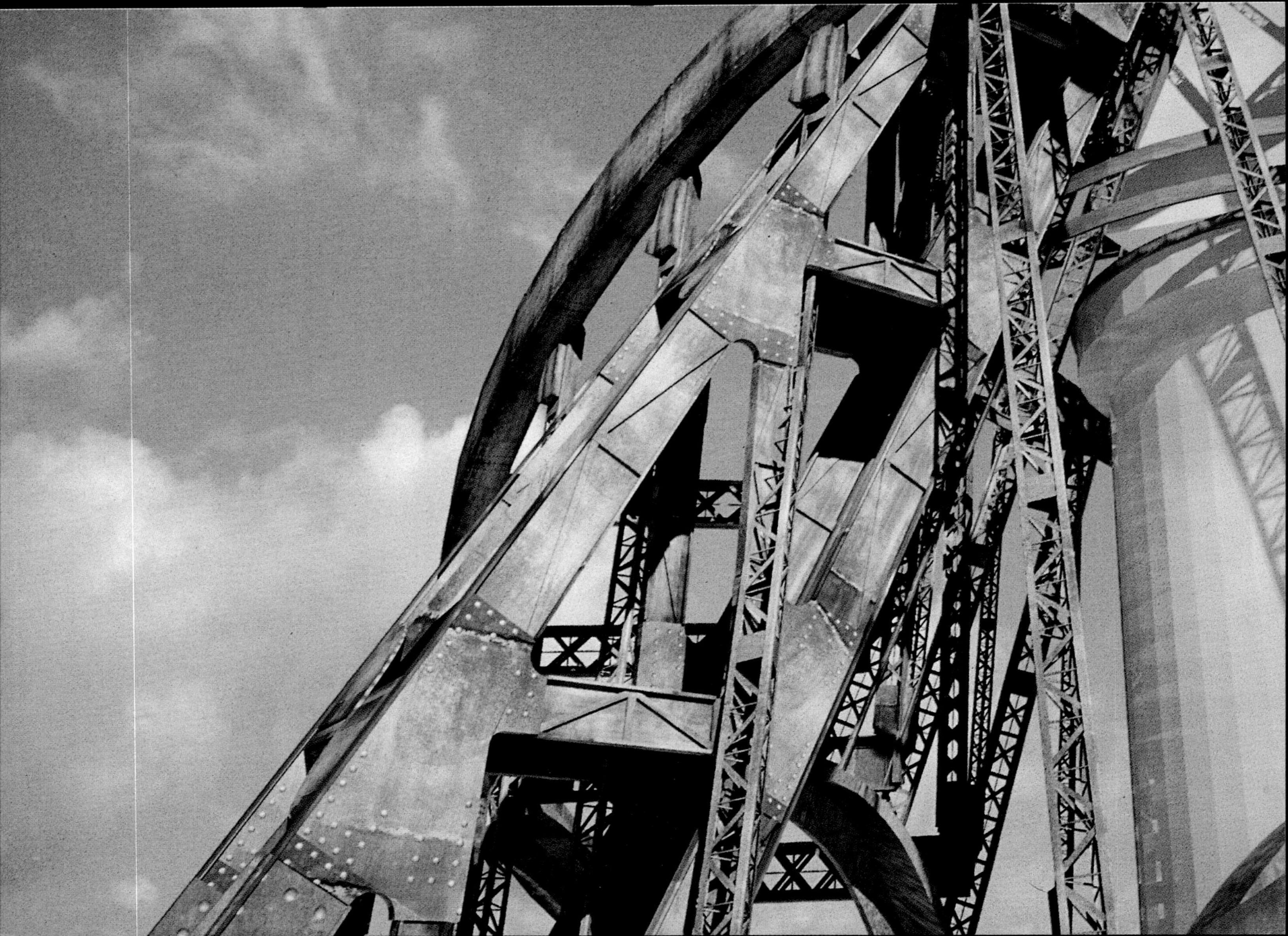

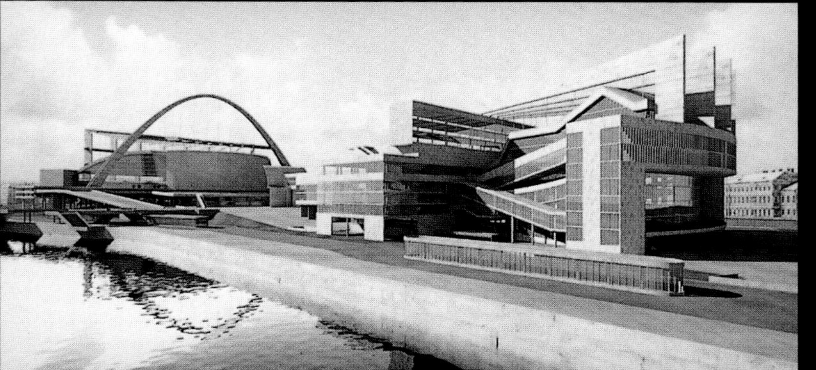

Palace of Soviets,
Le Corbusier, 1931, left
and below

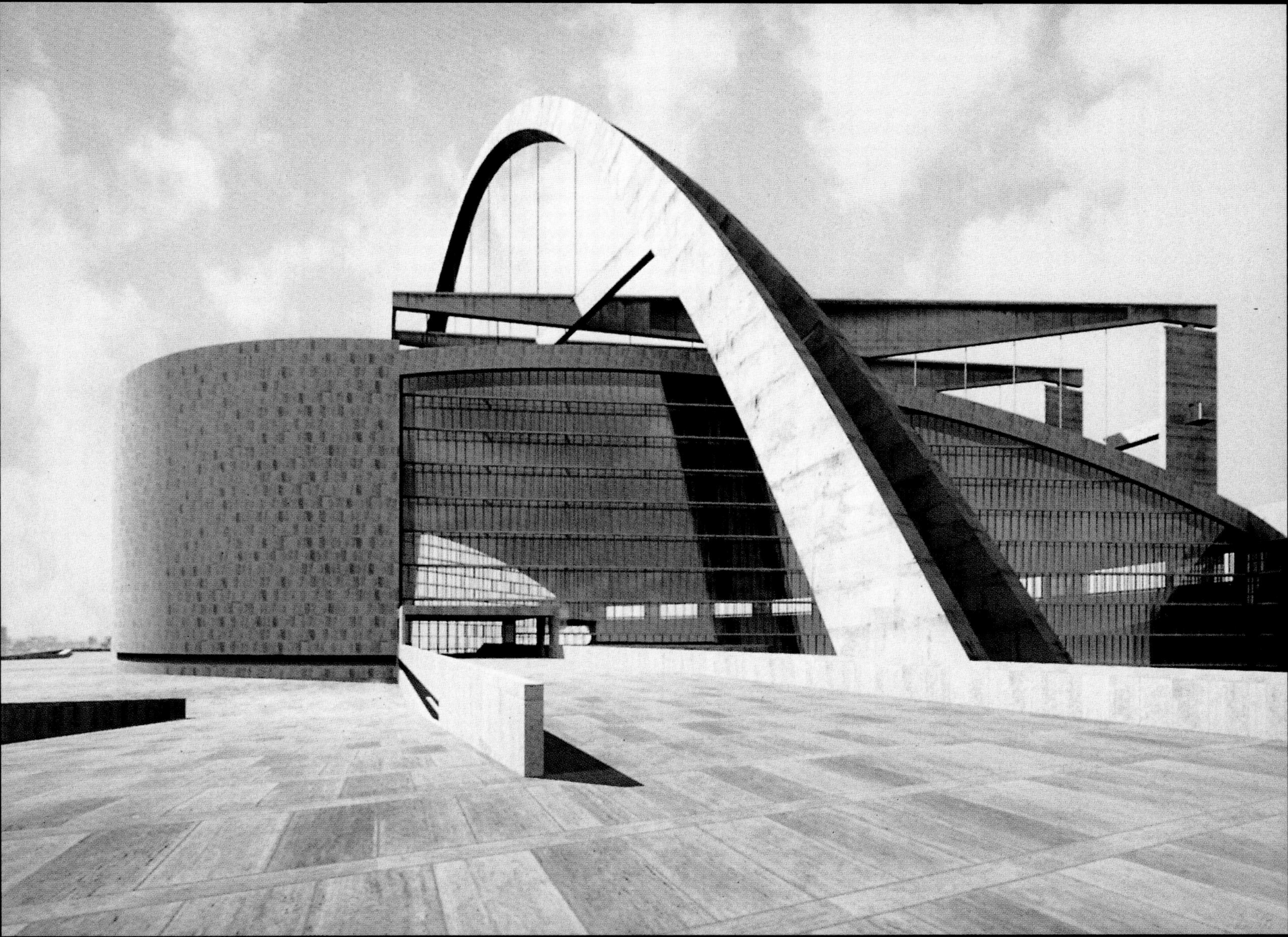

The Unbuildable
Sean Griffiths

A muscular man is dressed in his underpants. He stares out towards an imaginary viewer. He is holding a large lollipop. He occupies a room with two female companions. One is busy vacuuming the stairs. The other fondles her naked left breast with an expression of transcendent pleasure on her face. She is wearing what appears to be a lamp shade on her head. She sits on a sofa, in front of which is a coffee table. Upon the coffee table is placed, amongst other things, a large tin of processed ham.

Behind her is a television set which displays a talking head belonging to another beautiful female protagonist, who appears to be talking to her lover on the telephone, but is in fact acting a part in an advertisement for an unknown product. On the wall are two pictures: one a poster advertising a picture book called *Young Romance*, the other a photographic portrait of an American president from the nineteenth century. Illuminating the room is a large double-paned window. It is night time, and the window offers a view of a cinema which is showing the Al Jolson movie T*he Jazz Singer*, the very first talking picture. In the foreground of the scene is a reel-to-reel tape recorder.

Cut to a view of New York City seen from the East River. It is eight years later. The city is under attack. It's like something from HG Wells' *The War of the Worlds*. Gigantic scaly creatures with multiple orifices (are they eyes or anuses?) march upon the city. The creatures are able to look in all directions simultaneously. They have monstrous telescopic legs which reach out exponentially to find firm footing in the bed of the river. The city, this particular city, itself a fantastical and incredible piece of urban landscape, seems to stand aside in terror as these hideous creatures march by. It seems impotent by comparison.

Below: *Walking City*, elevation detail. Ron Herron, Archigram Group. Opposite: *Just what is it that make's today's homes so different, so appealing?* Richard Hamilton, collage, 1959

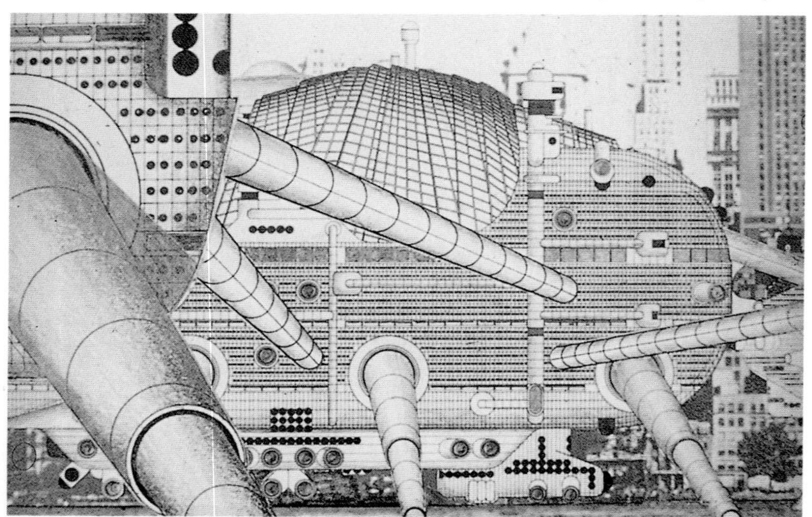

These could be scenes from some as yet unmade film, but they are not. One is an image which was intended as a design for a poster advertising an exhibition called *This is Tomorrow*, staged at the Whitechapel Art Gallery in London in 1956. The other is an architectural image dating from 1964. The images are Richard Hamilton's collage *Just what is it that makes today's homes, so different, so appealing?* and *Walking City* by Ron Herron and Archigram.

Both these images have long fascinated me. Both describe spaces that are unbuilt and which, as someone who practises architecture and therefore aims to build, I find strange and intriguing. This is because they speak of a different kind of desire to the desire one would normally associate with architectural drawings. For the architectural drawing is meant to be a representation of something to be. Its mystery lies in its pure inventedness. Unlike a depiction of a real scene, it represents something that does not exist. In this sense, all architectural drawings seem almost supernatural, having something of the quality of a premonition and of that sense of inevitability which is present in drawings by Piranesi.

In the two images I have described, this ambition does not exist. These are not images that represent a desire to build something. On the contrary, one is a poster design which became, by accident, an important work of art. The other is a work of art which attains this status by virtue of being an architectural image which refuses the traditional desire of the architectural drawing – the desire to become, to be realised.

I have always been thrilled by architectural drawings and trained to be an architect because it seemed to me that this career would satisfy my desire to draw. The drawing part of a project is always the bit that most interests me – far more than the construction process and the actual realisation of the work. It never really occurred to me that drawings of the unbuilt could be interesting precisely because they represented something that was meant to exist, but didn't. I have always preferred to see drawings as analogous to, and offering other interpretations of, some built reality. There is therefore always, nonetheless, an intense desire to build and a tremendous sense of disappointment when things are not realised, which of course happens more often than not. So in the context of these thoughts, my fascination with these two particular images, images of architectural spaces absent of the desire to become real, seems strange to me. But maybe the essence of the architectural drawing or image, which is suggestive of something that might come into being – even if the desire to come into being doesn't exist – is exhibited in another kind of desire. Perhaps it is also exhibited in desire's opposite – terror.

My own descriptions of these images make it clear to me that they contain elements of both desire and terror. Indeed, the battle for prominence between these conditions is what determines the meanings offered by these images. Is this what is at the heart of all architectural premonitions? And is this not particularly so when we know that they represent a terror of desire unrequited? Is this what makes representations of unbuilt projects particularly poignant?

I have to ask myself what it is that fascinates me about both of these images. What do I take from Herron's image? Its central idea – the notion that the cities should walk? This has always seemed silly to me, although it probably did not in 1964. When thinking about how this drawing proposes a future mode of living, it seems a tragic anachronism. But the basis of its proposal has never been the thing that has interested me about this image. Rather, the appeal lies in its evocation of certain aspects

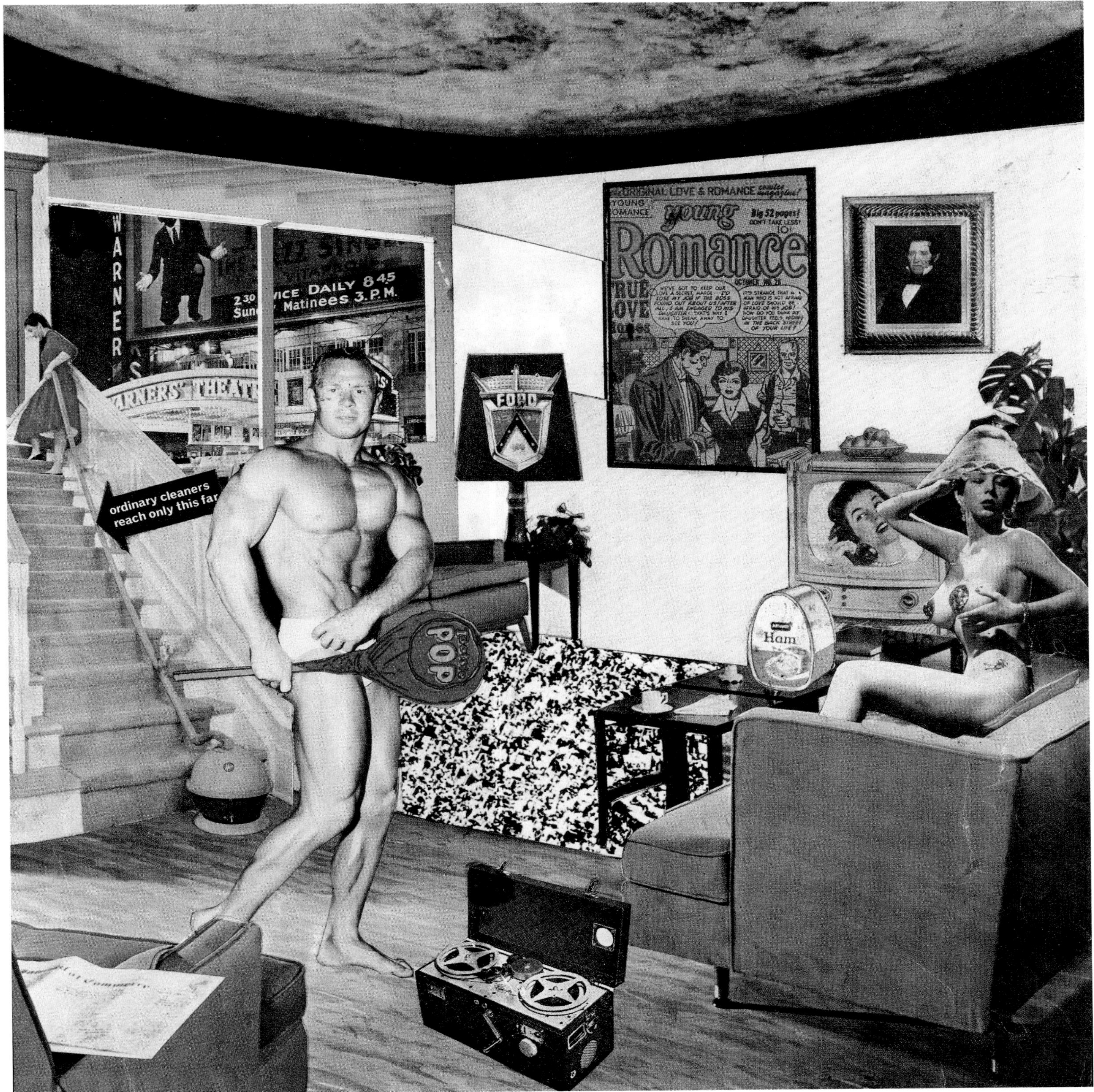
WARNERS
ordinary cleaners
reach only this far
FORD
ORIGINAL LOVE & ROMANCE comics magazine!
YOUNG ROMANCE
young Romance
Big 52 pages!
DON'T TAKE LESS!
10¢
WE'VE GOT TO KEEP OUR LOVE A SECRET, MARGE -- I'D LOSE MY JOB IF THE BOSS FOUND OUT ABOUT US! AFTER ALL, I AM ENGAGED TO HIS DAUGHTER! THAT'S WHY I HAVE TO SNEAK AWAY TO SEE YOU!
IT'S STRANGE THAT A MAN WHO IS NOT AFRAID OF LOVE SHOULD BE AFRAID OF HIS JOB! HOW DO YOU THINK MY DAUGHTER FEELS HIDING IN THE BACK STREET OF YOUR LIFE?
POP
Ham

of popular culture, of Saturday morning television repeats of 1930s American science fiction serials. Or of HG Wells' *The War of the Worlds*, serialised on radio, recorded on reel-to-reel tape, and replayed in school. It's almost funny how visions of the future translate so easily into nostalgia. But what really makes this image so memorable is its evocation of the terror that was always the attraction of that particular brand of popular science fiction. The essence of Ron Herron's image is therefore a nostalgia for fear, a fear we cannot experience in quite the same way in our post-war, post-nuclear age.

Something of this fear also exists in Richard Hamilton's image. This is an image of the Cold War, something which resonates with me because I am old enough to remember it. This image is also full of desire. It speaks, through its innocent abundance, of an austerity we cannot know today, of a desire for things, of an excitement and innocence in its view of technology. Its view of technology offers the same nostalgia tinged with fear. Its power also lies in a premonition of how technology would affect us, of the way in which the mass media and our desires distort our self image. It previews a scene from a David Lynch movie and so also, like the Archigram image, has something belonging to the realm of terror.

As proposals for environments, both are unrealisable, even allowing for their lack of desire to be so. The Hamilton picture is unrealisable due to the distorted nature of its perspective which, although beautifully crafted, could not be reproduced in real space, regardless of any future technological developments. Despite this, its distorted spatial characteristics bear an uncanny resemblance to those of Melnikov's realised Soviet pavilion for the Exposition des Arts Decoratifs, built in Paris in 1925, with its strange and impossible staircase, which distorts perspective in a manner very similar to the sampled domestic stair in Hamilton's image, which it pre-dates by thirty years. This project belongs to the era of the Russian Avant-Garde which is deemed politically acceptable. It is more or less contemporaneous with other visionary but unbuilt projects which have a poignancy as a result of their status as manifestations of a political ideal which became corrupted. Others one would include in this category are Tatlin's Tower and the Projects of Leodinov. One might also include Le Corbusier's Radiant City, a powerful conjunction of the respective imagery of technology and nature, which predates the merging of the man-made and the natural into a new ecology as propagated thirty years later by John McHale of the Independent Group (of which Hamilton was also a member) and Buckminster Fuller. All of these images exhibit something of the desire and exhilarating terror I think properly belongs to all unbuilt visionary projects.

But from where do these characteristic senses of desire and terror emanate? Perhaps there is something in the architect taking upon himself (and it is nearly always a him) the role of God that brings out these qualities. It is almost as if the representations of visionary projects, taken as they so often are from a God-like, overhead view, have been depicted by the architect occupying the highest perch of the tower.

Tatlin's Tower certainly has this quality. I think this has to do with the fact of its conception at a particular time, a time that was meant to constitute a new beginning. And this reinforces its resemblance to that earliest of visionary projects, the Tower of Babel, which beautifully articulates those qualities of terror and desire. By this I mean the tragic meeting of high and worthy aspiration with inevitable failure and the revealing of both the best of human intentions and the most monumental human folly. Herein lies the perfect expression of the meeting of desire and fear.

I have always felt the best visionary projects exhibited explicitly all of these characteristics and that their meaning was derived from the manipulation of them. This is certainly true of *Walking City*, which deals with terror through allusion to a child's exhilaration in a comic adventure. Other architects have dealt

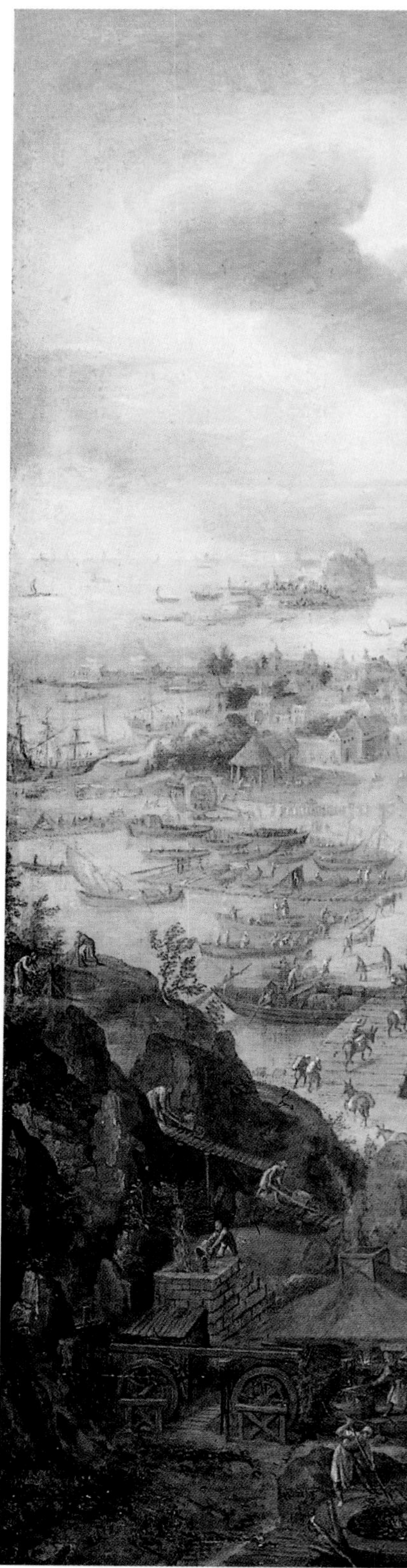

This page: *The Tower of Babel*, Maerten van Valckenborch, oil on oak, 1595.

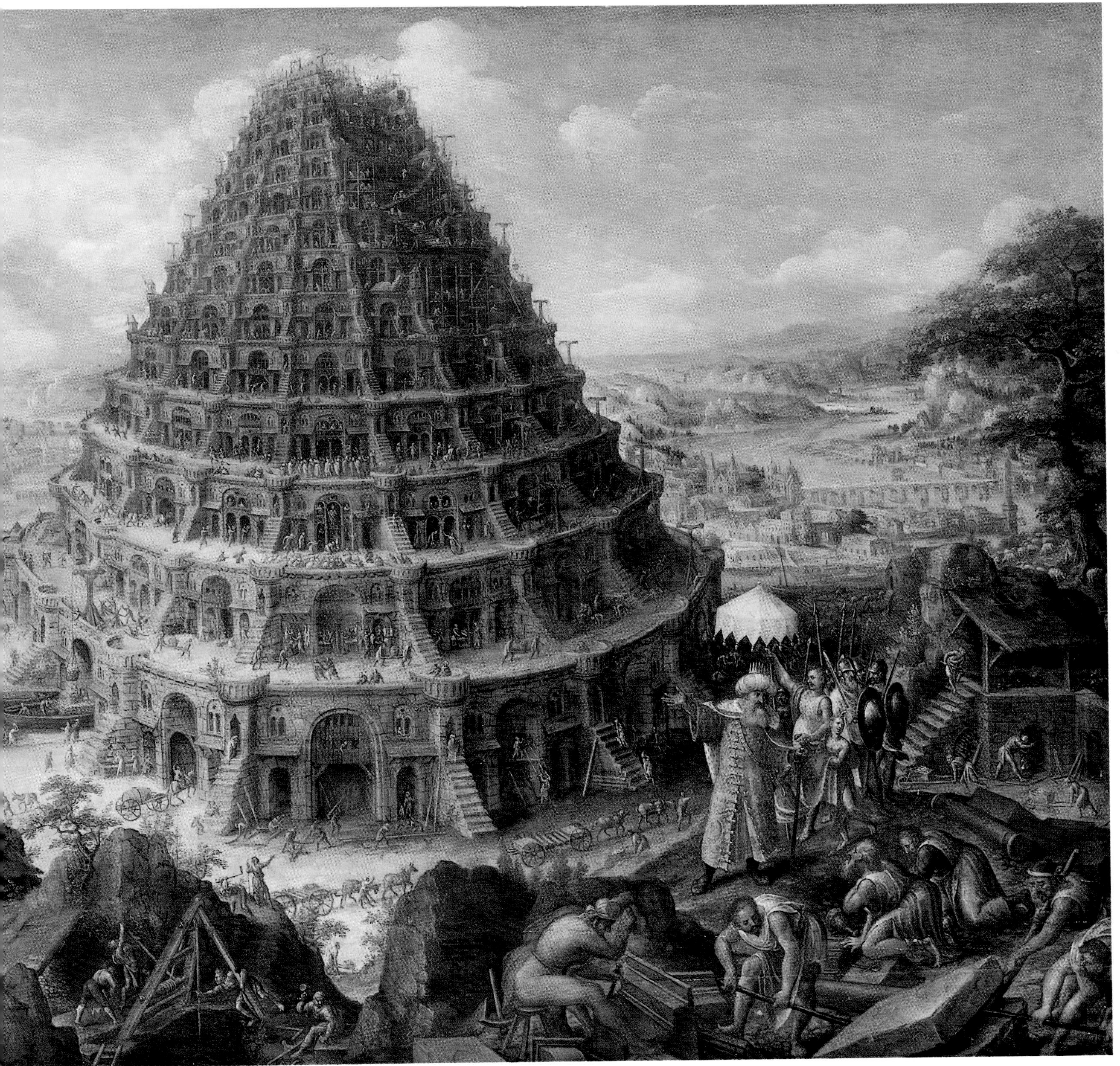

with it in a wholly different way.

Boullée's Cenotaph to Isaac Newton, dating from 1785, is a ludicrous but magnificent structure which is the centrepiece of what he himself called his 'genre terrible'. A gigantic unadorned sphere containing a suspended fire stands in tribute to scientific rationalism. Its terror lies in its evocation, despite the solid republicanism of its author, of an omnipotent abstract ruler, absent but ever present. Its poetic qualities lie in its aspiration and the inevitability of its remaining an image. It is a monument to an idea which can never be fulfilled in its purist form. In response, it offers a vision of terror as the only mechanism by which purity can be achieved, and which is therefore ultimately doomed to failure.

I think Melnikov was aware of this when he created the image of his proposal for the Ministry of Heavy Industry in 1934, which, anticipating the terror of the Stalin years, merges Babelonian ambition with an overwhelming totalitarian industrial symbolism. But this image speaks also of desire. Did the makers of the film *The Wizard of Oz*, a film at whose heart is the subject of adolescent terror and desire, ever see this image?

A gigantic stair rises to the centre of the image, terminating between two huge cylindrical blocks topped by giant wedges, which in turn support enormous statues of idealised workers. The entire view is framed by an enormous cylindrical industrial collar, mimicking Boullée's sphere. Behind the buildings dark clouds gather ominously. At the base of the stair, amongst other people, a man nonchalantly walks his dog. Such elements of apparent normality are included to counteract the terrifying sense of omnipotent force suggested by the image. But they also give it a black comic edge and an ironic optimism, characteristics that can be clearly read when the image is considered in the context of Melnikov's earlier work, projects that are bathed in the light of a purer optimism.

To conclude, I would like to return to the Richard Hamilton image. Apart from belonging to the realm of art rather than architecture, this image has significant differences from those of the architects. These differences are undoubtedly due in part to its status as art. This image does not have gargantuan scale and describes only one room. But from within that room, a view is offered that transcends the God-like view of the architect. For the ceiling of this room is made of an image of the earth taken from a space craft, an apparatus far more technologically sophisticated than anything dreamt up by Archigram. This apparatus is realised: it has been built. As well as being a visionary image itself, Hamilton's picture announces the tragic obsolescence of the visionary architectural project. For once God's own view has been replicated: there is no more need to represent it and the architect is finally emasculated.

Below: Newton's cenotaph, designed by Etienne-Louis Boullée (1728–1799), engraving. Opposite: Model of the planned monumental Congress Hall in Berlin, designed by Albert Speer in 1938/9, with next to it as a scale comparison the model of the Brandenburg Gate and the Reichstags.

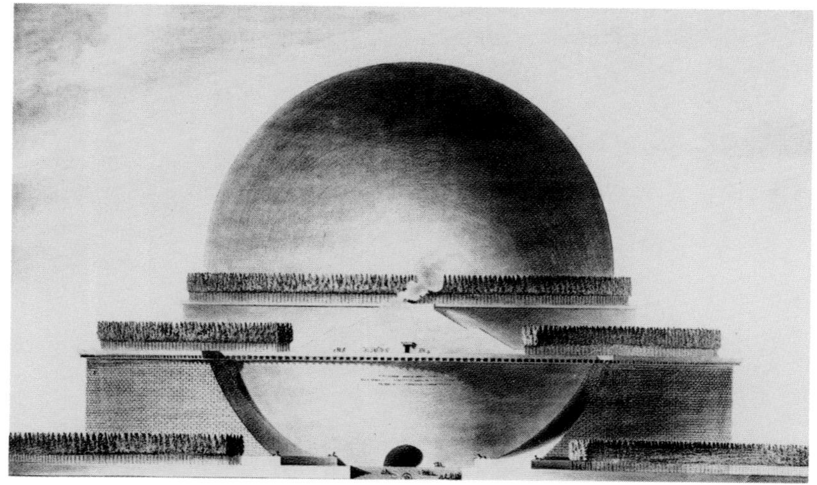

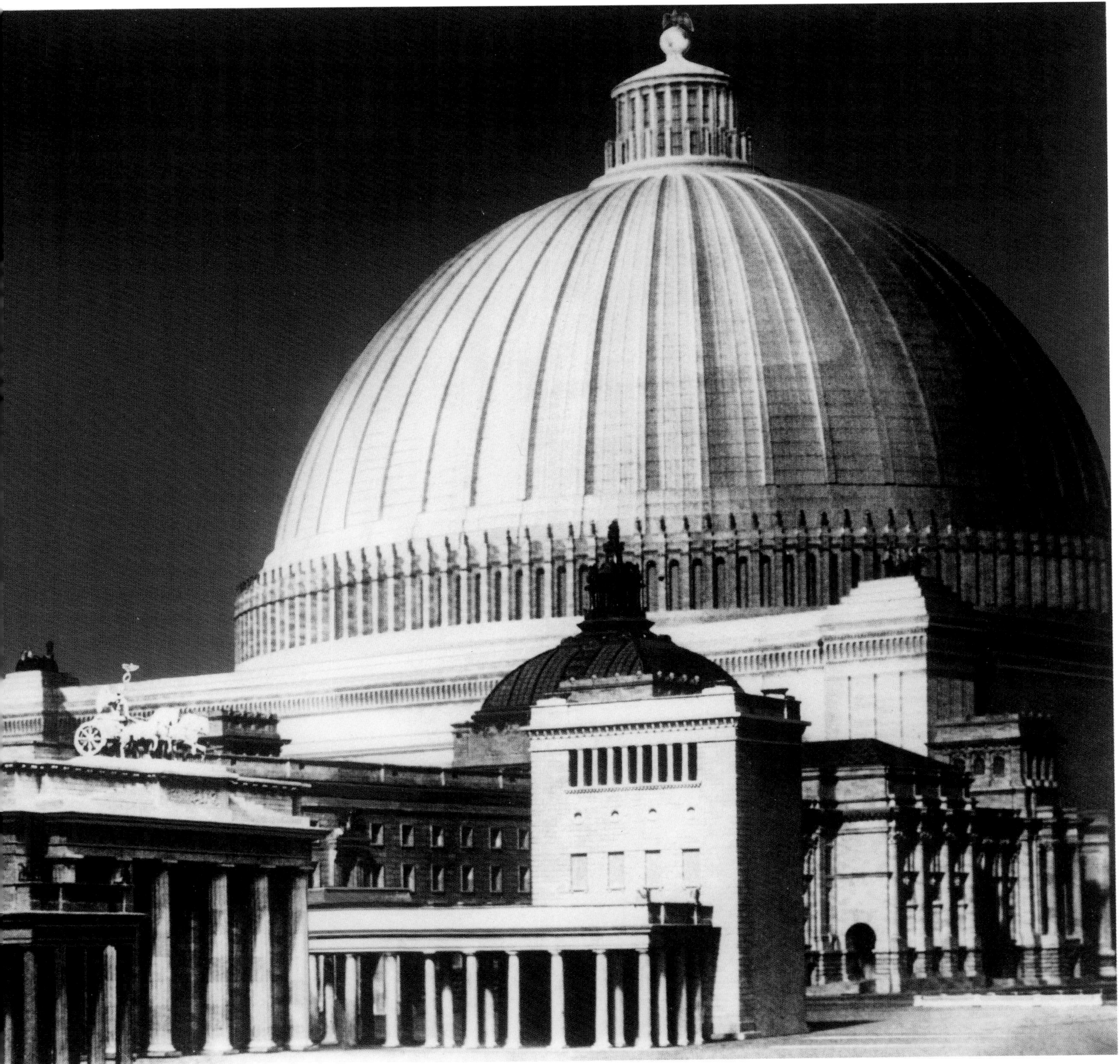

Xmas in Alabama
JJ Waller

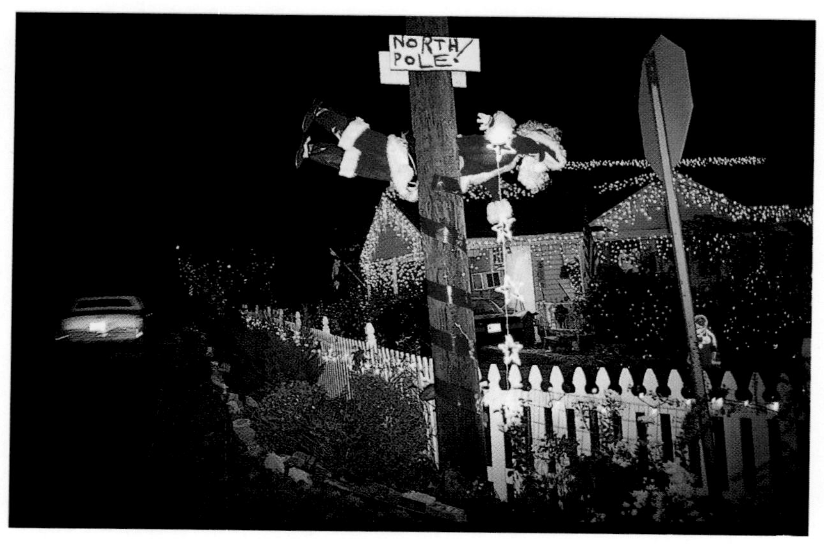

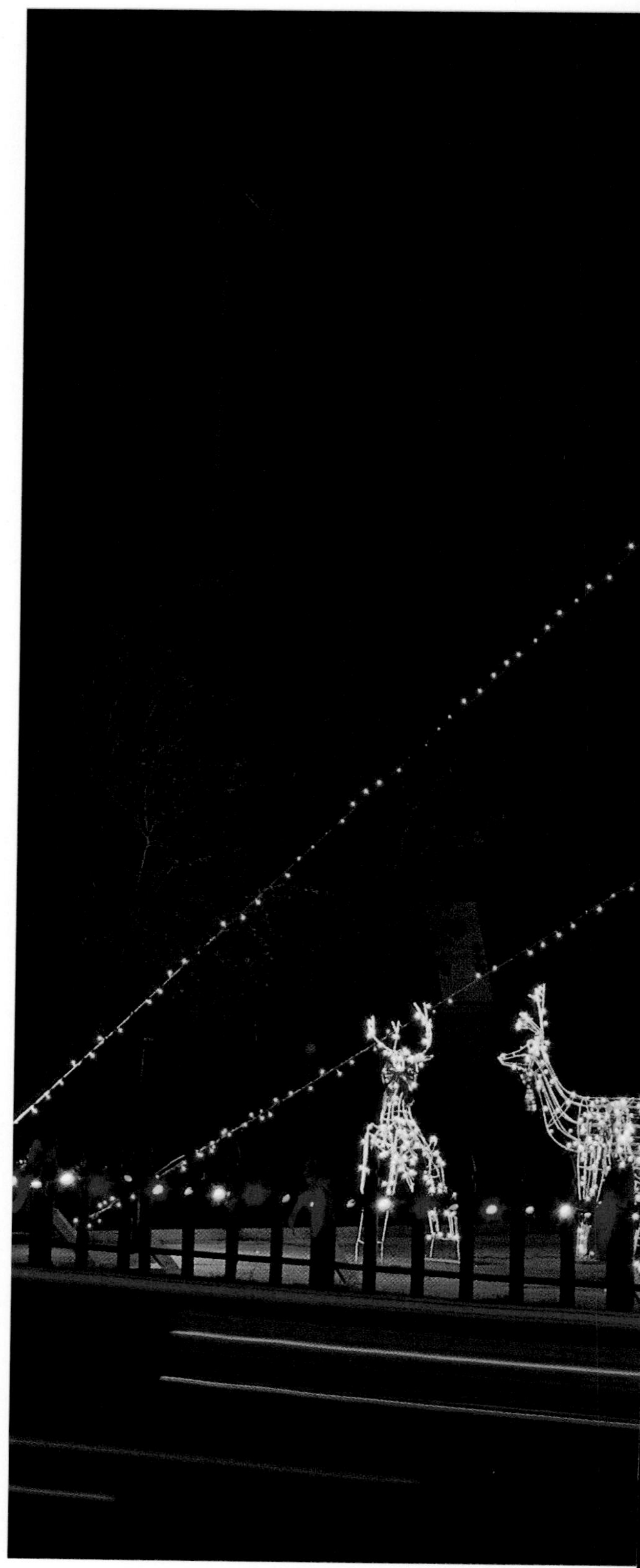

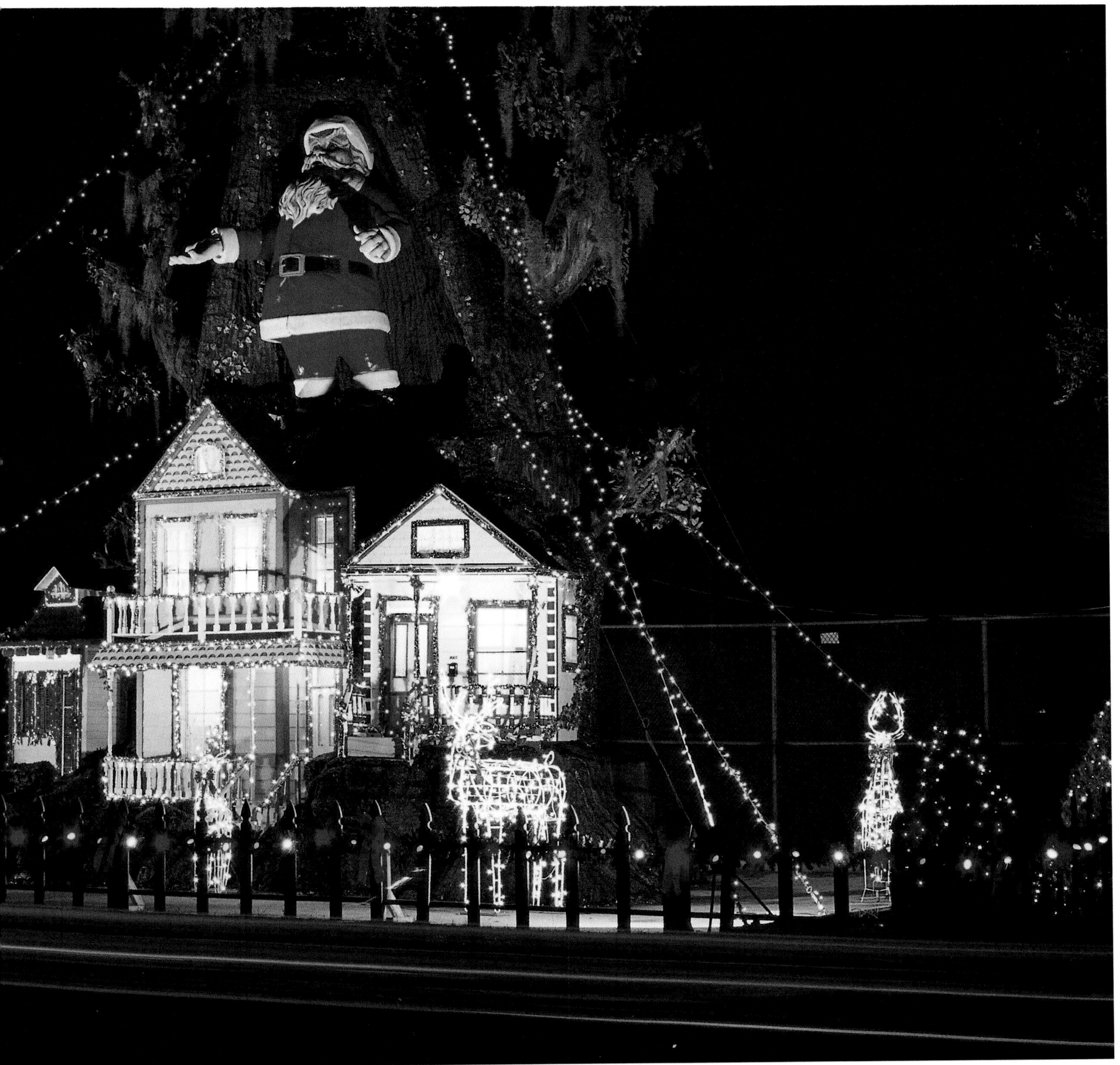

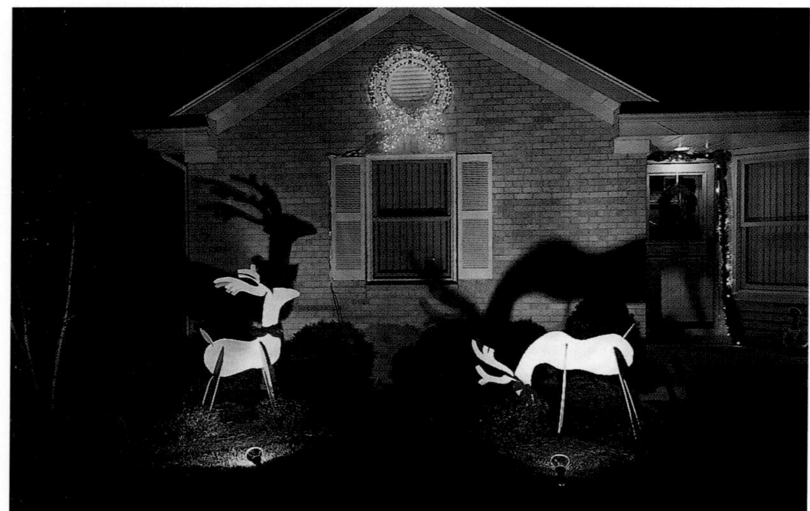

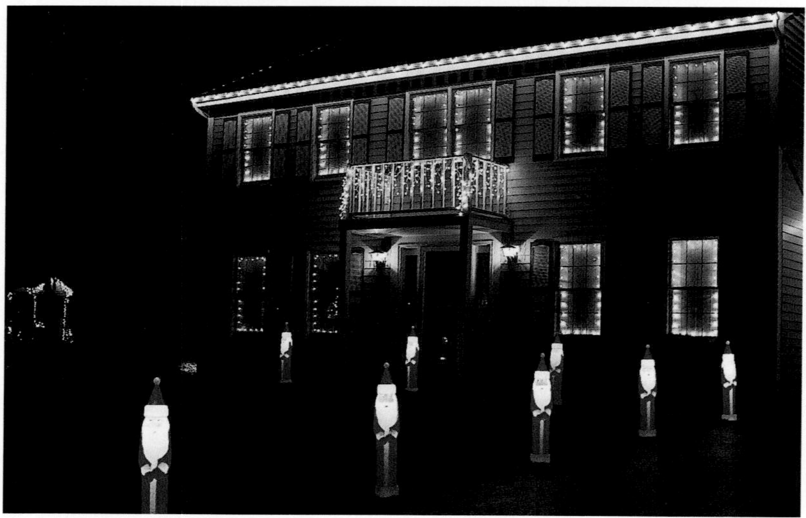

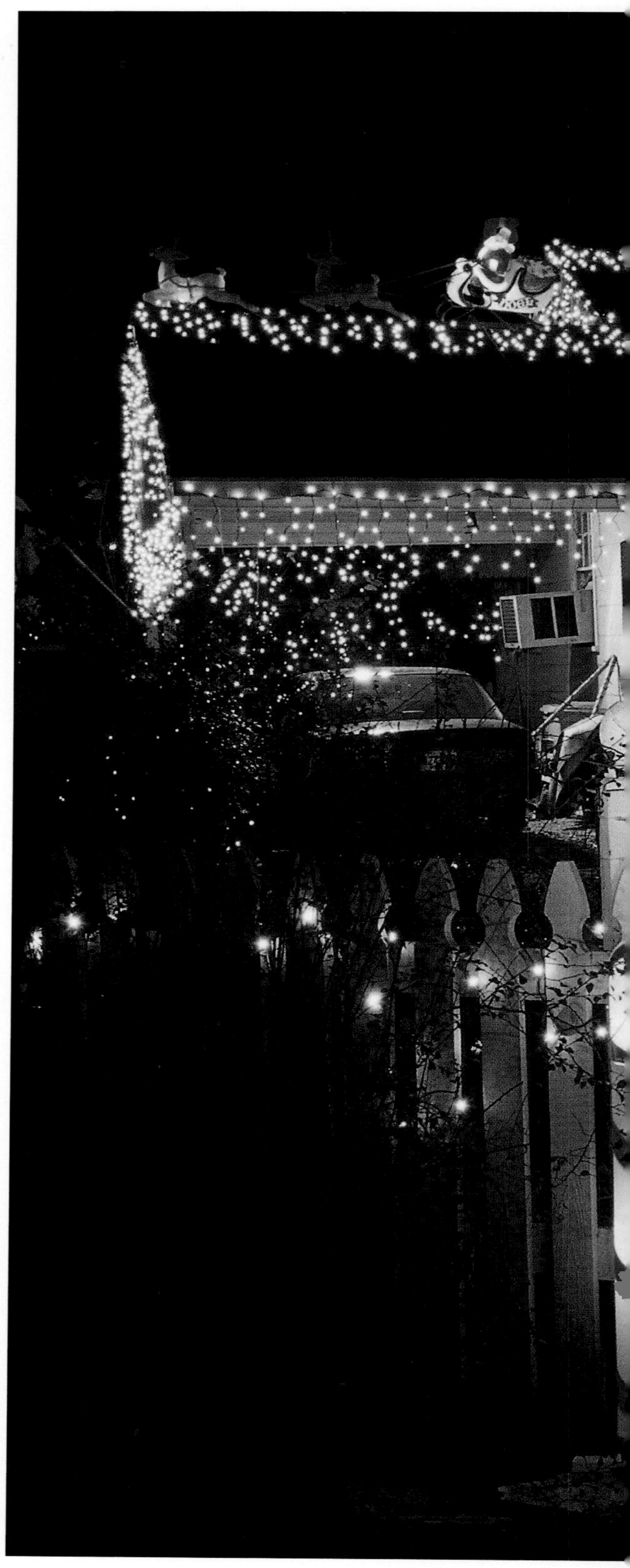

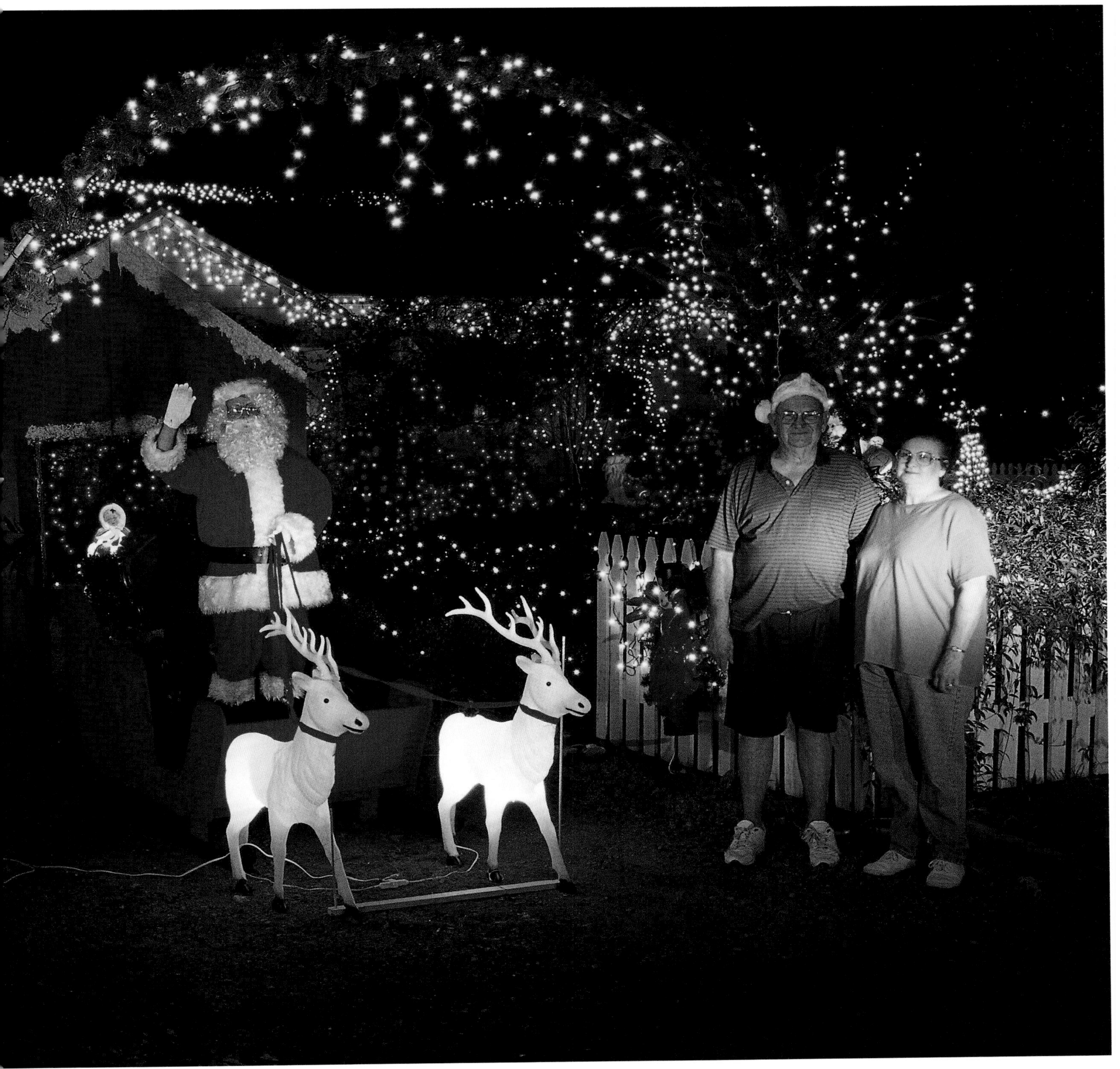

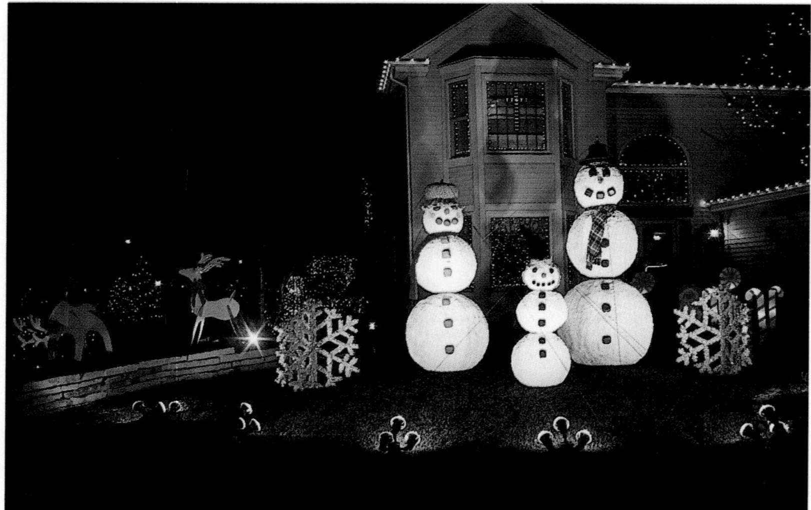

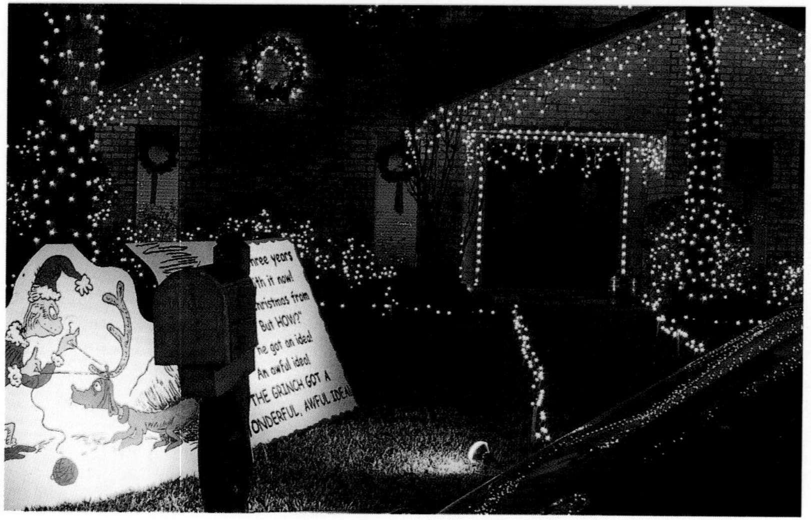
hree years
ith it now!
hristmas from
But HOW?"
he got an idea!
An awful idea!
THE GRINCH GOT A
ONDERFUL, AWFUL IDEA

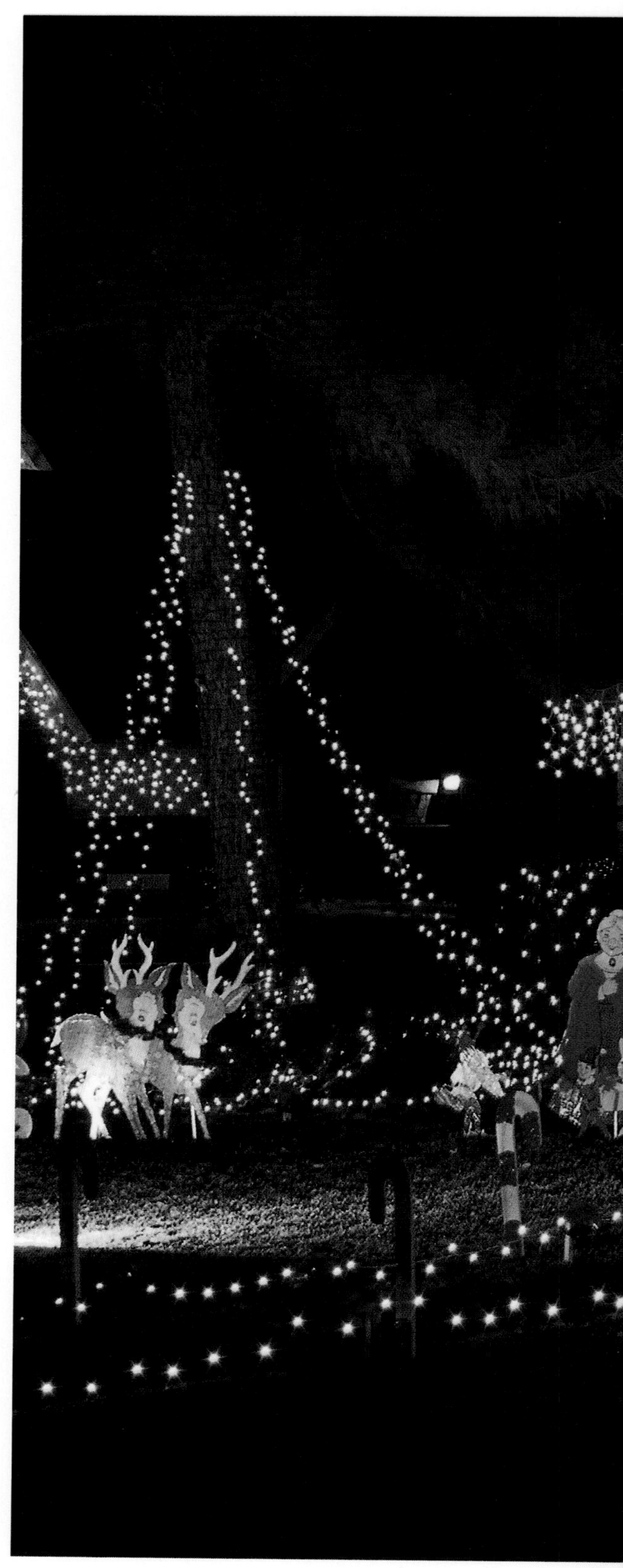

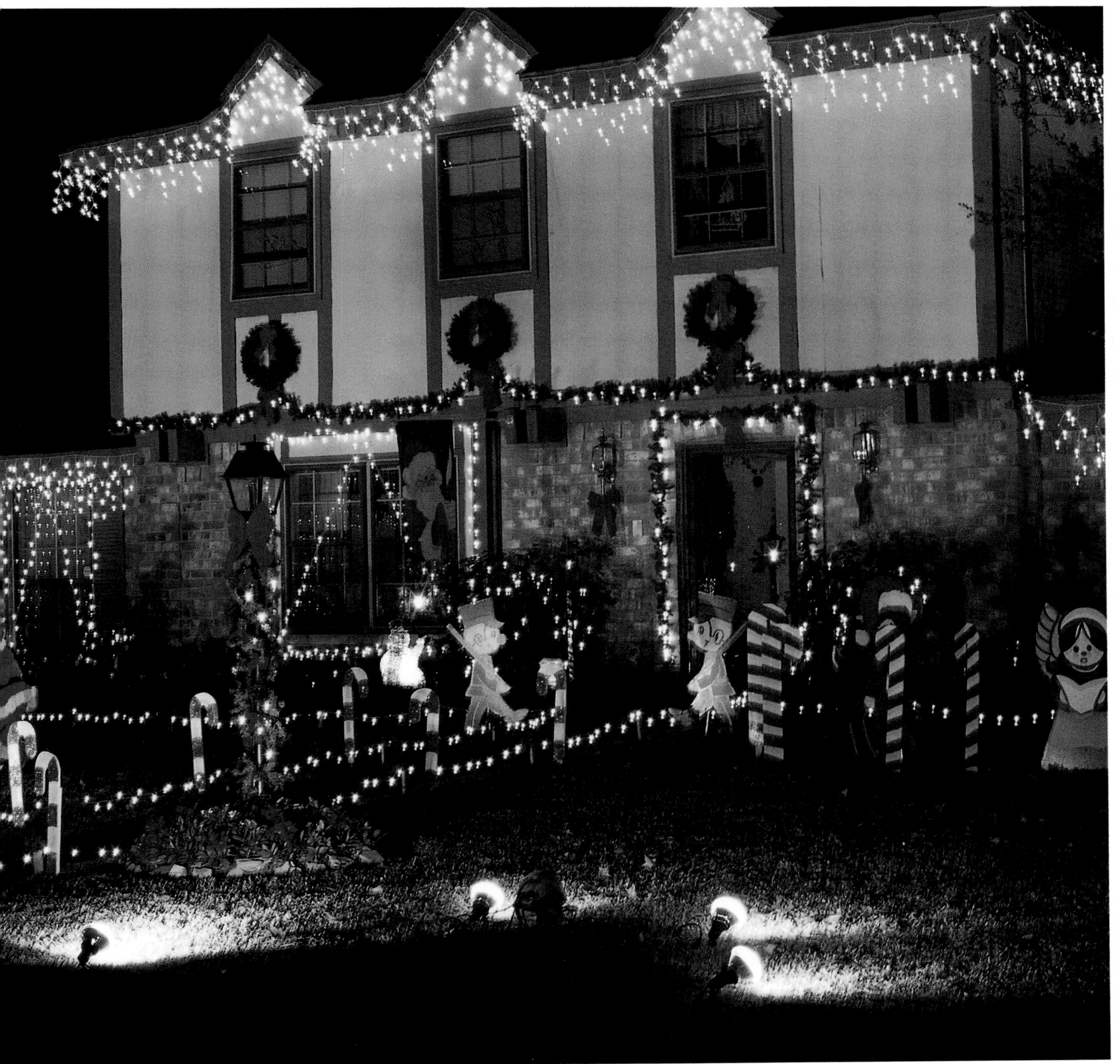

Photography Credits

Cover © Branson Coates Architects

INTRODUCTION
p.6: Chandigarh sign ©Juerg Gasser/Architectural Association Photo Library
p.7: Workers' Housing ©John Winter/Architectural Association Photo Library
p.9: Assembly Building ©Vandana Baweja/Architectural Assocation Photo Library
p.12–13: Courtesy Estate of Buckminster Fuller
p.14–17: Ecstacity images © Branson Coates Architects
p.20–23: Executing God © Office of ZahaHadid
p.24–25: Nobson Newtown All images Courtesy Maureen Paley/Interim Art

IDEALISM
p.26–27: Unité d'Habitation, Marseille © Paul Raftery/Arcaid
p.28: Courtesy of the Royal Society for the encouragement of Arts, Manufactures and Commerce
p.29: Lithograph. AKG London
p.30: Courtesy New Lanark Conservation Trust
p.33: Narkomfin © Ada Wilson/Architectural Association Photo Library
p.34: Unité d'Habitation © Paul Raftery/Arcaid
p.35: Unité d'Habitation © Paul Raftery/Arcaid
p.36 left: Lawn Road Flats, Courtesy the Pritchard Archive, University of East Anglia, Norwich
p.36 right: Lawn Road Flats, Courtesy the Pritchard Archive, University of East Anglia, Norwich
p.37: Lawn Road Flats, Courtesy the Pritchard Archive, University of East Anglia, Norwich
p.41: All pictures courtesy PRP Architects
p.42 top: Hanging lamps © Andy Keate/Sussie Ahlburg
p.42 bottom: Flats and grass © Andy Keate/Sussie Ahlburg
p.43 top: Courtesy de Rijke Marsh Morgan
p.43 bottom: Courtesy de Rijke Marsh Morgan
p.44–45: Courtesy de Rijke Marsh Morgan
p. 48–49: Kolonihavehus, The Royal Danish Library
p. 50: Model photos: Jens Lindke, courtesy arcspace
p.51–55: © Christian Richters
p.56–61: Photographs © Rick Poynor
p.62–63: Courtesy Landesmedienzentrum Hamburg
p.64–67: Courtesy Pendon Railway Museum
p.68: Modular House Mobile 1995/97. Photo AVL © Atelier van Lieshout/DACS, London 2000
p.69 top: The Good, the Bad + the Ugly, 1998. Photo Derk-Jan Wooldrik. © Atelier van Lieshout/DACS, London 2000
p.69 bottom: *Robber's Nest*, 1998. Photo Derk-Jan Wooldrik © Atelier van Lieshout/DACS, London 2000
p. 70 top: Atelier des Armes et des Bombes with Sleep/Study Ball, 1998. Photo AVL © Atelier van Lieshout/DACS, London 2000
p. 70 bottom: AVL Hospital, 1998. Photo Peter Foe. © Atelier van Lieshout/DACS, London 2000
p. 71: AVL Hospital, 1998. Photo Peter Foe. © Atelier van Lieshout/DACS, London 2000
p.72–75: Photos Alex Stetter
p.76–78: Courtesy Landesmedienzentrum Hamburg
p.81: Richard Prince, *Untitled (Cartoon)*, 1986. Courtesy Barbara Gladstone
p. 82–87: © Gunnar Knechtel

COMMERCE
p.88–89: Celebration photos © Joe Kerr
p.92: Bournville, courtesy Birmingham Central Library
p.94–95: Bournville, courtesy Birmingham Central Library
p.96: Courtesy Cornford and Cross/In the Midst of Things
p.97: Courtesy Birmingham Central Library/In the Midst of Things
p.98–99: Port Sunlight © Joe Kerr
p.102: Letchworth © Architectural Association Photo Library
p.103: Waterlow Court © Joe Kerr
p.103: Addison Way © Hazel Cook/Architectural Association Photo Library
p.103: Ruskin Close © Jane Beckett/Architectural Association Photo Library
p.104–105: British Architectural Library, RIBA, London
p.106: Frankfurt
p.109 bottom: Photo: Adrian Forty
p.114–117: Poundbury and Fairford Ley, Photos Jason Orton
p.107–125: All other images courtesy Joe Kerr
p.126–129: Photos: JJ Waller
p.130–131: Courtesy of Legoland Windsor
p.132–137: New Utopia, Photos Nigel Jackson
p.138–141: Courtesy Freedomship International
p.144: Oceandome, Courtesy Phoenix Resort Ltd
p147–148: Courtesy Harty and Harty
p.149–151: Courtesy Diller and Scofidio
p.152–157: Untitled series, 1993, © David Spero

VISIONS
p.158–176: Ronald Grant Archive
p.177, top: Ronald Grant Archive
p.177, bottom: © Fondation Le Corbusier, Paris/DACS, London 2000
p.178–179: © Martin Jones/Arcaid
p.180–181: Ronald Grant Archive
p.183, top: © Frank Gerssen/Architectural Association Photo Library
p.183, bottom: © Lewis Gasson/Architectural Association Photo Library
p.184–191: Courtesy Nathan Coley
p.192–193: The Drive-in House, Producer/Director: Takehiko Nagakura. Computer Graphics: Takehiko Nagakura, Marios Christodoulides. © Massachussetts Institute of Technology, 1998. Funding Support: Takenaka Corporation
p.194: Monument to the Third International, Producer/Director: Takehiko Nagakura. Computer Graphics: Andrzej Zarzycki, Takehiko Nagakura, Dan Brick, Mark Sich. © Massachussetts Institute of Technology, 1998. Funding Support: Takenaka Corporation
p.195: The Palace of the Soviets, Producer/Director: Takehiko Nagakura/Shinsuke Baba. Computer Graphics: Shinsuke Baba. © Massachussetts Institute of Technology, 1998. Funding Support: Takenaka Corporation
p.196: Walking City, Elevation detail, Archigram Group/Ron Herron, © Architectural Association Photo Library
p.197: © Kunsthalle, Tübingen, Germany/Bridgeman Art Library, London
p.199: photo AKG London
p.200: © Bibliotheque National, Paris/Bridgeman Art Library, London
p.201: photo AKG London
p.202–207: photos JJ Waller